Caring for People God's Way

Caring for People God's Way

Personal and Emotional Issues, Addictions, Grief, and Trauma

■ ■ ■

Edited by

TIM CLINTON, ED.D, LPC, LMFT

ARCHIBALD HART, PH.D., FPPR

GEORGE OHLSCHLAGER, J.D., LCSW

*A Joint Publication and Service Ministry of
the AACC and Thomas Nelson Publishers*

NELSON REFERENCE & ELECTRONIC
A Division of Thomas Nelson Publishers
Since 1798
www.thomasnelson.com

ISBN 10: 0-785-29775-8

Library of Congress Cataloging-in-Publication Data available upon request

Printed in the United States of America

3 4 5 6 7 — 10 09 08 07

In loving honor of my dad, James E. Clinton,
for 50 years of pastoral and helping ministry
and 80 years of a life well lived . . . .

and to the Executive Board of the
American Association of Christian Counselors
who have given so much to my life and the development of
Christian Counseling as we know it:
Dr. Diane Langberg
Dr. Ron Hawkins
Dr. Michael Lyles
Dr. Archibald Hart
Dr. David Stoop
Dr. Gary Oliver

# # #

To the scores of Christian Counselors all around the world
who minister to the deep wounds of broken people. Our prayer is that
God will bless its impact and empower all who read it to
become healing agents for the world.

To my students of every kind
and to my consultees with whom I work daily.
The future of Christian counseling is in your hands,
and the future looks very good from here.

Contents

Part 3: Addictions and Impulse Control Problems

Part 4: Counseling for Grief and Trauma

Acknowledgments

Those of you who write—and especially those who write books—know that many people are responsible for getting a finished book into the hands of the reading public. This book, in particular, had a very long gestation and, it felt at times, a rather torturous birth. It was begun many years ago as the natural sequel to our work on *Competent Christian Counseling*, and is tied closely to that seminal volume.

Great thanks is given to the many contributors to this volume—your tireless patience and continued encouragement to complete this work have been, in large part, the needed motivation to see this thing through to the end. The richness and higher value of these books are revealed by the expert contributions that so many of you made to this volume, and continue to make to our ever-growing field of Christian counseling. There is no way that we alone could have written a book of this quality—thank you all so much.

Special thanks to you, Arch Hart, for your inspiration and steady goading. And thank you, Greg Janz and Mark Laaser, for coming through at the near-midnight hour with excellent contributions that completed the subjects we needed for this volume.

We wish we had a "suffering servants" award for those of you who still have not seen your contribution in print. We can only ask for continued long-suffering patience with us, as we do have your work planned in future volumes. In fact, a fair share of the very best leaders in our field will have contributed to this series before it is done.

Special thanks and high praise for a job well done to Anthony Centore and Joshua Straub, our resident Ph.D. counseling students who have done a tremendous job at checking and cleaning up our references, building lists, and assisting us in the last-minute completion tasks that can be so overwhelming. Anthony also made written contributions to two chapters in the book, and is on his way to making a significant contribution in our burgeoning field.

One of the reasons this project took so long to fruition was our struggle to find the right publisher for this book and for the series. Thomas Nelson Publishers have come through with everything that we asked, and we are delighted to be back in partnership with the company that did *The Soul Care Bible*, the primary work that we are connecting to the entire series.

Finally, we are delighted to thank and acknowledge our wives and children—surely those who "long-suffered" the most in this project. Bless you, Julie, Megan, and Zachary, and you, Lorraine, Noelle, and her husband Josh Bronz, Justin, and Rea, for all that you mean to us. Thank you, always, for all the love and patience and succor that you pour out to us, even when it is not deserved.

Editors and Contributors

Tim Clinton, Ed.D., LPC, LMFT, is President of the 50,000-member American Association of Christian Counselors (AACC), the largest and most diverse Christian counseling association in the world; and is Publisher of the award-winning *Christian Counseling Today* magazine. He is Professor of Counseling and Pastoral Care, and Executive Director of the Liberty University Center for Counseling and Family Studies; and was recently Distinguished Visiting Professor in the Regent University School of Psychology and Counseling.

Licensed in Virginia as both a Professional Counselor (LPC) and Marriage and Family Therapist (LMFT), Tim is President and maintains a part-time counseling practice with Light Counseling, Inc., in Lynchburg, Virginia. He recently became Chairman of the Covenant Marriage Movement, and is a member of the Arlington Group, a national marriage policy leadership group based in Washington, DC.

Tim is Executive Editor and co-author of *Competent Christian Counseling:*

Foundations and Practice of Compassionate Soul Care (WaterBrook, 2002). He is lead author of *Attachments: Unlock the Secret to Loving and Being Loved* (Integrity, 2003). He was Executive Editor and a primary writer for *The Soul Care Bible* (2001), the NKJV Bible project by AACC and Thomas Nelson Publishers.

He has authored over 150 articles, chapters, notes, and columns on Christian counseling and on marriage and family life. He is co-author of *Baby Boomer Blues* in Word's Contemporary Christian Counselor series, and author of *Before a Bad Goodbye: How to Turn Your Marriage Around*, and the newly-released *The Marriage You Always Wanted*, both by Word.

Tim is a Liberty University honors graduate with B.S. and M.A. degrees in pastoral ministries and counseling. He then earned Ed.S. and Ed.D. degrees in counselor education from the College of William and Mary in Virginia.

Tim and his wife Julie have been married for 25 years, have two children—Megan and Zachary—and the family lives in Forest, Virginia.

Archibald D. Hart, Ph.D., is Senior Professor of Psychology and Dean Emeritus in the Department of Clinical Psychology at Fuller Theological Seminary in Pasadena, California. He was recently Executive Editor of International Relations for the AACC, and remains on AACC's Executive Board. Dr. Hart is a licensed psychologist, certified biofeedback practitioner, and is a board certified fellow in psychopharmacology. He is an internationally known speaker on Christian counseling and managing the stress of ministry.

Dr. Hart is best known for his research and writing on the hazards of ministry, depression, anxiety, divorce, stress, and sexuality. Among his numerous books are recent publications *Safe Haven Marriage* with daughter Dr. Sharon Hart May, *Unveiling Depression in Women* with daughter Dr. Catherine Hart Weber, *Unmasking Male Depression*, and *The Anxiety Cure*. He is now involved with these two daughters in the Hart Institute, an international caring and consulting ministry for the church. He is president of the International Association of Christian Counselors, a global umbrella group for national Christian counseling organizations.

Dr. Hart is an active member of the Prescribing Psychologists Register. A native South African, he holds the BSc from the University of South Africa, and the M.Sc. and Ph.D. from University of Natal.

He lives in Southern California with his wife Kathleen (they just celebrated 50 years together!), and he is surrounded by the love of his three daughters and nine grandchildren.

George Ohlschlager, J.D., LCSW, is Executive Director and Co-Founder of the American Board of Christian Counselors, the national Christian counselor credentialing and program accreditation agency affiliated with the AACC. He is Director of Policy and Professional Affairs for the AACC, and is Senior Editor and Writer of the award-winning *Christian Counseling Today* magazine, and the *Christian Counseling Connection* newsletter.

A Licensed Clinical Social Worker in California, George chairs the AACC Law & Ethics Committee, drafted and revised the *AACC Christian Counseling Code of Ethics,* and maintains a nationwide clinical, ethics, and forensic consulting and training practice. As a member of the Arlington Group, he does policy and political advocacy work in Washington, DC, on marital and family issues—especially to support the passage of a Federal Marriage Amendment to the U.S. Constitution. He teaches in the Ph.D. programs in professional counseling, and in pastoral care and counseling in the Liberty University Center for Counseling and Family Studies, and at St. Petersburg Theological Seminary.

George was honored as Consulting Editor and one of the primary writers of *The Soul Care Bible* (Thomas Nelson, 2001). He is Executive Editor and co-author of *Competent Christian Counseling* (WaterBrook, 2002), and also co-authored *Law for the Christian Counselor* (Word, 1992), and *Sexual Misconduct in Counseling and Ministry* (Word, 1995). He has authored and co-authored over 200 articles, chapters, columns, codes, reviews, memoranda and notes in his many fields of interest.

A B.A. psychology graduate of Humboldt State University in California, George holds an M.A. in counseling psychology and biblical/theological studies from Trinity Evangelical Divinity School (now part of Trinity International University). He then earned M.S.W. and J.D. degrees in a dual-degree, interdisciplinary studies program in social work and law at The University of Iowa.

George lives near Lynchburg, Virginia, with his wife, Lorraine, and they have three adult and teenaged children, Noelle, Justin and Rea—all are attending college.

Diane M. Langberg, Ph.D., is a member of the AACC's Executive Board and a Licensed Psychologist with *Diane Langberg, Ph.D. & Associates* in Jenkintown, Pennsylvania. She is also the author of *Counseling Survivors of Sexual Abuse* and *On the Threshold of Hope.*

Sharon Hart May, Ph.D., is Director of The Marriage, Family, and Relationship Institute at *La Vie Counseling Center* in Pasadena, California.

Catherine Hart Weber, Ph.D., is the co-author of *Secrets of Eve*, which reports on a recent national study of Christian female sexuality, and *Unveiling Depression in Women*. She serves on the International Board at C.A.R.E., a counseling resource for pastors and their families.

Anthony J. Centore, M.A., Ph.D. cand., is the Executive Assistant to Dr. Tim Clinton of the AACC, and works for the *Center for Counseling and Family Studies* at *Liberty University*, where he is a Ph.D. candidate in the Professional Counseling program.

Everett Worthington, Ph.D., is Professor of Psychology and Director of the Graduate Counseling Psychology Program at *Virginia Commonwealth University*, and he is Executive Director of *A Campaign for Forgiveness Research*.

Gary Stewart, D. Min., is a military chaplain trained in communications and crisis intervention. He is co-author of *Suicide: A Christian Response*.

Michael R. Lyles, M.D., is an AACC Executive Board Member and has a private psychiatric practice with Lyles & Crawford Clinical Consulting in Roswell, Georgia.

Mark R. Laaser, Ph.D., CCSAS, is Executive Director at Faithful and True Ministries in Eden Prairie, Minnesota.

Mark Crawford, Ph.D., is a Clinical Psychologist and a partner in Lyles & Crawford Clinical Consulting in Roswell, Georgia.

Siang-Yang Tan, Ph.D., is Professor of Psychology at the Graduate School of Psychology at Fuller Theological Seminary, and is also Senior Pastor of *First Evangelical Church* in Glendale, California.

Gary J. Oliver, Th.M., Ph.D. is Executive Director of The Center for Relationship Enrichment and Professor of Psychology and Practical Theology at John Brown University in Siloam Springs, Arkansas. He is a popular conference speaker and the author of numerous books including *A Woman's Forbidden Emotion* with H. Norman Wright.

Carrie Oliver, M.A., is a graduate of Denver Seminary, director of the University Relationships Initiative at JBU, a counselor specializing in marriage and family and women's issues, a conference speaker and an author. Gary and Carrie are parents of three boys and coauthors of *Raising Sons . . . and Loving It!*

Ian Jones, Ph.D., is Professor of Counseling and Director of the Baptist Marriage and Family Counseling Center at Southwestern Baptist Theological Seminary in Fort Worth, Texas.

Theresa Burke, Ph.D., LPC, is the Founder of Rachel's Vineyard Ministries and the author of *Forbidden Grief: The Unspoken Pain of Abortion*, as well as the *Rachel's Vineyard Weekend Retreat Manuals*, which serve as the basis for retreats offered in 45 states.

Greg Jantz, Ph.D., is a Psychologist, Author, Speaker, and the Founder of *The Center for Counseling & Health Resources*, which to date has helped almost 30,000 people. The Center has five locations in the Seattle, Washington area and an affiliate in Quito, Ecuador.

Linda Mintle, Ph.D., is a Virginia-based Therapist, Speaker, and Author of *A Daughter's Journey Home: Finding a Way to Love, Honor and Connect with Your Mother.*

Henry Virkler, Ph.D., has been training Christian Counselors at the graduate level for the past 25 years and is currently a Professor of Psychology at Palm Beach Atlantic University.

Mark Shandoan, LCSW, A.B.D., is a full-time Clinician at Light Counseling in Lynchburg, Virginia, and is completing his doctorate in Counseling Psychology at Argosy University of Sarasota.

Preface:

Introduction to the Book and the Series

On behalf of the American Association of Christian Counselors (AACC), we are delighted to announce our newest book and book series, *Caring for People God's Way*. This new ministry project is a joint publication venture of the AACC and Thomas Nelson Publishers, and follows the name and spirit of AACC's Caring for People God's Way video training series.

This highly usable, practice-oriented book, denoted as Volume 1A, is the bridging volume of our 2002 work on *Competent Christian Counseling* and the three volumes to follow in the format of this book. We intend this to become the Christian Counseling Practice Library for the 21st century, the leading edge of Christ-centered, research-savvy and user-friendly counseling books that takes Christian and pastoral counseling to a new standard of competent and caring delivery in this new millennium.

This entire Library is intended for professional Christian counselors, pastors and pastoral counselors, and anyone doing helping ministry in church-based ministry roles. The professional will appreciate the integration of biblical and psychosocial research material and the comprehensive way that treatment issues are covered, while the church-based helper will respond to the clear language and practical way that complex issues are defined and dealt with.

Each volume will present a discrete and clearly definable area of application—personal and emotional concerns, marriage, sexuality, trauma, addictions, grief, and loss, for example—and will cover the breadth of issues that are most commonly addressed in doing counseling in those arenas. In 20–22 chapters across 400+ pages, each volume is designed to cover material quickly and yet also comprehensively, honoring your busy schedules and need for practical, relevant data to assist you in your ministry or professional practice.

Christian Counseling has become so large and diverse that no one or two persons can write with expertise across the breadth of our burgeoning field. Beyond our own written contributions, we already have chapters for the various volumes written by over 30 of the best practitioner/teacher/writers in Christian counseling. Before this series is completed in 2007, we plan to invite over 60 people to contribute. Including *Competent Christian Counseling* with this series, you will be influenced by nearly 100 of the very best practitioners and leading academics we have in the field today.

Volume 1A, *Caring for People God's Way*, is foundational to the rest of the series. This new book encapsulates and advances the Paracentric counseling model of the earlier work on *Competent Christian Counseling* and presents it in a systematic, step-by-step fashion that outlines the process very practically for the reader. It is then applied to the most common issues faced by Christian counselors: personal and emotional issues, addiction problems, trauma disorders, grief, loss, and suicide.

This model is then superimposed on the counseling issues that are presented in each of the subsequent volumes, outlining the assessment, treatment planning and intervention strategies of the model for that area of application.

Volume 2 will address Christian counseling applied to marriage, divorce, family, and sexual issues, an arena where both the "cultural wars" and values issues in the counseling field are very hot topics right now.

Volume 3 tackles the tougher issues we all face as counselors, including counseling around medical and health care issues, working with more difficult personality disorders, and dealing with controversial treatment issues. Each of these areas is exploding as a major focus of training, research and practice throughout the world.

Finally, Volume 4 presents "The Ethical Helper." This last volume meets a crying need in the church by outlining the ethical, legal, and business issues related to Christian counseling in both professional and church-based settings, as well as delivering a "nuts-and-bolts" outline of counseling practice development in both church and clinic settings.

This library, this *Caring for People God's Way* project, intends to become the "must have" counseling and ministry resource for every professional therapist, pastor, pastoral counselor, and church-based lay helping ministry in the United States and throughout the world. We plan to finish this entire 4-volume series together so that the full project—all 4+1 volumes as a complete set—can be available for the first time by the 2007 AACC "No Greater Love" World Conference in Nashville.

Our hope—our prayer from this day forward—is that God will call you to loving service and anoint you with wisdom and power to lead others into that healing place that only He can transform. May this book and the volumes to come bless you for your work as Christian counselors in these last days.

TIM AND GEORGE
Forest, Virginia
August 2005

ARCH
Arcadia, California
August 2005

Caring for People God's Way

Part 1

21st-Century Christian Counseling

1

Introduction to Christian Counseling:
The 21st-Century State of the Art

Tim Clinton and George Ohlschlager

And we proclaim Him, admonishing every man and teaching every man with all wisdom, that we may present every man [and woman] complete in Christ.

COLOSSIANS 2:28

When good King Josiah died around 609 B.C., Israel was prosperous, strong, and safe in the world. Yet the people of Israel quickly declined both morally and spiritually, and their leaders grew corrupt. The whole nation refused to hear the prophets God sent, including Jeremiah, to call them to repentance and restoration.

Amid the ongoing search for the good life, a great terror was about to befall them—the complete destruction of Jerusalem and the forced slavery of the Jews by the Babylonians in 586 B.C.—but they would not turn their hearts. Jeremiah 6:14 captures the essence of that day, "They have healed the brokenness of my people superficially, saying, 'Peace, peace,' but there is no peace" (NASB).

Interestingly, as today's prosperous generations search for purpose, meaning and value, many are experiencing a pervasive sense of emptiness and isolation. And why shouldn't they? In a world flooded with distresses like father absence, abuse, violence, marital discord, and emotional problems there is a natural epidemic of escapism through consumerism, drugs, alcohol, sex, and suicide. Earnest Becker accents this thought concluding "Modern man is drinking or drugging himself to death...or he is shopping which is the same thing."[1]

Living in denial, today's powerful and pampered generations have become "tranquilized by the trivial," though they find neither solace nor healing—crying "'Peace, peace,' but there is no peace." Dallas Willard alludes to this modern journey in his book on spiritual disciplines and concludes, "Obviously, the problem is a spiritual one. And so must be the cure."[2] We agree.

In 1978, Scott Peck opened his near-classic work *The Road Less Traveled* with the profound truth assertion that "Life is difficult." In the quarter century following, everything has changed. Relativism, cynicism, and the deconstruction of traditional morality have run their course leaving a socio-cultural travesty in their wake. Hence, what was accurate and profound then, "Life is difficult," hardly grasps the needs or silent cries of many today; the trauma, loss, the present terror of neglect and abuse that touch the lives of so many.

Our pressing concern at the inception of the 21st century is that *people are hurting*—and searching frantically for hope and new life. If there is ever a time for godly leadership, servanthood and biblical counsel, it is now.

Consider the following facts about our modern world:

Marital Discord. Studies show 35% of persons who marry get a divorce, and 18% of those divorced are divorced multiple times. Currently, for African Americans, single-parent households outnumber married-couple families.[3] In addition, almost half (46%) of persons from the Baby Boomer generation have undergone a marital split, and millions more are expected to divorce in the next 10 years.[4]

It should be noticed that the destruction of the American family is troubling kids too. Reportedly, many children 10 to 15 years after the divorce of their parents continue to battle with resulting unhappiness.[5] In addition, younger generations are likely to reach record heights of divorce and it is estimated that somewhere between 40 and 50% of marriages that begin this year will end in divorce.[6]

Christians are far from exempt. According to The Barna Group, although churches try to dissuade congregants, rates of divorce among Christians are about the same as the non-Christian population. Moreover, data shows such divorces occur *after* the married persons have accepted Christ as their Savior. Also, multiple divorces are extraordinarily common among born again Christians, for 23% are divorced two or more times![7]

Fatherlessness. Each night, nearly 40% of children fall asleep in homes where their fathers are not present.[8] The deterioration of fatherhood in America—by 72.2% of the U.S. population—is considered by some our most serious social ill. Encumbering the development of youth, fatherlessness promotes mental disorders, crime, suicide, poverty, teenaged pregnancy, drug and alcohol abuse, and incarceration.[9]

A study of nearly 6,000 children found that youth from single-parent homes have more physical and mental health problems than children living with married parents, and another study confirms single-parent children are 2–3 times as likely to develop emotional and behavioral problems. In addition, almost 75% of children living in fatherless homes will experience poverty, and are 10 times as likely—as compared to children living with 2 parents—to experience extreme poverty.[10]

Sexual Abuse and Assault. The present evidence of widespread sexual abuse is daunting. By age 18, 1 in 3 girls and 1 in 6 boys will be sexually abused by someone they love or should be able to trust.[11] According to recent surveys, about 1 in 4 women during their college years, and 1 in 33 men, have experienced an attempted (or completed) rape. Moreover, according to a national survey of high school students, approximately 9% reported having been forced to have sexual intercourse against their will.[12]

Domestic Violence. Violence at the hand of an intimate partner occurs across all populations, irrespective of economic, religious, social, or cultural affiliation—and accounts for 20% of all nonfatal violent crime against women. The occurrence of nearly 5.3 million acts of domestic violence each year (among women 18 and older) results in almost 2 million injuries and 1,300 deaths. These deaths are not without warning, a staggering 44% of women murdered by their intimate partner enter emergency care within 2 years prior to the homicide, 93% seeking care for an injury.[13]

Suicide. A suicide occurs approximately every 20 minutes in the United States.[14] According to a 2004 study, over 30,000 U.S. residents commit suicide each year, and over 130,000 are hospitalized following a suicide attempt. For men, suicide is the eighth leading cause of death. For women (as compared to men), suicide attempts are 3 times as common. Also, suicide is the third leading cause of death for children 10–14, and adolescents 15–24.[15] These high rates of self-destruction are exacerbated by social isolation, being a victim of child abuse, having feelings of hopelessness, or sustained depression. Shawn Shea writes that suicide can be considered as an only option for those feeling deeply alone or ashamed.[16]

Alcoholism. In the year 2000 there were approximately 85,000 deaths in the U.S. attributable to either excessive or hazardous drinking—making alcohol the third actual leading cause of death. Recent studies show that approximately 40% of all crimes are committed under the influence of alcohol, 40% of persons convicted of rape or sexual assault state they were drinking at the time of the offense, and 72% of rapes on college campuses occur while victims are intoxicated to the point that they are unable to consent or refuse sex.

In addition, 50% of child abuse and neglect cases are connected with the alcohol or drug use of a guardian, two-thirds of domestic violence victims report the involvement of alcohol, and in 2001 there were 1.4 million arrests for driving under the influence of alcohol or narcotics: that is a rate of 1 out of 137 licensed drivers.[17]

Substance Abuse. The results of a 2003 poll show that 8.2% of persons 12 and older have used illicit drugs in the last month.[18] Though it is known that the motivation of substance use is to increase comfort of one's psychological state, less is known about what places one at risk for abuse. Genetics, learning, environment, intrapsychic issues, personal relationships, and early life experiences all seem to have influence, though there is no absolute determinant.[19]

Recently, in investigating these issues, it was found that 56% of substance abusers admitted for treatment met the diagnostic criteria for borderline disorder, a high percentage of abusers display self-damaging impulsive tendencies, and a recent analysis of literature involving the comorbidity of drug abuse and personality disorders shows that 80% of studies find a positive correlation.[20]

There are many abuse recovery treatments, which procure varying rates of success. Review of some programs has found treatment to be ineffective when compared to a control group. One study investigating inpatient care found a relapse of substance abuse in 90% of instances, if psychosocial intervention is not part of treatment.[21]

Depression. An estimated 20% of the U.S. population will experience clinical depression at some point in their lifetime.[22] More than just "the blues," clinical depression is distinct in that symptoms are of a severity that disrupt one's daily routine. Often ubiquitous, these symptoms include decreased energy, fluctuating body weight, depleted concentration, irritability, bouts of crying, and thoughts of suicide.

According to recent studies, depression appears to be on the rise—those born after 1950 are 10 times as likely to experience depression as compared to their predecessors. Currently, individuals between ages 25 and 45 occupy the greatest percentage of depression, though adolescent groups possess the fastest rate of depression growth.[23] Causing inestimable pain for both those enduring the disorder and persons closest to the sufferer, depression unnecessarily consumes and profoundly impacts both the life of the victim, and that of his/her family. Unfortunately, most sufferers do not seek treatment or believe their depression to be treatable.[24]

Anxiety. Maladaptive anxiety has become a common plague that affects approximately 19 million U.S. adults—or up to 25% of the general population—and is distinct in that it progresses to consume one with overwhelming irrational fear, panic and dread.[25] In many instances, symptoms are intense to the point that they cripple one's personal relationships, career, and quality of life.[26]

Even in its severity, anxiety can go misidentified by a sufferer, becoming deeply routed in one's personality. For example, currently 25% of persons who visit an emergency care unit presenting chest pain are actually suffering from Panic Disorder.[27]

Issues like financial setbacks, workplace demands, loss, unplanned pregnancies, cancer, obesity, and other physical problems and the stresses of our day quickly get overwhelming. Whoever described our times as "The Aspirin Age" didn't miss it by much.

But these problems are only one form of suffering in our groaning world. Demonic oppression is still rampant. Abject poverty and life-threatening disease beset nearly one-third of the world's population. Last year, AIDS became the largest pandemic of death in world history—exceeding the 75 million deaths of the Black Plague. The ongoing horror of terrorism and war has touched every corner of the world. Last but not least, political and religious persecution, torture, and murder affect half a billion people across the earth.

Global Recognition of Mental Disorders

We are also beginning to know a lot about mental disorders, not only in America, but around the world as well. In 2004, the World Health Organization presented the findings from its global study that analyzed data from 60,463 face-to-face surveys with adults in 14 countries—to estimate the prevalence, severity, and treatment of mental disorders.[28] All surveys used the World Mental Health-Composite International Diagnostic Interview (WMH-CIDI), a structured diagnostic interview to assess disorders and treatment. The surveys were conducted in the Americas (Columbia, Mexico, United States), Europe (Belgium, France, Germany, Italy, Netherlands, Spain, Ukraine), the Middle East and Africa (Lebanon, Nigeria), and Asia (Japan, separate surveys in Beijing and Shanghai in the People's Republic of China).

Mental health issues included anxiety disorders, mood disorders (i.e. depression), disorders with features of impulse control (i.e. the eating disorder bulimia), and substance abuse disorders. Treatment was also studied, and in the United States (US) treatment was found to be more strongly related to the ability to pay and less to the need for care, compared to other countries—many others having universal health insurance.

Despite differences in treatment, researchers found remarkably similar high proportions of mental disorders (17 to 29%, with the rates in the U.S. in the higher ranges at 26.4%), early age of onset (mostly childhood through the early adult years), high rates of chronic mental illness, and high levels of adverse effects on jobs, marriages, and other aspects of life.

Inadequacy of treatment. Over the last several decades, research studies have repeatedly proven the efficacy of counseling. Moreover, religious and faith-based psychotherapy have skyrocketed, showing again and again the great value that ensues when "faith meets counseling." What's sad is the gap between persons needing help, and the lack of trained individuals available to provide quality care.

For example, though there is a great client demand for spiritual care, a troublesome incongruity exists between Christian clients and mental health professionals. One survey shows that while 72% of the American population says religious faith is among the most important factors in their lives, only 33% of psychologists state the same.[29] Also, a Gallup poll suggests that above 60% of prospective clients prefer counselors with spiritual values, and 80% want their beliefs brought into the counseling process.[30] With a great many of mental health professionals deficient in an understanding of spiritual importance, the notion of finding suitable Christian counselors for all clients seems problematic, if not daunting.

Dr. Ronald Kessler, professor at Harvard Medical School, writes regarding the lack of counseling treatment in general, "The consistency of these patterns across a wide variety of countries is striking. Issue number one is that we can't wait as long as we do to get young people into treatment. Issue number two is that we have to do a better job of making sure patients are treated with the best available therapies once we manage to get them into treatment."[31]

In all countries, young, poorly educated males with serious mental disorders are the least likely to receive treatment, and it is suggested that school-based interventions in low-income school districts may help reach these young men to prevent progression from mild to more serious disorders. Early intervention is uncommon but important, according to the report, for "people with mild mental disorders, if left untreated, have a significant risk of future serious outcomes, such as attempted suicide, hospitalization, and work disability," the authors write.

Kessler said he and his coauthors were struck by the inadequate treatments in America stating, "This involves both medical care that fails to conform with accepted treatment guidelines, such as a homeopathic dose of a psychopharmacological medication prescribed by a family doctor, or care in some other sector of the treatment system, such as self-help or religious counseling, that has not been shown to be effective in treatment of clinically significant mental disorders."[32] In sum, there is a call for an increase in quality care, the necessity of which is inestimable.

Problems in the Pew

If the population in our pews is representative of the world around us, 1 in 4 of those pew-sitters in the U.S. wrestles with a diagnosable mental disorder with few receiving any help or direction. Moreover, churches involved in evangelism and outreach may show even higher rates of disorder because if they are succeeding in their job of fulfilling the Great Commission, then many entering these churches could be beset with chaos and trouble like the church has never seen.

A crisis of leadership. There is widespread acknowledgment that the American and Western Church is mired in a major leadership crisis. The Catholic Church's sexual abuse crisis, of course, immediately stands out for its severity and pervasiveness. Not only are there thousands of still-suffering victims of hundreds of serial sex-abusing priests, but the cover-up and shuffling of these priests to new parishes to replay their crimes over and over is a scandal that has implicated dozens of bishops and archbishops, and two American cardinals!

Not that the Protestant church has any reason to gloat or be smug about its own status. Nearly 6,000 Southern Baptist pastors leave the ministry prematurely every year. More than 200 pastors are fired every month! Former SBC president Jimmy Draper asserted that a third of the SBC's 62,000 churches have staff suffering from significant stress or emotional problems.[33]

Dr. Freddie Gage, former SBC evangelist and leader, pioneered a ministry to burned-out and abused pastors, called Wounded Heroes. After suffering from major bouts of anxiety and depression in his 40s, and receiving real help via psychiatric treatment, he worked for Rapha for many years as a liaison between that Christian counseling ministry and the SBC: "The majority of Southern Baptist ministers do not offer grace, compassion, and restoration to their fellow ministers. When a pastor stumbles, we purchase him a coffin and bury him," said Gage.[34]

Shooting our wounded leaders. The recent scandals of pastoral leadership only confound a wider issue: the abuse of church leaders by the church itself. A friend of ours was recently fired as pastor of his church. It was an unjust act—akin to shooting a bleeding soldier lying prone on the hospital cot rather than tending to his wounds and restoring him to health. Arguably, it was an act of soul-murder, and something that the conservative church does all too often, not just to its hurting people in the pews, but also to its wounded leaders.

This man—an author with a long history of successful pastoral ministry—wasn't caught in adultery, wasn't embezzling church monies, and wasn't engaged in fraud or wrongdoing of any kind. He simply got sick. He was stricken by a depression that adversely affected his ministry, no doubt about it, but in no way was a firing offense. His church should have rallied around, shown him love and mercy, given him a health-restoring sabbatical, and found him the resources to repair his life and return to ministry when able. Instead they wrote him off and kicked him out.

The great blessing for the woman caught in adultery was that she was hauled before Christ as the object lesson of a higher purpose—which was to entrap the Son of God in some violation of the law. For although the Pharisees had only one target audience—callously using this woman as if she didn't count, or even exist—Jesus never discounted her and always kept in view his two audiences, the abused woman and her powerful accusers. And it was surely the love of Jesus that intervened on her behalf, saved her life, and probably saved her soul with his merciful challenge to "go and sin no more."

The scandal of modern-day Pharisees who abuse and mistreat those needing mercy and a "safe-haven" is that these people are never brought before Christ. Instead, the abusers think they have the "mind of Christ" and those who suffer depression and chronic mental disorders—those among the "least of these" that Jesus calls us to special ministerial commitment—are often among the first that many churches scrub from their ranks.

Think about this being normative in the American church. The mentally and emotionally disabled are often too embarrassing and unrepresentative of the bright and shiny Christians the church wants to show off to the world. Stepping down to care for those with ugly dispositions and repulsive traits is exactly opposite to the step up we want to take in a life of ever-growing satisfaction with the abundant life that God promises on the other side.

No wonder Jesus wept. No wonder the scandal of the church shooting its wounded keeps growing. And no wonder there will be many expressions of shock and disbelief on judgment day when many will hear the Lord say, "Depart from me, for I never knew you."

However, it is also true that even some Pharisees and legalists in the modern church can be persuaded to provide care—even if it is condescending care—to the most needy and chronic sufferers. More and more people are understanding that many mental/emotional disorders are serious issues like cancer and diabetes. They understand the influence and mutual reinforcement of mental illness with poverty, illiteracy, family chaos and child abuse, drug abuse, and the like. And some people even understand the cyclical and repetitive nature of depression and various disorders that were once thought to be solely a product of sin or character defect.

But a pastor, a Christian leader, is expected to overcome trouble even if that trouble arrives through no fault of his own. A leader may suffer as any other mere mortal, but fault is attached if he does not overcome it, or carry through it with grace and aplomb.

The sad and harsh truth is that there is no room in Christian leadership for debilitating trouble. Tragically, there is no place to go for most—nowhere but down in flames and shame.

Living in a Hard-Hearted Age

We cannot escape the truth that we live in a cold and hard-hearted age. Without dedication, spiritual fullness, good health, good training, perseverance, and on occasion, a willingness to suffer with those one serves, helping ministry does not work all that well. Even with these things in place, it does not always work consistently, for there is one thing that must infuse and flow from the servant in order for counseling to be redemptive. That is the caring love of Christ, a love that must transcend the best love we can muster by ourselves.

Charles Colson and the TV interviewer. Years ago, in one of his columns for *Christianity Today*, Charles Colson tells the poignant story of an interview on PBS that demonstrates the power of caring, sacrificial love. In pointing out the limits of our best efforts to reform culture through political activism and persuasive argument, Colson asserts that "there is only one way people will genuinely 'hear' the gospel message: by observing how the church itself lives . . . They should see in the Christian community a unifying love that resonates with their own deepest longings—and points to a supernatural source." Then he told this wonderful story:

The interviewer had an aggressive manner and a hard expression under layers of make-up and mascara. "How can you be so sure about your faith," she challenged me. I answered by telling her a story of my time behind bars after Watergate, when several Christian men stunned me with a quality of love I had never known before.

> I'll never forget that day because one of them—Al Quie—called to say, "Chuck, because of your family problems, I'm going to ask the President if you can go home, while I serve the rest of your prison term." I gasped in disbelief. At the time, Al was the sixth-ranking Republican in the House, one of the most respected public figures in Washington. Yet he was willing to jeopardize it all out of love for me. It was a powerful witness that Jesus was real: that a believer would lay down his life for another.

As I retold the story for the cameras, the interviewer broke down and waved her hand, saying, "Stop, stop." Tears mixed with mascara were streaming down her cheeks. She excused herself, repaired her make-up, and—injecting confidence back into her voice—said, "Let's film that sequence once more." But hearing the story again, she could not hold back her tears. Later, she confessed that Al's willingness to sacrifice had touched her deeply, and she vowed to return to the church she had left years earlier.[35]

A Christian community united in love attracts attention in the most jaded culture. Sacrificial and caring love does offer up the best remedy to influence and change the hardest hearts. This is the difference that the love of Christ makes, and it is this kind of love that must make a difference in our service to hurting souls. When the love of Christ is truly shown the Spirit of God infuses it with power that changes lives.

Searching for God

Though it appears to be the worst of times, something else seems to be happening across America—people are searching for God. According to the work of George Gallup and Timothy Jones, 82% of Americans desire for a more intimate relationship with God: This is up 24% in just a 4 year period! Further, according to the research, in the last 24 hours some 66% had prayed to God seeking not only help but also direction in life. Some 50% had sensed a strong presence of God in their lives and had even gone out of their way to help another person with spiritual or religious issues.[36] A new Gallup book, *The Next American Spirituality*, cites how a spiritual movement in the hearts of Americans is contrasting what has become an overwhelming secular culture.[37]

With this we are reminded of Isaiah 6:8 when God asks, "And whom shall I send, and who will go for me?" We never cease to be amazed that God's desire is to send persons like you and each one of us to carry His message of hope in Christ to a searching and hurting world.

Preparing pastors, clinicians, paraprofessionals, and lay helpers. That is why we are so excited about what God is doing in and through the Christian counseling movement today, especially in the American Association of Christian Counselors (AACC), which is so dedicated to the entire community of care and to training and filling the church with lay helpers and caregivers beyond anything that has been done in history. Pastors and professional Christian counselors alone cannot possibly meet the needs that exist in the church and in the world today.

The helping ministry of the church must have *four* strong legs to properly function, to even begin to meet its ministry call in the 21st century world. Unless pastor, professional clinician, paraprofessional, and lay helper all work together—in harmony and with mutual respect and support for the role that each serves—the church will surely be overwhelmed by its sins and mental health troubles.

The Call to Care

Remember the story of Jesus' call to discipleship of Phillip and Nathanael in John 1? All he had to say to Philip was "Follow Me," and he did. Because of his great skepticism, Jesus did not approach Nathanael directly (he knew that a direct approach might likely yield a rejection of the call). Instead, he sent his friend Philip to persuade him to "come and see" the one that Moses and the prophets wrote about. And when Nathanael came, Jesus revealed to him his best character and self-perceptions, banishing all skepticism and leading him to exclaim, "You are the son of God! You are the King of Israel!" (John 1:43–50).

Are you called to Christian counseling? Are you called by God to lead others into a life-changing encounter with the living God? Just as God calls us and uses us to help others enter into a unique healing encounter with him, Jesus used Philip to draw his skeptical friend into a life-changing encounter with Jesus Himself.

God Will Make a Way

In a sense much like Paul's words in 1 Corinthians 4:1, "Let a man so consider us, as servants of Christ and stewards of the mysteries of God," we often assert in Christian counseling that "God never wastes a wound." Although he is not the author of evil or sorrow, he is wise to use every kind of wrong suffered and dream dashed to reach out to us to grab hold of his healing hand. He is the "God of all comfort, who comforts us in all our tribulation, that we may be able to comfort those in any trouble, with the comfort with which we are comforted by God" (2 Cor. 1:3b–4).

What a glorious circle of care! God comforts us, enabling us to turn and comfort others with that same care given by God, enabling both to worship God and give to others again. We are his agents, his regents, his care-giving disciples given to a call to "bear one another's burdens, and so fulfill the law of Christ" (Gal. 6:2).

Healing power in caring relationships. We believe, then, that Christian counseling and pastoral care is grounded upon the centrality of healing relationships with both vertical and horizontal dimensions. Like all counseling, it is dyadic in its horizontal dimension between at least two persons. As truly Christian counseling, it becomes uniquely triadic due to God's presence in the vertical, supernatural dimension. In Christian counseling, the Holy Spirit is the third person in every counseling situation. Since this vertical dimension is unique to Christian counseling, it is essential that we begin healing pursuits with the relational God—with Father, Son, and Holy Spirit.

Yes, the one God existing in three persons pushes beyond the boundaries of rational thought. God in three persons is the blessed Trinity, the spiritual lifeblood through which flows the meaning of our existence. It is to this triune God that we are called—wooed to participate in an intimate, lifelong relationship—now on this earth, and forever in a heavenly eternity. Come to the Father, Son, and Holy Spirit. When we encounter one, we encounter all three. When we worship one, we worship all.

Why does God exist this way? Why does He reveal himself to humanity in this difficult and complex manner? When it is so hard to understand God even in the best of circumstances, couldn't He have made it easier to know Him? Struggling with these questions, the disciples queried Jesus in John 14:8, "Show us the Father and that will be sufficient for us."

The cynic might say that God does this to confuse and distress us with mysteries we cannot understand, puzzles we cannot unravel. The believer might assert a simpler, more direct reason: *God does this to show us the beauty and value of relationship.*

Christian counseling reflects the Trinity. We tell of this important truth about the triune God of the Bible because it is an apt analogy for the development of Christian counseling, and of Christian counselors. Moving from a one or even two-dimensional practice to a triune, or three-dimensional practice means that one is maturing as a clinician in ways that more closely reflect the God who is there.

Counseling that Is Truly Christian

Christian counseling, then, may be defined as *a triadic healing encounter with the living Christ, facilitated by a helper who assists this redemptive, healing process, helping another get unstuck and moving forward on the path to spiritual maturity and psycho-social-emotional health.*

As with everything else in our triune approach here, this definition has three distinct clauses. To be "on the path to spiritual maturity and psycho-social-emotional health," focusing on the back end first, is to be committed to becoming like Jesus himself. It states the ultimate goal of sanctification, and hints at our ultimate state of glorification. God is at work at every turn in every Christian to make him/her more like Christ. The right metaphor is marriage, not cloning or robotics. Two travel on and become one in spirit and mutual purpose, all the while retaining their distinctive personalities and identities.

Secondly, getting "unstuck and moving forward" states a fundamental reason people come into counseling in the first place. Despite being panned by some recent critics, it is nonetheless true that people seek help and come into therapy on the basis of felt needs that go unresolved by the known efforts of the client.

Finally, the clients engage the counselor to assist them to experience a "healing encounter with the living Christ." Stated another way, the client should interact with and be touched by the Healer, who is Christ. Christ comes alive through the agency of the counselor, and makes himself dependent on the invitation of the people engaged in the process.

Christian counseling facilitates a supernatural encounter between the human spirit and the Holy Spirit wherein Christ is made alive in the life of the person in a fresh and healing way. The Holy Spirit is present to bring conviction and guide us into all truth (John 16:8, 13). And in this life the Holy Spirit comforts us (Acts 9:31), renews us (Titus 3:5), convicts of sin (John 16:8) and searches all things (1 Cor. 2:10). The apostle Paul proclaimed, "Likewise the Spirit helps us in our weakness. For we do not know what to pray for as we ought, but the Spirit himself intercedes for us with groanings too deep for words. And he who searches hearts knows what is the mind of the Spirit because the Spirit intercedes for the saints according to his purpose" (Rom. 8:26–27 ESV).

Embracing a Wisdom Theology of Caregiving

As we asserted in *Competent Christian Counseling*, every counselor has a theology—and a spirituality, bio-medical theory, and psychosocial theory—that directly influences the counseling process. We believe that Christian counseling is largely deficient in its theological roots and spiritual practices. Lamenting the current state of Christian counseling in this regard, Arch Hart, one of our pioneering leaders and co-author of this book, has challenged us:

> For some time now [speaking in 2001], experts have been telling us that the stock market is due for a major correction. Already we are beginning to see the economy "cool" with stocks jumping around like a cat on a hot tin roof. Well, I have the same fears about where we are headed in some of the things we do as Christian counselors, particularly our uncritical adoption of the secular psychological concepts. We have run ahead of our theological foundations in developing our understanding of a "Christian" approach to counseling—and we are due a major correction here as well![38]

A wisdom theology of caregiving, therefore, is especially commended to counselors, as it incorporates both the creation and redemptive visions of God and is most applicable to problems in daily living (see chapter 3). Consider this value as expressed in The Wisdom of Solomon:

> I called for help, and there came to me a spirit of wisdom. I valued her above sceptre and throne, and reckoned riches as nothing beside her...I loved her more than health or beauty, I preferred her to the light of day ...So all good things together came to me with her, and in her hands was wealth beyond counting, and all was mine to enjoy, for all follows where wisdom leads.[39]

Mark McMinn recently called attention to the importance of theology in counseling when he stated: "Effective Christian counselors also consider theological perspectives at the same time that they engage in the various psychological tasks of counseling. Historical and systematic theology, biblical understanding, and Christian tradition are all valued and considered essential components of counseling."[40] Effective counselors,

in McMinn's view, are those given to "multitasking"—the ability to utilize insights and skills gained from the study of theology, psychology
and spirituality simultaneously and appropriately for the benefit of the
client.

Allen Bergin[41] and Ev Worthington,[42] among others, have clearly shown
us that we cannot divorce counseling from its moral, theological and philosophical roots. All counseling and psychotherapy—especially that which
denies it—is deeply values-based. This makes it a given that we are all
doing theology when we practice counseling. The obvious questions, then,
are these: Are we doing theology well? Is the theology we are doing biblical
theology or bad theology?

Counselor competence is greatly enhanced when we build from a solid
theological foundation, for at theology's core is the study of God Himself.
Our hope is that Christian counselors will learn and impart to their clients a
living, caring, and experiential theology—revealing the truth of His Person
and His desire for relationship with us. Answering these questions and
reflecting upon the significance of the answers for counseling will provide
the structure for the rest of this chapter.[43]

Caring Enough to Challenge Transforming Change

A very significant area of study and debate in counseling today surrounds
the issue of change. Questions abound, like, What is meaningful change?
What is the true goal of counseling? Is it self-actualization? Helping people
become less dysfunctional? Cultivating more self-awareness? Becoming
unstuck? Getting in touch with the inner self? Personal congruence?
Enlightenment? If you have studied psychology you could probably easily
add to this list.

Most outcome research studies, however, simply hinge on symptom
reduction. An example would be; Johnny started out smoking two packs of
cigarettes a day and now only smokes one. While noble, change also needs
to go deeper and affect key issues of the heart. This is where the importance
of redeemed relationships and transforming change, versus change as mere
adjustment or "coped-with" relationships, spills over into our understanding of Christian counseling as caring ministry. A major challenge to Christian therapists is the incorporation of a biblical spirituality into counseling—

yielding ourselves and our work to the lordship of Christ in the counseling goal and process.

Yet we would also assert that counseling, by itself, is not enough. To revise, slightly, the language of Carl Rogers, counseling models that do not consciously set Christ at the center may be useful to some degree, but are insufficient models because clinically we have all encountered persons who, after years of work, are still stuck, still oppressed. There are many people who will not be freed without a healing *encounter* with the living God through the Holy Spirit. And most importantly, we assert true freedom only comes through faith in Christ.

Christ-empowered change, which can be understood as the power in counseling and psychotherapy, is transformative. It is not merely the process by which adaptive forces are placed in greater harmony, but the process by which "new life" itself is discovered and applied to one's existence.

Theologically, James Edwards has made a cogent case on the scandal of the Incarnation. Jesus—God come in the flesh—not only scandalizes the world and the acceptance of Christianity among the panoply of comparative religions, it is a scandal in the church itself. He argues that much of the church—in order to make the Christian gospel more palatable to the non-Christian world—shifts to and adopts a creation, rather than a redemptive theology.

A creation theology alone, in its acceptance of the natural order as God's created design, essentially denies sin and the need for a transforming redemption of the human personality. In this subtle sophistry, what is good and therefore must be affirmed and celebrated—redemption from sin and a Christ-transformed life—are not needed, nor are they wanted in a sin-denying/Jesus-rejecting world.

However, when God is truly present in counseling, sin can be redemptively accepted and honestly disclosed—as the Holy Spirit leads us. Wounds and traumas that still bind us—things we thought were resolved or that we simply live in denial about—can be revealed and washed away in supernatural healing. Jesus is magnified and glorified, and is known to us as a fellow sufferer and divine lover. God Himself is transformed in our perceptions of Him, becoming a divine object of attraction, rather than One of fear and avoidance. All things are genuinely possible when God is present in Christian counseling.

Caring vs. Curing

Systemically, in the same way that medicine is better balancing the demands of acute care and chronic care in the treatment of disease, Christian counseling must learn to do the same with its bio-psycho-social-spiritual interventions. In other words, we must learn to become much more focused on caring than solely on curing in our ministry work.

Of course, this is not a screed against counseling as a curative process. To be sure, many client problems are curable and will never beset that person again. This is especially true—and is far more possible in Christian counseling—because of the miraculous power of Christ. In fact, in this book we explicitly incorporate the necessity for supernatural healing encounters with the Holy Spirit as an essential part of true Christian counseling.

However, some of the issues that clients bring to us—including our dedicated Christian clients—are repetitive and long-term problems that appear over and over again in different contexts and at different times in the life of the client. While this borders on the definition of personality disorders (and personality quirks pushed to extremes by severe stress do exhibit many of these disorders), our point here is to acknowledge the chronic nature of many of the problems that are brought to us in counseling.

Problem chronicity demands a different approach, something other than the curative orientation of acute medicine. It demands a coping and caregiving approach that teaches problem management instead of cure. Theologically, this is about recognizing that we still live in a fallen world, and that sanctification should not be confused with glorification—as it often is in so much Christian advertising and book marketing. It is not the event of being made perfect by a major miraculous encounter with the risen Christ. It is about recognizing the distinction between acute and chronic care—that chronic pain, like the ongoing struggle for sanctification, has a quite different treatment from that applied to acute pain.

For example, most of the cases of depression that you will see will be seen again by you or someone else. For most sufferers, depression is a recurrent, even lifelong problem that erupts time and again at different junctures of living. Same with many anxiety disorders, social phobias, addictions, and anger and impulse control disorders. And, believe it or not, this is true with most of the Christians you will see in counseling, and in the church.

Moreover, our curative theology must change. Many Christians falsely believe that accepting a chronic understanding of a disorder is tantamount to a failed faith—even to a denial of Christ Himself. It is cure or nothing, as any alternative to a curative approach denies the power and desire of Christ to heal—and to heal now. We do not agree that this is a failed faith, but a failed hermeneutic, a distorted understanding of Scripture that is often reinforced by a "Pollyannish" view of God, and a "too magical" expectation about living. We certainly believe in soul healing but we also acknowledge that God sometimes chooses not to heal or that the healing comes in and through the pain.

Sanctification is a lifelong process of being made incrementally more like Christ as we travel the high road of Christian maturation. Or to state it from the negative reality: every one of us has chronic problems—including chronic sin problems—as detailed by Paul in Romans 7, that we will battle with at various stages throughout our lives. Also, the author of Hebrews (12:1) writes that we strive to "throw off everything that hinders and the sin that so easily entangles."

Therefore, much counseling has to do with problem management or reduction. To state this positively, much Christian counseling has to do with learning and applying the principles of kingdom living to the chronically recurring sins, fears, failures, and dark areas of our life.

The Foundation and Scope of this Book

We establish, once again in this book, the authoritative foundations for competent Christian counseling. For our purposes, in this book and in this library series, this authority is grounded on these four sources:

1. The revelation of God in Christ Jesus. Jesus is our Wonderful Counselor and the model for both therapist and client of that which calls us to maturity and excellence in life and in ministry. He is the Way, the Truth, and the Life, the guide upon whom we ground all our work as Christian counselors.

2. The preeminent role of the Bible (Old and New Testaments) and Scriptural truth as the final authority and primary revealer of Christ, of God's redemptive story on planet Earth, and his purpose for humankind, both individually and corporately.

3. The important, though secondary role of science and logic and also of history in the development of Christian counseling, as in all counseling.

4. The person of the counselor, including the training, experience, and credentials of the therapist. The helper's character and orientation to counseling, including primary values and ethical commitments, are central determinants in facilitating consistent, constructive, and ethical client change.

Therefore, as we did in *Competent Christian Counseling*, this work also melds together and takes further:

1. The foundations and teachings of Scripture, salted with the writings of the giants of church history on spiritual formation and pastoral care, with
2. some of the very latest research, theory, and practice in Christian counseling, in the broader fields of counseling and psychotherapy, and in the bio-psycho-social sciences, to
3. construct a biblically-based, strength-oriented, Spirit-directed, 21st century meta-model of Christian counseling—a model that is "counselor friendly," is effective in facilitating change, and is geared to help people mature in the ways and wisdom of Jesus Christ.

We also asserted in *The Soul Care Bible* that the church should become—that it is called by God and has the best people to be—a spiritual hospital in the best sense of that term: "The church is critical to the care and solace of those suffering with mental disorders. These people are very often isolated, fearful, confused, and in need of unconditional love of Christians to repair and return to vital living."[44]

This book, then, is not just about caring for people well, but *caring for people God's way*—the way revealed in the person and love of Jesus Christ. It is our hope—our prayer that goes out with this book—that you who are Christian counselors and pastors would renew your commitment to sacrificial love in service to hurting souls. We cannot do it alone, nor merely in the power of our own energies and desires.

By the Holy Spirit and bound together in Christ, however, it can and will be done. Be part of a redemptive revolution in this new millennium. It may not make the work of ministry any easier, but it surely will be a wonderful ride that bears great fruit for the kingdom of Christ.

Conclusion

Years ago the liberal religious magazine *Christian Century* told two stories of mainline church pastors who were transformed by Christ and became, in their words, "post-liberals." Embedded in both stories was the delightful telling of their conversions to Christ through their work in pastoral care, and the discovery of the wonder and power of the Scriptures. What you find in the stories are conversions to Christ that evince his healing love and wonder-working power.

These pastors became Christians as they witnessed Christ come alive in caring ministry to people who cried out for God's touch. Though we are committed evangelicals we recognize that God is at work mightily in the world far beyond evangelical boundaries. Whether Catholic, Orthodox, or Protestant "post-liberal," the church is being challenged by Christ himself and Christian counseling is called to serve it in all its varieties.

So then, let us renounce any dedications to dead religious formalism or hot new psychological programs and, instead, renew our relationships with the God of power and wonder. Jesus promised us that this kind of love freely given to the most wounded and desperate lives will move a jaded culture that has largely abandoned the Truth.

Christian counseling is wonderful, maddening, joyous work. Those called to walk with and serve the hurting are sometimes overwhelmed, often confused, and occasionally avoidant of walking committedly in this calling. We understand this because we ourselves know this joy and are beset, at times, with these very same struggles.

The wonder of it all is that Jesus sends the Spirit—all the time and in every way—to comfort us and to set us free of ourselves. Truly, our real life—and that of our clients and parishioners—is hidden with Christ in God. If we look for it, He always reveals it. Finding Him in the midst of every counseling situation—meeting Him in the midst of every need—is what this book is about.

ENDNOTES

1. Earnest Becker, *The denial of death* (New York: The Free Press, 1973).
2. Dallas Willard, *The spirit of the disciplines: Understanding how God changes lives* (San Francisco: Harper and Row, 1988), viii.

3. Population Reference Bureau, 2000 census data—living arrangements profile for United States, *Analysis of Data from the U.S. Census Bureau, for The Annie E. Casey Foundation.*

4. The Barna Group, Born again Christians just as likely to divorce as non-Christians, *The Barna Update* (8 September 2004) [journal online]; available from <http://www.barna.org.

5. Judith S. Wallerstein and Sandra Blakeslee, *The good marriage: How & why love lasts* (New York: Houghton Mifflin Company, 1995), 6.

6. Scott Stanley, Personal communication.

7. The Barna Group, Born again Christians just as likely to divorce as non-Christians, *The Barna Update,*(8 September 2004).

8. David Blackenhorn, *Fatherless America: Confronting our most urgent social problem* (New York: BasicBooks, 1995).

9. Rebecca O'Neill, *Experiments in living: The fatherless family,*<http://www.civitas.org.: The Institute for the Study of Civil Society, September 2002; The National Center for Fathering, *National surveys on fathers and fathering,* http://www.fathers.com/research/.

10. The National Center for Fathering, *The consequences of fatherlessness,* <http://www.fathers.com/research/consequences.html>.

11. D. Finkelhor, Hotaling, G., Lewis, I. A., and Smith, C., Sexual abuse in a national survey of adult men and women: Prevalence, characteristics, and risk factors, *Child abuse & neglect 14,* 19–28, (1990); C. Bagley, Development of a measure of unwanted sexual contact in childhood, for use in community mental health surveys," *Psychological Reports, 66,* 401–2 (1990).

12. National Center for Injury Prevention and Control, *Sexual violence: Fact sheet* (April 2005), <http://www.cdc.gov/ncipc/factsheets/svfacts.htm>.

13. National Center for Injury Prevention and Control, *Intimate partner violence: fact sheet* (November 2004), <http://www.cdc.gov/ncipc/factsheets/ipvfacts.htm>.

14. Shawn Christopher Shea, *The practical art of suicide assessment: A guide for mental health professionals and substance abuse counselors* (New York: John Wiley & Sons, Inc, 1999), 6.

15. National Institute of Mental Health, *In harm's way: Suicide in America* (2003), <http://www.nimh.nih.gov/publicat/harmaway.cfm>.

16. Shea, *The practical art of suicide assessment,*6.

17. National Center for Chronic Disease Prevention and Health Promotion, *General alcohol information* (September 2004), <http://www.cdc.gov/alcohol/factsheets/general_information.htm>.

18. National Center for Health Statistics, Health, United States, 2004: With chartbook on trends in the health of Americans(Hyattsville, Maryland: Author, 2004).

19. Lynn F. Ranew and D. A. Serritella, *Handbook of differential treatments for addictions* (Allyn and Bacon, 1992), 85.

20. Ibid.

21. Ranew and Serritella, *Handbook of differential treatments for addictions,* 33.

22. Archibald D. Hart and C. H. Weber, *Unveiling depression in women: A practical guide to understanding and overcoming depression* (Grand Rapids, MI: Fleming H. Revell, 2002), 23.

23. Hart and Weber, *Unveiling depression in women,* 23.

24. *Margaret Strock, et al., Depression,* National Institute of Health publication No. 00–3561 (2000): (originally published 1994 *as* Plain talk about depression) [journal online]; available from <http://www.nimh.nih.gov/publicat/depression.cfm.

25. National Institute of Mental Health, *Anxiety*, http://www.nimh.nih.gov/publi-cat/anxiety.cfm#anx1: (Author, 2000); Archibald Hart, *The anxiety cure: You can find emotional tranquility and wholeness* (United States: W Publishing Group, 1999); N. Short and N. Kitchner, Panic disorder: Nature assessment and treatment, *Continuing professional development*, Royal College of Nursing 5(7) (April 2002).

26. Carol M. Christensen, *Power over panic: Answers for anxiety* (Colorado Springs: Life Journey, 2003), 17.

27. J. Lee and L. Dade, The buck stops where? What is the role of the emergency physician in managing panic disorder in chest pain patients? *Journal of the Canadian Association of Emergency Physicians*, 5(4), (2003), 237–238; Hart, *The anxiety cure*; Short and Kitchner, Panic disorder: Nature assessment and treatment.

28. R. C. Kessler et al., The epidemiology of major depressive disorder: Results from the national comorbidity survey replication (NCS-R), *JAMA*, 289, (2003), 3095–3105.

29. A. E. Bergin and J. P. Jensen, Religiosity of psychotherapists: A national survey, *Psychotherapy*, 27, (1990), 3–7.

30. E. W. Kelly, *Religion and spirituality in counseling and psychotherapy* (Alexandria, VA: American Counseling Association, 1995).

31. Kessler et al., The epidemiology of major depressive disorder, 3095–3105.

32. Ibid.

33. Jeffrey Weiss, Wounded heroes, *The Dallas News* (7 March, 1998), <http://www.dallasnews.com>.

34. Ibid.

35. Charles Colson, "Wanted: Christians who love, *Christianity Today* (1995, October 2), 112.

36. George Gallup Jr. and T. Jones, *The next American spirituality: Finding God in the twenty-first century* (Colorado Springs, CO: Victor/Cook Communications, 2000).

37. George Gallup Jr., *The next American spirituality: Finding God in the twenty-first century* (USA: Chariot Victor Publishers, 2000).

38. Archibald Hart, Has self-esteem lost its way? *Christian Counseling Today* 9(1) (2001), 8.

39. The Wisdom of Solomon.

40. Mark R. McMinn, *Psychology, theology, and spirituality in Christian counseling* (Tyndale, 1996), 270.

41. A. E. Bergin, Values and religious issues in psychotherapy and mental health, *American Psychologist*, 46, (1991), 394–403.

42. Everett Worthington, Understanding the values of religious clients: A model and its application to counseling, *Journal of Counseling Psychology* 35(2) (1988), 166–174.

43. See R. Hawkins et al., in Timothy Clinton and G. Ohlschlager, *Competent Christian counseling, volume one: Foundations and practice of compassionate soul care* (Colorado Springs: WaterBrook, 2002).

44. Paul Meier, T. Clinton, and G. Ohlschlager, Mental illness: Reducing suffering in the church, *The Soul Care Bible*. (Nashville: Thomas Nelson, 2001), 364–365.

2

The Person of the Counselor:
Growing in Knowledge, Character, and Skill

Tim Clinton, George Ohlschlager, and Anthony J. Centore

As counselors, we should convene our sessions deeply aware of how
dependent we are on divine wisdom. We all live in a fallen world...

RON HAWKINS, IN *Competent Christian Counseling*[1]

I hadn't seen Eileen for nearly a year, so I was delighted when she called to
come back into counseling. Eileen had been a model client. She worked
diligently to understand her problem and her situation. She was intent to
incorporate and learn from my insights and interpretations, and was
always polite and thankful about gains she had made. The problem was
that she really didn't get any better.

She had come into counseling complaining of depression, anxiety, and
other symptoms that looked like a classic case of SAD—seasonal affective
disorder. Since she could trace the onset of tail-spin symptoms from
November onward the two previous years, I was convinced the diagnosis
was a no-brainer.

As a mild SAD sufferer myself who has struggled with it for numerous
winters, I was confident in both my assessment and treatment plan. Eileen
purchased a set of UV lights to work under in the evening, simplified and
focused her life, worked effectively at scrubbing some toxic "depresso-

genic" thinking out of her self-talk, and was praying and growing closer to the Lord in all this. She was doing everything right—and, I thought, so was I—but *she wasn't getting well.*

In fact, as the winter wore on, she complained of worsening depression and anxiety. I knew that anxiety was present in most depressive episodes, and, being the resourceful counselor I like to think I am, I thought I was dealing with a treatment-resistant form of depression that underlay the SAD disorder. I did what most good counselors do in this situation—I punted and referred Eileen to a local psychiatrist.

The psychiatrist diagnosed Eileen with a recurrent major depression, and a SAD disorder only secondarily. She prescribed Serzone, a stronger antidepressant that worked both serotonin and dopamine receptors in the brain. Eileen dutifully began the medication, worked through her body's adjustment to it, and showed some improvement in about two weeks. Now we were getting at the core of it—and it looked like a biological disorder at its root!

After a couple more sessions, Eileen's HMO benefits ran out and she decided to end counseling with me. We reviewed her progress—and lack of it—and Eileen was extremely grateful for all the help I had given her. We didn't discuss the nagging question that seemed to be in the back of both of our minds—that we were missing something. I think we still weren't quite sure what was going on—but, hey, we couldn't afford such expensive speculations anyway.

When she came in again, I was amazed how healthy and alive she was. My first thought was so self-inflated—that I really had helped her the year before, and the fruit of that work was shining a healthy glow in her face. She was happy to see me again and thanked me all over for the work that we had done together. I then queried what she had come in for, thinking there were some loose ends or unresolved issues that she was now ready to work on.

No, she replied, she had merely come to tell me what happened that last year—what the problem really was. That summer she had cleaned out an old storage room in her basement and had found stachybotris—black mold—covering most of a wall behind a large storage shelf. During the winter, when she had her house closed up, the heating system provoked mold growth and carried its microscopic spores throughout the house.

Eileen had been sick with black mold poisoning—something that, just like the course of SAD, got progressively worse as winter carried on—and cleared up each spring when she opened up her house. Eileen had the mold removed professionally and repainted her storage room—presto, mold gone and no more trouble.

I was dumbstruck as she told her story. I must have looked quite guilty, because at one point she stopped and said, "George, no, I'm not blaming you! If anyone is at fault it's my doctor and the psychiatrist who are probably most responsible for missing it. But I don't blame anyone here—who knew??!"

Who knew, indeed! This episode taught me that, as a clinician, it's more than what you know and don't know that counts for competence. Sometimes it's what you think you know that, in fact, you really don't.

The pearl-of-conclusive-wisdom to be drawn here is this: stay humble and be tentative about what you think you know in counseling. Just when you start to think you have it all figured out—that you're an expert and ready to start writing books on the subject—*bang*, along comes someone whom God uses to bring you down a few pegs on the humility scale. Life and counseling for that matter, are so complex, so full of mystery that over-confident assurance can be just as wrong, just as toxic for your patients as ignorance and a lack of confidence.

Becoming a Trustworthy Christian Counselor

As one studies and spends time doing counseling, it doesn't take long to learn that one of the most important ingredients in the counseling relationship is the counselor him- or herself. While empirical data now shows that client variables are most potent in affecting outcome, the counselor and the quality of the counselor-client relationship follows closely.[2] As a counselor, what you believe, how you feel and act, what you do and don't do, matters—a lot. Hence, building an effective caring and counseling ministry starts with you.

The essence of Christian counseling, as are all things Christian, is hidden in the person of Christ (Col. 1:26–27). The challenge of Matthew 22:42 (KJV) must be clearly understood and embraced by those who would call themselves a Christian counselor, "What think ye of Christ? Whose son is he?" It is a wonderful and, at times, elusive knowledge this revelation of Christ Himself, but one that is freely given to us when we seek it earnestly (Matt. 7:7–11). And our greatest calling/responsibility is to take Paul's words to heart as we seek to counsel: "follow my example, as I follow the example of Christ" (1 Cor. 11:1). We labor to outline this essence—the essence of Christ the caregiver—in this chapter, as well as the process by which Christian counseling works *in and through the person of the counselor.*

We do this so that Christian counselors are guided by a "road map" that helps them serve those in need in a way that honors Christ and brings unity to the church. This tall order we see as an important centralizing goal—in no way do we presume to fulfill it with this book or those that follow. We endeavor to be catalysts, acknowledging our small part in a growing field, pointing the way and encouraging action that will bring the ministry-movement to a fuller maturity.

Developing a Personal Style for Counseling Ministry

Making sense of all the counseling information, theories, and techniques now available; shaping them into a useful treatment approach, and applying it effectively and consistently in the lives of hurting people requires the adoption of a counseling model that is intensely personal at its core. As a counselor, "you can't treat what you don't see" and "you can't see what you don't understand." Therefore, cultivating a meaningful counseling relationship and process that answers core questions like "What works for this client, with this problem, in this situation, at this time in his life with you as the counselor under the direction of the Holy Spirit," is the challenge of your time together.

In fact, in the practice of ministry with people expecting or wanting change, the theoretical must be transformed into the personal. Clients are usually unwilling or are not interested in exploring the nuances and ramifications of some theoretical position that you, as a counselor, have embraced and are high about. Rather, they merely want to know "will this work for me and mine?"

On the other hand, they are almost always interested in you as a counselor—what you do, and say, and believe, which as we stated earlier really does affect counseling outcome. Constructing a personal model or style of intervention is a developmental process that every counselor must engage in to be fruitful in one's work.

Foundations of Christian Counseling

One cannot delegate responsibility without authority. How does a counselor establish a position of strength and authority in counseling? It all starts with a sure foundation—a foundation built on the Bible and cultivating an eternal perspective.

Scripture first. The foundation for Truth is given to us in the Bible—the standard by which everything else is evaluated. Second Timothy 3:16 boldly declares that "all Scripture is given to us by inspiration of the Holy Spirit and is profitable for teaching, for reproof, for correction and for training in righteousness."

Further, 2 Peter 1:3 reminds that "His divine power has granted to us all things that pertain to life and godliness, through the knowledge of him who called us to his own glory and excellence." If we are going to help people break free in this life, we start by knowing that "they are darkened in their understanding and separated from the life of God because of the ignorance that is in them due to the hardening of their hearts" (Eph. 4:18). Hence, new life is tied directly to one's relationship with God in Christ and that "the fear of the Lord is the beginning of wisdom" (Prov. 9:10).

The journey then becomes a life of faith that focuses on the washing and renewing of our minds and "destroying arguments and every lofty opinion raised against the knowledge of God, and to take every thought captive to the obedience of Christ" (2 Cor. 10:5). His way is not ours. Why? Because as Proverbs 16:25 declares, we naturally follow after our own ways and not necessarily God's ways: "There is a way that seemeth right unto a man but the ends thereof are the ways of death."

Hence an effective system for responsible Christian counseling involves the Chalcedonian pattern of logic. This occupies three features:

1. Two terms are placed in a relationship where they exist unaltered and autonomous.
2. The terms are related so that they coexist inseparably.
3. One term is deemed logically prior, given authority over the other.

When two disciplines conflict on some point (such as psychology and theology) the logically prior discipline (theology) prevails. For example, considering the purpose of prayer, in practice secular psychology often overrules theology (wrongly) and prayer is used primarily as a means to request healing.[3]

By using the Chalcedonian model, prayer is brought back to its proper (theological) main purpose—communion with God. One of the great dangers here would involve both disciplines—where truth is tainted by our fallible interpretations and understanding of it. The wise counselor will approach the pursuit of truth with both a spirit of expectation and humility.

Eternal perspective. Christians must also approach the counseling relationship with an eternal perspective of life, and of hope in Christ. Psalm 42:5 evinces this point: "Why are you downcast, O my soul? Why so disturbed within me? Put your hope in God, for I will yet praise him, my Savior..."

As Christians we believe that if a person struggles with emotional disorders, that the Lord is "near unto the brokenhearted and saves the crushed in spirit" (Prov. 34:18 ESV) whether in this life or in the one to come. However, if one dies without Christ the consequences are eternally devastating. As Christian workers, we wish to create better people on earth, so that they may serve God more fully. However, we do not wish to promote better-adjusted people at the expense of their salvation, or by denying their need for sanctifying growth.

A war of the mind and spirit. Christian counseling, in large part, is a war for the mind. Failure identity and negative thinking lead one with a serious drinking problem to think "I am an alcoholic" versus the truth "I am a child of God who struggles with alcoholism." Of course, we do not mean to minimize that man presents a fallen sin nature. First John 1:8 tells us, "If we say we have no sin we are deceiving ourselves and the truth is not in us."

However, there is a serious difference, as theologians teach, between *having* a sin problem and *being* sin (Col. 2:6–10; Rom. 6:11; Gal. 5:16; Eph. 1:18). This is an important distinction for Christian counselors. If we accept the theology that our clients *are* sin, there is no helping them. However, as we correctly show our clients that they are created in the image and glory of God and that sin is something that mars that image, help becomes a process of aiding a client to repent, accept forgiveness, and mature as a child of God.

Roles and Characteristics of Effective Counselors

As the counseling movement has matured and expanded, so have counselor roles and responsibilities. The following list is a general overview of the numerous roles in our modern-day profession:

1. Counselor—Although this word can be ambiguous, having multiple meanings (i.e. see wardrobe counseling), counseling generally focuses on helping clients navigate problem issues: relational, behavioral, spiritual, or emotional.

2. Consultant—Often understood as the role of an "expert guide," here a counselor helps the client to troubleshoot a situation or make important life decisions.

3. Teacher—Sometimes known as "psycho-education," teaching is a significant part of the helping process. With teaching, the counselor imparts insight into a client's issues and strategies for coping (i.e. answers to the questions "What is stress?" and "How can I decrease my stress?"). With Christian counseling, teaching also encompasses presenting solid biblical truths.

4. Supervisor—This is a professional-to-professional relationship where counselors participate in "peer-supervision," or it is where an experienced counselor oversees, and is held liable for, the practice and progress of a novice counselor.

5. Researcher—The practice of research is what allows counselors to know whether what they are doing is working, and is an empirical method of discovering the Truth of God. Research is what promotes positive revisions in counseling treatments, to meet changing contemporary needs for care.

Motivations for Becoming a Counselor

Counseling, as a profession, usually attracts kind and noble persons.[4] Healthy motivators for one pursuing a career in counseling, or a lay counseling ministry, include the desire to help others and a perceived "calling" that is confirmed by a body of Christian believers. However, not everyone in counseling is motivated by such pure desires; even the better counselors usually show a mixture of noble and not-so-noble motivations for their pursuits.

Therefore, before one makes the decision to pursue the practice of counseling, a prospective counselor is wise to complete some self-exploration. If you are considering a counseling ministry, a few of the major introspective questions include:

1. Do I have any unresolved personal issues I should "work on" before attempting to become a counselor?
2. Am I spiritually grounded and mature enough to lead others to a place of spiritual maturity?
3. Am I willing to be open, dependable, compassionate, and generally nonjudgmental—even when clients frustrate me?
4. Am I willing to repeatedly expose myself to the stress that is intrinsic to the counseling process?
5. Am I willing to provide care to clients that I do not like, and do I offer Christlike compassion when I struggle with those that I intensely dislike?
6. Do I understand that not everyone will improve through counseling?
7. Am I willing to undertake the necessary preparation, training, and supervision?
8. Am I willing to participate in ongoing continuing education for as long as I practice counseling?

Personality and Spirit

A Christian counselor's success depends on several distinguishing characteristics including personality, spiritual gifts, professional training, commitment to the gospel, and biblical worldview.

Personality. Regarding personal qualities, an effective counselor will often possess:

- a natural interest in and compassion for people[5]
- emotional intelligence and the ability to accurately assess feelings
- the facility to engage a variety of persons in conversation
- a disposition that allows one to listen well

- an understanding and mastery of empathy
- meaningful introspection and self-reflection
- the capacity to suspend one's personal needs to help others
- the ability to tolerate relational intimacy (therapeutic alliance)
- the ability to lessen, not increase, a client's anxiety
- the ability to establish healthy boundaries
- the aptitude to not let counseling relationships adversely affect the counselor's home life
- unwavering ethics and integrity

Spiritual gifts. It is true that God has equipped some people with gifts to be counselors (1 Cor. 12:7), and this calling is good motivation to become a counselor. However, as one writer states, "people helping is everybody's business,"[6] each of us has the ability through meaningful, empathic relationships to help someone every day of our lives.

Professional or other counselor training. Christian counselors, to truly be equipped, must be knowledgeable about a wide variety of topics and issues. They must be educated toward understanding the many needs and complaints that are prevalent today, as well as their treatment. This means formal education and specialized clinical trainings for anyone desiring to practice as a mental health professional. For the lay helper in church-based ministry, it demands some degree of structured training in basic helping skills and process to properly direct the gift that has already shown forth.

Second, for the helping professional particularly, one's training should involve learning how to see contemporary mental health issues in the light of Christian theology. Third, continuing education is key for a Christian counselor to stay current with his/her counseling approach! It is not only our strong recommendation—it is an important ethical standard.

Commitment to the gospel. Remember, the goal of Christian counseling is the restoration of the image of God in man, and maturity in Christ. Unlike secular psychology, the elimination of suffering is not necessarily the end-all of life's objective. Christian counselors must be dedicated not only to helping clients heal their emotional, maladaptive, and social problems, but also to restoring clients' relationship with God.

Biblical worldview. This characteristic involves an awareness of life and the world including, especially, the nature of the eternal, spiritual world as presented in Scripture. A discerning counselor accepts the truth about good and evil in the world, is able to clearly discriminate one from the other, engages in genuine warfare with the "enemy," and is willing and prepared to seek the Holy Spirit's guidance in the counseling process. The expert counselor also shows the facility to bring forth good fruit, and the wisdom to know when to convict and admonish, or when to comfort a client.

First Timothy 3:2–4 list qualities of a pastor that would benefit a Christian counselor. The character qualities, social relations, and circumspect behavior of a Christian leader are all noted herein:

> Now the overseer must be above reproach, the husband of but one wife, temperate, self-controlled, respectable, hospitable, able to teach, not given to drunkenness, not violent but gentle, not quarrelsome, not a lover of money. He must manage his own family well and see that his children obey him with proper respect.

A comprehensive biblical worldview also involves a clear and useful understanding of natural revelation—respect and facility with the world of science. This encompasses all useful knowledge of human emotions, thoughts, relationships, and physiology, as presented in clinical research, and is discussed in more depth later.

Integrating training, experience and character. This involves the amalgamation of one's scriptural knowledge and clinical education with practice. In metaphor, experience is the bridge between the understanding of art theory and creating great art.

Great art for Christian counselors is using biblically sound, research-based treatments at the right time, in the right way, with the right client. Moreover, it is encouraging the supernatural healing touch of God in counseling—fully expressing both sides of the Parakaleo philosophy, which is the ability to both admonish and give comfort as need requires. Lastly, great art is reinforcing a commitment bond with clients, building and maintaining strong rapport from intake to termination—and beyond.

The Interpersonal Environment

While there are many counseling approaches, theories, and techniques, and while the way a counselor engages a client will be influenced by situation and presenting needs, there is a series of core conditions for establishing an effective environment that are almost universally seen as important in the counseling relationship.[7]

Genuineness. In order to be effective, a counselor must live out the change he/she desires to see in a client. For example, a counselor with anger problems is not in suitable condition to counsel a client to better manage anger. Moreover, a counselor who is not living out his/her faith in Christ is not spiritually prepared to participate in Christian counseling (as a counselor, that is).

Warmth. This characteristic is simply necessary to promote a sense of comfort in the client. A counselor who comes off cold or abrasive will be ineffective in establishing relationship or rapport with those seeking help. Without rapport, the core of the counseling alliance is void.

Positive regard. Though this differs from the secular concept of "unconditional positive regard" where anything the client believes, desires, or does is acceptable, positive regard should be given universally to the *client as a person* created in the image of God. This is widely known as the principle of hating the sin, loving the sinner. In addition, Christian counselors need to know when to "hold off" on conviction for a time, and simply console and show compassion for a hurting client.

Support and challenge. There is an intricate balance of supporting clients through the "tough stuff" they are dealing with, while at the same time challenging their destructive beliefs and sinful choices. Counselors must strive to find a healthy balance in their relationship with clients; one where a client can approach the counselor with confession and feel *supported*, while at the same time be *moved to grow* in a healthy, Christlike direction.

Core Skills in Counseling Care

In *Competent Christian Counseling* we promoted 1 Thessalonians 5:14–18 as the penultimate biblical statement of Christian counseling:

> And we urge you, brothers, warn those who are idle, encourage the timid, help the weak, be patient with everyone. Make sure that nobody pays back wrong for wrong, but always try to be kind to each other and to everyone else. Be joyful always; pray continually; and give thanks in all circumstances, for this is God's will for you in Christ Jesus.

This extraordinarily powerful mandate should be the motto of every Christian counselor. In fact, when taken back to the full color of the Greek language this passage incorporates every Greek term that denotes the helping endeavor in the Scriptures, and reflects the many dimensions of counseling today:

Urge (*parakaleo*): Literally meaning to call to one's side, and incorporates a wider range of responsive behaviors in counseling, traveling among and between "comforting," "consoling," "encouraging," and "beseeching" or "admonishing."

Warn (*noutheteo*): Coming from the root meaning "mind," it is the seat of consciousness that includes "understanding," "feeling," "judging," and "determining." It is characterized by a confrontational style of directive challenge to root out sin and follow the right path.

Encourage (*paramutheomai*): Means to "comfort," "soothe," "console," or "encourage;" especially in connection with someone experiencing deep grief.

Help (*antechomai*): Refers to holding up or supporting someone who is weak and in deep need of assistance; to support something very fragile.

Be patient (*makrothumeo*): Literally meaning "long-tempered," this carries the idea of "forbearing," "suffering," and "enduring." It connotes the idea that we tend to be impatient and expect too much too quickly from those engaged in the change challenge.

Several other "core skills" of Christian counseling that are compatible with the theme of this passage include the following:

Active listening. Have you ever shared your heart with someone and it seemed his or her mind was a million miles away from you? In contrast, known also as "effective listening," active listening is a process where the counselor contains his/her biases, inner-conflicts, and disagreements as he or she focuses completely on the client. Active listening involves:

- verbal and nonverbal expressions to encourage the client to tell his/her story
- withholding of judgment (or revulsion) even while the client presents disquieting information
- attending to both what the client is saying and what the client is omitting (the ability to accomplish this will increase with training and experience)

- attending to a client's nonverbal communication and emotional themes
- waiting out moments of silence

Attending. This means to provide undivided attention to the counselee. In addition, the counselor attends by maintaining an open posture, eye contact (without staring), forward lean, and courteous gestures that assure the client the counselor is "present" in the counseling session.

Empathic response. This is responding to the client's dialogue in a way that reframes what the client has said and that focuses on the emotion being communicated. This assures the client that you are understanding what he/she shares in session, and it also provides the client with the therapeutic opportunity to hear his/her story told from another perspective.

Probing. This is the process of asking questions for the purpose of deepening the content of the therapeutic encounter (skills will greatly increase with continuing education and training). Probes often begin with the words *who, what, where, when,* or *how* (though not generally *why*) and should be designed in a way that the counselee can provide extensive feedback from a single query (i.e., When did you first feel depressed?).

Goal setting. Deciding the specific objective(s) of the counseling relationship: includes developing a course of action, and using research-supported biblically-based methods to lead the client from his/her current condition to a more functional, healthy, Christ-centered state.

Pitfalls and Ineffective Care

Robert Kellemen in his recent work *Soul Physicians* provides a vignette called "The Tale of Two Counselors" where two professionals are both ineffective in treatment of a client for different reasons. The first counselor (a pastoral counselor), after a client sobbingly tells him about the sexual abuse he endured at the hand of an uncle, responds with a 30 minute sermon on the client's sinfulness. The second (a professional Christian counselor) was equally ineffective, responding with empathy and compassion, but lacking any skills in helping the client "move forward" or deal pragmatically with his present relationship problems.[8]

Counseling is not simple, and there are many ways a counselor can go wrong in the (what should be) therapeutic process. Some mistakes are rooted in the motivation of the counselor, others in the counselor's approach.

Poor motivators for prospective counselors. Individuals become counselors for one of two reasons; either they wish to help others, or they wish to help themselves overcome their own issues. Most often it is a combination of the two. Prospective Christian counselors should examine their motivations for desiring to minister through the practice of counseling.

Simply put, Christian counselors must evince both emotional health and spiritual maturity to be effective. Even with proper education—or a clinical license—not everyone is prepared to serve as a counselor. Following are a few of the common pitfalls, motivators common to persons who decide to practice counseling.

1. *Hunger for Relationships:* Counselors must have their intimacy needs filled adequately if they intend to help clients with their interrelational problems. If a counselor is motivated by a need for intimacy, he/she will be inclined to use relationships with clients to fill emotional emptiness.

2. *Having a Messiah Complex:* Counselors (often novice counselors) believe they can heal everyone. This unfortunately is not the case. As a counselor you may find that some clients may not even like you and do not improve much, or at all. As a counselor, there may be areas that are not strengths for you. Learning to refer to another counselor, or even an inpatient program, then becomes a sign of maturity, not weakness. Hence, counselors need to accept their limits, and at times the limits of the counseling process.

3. *Needing to Have Control or Power:* For one desiring power or control over others, counseling is not the proper profession. Effective counselors operate under the premise that clients have rights and ultimately need to be in control of their own lives. Also, counseling is generally a collaborative process that operates upon a foundation of mutuality and collegiality, one not governed by the counselor as ultimate "authority."

4. *Living Vicariously:* Parents often try to live or relive their lives through their children. Likewise, counselors often try to fulfill their needs through the experiences and lives of clients.

5. *Vicarious Rebellion:* Sometimes counselors with unresolved issues will live out their rebellion through the dysfunction of their clients.

6. *Atonement:* Some may feel motivated to help others as a service of atonement—to compensate for some wrong one has done in his/her past. Counselors should first repent of their sins and fully accept the forgiveness given by God, before counseling.

7. *Self-Significance:* Wishing to make a difference in people's lives is different from desiring to be a counselor in order to be a person who has made a difference, for with the latter the focus is on the counselor, not the client. Counselors should understand their innate significance as children of God and not approach counseling as an avenue to becoming a significant person.

Mistakes in the Process of Counseling

Here is a list of several common mistakes that can be made in the counseling process:

1. *Rescuing*—Saving a client instead of empowering a client to save him/herself.

2. *Excessive Self-Disclosure and Transparency*—Extreme openness that moves the focus of the counseling session off of the client and onto the counselor.

3. *Assuming the Meaning of the Problem*—Presuming without adequate investigation, testing or data.

4. *Catching the Panic*—Instead of the counselor decreasing a client's anxiety, it is when the client's anxiety disrupts the stability of the counselor. Note: A client's crisis is *not* the counselor's crisis.

5. *Breaking the Silence*—Silence is sometimes more meaningful than words and is necessary for deep introspection. Counselors should not feel the need to fill the void of silence in counseling.

6. *Giving in to Demanding Clients*—Counseling is a mutual, collaborative engagement. Neither the counselor nor the client should have a disposition that is "demanding." Counselors should establish benevolent, though securely established, boundaries to protect themselves from overly demanding clients.

7. *Giving Advice*—Counseling is not advice giving. Instead, it is heavily rooted in empowering clients to advise themselves, to draw out and magnify the 'Truth of Christ' that lives in every believer.

8. *Not Setting Realistic Goals*—Setting grandiose goals will only discourage. Instead, create small objectives and encourage clients as they succeed.

9. *Being Controlled by One's Sexuality*—Healthy sexuality means the counselor deflects sexual advances made by clients.

10. *Lacking Empathy, and at Times Sympathy*—Remember, many people who enter counseling are broken and hurting. A counselor therefore must maintain an attitude of grace and sympathy to promote healing.

11. *Being Overly Emotionally Involved*—It is good to desire the best for your clients, and it is normal to feel upset when clients are hurting, or are not improving. However, counselors must establish emotional boundaries so that they can continue to objectively and effectively help clients.

You may be overwhelmed with all this, thinking to yourself "I am not this perfect!" Indeed, if this is the first time you have been exposed to these issues of motivation and competence and you are *not* beleaguered, reconsidering whether you should continue down the road of counselor training, something is wrong.

Counselors should be responsibly concerned about their competence, ability, stability, spirituality, and more. It is the constant introspection that makes them good counselors; and it is their prolonged growth that makes them great counselors. This is only the launching ground, and the journey is long for the person of the counselor: *for they are to be always growing in knowledge, character, and skill.*

ENDNOTES

1. Ron Hawkins, E. Hindson, T. Clinton, Theological roots: Synthesizing and systematizing a biblical theology of helping, in T. Clinton and G. Ohlschlager (eds.), *Competent Christian counseling* (Colorado Springs: WaterBrook, (2002), 101.

2. Timothy Clinton, and G. Ohlschlager, *Competent Christian counseling, volume one: Foundations and practice of compassionate soul care* (Colorado Springs: WaterBrook, 2002), 101.

3. Jay Adams, *Competent to counsel* (United States: Presbyterian and Reformed Publishing Company, 1970).

4. D. Hunsinger, An interdisciplinary map for Christian counselors, in M. McMinn & T. Phillips (eds.), *Care for the soul: Exploring the intersections of psychology and theology* (Downers Grove, Ill.: InterVarsity Press, 2001), 218–240.

5. S. T. Gladding, *Counseling: A comprehensive profession* (4th ed.) (Upper Saddle River, NJ: Prentice-Hall, 2005).

6. Gary R. Collins, *How to be a people helper* (Carol Stream, Ill.: Tyndale,1995).

7. Carl Rogers, *Client centered therapy* (Boston, MA: Houghton Mifflin, 1951); Carl Rogers, The necessary and sufficient conditions of therapeutic personality change, *Journal of Consulting Psychology* 21 (1957), 95–103; Carl Rogers, *On becoming a person* (Boston, MA: Houghton Mifflin, 1961); G. Egan, *The skilled helper: A problem-management approach to helping* (6th ed.) (Pacific Grove, CA: Brooks/Cole, 1998); S. Strong, Counseling: An interpersonal influence process, *Journal of Counseling Psychology* 15, (1968):215–224.

8. Robert W. Kellemen, *Soul physicians: A theology of soul care and spiritual direction* (Taneytown, MD: RPM Books, 2005).

3

Christian Counseling
and Essential Biblical Principles

Ian Jones, Tim Clinton, and George Ohlschlager

> True Christian counseling is "built upon a biblical understanding of people (Creation), problems (Fall), and solutions (Redemption). It focuses upon the process of sanctification—growing to reflect increasingly the relational, rational, volitional, and emotional image of Christ. Its goal is clear: the inner life of your spiritual friend is to look more and more like the inner life of Christ."
>
> ROBERT KELLEMAN, IN *Spiritual Friends*[1]

In his delightful book, *The Gift of Therapy*,[2] psychiatrist and Stanford professor Irvin Yalom tells the story of two master healers, Joseph and Dion, ancient desert characters from Hermann Hesse's classic novel, *Magister Ludi*. It is a story that, reframed once again by us beyond both Hesse and Yalom, encapsulates our hopes and dreams for the future of Christian counseling.

Joseph was the classic Christian psychologist, integrating the best Christian truth with the data of the psychosocial sciences. He was the empathic master, whose inspired listening and thoughtful responsiveness brought insight and healing to all who came to his tent. As Yalom tells it, "Pilgrims trusted Joseph. Suffering and anxiety [that] entered his ears vanished like water on the desert...and penitents left his presence emptied and calmed."

Dion was just as effective as Joseph in his healing work, but he worked from the directive orientation of the biblical counselor. His healing power was based on his ability to "divine their unconfessed sins" and guide the pathway to righteousness by his "active intervention." Dion treated his "penitents as children, he gave advice, . . . assign[ed] penance, ordered pilgrimages . . . , and compelled enemies to make up."

Though they had never met, Joseph and Dion knew of each other's stellar reputations, and secretly competed with each other for many years. Then came a time when Joseph fell ill in mind and spirit. He became filled with despair and thoughts of suicide that he could not shake. Unable to heal himself, he set out on a journey to find Dion and seek his help. While resting at an oasis, he recounted his search to a fellow traveler, who immediately offered his help to find Dion. After many days of continued journey together, the traveler revealed to Joseph that he was, in fact, Dion.

Joseph went home with Dion and found healing under his tutelage and care. He continued to live in Dion's home for many years, eventually becoming his most trusted and valued healing colleague. For years they worked collaboratively and found great success, far beyond that which either knew on his own.

Then one day Dion fell ill and, bereft of any recovery, called Joseph to his side to make to him a deathbed confession. He told Joseph that he, too, isolated and living alone, had become sick of heart and was on his way to find Joseph when they had met years before. As Joseph's eyes flared in question and surprise, Dion confessed how empty and despairing his life had become and what a miracle it had been to meet Joseph and become partners in the way it had all come about.

Dion told Joseph how he had been healed of his own sickness by his care for Joseph. He admitted how proud he had been—a pride that God had healed by Dion making Joseph his healing colleague. Before he died, he thanked Joseph for his love and friendship, who expressed the same to Dion. At the end, they had become fully honest, fully transparent, fully friends.

True metaphor? Are we at an end, and at a new beginning, in Christian counseling? Although tension between the two main rival camps in Christian counseling remains, we are heartened by the way the diverse development of our increasingly complex discipline is already resolving this dispute.[3] It is a dispute being resolved not so much by the assertion of bridge-building models—which we do present in this chapter—but by the goodwill and mutual commitments of bridge-building people. A new generation of leaders is arising on both sides of this increasingly fading divide and is coming together because of our common bond in Christ and mutual recognition that our real war is "out there," and not within the fences of our own camp.

Necessary but Deficient Roots

Christian counseling has far too long suffered the conflict between biblical counseling and the integrationist movement. And in denying the influence of twelve-step, lay counseling models, and the inner healing and prayer ministries—other prominent lines in our history—this dichotomy was not even an accurate picture of Christian counseling at the height of the debate.

Furthermore, in *Competent Christian Counseling*, we challenged this false dichotomy by indicating at least ten distinctive counseling theories or identities across the nearly 50,000 members of the American Association of Christian Counselors.[4] We now torpedo this false dichotomy one last time in this volume by presenting a theoretical perspective, a unitary model of Christian counseling that we believe both fair-minded biblical counselors and integration therapists can embrace.

Nouthetic roots and biblical counseling. Jay Adams brought a biblical revolution to Christian and pastoral counseling in the 1970s, challenging a field that was racing toward rancor, even dissolution by its fascination with all manner of anti-Christian psychobabble.[5] The clarion call to maintain theological orthodoxy, the centrality of Scripture in counseling and pastoral care, and the necessity of holy living by dealing with sin and overcoming evil were its prophetic markers in a larger counseling movement that too easily forgot such truths.

However, its reliance on *noutheteo*—confrontational warning about sin and wrongdoing—as the near-exclusive means to godliness was a fatal flaw that denied it wider acceptance among even evangelical counselors. That and the fact that some of its leaders maintained an adversarial, inflammatory style and ongoing animus toward integration over the years has deeply limited its reach as an intervention model.

We believe that *parakaleo*—coming alongside someone to offer encouragement and succor as well as godly challenge—is a more normative New Testament value, and offers a unique basis for Christian counseling ministry.[6] Parakaleo not only includes the role of admonishment and confrontation about sin that noutheteo exclusively promotes, but also includes the roles of comfort, consolation, and encouragement for the brokenhearted souls in one's care.

A recent article on treating sexual abuse victims reveals the challenge of an exclusive use of a sin-confrontation approach in all of one's caregiving. Many in the biblical counseling field today are moving beyond mere proclamation to living lives of caring demonstration—one that is inherently challenging of the truth—and attractive in the way that love is shown to be true.

> Sarah is five. Her parents drop her off at Sunday school every week. She learned to sing, "Jesus loves me, this I know, for the Bible tells me so," "Little ones to Him belong," and "They are weak but He is strong." Sarah's daddy rapes her several times a week. Sometimes she gets a break because he rapes her sister instead. The song says Jesus loves her. It says He is strong. So Sarah asks Jesus to stop her daddy from hurting her and her sister. Nothing happens. Maybe Jesus is not so strong after all. Or at least, He is not as strong as her daddy. Nothing, not even Jesus, can stop her daddy. The people who wrote the Bible must not have known about her daddy.
>
> . . . You do not have to know very much about learning theory to grasp the profound impact of such experiences on a life. The abuse, due to the intensity of the traumatic experience, shapes the control beliefs by which all other information is processed.
>
> What response can a counselor or pastor give that will be powerful enough to overcome such obstacles? If simply speaking or teaching the truth is not sufficient, then what else is required? I believe that those members of the body of Christ who have been called to walk with survivors become the representative of God to them. The reputation of God is at stake in our lives. We are called to live out in the seen, in flesh and blood, what is true about who God is. . . .
>
> In other words, we are to demonstrate in the flesh the character of God over time so that who we are reveals the truth about God to the survivor. This is not in any way to deny or underestimate the power of the Word of God. However, often that Word needs to be fleshed out and not just spoken for us to truly grasp what it means.[7]

Christian cognitive-behavior therapy. Much Christian counseling is now done as a variant of cognitive-behavioral therapy. This seems to certainly be the common preference of those who have identified with the integration movement. It is also the most preferred model of practice among members of the American Association of Christian Counselors.[8]

At the core of this practice is the process of assessing, identifying, and renouncing faulty thinking, adopting instead the truths and insights of Scripture and right thinking. Exposing the "lies" clients still live by after regeneration and exchanging them with the truths of Scripture is a central method of numerous models of Christian therapy now being practiced.[9] The best Christian cognitive therapists have incorporated Christ and the centrality of Christian maturity in the counseling goal and process. And whether they recognize it or not, many nouthetic counselors are essentially practicing a form of cognitive-behavior therapy in the name of biblical counseling.

Yet we would also assert that the best cognitive therapies are not enough. In the classic language of Carl Rogers, cognitive-behavioral models are necessary but insufficient for a full Christian counseling. Changed thinking is not enough—a changed heart is also required. In fact, it can be cogently argued that changed thinking flows primarily from a transformed heart in the process of Christian maturity. From a theological perspective, a purely cognitive therapy would be like counseling without the Holy Spirit, or lacking the Spirit's fullness and power. Systemically, however, the order of influence is not as important as recognizing the cyclical, mutually reinforcing influence that both a change of heart and a transformed mind have on each other.

Clinical and pastoral experience, moreover, reveals this insufficiency. For example, most pastors and clinicians have encountered Christians who, after years of Bible study and growth in Truth by the Scriptures, are still stuck, still oppressed. And this has nothing to do with the limits of salvation or the "need for" something more than the Bible—the Scriptures are complete in themselves, revealing all the truth that we need.

From proposition to encounter. Transformative change becomes a matter of translating the Truth from a proposition to an encounter—oftentimes a series of life-changing encounters—with the living God. There are many people who will not be freed—including freed enough to grow into maturity—without a supernatural healing encounter with the Holy Spirit. Russ Willingham states this truth well in the context of sexual addiction treatment:

No one is transformed by a purely cognitive approach, even if that approach is biblical. Healing of the self *requires a spiritual-emotional attachment to a nurturing parenting figure* . . . Identity formation . . . comes about as the sexually broken person *learns to attach to Christ subsequent to conversion.*

Contrary to popular evangelical belief, this doesn't happen solely through the accumulation of biblical facts or by religiously following the propositions and instructions of Scripture. This happens by interpersonal interaction with Christ, similar to the interaction between parent and child in a healthy family . . . The processes are identical, yet obviously different, in that Christ will not literally take a person up in his lap and speak audibly into his ears . . . But a *similar work must be accomplished by the indwelling Spirit, which is no less real.*

In addition, since attempts to form a Christian identity are often based on the learning and memorization of biblical truths—largely an impersonal acquisition of facts—this also will not suffice. Please don't misunderstand me here, as I am dedicated to the study and learning of the Bible—God's revelation of Himself to us. *What I am opposed to is the mere learning of facts about God, and substituting that for a relationship, the intimate knowing of God. Far too many Christians, and most addicts, make this basic mistake.*[10] (emphases ours).

So then, do we forsake both biblical counseling and cognitive-behavior therapy and turn wholesale to inner healing strategies, a twelve-step program, or ministry? Not at all. Sole reliance on these interventions (eventually) tends to rigidly program the uncontainable movement of the Holy Spirit, and often fail to attend to the aftercare dimensions of growth and maturity. Whether the fault of the practitioner or recipient, there is often the false expectation that the dramatic healing encounter is all that is needed—that healing and maturing growth are included in the same touch. The hard work of discipleship or the ongoing challenge of spiritual formation and godly maturity revealed in the Bible is too often forsaken by a quick and easy approach that mirrors the "you can have it all and have it now" lie of the culture.

However, we must incorporate inner healing—facilitating true and life-changing encounters with the risen Christ—into our Christian counseling regimen. Such ministry not only is necessary for some who need a profound healing touch, but it is the growing currency for reaching a postmodern generation that is no longer moved by modernist approaches to the Truth—empirical evidence and rational persuasion. Those opposed to this because "an unbelieving generation always seeks a miraculous sign" (Matt. 12:39) end up denying the fact that while Jesus rightly challenged such unbelief, he then went ahead and performed many miracles.

In fact, we now believe that critical aspects of all three approaches are necessary for a complete and comprehensive Christian counseling. In this book *biblical counseling, Christian cognitive-behavioral therapy* approaches, and *inner healing* therapies are all incorporated into the construction of a new-century model for Christian counseling.

A Comprehensive Orientation

Christian counseling has perpetually searched for a comprehensive theory—a metaperspective that can help integrate biblical wisdom, personality theory, developmental constructs, psychopathology, and spiritual formation. Such a theoretical perspective would help us better understand how people grow, not only emotionally and psychologically, but spiritually. A metaperspective would also offer us more powerful insights into how normal development can go awry, leading to psychopathology and a wide array of spiritual maladies (i.e., psycho-spiritual pathology) such as spiritual apathy, turning-away from God, and chronic doubt.

Most important, this theory would guide counseling practice in a dynamic way, becoming wedded to practice so that each realm helps shape the other as both theory and practice grow to maturity. Christian counseling needs a metaperspective that will help guide our helping efforts, especially as many of us try to sort our way through a myriad of counseling schools, or theoretical perspectives. A biblically sound metaperspective would not necessarily compete with any one theory of counseling so much as it would help us make sense of how each theory can offer unique insights into a particular client's problems.

Finally, a useful metaperspective would be an empirical one—using clinical science to help Christian counselors devise and deliver more effective intervention programs. A Christian perspective on empirically-supported treatments (EST's) could be known as the BEST interventions—biblically-based, empirically-supported treatments. Such a model will never be slavish to empiricism or a naturalistic worldview, but will be open to supernatural intervention, with methodologies constructed to allow for and observe those interventions in practice.

In addition, we hope this metaperspective would encourage churches to focus more attention on prevention and wellness, incorporating the best of the bio-psycho-social sciences and the positive psychology movement. Understanding how to promote healthy relationships and God-honoring psycho-spiritual behavior, and how to prevent the development of unhealthy and potentially detrimental outcomes would seem to us to have a profound future in the Church.

A Model for Christian Churches

The importance of the church for promoting spiritual and emotional health, and for the development of meaningful counseling that disciples its members can hardly be overstated.[11]

For this endeavor, Larry Crabb has suggested a comprehensive, three-tiered model.[12]

Encouragement. Regarding the first tier, encouragement, all church members can and should be involved with providing counseling at this basic level, which will help in subduing problem feelings. Though persons are often hurting, and though Christians share a profound unity in membership with Christ's body, interaction is usually—though friendly—shallow and utterly trivial. Stated, Christians warmly shake hands each Sunday with those who are about to come apart at the seams—people who could be drastically helped by the encouragement of ordinary people who care.[13]

From a clinical perspective, this first tier is an example of the church providing proactive "primary care" to its congregants. In brief, the level one counselor in the church maintains awareness in regards to brothers or sisters, and notices counseling need; uncharacteristic quietness, distant or strained conversation, a gloomy or indefinably different affect. Then the level one counselor engages such a person in meaningful conversation, to help him/her.

Exhortation. The second tier, which concerns problem behaviors, implements counseling by exhortation. Candidates for level two counseling include elders, deacons, Sunday school teachers, and pastors. Level two counseling requires knowledge of Scripture, an ability to reflect feelings accurately (empathic response), counseling technique, and (most importantly) a strong interpersonal connection. The approach of the second level counselor will be accepted well by the client if his or her motivation strongly includes wanting to please God.

This second tier aligns well with what is clinically known as "secondary care," the providing of counseling in milieu of a presenting problem.

Enlightenment. The third, and highest tier, concerns problem thinking, and counseling is implemented by enlightenment. Accordingly, only a few select persons can be equipped to handle these more drastic, complicated issues, for training should be more extensive: a recommended three hours per week for six months to a year. In level three counseling, to observe a person's erroneous thoughts, one must look under the existing problem behaviors. It is said to change a behavior, first belief must be modified. This includes the understanding of the gospel, which also directly effects one's commitment to Christ.

Categorized clinically, the third tier of help in the church provides a type of "tertiary care," which is counseling amid more serious problems, or a client's personal crisis.

Biblical Principles in Counseling Theory and Practice

How do you evaluate the biblical authenticity of the variety of counseling theories and practices that lay claim to a biblical or Christian foundation? The field of Christian counseling has come a long way from a time when its theoretical development reflected either secular models baptized in a biblical framework or narrow exegetical models of biblical terms and phrases, lacking rigorous hermeneutical examination or empirical validation. The robust nature of the field has yielded numerous approaches to caregiving, with an assortment of techniques and interventions.

Scripture as Foundation

As we indicated earlier, 2 Timothy 3:16–17 states, "All Scripture is given by inspiration of God and is useful for teaching, rebuking, correcting and training in righteousness, so that the man of God may be thoroughly equipped for every good work." Hence, the foundation for Truth by which everything else is evaluated is the Bible, and the Scriptures in themselves provide us with a plethora of information in instructing one on how to live a proper life.

For example, a man comes to his pastor with a confession of adultery, and is consumed in guilt and depression over his error. The best and most proper way to help the client in such a case is the traditional biblical design that includes "the classic interventions of compassionate and humble listening; confrontation over sin; consolation, comfort and companionship in despair; receiving of confession, assurance of pardon, and reconstruction of that man's life in accord with proper virtues of self-control, fidelity, respect for life and so forth."[14]

The Bible provides the singular authoritative standard for both generating and evaluating a caregiving ministry. The essential qualities of a complete Christian counseling theory and practice should incorporate our creation in the image of God, the model of Jesus Christ, and the empowerment of the Holy Spirit. The components necessary for an adequate model of personality and counseling include an explanation of (1) our origin, (2) our essential nature or the things that we all share in common, (3) our current condition or a diagnosis of what is basically wrong with mankind, and (4) a prescription for remedying our problems based on an adequate understanding of human motivation, development, and the processes of change.[15]

Christian counselors help people to find their location in relationship to God, self, and others. They accept the authority of Scripture, recognize the uniqueness of human creation in the image of God and the effects of sin, acknowledge the redemptive initiative of God, and help people to find and follow a godly plan for healing. The Greatest Commandment guides them in their communication and service to others, as they seek to discover the provision and goodness of God in every situation. Such counselors try to model the example of Christ, the Messiah and Master Counselor, in wisdom and understanding, planning and power, and the knowledge and fear of the Lord, as they engage in the theory and practice of caregiving.

Christian counselors allow the Holy Spirit to do His work through the ministry of counseling. They nurture the fruit of the Spirit, the gifts of the Spirit, biblical traits, and spiritual disciplines. In the process, they draw others to God and build up the church, the body of Christ.

Creator and Creation: The Bedrock

There is a temptation to align ourselves with the familiar. Our ethnocentric predisposition draws us toward counseling models that reflect our own needs and interests. Indeed, modern secular counseling theories often mirror the culture, historical context, and biographical character of their creators. Christian approaches to counseling generally mirror preferred theological orientations along with supporting verses from Scripture, usually from the New Testament and, in particular, from the Pauline epistles.[16] The challenge for all Christian counselors who desire to be truly biblical is to develop counseling approaches that embrace foundational principles of caregiving cultivated and mined out in Scripture, from Genesis to Revelation.

Our Design and Purpose

An understanding of our divine origin is essential to the development of a fully Christian counseling theory and practice. The opening chapters of the book of Genesis reveal that all creation owes its existence to God. Humans are unique among creation in that they bear a special imprint of their Creator. They were originally designed for the purpose of having communion with Him and being caretakers over His world. We bear the image (Hebrew: *tselem*) and likeness (Hebrew: *demuth*) of our Creator (Gen. 1:26–27), but our relationship with God has been broken due to sin.

Created for relationship. We are designed by God for fellowship with Him and with other people. The desire for relationship is a basic component of our human nature, and this quality is found in the nature of our triune God.[17] We do not exist as a result of chance or arbitrary genetic mutation. Each person is part of a divine design and plan. Knowing our Creator and having relationship with Him is the primary task of all people, including biblical counselors.

Our fallen nature. Adam and Eve's decision to listen to an authority other than God's and reject His will has resulted in a fallen world, filled with deception and disobedience. Our original purpose of relationship with God and with others has been shattered. Sin has led to disobedience to the Word of God, destruction of the unique relationship with our Creator, and to conflict in our relationships with others. Only through the initiative, grace, and power of God will we find the ultimate solution to our dilemma. We are incapable of resolving these problems ourselves.

All secular counseling theories present an incomplete picture of human nature. They are unable to account adequately for both our attraction to the eternal, the spiritual, and the altruistic, and our pull toward the temporal, evil, and the selfish. These theories will emphasize either a basic goodness (e.g., Carl Rogers) or a basic depravity (e.g., Freud) in the soul. These counseling models place the individual self, social forces or biological drives at the center of all change.

Such theories may rest upon a belief in free will or biological or social determinism; cognitive, affective, or behavioral reprogramming; a problem-solving or solution-focused orientation; depth analysis or minimalist intervention. Ultimately, they all seek resolution of human dilemmas in some expression of personal or social power. Mankind is central, while God is relegated to a peripheral function. He is created in the image and for the needs of humanity or He is entirely ignored. The result is a form of idolatry or a cult of self worship.[18] Christian counselors understand that all biblical care giving and assistance falls within the larger plans and purposes of God, and that Christian counseling should begin with God and model His actions.

The Genesis Model of Intervention

The first question asked by God in human history occurred in the context of a crisis counseling situation. Adam and Eve had listened to a different voice of authority and their disobedience led to a breakdown in fellowship with God, as well as their relationship with each other (Gen. 3:1–19). They were in a state of spiritual and relational crisis, with their very souls at stake. Adam blamed both God and Eve ("The woman whom You gave to me" [Gen. 3:12]), while Eve accused the serpent of causing the problem. The communion between the couple and their Creator was broken and a dissonance had entered the relationship between the man and the woman.

The initiative of God. The response of God to the Fall serves as a model for the church and its ministry, particularly in the fields of evangelism, discipleship, service and counseling. God took the initiative in reestablishing contact with Adam and Eve. He is a pursuing God.

"Then the Lord God called to the man, and said to him, 'Where are you?'" (Gen. 3:9 NASB). This passage is one of the most interesting, and perhaps one of the most significant in all of Scripture. Humans had just freely chosen to turn their backs on their Creator and reject His Word and authority. They were in a state of sin. We would expect God to react to their behavior with righteous judgment, condemning them for their sin, demanding repentance, and dictating their punishment. Although the consequences of their sin was revealed, God did not open His conversation with words of condemnation. Instead, we see Him beginning His intervention with a question: "Where are you?" (Gen. 3:9).

The importance of location. The question of location is basic to a biblical model of Christian counseling. If you have ever been lost, then you will understand the importance of knowing your location. Your very survival may depend upon such knowledge. There are three things that you need to know to reach safety when you are lost: your current position, the place of safety or your goal, and the path(s) that will lead you safely to your destination. Effective Christian counseling addresses these three areas.

The temptation for Christian counselors is to step into a counseling situation and direct people toward answers based upon a particular theory or selective verses from the Bible without taking the time to get to know the people in need and to allow them to define their situation. Often, we expect people to conform to our interpretation of the problem and to act on our terms. God shows us a different approach. His question gave Adam an opportunity to define his current condition and accept responsibility. Jesus followed this approach on a number of occasions.[19]

The application of location and relationship in counseling. Christian counseling seeks to discover a person, family, or group's position in relationship to God, self, and others. Locating clients becomes difficult when they are overwhelmed by their problems, being deceptive or deceived, hiding from or unwilling to accept the truth of their condition, or confused by their situation. Effective counseling focuses on the three dimensions of relationship (God, self, and others) and the client answering the following basic questions concerning location.

Current Location, Problem Definition

- Where do you say that you are located? What do you believe is the problem?
- Where do others say that you are located? What do they say is your problem?
- Where does God say that you are located? What is the biblical view of your situation?

Goal, Destination, or Solution

- Where do you believe that you want to be? What is the solution to your problem and what changes do you want? Where do you have control? What changes are you willing and able to make?
- Where does your counselor and others say that you need to be? What do they suggest?

- Where does God say that you need to be? What does Scripture say is the solution to your problem and what changes does God expect?

Plan for Change

- How do you propose to get to your goal? What resources do you have?
- What suggestions do your counselor and others have for reaching your goal?
- What is God's plan for your life in this situation? What spiritual resources has God provided for you?[20]

In the ideal counseling situation, there is complete agreement between a counselee, the counselor, and the Word of God on the answers to these questions. Of course, not every case works an ideal result.

The Greatest Commandment: Guiding Principle for Treatment and Healing

Christian counseling follows the biblical model of caregiving by seeking to achieve healing in the relationship with an individual, family, or group and God, the self, or others. The guiding principle that provides the spiritual and ethical standard of practice in this task of healing is the Greatest Commandment. Jesus identified the greatest commandment as *the call upon us to love God with all our hearts, souls, minds, and strength, and to love other people as much as we love ourselves* (Matt. 22:34–40; Mark 12:28–34; Luke 10:25–28). The commandment summarizes the message of the Ten Commandments into two distinct dimensions, our relationship to God and our relationship to others.

The Three Dimensions of Healing

Jesus proclaimed that the kingdom of heaven was at hand. He revealed the healing and redemptive activity of God in the world and in the process addressed the essential issue of Eden: our location and lostness in relationship to God, to self, and to other people. Biblically-based therapy needs to address a client's current spiritual, cognitive, social, behavioral, and affective condition in relationship to these three dimensions. We find this subject clearly presented in the theme of the Greatest Commandment.

Our priority must be to seek and love God, placing Him first in our lives (Deut. 6:5, 10:12, 30:6). We show our devotion to God by accepting His love for us. The godly love of self is not an egoistic selfishness; rather, it is the recognition of our creation in the image of God. We show a true love of self by seeking the best for ourselves, by answering His call and being obedient to His will. We express our love toward God by joining with Him in loving others (Lev. 19:18; Rom. 13:9; Gal. 5:14; James 2:8).

Adjusting interventions to individual location and needs. Jesus gives us an example of finding the location of people in need and adjusting His intervention when, on two occasions, He is asked a question related to the Greatest Commandment. Both the rich young ruler and a scribe or lawyer approached Jesus with the same question, "What must I do to inherit eternal life?" (Luke 18:18–21, 10:25–28), but He gave different responses to each of His inquirers. The two situations provide insight into the biblical counseling principles of location and intervention.

1. *Address the questions raised by the clients and begin with their understanding of the problem.* Jesus responded to the questions raised by the young ruler and the scribe. Since they were interested in a theological issue, Jesus focused on this area. If they had asked a question on some other matter, then we can assume that Jesus would have shifted His response to meet their needs as they defined them.

2. *Look for ways to connect or join with clients.* Jesus responded to the youthful zeal of the young ruler with warmth and affection (Mark 10:21). With the scribe, He deferred to the status of the scholar by asking him to answer the question. When the scribe correctly cited the Greatest Commandment, Jesus affirmed the man's knowledge of the Law.

3. *Do not assume that people who ask the same question have the same problem.* Jesus understood that while these two men were asking the same question, they, nevertheless, were wrestling with different fundamental issues in their relationship with God and with others. We see these issues revealed as Jesus adjusted His intervention according to the theological and spiritual position or location of each of the men.[21]

4. *Begin interventions, if possible, at the points of agreement.* If our relationship to God is more important than our love of neighbor, then why did Jesus begin His response to the young ruler by referring to the second table of the Ten Commandments? Surely a pious and godly biblical counselor must start every counseling session by focusing on God and insisting that the client start there also! Yet, Jesus did not begin by identifying the first commandments. Instead, He listed commandments that dealt with adultery, murder, stealing, false witness, and honoring parents.

     The young ruler's claim that he had kept all these commandments gives us a clue to the strategy of Christ. He connected with His inquirer by focusing first upon the person's spiritual and relational strengths. Beginning with areas of agreement lessens the likelihood of rancor, defensiveness, and debate. Instead, it increases the chances that a client will be open and receptive to the truth. The young ruler's problem lay elsewhere, with the first commandment and his relationship to God. In contrast, the scribe did not have a problem with the first commandment and the importance of placing God first in his life. Jesus seemed to agree with the scribe on this point, but His response elicited a question from the man that went to the heart of his real problem: "Who is my neighbor?" (Luke 10:29).

5. *Encourage clients to wrestle with the truth using techniques that illuminate biblical principles as clearly as possible for them.* The young ruler's problem was a common idolatry for many of us today. He was placing his material wealth before God. Jesus used a direct approach to test the man and prove the point. He told him to sell his possessions and give all he had to the poor. In the case of the scribe, Jesus told him the story of the Good Samaritan and concluded with a question (Luke 10:30–36) designed to reveal the scribe's inadequate understanding of the biblical view of neighbor.

6. *Allow clients to take personal responsibility and apply biblical truths to their lives.* The young ruler was faced with a choice, and he went away sad, because he was very wealthy and he was unwilling to express his total commitment to God (Luke 18:22–24). The scribe revealed his struggle with biblical truth by identifying the true neighbor only as "the one who showed mercy" toward the victim

of the attack (Luke 10:37). He still could not bring himself to say the word "Samaritan." Jesus challenged him to show the same mercy toward all people.

Not all clients will make the right decision, or even arrive at one. Counselors cannot decide or act for their clients, but they look for the most effective means of joining with clients and revealing the paths to truth in ways that make the most sense to them. If a counselor can facilitate a client encounter with God, wrestling with His way, then much is accomplished, and a holy seed has been planted that God will water and nurture.

The Messianic Example

If Jesus Christ is the perfect and only answer to the problem of sin, then He is also the supreme model for counseling. While it is beneficial to study the examples of caregiving found in the ministry of Jesus, we find the foundation for His ministry in the Old Testament, and, in particular, in the messianic passages. Isaiah 9:6 gives us an overall description of the Messiah:

> For a child will be born to us, a son will be given to us;
> And the government will rest on His shoulders;
> And His name will be called Wonderful Counselor, Mighty God,
>   Eternal Father, Prince of Peace (Isa. 9:6, NASB).

The Authority of Jesus

"I have been given *complete authority in heaven and on earth*. Therefore, go and make disciples of all the nations, baptizing them in the name of the Father and of the Son and of the Holy Spirit. Teach these new disciples to obey all the commands I have given you. And be sure of this: I am with you always, even to the end of the age."

This Great Commission of Christ, His last words recorded in Matthew's Gospel (24:18–20), are much more than a charge to evangelize the world. He reveals that God the Father has given Him all authority over all the powers of heaven and earth. From this power the disciple-making challenge is possible—the very same power to lead the church into maturity in Christ. Christ is the Source of this power, and He promises to be always available to accomplish this task—He is the Source of all authority, and He will never leave us!

The Messiah will come as a gift from God (cf. John 3:16), as a child who will be given all authority in heaven and on earth (Matt. 28:18). We will find His authority and His character revealed in His names.

Wonderful Counselor. The Hebrew word for counselor (*yaats*) should not be confused with the formal concept of modern psychotherapy; rather, it conveys the incomprehensible vastness of the wisdom and knowledge of the Messiah. He will be able to discern the truth in all situations and determine the appropriate way to proceed. The term "wonderful" (Heb: *pali*) is a descriptive adjective, and accentuates the supernatural nature of the Messiah, indicating that His counsel will lie beyond our comprehension and ability. It will be so exceptional that human wisdom would appear as foolishness by comparison (1 Cor. 1:25, 3:19).[22]

Mighty God. The Messiah will express the creative and miraculous power of God. His authority will extend over heaven and earth, body and spirit, and the temporal and eternal.

Eternal Father. The Messiah will express the nature of our heavenly Father, our Creator and Redeemer. He will come as an everlasting presence with whom we may share a personal relationship as adopted children (Rom. 8:15, 23; Gal. 4:5; Eph. 1:5).

Prince of Peace. The Messiah will bring eternal peace and salvation (Luke 2:14). He will be the One who brings reconciliation between God and fallen mankind (Eph. 2:14–19). His peace will be beyond any peace that the world can offer. It will be capable of calming all fears and bringing the grace of God and His redeeming presence into all situations (John 14:27).

The Messiah will come as Savior. He will locate us in our sin and provide us with the only path to salvation. In so doing, He will serve as the standard or model for counseling intervention.

The "Spirit of the Lord" in Christian Counseling

The nature of the Messiah is revealed in the form of three spirits, each spirit having two characteristics.

> Then a shoot will spring from the stem of Jesse,
> And a branch from his roots will bear fruit.
> The Spirit of the Lord will rest on Him,

The spirit of wisdom and understanding,
The spirit of counsel and strength,
    The spirit of knowledge and the fear of the Lord (Isa. 11:1–2 NASB).

The three spirits (wisdom and understanding, counsel and strength, and knowledge and fear of the Lord) are all expressions of the one Spirit of Jehovah. The three groupings and the pairing of characteristics indicate distinct dimensions with overlapping meanings.[23] The six terms give us insight into the personal nature of the Messiah. They provide us with an ideal picture not only of God, but also of the perfect Man, unblemished by sin. The six characteristics are expressed in the life of Christ, and through His example, they provide us with a framework for developing a model of care and counseling.

Wisdom (Hebrew: *hokmah*; LXX: *sophias*).[24] The Messiah will not make judgments based on external appearances and circumstances (Isa. 11:3–5). Instead, He will possess a divine awareness of the broader context of a situation as well as supernatural insight into the true nature of a person. Godly wisdom is the ability to see into the heart of a matter, beyond the visible and superficial, and correctly discern the most appropriate response.

In the context of a counseling ministry, this godly wisdom indicates the need for a comprehensive theoretical basis for caregiving that encompasses a full awareness of human nature, including the social, cognitive, behavioral, affective, and spiritual dimensions. Such complete wisdom is not accessible outside of the guidance of God (Job 28:12–28). Proverbs 8:1–36 connects this wisdom to four other expressions in Isaiah 11:2: knowledge (*daath*), sound advice (*etzah*), understanding (*binah*) and strength (*geburah*).

Jesus kept increasing in wisdom (Luke 2:52). His wise counsel is expressed in the Sermon on the Mount (Matt. 5–7) and the many occasions when He looked beyond external appearance and circumstances to see the broader spiritual, social, and psychological factors in a situation.

Understanding (Hebrew: *binah*; LXX: *suneseos*). The Messiah will possess a deep and practical understanding of individuals and events. Understanding is the ability to discern and discriminate between the various parts of a situation; to know how the different components relate to one another. In counseling, we need such understanding to look beyond the external and the superficial and to identify the motivations and complex social forces that influence human interaction and individual behavior.

We find an example of such understanding in King Solomon's order to divide a child in two when two mothers both had claimed the same baby (1 Kin. 3:16–28). Solomon knew the true mother would relinquish her claim rather than see her child harmed. He understood the motivating forces and emotions at work in both the biological mother and the false claimant, and he used this knowledge to reveal the truth.

Jesus understood human motivation and what lay in the heart of a person (John 2:25). He used this understanding with His disciples, people in need, and others who opposed Him. In the case of the woman caught in adultery, His awareness of the motives, needs, and attitudes of the Pharisees and the woman enabled Jesus to join relationally with both the accusers and the accused, deescalate a dangerous situation, biblically confront the religious authorities, save a woman from physical harm and minister to her spiritual needs (John 8:3–11).

The brilliance of His counseling intervention was revealed in His ability to address the issues in a way that revealed the therapeutic path for both parties. Both the Pharisees and the woman were confronted with a choice. How they responded was their personal responsibility.

Counsel or Knowledge (Hebrew: *etzah*; LXX: *boules*). The Messiah will have a spirit of knowledge that will enable Him to evaluate a situation correctly in order to determine the appropriate response and develop the best plan. The Hebrew word *etzah* conveys the idea of giving counsel or advice based upon wise planning and an accurate assessment of a situation.

Both appropriate and inappropriate counsel is found in the story of Rehoboam, who chose to ignore the recommendation of his older counselors for reform by lightening the burden of the people. Their advice (*etzah*) was based upon their knowledge of the hearts of the people and insight into the political climate. Instead, Rehoboam listened to his young and immature peers who argued for further oppression. Their counsel did not reflect a careful examination of the situation nor wise planning. The king's decision had disastrous consequences (1 Kin. 12:13–14).

Wise Christian counselors gather and examine all the data in a situation. They carefully identify the important information and they assist people in designing a course of action that accounts for the circumstances, possible dangers, and abilities of the person or people in need. Such counsel, however, wisely acknowledges that behind every situation God is still in control. Consequently, it is imperative that a godly path be chosen. "Many plans (plots, thoughts, schemes) are in a man's heart, But the counsel (*etzah*) of the Lord will stand" (Prov. 19:21).

Jesus clearly articulated His mission plan in Luke 4:18 where He quoted from Isaiah 58:6 and Isaiah 11:3–4: "The Spirit of the Lord has come to me because he has chosen me to tell the good news to the poor. The Lord has sent me to announce freedom for prisoners, to give sight to the blind, to free everyone who suffers, and to proclaim that this is the year the Lord has chosen." His Great Commission outlined His plan for all Christians (Matt. 28:18–20).

Christians have the promise of Christ's power, presence, and authority. As we obey Christ's call, the Holy Spirit, our Divine Comforter and Counselor, will guide and help us. An important role of the Holy Spirit is to reveal to us the true nature of things, teaching us, reminding us, and helping us to witness for Christ (John 14:15–17, 26; 15:26–27). All Christian counselors possess at least one of God's many gifts to be used in service to others and for His glory (1 Pet. 4:10–11). In addition, God has given us a Spirit of power and of love and of a sound mind to care for others (2 Tim. 1:7).

Christian counselors assist their fellow believers to grow and mature in Christ and in their relationship with other people. Such counseling also provides Christians with an opportunity to represent Christ in a therapeutic encounter with non-believers. The process of revealing Christ is an essential component of competent Christian counseling; however, it must be done in a way that honors client choice and follows accepted ethical practice.[25]

Christian counselors must seek the Spirit of Knowledge, but wise planning is not enough to ensure that changes will take place in a person's life. There must be a source of power strong enough to execute the plan and produce change.

Power (Hebrew: *geburah*; LXX: *ischuos*). Power is the strength or might to produce change; the ability to execute a plan; and the capacity to remain firm and constant in a situation, despite opposition. The Bible calls upon us to recognize and sing praises to the power and strength of God (Ps. 21:13). Job acknowledged his complete dependence upon God, who possessed wisdom (*hokmah*), strength (*geburah*), counsel (*etzah*), and understanding (*binah*) (Job 12:13). God knew human nature. He understood the strengths and limitations of Job and the dilemma that he faced. God's message to Job was that He also had the power to deal with any problem or situation and to determine the future.

This power is found in Christ, who worked in the power of the Holy

Spirit (John 4:14), and who was given all power and authority in heaven and on earth (Matt. 28:18). His power is revealed clearly in John 10:17–18, where He proclaimed that He not only had the power to lay down His life for others, but He also had the power to take it up again. Jesus had power over death. He had the plan for salvation and the power to execute the plan. Christian counselors have access to the supernatural power of Christ, who has the strength to overcome all the forces, authorities, and rulers in the world (Eph. 1:17–23).

Many plans fail because people lack the strength to implement them. Wise counselors consider the skills and abilities of their clients in the process of developing treatment plans. Attempts to impose changes and place unrealistic expectations upon clients can leave people feeling frustrated and overwhelmed. Repeated failures due to poor planning and inadequate power resources can lead people to experience habitual or learned helplessness. They just give up.[26] Consequently, it is essential that each client's location in relationship to God, self, and others is determined and that an assessment is made of the resources available to the one in need.

The Knowledge of God (Hebrew: *daath*; LXX: *gnoseos*). The Messiah will possess a perfect understanding of the will of God. The knowledge of God is the ability to see a situation through the eyes of God who is all knowing, and to possess the information necessary to determine God's intention or direction. Proverbs 2 tells us that we will understand the fear (*yir'ath*) of Jehovah and the knowledge (*daath*) of God if we bow our ears to wisdom (*hokmah*), extend our hearts to understanding (*binah*), cry out and seek discernment (*binah*), and lift up our voices for understanding (*binah*).

The Messiah possessed this knowledge of God (cf., Isa. 53:11) and Christ embodied this knowledge as the Way, the Truth, and the Life (John 14:6). Christians have access to the knowledge of God through their relationship to Jesus Christ and the presence of the Holy Spirit in their lives. The Spirit enables Christian counselors to commune with God and access the knowledge of God revealed in Scripture.

The Fear of God (Hebrew: *yirath*; LXX: *eusebeias*). The fear of God is a holy reverence of and respect or honor toward God. It is the loyalty and duty that we owe God by placing Him first above everything else. The fear of God in its fullness represents a perfect relationship with the Creator. "The fear (*yirath*) of the Lord is the beginning of knowledge (*daath*); fools despise wisdom (*hokmah*) and instruction" (Prov. 1:7). Wisdom and knowledge begin when God is placed first in our lives and we seek to live our lives in accordance with His will.

Fear of God and obedience to His Word allows us to make sense of this world (Eccl. 12:13–14). True fear is based upon an awareness of who God is and a desire to find Him in every situation in life. The true believer continually seeks the will of God and fears the possibility of ever losing sight of God. False fear is rooted in a doubt of God's existence (Ps. 14:1, 53:1) and the subsequent dread of death and a future judgment. Such people live their lives in rebellion to the will of God. [27]

Godly people express their fear of the Lord by refusing to engage in sinful attitudes and actions. Jesus perfectly manifested the fear of God, as He lived a perfect and sinless life. He was in the Father and the Father was in Him (John 14:10). He was in His very nature God (Phil. 2:6–11). "I and the Father are one," He said (John 10:30). His life exemplified a person who never took His eyes off the Father, one who reflected the absolute holiness of God and the rejection of evil.

> The fear of the Lord is to hate evil;
> Pride and arrogance and the evil way
> And the perverted mouth, I hate.
> Counsel is mine and sound wisdom;
>   I am understanding, power is mine (Prov. 8:13–14 NASB).

Counselors need to help people distinguish between true and godly fear and the false fears that mislead and debilitate. An important role of biblical counselors is to represent Christ and to look for the hand of God working in every counseling situation.

The Holy Spirit and Spiritual Gifts in Counseling

Jesus said that He would ask the Father to give His followers another Counselor or Helper (Greek: *parakletos*), the Spirit of Truth, to abide with them and teach them (John 14:26). As the Divine Advocate or representative of Christ (John 15:26) in the life of Christian counselors, the Holy Spirit strengthens and directs them. The traits attributed to the Messiah in Isaiah 11:2 (wisdom, understanding, knowledge, power, the knowledge of God, and the fear of God) are now expressed through the Holy Spirit.

Christian counselors are filled with the Spirit (Eph. 5:18), bear the fruit of the Spirit (John 15:16; Gal. 5:22), and receive the gifts of the Spirit. The fruit of the Spirit (love, joy, peace, patience, gentleness, goodness, faithfulness, meekness and self-control) are necessary components of mature Christian counseling (Gal. 5:22–23). They are more accurate measures of our identity in Christ than the possession of gifts, which can be misused.

The spiritual gifts reveal God and the eternal presence of His Spirit, as well as minister to and edify the believer and others. Paul identified nine gifts in 1 Corinthians 12:8–10: the word of wisdom, the word of knowledge, special faith, healing gifts, the working of miracles, prophecy, discernment between spirits, tongues, and the interpretation of tongues. Paul clearly stated that the gifts were not distributed equally and that certain Christians were blessed with particular gifts of the Spirit.

Additional gifts include service to others and helping, teaching, encouragement, giving, leadership, mercy, apostleship, missionary evangelism, and pastoring (Rom. 12:6–8; 1 Cor. 12:28; Eph. 4:11). We are expected to speak the words of God accurately and to work in the power of the Spirit as we minister to others with our gifts (1 Pet. 4:10–11).

The Spiritual Disciplines in Counseling

Christian counselors need to develop the biblical traits and spiritual disciplines associated with caregiving. One survey identified nearly 50 biblical traits and 20 spiritual disciplines that are related to counseling, including the traits of patience, gentleness, self-control, compassion, truthfulness, approachableness, ability to teach, discernment, empathy, giving comfort and encouragement, confrontation, integrity, thoughts obedient to Christ, hope, ability to relate well to others, a longing for God, and an example to those served. Spiritual disciplines included prayer, service, maintaining purity, compassion, accountability, forgiveness, obedience, confession and repentance, wisdom, agape love, listening and guidance.[28] Such encounters with the living God changes everything for both counselor and client.

Conclusion

We are honored that our friend and colleague, Professor Ian Jones of Southwestern Baptist Theological Seminary joined us in this chapter and consented to contribute the essence of his soon-to-be-published manuscript as the core content here. His careful exegesis of the "whole counsel of God" on the counseling endeavor has yielded a rich treasure of revelation that will guide our field in our research, practice, and theory-building for the rest of this century.

ENDNOTES

1. Robert W. Kellemen, *Spiritual friends: A methodology of soul care and spiritual direction,* (Taneytown, MD: RPM Books, 2004), 77.
2. Irvin D. Yalom, *The gift of therapy: An open letter to a new generation of therapists and their patients* (NY: HarperCollins, 2002).
3. Timothy Clinton, and Ohlschlager, G., *Competent Christian counseling, volume one: Foundations and practice of compassionate soul care* (Colorado Springs: WaterBrook, 2002), chapter 3.
4. Timothy Clinton, and Ohlschlager, G., *Competent Christian counseling, Volume One.*
5. Jay Adams, *Competent to counsel* (Presbyterian and Reformed Publishing Company, 1970).
6. Timothy Clinton, and Ohlschlager, G., *Competent Christian counseling, Volume One.*
7. Diane Langberg, *On the threshold of hope: Opening the door to healing for survivors of sexual abuse* (Wheaton, IL: Tyndale, 1999).
8. AACC members survey.
9. W. Backus, *Telling the truth to trouble people: A manual for Christian counselors* (Minneapolis: Bethany House, 1985); W. Backus, *What your counselor never told you: Conquer the power of sin in your life* (Minneapolis, MN: Bethany House, 2000); L. Vernick, *The TRUTH principle: A life changing model for spiritual growth and renewal* (Colorado Springs: WaterBrook Press, 2000); C. Thurman, *The lies we believe* (Nashville: Thomas Nelson, 1989).
10. Russ Willingham, *Breaking free* (Downers Grove, IL: Intervarsity, 1999).
11. Mark McMinn, and A. Dominguez, Psychology collaborating with the church, *Journal of Psychology and Christianity,* 22(4), (2003), 291–294.
12. Larry Crabb, *Effective biblical counseling: A model for helping caring Christians become capable counselors* (Grand Rapids, MI: Zondervan, 1977).
13. Larry Crabb, *Connecting* (Nashville: W Pubishing Group, 1997), 25.
14. This section is a summary of the biblical foundations of counseling addressed in Ian F. Jones, *The counsel of heaven on earth* (Manuscript submitted for publication, 2003).
15. Leslie Stevenson, *Seven theories of human nature,* second edition (New York: Oxford University Press, 1974), 5–7; Mary Stewart Van Leeuwin, *The person in psychology: A contemporary Christian appraisal* (Grand Rapids, MI: Eerdmans, 1985), 46. The four features of a complete theory of human nature are identified by Stevenson and developed by Van Leeuwin within a Christian worldview. They overlook the crucial fifth criterion: a clear articulation of the source of authority for the truth claims.

16. A challenge for all Christian counselors is to examine their preferred counseling model in light of their personal history, personality, and culture. Failure to do so is likely to result in a theory that inadvertently reflects the needs, character, and experiences of individual theorists, who then assume that their particular approach is universally applicable for all people at all times—a fault found, in particular, among the pioneers in secular psychology and counseling. Subsequently, any other approach encountered by these Christian counselors must be, by their own definition, less than biblical.

17. Francis Schaeffer argues that the Christian doctrine of the Trinity is essential, in that it reveals that God has no need for relationship outside of Himself. He was not compelled to create us in order to have fellowship, but we are absolutely dependent upon Him for our existence and survival. See Francis A. Schaeffer, *He is there and He is not silent* (Wheaton, IL: Tyndale, 1972), 14–17.

18. See Paul Vitz, *Psychology as religion: The cult of self worship*, second ed. (Grand Rapids, MI: Eerdmans, 1994).

19. Variations on the question of location are found in the response of Jesus to people seeking healing and many of the questions He asked and discussions He had with His disciples. Most of His post-resurrection appearances are examples of God locating people in need and directing them toward an understanding of His will and truth.

20. These questions reflect general areas of inquiry in counseling. They should not be used in a rote manner, without considering the location of the client in terms of language, temperament, concerns, context, and physical, spiritual, social, and emotional condition.

21. Counselors need to be cautious about automatically responding to an identified problem with a pre-selected technique or verse of Scripture, without investigating a client's location in such areas as context and motives.

22. If the terms *Wonderful* and *Counselor* are considered to be separate names or titles, as some translations prefer [e.g., King James Version], then "Wonderful" conveys a sense of the incomprehensible and mysterious nature of God.

23. Isaiah is not describing three or even six different entities in the passage, but a single Spirit manifest in different attributes. While parallelisms involving synonyms that convey identical meaning are used in Hebrew literature, the terms used in this passage appear to have discrete, although overlapping meaning. See, e.g., Joseph Addison Alexander, *The earlier prophecies of Isaiah* (New York: Wiley and Putnam, 1846), 220; and Edward J. Young, *The book of Isaiah: The English text, with introduction, exposition, and notes, New International Commentary on the Old Testament*, ed. by R. K. Harrison (Grand Rapids, MI: Eerdmans, 1965), 380–381.

24. LXX refers to the Septuagint—a Greek translation of the Old Testament.

25. George Ohlschlager and Clinton, T., Inside law and ethics: The ethics of evangelism and spiritual formation in professional counseling, *Christian Counseling Connection* (Issue 1, 2000), 6–7.

26. Martin E. P. Seligman, *Helplessness: On depression, development, and death* (San Francisco: W. H. Freeman and Company, 1975), 21–44.

27. Blaise Pascal, *Pensèes and the provincial letters* (New York: The Modern Library, 1941), 92, (Pensèe #262).

28. Kevin Scott Forrester, Determining the Biblical traits and spiritual disciplines Christian counselors employ in practice: A delphi study, PhD diss., Southwestern Baptist Theological Seminary, (2002), 151–157. The biblical traits were love, joy,

peace, patience, kindness, goodness, faithfulness, gentleness, self-control, compassion, living in the Spirit, humility, forgiveness, truthfulness, holding others accountable, approachable, wisdom, self-giving, able to teach, meekness, hunger and thirst for righteousness, merciful, pure in heart, peacemakers, walking with the Lord, prayerful attitude, giving God the glory, discernment, thankfulness, empathy, respect, biblical morality, giving comfort and encouragement, confrontation, integrity, renewed mind, thoughts obedient to Christ, using the armor of God, knowledge of God's Word, endurance, hope, acceptance, ability to relate well to others, a longing for God, knowing self, avoiding quarrels, work toward biblical goals, an example to those served, and not practicing worldliness. The spiritual disciplines were prayer, listening prayer, service, Scripture: counselor proactive, maintaining purity, compassion, praise, being an example, accountability, forgiveness, discernment, obedience, confession/repentance, wisdom, agape love, growth, caring, listening and guidance, thought life, and ministering to all needs.

4

Christian Counseling Process:
Goals, Traits, Stages, and Plan

George Ohlschlager and Tim Clinton

The path of life runs in and out of darkness, confusion, uncertainty, loss, and heartache—not a path we would choose naturally. It compels us to walk as aliens and strangers through the desert and through the valley of the shadow of death.

DAN ALLENDER, IN *The Healing Path*[1]

This chapter is for the analyst, the rational logician in every reader. It delivers the cognitive road map of competent Christian counseling—a map that will assist you when you get stuck in counseling, and one that you will necessarily teach to many of your clients. This chapter outlines the structural matrix of Christian counseling—a perspectival grasp of the track, traits, goals, and session-by-session plan of counseling—that easily facilitates left-brain understanding and analysis.

Novice helpers will want to study this chapter—all five chapters in this first section—carefully and in depth, working to engrave this matrix into your thinking until it becomes "second nature" to your own analytical process. Experienced helpers will want to return and review these chapters from time to time as a refresher, to remember what should never be forgotten in the counseling endeavor.

Knowing the road map richly and in great detail will always serve your mission as a helper in all kinds of cases, and will mark you as a wise counselor and a confident teacher. This, of course, is true about any life journey, not just counseling. Let's begin with a common dilemma in counseling—misunderstandings between counselor and client.

The client was devastated. We were near the end of our eighth session and I had just raised the question of terminating counseling with her. A divorcee in her mid-thirties with two children she was raising on her own, she had brought a thorny relationship problem with her new fiancé into counseling. She had worked through most of the trouble she originally presented with courage and, it seemed, real success. Termination was a natural and logical step to now consider.

Her reaction surprised me, or I should say that the strength of her reaction was the surprise, as termination issues are often fraught with strong emotions. Though I raised it as a tentative question, as I had long ago learned to do, it was clear she had heard it as a threat, as an inflexible demand to end our relationship as soon as possible. First she was hurt, then she became increasingly angry as she talked about ending counseling (triggering some abandonment questions in my mind that came out later in therapy, as she explored her fear of and resistance to remarriage).

Client: I *can't believe* you want to terminate me now. I thought we were starting to work together really well.

G.O.: We are working well together... In fact, it's working so well that you are telling me, in effect, that you've accomplished most of what you wanted when you came in.

Client: Well if I have given you that impression, I am sorry. There is so much more to do... and then you broadside me with talk of ending counseling.

G.O.: Termination is a proper subject to consider when you've reached your goals... but if there is something else?... [I left it hanging as a question.]

Client: Well... there is something... something that I hadn't planned on bringing up in counseling... at least not when I started...

G.O.: And maybe you're wondering whether you should bring it up now?...

Client: Yea, I'm afraid that things could spin out-of-control if I do... I mean I KNOW you're a mandatory reporter and all....

G.O.: Oh, and if you tell me about some child abuse situation or some-thing...I'm going to have CPS (child protective services) all over you and your boyfriend.... [Again, I left the question hanging.]

Client: Yea, something like that....I mean I know I need to talk to someone about this, and I really do trust you to do right by me...but I don't want to lose....[her voice started to crack and tears welled up.]

G.O.: [I sat back and went as soft and non-threatening as I possibly could.] You know, most clients fear the worst will happen, and it rarely does. I know some people at CPS who are very good at what they do, and are committed to maintaining the integrity of the marriage and family...Compared to carrying this thing any further all by yourself, sometimes the best thing to do is to get it out and let others take on the burden with you...

That was all it took for the story I hadn't yet heard to come pouring out. As it happened, I did have to make a report, but CPS in Northern Califor-nia is so overwhelmed with truly horrendous cases that they did not get involved in the matter. I ended up continuing to work with this client, her husband-to-be, and their blended family-to-be for another two and a half years, including a year after they were married.

Getting and Staying Oriented to Your Client's World

Counselors will often find themselves backing off going forward—pausing instead to find common ground with their clients in our increasingly plu-ralistic world—a world where common understanding of issues and terms is less and less likely as we proceed into the 21st century. Not only is it get-ting difficult to establish a common cultural understanding in America, but a common Christian culture is harder and harder to agree upon. Helpers will necessarily borrow the language of science to "operationalize" terms—to define common meanings that will resonate in mutually understood lan-guage and goals with their clients.

All counselors need to deeply understand their clients—to get oriented to their clients' ways of perceiving and understanding the world—and to reinforce this understanding by adapting to the language that they use. Some have suggested that focusing on how people think, feel, and act is essential for increasing counseling effectiveness.[2] Such a belief led Hutchins and colleagues to espouse a model called the "TFA System."[3] His model is designed as a means for "examining theories, techniques, behavioral problems, and interactional patterns that exist between people."[4]

Thinking orientation. Generally, thinking persons are characterized by intellectual, cognitively-oriented behavior. They tend to behave in logical, rational, deliberate, and systematic ways. They are fascinated by the world of concepts, ideas, theories, words, and analytic relationships. The range of behavior in this category runs from minimal thought to considerable depth in quality and quantity of thinking. Organization of thoughts ranges from scattered to highly logical and rational.

Counselors with this orientation tend to focus on what clients think and the consequences. Special attention is paid to what the client says or does not say. Frequently, illogical, irrational thinking is seen as a major cause of client problems. A primary goal of this approach is to change irrational thinking, thus enabling the client to see things more rationally and to resolve problems. Counselors who use this approach are likely to be influenced by the work of Ellis (Rational-emotive therapy), Beck (Cognitive therapy), Maultsby (Rational behavior therapy), and Meichenbaum (Cognitive behavior modification).

Feeling Orientation. Feeling persons generally tend to behave in emotionally expressive ways. They are likely to go with their feelings in making decisions: "If it feels good, do it!" The expression and display of emotions, feelings, and affect provide clues to people with a primary feeling orientation. A person's look can range from angry, anxious, bitter, hostile, or depressed to one of elation, joy, or enthusiasm. One's emotional energy level can vary from low to high.

Counselors with this orientation are likely to be regarded as especially caring persons. They tend to focus on the client's feelings, paying special attention to the expression of emotion by how the person talks. Knotted and tangled emotions are seen as a major source of the client's problems. These counselors help the client describe, clarify, and understand mixed up and immobilizing emotions. As emotional distress is straightened out, the client is frequently able to perceive things more clearly (insight). Counselors using this approach are likely to be influenced by the work of Rogers (Non-Directive/Client-Centered/Person-Centered Therapy), Perls (Gestalt Therapy), Maslow, and a host of phenomenological, humanistic, and existential writers.[5]

Acting Orientation. Acting persons are generally characterized by their involvement in doing things, and their strong goal orientation. They are frequently involved with others, and tend to plunge into the thick of things. Action types get the job done, one way or another. To them, doing something is better than doing nothing; thus, they are frequently involved in a variety of activities. Their behavior may range from loud, aggressive, and public-oriented, to quiet, subtle, and private.

Counselors with an action orientation tend to see client problems as arising from inappropriate actions or lack of action. These counselors focus particularly on what the client does or does not do, and they tend to encourage clients to begin programs designed to eliminate, modify, or teach new behavior. An action-oriented counselor is likely to be influenced by the work of Bandura (Behavior Modification), Wolpe (Behavior Therapy), Krumboltz and Thoresen (Behavioral Counseling), and others espousing a behavioral approach to change.

A more learned expression of these modes would be in the form: cognition/affect/behavior. A cognitive person is a thinker, a feeling person is very affective, and behavior and action are obviously synonymous terms.

Proposed Correlates for Christians

We would encourage this next generation of Christian counselors to develop client-centered models of understanding based on the religious and cultural traditions of various Christian populations that we tend to work with most heavily. Two ideas, for example, that may have some merit for future research and theory building are noted below.

Theology/Spirituality/Religion. The religious correlates to the thinking/feeling/acting aspects of a psychological orientation are proposed as theology/spirituality/religion. Theology literally means the knowledge of God and correlates to thinking or cognitive modes. Spirituality is more feeling oriented—an affective mode of perceiving and understanding the world. Religion correlates with action—the behavior of belief.

Head/Heart/Hands. The body orientation of many clients might express itself by way of head/heart/hands. The head obviously correlates with thinking and theology—with a cognitive orientation. Heart is the grand metaphor for feeling, for affect, and for spiritual life. And hands have to do with action and behavior—they are the prime tools (along with our feet) by which we take action and get things done.

Motivation from the Client's Perspective

Client motivation is a huge issue in successful counseling. There has been some significant research done on identifying the motivation levels and developmental progression of counseling as experienced by the client.[6] Again, this can vary depending on specific circumstance. However, this general six-stage outline provides a useful introduction to this important work.

Pre-contemplation. Though a client can be in counseling and in this stage, the client in pre-contemplation has little desire for change, or does not believe change is necessary. A case example of this is someone mandated by a court of law to participate in counseling, or a husband pressured to see a counselor by his spouse.

Contemplation. In this phase a client observes that he/she needs to change, though may not be convinced he/she wishes to exert the effort to do so. In essence the client is weighing the pros and cons of taking steps to change. It is said persons can spend years in this stage, and often counselors mistake a client's "contemplation" for the next phase, "preparation."

Preparation. With preparation, clients have made the decision to begin working toward their goals within one month's time. Nothing has technically been "done" in terms of progress, except that the client has agreed to and intends to carry out a plan of action.

Action. Here a client actively makes steps to change. Whether it is outward behavior modification (i.e. stop drinking; begin attending Bible study) or inward (i.e. establish a healthy thought life; use positive thinking), the results of this stage are the most obvious—the most observable change takes place.

Maintenance. This involves the establishment of a "post-treatment program," which is designed to solidify the positive changes and actions that have taken place in the preceding stage. In essence, the maintenance stage is concerned with preventing relapse.

Termination. Termination involves looking back at the journey that was made, and concludes the counseling relationship while at the same time establishing that the counselor is available later, if necessary for the client. Moreover, some counselors schedule a "checkup" appointment about 3 to 6 months after termination to help the client address any related issues that may manifest after the end of therapy. In general however, termination after successful counseling is a time of reflection and celebration of the change, maturity, and healing that have taken place.

The Goals and Traits of Christian Counseling

Christian Counseling Goals

Constructive client change—improving how to think, feel, and act in a goal-directed way—is the primary mission of all counseling. Christian counseling would qualify or add to this universal goal statement to assert the importance of improved belief or better faith in Christ—growing up into Christian maturity. The definition of these goals must ultimately be stated and owned by the client, with the counselor's help. Proverbs 27:19 reveals that, "As in water, face reflects face, so the heart of a man reflects a man."

Counseling, it could be argued, is a process of shifting the locus of one's dreams from the present into the future. That is, the counselor helps the client overcome their obsessions with the past and directionless daydreaming and fantasy to honestly locate themselves in the present, while they define an attainable goal they are willing to pursue into the future. Clients must be able to honestly admit their current status—their present location, as we argued in the last chapter—while assessing the resources and barriers to goal attainment.

A client who has come to pursue God's will in their life as the biggest dream they have, as the most important thing in their life, is far down the road of sanctification, of Christian maturity. "The good person out of the good treasure of his heart produces good; and the evil person out of his evil treasure produces evil, for out of the abundance of his heart his mouth speaks." (Luke 6:45)

A key challenge, then, in Christian counseling goal discussion and negotiation is to influence—to artfully argue for and persuade—a client to "turn your eyes upon Jesus," as the famous hymn states. This demands a maturity in the counselor that clearly distinguishes the unethical imposition of values and, at the other extreme, acceding to "anything goes" from the client, from exposition of the goodness of God and the high road of following Christ. Consistently seeing the relationship between the client's immediate interests and goals and the higher goals of Christ takes an experienced wisdom forged over many years of practice.

Short term and long-term goals. Distinguishing short and long-term goals is an effective way for counselors to resolve the otherwise incompatible conflicts that arise in defining client goals and God's will in a person's life, between merely coping in this life versus liberating the heart of man. As Proverbs 9:10 states, "The fear of the Lord is the beginning of wisdom." The wise counselor learns to connect client goals in the present with God's long-term design for the sanctified life.

We know biblically that the primary issues in life are related to brokenness in relationship with God and others (insecurity and lack of safety). Attachment wounds affect our core relational beliefs about God, self, others and the world in which we live. If we can understand that our emotional life and hence, our goals in living, are directly tied to our sense of safety and stability in relationships with God and others, it is easier to see how a client's short-term goals are linked to God's design.

Some clients are in open rebellion toward God, and destructive to themselves and others. Ephesians 4:18, "They are darkened in their understanding and separated from the life of God because of the ignorance that is in them due to the hardening of their hearts." Warnings and admonishment are more often the challenge for helpers in such cases. Second Corinthians 10:5 states it best: "We destroy arguments and every lofty opinion raised against the knowledge of God, and take every thought captive to obey Christ. . . . " believing that "I am a child of God, the evil one cannot touch me . . . " (1 John 5:18) for what the heart takes in also tends to become its master . . . "A characteristic of the heart and the center of man is its propensity to give itself to a master and to live toward some desired goal."[7]

Seven Synthesizing Traits

Competent Christian counseling can also be described by its most salient traits. These seven synthesizing S traits are the features of this counseling model with which every learner should become most familiar.

Scripturally anchored. True Christian counseling is as dependent on Scripture as people are on food and water to live. The Scriptures are the food and water of spiritual life, and the resource to be constantly tapped in the practice of helping others grow to Christian maturity. As we cogently argued in the last chapter, reliance on the Bible must be based, not on a few proof texts, but on the entire revelation of God from Genesis to Revelation.

Spiritual-forming. As we highlighted in Chapter 2, Christian counseling at some level involves growth toward Christian maturity. Christian counselors are called to help form the Spirit of God into the lives of those who come for help. Whether such a goal is explicit and mutually agreed between counselor and client, or more covert, linked to a long-term strategy and prayer on behalf of the client, spiritual formation and growth in faith is central to this Christian counseling endeavor.

Short-term (initially). Modern Christian counseling, like all other counseling, is bending to the realities of the marketplace. It is transforming into a brief counseling modality, one in which the majority of cases are concluded in ten sessions or less. Acknowledging the marketplace is not merely a recognition of the influence of managed care on modern mental health practice. It reflects, primarily, the growing consumer reality that most clients also conclude counseling themselves in less than ten sessions. Most clients today do not want to be in counseling interminably; counseling, like everything else in our frenetic existence, must yield to the demands of busy, modern lives.

Therefore, we restate and emphasize here the two-phased model of counseling we introduced in *Competent Christian Counseling:* Brief therapy is mandatory for every client, with long-term therapy being a discretionary option for those who want and can afford it.[8]

Solution-focused. Brief therapy is necessarily focused on finding solutions—solutions that are often based (incorporating the next section) on targeting and building upon selected client strengths. It is not merely that there is not enough time to explore and reduce or scrub away the problems or pathological elements of a person's life. It is a recognition that, often, the most effective way of doing that is to seek strength-based solutions, concentrate on and grow them stronger, and let them constructively compete with and replace the problems that exist.[9]

Strength-based skills. Another essential aspect of brief Christian therapy is its strength-based approach to change. In its essence, a strength-based orientation de-focuses problems and pathology in order to highlight, to strengthen the best and most constructive things going on in a person's life.

Pragmatically, this means that much problem solving involves helping others focus on and do more of what they are already doing well and right. Since most Christian counselors practice cognitive-behavioral therapy, there is widespread recognition that change involves an educative/learning process that concentrates the acquisition and mastery of current and new skills.

Storied narratives. Years ago, the editors of *Futurist* magazine made the outlandish prediction that "Story-tellers will be the most valued workers of the 21st century." The further we travel into this very young new century, the more we believe this to be true. Narrative, in fact, is the way we live, the way we reveal ourselves and understand the story of our lives. We are story-tellers and story-sharers from the earliest times of our lives right through to the day of our death.

Narrative—and especially relationship narrative—is the way God tells us His story in the Bible. Yes there are wonderful books laid out in the form of precepts and propositions—Scripture covers all the ways that truth can be revealed—but it is primarily a book of stories. God is revealed as the Author and Finisher of our faith, the grand Narrator who is writing our lives into a beautiful story of faith, redemption, hope, and courage.[10]

Scientific. All Christian counseling is being called to an empirical accountability. We heartily support this and invite any and all aspects of this model to be applied and tested empirically. We want to encourage the 21st century development of BEST interventions—biblically-based, empirically-supported treatments. Again, we are not slavish to empiricism or a naturalistic worldview, as we actively invite supernatural intervention by God, hoping to observe, record, and then replicate these interventions in practice. But we are committed to empirically test and validate all our models of Christian intervention.

The Process and Content of Christian Counseling

In our first volume we introduced a brief, solution-focused, two-phased model of eclectic therapy that fits the counseling process to the motivation and needs of the client. This model, in the first and mandatory phase of counseling, ordinarily accomplishes essential counseling goals in five to ten sessions. It is action-oriented, directed toward solutions that enhance spiritual maturity in Christ, and relies heavily on specific, task-related questions to assess client need and direct client behavior (see the last section of this chapter).

At the end of the short-term phase of brief therapy, clients should be able to report positive change in the direction of their goals and accomplishment in their lives, coupled with noticeable problem/symptom reduction.

The second phase of our model is longer-term and discretionary, oriented toward a deeper level of healing and characterological change. This is depth therapy that can run anywhere from ten to fifty or more sessions—running from a few months to a few years to accomplish stated goals. This therapy is discretionary in that both the costs and the time incurred by clients is substantial, and most if not all of these costs are borne by the client alone. Therefore, since managed care and insurance no longer pay for this kind of long-term care, consent to such care is an important discretionary choice by the client. The transition from one to the other comes about in a hundred different ways—even in the revelation of child abuse that will not be revealed until there has been a successful period of counseling on another issue.

A Seven-step Process

The counseling relationship can take many forms depending on the counseling theory the counselor maintains, the presenting problem(s) of the client, and the unique style of the interpersonal relationship that counselor and client develop. Despite these differences, there is a series of stages in the process of counseling that are generally consistent across the spectrum of differing theories. The process of Christian counseling tracks through these seven interrelated and overlapping steps. Competent helpers should be able to locate themselves and their client at the proper stage along this road map, and to be able to define the necessary work to be done to move the process along to the next stage.

Intake. Remember that well-worn adage: "You never get a second chance to make a first impression." Since many people come into counseling with some anxiety and skepticism, first impressions by counselors and their staff are vitally important.

You want to do everything you can to reduce anxiety, inspire hope, and promote confidence in others who may be looking for any excuse to turn and run. It has long been accepted that the rapport between client and counselor is the most important part of the counseling process. Known as the "therapeutic alliance," relationship formation includes a commitment on the part of the client and counselor to participate in therapy, and a mutual perception that both can communicate effectively. These are critical to the construction of a bond of interpersonal trust, and that begins with the first contact.

Assessment. Counseling is much like medicine in that it involves an accurate assessment of the patient's problems, goals, and abilities and deficits that will impact the process of goal attainment. There are many different methods for assessment of a client's situation. These range from psychological testing, to neurological CAT-scans that show cross sections of the brain, to an in depth counseling interview. Some of the most basic questions a counselor can ask a client are:

1. What do you want? What kind of changes are you hoping for?
2. What are you doing to get what you want?
3. Is it working? Or what's working and what's not? and
4. If not, what do you have to think/do/maintain/relate differently to make it work?

Gaining insight, or improving support-building, explanation and understanding. Support-building combines both the intangible qualities of relational trust with the practical enrichment of professional and social support that is built around the client during therapy. The supportive aspects of an ever-increasing trust relationship allows the therapist to explain, to challenge, even to goad the client toward a deepening understanding of avoided pain and change-oriented risk-taking.

Though identifying the problem begins early on, understanding develops progressively throughout the counseling process until genuine insight into life—especially God's invisible interior life—is attained. For example, a woman in counseling is diagnosed with depression, and may begin to understand some causes of her depression. However, only after continued counseling does she understand the full root source of the problem. It should be noted—from a pastoral aspect—it is in this part of the counseling relationship that confession and repentance take place.

Yielding to His healing touch. Can counseling be truly Christian without an encounter with the living God? We think not. We believe that the essential experience in Christian counseling—and that which produces lasting, even eternal change—is a result of encountering God via the relationship between Christian counselor and client. Christian counselors, when functioning at their highest, are truly the healing regents of the living God, and are engaged in the triadic relationship we defined and described in Chapter 1. The Christian counselor, as an agent of supernatural change, guides the helpee into that otherwise scary zone of meeting and yielding to the Master of all healing. This reminds us of 1 Corinthians 4:1–2 where Paul writes, "So then, men ought to regard us as servants of Christ and as those entrusted with the secret things of God. Now it is required that those who have been given a trust must prove faithful."

Active change (brief counseling for all). Interventions that facilitate client change in thinking, decision making, and goal-directed behavior reach their peak during this phase of active change. This mandatory and, for most, only time in counseling requires skillful treatment planning and goal setting. Treatment planning involves pinpointing an end goal—the purpose of the counseling—and then developing a course of action for achieving said goal. A good treatment plan will be research based and present many small objectives on the course to an end goal.

Implementation is the effort to carry out the treatment plan. Here the counselor may assign specific tasks for the completion of small objectives in pursuit of the final treatment goal.

Transformative change (long-term therapy for some). The focused time spent in active change (brief therapy) will, for many clients, cascade into a longer period of transformative change. This will come about, essentially, in two ways. Some clients will elect to continue in long-term therapy, with a goal of effecting deep healing and core characterological change. Others will terminate counseling but will seek out a coach or pastor or spiritual guide to engage more fully the journey of spiritual formation and life transformation.

Counseling as discipleship. The final step of the model involves the very natural progression of counseling to discipleship. We recognize and strongly support the view of Christian counseling as a necessary and very effective form of intensive discipleship in the overall plan of God to bring the entire church to maturity and service. This is God's universal goal—and His constant work through the Christian counseling endeavor—to help us become more like Christ and to motivate us to give that same gift away to others.

The Outline of Brief Christian Therapy

Since most clients terminate counseling within 8-to-10 sessions, and since managed care rarely authorizes more, we have developed a 10-session outline of Christian counseling that addresses both content and process issues a counselor will most commonly face. Bathing each session and the client in prayer, we begin with:

1. First Contact: First Impressions Always Count

- The first phone call: Take basic information and build rapport.
- Maintain calm in client crisis, while countering skepticism and promoting optimism.
- Convey to clients the likelihood of a successful outcome (to build confidence).
- Is the client presenting a problem I am competent to work with? Do I need to refer now?
- Schedule an appointment and pray to invite God to begin change now.

FIRST SESSION

2. Trust Building and Beginning Assessment

- *Directed facilitation:* Striking the balance between relationship building and intentional interviewing to gain both rapport and necessary information about the client and his/her life.
- *Facilitating client storytelling and collecting client information.* Beginning a mental status exam and collecting data on personal history, family history, medical history (and medications), and psychosocial treatment history.
- *Assessing suicide and dangerousness, and religion and spirituality.*
- Is the client a danger to himself or others? Is the risk severe and immediate?
- Has the client reported the abuse of a child, the elderly, or a handicapped individual?
- Does the client find solace or pain in his/her religious faith?
- Is the client striving toward spiritual obedience and maturity?

- *Informed Consent:* Begin to tell the client about the treatment/ services you provide, and about the rights and limits of confidentiality

3. Life-enhancing Goal Setting (LeGS)

- *Understanding ultimate and immediate goals.* What is the Christ-centered end goal, and what are the smaller, client-stated objectives to be obtained along the way?—assess and link the two!
- *Facilitating client goal-setting:* Does the client claim ownership of the treatment goals and have they made a firm resolve to participate in treatment?
- *Using the miracle question:* Ask, "If you woke up tomorrow and everything was perfect, what would it look like?"
- *Fee-setting and service contracting*: Be very specific about your counseling rates, cancellation policy, time of payment due, warranties, and other financial matters.
ACTION 1: SHOW the client the beginning way out by giving them a Simple Homework task that Overcomes the World—that begins to resolve the problem.

SECOND SESSION

4. Comprehensive & Diagnostic History-taking

Using the BECHRISTLIKE Christ-centered Multimodal Assessment tool

B—*Behavior:* Focuses on observable behavior and assesses whether helpful or harmful. Defines key behavior patterns around problem issues. Assesses antecedents and consequences of behavior. Notes behavioral strengths and deficits.

E—*Emotions:* Assesses primary emotional disturbance and the emotional patterns. Describes desired feelings. How does client value emotions in relation to beliefs, thoughts, and behavior? How do emotional themes reveal relations with God?

C—*Cognition:* Assesses thought content and process. What are the lies and distortions that animate this client? Reasoning ability? Psychotic or delusional symptoms? Self-talk? Is client imagery helpful vs. traumatic? What is imagery content, intensity, and frequency?

H—*Health:* What is client's overall health status? Notes medical problems, and whether or not under a physician's care. Notes sensory/somatic complaints and psychosocial interactions, whether for better or for worse. Assesses sleeping, eating, and exercise habits and conditions. Is MD referral called for?

R—*Religion:* Where is the client in Christ? Saved or not? Maturing or not? Assesses church life and Christian practices. Conducts a biblical analysis of problem behavior. Assesses receptivity vs. resistance to spiritual interventions.

I—*Idols and false beliefs:* What desires and values compete with God, with God's priorities? What values line up biblically and need strengthening? How is problem related to value conflicts and discrepancies, biblically understood?

S—*Substances:* Assesses what drugs client is taking, both prescribed and/or illicit. What are drug interactions? Does client need MD referral for psychotropic meds? Does client need a program for detox and substance abuse treatment?

T—*Teachability:* Is client motivated or resistant, and is it global or specific, dependent on problem or other variables? Hope vs. hopelessness? Does client trust the counselor? Are there racial, ethnic, or gender differences that need to be bridged?

L—*Law/ethics:* Assesses whether client is a danger to self or others. Any current legal trouble? Any other red-flag issues that demand immediate attention? Does client need to be referred to a lawyer?

I—*Interpersonal relations:* Describes current issues and history with family and friends—rich web or deficient? Who is best and worst family member? Best and worst friend? Best and worst traits in father and mother? Describe spousal relations, satisfying and dissatisfying. Describe sexual behavior and problems.

K—*Knowledge:* Does client have sufficient knowledge/skill to change? Assesses skill strengths and deficits. Notes formal education and what, if anything, client does to improve knowledge. Considers resources for further learning, formal and informal.

E—*Environment:* What are the external obstacles and reaction triggers? What are strengths and resources available to client? What is client's locus of control—does s/he perceive they are controlled by events or free to influence them?

See our text on *Competent Christian Counseling*, for a more in depth discussion of this anagrammatic tool. Through interview or testing, obtain a diagnostic analysis of the client.

Screening for psycho-social problems, and for addictions and psychosis, and for medical/legal referral. Complete mental status exam with clear indications of any referrals and with a narrowing focus on the treatment goals that you will be working toward with your client.

ACTION 2: Review homework from week one and build on what was done well, or evaluate why nothing was completed and recalibrate homework task.

THIRD SESSION

5. Treatment Planning and Ongoing Prayer

- *Making a DSM diagnosis:* Usually for the process of insurance reimbursement; include axes 1–4 even if *diagnosis is deferred.*
- *Translating goals and data into a plan:* A research-based treatment protocol should be used to treat the presenting problem.
- *Continual prayer for wisdom, discernment, guidance:* Do not overlook the healing touch and spirit of God by taking a fully cognitive approach to therapy.

ACTION 3: Review week two homework and continue to build on what was done well, generalizing this initial success to another, more central issue of concern.

THIRD/FOURTH SESSION

6. Working from the Therapeutic Frame

- *Therapy rules that enhance client safety and motivation:* Instituting structure and boundaries in the counseling process is an important part of treatment.
- *Working toward goals that will likely succeed:* Do not set your clients up for failure by establishing unreasonable or grandiose goals (small steps in the right direction make more sense than big ones in the wrong).

- *Fostering attachment to God in Christ:* The goal of Christian counseling is not symptom relief but reestablishing the image of God in man, and maturity in Christ. Is your treatment promoting this objective?
- *As you think, so shall you act:* From the good treasure stored up in the client's heart—thus says Luke. Clients must experience internal sanctification if they are going to sustain a positive external change.

ACTION 4: Review last session homework, praising and reinforcing any success shown and pointing its effects across the bio-psycho-social-spiritual spectrum of the client's life. Move further in the generalization of successful to other, more difficult problems.

FIFTH–TENTH SESSIONS

7. Working with Client Resistance and Dependency

- *Resistance is normal—use it, don't fight it.* When resistance occurs, use the opportunity to investigate what is keeping the client "stuck."
- *Client phone calls—emergencies or dependencies.* It is not uncommon for clients with attachment issues or borderline tendencies to call counselors under the ruse of a crisis, as a way to attempt to control or sabotage a counseling relationship. Counselors must handle these clients with boundaries, and also with compassion—for their intrusiveness is rooted in need and dependency.
- *Dealing with no-shows and late arrivals.* Payment for missed sessions omitted, counselors should communicate with clients their policy of starting counseling sessions late, and the issue of no-shows. Sometimes missed sessions are an action used by clients to regain control of a dynamic, or to avoid progress of the counseling endeavor.

ACTION 5: Review last session homework, praising and reinforcing any success shown and pointing out and strengthening its effects across the bio-psycho-social-spiritual spectrum of the client's life. Address any issues of entropy or resistance by talking and working through them.

8. Working through Your Lapses and Frustrations

- *Boredom and empathic lapses.* A good counselor can set aside his or her needs and be completely present for a client. This includes the counselor's needs for fun and emotional rest. Counseling is a draining process for all parties involved; counselors should prayerfully ask for strength to remain empathetic and involved amid a long day of sessions.
- *Managing frustration with clients.* Clients can frustrate counselors through their lies, deceit, and sin. Others will purposefully attempt to frustrate counselors, for doing so is part of their dysfunction. In addition, counselors are not immune to counter-transference issues, and react to client traits and behavior with annoyance and avoidance or denial.
- *Maintaining constructive work.* The counselor should A) assess if they are able to work with the frustrating type of client (i.e. some counselors will not work with men who abuse) and B) should work diligently to be supportive and therapeutic of frustrating clients they do agree to work with.
- *Using your anger wisely.* Anger is not a sin but a God-given response to a real or perceived injustice or wrong. Used wisely anger is gently assertive, and takes into account the needs of the client. Counselors should understand healthy and constructive expression of anger.

ACTION 6: Review last session homework, praising and reinforcing any success shown and pointing its effects across the bio-psycho-social-spiritual spectrum of the client's life. Address any issues of entropy or resistance by talking and working through them.

9. Managing Ethical Tasks and Dilemmas

- *Knowing when consent is withdrawn.* Consent is more than merely a formal legal construct—clients may withdraw it psychologically and show, by resistance maintained or refusing to return to therapy—that they have disengaged altogether.
- *Confidentiality and reporting duties.* Make sure you follow through

with these demands in a timely fashion, giving your client notice
of intended action.

- *When clients want to see their records.* Give them a summary statement of their records. If they want more, set a date to copy and
  give clients what they are due.
- *Dealing with sexual feelings in therapy.* Acknowledge them, pray
  about them, and DON'T ACT THEM OUT WITH YOUR CLIENT.
  If they persist, go find a trusted colleague of the same sex, and talk
  them through with honesty and wisdom.

ACTIONS 7/8/9: Review last session homework, same as before, praising and reinforcing any success shown and pointing its effects across the
bio-psycho-social-spiritual spectrum of the client's life. Address any issues
of entropy or resistance by talking and working through them. Continue to
encourage and assist client along to goal acquisition.

LAST SESSION

10. Terminating Treatment

- *Don't abandon your clients.* When counselors can no longer provide
  service, they are ethically obligated to refer clients to another mental health service provider.
- *When the client simply drops out of counseling.* This is not uncommon, and preventing dropout is often outside the power of the
  counselor. Counselors should discuss a dropout policy with
  clients during the intake process that answers questions like "Are
  clients welcome to return if they drop out of counseling?"
- *When ending counseling is raised in-session.* Clients can have apprehension about ending counseling, even when the goals have been
  achieved. Counselors should reinforce their client's independence
  while also making themselves available in the instance of client need.
- *Once a client, always so?* Counselors maintain some ethical and
  legal responsibility long after the counseling relationship ends.
  For example, if a client commits violence against himself or others
  after termination, the counselor may be called into question. Also,
  romantic relationships and other dual roles are typically forbidden with past clients.

ACTION 10: Review the entire course of counseling, discussing what went well and what didn't. Discuss and secure client commitment to continue in working and maintaining change. Terminate with a clear invitation to return in the future if needed.

Documentation

A final word must be said about note taking and documentation. This is a very important part of the counseling process that should begin with the first contact by a client (or prospective client) and continue until termination. Counselors are ethically responsible to maintain a client record for each person they counsel: including a diagnosis, treatment plan, progress notes, etc. Some counselors will make parts of the file available to clients, while others will provide an interpretation of the record upon a client's request. For pastoral counselors and lay helpers, a full record may not be necessary, though one should check with the practice laws in his/her state of residence.

ENDNOTES

1. Dan B. Allender, *The healing path: How the hurts in your past can lead you to a more abundant life* (Colorado Springs: Waterbrook, 1999), 19.

2. G. Corey, *Theory and practice of counseling and psychotherapy 6th.ed* (Pacific Grove, CA: Brooks/Cole, 2000); Albert Ellis, *The Albert Ellis reader: A guide to well-being using rational emotive behavior therapy* (NY: Citadel Press, 1998); L. L'Abate, Classification of counseling and therapy, theorists, method process, and goals: The E-R-A model, *The Personnel and Guidance Journal,* 59 (1981), 263–265.

3. D. Hutchins, and Cole, C., Helping relationships and strategies 2d ed. (Pacific Grove, CA: Brooks/Cole, 1992); D. Hutchins, Improving the counseling relationship, *The Personnel and Guidance Journal,* 62(10), (1984), 572–575.

4. D. Hutchins, Improving the counseling relationship, *The Personnel and Guidance Journal,* 62(10), (1984), 573.

5. Ibid.

6. Timothy Clinton, and Ohlschlager, G., *Competent Christian counseling, volume one: Foundations and practice of compassionate soul care* (Colorado Springs: WaterBrook, 2002), 101; James O. Prochaska, Norcross, J. and DiClemente, C., *Changing for good* (NY: Avon Books, 1994).

7. Neil Anderson, *Discipleship counseling* (Ventura, CA: Regal Books, 2003), quote by Robert Jewett.

8. Timothy Clinton, and Ohlschlager, G., *Competant Christian Counseling, Volume One: Foundations and Practice of Compassionate Soul Care* (Colorado Springs: Waterbrook, 2002).

9. Gary J. Oliver, Hasz, M., and Richburg, M., *Promoting Change Through Brief Therapy in Christian Counseling,* (Wheaton, IL: Tyndale House, 1997).

10. Dan B. Allender, *To be told* (Colorado Springs: WaterBrook Press, 2005).

5

Christian Counseling Ethics:
Honoring a Clear Moral Structure

George Ohlschlager and Tim Clinton

Counseling is often a moral, legal and emotional "minefield." Pastors and lay helpers should not attempt long-term, in-depth counseling and psychotherapy unless they are specifically trained to do so. The subtle but powerful moral conflicts and ego dynamics inherent to counseling have trapped many well-meaning pastors and their counselees in moral compromise and spiritual defeat...I recommend that pastors develop and honor a three-part policy of pastoral counseling and referral. (1) Set clear limits to the time, number of sessions, and kinds and depth of problems that you will work with, referring parishioners when these limits are reached...(2) Develop and train lay ministers for both one-to-one help and, especially, small support group ministry that can be a first source of referral...(3) Finally, refer the more difficult and long-term problems to ...professional Christian counselors.

Pastor Amos Clemmons[1]

As Christian counseling is drawn into greater intimacy with God and service to the church, not only are professional Christian counselors serving more frequently in church staff and consultative roles, but pastoral counseling and lay helping ministry is mushrooming. This is a wonderful development, and goes far toward fulfilling the promise of Christian counseling in the 21st century.[2]

However, there is increasing concern over the ethical-legal issues of Christian counseling from a number of power centers—the church and the law being the two most obvious. Calls to the AACC for consultation, mediation, and training about the ethical practice of Christian counseling has seen an exponential rise in recent years. We believe that if every pastor honored the framing ethic of pastoral counseling practice stated above by Pastor Clemmons, then the church's entire helping ministry would operate like a well-oiled machine.

Some look at ethical codes, state and nationally legislated counseling laws, and all the "legalese" present for the practice of counseling, and cringe! However, in truth such guidelines are designed just as much for the protection of the *counselor* as they are for the *client*. Anyone looking to function in the role of Christian counselor should be familiar with (at least) the major counseling ethical standards.

Also, ethical decision-making is mired in crisis and confusion in our values-relative and pluralistic world. The moral elasticity of our postmodern, post-Christian culture has even infected the church. Whether it is pulpit exaggeration, printed hyperbole, the abuse of conferred power, sexual misconduct, or other serious forms of client/parishioner exploitation, too many church leaders and counselors today are losing the battle of moral purity and ethical integrity. As a result, Christians are ridiculed, and the cause of Christ suffers.

Although we are witnessing an increasing frequency of lawsuits against counselors and clergy, we believe that the majority of these lawsuits are preventable. We noted in *Law for the Christian Counselor*[3] that most suits were a function of these problems:

1. Sexual involvement with a counselee—still the most frequent source of trouble, by far.
2. Counseling beyond your competence, ability, or training.
3. Advice against medical or psychological treatment, including medications.
4. The administration, interpretation, and scoring of personality and psychological tests.
5. Inadequate records or the improper care of records.
6. Inadequately trained and supervised lay and pastoral counselors.
7. The failure to give credence to violent intentions or statements.
8. Misdiagnosing psychotics (or others) as demon-possessed.
9. Misrepresenting one's title, position, degrees, or abilities.
10. Recommending for or against divorce.
11. Violations of confidentiality (in both clinical and church settings).
12. Denial of the existence or severity of a psychological or psychosomatic disorder.

13. The belief that all problems are spiritual or physical with denial of the psychological dimensions.

14. The belief that pastoral and lay counselors need only biblical training to solve such severe problems as neuroses, psychoses, suicide issues, and the like.

Getting Oriented to Christian and Counseling Ethics

Webster defines "ethics" as the "study of standards of conduct and moral judgment," and the "system or code of moral conduct of a particular person, religion, group, profession, etc." Corey, Corey, and Callanan further distinguish ethics from values: "Although values and ethics are frequently used interchangeably, the two terms are not identical. Values pertain to beliefs and attitudes that provide direction to everyday living, whereas ethics pertain to the beliefs we hold about what constitutes right conduct. Ethics are moral principles adopted by an individual or group to provide rules for right conduct..."[4]

A code of ethics is a systematic statement of ethical standards that represent the moral convictions and guide the practice behavior of a group—in this case, the pastoral and lay counseling ministry of the church. Every one of the primary counseling disciplines—psychiatry, psychology, social work, marriage and family therapy, and professional counseling—has an ethics code. These codes are revised and updated every few years to stay current with emerging issues and to develop a refined sense of ethical clarity and direction. Christian counseling has developed ethical codes, including the *AACC Christian Counseling Code of Ethics* (Code), parts of which are detailed in the remainder of this chapter.[5]

Accountability is central to our consideration of what it means to be an ethical helper. Jesus practiced a divine accountability to His Heavenly Father at every step of His public ministry—and He asserted that, in similar fashion, His disciples were accountable to Him and His Father as well. "All those who love Me will do what I say. My Father will love them, and We will come to them and live with them. And remember, My words are not My own. This message is from the Father who sent Me." (John 14:23–24) The most powerful being in the universe was dedicated, not to His own agenda, but constantly yielded to He who sent Him. Imagine it. We are to do no less.

Ferment over Ethical Foundations: Three Views

Ethical decision making in the modern world is now influenced by three major orientations:

1. *Divine revelation yielding moral absolutes.* For two millennia of church and Western history, most ethical systems have been rooted in Judeo-Christian values flowing out of God's revelation in the Scriptures. This view asserts that the infinite-personal God of the Bible has revealed the perfect law—a transcendent and universal order of right and wrong—and has given us grace through Jesus Christ to know and attain it.

God's moral absolutes are held to be universal, not culture or time-bound, but applicable across all space and time. With the Law of Moses, the ethics of Jesus Christ—revealed in their highest form in the Sermon on the Mount—are the basis of ethical, legal, political, and economic principles that have shaped the development of Western history and culture. Honoring these ethics promises to bring order, peace, prosperity, and dignity to the people and cultures that do so. Transgressing these ethics results in personal distress, interpersonal conflict, political and cultural decline and, if not halted and godly ethics restored, national anarchy and dissolution.

2. *Radical individualism yielding moral relativism.* The ethical history of the 20th century reveals the incremental and systematic rejection of divine authority and the rise of secular humanism. Individual autonomy is supreme in this worldview and moral relativism—"do your own thing, just don't hurt me doing it"—is the result. The root value of this perspective is that "man is the measure of all things" including his or her own judgment about right and wrong. Also known as subjectivism, or "situational ethics" as an applied practice, this view yields an extreme form of moral relativism—"I will decide for myself what is right and wrong; whatever is right for you may not be so for me."

Proponents of this view consider personal freedom to be the ultimate value and autonomous living the grand pursuit. Hence the value of individualism is radicalized—placed above and over all other values—and any recourse to social convention or moral absolutes is denied. Laws, custom, and social convention is held to be a constraining, even oppressive force that only serves to unjustly inhibit personal freedom.[6] Politically, anarchy is the result of this view when pushed to its systemic conclusion.

3. *Social constructionism yielding moral consensus.* A third model gaining

current force is influenced by family and social systems theory as well as our democratic political tradition. The social constructionist view posits that ethics are forged in the interactive consensus-building process of people and systems in relationship. By negotiation, mediation, and arbitration, derived ethics reflect a group or social consensus whereby the best values as agreed upon by the participants in the process are expressed as ethics and codified into law.

Moral absolutes are not controlling in this approach, but may be reflected in the consensus values and ethics that are reached by majority rule. Biblical values may or may not survive this process of ethical and legal decision-making. The group or the "body politic"—whatever its size and function—is the creator of the moral consensus, and the final arbiter of right and wrong. This view seems to be ascendant among those who recognize the social and political risks of a purely subjective and individualized ethic, but do not want to adhere to the revealed ethics flowing from God's revelation.

1. Above All, Do No Harm

The first rule of ethics in any profession—especially the counseling professions—that serves human need is: do no harm. At first blush this may seem absurdly obvious and simple. On reading and reflection the depth and importance of this rule comes to light. Consider both our general statement and one of its applications—euthanasia and assisted suicide:

> 1–100 Christian counselors acknowledge that the first rule of professional-ministerial ethical conduct is: do no harm to those served.
>
> 1–101 Affirming the God-given Dignity of All Persons
>
> Affirmatively, Christian counselors recognize and uphold the inherent, God-given dignity of every human person, from the pre-born to those on death's bed. Human beings are God's creation—the crown of His creation—and are therefore due all the rights and respect that this fact of creation entails. Therefore, regardless of how we respond to and challenge harmful attitudes and actions, Christian counselors will express a loving care to any client, service-inquiring person, or anyone encountered in the course of practice or ministry, without regard to race, ethnicity, gender, sexual behavior or orientation, socio-economic status,

education, denomination, belief system, values, or political affiliation. God's love is unconditional and, at this level of concern, so must that of the Christian counselor.

1–120 Refusal to Participate in the Harmful Actions of Clients

Christian counselors refuse to participate in, condone, advocate for, or assist the harmful actions of clients, especially those that imperil human life from conception to death. This includes suicidal, homicidal, or assaultive/abusive harm done to self or others—the protection of human life is always a priority value. We will not abandon clients who do or intend harm, will terminate helping relations only in the most compelling circumstances, and will continue to serve clients in these troubles as far as it is possible.

1–122 Application to Euthanasia and Assisted Suicide

Christian counselors refuse to participate in, condone, advocate for, or assist clients in active forms of euthanasia and assisted suicide. We may agree to and support the wish not to prolong life by artificial means, and will often advocate for hospice care, more effective application of medicine, and other reasonable means to reduce pain and suffering.

Regarding patients or clients who wish to die, we will not deliver, nor advocate for, nor support the use of drugs or devices to be utilized for the purpose of ending a patient's life. We recognize that the death of a patient may occur as the unintended and secondary result of aggressive action to alleviate a terminally ill patient's extreme pain and suffering. So long as there are no other reasonable methods to alleviate such pain and suffering, the Christian counselor is free to support, advocate for, and participate in such aggressive pain management in accordance with sound medical practice, and with the informed consent of the patient or patient's representative.

For physicians the call to "do no harm" may translate into doing nothing medically, or always considering the least intrusive action first. Christian counseling ethics also presumes this all-encompassing first rule: that to help someone, we must first ensure that we do not harm them. This is not as easy or as obvious as it seems. Understanding that harm is possible in any kind of human intervention yields an ethic enlightened and humbled by the fact that even though saved by Christ and sanctified by the Spirit, humans remain susceptible to sin and wrongdoing (and do frequently sin on a regular basis).

Research indicates that negative outcomes affect a stubborn minority of all counseling cases, and hurtful yet unintended consequences are unyielding phenomena of human interaction. We give children the grace to continually say, "But I didn't mean to hurt them." As adults, we are usually allowed only one or two such excuses before we are barred from doing the thing we hope will be helpful, not harmful.

2. Supervision and Training in the Church

We state in the preface to this section to Christian counseling leaders that "Some Christian counselors serve in senior professional roles—as administrators, supervisors, teachers, consultants, researchers, and writers. They are recognized for their counseling expertise, their dedication to Christ and the ministry or profession to which they belong, and for their exemplary ethics. These leaders are responsible for the development and maturation of the Christian counseling profession, for serving as active and ethical role models, and for raising up the next generation of Christian counselors and leaders."

We are opposed to all forms of "lone ranger" ministry, and do not advocate for or distribute our lay helper training programs without a commitment to pastoral oversight and supervision in the church. Pastors and counseling professionals in the church should be involved in every step of the selection, training, and supervision of lay helpers and church counseling staff.

2–110 Ethics and Excellence in Supervision and Teaching

Christian counseling supervisors and educators maintain the highest levels of clinical knowledge, professional skill, and ethical excellence in all supervision and teaching. They are knowledgeable about the latest professional and ministerial developments and responsibly transmit this knowledge to students and supervisees.

2–111 Preparation for Teaching and Supervision

Christian counseling supervisors and educators have received adequate training and experience in teaching and supervision methods before they deliver these services. Supervisors and educators are encouraged to maintain and enhance their skills through continued clinical practice, advanced training, and continuing education.

2–120 Supervisors and Educators Do Not Exploit Students and Trainees

Christian counseling supervisors and educators avoid exploitation, appearances of exploitation, and harmful dual relations with students and trainees. Students and trainees are taught by example and by explanation, with the mentor responsible to define and maintain clear, proper, and ethical professional and social boundaries.

3. Competent Counseling: Doing Well at Consultation and Referral

Being a competent Christian counselor means that one is highly aware of and honors the limits of his/her counseling knowledge and skill. Lay helpers must embrace this rule with enthusiasm, and most pastors do so out of necessity due to the myriad demands of pastoral life. Here is an excerpt of this ethical rule.

210 Honoring the Call to Competent Christian Counseling

Christian counselors maintain the highest standards of competence with integrity. We know and respect the boundaries of competence in ourselves and others, especially those under our supervision. We make only truthful, realistic statements about our identity, education, experience, credentials, and about counseling goals and process, avoiding exaggerated and sensational claims. We do not offer services or work beyond the limits of our competence and do not aid or abet the work of Christian counseling by untrained, unqualified, or unethical helpers.

1–220 Duties to Consult and/or Refer

Christian counselors consult with and/or refer to more competent colleagues or supervisors when these limits of counseling competence are reached: (1) when facing issues not dealt with before or not experienced in handling, (2) when clients need further help outside the scope of our training and practice, (3) when either counselor or clients are feeling stuck or confused about counseling and neither is clear what to do about it, or (4) when counselees are deteriorating or making no realistic gain over a number of sessions. Christian counselors shall honor the client's goals and confidential privacy interests in all consultations and referrals.

1–221 Consultation Practice

When counseling help is needed, and with client consent, consultation may be attempted first, when in the client's best interest and to improve helper's knowledge and skill where some competence exists. Counselors shall take all reasonable action to apply consultative help to the case in order to gain/maintain ground toward client objectives. The consultant shall maintain a balanced concern for the client discussed and the practice/education needs of the consultee, directing the counselor-consultee to further training or special resources, if needed.

1–222 Referral Practice

Referral shall be made in situations where client need is beyond the counselor's ability or scope of practice or when consultation is inappropriate, unavailable, or unsuccessful. Referrals should be done only after the client is provided with informed choices among referral sources. As much as possible, counselors referred to shall honor prior commitments between client and referring counselor or church.

1–223 Seek Christian Help, If Available

When consulting or referring, Christian counselors seek out the best Christian help at a higher level of knowledge, skill, and expertise. If Christian help is not available, or when professional skill is more important than the professional's beliefs, Christian counselors shall use the entire network of professional services available.

1–224 Avoid Counsel Against Professional Treatment

Christian counselors do not counsel or advise against professional counseling, medical or psychiatric treatment, the use of medications, legal counsel, or other forms of professional service merely because we believe such practice is per se wrong or because the provider may not be a Christian.

Dr. Gary Collins,[7] one of the pioneers of our field who trained and mentored us both, advocates that, "Sometimes we help counselees most by referring them to someone else whose training, expertise and availability can be of special assistance... referral can reflect the counselor's concern for the counselee, and can show that no one person is skilled enough to counsel everyone."[8] The counselor has the moral, ethical and professional responsibility to admit to herself, and to her client, when the relationship fails, or the client's situation exceeds her ability to help.

It is not always the counselor's lack of expertise that is the determining factor for a referral. Therapeutic relationships can fail when:

1.   Counselor and client have incompatible personalities
2.   Transference or counter-transference issues occur that cannot be resolved (such as sexual attraction)
3.   When there is incongruity between counselor's and client's beliefs or values
4.   When the counselor is unable to break through a client's resistance to change
5.   Dual roles manifest (such as a client becoming a college student of the counselor)

Lastly, the responsibility to refer implies counselors be familiar with all resources and persons available for referral.

4. Informed Consent for Church-based Counseling

The need for informed consent increases as intervention increases or as a specialized kind of counseling method takes place (i.e a brief meeting vs. biofeedback therapy). Pastoral and lay helpers should use a simple one-page agreement that covers some of the issues (in 1–320 below) and indicates that the clients understand they are engaged in pastoral or lay helping, not professional counseling.

1–310 Securing Informed Consent

Christian counselors secure client consent for all counseling and related services. This includes the video/audio-taping of client sessions, the use of supervisory and consultative help, the application of special procedures and evaluations, and the communication of client data with other professionals and institutions.

Christian counselors take care that (1) the client has the capacity to give consent; (2) we have discussed counseling together and the client reasonably understands the nature and process of counseling; the costs, time, and work required; the limits of counseling; and any appropriate alternatives; and (3) the client freely gives consent to counseling, without coercion or undue influence.

1–320 Consent for the Structure and Process of Counseling

Christian counselors respect the need for informed consent regarding the structure and process of counseling. Early in counseling, counselor and client should discuss and agree upon these issues: the nature of and course of therapy; client issues and goals; potential problems and reasonable alternatives to counseling; counselor status and credentials; confidentiality and its limits; fees and financial procedures; limitations about time and access to the counselor, including directions in emergency situations; and procedures for resolution of disputes and misunderstandings. If the counselor is supervised, that fact shall be disclosed and the supervisor's name and role indicated to the client.

1–321 Consent from Parent or Client Representative

Christian counselors obtain consent from parents or the client's legally authorized representative when clients are minors or adults who are legally incapable of giving consent.

1–330 Consent for Biblical-Spiritual Practices in Counseling

Christian counselors do not presume that all clients want or will be receptive to explicit spiritual interventions in counseling. We obtain consent that honors client choice, receptivity to these practices, and the timing and manner in which these things are introduced: prayer for and with clients, Bible reading and reference, spiritual meditation, the use of biblical and religious imagery, assistance with spiritual formation and discipline, and other common spiritual practices.

1–331 Special Consent for More Difficult Interventions

Close or special consent is obtained for more difficult and controversial practices. These include, but are not limited to: deliverance and spiritual warfare activities; cult de-programming work; recovering memories and treatment of past abuse or trauma; use of hypnosis and any kind of induction of altered states; authorizing (by MDs) medications, electroconvulsive therapy, or patient restraints; use of aversive, involuntary, or experimental therapies; engaging in reparative therapy with homosexual persons; and counseling around abortion and end-of-life issues. These interventions require a more detailed discussion with patient-clients or client representatives of the procedures, risks, and treatment alternatives, and we secure detailed written agreement for the procedure.

5. Multiple Clients: Working with Groups, Couples, and Families

Most pastors work with couples and families, and church-based counselors lead all kinds of groups—counseling groups, Bible study groups, growth groups, spiritual formation groups, 12-step and recovery groups, supervision groups, and education groups of all sorts. Here are our ethical guidelines for group work.

1–540 Working with Couples, Families, and Groups

Christian counselors often work with multiple persons in session—marriage couples, families or parts of families, and small groups—and should know when these forms of counseling are preferred over or used as an adjunct to individual counseling. In these relationships we will identify a primary client—the group as a unit or the individual members—and will discuss with our client(s) how our differing roles, counseling goals, and confidentiality and consent issues are affected by these dynamics.

1–541 Safety and Integrity in Family and Group Counseling

Christian counselors will maintain their role as fair, unbiased, and effective helpers in all marital, family, and group work. We will remain accessible to all persons, avoiding enmeshed alliances and taking sides unjustly. As group or family counseling leaders, Christian counselors respect the boundary between constructive confrontation and verbal abuse, and will take reasonable precautions to protect client members from any physical, psychological, or verbal abuse from other members of a family or group.

6. Confidentiality and Its Exceptions

Since confidentiality reaches the very core of the maintenance of trust in helping relationships, we recommend that pastors and lay helpers take it as seriously as do professional therapists. Here are the primary rules that govern modern-day confidentiality and privilege.

1–410 Maintaining Client Confidentiality

Christian counselors maintain client confidentiality to the fullest extent allowed by law, professional ethics, and church or organizational rules. Confidential client communications include all verbal, written, telephonic, audio or video-taped, or electronic communications arising within the helping relationship. Apart from the exceptions below, Christian counselors shall not disclose confidential client communications without first discussing the intended disclosure and securing written consent from the client or client representative.

1–411 Discussing the Limits of Confidentiality and Privilege

Clients should be informed about both the counselor's commitment to confidentiality and its limits before engaging in counseling. Christian counselors avoid stating or implying that confidentiality is guaranteed or absolute. We will discuss the limits of confidentiality and privacy with clients at the outset of counseling.

1–420 Asserting Confidentiality or Privilege Following Demands for Disclosure

Protecting confidential communications, including the assertion of privilege in the face of legal or court demands, shall be the first response of counselors to demands or requests for client communications and records.

1–421 Disclosure of Confidential Client Communications

Christian counselors disclose only that client information they have written permission from the client to disclose or that which is required by legal or ethical mandates. The counselor shall maintain confidentiality of client information outside the bounds of that narrowly required to fulfill the disclosure and shall limit disclosures only to those people having a direct professional interest in the case. In the face of a subpoena, counselors shall neither deny nor immediately comply with disclosure demands, but will assert privilege in order to give the client time to consult with a lawyer to direct disclosures.

1–430 Protecting Persons from Deadly Harm: The Rule of Mandatory Disclosure

Christian counselors accept the limits of confidentiality when human life is imperiled or abused. We will take appropriate action, including necessary disclosures of confidential information, to protect life in the face of client threats of suicide, homicide, and/or the abuse of children, elders, and dependent persons.

1–431 The Duty to Protect Others

The duty to take protective action is triggered when the counselor (1) has reasonable suspicion, as stated in your state statute, that a minor child (under 18 years), elder person (65 years and older), or dependent adult (regardless of age) has been harmed by the client; or (2) has direct client admissions of serious and imminent suicidal threats; or (3) has direct client admissions of harmful acts or threatened action that is serious, imminent, and attainable against a clearly identified third person or group of persons.

1–432 Guidelines to Ethical Disclosure and Protective Action

Action to protect life, whether your client or a third-person, shall be that which is reasonably necessary to stop or forestall deadly or harmful action in the present situation. This could involve hospitalizing the client, intensifying clinical intervention to the degree necessary to reasonably protect against harmful action, consultation and referral with other professionals, or disclosure of harm or threats to law enforcement, protective services, identifiable third-persons, and/or family members able to help with protective action.

1–433 Special Guidelines When Violence Is Threatened Against Others

Action to protect third-persons from client violence may involve or, in states that have a third-person protection (Tarasoff) duty, require disclosure of imminent harm to the intended victim, to their family or close friends, and to law enforcement. When child abuse or elder abuse or abuse of dependent adults exists, as defined by state law, Christian counselors shall report to child or elder protective services, or to any designated agency established for protective services. We shall also attempt to defuse the situation and/or take preventive action by whatever means are available and appropriate.

When clients threaten serious and imminent homicide or violence against an identifiable third-person, the Christian counselor shall inform appropriate law enforcement, and/or medical-crisis personnel, and the at-risk person or close family member of the threat, except when precluded by compelling circumstances or by state law.

When the client threat is serious but not imminent, the Christian counselor shall take preventive clinical action that seeks to forestall any further escalation of threat toward violent behavior.

1–470 Advocacy for Privacy Rights Against Intrusive Powers

Christian counselors hear the most private and sensitive details of their clients' lives—information that must be zealously guarded from public disclosure. Rapidly expanding and interlocking electronic information networks are increasingly threatening client privacy rights. Though federal and state laws exist to protect client privacy, these laws are weak, are routinely violated at many levels, and the record of privacy right enforcement is dismal. Accordingly, Christian counselors are called to wisely protect and assertively advocate for privacy protection on behalf of our clients against the pervasive intrusion of personal, corporate, governmental, even religious powers.

Clients rightly expect that whatever they reveal to the counselor will be kept confidential. But competent counselors must be aware of limitations, and they have a responsibility to advise clients of these up-front. As you can see, we have incorporated Tarasoff principles into our ethics code—referring to the now-famous California Supreme Court decision establishing the duty to warn others if a client threatens homicide. We did so because the policy behind Tarasoff—that human life is more important than confidentiality—is good biblical ethics and law.

In addition, counselors will need to familiarize themselves with: (1) individual state laws concerning responsibilities related to suicide, child and elder abuse, abuse of the handicapped, and threats of violence; (2) available resources in their areas for emergency action regarding suicidal and homicidal clients; (3) who to contact regarding child and elder abuse reports; and (4) information regarding AIDS reporting and limits, which is increasingly regulated by state statutes that affect all health care professionals.

7. Dual and Multiple Relations in Church-based Counseling

No area of ethical development has given us more trouble. Defining the principle and the boundaries of dual relations is highly dependent on the application of the rule—whether in a church or in a professional clinical setting. The ethical guidelines concerning this are as follows.

1–140 Dual and Multiple Relationships

Dual relationships involve the breakdown of proper professional or ministerial boundaries. A dual relationship is where two or more roles are mixed in a manner that can harm the counseling relationship. Examples include counseling plus personal, fraternal, business, financial, or sexual and romantic relations.

Some dual relationships are not unethical—it is client exploitation that is wrong, not the dual relationship itself. Based on an absolute application that harms membership bonds in the body of Christ, we oppose the ethical-legal view that all dual relationships are per se harmful and therefore invalid on their face. Many dual relations are wrong and indefensible, but some dual relationships are worthwhile and defensible (per 1–142 below).

1–141 The Rule of Dual Relationships

While in therapy, or when counseling relations are imminent, or for an appropriate time after termination of counseling, Christian counselors do not engage in dual relations with counselees. Some dual relationships are always avoided—sexual or romantic relations, and counseling close friends, family members, employees, or supervisees. Other dual relationships should be presumed troublesome and avoided wherever possible.

1–142 Proving an Exception to the Rule

The Christian counselor has the burden of proving a justified dual relationship by showing (1) informed consent, including discussion of how the counseling relationship might be harmed as other relations proceed, and (2) lack of harm or exploitation to the client. As a general rule, all close relations are unethical if they become counselor-client or formal lay helping relations. Dual relations may be allowable, requiring justification by the foregoing rule, if the client is an arms-length acquaintance—if the relationship is not a close one. This distinction is crucial in the applications below.

1–143 Counseling with Family, Friends, and Acquaintances

Christian counselors do not provide counseling to close family or friends. We presume that dual relations with other family members, acquaintances, and fraternal, club, association, or group members are potentially troublesome and best avoided, otherwise requiring justification.

1–144 Business and Economic Relations

Christian counselors avoid partnerships, employment relations, and close business associations with clients. Barter relations are normally avoided as potentially troublesome, and require justification; therefore if done, barter is a rare and not a common occurrence. Unless justified by compelling necessity, customer relations with clients are normally avoided.

1–145 Counseling with Fellow Church Members

Christian counselors do not provide counseling to fellow church members with whom they have close personal, business, or shared ministry relations. We presume that dual relations with any other church members who are clients are potentially troublesome and best avoided, otherwise requiring justification. Pastors and church staff helpers will take all reasonable precautions to limit the adverse impact of any dual relationships.

1–146 Termination to Engage in Dual Relations Prohibited

Christian counselors do not terminate counseling to engage in dual relationships of any kind. Some counselors and their former clients will agree that any future counseling will be done by someone else if, after legitimate termination, they decide to pursue another form of relationship.

8. Sexual Misconduct: Getting Under Control or Going Underground?

Nothing is more harmful to clients than to be exploited sexually by a therapist that one has hired to help with the most private secrets and sensitive life issues. It is a betrayal like no other in counseling and is being criminalized by a growing number of states as a grave and serious offence.[9]

1–130 Sexual Misconduct Forbidden

All forms of sexual misconduct in pastoral, professional, or lay relationships are unethical. This includes every kind of sexual exploitation, deception, manipulation, abuse, harassment, relations where the sexual involvement is invited, and relations where informed consent presumably exists. Due to the inherent power imbalance of helping relationships and the immoral nature of sexual behavior outside of marriage, such apparent consent is illusory and illegitimate.

Forbidden sexual activities and deceptions include, but are not limited to, direct sexual touch or contact; seductive sexual speech or nonverbal behavior; solicitation of sexual or romantic relations; erotic contact or behavior as a response to the sexual invitation or seductive behavior of clients; unnecessary questioning and/or excessive probing into the client's sexual history and practices; inappropriate counselor disclosures of client attractiveness, sexual opinions, or sexual humor; advocacy of the healing value of counselor-client sexual relations; secretive sexual communications and anonymous virtual interaction via the Internet or other electronic and informational means; sexual harassment by comments, touch, or promises/threats of special action; and sexual misconduct as defined by all applicable laws, ethics, and church, organizational, or practice policies.

1–131 Sexual Relations with Former Clients Forbidden

All sexual relations as defined in 1–130 above with former clients are unethical. Furthermore, we do not terminate and refer clients or parishioners, even at first contact, in order to pursue sexual or romantic relations.

1–132 Counseling with Marital/Sexual Partners

Christian counselors do not counsel, but make appropriate referral, with current or former sexual and/or marital partners.

1–133 Marriage with Former Clients/Patients

Since marriage is honorable before God, the lone exception to this rule is marriage to a former client, so long as (1) counseling relations were properly terminated, and not for the purpose of pursuing marriage or romantic relations, (2) the client is fully informed that any further counseling must be done by another, (3) there is no harm or exploitation of the client or the client's family as a result of different relations with the counselor, and (4) the marriage takes place two years or more after the conclusion of a counseling or helping relationship.

9. Ending Counseling: Termination, Abandonment, and Inept Care

Ending counseling is as important as beginning it—doing it well means clients leave with hope and encouragement that they can carry on the change they have experienced. Consequently, poor termination has become a troublesome ethical issue.

1–560 Continuity of Care and Service Interruption

Christian counselors maintain continuity of care for all patients and clients. We avoid interruptions in service to clients that are too lengthy or disruptive. Care is taken to refer clients and network to provide emergency services when faced with counselor vacations, illnesses, job changes, financial hardships, or any other reason services are interrupted or limited.

1–570 Avoiding Abandonment and Improper Counseling Termination

Christian counselors do not abandon clients. To the extent the counselor is able, client services are never abruptly cut-off or ended without giving notice and adequately preparing the client for termination or referral.

1–571 Ethical Termination of Counseling

Discussion and action toward counseling termination and/or referral is indicated when (1) counseling goals have been achieved; (2) when the client no longer wants or does not return to counseling; (3) when the client is no longer benefiting from counseling; or (4) when counseling is harmful to the client. Christian counselors shall discuss termination and/or referral with clients, offer referral if wanted or appropriate, and facilitate termination in the client's best interest. If crisis events alter, even end counseling prematurely the counselor, if it is safe and proper, should follow-through with the client to ensure proper termination and referral.

It is time to consider termination when clients (1) have achieved their therapeutic goals; (2) appear stable emotionally, psychologically and spiritually; (3) maintain behavioral changes or goals for a reasonable amount of time; (4) possess a new perspective of their world as a whole; (5) appear to have taken control of their lives; (6) personal relationships have improved; and (7) tell you they believe it is time to go.

Termination should be a gradual process when possible, and often is not absolutely final. Some clients return off and on for years; some for a periodic "check up." Others soar to new emotional, psychological and spiritual heights and never return. Kottler asserts, "There is nothing like that feeling of elation we sometimes experience when we know beyond a shadow of a doubt that our efforts have helped redeem a human life."[10]

10. Values Conflicts with Parishioners and Clients

We show in this book a variety of ways that counseling is a values-laden experience, one that we believe requires that the values of every counselor be made known, if possible, at the start of counseling.

1–550 Working with Persons of Different Faiths, Religions, and Values

Christian counselors do not withhold services to anyone of a different faith, religion, denomination, or value system. We work to understand the client's belief system and always maintain respect for the client. We strive to understand when faith and values issues are important to the client and foster values-informed client decision-making in counseling. We share our own faith only as a function of legitimate self-disclosure and when appropriate to client need, always maintaining a humility that exposes and never imposes the way of Christ.

1–551 Action If Value Differences Interfere with Counseling

Christian counselors work to resolve problems—always in the client's best interest—when differences between counselor and client values become too great, adversely affecting counseling. This may include discussion of the issue as a therapeutic matter, renegotiation of the counseling agreement, consultation with a supervisor or trusted colleague or, as a last resort, referral to another counselor if the differences cannot be reduced or bridged.

We recognize a continuum of Christian counselors who emphasize varying degrees of Christian practices in counseling. At one pole is the helper who plans and practices every session as a discipling experience—praying overtly with clients in every session, referencing Scripture, encouraging yieldedness to Christ, exhorting confession and forgiveness, and reinforcing any movement toward Christian growth.

At the other pole is the helper who, although confessing Christ, believes that inclusion of Christ in therapy is an unjust imposition of religious values, one that violates client self-determination. Although some may engage in Christian practices with Christian clients who ask for it—especially prayer—these brothers and sisters emphasize a psychological practice where evangelism and overt forms of spiritual exhortation and advocacy of Christ are not done.

While our bias is clearly toward Christian counseling that incorporates spiritual disciplines, we take an inclusionary approach and see all believers as welcome within Christian counseling's "big tent." We suggest that excellence and positive outcome is better correlated with an active inclusion of Christ and Christian principles, but one that respects the working environments and the limits, capabilities, learning styles, and the readiness of clients. What good is forcing a message upon deaf ears? Then again, what good is mere psychological adaptation if one adapts better to evil ways? Both polar extremes are too doctrinaire, putting ideology, absolute ethics, and rigid theology above people. Nonetheless, we recognize all practitioners who name the name of Christ as citizens of God's kingdom and want to encourage them as brothers and sisters in the Christian counseling fold.

Moving from Law to Love: Helping Others Be Like Christ

In their 1998 volume, Corey, Corey, and Callanan discuss two basic kinds of ethics in counseling—what they call principle ethics and virtue ethics. Principle ethics are specific and applied; virtue ethics are global and aspirational. Therefore, a respect for client privacy is a virtue ethic; when and how to responsibly breach confidentiality is a principle ethic. I (George) followed this distinction—one that is rooted first in the Scriptures—in an article that revealed the zone of ethical behavior between conforming ethics and transforming ethics.[11] Essentially, it is a study on the differences and relationship between law and love.

Conforming (or principle) ethics are the baseline standards, the floor below which no one should fall in their practice with others. Transforming ethics are the ethical ideals reflected in the law of love that Christ Himself showed toward us by willingly going to a cross to die on our behalf. These are the perfect virtue ethics toward which all Christian counselors should strive.

Remember that when a counselor is dedicated to fully revealing the love of Christ—against this kind of love there is no law. In this love, there is no harm to another. Because of this love, people's lives are transformed into something beautiful and holy. This is the love of Jesus, and the Holy Spirit just loves to pour it out to those who seek it. The relationship between the two kinds of ethics is suggested in the Christian Counselor's golden rule expressed below.

The Christian Counselor's Golden Rule

This Christian counselor's application of the Golden Rule is adapted from Romans 13:8–10. It expresses the cardinal values and core rules of Christian counseling ethics.

Christian counselor, hear this:

Do not be indebted to any client or parishioner, except the debt to love them.

For if you love your clients, you honor all your professional and ministerial duties.

You know the rules of counseling and pastoral care:

Do not engage in any form of sexual misconduct with your clients, whether current or past.

Do not, as far as is possible with you, let them kill or harm themselves or anyone else.

Do not steal your clients' money or disregard your time with them.

Do not harm, or envy, or look down on, or manipulate, or fight with,
or in any way exploit those Christ has sent to you for help.

In fact, to sum it up and state it conclusively:

Practice the Golden Rule with all wisdom and grace.

Love your clients as yourself.

Don't do anything to your clients or those they love
that you wouldn't want done to yourself.

For love does no wrong to any client.

Therefore, to love your clients as Christ loves you
is to fulfill all your obligations—all your moral-ethical-legal duties—as a
Christian counselor.

ENDNOTES

1. Amos Clemmons, The pastor and the institute, *Parakaleo* (Eureka, CA: The Redwood Family Institute, 3, 1991), 1–2.
2. Tim Clinton and Ohlschlager, G., *Competent Christian counseling: Practicing and
   pursuing compassionate soul care* (Colorado Springs: WaterBrook Press, 2002).
3. George Ohlschlager and Mosgofian, P., *Law for the Christian counselor: A guidebook
   for clinicians and pastors* (Dallas: Word, 1992) and adapted from Thomas Need-
   ham, Helping when the risks are great, in *Clergy malpractice*, 89–90.
4. G. Corey, Corey, M., and Callanan, P., *Issues and ethics in the helping professions* 5th
   ed. (Pacific Grove, CA: Brooks/Cole, 1998).
5. American Association of Christian Counselors, *AACC Christian counseling code of
   ethics* (Forest, VA: AACC, 2001).
6. See *Lawrence v. Texas*, 2003, on the establishment of the right to homosexual
   sodomy via the elevation of the Autonomous Self, for an extreme example of this
   ethic being anchored into American law by the U.S. Supreme Court.
7. Gary R. Collins is another pioneer who taught and mentored us both.
8. Gary R. Collins, *Christian counseling: A comprehensive guide*, rev. ed.(Nashville: W
   Publishing Group, 1988), 54.
9. Glenn Gabbard, *Sexual exploitation in professional relationships* (Washington: American Psychiatric Association, 1989); George Ohlschlager, and Mosgofian, P., *Law
   for the Christian counselor*; Kenneth Pope, Sonne, J., and Holroyd, J., *Sexual feelings
   in psychotherapy* (Washington: American Psychological Association, 1993).
10. Jeffrey Kottler, *On being a therapist* rev. ed. (San Francisco: Jossey-Bass, 1993), 46.
11. George Ohlschlager, Avoiding ethical-legal pitfalls: embracing conformative
    behavior and transformative virtues, *Christian Counseling Today*, 7(3), (1999),
    40–43.

Part 2

Counseling for Personal and Emotional Issues

6

Helping People Forgive:
Getting to the Heart of the Matter

Everett L. Worthington Jr.

Be kind one to another, tender-hearted, forgiving one another, as God in Christ has forgiven you.

EPHESIANS 4:32 (ESV)

We can forgive because we have been forgiven.

At age 8, little girls are *not* supposed to be raped or molested by their fathers. It is one of the most horrific experiences imaginable. We hear an adult molested as a child affirm, "I can't forgive him!" She clenches her fists, looks you square in the face, and asserts with certitude, "I *won't* do it." More often than not, we find ourselves automatically shaking our heads in agreement. For how can anyone forgive—and then be reconciled—to a sex offender who was supposed to be the child's primary defender in life? The thought is reprehensible, beyond the pale. Yet forgiveness is the centerpiece of Christianity—and of effective Christian counseling.[1]

We are impelled by two motivations to forgive. On one hand, we are commanded to forgive. Jesus clearly says that if we forgive, we will be forgiven, but if we do not forgive, we will not be forgiven (Matt. 6:12, 14–15; Luke 6:37–38). The parable of the unforgiving servant encourages us to forgive because God holds us accountable for forgiving (Matt. 18: 23–35). So duty, responsibility, accountability, desire to please God, and desire to avoid displeasing God motivate us to forgive.

On the other hand, we are admonished to forgive spontaneously and emotionally as Christ forgave us (Eph. 4:31–32), and as God forgives (Jer. 31:34; Heb. 8:12, 10:17; Ps. 103:12). We see examples in Scripture of forgiveness from the heart—like Jesus on the cross (Luke 23:34) and Stephen facing his executioners (Acts 7:55–56). We see parables of unfathomable grace, like the prodigal son, in which the father's heart of forgiveness is almost incomprehensible (Luke 15:11–32). On that hand, forgiveness is an altruistic gift we freely give to those people who harm us and who do not deserve forgiveness.

With those two motivations to forgive, and the believer's experience of God's mercy and grace in giving Jesus freely to die for us (Rom. 5:1; Col. 2:13–14), Christians should hope that all Christians are ever-merciful—always forgiving. Yet, mostly, we see with great sympathy Peter, plaintively whining to Jesus, "How many times must I forgive one who harms me?" (Matt. 18: 21–22; see also Luke 17:3–4). How many, Lord? We identify with Peter. We almost daily catch ourselves judging others for not forgiving. We feel the deserved shame of knowing how short we fall of forgiving anyone 70 times 7 (Luke 17:5).

As helpers, people come to us and pour out their woes, their unforgiveness, their sorrow at the pain of relationships ruined. They ask us to help them find solace. Yet, their pleas inform us of how far we are from being examples of forgiveness.

I know in my heart how much resentment I harbor, and I know that my heart is deceitful so that I am not aware of much of my own sin (Jer. 17:9–10). My intentions are often good. I want to forgive. Yet I repeatedly fail. How can I help someone forgive?

I can forgive and help others to do so only by the grace and mercy of God. I am an unworthy vessel. I know that what might flow from me is muddy clay-stained water, not pure cleansing water. Yet, somehow a profound mystery exists. I am part of Jesus' church (Eph. 1:22–23), and the mystery is that despite the muddy water flowing from me, people can often be cleaned.

There is no mystery in counseling techniques. Counseling techniques cannot help people forgive any more than a physician can heal a person's body. Counseling techniques, like a physician's tools, are merely structures through which God sometimes sovereignly acts. He acts more often through some structures than through others. He brings more forgiveness about through counseling than through football, for example.

In this chapter, my goal is to provide one structure that I hope will help counselors assist people to forgive after a transgression and to become more forgiving people. To accomplish this, I will combine the Scriptures about forgiveness with the scientific studies done in our lab and elsewhere to provide an understanding of unforgiveness and forgiveness that complements and fleshes out what is said in Scripture. I describe a method of helping people forgive—which I describe first within a psychoeducational group,[2] and second show its use within a counseling session with a couple.[3]

The ideas I will talk about in this chapter are useful at a number of levels. They might help readers to understand forgiveness and to forgive more successfully in their own lives. They might help readers to counsel others in ways that promote forgiveness and reconciliation. These applications might occur in psychoeducational groups. We can teach forgiveness in Bible studies, Sunday school classes, teaching seminars in church or other settings, adjunct groups to psychotherapy, psychoeducational groups aimed at a particular problem like romantic betrayals, forgiving a more general collection of offenses, or abuse, or psychoeducational groups aimed at becoming a more forgiving person.

We can also teach forgiveness in individual, couple, family, or group counseling or therapy. These interventions can be conducted by laypeople, clergy, or professional therapists. Even community interventions such as disseminating the information through sermons or to community organizations could produce change in larger bodies of Christians.

Understanding Unforgiveness and Forgiveness

When people are wronged or hurt, they experience an "injustice gap"—the difference between the way the person would like a transgression to be resolved (i.e., desired outcome) and the way things are perceived to be currently (i.e., current outcome). They also respond with immediate anger in response to perceived offenses or wrongs, or they respond with anger plus fear in response to perceived hurts.[4] They might inhibit their motivations to act in revenge or avoidance. McCullough, Fincham, and Tsang call that inhibition of expression of negative motivations, "forbearance."[5]

There are two types of forgiveness. First, "decisional forgiveness" can cancel an interpersonal debt caused by a transgression. A person simply decides to forgive. Often this occurs because people feel that it is their duty to forgive, that God holds them accountable for forgiving, that they are responsible for forgiving. Their decision to forgive is a statement of intent not to pursue the natural motivation to seek revenge or avoid the person who harmed one. Once it is made, that decision prescribes some behaviors (like acting as one did prior to the transgression) and proscribes other behaviors (like retaliating). Decisional forgiveness does not deal with the emotions. It reflects a preference for or understanding that duty, accountability, and responsibility—what we call "conscientiousness-based virtues"—are highly valued.[6]

Second, when people are hurt or offended, they respond in immediate anger or fear or a combination. They might ruminate about the event and the consequences to the victim until they develop emotional feelings of "unforgiveness," which is a combination of resentment, bitterness, hostility, hatred, anger, and fear.[7] In tandem, rumination produces motivational desires to act on that unforgiveness (even though they may have struggled to forbear or have foresworn revenge and avoidance in a decisional statement of forgiveness). Those emotional feelings of unforgiveness (and associated negative motivations) will eat at a person who does not reduce those negative emotions in some way.

"Emotional forgiveness" juxtaposes positive emotions toward the offender such as empathy, sympathy, compassion, agape love, or romantic love against the negative unforgiving emotions. Emotional forgiveness is born out of a valuing of the "warmth-based virtues" (such as love, compassion, gratitude, humility, sympathy, and compassion)[8] in contrast to the conscientiousness-based virtues that motivate decisional forgiving. The emotional juxtaposition first neutralizes negative emotions and second builds in positive emotions such as a net positive love, until emotional replacement occurs.

Because emotions and motivations are so closely linked, with emotions stirring up motivations on occasion and changes in motivation changing emotions on other occasions, motivations are inevitably changed as emotional forgiveness occurs. Emotional forgiveness is indeed both a change in emotions and motivations simultaneously. (Parenthetically, there are numerous ways to reduce unforgiveness—such as seeing civil, criminal, or personal justice done, turning the matter over to God, renarrating the event to excuse or justify the transgression, or defending against the threat psychologically).[9]

Decisional forgiveness and emotional forgiveness are related, but they respond to different rules. Different circumstances can promote or inhibit each one separately. Michael McCullough and I have, together and separately, described emotional forgiveness. McCullough has concentrated on the motivational aspects of emotional forgiveness.[10] I have concentrated on the emotional aspects.[11]

Emotional forgiveness changes over time. Emotions may change, and associated motivational desires to avoid or to seek revenge against a person may also decay as time passes. This is especially true if intervening events do not intercede to make things worse. When positive events occur (such as receiving a sincere apology or restitution), those events can help neutralize negative unforgiving emotions, increase positive forgiving emotions, reduce the motivation for avoidance and for revenge, and increase the motivation for conciliation even further.

Helping People Forgive Using a Psychoeducational Group

Under normal circumstances people forgive in many ways. They might forgive in response to God's prompting, to worship, to reading a book, to their own prayer or meditation, to conversation with a friend, upon the advice of a pastor, or because they were exposed to some intervention. Therefore under normal circumstances, God has an amazing array of avenues by which He can move people from the state of unforgiveness to the state of forgiveness.

These avenues are as numerous as the possible routes one could use in moving from the state of Virginia to the state of California. Helpers take many routes to guide people through a process of forgiving. We have examined the published research on interventions to promote forgiveness.[12] Through that review of the literature, we have discovered that almost every program that helps people forgive, whether it is psychotherapeutic or psychoeducational, leads people through similar events. This is similar to saying that leading people from Virginia to California can be done through many routes; however, these routes pass through the same six or seven cities as a person navigates across the country.

I have been conducting research on how to help people forgive using psychoeducational and therapeutic methods in a variety of formats since the mid-1980s. This has culminated in a method that I call a Pyramid Model to REACH Forgiveness, where REACH is an acrostic in which each letter stands for one of the five major steps. Below, I will describe the steps in helping people reach emotional forgiveness using my Pyramid Model to REACH Forgiveness as a way of structuring the steps.[13] However, I must point out that other people put these elements together in different orders and different ways. So there is a freedom involved in how people organize and present these steps.

The steps to REACH forgiveness can be used in psychoeducational groups and in counseling. First, I will describe one way to conduct a psychoeducational group (based on my book, *Forgiving and Reconciling*, plus additional exercises derived from my experience since I wrote the book). Then, I will illustrate how to use it in couples counseling.

Who Should Participate in Forgiveness Groups?

People who can benefit from an intervention to help them forgive are those who want to forgive but have not been able to do so. They might have tried repeatedly to forgive or they forgave and back-slid. Sometimes we helpers want to take over one of the roles of the Holy Spirit and convict people that they need to forgive. We quote Scripture and admonish people to be responsive to God's Word. These methods to follow, however, help people experience emotional forgiveness. This group is aimed at 13 one-hour sessions—making up a Sunday school quarter or 13 hourly counseling sessions.

Agreement on Goals and Definitions

Goal setting (Hour 1). Because people understand forgiveness in many ways, and those ways can result in disagreement, begin the group by stating the goal of the group. The goal might be aimed at three levels. At level one, we hope to help people forgive a single past or current transgression. At level two, we hope to help people learn *how to* forgive transgressions. These skills cannot be effectively taught in the abstract. They must be learned by applying them to one event and by being explicit as to how that event is forgiven. At level three, we hope to help people become more forgiving people. Just as skills to forgive a transgression cannot be learned in the abstract, people cannot learn how to become more forgiving people in the abstract. Rather, people must forgive transgression after transgression and person after person.

The leader should solicit from group members their goals. After everyone has shared, the group leader can describe the three levels of forgiveness. The leader either states the advertised purpose of the group, or decides on the goal based on the sharing of the members.

At whatever level of goal is aimed at—forgiving a particular hurt, learning how to forgive better, or becoming a more forgiving person—the person must learn to forgive one transgression. The steps will then be applied more generally and more repeatedly if more levels are addressed. Therefore I will describe carefully how to help people forgive one transgression.

Definitions of forgiveness (Hour 2). The leader should circulate a list of definitions of forgiveness. Most are incorrect definitions such as "forgiveness means forgetting," "forgiveness means excusing the person for having done something wrong," or "forgiveness means realizing that the person was justified in transgressing." Two of the definitions within the list might be those that will be used in the group. Decisional forgiveness will be identified with the definition "forgiveness involves declaring that one is not going to seek revenge or avoid the other person but will do his or her best to get along in the future." Emotional forgiveness will be identified with the definition, "forgiveness involves a change of heart in which one replaces negative emotions of resentment, bitterness, hostility, anger, hatred, and fear with more positive emotions toward the person, such as empathy, sympathy, compassion, or love."

Group members discuss in triads which definitions of forgiveness they consider to be correct and incorrect, and why. After three-person discussion, the group reconvenes. Group discussion is held. The group comes to agree on the two definitions as being forgiveness. The leader should differentiate between decisional and emotional forgiveness. The leader suggests that the group will be aimed at forgiving from the heart (i.e., emotional forgiveness)—and depending on the goal, on building skills to forgive or being a more forgiving person.

Christian views of forgiveness. Scriptures pertaining to the two types of forgiveness are considered by asking people to contrast the parable of the unforgiving servant (Matt. 18:23–35) with the parable of the prodigal son (Luke 15:11–32). The leader makes it clear that there are two distinct types of forgiving—with decisional forgiveness governed by duty, accountability, and responsibility, and emotional forgiveness governed by love.

Unforgiveness (Hour 3). In the group, people describe what it feels like to be unforgiving. The group leader lists emotion-words as members discuss. The leader refers to the definition of emotional forgiveness, which describes the six negative emotions that make up unforgiveness, and then defines unforgiveness. The leader draws a flow path that describes how people develop unforgiveness after a transgression. A transgression leads to a perception of a hurt or offense, which generates an immediate emotion of anger, fear, or their mixture. Rumination—continual replaying of the event—leads to unforgiveness. The group lists physical, mental, and relational effects of unforgiveness. The leader briefly refers to research on the effects of unforgiveness on physical, mental, and relational health.

R = Recall the Hurt

The leader directs each person to describe (in writing) the event that he or she hopes to forgive. The Transgression-Related Inventory of Motivations (TRIM) scale should be completed, the single-item measure of forgiveness, and the Forgiveness-Perceptions, Emotions, Actions, and Cognition (F-PEAC) should be completed[14] (see Table 1).

People discuss the event in dyads. They are directed to discuss how their unforgiveness developed over time, using stimulus questions about the kind of emotion they felt in the beginning, whether they could turn loose of the event, or how they tried to deal with the event and their feelings? The leader reconvenes the group. Three volunteers share their experiences.

Participants are asked to focus on how they have tried to deal with the event and their emotions. The leader defines the injustice gap as the difference between desired and current outcomes. The group lists ways that people attempt to close the injustice gap and reduce unforgiveness. The list is compared with a table of ways to reduce unforgiveness.[15] Ways that better the current situation include (1) receiving an apology or restitution, (2) understanding the transgressor better, and (3) seeing civil or divine justice enacted. Ways to lessen expectations of desired outcomes include accepting the transgression and moving on with one's life or giving the judgment to God. Group members discuss which methods are biblical (the answer is that all are consistent with Scripture) and whether people who have tried them have found them to work.

The leader tells the group that recalling the hurt is effective, but only if people move past feeling how badly we have been victimized or what a jerk the other person is. Group members must express themselves but then work toward a different understanding of the transgression.

E = Empathize with the Transgressor (Hours 4 through 7)

To forgive the transgressor, victims must change negative unforgiving emotions to less negative or more positive emotions. Typically, people will not jump from a negative to a positive emotional state, but will reduce negative emotions gradually by neutralizing them as they experience positive emotional states.

Empathy. If people who feel unforgiveness can empathize with the transgressor temporarily, then empathy can erode some unforgiveness. If people can sympathize with, feel compassion for, or experience love toward the transgressor, they will reduce their unforgiveness. Finally, they might feel more positive emotions toward the transgressor. Because people forgive as they feel positive emotions while thinking about the transgression, group members must be helped to experience positive emotions toward the transgressor.

We first take people through several methods to help them understand more about what might have been going on in the transgressor's life. Each group member writes some notes about what he or she thought might be going on in the transgressor's life. In dyads, partners share with each other. The facilitator demonstrates the empty-chair technique—moving from chair to chair in a mock conversation between transgressor and victim, which stimulates understanding and empathy. Members of dyads take turns enacting empty-chair dialogues while the dyadic partner observes. After the empty-chair conversations are complete, the group is reconvened and members share reactions.

We assign homework: each group member should write a letter giving an account of the transgression as if he or she were the transgressor. The letter should describe the thoughts, feelings, and motivations of the transgressor, who usually had positive intentions yet offended or hurt the group member because things seemed to just "go wrong." In the following session, people read their letters to a partner. We reconvene the group and ask two or three people to read their letters to the group. We ask how successful group members were in empathizing with the transgressor. At this point, some people raise objections—they could not empathize or empathy had only a small effect. Others were more successful in empathizing.

Sympathy, compassion, and agape love. Because several positive emotions can replace unforgiveness, we ask that people sympathize with the transgressor. Empathy is merely feeling what the transgressor felt; sympathy is also feeling sorry for the transgressor. We process the results of the sympathy discussion. We ask people whether they can feel compassion for the other person. Compassion is empathy plus sympathy plus a motivation to do something for the person. Finally, we ask people whether they can experience agape love for the other person. Perhaps the love might be motivated by Christian commands to love one's enemies (Matt. 5:44; Luke 6:27–28) or one's brother (1 John 4:20–21). We discuss what this love would look like and if the person were to love one's enemy, how would each person act?

Symbolizing positive feelings for the transgressor. These interventions have been aimed at helping people experience positive emotions that replace unforgiveness. In the group, we ask people to discuss how successful this was. People readily symbolize the extent of emotional replacement for the person who transgressed against them.

In advance, we prepare two dark pieces of construction paper with a piece of golden construction paper inside, and we cut the three pieces of paper, together, into the shape of a heart. They are taped into a three-layered heart. Group members are given one of the hearts. They look at the dark exterior and think about their judgment toward the person who hurt them and the times they had wished that person ill. They are then told that if they have now become more empathic, sympathetic, compassionate, or loving toward the person, their hearts have been lightened. They tear away the dark exterior and reveal the heart of gold (sunshine) within.

A = Altruistic Gift of Forgiveness (Hour 8)

People forgive best if they are motivated to forgive altruistically—to bless the other person—rather than to get a blessing for themselves (such as better physical or mental health). People recall a time when they transgressed against someone who forgave them. We give people time to reflect on that and to write a description of the event. In dyads, people describe the event. We convene the group and ask two or three people to share with the entire group. People report feeling free and unburdened when they received forgiveness.

We then say, "You have now empathized with (and perhaps sympathized with, felt compassion for, and experienced love for) the person who hurt you. You also now have realized how good you felt when you received forgiveness. Would you like to give that gift to the person who had hurt you so that person could feel forgiven?" Some people forgive totally, but others answer that they are not yet ready to fully forgive. We accept anything as a valid answer and ask each person to quantify how much forgiveness they are willing to grant—10%, 25%, 50%, 75%, or whatever. They answer aloud within the group.

C = Commit Publicly to the Forgiveness One Experiences (Hour 9)

To assist in maintaining the forgiveness, when almost unavoidable doubts about whether one has completely forgiven occur, we ask people to commit publicly to the forgiveness they have experienced. People write a certificate of forgiveness stating the degree of forgiveness experienced. They share the certificate with others in the group as they talk about the forgiveness that they have experienced. This provides another public commitment that they have forgiven to some degree.

We solicit expression of the roadblocks to complete forgiveness. Group members discuss what it would take to help them forgive. We note that there are many paths to forgiveness. Some say that they would forgive if the other person simply apologized or made restitution. We agree with them. Then we say, "Are you going to allow your transgressor to dictate whether you will experience perhaps years of unforgiveness?" We suggest decisional forgiveness, trusting God to then change the feelings as they act as if they had forgiven the transgressor. We also might recycle through steps E and A, and then again ask people to rate the degree to which they had forgiven.

In a group, some people will have fully forgiven, but others not. We invite the people who have forgiven to take a different transgression by the person or even a different person's transgression while others work further on the initial transgression.

We symbolize the forgiveness people have experienced through a ceremony. We might have each person bring in a rock weighing about two pounds. People hold the rock at arm's length as we discuss the weight of unforgiveness that people have carried. As arms droop, we invite people to symbolize their forgiveness by putting down the rock—laying down the burden of unforgiveness they have carried for so long.

Another way of symbolizing the forgiveness is through writing a brief description of the offense and burning it or pinning it to a cross. Still another way of symbolizing the forgiveness is to write a word describing the offense on the person's hand, then try to wash the hand clean. We note that the ink does not come off easily. It lightens as the soap of forgiveness cleanses the person's feelings, but it will take time before the word is gone.

H = Hold on to Forgiveness When You Doubt (Hour 10)

Maintenance of gains of forgiveness is always difficult. People who feel that they have fully forgiven an offender can merely see the offender and feel anger and fear stir their hearts. Usually people will then conclude that they have not really forgiven, because *if I had really forgiven*, they think, *I should feel no anger or fear toward the transgressor*. However, this is not a true perception. Anger and fear are their God-given natural bodily mechanisms to protect them from a harmful situation.

We explain an analogy to help people remember and understand this. "Assume that you burn your hand very badly on a stove. After it has healed, your hand passes near a hot eye again. Immediately a fear rushes back into your entire body. It is not that you are unforgiving of the stove eye for "burning" you. Rather, the fear and anger is a natural bodily response to having been injured. This is what happens when a person has been transgressed against and suffered a psychological or physical injury and forgives, and then sees the person and transgressor again.

Unforgiveness might be rekindled if the person ruminates about the event. Rumination is persevering on the negativity and negative consequences of the event. So the person needs to have some mechanisms to get his or her mind off the rumination. Daniel Wegner's white-bear studies illustrate the almost impossibility of stopping intrusive thoughts consciously. In Wegner's studies, people are told *not* to think about white bears. If they fail at the task (and thus think about white bears), they must ring a bell. The command to try to inhibit thoughts increases the thoughts rather than decrease them. Thus, people must not merely seek to stop rumination but think of other things in place of the negative thoughts. For example, they might think positively of the person, or simply distract themselves to think of something else altogether.

Talking About Transgressions (Hours 11 and 12)

Content of the teaching. The way people talk about transgressions can affect forgiving. If people talk destructively about transgressions, unforgiveness multiplies. We teach two skills. One is to make good reproaches. A reproach is a request for an explanation if a person believes that he or she has been transgressed against. A good reproach assumes that the transgressor had positive motives and love for the victim. It does not blame and accuse the transgressor. A good reproach says, "Usually, you are very sensitive. I was puzzled when you [forgot our anniversary]. I didn't understand; that doesn't fit my concept of you. Can you help me understand what was going on with you that caused you to [forget]?"

Once a victim reproaches, the offender tries to make a good account of the behavior. There are four types of accounts. One type is a denial. A denial says, "I did not do what you're accusing me of." A second type of account is a justification, which admits transgressing but claims that the transgression was justified (usually because of what the other person did to provoke the act). Denials and justifications are called aggravating accounts. They make matters worse.

Mitigating accounts make things better. One type of mitigating account is an excuse. An excuse admits to the wrongdoing but tells the pressures and stresses that make the behavior more understandable. Importantly, the timing of the excuse is crucial. Excuses should not be given right away, but instead should be given only after a good confession is made. The person can then say, "Would it help your consideration of forgiving if I described what was happening so that you understand what was going on with me?"

A confession is an admission of wrongdoing without excuse. Again, from my book, *Forgiving and Reconciling,* we use an acrostic to structure the confession.

- C = Confess without excuse
- O = Offer an apology (and it must be believable and sincere)
- N = Note the other person's pain (i.e., communicate your empathy)

- F = Forever value the person (i.e., say that repairing the relationship is more important to you than being "right")
- E = Equalize the situation (i.e., make restitution if appropriate)
- S = Say, "I'll try to never do it again."
- S = Seek forgiveness

Introduce the topic. Set up a role-play for people to demonstrate the worst possible communication. Describe the scenario—a forgotten anniversary. Let volunteers act out an example of terrible communication. Have group members describe ways that communication was poor. Describe in general what reproaches and accounts are.

Teach reproaches. Solicit ideas about what makes a good reproach. Demonstrate a good reproach. Have dyads practice making a good reproach.

Teach accounts. Describe aggravating accounts and refer back to the terrible-communication role-play for examples. Teach about excuses (and their proper timing) and making a good confession. Solicit discussion that identifies elements of a good confession. Summarize by teaching the CONFESS acrostic. Give people a handout summarizing CONFESS. Demonstrate a good confession. Have dyads practice giving a good confession to each other.

Discussion. Numerous issues arise as group members discuss how and when to make good reproaches and confessions. These often revolve around the other person not apologizing, not making a good confession, or not seeming sincere or regretful. People complain of the transgressor repeatedly confessing (and seeming to mean well) but continuing to offend. People describe times in which the transgressor intentionally hurts or offends. They talk about how the transgressor may be unwilling to stop the offenses. They describe having forgiven repeatedly, and they ask when it is enough.

Usually, the discussion boils down to a realization that one cannot be responsible for the other person. Rather, a group member is responsible only for his or her own behavior. On the other hand, the necessity of setting limits arises. Forgiving does not mean being a doormat. Nor does it mean putting oneself in harm's way if the transgressor is likely to inflict permanent physical or psychological damage.

Often, there are no good answers to the really difficult issues with which people must deal. The leader of the group must not feel that he or she must satisfactorily answer every question and erase all objections. Some things must simply be matters of conscience between the group member and God.

Becoming a More Forgiving Person (Hour 13)

Despite the practical objections that surface, most people want to become a more forgiving person. So, in the last session, the leader attempts to leave the person with positive motivation to practice forgiving. Becoming a more forgiving person requires that the person practice forgiving many different transgressions with many different people. However, part of becoming a more forgiving person involves having a motivation, or increasing one's motivation, to be a more forgiving person. This means that people will need to cue themselves to forgive when they become angry. Besides practicing repeatedly, there are several ways that we help people try to become a more forgiving person. One of those is to have them reflect on the Scriptures prayerfully. People can be given a list of Scriptures to meditate on, and can pray through those Scriptures. This can increase the person's desire to be more forgiving.

Another way to become a more forgiving person is to adopt a journal and each day reflect on forgiveness. A third way to become more forgiving is to get a good book on forgiveness and read it for morning or evening devotions. Each of these ways is aimed at getting people to think about forgiveness in more situations in their lives throughout the day, and sustain that interest and attention over time.

Helping People Forgive Using Couple Therapy

I have described how we conduct the Pyramid Model to REACH Forgiveness using psychoeducational groups. However, it can also be used within counseling, as I show below. The flow is not as linear as in psychoeducation. Counseling simply cannot be controlled as well as a structured group. Also, in counseling, the problems have usually become more chronic and more distressing and might be entangled with other issues. For the transcript below, W = Worthington, R = Ron, and C = Cindy.

The situation: A year before counseling began, Ron signed up for a class at a health club. Ron knew that Cindy did not approve. When the health club sent a bill for $1,000, Cindy opened it and hit the roof. After the argument settled down, both partners brought it up periodically. Now, after counseling had worked on their communication and resolution of conflicts within the hope-focused marriage framework,[16] they identified that event as the hurt that generated the most unforgiveness in each.

Counseling Transcript

W: Ron, tell me more about this issue. *(Comment: I encourage them to R=Recall the Hurt. I will work with one person at a time.)*

R: We were back in this time when we were really fighting. I felt I needed to be in a health club, so I felt justified in joining. We were at the point where if Cindy said she thought something— anything—was a bad idea, that meant I would almost certainly do it. I only went to the spa about 3 weeks. I know that decision was a pretty large screw-up. I've admitted that. I've asked for forgiveness. I recognize my fault.

W: And yet...

C: And yet, we still had to deal with a $1,000 bill, which meant our vacation plans for that summer were changed. We had to readjust some priorities. I was not happy about that at all.

R: That's putting it mildly.

W: I understand that this has not been one-sided. Ron, you felt like once you apologized, said you were sorry, and admitted to messing up, that should end it. But that didn't end it.

R: Right. I felt like I went as far as I could go. Yet it's still an issue. It's frustrating. I find a lot of anger building up as that issue keeps resurfacing.

W: So you said last week that you were having trouble forgiving *her* for not forgiving you.

R: Right. It's a big spiral. I did something wrong. She recognized that and accused me of it. I came around to seeing some of her side of it. But she can't let it go. So now, I don't like her response. I was being humble. I made myself vulnerable. I did what was right. But we still haven't resolved anything.

W: So both of you feel unforgiving but for different reasons. Today, let's see whether we can make some progress toward a more forgiving spirit for each of you. Ron, I think I'll start with you. Would you pretend for a minute that you are Cindy? *(Comment: In this couple, Cindy seemed a bit more insightful, so I wanted to begin with Ron. I hope to help Ron empathize with Cindy. E=Empathize with the one who hurt you.)* As "Cindy," tell "Ron" there [points to Cindy] what you have felt about all this. What are your feelings about what Ron did?

R: That's hard. I'm an intellectual person. I rationalize and justify. Now you're asking me to put aside my understanding of what's right and be somebody else.

W: I know you can do this.

R: Okay, from me being "Cindy": I saw Ron act irresponsibly. He didn't consider us as a couple. He was financially irresponsible. It just wasn't a very smart choice.

W: And what was your emotional reaction? *(Comment: Because I want to help him eventually replace his negative unforgiving emotions with more positive emotions—like empathy and love—I pay a lot of attention to his emotions.)*

R: That jerk.

W: Anger.

R: Anger at stupidity. Offended. My values weren't considered. What else can I say?

C: *I know.* [Cindy raises her hand.]

W: Wait a minute, let's let "Cindy" here tell us more. "Cindy," did you only feel anger? Nothing else?

R: That's tough. Sure. It wasn't just anger; it was irreverence towards me, "Cindy's" person, disregard or disrespect. I don't know what other words to put on there.

W: It's like a wound that's been dealt to you. *(Comment: Both anger and hurt are mixed. Because Ron is aware of and sees Cindy's anger, I want to call attention to the other side, so that he sees her reaction as "softer" toward him. If he had attended to the hurt, I probably would have mentioned the anger briefly, but I would have gone back and focused on the hurt—the softer emotion. Accurate empathy demands that he see both sides, but the therapeutic use of empathy demands that he focus on the softer emotion if he is to forgive.)*

R: Sure.

W: So what kind of emotion would you think having been *hurt* by this …

R: I was going to say, "hurt." What kind of emotion? I don't know if this counts as an emotion but a kind of deflated feeling—like "that guy doesn't see the worth in me."

W: So, "Cindy," you feel sadness, depression, lower self-esteem because of this.

R: Right. Yeah, that certainly causes me to evaluate who I am. Am I really insignificant like "Ron" keeps telling me I am.

W: Now, Ron, this has gone on awhile. Why would this go on? What might she be feeling? Or, I should say, what might *you* be feeling "Cindy" that would make this last so long. (Pause) There's anger, there's hurt, depression.

R: It's a big anger and a deep wound. And I'm trying to deal with it using a little Band-Aid.

W: So, "Cindy," you feel helplessness, thinking *What we can do? That apology wasn't enough.*

R: Sure, a big gap, a big divide that never did get bridged.

W: So, "Cindy," if you didn't care about Ron, it seems to me that this wouldn't bother you at all. But somehow it bothers you a lot.

R: Hmm, that's true.

W: So, you must care a lot about him to be so worried, so afraid that this might happen again, and so distraught and distressed. Do you think that might…?

R: That sounds right. I'm trying to put myself in Cindy's shoes, but you got me thinking.

W: Let me change. You're Ron again here for a minute.

R: I can do *him* better.

W: Would you think a minute about your relationship with Cindy. Can you recall whether you've seen somebody, not you, hurt her. *(Comment: I want him to experience even more empathy for Cindy— and to show her that he can understand her.)*

R: We work at church and she was in charge of the nursery. There was another Mom that lit into her one morning about something. I don't even remember why.

C: About her child.

R: She let everybody know—loudly—that she thought Cindy really screwed something up. It was a very personal and public attack. The issue was insignificant. I don't remember what it was.

W: But it certainly was a *personal and public* attack. And how did that make you feel—as her husband?

R: Oh, wow, a mixture of things. Part of me, the angry male, wanted to go plunk (that woman) on the head and say, "Quit being an idiot!" Part of me wanted to put my arms around Cindy and say. "That wasn't accurate. It didn't treat you fairly, honestly, and correctly." Protect her. *(Comment: He is directly telling her of his love.)*

W: You could sense the way that y'all are tied together as one flesh. That attack on her was...

R: It was on me, too [overlapping].

W: ... was an attack on you.

R: Yeah.

W: *(Comment: Ron seems "softer" toward Cindy after expressing his love for her. I sense that it might be good timing to try to get him to give a good apology.)* You know you've said that you have confessed your part in this betrayal with the health club before. And thinking about what she's gone through, I wonder if you'd be willing to tell her again, in my presence, how you feel about your part in the health-club incident.

R: Part of me feels like she attacked me over it, and so I'm defensive. She might attack again. Also I don't want to admit I've been so wrong. I feel really guilty. But [turns to Cindy], I guess what I really want to try to say is I never meant to do something so personally hurtful to you. It wasn't about *you*. I don't want that to stay between us.

W: So, can you tell her that what you did was wrong?

R: I knew it was wrong when I did it. Even more, over the last year. But today, I realized that this affects you in a very deep and personal way. I know how deeply it hurt you. What I've been writing off as a small incident is really a big and important one to you. *(Comment: He expresses his empathy, but he has trouble using "feeling" words. I encourage him.)*

W: I can hear in your voice real sorrow and regret. Can you express how sorry you are?

R: I can't find the words that could capture it, other than "a lot."

W: I guess, let me say that eventually if Cindy is going to be able to forgive this, she needs to know what impact it had on you. She needs to believe how sorry you are that this happened.

C: That would help.

R: As I sit here right now, I recognize that we aren't talking about $1,000. We aren't talking about it was only a few weeks. We are talking about *I hurt you*. And that's a big difference. You weren't supported.

W: I think that seemed to me to be a wonderfully sincere expression of your feelings. I don't know whether it felt that way to you, Cindy?

C: I hear he understood. It feels more now like he understands than he ever did. But he chose to do something without me knowing. And that hurt. *(Comment: Cindy wants reassurance.)*

W: Ron, I guess if I were Cindy and had worried for a year about this betrayal, I might think, *Oh, my, what if it happened again? That would be horrible if it happened again.* Do you think something like this could happen again?

R: I know something now that I didn't before. It could never happen *this way* again. But I guess there's a real fear in there too. I could still screw up again and hurt you by accident—not *planning* to hurt you, or not *trying* to hurt you. *(Comment: Ron waffles on giving unconditional reassurance, so I must put as good a spin on it as possible.)*

W: You're saying you really want to *try* never to do anything like this again. But you also are aware of your own *humanness*, that you might mess up. You know it could happen, but you don't *want* it to happen. *(Comment: I want to positively reframe Cindy's reluctance to turn loose of the incident, in order to bring out their love, which will foster more forgiving.)* Let me shift gears a little. Can you see why Cindy might have continued to bring this up repeatedly?

R: Sure. I was addressing the superficial issues, not the real deep ones, the ones that really hurt, the ones that affect her personally.

W: But also she was worried. She loved you. And she didn't want to lose the relationship. She was coming out of a position of love over this.

R: It was harder to see when I felt I was getting emotionally blasted.

W: That's right, her anger made a lot of noise and fireworks. It was hard to see in the darkness behind those fireworks.

R: Right. *(Comment: Remember, we are working on helping Ron forgive Cindy for bringing this up repeatedly. He has demonstrated some empathy for her, sees his part in provoking her, but he might not be ready to forgive her by giving her an altruistic gift of forgiveness.)*

W: Can I get you to do one other thing for me? I would like for you to think back on your life. Can you recall a time when you might have hurt somebody else—not Cindy—but somebody from your past? Yet they forgave you for it and told you.

R: I can think of a fairly recent one. It was my son. He's 11. He broke a lamp. I let him have it, just verbally. I didn't throw him across the room or anything, but I really tore into him about watching what he was doing, paying attention, quit being irresponsible— the whole spiel. And it was obvious looking at him that I was hurting him. It took me several hours to go back and tell him that I knew I overreacted. I told him that compared to a lamp he was infinitely more important. So I told him I was sorry. He didn't hesitate at all. He just put his arms around me and said, "I forgive you, Daddy." I felt like somebody who was really wrong. Yet when I said I was sorry, he said "That's okay." He forgave me, and we could still love each other.

W: You could really *feel* that forgiveness. When he granted forgiveness and hugged you, you knew it was okay. It was a freedom for you.

R: Oh, absolutely. Yeah, very much.

W: As you've talked through your health-club incident here, you've thought about how Cindy brought this up many times. You see now what was going through her head. You said you were holding some unforgiveness about this.

R: Yes.

W: And you have understood that she was bringing it up because she loves you and was worried about your relationship. Also, you saw that when you received forgiveness from your son how good and free it made you feel. I was just wondering if you'd want to give that gift of the freedom of forgiveness to Cindy—if you really *feel* forgiving, that is. *(Comment: I ask him to give A=Altruistic Gift of Forgiveness.)*

R: I'd like to do that. [Faces Cindy] I know you love me. I love you very much. I see now that your mentioning my having hurt you often was saying that you care for me, for us. I want you to know that I forgive you for bringing this up. In a way, I'm glad that you did 'cause I didn't honor you when I tried to deceive you. I'm sorry I did that. I'm glad I could say that to you. Anyway, I love you. [They kiss and hug] *(Comment: Ron commits in front of Cindy—and in front of me—to the forgiveness he experienced in his heart. C=Commit publicly to the forgiveness.)*

Conclusion

Scripture and counseling practice coincide. Some aspects of forgiveness require us to forgive simply because we know it is the right thing for Christians to do. Other aspects of forgiveness require a gradual change in emotions over time. I have provided an understanding of unforgiveness and two types of forgiveness, and have outlined an organized structure that can be used to help people forgive.

I end this chapter the same way I began it. Forgiving others their sins and transgressions is not due to technique. In shaping the graceful steel of a beautiful Christian character, psychoeducational or therapeutic actions by group leaders, teachers, or therapists are merely the hammer and anvil. Life experiences supply the heat that makes us malleable, and God's hands provide the material and use us as tools to shape His church into something beautiful.

ENDNOTES

1. Martin E. Marty, The ethos of Christian forgiveness, in E.L. Worthington, Jr. (ed.), *Dimensions of forgiveness: Psychological research and theological perspectives* (Philadelphia: The Templeton Foundation Press, 1998), 9–28.
2. Michael E. McCullough, and Worthington, E. L., Jr., Promoting forgiveness: A comparison of two psychoeducational group interventions with a waiting-list control, *Counseling and Values, 40*, (1995), 55–68; J.S Ripley, and Worthington, E.L., Jr., Comparison of hope-focused communication and empathy-based forgiveness group interventions to promote marital enrichment, *Journal of Counseling and Development, 80*, (2002), 452–463; E. L. Worthington, Jr., Kurusu, T., McCullough, M.E., and Sandage, S., Empirical research on religion and psychotherapeutic processes and outcomes: A 10-year review and research prospectus, *Psychological Bulletin, 199*, (1996), 448–487; S.J. Sandage, *An ego-humility model of forgiveness: A theory-driven empirical test of group intervention*, PhD diss., Virginia Commonwealth University (1997); for the best summary see E.L. Worthington, Jr., *Forgiv-*

ing and reconciling: Bridges to wholeness and hope (Downers Grove, IL: InterVarsity Press, 2003), which summarizes and discusses the full model.

3. Everett L. Worthington, Jr., An empathy-humility-commitment model of forgiveness applied within family dyads, *Journal of Family Therapy, 20,* (1998), 59–76.

4. Everett L. Worthington, Jr., Is there a place for forgiveness in the justice system? *Fordham Urban Law Journal, 27,* (2000a), 1721–1734.

5. Michael E. McCullough, Fincham, F.D. and Tsang, J-A., Forgiveness, forbearance, and time: The temporal unfolding of transgression-related interpersonal motivations, *Journal of Personality and Social Psychology, 84,* (2003), 540–557.

6. Everett L. Worthington, Jr., Berry, J.W., and Parrott, L. III., Unforgiveness, forgiveness, religion, and health, in T. G. Plante and A. Sherman (eds.), *Faith and health: Psychological perspectives* (New York: Guilford Press, 2001), 107–138.

7. Everett L. Worthington, Jr., and Wade, N.G., The social psychology of unforgiveness and forgiveness and implications for clinical practice, *Journal of Social and Clinical Psychology, 18,* (1999),385–418.

8. See Everett L. Worthington, Jr., Berry, J.W., and Parrott, L. III., Unforgiveness, forgiveness, religion, and health. In T. G. Plante and A. Sherman (eds.), *Faith and Health,* 107–138.

9. See Nathaniel G. Wade, and Worthington, E.L., Jr., Overcoming interpersonal offenses: Is forgiveness the only way to deal with unforgiveness? *Journal of Counseling and Development, 81,* (2003a), 343–353; E. L. Worthington, Jr., Unforgiveness, forgiveness, and reconciliation in societies, in Raymond G. Helmick and Rodney L. Petersen (eds.), *Forgiveness and reconciliation: Religion, public policy, and conflict transformation* (Philadelphia: The Templeton Foundation Press, 2001a), 161–182.

10. Michael E. McCullough, Bellah, C. G., Kilpatrick, S. D., and Johnson, J. L., Vengefulness: Relationships with forgiveness, rumination, well-being, and the big five, *Personality and Social Psychology Bulletin, 27,*(2001), 601–610; M. E. McCullough, Fincham, F.D. and Tsang, J-A., Forgiveness, forbearance, and time: The temporal unfolding of transgression-related interpersonal motivations, *Journal of Personality and Social Psychology, 84,* (2003), 540–557; M. E. McCullough, Rachal, K. C., Sandage, S. J., Worthington, E. L. Jr., Brown, S. W., and Hight, T. L., Interpersonal forgiveness in close relationships II: Theoretical elaboration and measurement, *Journal of Personality and Social Psychology, 75,* (1998), 1586–1603; M.E. McCullough, Sandage, S. J., and Worthington, E. L., Jr., *To forgive is human: How to put your past in the past* (Downers Grove, IL: InterVarsity Press, 1997); M. E. McCullough, Worthington, E. L. Jr., and Rachal, K. C., Interpersonal forgiving in close relationships, *Journal of Personality and Social Psychology, 73,*(1997), 321–336.

11. Nathaniel G. Wade, and Worthington, E.L., Jr., Overcoming interpersonal offenses: Is forgiveness the only way to deal with unforgiveness? *Journal of Counseling and Development, 81,* (2003a), 343–535; E. L. Worthington, Jr., On chaos, fractals, and stress: Response to fincham's 'Optimism and the Family,' in J. Gillam (ed.), *The science of optimism and hope* (Philadelphia: The Templeton Foundation Press, 2000b), 313–318; E. L.Worthington, Jr., Unforgiveness, forgiveness, and reconciliation in societies, in Raymond G. Helmick and Rodney L. Petersen (eds.), *Forgiveness and reconciliation: Religion, public policy, and conflict transformation* (Philadelphia: The Templeton Foundation Press, 2001a), 161–182; E. L.Worthington, Jr., *Five steps to forgiveness: The art and science of forgiving* (New York: Crown Publishers, 2001b); E. L. Worthington, Jr., and Scherer, M, Forgiveness is an emotion-focused coping strategy that can reduce health risks and promote health

resilience: Theory, review, and hypotheses, *Psychology and Health, 19*, (2003), 385–405; E. L. Worthington, Jr., and Wade, N.G., The social psychology of unforgiveness and forgiveness and implications for clinical practice, *Journal of Social and Clinical Psychology, 18*, (1999), 385–418.

12. Nathaniel G. Wade, and Worthington, E.L., Jr., Overcoming interpersonal offenses: Is forgiveness the only way to deal with unforgiveness? *Journal of Counseling and Development, 81*, (2003a), 343–353; Nathaniel G. Wade, and Worthington E.L., Jr., Content and meta-analysis of interventions to promote forgiveness, Manuscript under editorial review, Virginia Commonwealth University (2003b).

13. Everett L. Worthington, Jr., *Five steps to forgiveness: The art and science of forgiving* (New York: Crown Publishers 2001b); E. L. Worthington, Jr., *Forgiving and reconciling: Bridges to wholeness and love* (Downers Grove, IL: InterVarsity Press, 2003).

14. Michael E. McCullough, Rachal, K. C., Sandage, S. J., Worthington, E. L. Jr., Brown, S. W., and Hight, T. L., Interpersonal forgiveness in close relationships II: Theoretical elaboration and measurement, *Journal of Personality and Social Psychology, 75*,(1998), 1586–1603; E. L. Worthington, Jr., Sandage, S. J., and Berry, J.W., Group interventions to promote forgiveness: What researchers and clinicians ought to know, in M.E. McCullough, K.I. Pargament, and C.E. Thoresen (eds.), *Forgiveness: Theory, research and practice* (New York: Guilford Press, 2000), 228–253; Nathaniel G. Wade, and Worthington, E.L., Jr., Overcoming interpersonal offenses: Is forgiveness the only way to deal with unforgiveness? *Journal of Counseling and Development, 81*, (2003a), 343–353.

15. Everett L. Worthington, Jr., Unforgiveness, forgiveness, and reconciliation in societies, in Raymond G. Helmick and Rodney L. Petersen (eds.), *Forgiveness and reconciliation: Religion, public policy, and Conflict Transformation* (Philadelphia: The Templeton Foundation Press, 2001a), 161–182.

16. Everett L. Worthington, Jr., *Hope-focused marriage counseling* (Downers Grove, IL: InterVarsity Press, 1999).

7

Depression and Bipolar Disorders

Siang-Yang Tan and Michael Lyles

Hear my prayer O Lord, and let my cry come to You. Do not hide your face from me in the day of my trouble . . . For my days are consumed like smoke, and my bones are burned like a hearth. My heart is stricken and withered like grass, so that I forgot to eat my bread . . . I lie awake . . . for I have eaten ashes like bread, and mingled my drink with weeping.

PSALM 102:1–9

Jim awoke with a groan and rolled over and checked his clock on the bed stand: 1:30 in the afternoon. Not that time or routine meant anything anymore, as he was as likely to be wide awake at 1:30 A.M. as asleep in the middle of the day.

Jim had lost his job at the sawmill three months earlier due to his chronic depression. His boss could no longer count on him showing up, let alone accomplishing a solid day's work when he was there. Jim decided to go into business for himself—he made fine redwood boxes and gifts in his shop—but his shop was a chaotic mess and his lack of attention to business detail made it nearly impossible for others to count on timely delivery of goods.

Thankfully, his wife worked full time or they'd be in serious financial trouble. However, she was complaining of leaving him due to being overwhelmed with the hopeless job of caring for him and carrying all the family responsibilities. Jim had felt alienated from her for some time now—in fact, he noticed that all social relations were a real chore and he was systematically avoiding them, lost increasingly in his own dark thoughts.

When Jim thought about all this, he felt nothing—he was numb. He knew this was odd and a real change from the frustration and anger that he experienced over his conditions in the early months of "the black cloud" (as he had long described it). He noticed, now, that he would just shrug his shoulders, as if he were witnessing his own demise in a dreamlike stupor that he could neither shake himself out of nor did he really care to do so.

Jim also noticed that he was no longer overeating and drinking heavily, which he had done for the first 7 to 8 months of his depression. His appetite for food—in fact, for anything enjoyable—had dried up almost completely. He smiled at the irony of it all. Although he was no longer so angry, even violent at times, he had broken so many good relationships then that he had no one around to enjoy his newly detached self. Sad thing was, he told himself, that he didn't really care—about anything.

Jim had long since overcome his denial of naming his problem correctly. He knew he was depressed and had long accepted the fact that he was in deep suffering. He had visited his pastor, and much prayer had been given on his behalf, but he had refused to see a counselor, believing for a long time that he merely had a case of "the blues" that would eventually pass. He did see a physician, who prescribed Prozac, but Jim quit the drug after a week because he "felt weird" and it wasn't helping him get better (he had shut out his wife's nag that the doctor said it would take 3–4 weeks to work).

Now he was plagued by thoughts of suicide, and wondered whether it would simply be easier to just shoot himself and end this unending misery for himself and his family. Of course, he told no one about this. He didn't want anyone to think he was beginning to "go crazy."

A Most Prevalent Disorder

Depression is one of the most prevalent and serious mental disorders in the United States. It has been called the common cold of emotional disorders and appears to be on the rise, affecting up to 20% of the population at some time in their lives, with women being twice as likely as men to suffer from major depressive and dysthymic disorders (a milder form of chronic depression), but *not* bipolar disorders.

More specifically, major depressive disorder as one type of clinical depression is the most frequently diagnosed adult psychiatric disorder in the United States, with lifetime prevalence rates of 20 to 25% for women and 9 to 12% for men or point prevalence rates of about 6% for women and 3% for men.[1] In fact, the National Institute of Mental Health (NIMH) has noted that over 19 million adult Americans will experience some form of depression each year, with depression being the leading cause of disability and annual associated costs totaling more than $30 billion! Depression also increases the risk of heart attacks and is a serious and frequent complicating factor in stroke, diabetes, and cancer.[2]

Bipolar disorder (previously called manic-depressive disorder) with extreme mood swings or ups and downs, and a vulnerability to future episodes has also received increasing attention in recent years. It is estimated that about 1.5% of the adult population has classic bipolar disorder, affecting men and women equally, but with the inclusion of subtypes the prevalence can be as high as 5%[3] or even 6.5%![4] Both depression and bipolar disorder are therefore crucial ones to understand in order to be of effective help to the many who suffer from these conditions.

Diagnosing Depression and Bipolar Disorder

Misdiagnosis of depression is very common at both ends of the spectrum. Not only do a lot of laypeople mislabel a variety of sadness and grief reactions as depression, but many physicians will misdiagnose depression as anxiety (a common affect with many depressions) or other mood disorders. Accurate assessment is the first step to proper treatment.

(a) Depression

Depression can have a variety of meanings because there are different types of depression. Clinical depression as a disorder is not the same as brief mood fluctuations or the feelings of sadness, disappointment, and frustration that everyone experiences from time to time and that last from minutes to a few days at most. Clinical depression is a more serious condition that lasts weeks to months, and sometimes even years.

The *DSM-IV* (American Psychiatric Association, 1994), or more recently the *DSM-IV-TR* (American Psychiatric Association, 2000), identifies five major categories of mood disorders: depressive disorders, bipolar disorders, mood disorders due to a general medical condition, substance-induced mood disorders, and mood disorders not otherwise specified.[5] This chapter will focus on depressive and bipolar disorders.

In order for *Major Depressive Disorder* to be diagnosed, one or more major depressive episodes must have occurred. This means that the depressed person must have experienced at least two weeks of depressed mood (or irritable mood in children or adolescents) or loss of interest or pleasure in almost all activities, together with a minimum of four other symptoms of depression (only three if both depressed mood and loss of interest or pleasure occur) such as: (1) marked weight loss when not dieting, weight gain, or change in appetite; (2) insomnia or excessive sleep; (3) slowed movements or agitation; (4) decreased energy or fatigue; (5) feelings of worthlessness or inappropriate or excessive guilt; (6) indecisiveness or decreased ability to concentrate; and (7) recurrent thoughts of death or suicide. These symptoms (the second to the sixth) must occur almost every day.

A milder form of a depressive disorder is *dysthymic disorder.* Here the depressive symptoms are not serious enough to meet the criteria for major depressive disorder, but the person has a depressed mood more days than not for a minimum of two years. The other category of depressive disorder is *depressive disorder not otherwise specified.*

(b) Bipolar Disorder

DSM-IV lists 4 major types of bipolar disorder: Bipolar I Disorder, Bipolar II Disorder (Recurrent Major Depressive Episodes with Hypomanic Episodes), Cyclothymic Disorder, and Bipolar Disorder Not Otherwise Specified.

In order for *Bipolar I Disorder* to be diagnosed there must be: (1) one or more *manic episodes* in which the patient feels hyper, extremely "high," wired, or unusually irritable, and gets into trouble, is unable to function at school or work, or ends up being hospitalized; (2) during the *manic episodes*, at least 3 of the following symptoms present: feeling overly self-confident or even grandiose; needing significantly less sleep than usual; being unable to stop talking; having racing thoughts; being easily distracted; being much more active socially or sexually, or being much more productive at work or at school than usual, or feeling agitated much of the time; getting involved in pleasurable activities without thinking of the consequences (e.g., buying things that are not affordable or having unprotected sex with a stranger);

and (3) one or more *depressive episodes* as described earlier for *major depressive disorder*.

In order for *Bipolar II Disorder* to be diagnosed, there must be: (1) one or more *depressive episodes* as described for *Major Depressive Disorder*; and (2) one or more *hypomanic episodes* which are similar to manic episodes but are not as impairing or severe. The hypomanic episodes usually last two to four days, causing Bipolar II patients to have far more depression than hypomania. They are often misdiagnosed with Major Depression but are worsened by antidepressant treatments. The suicide rate for this disorder is slightly higher than the rate for Major Depression.

In order for *Cyclothymic Disorder* to be diagnosed, there must be: (1) mood swings that are unpredictable, with the "ups" less severe than manic episodes and the "downs" less severe than major depressive episodes; (2) reduced productivity and unreliability in the patient due to the unstable mood even though it does not cause significant problems per se.[6]

What Causes Depression?

There are various possible causes of depression. Different authors emphasize different causes depending on their theoretical viewpoints, but in general the possible causes (which are not mutually exclusive) can be grouped into six categories or factors: biological-genetic, physical, spiritual, personality and psychological, interpersonal, and environmental or societal.[7]

Biological or Genetic Factors

Biologically oriented counselors and psychiatrists often view severe depression and bipolar disorders as being due to imbalances in brain biochemistry. These may be related to genetic influences and/or constitutional predispositions, as well as to environmental and life stress. More specifically, depression may be due to a deficiency in norepinephrine, dopamine, or serotonin, neurochemicals needed for proper brain functioning. Medical treatments such as antidepressants and/or electroconvulsive shock treatment are often recommended for severe depressive disorders. Antidepressants differ in mechanisms of action and side effect profile, leading patients to respond to some better than others. Mood stabilizers or medications such as lithium, depakote (divalproex), lamictal (lamotrigine), and atypical neuroleptics such as abilify (aripiprazole), geodon (ziprasidone), seroquel (quetiapine), and risperdal (risperidone), are crucial to the treatment of bipolar disorder. An interesting recent development is the use of mega-3 fatty acids (or fish oils) for bipolar disorder.[8] Antidepressants can worsen bipolar disorder and should be used sparingly and with a mood stabilizer.

It takes antidepressants four to six weeks to work. Mood stabilizers and atypical neuroleptics tend to work quicker to stabilize acute symptoms. However, they also can take four to six weeks to begin to maximize the benefit. Neither antidepressants nor mood stabilizers/atypical neuroleptics are addictive. They do, however, need close monitoring to avoid side effects or medical complications.

Physical Factors

Lack of sleep, lack of regular exercise, poor diet or nutrition, substance abuse (e.g., cocaine, alcohol), overwork or exhaustion, some physical illnesses and conditions (for example, an underactive thyroid, chronic illness, or traumatic injuries), or certain types of medication (e.g., tranquilizers, steroids) can contribute to depression. Postpartum depression is an example of how physical or biological factors can lead to depression. It occurs after childbirth in about 10–15% of all deliveries. Another example concerns sunlight exposure and its effects on our biological systems. Seasonal affective disorder, or SAD, is an acute form of winter depression. It affects about 5–6% of the population, and exposure to sunlight is a natural and effective treatment. Artificial sunlight fixtures that mimic full spectrum bright sunlight are useful for this population.

Spiritual Factors

Sin. Does sin cause depression? There are cases where depression appears to be a consequence of sin in a person's life, although this does not mean that depression is always due to personal sin. Possible sin-related causes of depression include negative attitudes or feelings like bitterness and hatred, guilt and lack of repentance over sinful behavior or attitudes, turning away from God and His Word, fear of the future and lack of trust in God as sufficient Provider, and unbelief in general.

God-sent trials. Difficult, painful, stressful times of trial or struggle may lead to periods of depression. Such God-sent trials are meant, however, to prune or purify us, so that we can bear more fruit (John 15:2; 1 Pet. 1:6–7).

Demonic attacks. Satan and his demonic forces may attack and oppress people. This in turn may sometimes lead to depression. Inner healing prayer and prayer for deliverance may be helpful.

Existential vacuum. At times depression may be due to feelings of meaninglessness and emptiness—an existential vacuum in life. Milder depression, experienced by almost every person at times, may come from the pain of being human in a fallen world.

"Dark night of the soul." There are times when depression is associated with spiritual dryness and an experience that St. John of the Cross called "the dark night of the soul" (Isa. 50:10). Richard Foster, in his excellent book, *Celebration of Discipline,* describes it: "The 'dark night'...is not something bad or destructive....The purpose of the darkness is not to punish or afflict us. It is to set us free....

What is involved in entering the dark night of the soul? It may be a sense of dryness, depression, even feeling lost. It strips us of overdependence on the emotional life. The notion, often heard today, that such experiences can be avoided and that we should live in peace, comfort, joy, and celebration only betrays the fact that much contemporary experience is surface slush. The dark night is one of the ways God brings us to a hush, a stillness, so that he can work an inner transformation of the soul....Recognize the dark night for what it is. Be grateful that God is lovingly drawing you away from every distraction so that you can see him."[9]

Personality and Psychological Factors

Temperamental vulnerability (Depression-prone personality). Are some people innately prone to being depressed? Two decades ago, Frederic Flach described the depression-prone person who has a temperamental vulnerability to depression. Such people often have experienced loss early in life, such as the death of a parent. They are conscientious and responsible, with high morals and a tendency to feel guilty even when they have done nothing wrong. When they are not depressed, they may be energetic and competitive. They are introspective but concerned with the feelings of others, often to the point that they try hard to avoid hurting anyone's feelings.

Many are overinvolved in activities and overly dependent on others. They are easily hurt, sensitive to rejection and loss of self-esteem, and have a high need for control. Often they are not aware of the intense anger they feel and have trouble expressing anger appropriately when necessary. [10]

Although this description is somewhat general, it is a helpful reminder that some people are more susceptible than others to depression. These people may need to take special steps to avoid depression-producing situations or relationships.

Loneliness. Sometimes loneliness is seen as the consequence of a fear of love or a fear of rejection. This can result in depression if a person withdraws from much needed fellowship and interaction with friends.

Triggering situations. A number of situations can trigger depression or depressive reactions. These include insult, rejection, or failure; loss—especially of a loved one or object; life stress and change, especially if it occurs too often or too quickly; lack of positive, reinforcing, or rewarding events (or loss of the power of such events); success (when it is very taxing or stressful, or sometimes just before a success occurs); or learned helplessness, in which a person discovers, as a result of numerous experiences, that he or she can do nothing to change life events.

Irrational, unbiblical self-talk, or misbeliefs. Cognitive therapists have emphasized that triggering situations do not cause depression per se. Instead, depression is due to a person's mental attitude or self-talk (reactions, interpretations, expectations, and implicit beliefs) in response to such situations. Perfectionistic and rigid ways of thinking, often with logical errors (for example, blowing things out of proportion, taking things too personally, focusing only on the negative, jumping to conclusions) can distort views of oneself, the world, and the future. Depression follows and is likely to persist unless such distorted thinking is challenged and corrected, sometimes with the help of a counselor.

Anger turned inward against the self. Some mental health professionals, especially those with a more psychodynamic (Freudian) perspective, suggest that unresolved anger turned inward against oneself can result in depression. Such anger initially may have been directed toward a loved one or object that has been lost. Hurt may underlie the anger, and eventually this results in depression.

Interpersonal Factors

Serious interpersonal disturbance or relationship problems also may lead to depression. For example, about 50% of depressed people also experience chronic marital discord. Recent research has shown that marital difficulties and family dysfunction have a significant impact on the course of depression. Relapse following therapy is more common among individuals whose families have high levels of criticism in their communication. Marital counseling can be a crucial approach to helping depressed individuals.

Environmental or Societal Factors

Larger environmental, societal, and cultural factors like political unrest, economic recession, modernization and industrialization, high divorce rates, and poverty also may contribute to higher rates of depression. In addition, the ways people express their depression in terms of specific symptoms is affected by ethnic and cultural influences. For example, Asians tend to "somaticize" their depressions, showing physical symptoms, including loss of appetite, sleep difficulties, and headaches or other aches or pains.

What Causes Bipolar Disorder?

Briefly, as Miklowitz has pointed out, genetics, biological vulnerabilities, and, to a lesser extent, stress, may all be possible causes of bipolar disorder. The biological vulnerabilities may include disturbances in the production and chemical breakdown (catabolism) of neurotransmitters such as norepinephrine, dopamine, glutanate, serotonin, and abnormal production of hormones like cortisol when under stress. The tendencies toward these biological vulnerabilities appear to be genetically mediated. While stress does *not* cause bipolar disorder per se without the crucial roles played by genetics and biological vulnerabilities, stress may increase the likelihood of having another episode of mania or depression for someone who already has bipolar disorder. Three kinds of environmental stress may be particularly significant: major life change (positive or negative), sleep-wake cycle disruptions, and conflicts with significant others.[11]

Psychosocial Treatments for Major Depressive Disorder

Our goal here is to outline a reliable treatment approach to depression that combines biological, psychosocial, and spiritual elements of care. The good news is that depression is very treatable, if it is accurately recognized and rightly approached by caring family, pastors, and professional helpers.

Behavior therapy, cognitive-behavior therapy, and *interpersonal psychotherapy* have all been found to be effective psychosocial treatments for major depressive disorder. Psychosocial and pharmacological interventions for major depressive episodes appear to be equally effective, with some support found for the superior effectiveness of combined psychosocial and pharmacological treatments, although this is less clear for *severely* depressed patients.[12]

The following are some helpful books that provide clinical guidelines and methods for the psychosocial treatment of depression: Martell, Addis, and Jacobson on *Behavioral Activation, an approach to Behavior Therapy*, and McCullough on *Cognitive Behavioral Analysis System of Psychotherapy*; Beck, Rush, Shaw, and Emery, Klosko and Sanderson, and Persons, Davidson, and Tompkins, on Cognitive Therapy or *Cognitive-Behavior Therapy*; and Klerman, Weissman, Rounsaville, and Chevron, as well as Weissman, Markowitz, and Klerman on *Interpersonal Therapy*.[13]

A Spiritually Oriented Psychosocial Approach to Treating Depression

In a short-term structured approach to strategic pastoral counseling with depressed parishioners or clients, Tan and Ortberg[14] have integrated some of the main aspects or components of behavior therapy, cognitive-behavior therapy, and interpersonal therapy within a biblical or spiritual perspective as follows:

A. (Affect): *Strategies for Exploring and Dealing with Feelings Associated with Depression*

1. *Permission-Giving* to clients to talk openly about their struggles with depression
2. *Attentive Listening*
3. *Empathic Responding*
4. *Use of Feeling Words, Imagery, and/or Role-Playing* to help clients better express their feelings
5. *Appropriate Self-Disclosure*
6. *Identifying Losses and Working Through the Grieving Process*
7. *Inner Healing Prayer* for past hurts and painful memories, using a 7-step model developed by Tan: (a) begin with prayer for the Lord's guidance and blessing as well as protection; (b) use a relaxation strategy (e.g., slow, deep breathing, calming self-talk, and pleasant imagery, prayer, and biblical imagery or verses) to help

the client relax deeply; (c) once deeply relaxed, guide the client to go back in imagination to reenact a past event that is particularly painful or hurtful still. Ask the client at appropriate times, "What's happening right now? What are you feeling or experiencing?"; (d) after sufficient time has gone by, pray aloud for the Holy Spirit to come and minister His healing grace to the client in whatever way is needed or appropriate; (e) after some waiting, ask the client again, "What's happening? What are you experiencing or feeling now?"; (f) close with a brief prayer by both the counselor or client if possible; and (g) debrief the inner healing prayer experience with the client, and assign homework inner healing prayer to the client if appropriate.

B. (Behavior): *Behavioral Interventions for Treating Depression*

1. *Self-Monitoring,* using a Weekly Activity Schedule or Log, and rating activities engaged in with a Mastery (sense of achievement) and Pleasure (sense of enjoyment) scale of 0–5, gradually scheduling in more pleasant activities and events over time (Activity Scheduling).
2. *Use of Graded Task Assignment,* breaking down bigger tasks into smaller, more "doable" or manageable units.
3. *Use of a "Behavioral Experiment"* to overcome perfectionism or shame (e.g., by intentionally losing at a board game).
4. *Assertiveness Training,* using role-playing and modeling of appropriate, assertive responses.
5. *Relaxation/Coping Skills Training* to reduce tension and help to control negative thinking and feelings.
6. *Listening to Music and Engaging in Other Pleasant Activities.*
7. *Taking Care of the Body* (e.g., with good nutrition, regular exercise, and adequate sleep of 8 hours a night).
8. *Use of "light boxes" or special light bulbs* if the client is suffering specifically from Seasonal Affective Disorder (SAD).

C. (Cognition): *Helping Depressed People Change Distorted Thinking*

1. *Use of an "ABC" Diary,* with A for Activating Event or Situation, B for Belief or Self-Talk, and C for Consequences (Feelings and Behaviors).

2. *Thought-Stopping* to temporarily stop recurrent negative thinking by shouting "STOP" and eventually saying "STOP" sub-vocally to oneself.

3. *Cognitive Restructuring,* the mainstay of cognitive therapy, to help the client change negative, distorted thinking into more accurate, realistic, biblical thinking, with the following helpful questions:

- On what basis do you say that? Where is the evidence for your belief or conclusion?
- What's another way of looking at the situation? (alternative interpretation)
- Assuming that your conclusion or belief is correct, what then does it mean to you? (the "so what" question)
- What do you think God's view of this might be? What does the Bible have to say?

4. *Prayer with Thanksgiving* (Phil. 4:6–7)
5. *Use of humor*
6. *Bibliotherapy (Homework Reading)*
7. *Use of Contemplative Prayer and Meditation on Scripture and Other Spiritual Disciplines for Learning to Rest in the Lord.*[15]

Psychosocial Treatments for Bipolar Disorder

Psychosocial treatments for bipolar disorder are *adjunctive* or secondary to the primary treatment involving pharmacological interventions or medications. Psychosocial treatments have the potential to increase medication adherence, improve quality of life, and enhance strategies for coping with stress. Combining pharmacotherapy and psychosocial treatments for bipolar disorder may therefore significantly lower the risk of relapse and rehospitalization, and improve the quality of life for patients.

Psychoeducation, involving the provision of information about bipolar disorder and its pharmacological treatment and treatment side effects to patients and their families, has been found to increase medication adherence.

Cognitive-behavior therapy as an ancillary or adjunctive treatment is effective in increasing medication adherence, decreasing rehospitalizations, and improving occupational and social functioning. *IPSRT* (a combination of Interpersonal Psychotherapy or IPT and Social Rhythm Therapies or SRT) has demonstrated its greatest impact on symptoms of depression. Consistency of psychosocial treatments over time may also be an important factor in the effective helping of bipolar patients.

Finally, *marital/family therapy* can be successfully combined with pharmacotherapy to decrease recurrences of bipolar disorder and improve occupational and social functioning.[16]

The following are helpful books that contain clinical guidelines and methods for the psychosocial treatment of bipolar disorder: Newman, Leahy, Beck, Reilly-Harrington, and Gyulai, Basco and Rush, and Lam, Jones, Hayward, and Bright on *Cognitive Therapy or Cognitive-Behavior Therapy*; Weissman, Markowitz, and Klerman on *Interpersonal Therapy and Social Rhythm Therapies* or IPSRT; and Miklowitz and Goldstein on a *Family-Focused Treatment Approach*.[17]

A Spiritually Oriented Psychosocial Approach to Treating Bipolar Disorder

Many of the strategies covered for treating depression also apply to bipolar disorder, especially the "downswings" of the disorder. Miklowitz[18] has provided the following more specific aspects or components of effective psychosocial treatments (i.e., psychoeducation, cognitive-behavior therapy, IPSRT, and a family-focused treatment approach) for bipolar disorder, aimed at reducing risk factors and enhancing protective factors for the client:

A. *Reducing Risk Factors such as:*

1. *Stressful Life Changes*
2. *Alcohol and Drug Abuse* (and Caffeine Use)
3. *Sleep Deprivation* (e.g., jet lagging or changing time zones, staying up all night, sudden changes in sleep-wake cycles)
4. *Family Distress or Other Interpersonal Conflicts* (e.g., high levels of criticism from a spouse or parent, hostile interactions with coworkers or family members)
5. *Inconsistency with medication* (e.g., frequently missing one or more dosages, suddenly stopping taking mood stabilizing medication)

B. *Enhancing Protective Factors such as:*

1. *Observing and self-monitoring of client's mood and triggers for mood swings* (e.g., by keeping a daily mood chart or social rhythm chart)
2. *Maintaining regular daily and nightly routines* (e.g., by having a predictable or stable social schedule and going to bed and waking up around the same time each day)
3. *Relying on family and social supports* (e.g., by clearly communicating with family or relatives and asking for their help in emergencies)
4. *Receiving regular medical and psychosocial treatment* (e.g., by taking medications regularly, attending support groups, and by seeing a psychotherapist or counselor)

Miklowitz also listed the following objectives of psychotherapy for persons with bipolar disorder: to help the client make sense of current or past bipolar episodes; to do long-term planning, given the client's vulnerability to future episodes; to help the client accept and adjust to a long-term medication regimen; to identify and develop strategies for effectively coping with stress; to improve the client's functioning at work or in school; to help the client deal with the stigma of having bipolar disorder; and to improve family or marital/romantic relationships.[19]

Depression, Bipolar Disorder, and Suicide

It is well known that severe depression and bipolar disorder have a high risk for suicide. Some have described suicide as a current "epidemic," especially among children, prisoners, the elderly, young adults, and particularly teenagers. Risks are highest among men, especially those over 65, people who feel hopelessness, and those who have experienced severe stress. Other factors associated with a high suicide risk include a prior history of suicide attempts, alcoholism, the presence of an organized and detailed plan for killing oneself, the lack of supportive family or friends, rejection by others, and, for many, the presence of a chronic, debilitating illness.

Most counselors are aware that when counseling depressed individuals or those with bipolar disorder who may be at risk for suicide, it is crucial to ask openly whether they have been thinking of taking their lives, and if so, whether they have specific plans. Open discussion, sometimes followed by hospitalization or referral, can reduce the likelihood of suicide.

Within recent years depression has become so common, within the church and without, that many people are aware of its symptoms and potential for impacting lives and families. Bipolar disorder involving extreme mood swings is also beginning to receive more attention. Helping others to understand the basics of depression and bipolar disorder can be a first step toward effective treatment for people suffering from these disorders.

After many years of denial and misunderstanding, Christians are coming to recognize that depression and bipolar disorder are complex conditions. They can be effectively treated, but they are not likely to be dismissed by simplistic explanations or approaches to treatment.

When God Comes Near

Elijah is a great example of how depression can strike even the boldest and most godly of men. He became so stricken he retreated to a cave and wanted to die (1 Kin. 19:4). Yet God—in contravention of the common belief among depressives that He is angry with or doesn't care about the depressed sufferer—came and ministered to Elijah's every need. God provided him with food, sent angels to minister to his loneliness, and called him a godly rest. Elijah received God's loving care and was eventually restored in strength and purpose. God ministers the very same way today to anyone who suffers in the dark places of depression.

ENDNOTES

1. W. E. Craighead, Hart, A. B., Craighead, L.W., and Ilardi, S.S., Psychosocial treatments for major depressive disorder, in P. E. Nathan and J. M. Gorman (eds.), *A guide to treatments that work*, second edition (New York: Oxford University Press, 2002), 245–261. Also see I. H. Gotlib and C. L. Hammen (eds.), *Handbook of depression* (NY: Guilford, 2002).
2. National Institute of Mental Health (NIMH), *The numbers count*, NIH Publication No. NIH 99–4584, (1999) [Online]. Available:<http://www.NIMH.NIH.gov/pulicat/members.CFM
3. M. Maj, Akiskal, H.S., Lopez-Ibor, J.J., and Sartorius, N. (eds.), *Bipolar disorder* (New York: Wiley, 2002).
4. M. R. Lyles, Will the real mood stabilizer please stand up? *Christian Counseling Today*, 9(3), (2001), 60–61.
5. American Psychiatric Association, *Diagnostic and statistical manual of mental disorders, fourth edition* (Washington, DC: American Psychiatric Association, 1994), 317–391. Also see American Psychiatric Association, *Diagnostic and statistical manual of mental disorders, fourth edition, text revision* (Washington, DC: American Psychiatric Association, 2000), 345–428.

6.   See A. Frances and M. B. First, *Your mental health: A layman's guide to the Psychiatrist's Bible* (New York: Scribner, 1998), 59–78.

7.   Some of the material in this chapter is based on a more detailed description of depression and strategic pastoral counseling found in S.-Y. Tan and J. Ortberg, Jr., *Understanding depression* and *Coping with depression,* (Grand Rapids, MI: Baker, 1995). From a Christian perspective, also see: A. Hart, *Counseling the depressed* (Waco, TX: Word, 1987); A. Hart, *Unmasking male depression* (Nashville: W Publishing Group, 2001); A. Hart and Weber, C.H., *Unveiling depression in women* (Grand Rapids, MI: Revell, 2002); F. Minirth and Meier, P., *Happiness is a choice,* second edition (Grand Rapids, MI: Baker, 1994); P. Meier, Arterburn, S. and Minirth, F., *Mood swings* (Nashville: Thomas Nelson, 2001).

8.   A. L. Stoll, *The Omega-3 connection* (New York: Simon & Schuster, 2001).

9.   R. Foster, *Celebration of discipline* (San Francisco: Harper & Row, 1978), 89–91.

10. F. F. Flach, *The secret strength of depression* (Philadelphia: Lippincott, 1974), 41–42.

11. D. J. Miklowitz, *The bipolar disorder survival guide* (New York: Guilford Press, 2002), 73–97. Also see E. F. Torrey and Knable, M. B., *Surviving manic depression* (New York: Basic Books, 2002); J. Fawcett, Golden, B., and Rosenfeld, N., *New hope for people with bipolar disorder* (Roseville, CA: Prima Publishing, 2000); F. M. Mondimore, *Bipolar disorder* (Baltimore: Johns Hopkins University Press, 1999); J. Scott, *Overcoming mood swings* (New York: New York University Press, 2001); D. Papolos and Papolos, J., *The bipolar child* (New York: Broadway Books, 1999). For secular self-help books on depression see: D. Burns, *Feeling good* (New York: William Morrow, 1999); D. Greenberger and Padeskey, C.A., *Mind over mood* (New York: Guilford Press, 1995); P. M. Lewinsohn, Munoz, R.F., Youngren, M. A., and Zeiss, A.M., *Control your depression* (New York: Fireside/Simon and Schuster, 1992); D. Papolos and Papolos, J., *Overcoming depression,* third edition (New York: Harper Collins, 1997); M. Broida, *New hope for people with depression* (Roseville, CA: Prima Publishing, 2001); M. E. Copeland, *The depression workbook,* second edition (Oakland, CA: New Harbinger, 2001).

12. Craighead, Hart, Craighead, and Ilardi (see note 1), 245. See also R. J. DeRubeis, S. D. Hollon, J. D. Amsterdam, R. C. Shelton, P. R. Young, R. M. Salomon, et al., Cognitive therapy vs. medications in the treatment of moderate to severe depression, *Archives of General Psychiatry,* 62 (2005): 409–416, and S. D. Hollon, R. J. DeRubeis, R. C. Shelton, J. D. Amsterdam, R. M. Salomon, J. P. O'Reardon, et al., Prevention of relapse following cognitive therapy vs. medications in moderate to severe depression, *Archives of General Psychiatry,* 62 (2005): 417–422.

13. See C. R. Martell, Addis, M.E. and Jacobson, N. S., *Depression in context: Strategies for guided action* (New York: W. W. Norton, 2001); J. P. McCullough, *Treatment of chronic depression: Cognitive behavioral analysis system of psychotherapy* (New York: Guilford Press, 2000); A. T. Beck, Rush, A.J., Shaw, B.F., and Emery G., *Cognitive therapy of depression* (New York: Guilford Press, 1979); J. S. Klosko and Sanderson, W.C., *Cognitive-behavioral treatment of depression* (Northvale, NJ: Jason Aronson, 1999); J. B. Persons, Davidson, J., and Tompkins, M.A., *Essential components of cognitive-behavior therapy for depression* (Washington, DC: American Psychological Association, 2001); G. L. Klerman, Weissman, M. M., Rounsaville, B. J., and Chevron, E.S., *Interpersonal psychotherapy of depression* (New York: Basic Books, 1984); M. M. Weissman, Markowitz, J.C., and Klerman, G. L., *Comprehensive guide to interpersonal psychotherapy* (New York: Basic Books, 2000).

14. S.-Y. Tan and J. Ortberg, *Understanding depression* (see note 7). See also Tan and Ortberg, *Coping with depression*, rev. ed. (Grand Rapids, MI: Baker, 2004).

15. See S.-Y. Tan and Gregg, D.H., *Disciplines of the Holy Spirit*, (Grand Rapids, MI: Zondervan, 1997); and S.-Y. Tan, *Rest: Experiencing God's peace in a restless world* (Ann Arbor, MI: Vine Books, 2000).

16. W. E. Craighead, Miklowitz, D. J., Frank, E., and Vajk, F.C., Psychosocial treatments for bipolar disorder, in P. E. Nathan and J. M. Gorman (eds.), *A guide to treatments that work*, second edition (New York: Oxford University Press, 2002), 263–275.

17. See C. F. Newman, Leahy, R. L., Beck, A.T., Reilly-Harrington, N. A., and Gyulai, L., *Bipolar disorder: A cognitive therapy approach* (Washington, DC: American Psychological Association, 2002); M. Basco, and Rush, A. J., *Cognitive-behavioral therapy for bipolar disorder* (New York: Guilford Press, 1996); D. H. Lam, Jones, S. H., Hayward, P., and Bright, J. A., *Cognitive therapy for bipolar disorder: A therapist's guide to concepts, methods, and practice* (Chichester, UK: Wiley, 1999); Weisman, Markowitz, and Klerman (see note 13); D. J. Miklowitz, and Goldstein, M. J., *Bipolar disorder: A family-focused treatment approach* (New York: Guilford Press, 1997).

18. Miklowitz, *The bipolar disorder survival guide* (see note 11), 153.

19. Ibid., 122.

8

Stress and Anxiety

Archibald Hart and Catherine Hart Weber

The only thing we have to fear is fear itself.

FRANKLIN D. ROOSEVELT

At first John enjoyed the excitement, the exhilaration and rush of the adrenaline surges. He felt a sense of profound urgency that propelled him to long working hours. He missed lunch often and had little time for his declining marriage and activities such as exercise and recreation. He had to focus. There were a lot of changes his business was going through, reorganizing and integrating many new systems.

His symptoms were subtle at first, nothing to be alarmed about, just annoyance. A low-grade sense of discomfort hovered over his life. Physically, he battled frequent colds. He didn't eat well and battled exhaustion. He masked the unresolved grief of several losses in his life. Drinking and other addictions had been temporary solutions to dealing with his pain. And then there was the occasional pounding heart, pains in his chest and muscle tension. Insomnia kept him awake at night, which gave opportunity for his mind to strategize anxiously and worry.

He tried to trust God and let go, but his faith and hope were clouded by a stronger force that had hold of him. He withheld his feelings of being overwhelmed, helpless, frustrated and disconnected, even from his wife.

Then, on a Friday afternoon, out of the blue, while driving home from work, John started having severe pains down his left arm and across his chest. He started to hyperventilate and panic. Tearfully, in desperation he called his wife on the cell phone. "Honey, I'm having a heart attack! I'm going to die!" She calmly instructed him to hang up and call 911. But he decided to drive himself to the nearest emergency room, stumbling in a state of fear and panic declaring he was having a heart attack.

He got immediate response, with extensive testing. No, it was not a heart attack, but a close resemblance: a panic attack (also known as a "stress attack" or "anxiety attack"). That is when he realized he needed to get some help.

Epidemic Disorders

Behind the emotional pressure, fear, worry, catastrophizing, wandering thoughts and physical discomfort of stress and anxiety that John and millions of others experience was a powerful and intricately designed system created by God and centered in the mind, nervous system, and the brain. While this natural defense mechanism is designed to alert us to danger, keep us growing, vigilant and productive, it can also be pushed too far and become toxic.

When the immediate threat or call for action is long gone, the nervous system can sometimes continue to stay activated, intensifying symptoms resulting in stress or anxiety disorders, depression and many other health problems. Quite simply, our bodies and being aren't physiologically capable of dealing with the prolonged pressures of modern-day living that so many are experiencing.

Stress, anxiety, and related depression are now considered epidemic and the leading mental health disorders in our nation. Christian counselors will increasingly be challenged with connecting this array of overlapping and sometimes confusing symptoms with understanding the underlying causes and providing effective comprehensive treatment that brings complete healing to the whole person, not merely eliminating symptoms.

Christian counseling can provide effective lasting recovery through utilizing a combination of approaches in caring for the whole person. Effective counseling will augment conventional psychotherapy addressing areas of change and growth, cognitive-behavioral and medication treatments along with other complementary approaches.

Stress

First, let us examine the nature of stress. Hans Selye, Ph.D., the Canadian endocrinologist who first discovered "the stress response" in the mid-1930s, clearly described the physiological changes that occur when a person experiences difficulties or pressures in life. Science has made much progress since then in understanding the stress response and long-term effects. We now know that it is not stress itself that is the problem, but our *responses* to stress, the sense of *helplessness*, the *duration* of the stress, and the *lack of recovery* from the stressors bombarding us which cause damage emotionally and physically.

Eustress, or so-called normal healthy stress, is an essential natural part of life enabling us to change, grow, and produce good results in our lives. God uses times of difficulty and adversity to stretch us and develop our character. This mechanism also keeps life exciting, enabling us to be creative and productive. *Acute*, short-lived stress keeps us alert to the protective response, equipping us to deal with challenges, unless they are too traumatizing. However, when any stress is prolonged (good or bad), *chronic*, excessive and intense—when we aren't able to recover, or remove ourselves from it, there is a transition into *distress* (stress disease). This causes adrenaline exhaustion and begins to erode the foundations of mental and physical health. The mind and body are not equipped to handle the process of ongoing chronic stress.

Causes and Symptoms of Stress

So what is causing this epidemic of stress? The source of stress can come from external or internal factors.

External Stressors include adverse physical conditions such as pain, illness, extreme temperatures, noise, foul air, hurried schedule; or stressful psychological environments such as work demands, abusive or conflictual relationships, the environment and unpredictable events.

Internal Stressors can also be physical such as infections, inflammation, hormonal imbalances, poor health habits; or psychological such as intense worry about finances, work, family and relationship problems, worrying about a harmful event that may or may not occur, an emptiness, lack of fulfillment, irresponsible behavior, unrealistic expectations, negative attitudes and feelings, personality traits such as perfectionism, trying to do too much, change and loss.

Whether seeking help for primarily psychological or physical ailments, doctors say that their patients complain about stress, anxiety and other related emotional and physical symptoms more than anything else.[1, 2] An estimated 20 million Americans are experiencing nervous tension, sleep disturbances, physical aches and pains and many other symptoms due to these conditions.

In Table 1, we provide a way to differentiate some of the symptoms of stress from anxiety. Table 2 differentiates symptoms of depression from the stress/anxiety complex. Although some of these symptoms also overlap with other physical and psychological conditions, many have been overlooked as evidence of stress, anxiety and depression, resulting in patients being frustrated with undiagnosed conditions and unhappy lives. Others are shocked to realize that the numbness in the limbs or frequent urination are actually the result of stress and anxiety. Encourage clients to not merely focus on symptom relief, but what these symptoms are alerting them to. Once they understand the underlying cause(s), complete, lasting recovery is then possible.

The Stress Response

To expand your understanding and assist you to effectively counsel those who suffer from excessive stress, here is a brief summary of the stress response. The stress response starts in the brain. When a stressor is detected as a threat, the *amygdala, hypothalamus,* and *pituitary glands* trigger the "flight-or-fight" stress response. The *sympathetic nervous system* activates several different physical responses to mobilize for action. The *adrenal glands* increase the output of *adrenaline* (also called *epinephrine*), *cortisol* and other *glucocorticoids*. These are the stress hormones. In turn, nerve cells release *norepinephrine*, which tightens and contracts the muscles and sharpens the senses to prepare for action.[3]

An outpouring of these stress hormones impacts virtually every system

TABLE 1:

DIFFERENTIATING STRESS FROM ANXIETY

Symptoms of General Stress
(Consult the DSM-IV for criteria of specific stress disorders)

Physical Discomforts (which are not due to another illness):
Muscle and skeletal problems such as tics, headaches, dizziness, aches and pains due to muscle tension, trembling. Gastrointestinal difficulties such as indigestion, nausea, stomach aches, diarrhea. Cardiovascular changes—pounding heart, high blood pressure, fatigue, lack of energy, insomnia, weight gain—especially around the abdomen.

Behavioral changes: Withdrawal. Avoidance. Increased alcohol and/or substance use, change in eating habits, appetite and weight. Change in sleeping habits. Sleep disturbances.

Social, Emotional, Mental uneasiness: Chronic fatigue, irritability, feeling out of sorts, interpersonal conflict, reduced concentration, lower levels of creativity, negative, pessimistic thinking, depression, an inability to switch off and relax.

Symptoms of General Anxiety
(Consult the DSM-IV for criteria of specific anxiety disorders)

Physical, mental, emotional changes: Heart palpitations, mitral valve prolapse, sensations of smothering/ choking, stabbing pains, chest pain, headaches, back pain, muscle spasms, sweating (hot or cold), constant need to urinate or defecate, apprehension, nervousness, worry, uncertainty, jitteriness, fear or panic, feeling of doom, dizziness, nausea, diarrhea and stomach problems, depersonalization, paresthesias (arms, legs, mouth), preoccupation with symptoms, irrational fears about: dying, losing control, losing your mind, embarrassing yourself, having a heart attack.

Behavioral and social changes: Erratic or consistent impairment in functioning, hostile angry outbursts, verbal and emotional attacks, social withdrawal, dependent clingy behavior, compulsive behaviors, phobic fears, self-destructive irrational behavior.

Indications for anxiety in children: Refusing to go to school; overly clinging behavior; frequent stomach aches; headaches and other physical complaints; persistent nightmares; not getting work completed.

Indications for anxiety in adolescents: Substance abuse; frequent truancy; risk-taking behavior; "acting out"; decline in academic performance; inability/ fearfulness of engaging in social relationships.

> ### Symptoms of General Stress and Anxiety
>
> Fast heart rate, rapid or shallow breathing; increased muscle tension; loss of concentration; diarrhea; substance abuse; avoidance behaviors; sleep disturbances; appetite disturbance; repetitive behaviors; intrusive thoughts; interpersonal conflict; depression.
>
>   Also listen for some common complaints such as:
>
>   Tension, feeling on edge, up-tight, hassled, nervous, jittery, jumpy, wound up, scared, terrified, insecure, pressured, alarmed, anxious, worried, dreading what might happen, uncertainty, vulnerability, apprehension, edgy, troubled.

of the body. Four main systems respond to stress and can be compromised by prolonged stress: the cardiovascular system, immune system, nervous system, endocrine or glandular system and metabolic response. The heart and pulse rate increase, breathing becomes shallow and rapid, muscles get tense, the digestive system shuts down and the hands and feet become icy cold. Eventually, when the danger or pressure passes, the level of stress hormones drop.

Negative consequences of chronic stress. However, chronic low or high levels of stress can keep the *glucocorticoids and catecholamines* (stress hormones) in circulation, causing all systems involved in the stress response to be compromised. Fatigue, exhaustion and illness results when the body doesn't get enough rest, relaxation and recovery time to restore equilibrium. The body also forms free radicals that are associated with degenerative diseases, illness and acceleration of the aging process. Table 3 presents a list of some of the negative consequences of prolonged, chronic stress.

Diagnostic Criteria for Stress

Most stress related problems would be categorized under the heading of Adjustment Disorders in the DSM-IV. The first criteria states: "The development of emotional or behavioral symptoms in response to an identifiable stressor(s) occurring within 3 months of the onset of the stressor(s)." Here is the range of classifications:

TABLE 3

CONSEQUENCES OF PROLONGED STRESS

Negative consequences of prolonged, chronic stress

Physical and emotional exhaustion, Anxiety, Depression, Heart disease, Stroke, Depletion of calcium from the bones, Immune system vulnerability, Immune disorders, Cancer, Gastrointestinal problems, Eating problems, Weight gain—especially around the abdomen, Diabetes, Pain, Sleep disturbances, Sexual and reproductive dysfunction, Self medication and unhealthy lifestyles, Damage to the brain causing Hippocampal atrophy, killing of brain cells, memory loss and diminished concentration.

Adjustment Disorders

309.0	With Depressed Mood
309.24	With Anxiety
309.28	With Mixed Anxiety and Depressed Mood
309.3	With Disturbance of Conduct
309.4	With Mixed Disturbance of Emotions and Conduct
309.9	Unspecified

The nature of the stressor can be indicated by listing it on Axis IV (e.g., Divorce).

Categories of Stress

Serious stress disorders can be divided into two main categories:

Acute Stress. This is the reaction to an immediate threat, danger or loss eliciting the fight or flight response. Acute stress meets the diagnostic criteria if it lasts less than 6 months. It is sudden in onset then usually diminishes once the threat is over.

Chronic Stress. Constant ongoing stressful situations, even seemingly minor ones, that are not short-lived can cause continual pressure that then become chronic. This is a more serious form of stress disorder, even though it may not seem as intense as acute stress. Ongoing highly pressured work, long-term relationship problems, loneliness, complicated bereavement, persistent financial worries—all could meet the diagnostic criteria if these disturbance lasts for 6 months or more. Eventually this form of stress can weaken the immune system and have many damaging effects to health and well-being.

Anxiety

Now, let us examine the nature of anxiety. Anxiety results from a combination of chemical reactions in the brain to a stimulus, fearful and worrisome thinking, troubled feelings and an exaggerated and persistent stress response. Anxiety, in effect, can be a stressor OR can be caused by stress. There is a body-mind connection where every change in the mind (anxiety) produces a corresponding change in the body (alarm and stress) and vice versa. This reaction impacts every part of a person's being all at once.[4]

Anxiety, like stress is an inevitable part of life. Symptoms and intensity range from a "mild" response to stressful or challenging situations to "intense" fear and a troublesome disorder, which interferes with daily functioning and a sense of well-being.[5] Some people have a lower threshold for stress and are more susceptible to develop anxiety. For example, in some people, stress hormones remain elevated instead of returning to normal levels. This may occur in highly competitive athletes or people with a history of depression, or early childhood anxiety. Anxiety can result from a number of other factors such as: genetic predisposition, a painful childhood, major stress or trauma, medical illness, alcohol or drug abuse—and can also occur for no obvious or apparent reason.

The Anatomy of Anxiety

When faced with a stressful, anxious thought, feeling or startling sensory trigger, the emotional and fear center in the brain, the *amygdala* is activated and alerts other parts of the brain for a *fear response*. This powerful mechanism, begins in the brain, and also involves the spinal cord and the peripheral nerves. The *locus ceruleus* receives signals from the amygdala initiating many responses in the body's *sympathetic nervous system*, such as sweaty palms, rapid heartbeat, increased blood pressure and pupil dialation. The *hypothalamus and pituitary gland* signals the adrenal glands to pump out high levels of the stress hormone *cortisol*.

The physiological response to anxiety or stress is the same no matter what the initial stressor is (physical danger or imaginary threat). After the initial fear response, the conscious mind is activated. Some of the sensory information through sight, sound and smell doesn't go directly to the amygdala but takes a route through the *hypothalamus, hippocampus* then the *cortex*, where the threatening or traumatic stimuli it is analyzed. If the decision is yes, then the cortex signals the *amygdala* and the body stays on alert. The *bed nucleus of the stria terminalis* in the brain perpetuates the fear response, causing the symptoms typical of anxiety.[6]

Each anxiety response and disorder has its own distinct features, but they are all bound together by the common theme of excessive, irrational fear and dread. Presented below are the primary types of anxiety disorders and the diagnostic categories, which are outlined in the DSM-IV under *Anxiety Disorders*. Each has distinct criteria, requiring specific treatment.

Diagnostic Categories for Anxiety

300.01	Panic Disorder Without Agoraphobia
300.21	Panic Disorder With Agoraphobia
300.22	Agoraphobia Without History of Panic Disorder
300.29	Specific Phobias
300.23	Social Phobias (Social Anxiety Disorder)
300.3	Obsessive-Compulsive Disorder
309.81	Post Traumatic Stress Disorder
308.3	Acute Stress Disorder
300.02	Generalized Anxiety Disorder
293.89	Anxiety Disorder Due to...(indicate the General Medical Condition)

Substance-Induced Anxiety Disorder

300.00	Anxiety Disorder Not Otherwise Specified

Comorbidity Between Stress, Anxiety and Depression

Many who suffer from stress and anxiety slowly become depressed to some degree. Comorbidity between depression and any of the anxiety disorders is well over 50%. This has crucial implications for accurate diagnose and effective treatment for those experiencing both anxiety and depression.[7] According to the National Institute of Mental Health, anxiety disorders can also co-exist with eating disorders, substance abuse, depression, other anxiety disorders and illnesses such as cancer or heart disease. Anxiety disorders can precede the onset of depression or follow it, and successful treatment of an anxiety disorder may delay or minimize the severity of depression.

A combination of determinants work together to predispose someone to stress, anxiety and depression disorders: life events, childhood experience (brain becomes vulnerable to depression), faulty parenting, heredity, individual personality (inhibited, introverted), cumulative chronic stress, lifestyle, interpersonal conflicts, biochemical imbalance in the brain, abnormalities in the emotional processing center of the brain (the amygdala). Other complicating problems can increase symptoms of depression such as hypoglycemia, premenstrual syndrome and alcoholism.[8] These causes and the factors that maintain the disorders are varied and experienced in every level of life.

Treating Stress and Anxiety: A Comprehensive Approach

For lasting healing in treating stress and anxiety, an integrative combination of approaches in caring for the whole person and the full range of contributing factors has proven to be most effective. The physiological response, cognitive, emotional, relational, behavioral, spiritual and lifestyle factors all interact to trigger and overcome the causes and effects of stress and anxiety. Clinical practice usually utilizes the conventional scientifically proven combination of cognitive-behavioral therapy along with medication, for more moderate to severe anxiety disorders. However, although these treatments are helpful, not everyone is able to achieve complete recovery, or may get better for a while and then relapse, because treatment wasn't sufficient for complete healing.[9]

To ensure lasting recovery, the *whole person* and their *whole life* need to get better. Effective treatment will go beyond learning specific strategies and techniques to reduce symptoms of physiological anxiety, redirecting fear-provoking thoughts and overcoming negative behavior. As an integrative Christian counselor, address other areas of change and growth such as a healthy lifestyle, diet and exercise, overcoming anxiety-prone personality traits, interpersonal conflicts, grieving, spiritual hope, strategies for reducing and managing stress.

Treatment Summary

Treatment of stress and anxiety problems will require a specific treatment plan for each client depending on their diagnostic features. Utilizing conventional and integrative resources will most-likely span several interventions and disciplines. Here is a summary of primary considerations:

1. *Do a comprehensive diagnostic evaluation.* Review *current problems and concerns,* and their perceptions (such as helplessness and hoplessness). Depending on the presenting issues, use whatever *measures* for determining levels of stress, anxiety and depression you are trained to use. If you are not trained to do assessment, refer to someone who is. Identify typical as well as atypical signs and symptoms and the underlying cause(s). (The client might be more comfortable describing physical symptoms than admitting to emotions associated with depression or anxiety.)

Take a complete *patient history,* as well as family of origin. Assess for *medical conditions, genetic factors, medical history and underlying causes of stress* as well as *negative coping patterns* such as substance abuse, alcoholism, addictions, eating disorders, excessive behavior, anxiety disorder, depression and suicide. Anxiety disorders are not all treated the same and coexisting conditions will determine treatment. Establish the specific problem before continuing treatment. A condition such as alcoholism would need to be treated before or along with anxiety disorder.

2. *Refer client to their primary physician for an updated complete physical.* This should include a blood workup to rule out a physical illness and medications. Get a release to access their past medical and psychiatric history as well.

3. *For severe symptoms of anxiety, refer to a psychiatrist.* Consider further testing and possible prescription medications to be combined along with cognitive-behavioral therapy for the best results. Medication is critical in treating those with severe symptoms of panic attacks, agoraphobia, obsessive compulsive disorders or those who do not respond to other treatments. Anxiety is considered "severe" when the client meets one of the following criteria:

- Anxiety is disruptive to their life, prohibiting functioning at work.
- Anxiety interferes with their ability to be in relationship with others.
- Anxiety causes distress at least 50% of the time they're awake.

4. *Develop a comprehensive treatment plan for recovery.* This plan is customized to the specific needs of your client. Work with them to outline changes and strategies for each area of their life, as well as treating any co-existing disorders. Physical—Mental—Emotional—Spiritual—Behavioral—Social. Begin with progressive, practical action strategies that moves them toward overcoming a sense of helplessness, but is not overwhelming. Educate client on the stress response—what is normal, how to discern when it is not. For successful recovery, use practice and repetition to strengthen the longevity of skills and resources gained in therapy.

5. *Consider consultation with a dedicated treatment team.* If the case is complicated indicating comorbidity with other disorders such as substance abuse, and/or physical illness, you will need to work together with a team of health professionals. This might include their primary physician, psychiatrist, specialist, nutritionist, outpatient rehab, pastor or social worker. Get consultation and utilize support networks in order for the client to receive the most comprehensive effective treatment.

6. *Help your client understand the nature of the underlying cause(s) of stress/anxiety.* They might deny that they are even "stressed out". Regard symptoms as a signal with a message, to assist them to understand themselves more and make changes. *What are my body and mind trying to tell me? What is causing me stress? How am I alleviating and recovering from stress? What is behind my developing the anxiety? What led to my developing these symptoms? What changes are necessary in order for me to recover? What can't I change, but learn to live with better? How can I gain a more optimistic sense of control?*

The goal may be to reduce stress, resolve relationship conflict, grieve a loss, change personality patterns, grow in trust and faith spiritually or make healthier lifestyle changes. When they are able to heed the symptom's warning signals and identify and make the necessary underlying changes in all areas of life, not only will the stress, anxiety and depression symptoms improve, but their whole life will get well. Address each coexisting diagnosis separately, treating each progressively along with the overall treatment goals.

7. *Help treat the milder physical symptoms.* Milder physical symptoms of

pain, headaches, stomachaches, tension and insomnia could be managed by over-the-counter medications or calming herbs such as Kava Kava, if their physician permits.[10]

8. *Practice the best Christian cognitive-behavioral therapy you can.* Conventional interventions that have been found effective in treating stress and anxiety are cognitive-behavioral therapy along with medication (for moderate to severe anxiety). If you are not trained in these techniques, seek consultation. (See a brief description following.) In order to get the benefit from cognitive-behavioral therapy, it takes consistent effort and time practicing these basic strategies and techniques. This can be difficult to do, especially after therapy is terminated. To ensure ongoing recovery, you could suggest the use of cassette tapes and occasional sessions with the client after termination, in order to brush up and stay on track with the strategies they learned. Referral to an anxiety support group will also enhance recovery.

9. *Address personality and other issues.* There are often issues that go beyond fears and distorted thinking that contribute to stress and anxiety problems. *Personality traits most associated with stress, anxiety and depression are*: excessive need to please (fear of rejection); anger, hostility; over-control; perfectionism; over-cautiousness (fear of illness, injury or death); fear of confinement; extremely analytical; emotionally sensitive; over reactive; low self-esteem; and being guilt ridden. Equip and empower clients to overcome these challenges with resources such as: assertiveness training, anger management, healthy emotional expression, learning to trust and let go, positive self-talk, dealing with disappointments guilt and worry, overcoming an emotional sense of helplessness and gaining a sense of control.

10. *Encourage optimism and a sense of control.* Acute and chronic stress can have negative effects, but what really determines the toll on health is the extent to which one feels an emotional sense of being *helpless* and *hopeless*. The stressor isn't usually the problem, but the perceived *sense of control*. This helplessness can lead to physical and emotional degeneration including depression. It is essential then, to help clients be optimistic, to do something—anything against the chronic stressor to reduce helplessness and being overwhelmed. If there is some way to contribute to and predict what will happen next, to remain optimistic, there is a higher resistance to hopelessness. Learning a relaxation response, exercising regularly, prayer, meditation on the Word and hope in God—all contribute to gaining a sense of

control over the stressor and damages from chronic exposure of stress-induced chemicals.

11. *Spirituality is important for complete healing.* In addition to counseling and medication, the healing power of relationship with God, the Bible, prayer and connection with others are essential. As a Christian counselor you are uniquely equipped to be sensitive to the client's spiritual experience and issues that could be contributing to the root of anxiety. Do they feel distant from God, empty, lacking meaning, vision, and purpose, confused, fearful, directionless, unloved, not knowing their unique gifts or creativity? Are they experiencing a spiritual battle in their mind? Peace of mind, tranquility, hope, and unconditional love can be viewed as the ultimate remedy for fear, worry, and anxiety. Explore with them ways they can strengthen their relationship with God through spiritual direction resources of reading, applying Scripture to their life, prayer, meditation, and connection with others.

12. *Adopting a healthy lifestyle, with proper self-care should be encouraged.* Even if the client is receiving good care through conventional medication and therapy, full recovery will be limited if they fail to place importance on their peace of mind, practical lifestyle, reducing and managing stress, and staying aware of their vulnerability to external and internal stress that can lead to anxiety and depression. Encourage them to:

   a.   Eat well-balanced, nutritious meals. Eliminate harmful substances.
   b.   Learn mind-body techniques to help relax and reduce stress response.
   c.   Get enough sleep, rest and relaxation.
   d.   Develop a relationship with God. Practice prayer and Christian meditation.
   e.   Exercise regularly. At least 30–45 minutes of exercise a day.
   f.   Counteract negative self-talk and mistaken beliefs with positive reality and God's Word.

12. *Address stress management and anxiety reduction interventions.* Relaxation techniques and stress reducing outlets are absolutely essential to recovery. An essential passive way to counteract the physiological stress response is to elicit a relaxation response. The body can't be relaxed and

tranquil as well as tense and anxious at the same time. An active lifestyle including regular exercise is another effective antidote to recovering from the physiological strain of stress and anxiety. Explore how the client can reduce stressors—what they can change, what they cannot. Infuse a *sense of control* over the stressor and stress response through these following strategies, which counteract helplessness and hopelessness.

Deep breathing exercises:

    a.   Progressive muscle relaxation
    b.   Prayer and Christian meditation
    c.   Mindfulness training
    d.   Biofeedback
    e.   Massage therapy
    f.   Exercise

13. *Strengthen or establish the client's support network.* Meaningful connection with others and safe, trustworthy people can be helpful in difficult times. Discourage isolation, which is a symptom of depression, and only further complicates the healing process. Encourage connections with family, friends, church, community, and support groups.

Integrative Therapeutic Interventions

In closing this chapter let us review in more detail the primary therapeutic interventions that need to be utilized in treating stress and anxiety problems.

Cognitive-Behavioral Therapy

Cognitive-behavioral therapy (CBT) is solution focused psychotherapy enabling the client to learn skills that they can continue to utilize and improve the quality of their life. From a Christian perspective, cognitive therapy can be integrated as an effective resource for those seeking answers in their life, and as a means of changing and gaining control over faulty thinking and behaviors. A combination of the following strategies have been proven to be effective therapeutic treatments for stress and anxiety disorders:

- Abdominal breathing training,
- Muscle relaxation training,
- Cognitive restructuring,
- Systematic desensitization, and
- In vivo exposure.

The cognitive therapy process identifies distorted thoughts and perceptions which contribute to the anxiety, and are then challenged and redirected. Here are some of the basic fundamentals:

1. Help the client identify the sources of stress and anxiety by asking the client to keep a journal of daily events, activities and thoughts, feelings, physical discomfort and the severity. This helps to make connections between negative thoughts, and the resulting emotions and behaviors.

2. Once a list of automatic distorted thoughts and fears are identified, begin to teach clients to monitor and challenge these with contrary evidence and reality. Using the Word of God is a helpful mainstay for this process.

3. Teach strategies to dispute the negative irrational thinking, substituting new ways of thinking, believing and responding, and help them deal with reality.

4. The client then learns how to monitor their negative thinking, ruminating and self-talk by having better control of their thoughts and thus over their lives.

5. Then they are able to identify, question and change the irrational thinking and replace them with empowering, positive thoughts and beliefs.

Antidepressants

SSRI's such as Paxil, Zoloft, Buspar or Celexa are often used in the treatment of anxiety. A new group of antidepressants known as serotonin-norepinephrine reuptake inhibitors (SNRI's), are being considered to be even more effective in treating anxiety disorders. These newer antidepressants act on both serotonin and norepinephrine and are preferred medications in the treatment of comorbid anxiety and depression disorders due to their broader spectrum of effect on multiple neurotransmitter systems. The effectiveness is due to being able to target several neurotransmitters, which can stabilize mood as well as the fight-or-flight response. These can be used for long periods of time provided patients have regular liver function tests.

When treating anxiety, in order to avoid relapse, clients will need to take antidepressant medication at least eighteen months or longer. Staying on the medication longer enables the brain to rest, regenerate and recover from the initial trauma of severe anxiety symptoms. Relapse is higher for those who take medication for a shorter period of time, especially without psychotherapeutic resources.

Tranquilizers

Faster acting relaxants can be used as short-term temporary intervention until the longer-acting medications kick in, but only under very limited and severe circumstances. Benzodiazephines such as Xanax, Ativan or Klonopin must be used for a limited time under strict limit refills because they can be addictive, and can be harmful if not used properly.

Alternative Therapies

There is increasing interest in exploring alternative approaches either instead of prescription drugs, or along with conventional treatment.[11] Herbs, supplements and deep relaxation approaches have been found to be helpful in treating mild to moderate anxiety and depression and can be used in conjuction with therapy. Natural tranquilizers having a calming effect are Kava, Valerian, and passionflower. For mild depression accompanying anxiety, Sam-e, tryptophan and St. John's Wort can be helpful.[12] Other helpful herbs are Gotu Kola and Ginkgo Biloba. Amino acids used to treat anxiety and mood disorders are Tryptophan, Gamma Amino Butyric Acid, DL-Phynylalanine and Tyrosine. Natural hormones such as melatonin is used to help with sleep and DHEA, which improves mood. Due to the lack of getting adequate nutrients from food, and the wear and tear on the body, stress and anxiety patients need vitamin supplements to replace the deficiencies. The following is recommended: Vitamin B complex, Vitamin C, Calcium and Magnesium, Zinc, Chromium and Iron.

If your clients are exploring these, caution them regarding not self-medicating by taking more than is recommended, taking natural pharmaceuticals along with other medications and the exposure to "new age" practices that often accompany alternative remedies. A helpful resource to guide clients through alternative treatments is the book *Christian Guide to Alternative Medicine.*

Healthy Lifestyle Changes

Eat well. Food does impact mood and is essential for fueling the body, enhancing recovery and reducing symptoms of stress and anxiety. Here are the essential considerations:

1. Eat five to six small, balanced mini-meals throughout the day, to help keep blood sugar stabilized. Don't skip breakfast.
2. Use olive and canola oil, but no hydrogenated oil products.
3. Eat whole, unprocessed foods, organic when possible. Choose brightly colored fruits and vegetables.
4. Eat balanced meals including lean protein and complex carbohydrates at every meal.
5. Take a good quality vitamin and mineral supplement, and adequate amounts of calcium, magnesium, folic acid, selenium and vitamin B complex.
6. Avoid or eliminate substances and stimulants such as caffeine, refined foods, sugar, MSG, saturated animal fats and foods that cause allergies. Check with primary physician regarding any prescription drugs being taken, to see if they could be contributing to symptoms.
7   Drink 8–10 glasses of water a day.

Exercise. Regular exercise is a beneficial form of stress, as it is an effective way to train the body to actively withstand and recover from stress.[13] Chemical and hormonal changes released while exercising have a positive impact on emotions. Physical activity also protects against possible health problems associated with stress, anxiety and depression such as obesity, heart disease and cancer. The most effective form of exercise is interval training—when waves of energy expenditure are followed by recovery. Raise and lower the heart rate between 60%–75% of maximum, creating cycles of stress and recovery during the activity. Two 12–20 minute sessions can be done a day, or one 45–60 minute session. As physical endurance improves, so will endurance for dealing with stress.[14]

Prayer and Biblical Meditation

"Anxiety in the heart of man causes depression, but a good word makes it glad." *Prov. 12:25*

"The Lord God has given Me (Jesus) the tongue of the learned . . . that I should know how to speak a Word in season to him who is weary." *Isa. 50:4*

Scientific research is now validating the power of prayer in healing and recovery. Why worry, when you can pray? Take it to the Lord in prayer. Besides, worry never changes anything, but prayer does. And we have proof. Regular prayer and biblical meditation leads to increased peace and tranquility, a very effective passive approach for reducing worry and generalized anxiety. However, the benefits of the power of prayer and meditation are more profound than the calming effect on our body, mind and emotions. Like the healing infusion of hope and encouragement that builds faith knowing people are praying for us. The ultimate transformation comes as we come into relationship and a complete encounter with the living God, Christ His Son, the Holy Spirit and the changing power of His Word. He sets us free from the wounds and strongholds of the past, bringing reconciliation with Himself, ourselves and others.[15]

The discipline of Christian meditation on Christ and the Word is an important heritage since the first days of the church, but misunderstood and distorted by new age and eastern religions. It is a dynamic way to change the thought life by focusing on God and His Word, and thus changing the rest of life—and can be utilized effectively into cognitive therapy. It instills a sense of control, optimism and hope. Direct your clients to learn more through Christian resources such as the books *Biblical Meditation for Spiritual Breakthrough* by Elmer L. Towns, *Praying God's Word* by Beth Moore, and the Christian relaxation tape available through *The Anxiety Cure* by Dr. Archibald Hart.

ENDNOTES

1. Susan M. Lark, *Anxiety and stress* (Berkely, CA: Celestialarts,1996), 10.
2. Richard A. Swensen, *Margin* (Colorado: NavPress, 1995), 20.
3. Michael Lemonick, How stress takes its toll, *Time*, special issue (20 January 2003), 67.
4. Harold H. Bloomfield, *Healing anxiety naturally* (New York: HarperPerennial, 1998.), 31.
5. Archibald D. Hart, *The anxiety cure* (Nashville: Word, 1999), 5.
6. Christine Gorman, The science of anxiety, *Time* (10 June, 2002), 46.
7. Steffany Fredman, and Rosenbaum, G. F., Treatment of anxiety disorders with co-morbid depression, available from <http:// www.medscape.com>.
8. Archibald D. Hart, *The anxiety cure* (Nashville: Word, 1999), 170.
9. Edmund J. Bourne, *Beyond anxiety and phobia* (Oakland: New Harbinger, 2001), 6.
10. N.D. Murray, and Pizzorno, N.D., *Encyclopedia of natural medicine* (Rocklin, CA: Prima Health, 1998).
11. Donal O'Mathuna, and Larimore, W., *Alternative medicine: The Christian handbook* (Grand Rapids, MI: Zondervan, 2001).
12. Archibald D.Hart, and Hart Weber, C., *Unveiling depression in women* (Grand Rapids, MI: Fleming H. Revell, 2002), 165–185.
13. Robert M. Sapolsky, *Why zebras don't get ulcers* (New York: W.H. Freeman and Company, 1998), 321.
14. Nicholas Hall, Stress: A psychoneuroimmunological perspective, available from <www.psychjournal.com/interviews>; Stress and exercise, available from <http://www.saluminternational.com/articleshall.htm>.
15. Archibald D. Hart, *Adrenaline and stress*, (Dallas: Word, 1995), 201.

9

Perfectionism and Obsessive-Compulsive Disorders

Mark E. Crawford

> Few ways of thinking are as harmful as perfectionism. Perfectionists
> believe that they should never make mistakes and that it is a catastrophe
> when they do. They tend to become quite upset when people or situations
> are out of their control and don't go the way they "should." They expect
> more from themselves and others than is reasonable and often become
> angry and bitter as a result. Though perfectionism in people is fairly com-
> mon, it carries a high price tag in terms of causing emotional problems,
> relationship difficulties, and spiritual burnout.
>
> CHRIS THURMAN[1]

Dr. Molar returned to his office six times that weekend to check whether or
not his doors were locked and the security system turned on. The robbery
of his thriving dental practice just a few months before was constantly on
his mind, distracting his thoughts and disturbing his sleep like nothing
ever had before.

His wife was not aware of how many times he had checked that weekend, but this fifth visit (he checked again that evening) did get her notice.
He drove all the way across town before church on Sunday morning to
check things again, and they ended up being a half-hour late for church.
That made her upset, as she did not understand why he couldn't wait until
after church to check things out. His reasoning made perfect sense to him,
however, "My office manager had been there Saturday night to pull charts
for Monday, and may have left things open." He had almost gotten into his

car to drive over to check the office at 3 A.M. because he was up pacing and obsessing about it most of the night.

Dr. Molar was a prompt and meticulous professional, who demanded of himself and his staff near perfection in the operations of his dental practice. His staff, more afraid of his wrath for anything done out of order, joked about him being "an obsessive sicko." The past month had been no joke, however, as Dr. Molar so constantly complained and pushed on their behavior that half the staff were on the lookout for a better job.

Molar's wife and family had also lived a miserable month with their insufferable husband and father. Mrs. Molar began to suspect something more, however, that Sunday while the family was out to dinner after church. Her husband had not only left church at the beginning of the sermon to check whether or not the car was locked, he did the same thing in the middle of dinner. She wasn't sure how to broach the subject, for she knew how well defended and hyper-rational her husband was, but she took a deep breath and plunged in anyway, "Honey?...."

Defining Our Terms

"Perfectionistic," "compulsive," and "obsessive" are all terms that most of us have used to describe our own or others' behavior at one time or another. For example, a person who may be preoccupied about an upcoming project may be described as obsessing about it. I have heard many parents tell me that their child "compulsively" played video games. A person who is very conscientious about his performance at work or a homemaker who is fastidious regarding housework may be described as perfectionistic in these roles. However, much of the time, these behaviors or traits do not represent pathological behavior.

The functional/dysfunctional continuum. But like most human traits and behaviors, these aspects of functioning exist on a continuum. When they increase to a level that *begins to interfere with effective daily functioning, then they can be considered pathological.* Obsessive-compulsive disorder (OCD) is the term for a specific clinical disorder that significantly interferes with daily living, and is characterized by two primary symptoms: obsessive thoughts or images and compulsive behaviors. Defining these terms is essential to proper understanding, diagnosis, and treatment of this disorder.

Obsessions

Obsessions refer to intense thoughts, worries, or images that are experienced as intrusive and unwanted. These obsessions cause great anxiety for an individual. One of the simplest ways to describe an obsession is an unrealistic or over-exaggerated worry or concern about something. The person experiencing an obsessive worry will frequently describe a thought or concern that sounds magnified or "catastrophized" to others. In other words, they will talk about a fear or worry that is far beyond what most people consider "normal."

In fact a person with OCD can sometimes tell you that they realize that their fears or worries are irrational or illogical. However, the anxiety is very real and overpowering. I've talked with many patients who tell me that they know their worries are irrational; however, they can't control the overwhelming fear and anxiety that these obsessive thoughts produce.

In his book, *Secret Thoughts and Tormenting Rituals* by Ian Osborn,[2] Dr. Osborn states that four qualities distinguish obsessive thoughts from everyday preoccupations, temptations, and worries. These four qualities include: 1) the thoughts are *intrusive*; 2) the thoughts are *unwanted* by the individual; 3) the thoughts are *recurrent*; and 4) the thoughts are *inappropriate*. In OCD, obsessions often fall within one of several categories including, but not limited to:

Contamination obsessions: worries about being contaminated by germs, toxins, or diseases. These worries frequently involve being contaminated by everyday contact with the outside world (doorknobs, money, handshakes, etc.). The person may also worry excessively about contaminating others.

The need for symmetry or exactness: a need for things to be "even" or symmetrical in their environment or on one's body. Examples include needing to have the same number of objects on each side of one's desk; needing to have one's shoes tied to the same tension on each foot; or having to tap or touch the left arm if one accidentally bumps the right one.

Violent or aggressive obsessions: these include either being bothered by intense and troubling images of violence or aggression and/or worries or fears that one may suddenly act out violent or aggressive impulses. Examples include sudden thoughts or images of horrible or violent things happening, particularly to a loved one and fears that one may act out in a violent or aggressive manner, such as hurting someone or oneself.

Sexual obsessions: these types of obsessions involve experiencing severe anxiety regarding normal sexual thoughts or feelings. These symptoms are particularly common among adolescents who may become very anxious about normal sexual thoughts and feelings.

Doubting obsessions: As in Dr. Molar's case, this category involves excessive questioning oneself regarding thoughts or behaviors. For example, a person may question whether they locked the door or turned off the stove.

"Just so" obsessions: this includes the need to do something in a particular manner that is known only to the individual. In other words, only they know when they have completed the activity "just right."

Blasphemous obsessions: obsessive thoughts and worries about possible blasphemy are common among patients with OCD. These obsessions include worries that one may have committed the unpardonable sin or blasphemed the Holy Spirit.

Disturbing religious imagery: many people with OCD report intrusive images that involve spiritual or religious themes, but include inappropriate or blasphemous imagery.

Obsessing about losing salvation: many Christians with OCD report being plagued by the fear that they have lost their salvation.

These are just a few examples of the types of obsessions that are common among OCD patients. However, obsessions can take any form and include any type of content. Remember, the definition of an obsession is any thought, worry or image that is experienced as intrusive, unwanted, recurrent, and inappropriate to the person.

Compulsions

Compulsions are behaviors that are usually done in an attempt to decrease the anxiety caused by obsessive thoughts. These behaviors typically feel like they "must be done." Consequently, the person with OCD feels unable to control them. Usually, compulsions are done to accomplish one of the following:

1. to prevent something bad from happening
2. to "undo" the thought or feeling associated with an obsession
3. to minimize or temporarily eliminate the anxiety caused by an obsessive thought

ON PERFECTIONISM, BY CHRIS THURMAN[3]

What is Perfectionism?

Two perspectives are helpful to consider when defining perfectionism.

Theologically, perfectionism is the destructive belief that people can be equal to God. Specifically, perfectionistic people think they should be all-knowing (omniscient), all-powerful (omnipotent), and everywhere at once (omnipresent). When people think they should know everything, they beat themselves up for mistakes. When they think they should be totally powerful, they become upset when things are out of their control. When they believe that they should accomplish the work of ten people in a given day, they become depressed and discourage over what "little" they did accomplish. While God calls us to be "perfect," it is an ideal that He is asking us to move in the direction of, not something we can literally be. Only God knows it all, controls it all, and fills up the universe with His presence. Finite human beings know very little, can't control others, and can only accomplish the work of one person on a given day. God accepts that about us, and we need to as well.

Psychologically, perfectionism has several facets as well. Perfectionists are idealistic in that they frequently think about how things "should" be, not how they really are. Perfectionists set *impossibly high goals* which lead to discouragement, failure, and ultimately quitting. They are *product-minded*, believing that contentment, happiness, and a sense of accomplishment are not permissible until their current project or activity has been completed. The "process" is overlooked because the end result has not been reached, thus there is no "joy in the journey." Perfectionists often feel that they have to be the best at what they do. To simply do one's best is not good enough. Perfectionists also *equate their worth with their performance.* They only feel worthwhile as people if they perform well. Since day-to-day performance in various areas of life fluctuates, a perfectionist's sense of worth fluctuates as well.

The theological and psychological components of perfectionism destroy any chance at an emotionally and spiritually healthy life. So what can be done to help the perfectionist?

How to Defeat Perfectionism

Several steps can be taken to help perfectionists become more realistic in their view of life and personal abilities.

- *Be humble*—Perfectionists must humble themselves before God and repent of being prideful enough to think they can be His equal.
- *Be reality-focused*—Perfectionists need to face life as it really is, not focus on how it "should" be.

- *Set attainable goals*—Perfectionists need to set goals that are small, realistic, and achievable in the here and now. Long-term goals need to be broken into short-term, tangible goals.
- *Set reasonable time limits*—Spending too much time on an activity in order to do it perfectly needs to be replaced with prioritizing activities so that each is given a reasonable amount of time.
- *Accept doing "good enough" on certain tasks*—Given the number of tasks people must complete each day, not every one of those tasks has to be, or can be, done exceptionally well. In areas of less importance, perfectionists need to allow themselves to do "good enough" and move on to the next task.
- *Stop black-white thinking*—Thinking in all-or-nothing terms often makes perfectionists miss the shade of gray in a given situation. By not thinking in extremes, perfectionists can have a more accurate perspective.
- *Learn from mistakes*—Everyone makes mistakes. The key is to learn from the mistakes.
- *Confess sin to others*—Acknowledging imperfections to others (rather than keeping them secret) can help release people from perfectionism. By sharing moral imperfections and personality flaws, perfectionists invite others to see them as they really are. Living a more transparent life builds healthy relationships and is critical for personal growth.
- *Find joy in the journey*—Becoming more like Christ is a process. Each step people take toward being more mature is pleasing to God and is a step further than where they were before. Perfectionists need to take time to stop and enjoy where they are in life.
- *Find worth in God*—Perfectionists need to find their worth not in what they do or how well they do it, but in being God's creation.

Knowing the theological and psychological aspect of perfectionism is only the beginning. Perfectionists must continue to grow in their knowledge of and love for Christ. Perfectionists must remember Paul's words, "Not that I have already attained, or am already perfected; but I press on" (Phil. 3:12). God will bless them as they seek to live for Him every day.

Compulsions often must be done in a certain manner, and at times, must be repeated over and over. They can be behavioral or mental in nature and typically fall under these categories:

Cleaning/Washing Compulsions: this involves cleaning or washing excessively in response to the fear of contamination. Common examples include excessive hand washing or compulsively cleaning one's home or environment. In fact, some people wash their hands so frequently, they develop severe skin irritation.

Checking compulsions: this includes the need to check and recheck things e.g., making sure appliances have been turned off; doors have been locked; or that something was done (an entry was made in a checkbook) or *not* done (making sure someone was not hurt by an action). Checking once does not bring reassurance; consequently, checking is done repeatedly.

Repeating compulsions: repeating compulsions are similar to checking in the repetitive nature of the behavior. However, unlike checking, the compulsion may not be in response to a doubting obsession. Repeating compulsions may appear more random. Examples include rewriting letters or words; retracing steps; or repeating words or phrases.

Hoarding compulsions: the hallmark of this type of compulsion is the inability to discard useless or worn out items. Patients with hoarding compulsions become "pack rats," compiling piles of useless "junk."

Ordering/Arranging Compulsions: this type of compulsion refers to the need for objects to be placed in a specific manner. Frequently, items are arranged or catalogued alphabetically or chronologically. Inanimate objects may be lined up or spaced perfectly or symmetrically. At times, objects must face a certain direction.

Rubbing, touching, tapping compulsions: these types of compulsive behaviors involve touching or tapping objects for no better reason than not doing it causes significant anxiety and distress. Often, there is no obvious or logical reason for touching or tapping the object. However, *not* doing it can cause a nagging or persistent preoccupation that it *should* have been done, and the OCD sufferer fears that if they don't touch, rub, or tap the object, they will never be able to get the thought out of their head.

Blinking or staring compulsions: this involves the need to stare at objects for a certain period of time or blink a certain number of times or in a certain pattern.

Counting compulsions: this is a common compulsive behavior and includes the need to count things such as the number of stairs climbed; count the number of steps taken; or count the number of mailboxes passed on a car trip.

Compulsive confessing: this compulsive behavior involves the need to confess any and all behaviors that the person feels may have been wrong. It differs from normal or healthy disclosure of genuine misbehavior. In compulsive confessing, the person "confesses" normal behavior that is neither wrong nor inappropriate.

Compulsive prayer: this differs from the type of genuine prayer that is essential for all Christians. Compulsive prayer is simply a ritualistic type of prayer that the person feels they *must* recite—much like a magic phrase.

Compulsive behaviors are behaviors that are typically done in response to anxiety caused by obsessive thoughts. The person feels unable to resist the urge to perform the compulsive behaviors and experiences severe anxiety if they do not perform the compulsions.

According to the *Diagnostic and Statistical Manual of Mental Disorders— Fourth Edition (DSM-IV)*,[4] in order to receive a diagnosis of OCD, one must have either obsessions, compulsions, or both (as described above). A person must recognize that these symptoms are excessive or unreasonable (except in children), and the symptoms cause significant distress; are time consuming (taking more than one hour per day); and significantly interfere with the person's normal routine. In addition, the symptoms cannot be due to another medical condition or the physiological effects of a substance.

Prevalence, Course, and Causes

According to research, approximately 1 in 40 adults (2.5% of the general population) suffers from OCD at some point in their lives. This makes OCD one of the most common psychiatric disorders. OCD affects both adults and children. While some individuals report that OCD symptoms first manifested in adulthood, it is common for symptoms to begin in childhood. Some studies indicate the average age of onset of OCD in children to be around 10 years of age. However, many children show symptoms much earlier.

The typical course of OCD is a waxing and waning of symptoms throughout one's lifetime with exacerbation of symptoms when the person is experiencing significant stress. People typically wait several years after experiencing symptoms before seeking help for the disorder. In fact, on average, a person waits 7 years after the emergence of symptoms before seeking help from a professional.

OCD is frequently misunderstood. Many people mistakenly believe that OCD is caused by unconscious and unresolved psychological conflicts. Because the symptoms frequently manifest with religious or spiritual themes, some people erroneously attribute disorder to spiritual determinants such as unconfessed sin and even demonic activity. *It is essential to understand that OCD is now primarily understood and treated as a biological disorder that is the result of abnormal brain activity.*

Genetic studies clearly support the fact that OCD runs in families. In fact, genetic researchers have suggested that OCD is approximately 60% genetically caused. If a person has OCD, the chance of a first degree relative having the disorder is approximately 10–25%. In twin studies, the concordance rate of OCD in identical twins is approximately 67% and in fraternal twins is approximately 47%. Like most disorders with a genetic component, it is believed that OCD is best explained using a diathesis-stress model. In other words, one may inherit a genetic vulnerability or predisposition towards OCD which interacts with other variables (particularly stress) to result in the presence of the disorder.

Brain imaging studies have been helpful in identifying which areas of the brain appear to be implicated in OCD. Both the basal ganglia and orbital frontal regions of the brain appear to be over-stimulated in individuals with OCD. The basal ganglia is an area of the brain involving several structures. These areas work together to control initiation and modulation of movement, and to process and filter information that is fed back to help control behavior and thinking. The primary functions of the orbital frontal region of the brain include filtering, prioritizing, and organizing information received by the brain; inhibiting responses to irrelevant stimuli; engaging in logical and consequence-based decision making; and regulating movements and complex behaviors activated by the basal ganglia.

Finally, the most helpful discovery regarding the causes of OCD has been the understanding of the role of the neurotransmitter serotonin. Neurotransmitters are chemicals in the brain that are essential for communication between the nerve cells of the brain. Patients with OCD have a significant decrease in serotonin activity. Numerous studies indicate that treating OCD with medications that enhance serotonin activity decrease OCD symptoms while giving a patient with OCD a substance that opposes serotonin activity in the brain worsens symptoms.

Comorbid Disorders

There are a number of other disorders that frequently exist *with* OCD. These are known as comorbid disorders. These include the following:

Tourette's disorder: Tourette's disorder is defined as the presence of multiple motor tics and one or more vocal tics which occur many times daily nearly every day for a period of more than a year. A tic is a sudden, rapid, recurrent, stereotyped motor movement or vocalization. Tics are experienced by individuals as irresistible; however, they can be suppressed for some time. Motor tics take many forms: eye blinking; eye rolling/squinting; finger tapping; head jerking/ rolling; nose twitching; eye twitching; facial grimacing; hand clenching/unclenching; jaw/mouth moving; lip licking/smacking; muscle flexing/unflexing; shoulder shrugging/ rolling; teeth clenching/unclenching; and tongue thrusting.

Vocal tics also manifest in myriad ways including: barking; belching; coughing; throat clearing; sniffing; grunting; humming; making animal noises; making "tsk," or "pft" noises; making guttural sounds; screeching; shouting; calling out; snorting; moaning; blowing noises; shrieking; and whistling. Studies show that approximately 1 in 5 of OCD patients also have a diagnosis of Tourette's disorder. This is in contrast to rates of 1 in 100 boys and 1 in 600 girls in the general population.

Attention-Deficit Hyperactivity Disorder: ADHD is a neurological disorder that consists of difficulties in the areas of sustained attention and concentration and/or impulse control. ADHD affects approximately 5% of the general population. However, it is a frequent coexisting disorder among OCD patients—15–30% of ADHD patients also have OCD.

Trichotillomania (TTM): Trichotillomania is a disorder that involves the recurrent pulling out of one's hair resulting in noticeable hair loss. This typically begins in childhood with onset beginning around age 5–8 years. In some cases, children may show transient periods of hair pulling that stop with no intervention. However, some individuals experience hair pulling into adulthood. For some, hair pulling is continuous while for others, it may be episodic (e.g., symptoms may come and go for weeks, months, or years at a time).

Body Dysmorphic Disorder (BDD): BDD is a disorder diagnosed when a person develops a preoccupation with what they believe to be a defect in the way they look. Patients with BDD become focused on a slight or imagined defect in their physical appearance. They may become preoccupied by the belief that an aspect of their body is asymmetrical; that a body part is too large or too small; that a certain aspect of their body is misshapen; etc. There is no specific aspect of appearance on which patients with BDD might focus. In fact, patients with BDD may change the focus of their distress over time.

Compulsive Skin Picking: While this is not a disorder listed in the DSM-IV, in his book *Obsessive-Compulsive Disorders: A Complete Guide to Getting Well and Staying Well*,[5] Fred Penzel lists compulsive skin picking as one of the *obsessive-compulsive spectrum disorders* along with BDD, TTM, and Tourette's disorder. Compulsive skin picking is defined as picking to the point of creating open sores and then picking at the scabs that result. It also includes squeezing and digging at pimples and blackheads with fingers or other implements to the point of causing infections and scarring of the tissue. Compulsive nail biting is defined as biting the nails to the point of bleeding and disfigured fingertips. Infections are often the result.

Depression: Clinical depression also co-occurs with OCD. Studies have found that approximately 25% of OCD patients meet criteria for a major depressive episode. Left untreated, the symptoms of OCD can lead to the development of clinical depression.

Substance Abuse: Some patients with OCD attempt to relieve the anxiety associated with the disorder through alcohol or other illegal or non-prescribed drugs. Marijuana is a drug that is frequently used to "self-medicate" the anxiety associated with OCD. At times, patients develop substance abuse problems due to overuse of these substances.

Treatment

The good news for patients with OCD is that it is a treatable disorder. In fact, studies show that with appropriate treatment, 80–90% of OCD patients show significant improvement and 75% show long-term improvement in their symptoms. There are two main types of treatment, and combinations of treatment, that have been shown to be effective for the treatment of OCD: cognitive-behavior therapy and medication.

Cognitive-Behavior Therapy (CBT)

Cognitive-behavior therapy involves several components: education; exposure and response prevention; cognitive restructuring; and the 4 R's.

Education. It is imperative to educate patients about OCD. Patients need to understand that OCD is primarily a biological disorder caused by abnormal brain functioning. They need to see their symptoms as *external* to themselves. Treatment goals must be realistically explained and realistic goals must be established. Analogies can be helpful such as explaining obsessive thoughts as similar to junk mail; spam e-mail; or a heckler at a sporting event. This often helps patients to learn to respond differently to their obsessive thoughts.

Education should also discuss outcome, as some patients are resistant to treatment due to their *dichotomous thinking* about the outcome. Dichotomous thinking refers to the tendency to see the world in terms of one extreme or the other. Many individuals see their OCD tendencies as adaptive, describing their punctuality, orderliness, and attention to details as valued functions. They mistakenly see these as part of their disorder and believe that if treatment works, they will move to the opposite end of the continuum of these traits. Instead of being obsessively punctual and perfectionistic, treatment will make them chronically late, hopelessly disorganized, and laissez faire or careless about everything.

It is important to remind these individuals that virtually all characteristics of human functioning exist on a continuum. I often draw a continuum that looks something like this:

I explain that the OCD end is that area that includes all of their OCD symptoms including all of the obsessive thoughts and worries and compulsive behaviors that currently cause them such misery. The anti-OCD end of

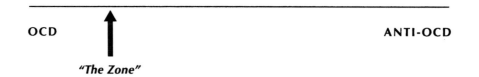

OCD   **ANTI-OCD**

"The Zone"

the continuum includes the opposite traits—disorganization, carelessness, tardiness, lack of scruples, messiness, etc. The fear for many OCD patients is that if they let go of the OCD end, they will automatically swing to the other end. This, of course, is unacceptable.

I point out that it is perfectly acceptable to live a healthy and happy life closer to the OCD end, as long as they are not on the extreme end. I explain that it is even fine to be closer to the OCD end than to the middle. Many high functioning people show a tendency toward obsessiveness or compulsiveness, but do not suffer from OCD. I call this area "the zone" and indicate that the goal of treatment can be to eliminate or reduce the OCD symptoms without decreasing their effectiveness or productivity. In fact, by eliminating or reducing the OCD symptoms and staying in "the zone," they will actually become *more* effective and productive.

Exposure and response prevention. Current research indicates that the most effective form of non-pharmacological treatment for OCD is Exposure and Response Prevention (E/RP). This consists of a therapist and patient cooperating together to gradually expose the patient to anxiety provoking obsessive thoughts while resisting the urge to engage in the compulsive behaviors that serve to decrease the anxiety that follows the obsessive thoughts. When done correctly, this form of treatment is highly effective in reducing obsessive thoughts and compulsive behaviors, and the improvement lasts over time.

The initial phase of this approach requires the patient to "rank" anxiety producing situations (those that elicit obsessive thoughts) from least to most severe. It is usually helpful to ask the patient to assign a number value from 1 to 100 with 1 being a non-anxiety situation and 100 being the worst type of anxiety possible. This is helpful for both the patient and the therapist to communicate with each other about anxiety producing situations.

The technique of E/RP is relatively simple, but wonderfully effective. The patient starts out by resisting the typical compulsive behavior associated with their least anxiety producing situation. I use the diagram below to illustrate how it works:

Response Prevention

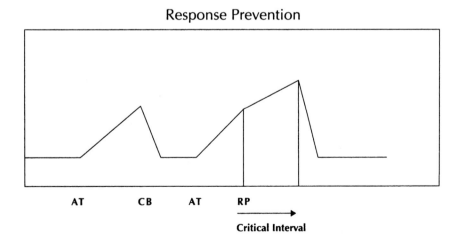

In the diagram, the x-axis represents the passage of time while the y-axis represents anxiety levels from low to high. AT refers to an "anxiety thought." This is any situation that results in the type of obsessive doubt, worry, thought, image, etc. which begins to raise anxiety. CB represents any type of compulsive behavior (e.g., washing, checking, compulsive praying; etc.). As the diagram shows, performing a compulsive behavior immediately results in a reduction of anxiety to same level as before the anxiety thought occurred. Prior to treatment, this pattern would continue ad infinitum. The patient may have different anxiety producing thoughts and perform different compulsive behaviors. However, the pattern would continue in the same predictable way.

On the diagram, the second AT still refers to an anxiety producing thought. However, in this example, at the point the patient would previously perform a compulsive behavior (CB), I ask them to resist the compulsive behavior (Response Prevention or RP). At this point, you see that the anxiety level actually increases beyond the point the patient normally allows anxiety to rise. It is important to predict this rise in anxiety and to explain that this is to be anticipated. The graph also shows that if the patient continues to resist the urge to perform the compulsive behavior, their anxiety level will ultimately decrease spontaneously and will return to the normal level without having to perform a compulsive behavior.

I have labeled the time from the moment the patient resists the compulsion (RP) to the time when the anxiety level falls as the *critical interval.* This is the interval of time that *must be endured* in order to break the pattern of OCD. Without fail, most patients who attempt to do this on their own are unable to endure the critical interval. Many patients erroneously believe that their anxiety may continue to rise to an intolerable level, or that their anxiety will never decrease unless they perform the compulsive behavior. Most patients who successfully endure the critical interval tell me that it normally takes only about 10–20 minutes before their anxiety begins to fall. This may sound like a brief time, but for the patient with OCD, it can seem like an eternity. This is particularly true if the fear is that their anxiety may never stop.

I have found that it is much easier to make it through the critical interval if the patient has something to distract him during this time. I often instruct the patient to have something else that they can get involved in to help them not to sit and dwell on the fact that they are anxious. If a patient can make it through a critical interval without performing a compulsive behavior, it is a great success which should be celebrated. Each time a patient is successful with E/RP, he is in fact weakening the grip of OCD on his life.

Cognitive restructuring. Most people with OCD are able to identify thoughts or beliefs that are extreme or slightly distorted. These thoughts and beliefs are referred to as errors in thinking and need to be identified and modified in order to effectively treat OCD. Examples of common cognitive errors include:

1. *Emotional reasoning:* this refers to reaching conclusions based upon feelings rather than facts. For example, a person with OCD shakes hands with a person he just met and *feels* contaminated, therefore he believes that he *is* contaminated.
2. *Catastrophizing:* this refers to imagining the worst case scenario of a situation and reacting to the imagined "catastrophe" rather than the actual situation.
3. *Dichotomous thinking:* this refers to the tendency to think in absolute terms (either-or thinking). This is often the origin of perfectionism. A person may have unrealistic standards for performance. Anything short of perfection is experienced and viewed as a failure.
4. *Selective Attention:* this type of cognitive error refers to the tendency of a person to notice and consider only certain aspects (usually negative) of a situation.
5. *Personalization:* this belief refers to the tendency to make everything that happens somehow related to the person (i.e., "everything's my fault").

These are just a few of the cognitive distortions related to OCD. For a person with OCD, cognitive distortions typically involve such areas as overestimating negative outcome in situations; exaggerations of "normal" concerns about situations; owning too great a share of responsibility for the outcome of situations; and having unrealistic expectations for performance.

Biblical Thought Modification

Scripture tells us in John 8:31–32, "If you hold to My teaching, you are really My disciples. Then you will know the truth, and the truth will set you free."

Second Corinthians 10:5 tells us, " . . . we take captive every thought to make it obedient to Christ." I use these Scriptures to help patients understand the importance of cognitive therapy in the treatment of OCD. It is important to recognize the truth of our thinking as opposed to simply accepting our cognitive distortions as fact. Also, we do have the ability to "take our thoughts captive," i.e., we can control what we think if we work at it. For specific cognitive errors, the following modifications may be helpful:

Emotional Reasoning: Your feelings are like a faulty navigation system on an airplane. Most pilots know that you can fly an airplane by determining your direction and location from objects on the ground, or by using instrumentation on the control panel. At night, or in inclement weather, you don't have much choice but to rely on instrumentation. I explain that feelings are an unreliable source for drawing conclusions. Recall that in emotional reasoning, a person reaches conclusions based upon how they feel rather than on facts. Therefore, I encourage patients to question their feelings and to make sure that they draw conclusions about situations based on the facts rather than on their emotions which will often lead them astray.

Catastrophizing: Recall that this refers to reacting to the imagined worst-case scenario. I encourage my patients to make sure that they are living in the *"what is"* instead of in the *"what if."* Many people with OCD find themselves living in the future rather than in the present. At least 90% of the things people with an anxiety disorder worry *might* happen never do. I think Jesus illustrated this point best when He said, "Therefore do not worry about tomorrow, for tomorrow will worry about itself. Each day has enough trouble of its own." (Matt. 6:34)

Another tool that is useful for people who tend to "catastrophize" is called *probability estimation.* In probability estimation, the person is asked to estimate the likelihood that a particular event will actually occur. Through logically evaluating the probability of something happening, the person often reaches the conclusion that they are worrying about something that has a remote chance of actually happening.

Dichotomous thinking: For people who tend to think in only two categories, I try to help them create a "third file" for thinking about things. I explain that it is as if they have just two files—one for one extreme and one for the other extreme. Most things in their lives actually fit best into a third file that is somewhere between the two extremes. One example of this involves performance expectations. As we discussed earlier, OCD patients often have perfectionistic tendencies. They see their performance in a diagram that looks something like this:

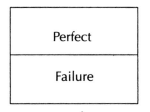

In the diagram, there are only two categories of performance: perfect and failure. Because perfection is difficult, and sometimes impossible to attain, these individuals usually feel that their performance is a failure. I explain that this model is unrealistic and needs to be modified to create a third category:

In the revised diagram, a third category called "good enough" has been added to the model. In this model, perfection is still present, as is failure. However, failure is a much smaller category now, and the largest area is "good enough." Most of our performance is, in fact, good enough—not perfect, but certainly acceptable. Creating a third category enables the perfectionist to accept their less than perfect performance without feeling like a failure. For patients with OCD, third categories need to be established in many different areas in order to avoid the dichotomous thinking errors that exacerbate anxiety and obsessiveness.

Personalization: For this type of error, I help patients challenge the belief that all things that happen are related to or caused by them. I encourage patients to consider whether there is sufficient evidence to indict them for the crime they feel they committed. I use the example of "putting OCD on trial" instead of them. Most of the time, a person with OCD will feel responsible for something when there is no evidence that they are responsible. They need to reconsider the evidence, to rationally and logically evaluate their conclusion that they are somehow always responsible for the negative outcomes in their lives.

Selective attention: For this type of cognitive error, it is important to get and keep a perspective. Recall that in selective attention, the person has a filter that results in ignoring some aspects of a situation and focusing only on the negative aspects of it. I explain that selective attention is like viewing a situation through a camera lens that is focused to only one small aspect of the picture. In this case, the only thing the person is going to see is what the camera lens is focused on. It is important to back up the lens in order to allow the picture to contain all aspects of the scene in order to get an accurate view of the situation.

The Four R's

Because E/RP and cognitive therapy have been found effective for treatment of OCD, I always use both techniques to treat patients. I have developed a technique known as the Four R's to help patients remember the essential elements of beating OCD.

Recognize: This step uses cognitive therapy tools to enable the patient to identify the thinking that is behind the anxiety. In treating OCD, this inevitably results in identifying the obsessive thought, worry, or image and correctly defining it as an irrational obsessive thought.

Resist: This step refers to RP in the Response Prevention diagram. In this step, the patient is aware of the urge to perform a compulsive behavior. He has been educated regarding the importance of employing RP as essential in breaking the power of OCD and is prepared to resist the urge to perform the compulsive behavior.

Replace: In step 3, the patient begins the process of modifying the obsessive thought or worry with one that is based on truth.

Redirect: In the final step, the patient is taught to use the tools mentioned earlier to get through the critical interval of response prevention until the anxiety passes and the pattern of obsessive thoughts followed by compulsive behaviors is weakened.

The Four R's sounds easy, but is actually a simplified model that requires the individual to have a great deal of knowledge about the techniques used to treat OCD, including understanding the principles behind response prevention as well as the theory of cognitive therapy. Once a patient becomes familiar with these concepts, the Four R's is an easy way to remember how to employ these new tools. Learning this method of treatment requires homework assignments, keeping journal entries of thoughts and behavior patterns, and much trial and error. It is a process that takes time, but is ultimately effective in treating OCD.

Medication

Because of the biological basis of OCD, medications that enhance serotonin activity are essential to treating this disorder effectively. While there are several medications used to treat OCD, the ones most often used include the following: Prozac (fluoxetine); Zoloft (sertraline); Paxil (paroxetine); fluvoxamine; and clomipramine (the latter two are available in generic form only. These medications are typically used in combination with CBT. Treatment using a combination of medication and CBT is highly effective.

Treatment with medication alone is effective in symptom reduction. However, if medication is used without CBT; there is a high likelihood of a return of symptoms after medication is discontinued. Medications used to treat OCD do have some side effects, the most common of which include sexual side effects (decreased libido and responsiveness); weight gain; and fatigue. The decision to use medication is ultimately made by a physician. It is recommended that medication be used (rather than CBT alone) when a person is having difficulty with normal daily activity; when they may not be able to complete CBT without medication; or when comorbid depression is severe. Medications are typically taken from 12–18 months. They usually take 4–6 weeks before results are realized.

Summary

OCD is a neurological disorder that is the result of abnormal brain functioning. Symptoms can be confusing and debilitating for individuals. Many, but not all people with OCD manifest pockets of perfectionism in their lives as a result of dichotomous thinking. Correctly diagnosing OCD can bring immediate hope for recovery. OCD does respond well to treatment, which is often a combination of cognitive-behavior therapy and medication.

ENDNOTES

1. Chris Thurman, Perfectionism, in T. Clinton, Hindson, E. and Ohlschlager G. (eds.), *The soul care Bible* (Nashville: Thomas Nelson, 2001).
2. Ian Osborne, *Tormenting thoughts and secret rituals: The hidden epidemic of obsessive-compulsive disorder* (New York: Dell, 1998).
3. Chris Thurman, Perfectionism, in T. Clinton, Hindson, E., & Ohlschlager, G. (eds.), *The soul care Bible* (Nashville: Thomas Nelson, 2001).
4. American Psychiatric Association, *Diagnostic and statistical manual of mental disorders*, 4th ed. (Washington, DC: Author, 1994).
5. Fred Penzel, *Obsessive-compulsive disorder: A complete guide to getting well and staying well* (New York: Oxford University Press, 2000).

10

Managing Your Anger

Gary J. Oliver and Carrie E. Oliver

Don't sin by letting anger gain control over you. Don't let the sun go down
while you are still angry, for anger gives a mighty foothold to the Devil.

EPHESIANS 4:26–27 NLT

David Augustus Burke's last words were tainted by vengeance. "Hi, Ray, I
think it's sort of ironical that we end up like this," he scribbled on an air
sickness bag. "I asked for some leniency for my family, remember. Well I
got none and you'll get none."

His last telephone message was tinged with love. "Jackie, this is David.
I'm on my way to San Francisco, Flight 1771. I love you. I really wish I
could say more, but I do love you."

No one knows what Ray Thomson told David Burke when he fired him
November 19 for allegedly pocketing $69 of in-flight cocktail receipts.
Those who knew Thomson described him as quiet but confident, the kind
of guy who didn't take guff. Whatever Thomson said, Burke didn't buy it.
Unemployed, spurned by his girlfriend, he apparently began making quiet
but methodical preparations for a bizarre murder-suicide mission that
would kill a planeload of people.

On Monday all of the rejection, all of the suppressed and hidden anger exploded 22,000 feet over Central California. Shots splintered the calm of a routine commuter flight, and if his calculated death plan of revenge succeeded, at least one shot probably tore into Thomson.

The pilot radioed, "I have an emergency . . . gunfire." Sounds of a tremendous scuffle would be heard later on a cockpit voice recorder tape. A groan. A gasp. Then PSA Flight 1771 plunged nose-first into a cattle ranch in San Luis Obispo County.

A few days later, David's father, Altamont Burke, tried to make sense of the dichotomy. "My son was a gentle guy, *but don't talk any trash to him,*" he said. Burke, Thomson and 41 other persons died, their bodies ripped apart and flung across acres of green hillside. Lying in the rubble was the .44 caliber magnum that Burke had borrowed from a friend with six cartridges spent.

Also found in the horrid carnage was the air sickness bag that spelled out the apparent motive for mass murder.[1]

From many of the newspaper reports and interviews with family and friends it was clear that David Augustus Burke did not appear to be the "typical" angry person. You might be asking yourself just what do we mean by a "typical angry person"? That's an important question! But let's turn it around. How would YOU describe the "typical" angry person? When you think of anger or angry people what comes into your mind? Who do you think of first? A father or mother, a brother or sister, a husband or wife, a good friend . . . yourself? What do angry people look like? What do angry people sound like? What does it FEEL like to be around someone who is frequently and visibly angry?

For over twenty years we've had the privilege of helping people understand that being made in the image of God means that we have emotions, and that includes the emotion of anger. In our seminars people ask us: What is the emotion of anger? Why did God create it? How can anything good come from anger? Where does my anger come from? Why is anger such a difficult emotion to deal with? Why are my anger responses so hard to change? How can I make my anger work for me rather than against me?

In this chapter you will find practical answers to each of these questions. The essential starting place is to define this emotion. If we are going to learn how to make anger work for us rather than against us there are a few things we need to understand.

Anger Is a God-Given Emotion

We were amazed to discover how much the Bible has to say about anger. God clearly acknowledges the significance of this powerful emotion. In fact, the only emotion the Bible mentions more than anger is love. Anger first appears in Genesis 4:5 and the last reference to anger is found in Revelation 19:15. In the Old Testament alone, anger is mentioned 455 times, with 375 of those references dealing with God's anger. [2]

The New Testament uses several Greek words for anger. It is critical to understand the distinction between these words. We have had many people remark that Scripture appears to contradict itself because in one verse we are taught not to be angry and in another we are admonished to "be angry and sin not." Which is the correct interpretation and which should we follow?

The most common New Testament word for anger is *orge*. It is used forty-five times and means a more settled and long-lasting attitude of anger, which is slower in its onset but more enduring. This kind of anger is similar to coals on a barbecue slowly warming up to red and then white hot and holding this temperature until the cooking is done. This kind of long-lasting anger often includes revenge.

There are two exceptions where this word is used and revenge is not included in its meaning. In Ephesians 4:26a we are taught to not "let the sun go down on your anger." Notice that the anger in the first part of this verse (*orge*) is different from the anger in the second half (*parorgismos*) where we are told not to let the sun go down upon this anger. Mark 3:5 records Jesus as having looked upon the Pharisees "with anger." In these two verses the word means an abiding habit of the mind that is aroused under certain conditions against evil and injustice. This is the healthy type of anger that Christians are encouraged to have—the anger at wrongdoing and evil that includes no revenge or rage.

Another frequently used word for anger in the New Testament is *thumas*. It describes anger as a turbulent commotion or a boiling agitation of feelings. This type of anger blazes up into a sudden explosion, whereas in *orge* there is an occasional element of deliberate thought. It is an outburst from inner indignation and is similar to a match that quickly ignites into a blaze but then burns out rapidly. This type of anger is mentioned eighteen times (see for example Ephesians 4:31 and Galatians 5:20) and is the type of anger we are called upon to control.[3]

Anger as a Secondary Emotion

Most people have no idea that anger is a secondary emotion that is usually experienced in response to a primary emotion such as hurt and fear. Anger can be an almost automatic response to any kind of pain. It is the emotion most of us feel shortly after we have been hurt. When you trip and fall or drop a hammer on your toe, it hurts, and you may experience mild anger. When your son corrects or talks back to you in public, it hurts, and you may respond to him (probably in the car on the way home) in anger.

Anger is usually the first emotion we see. For males it's often the only emotion that they are aware of.[4] However, it is rarely the only one they have experienced. Just below the surface there are almost always other, deeper emotions that need to be identified and acknowledged. Hidden deep underneath that surface anger is the fear, the hurt, the frustration, the disappointment, the vulnerability, and the longing for connection.

At a very early age many people learn that anger can help them divert attention from these more painful emotions. Anger is safer. It provides a sense of protection for the frightened and vulnerable self. Angry people respond verbally or physically to their seeming helplessness. It doesn't take long for some people to learn that it's easier to feel anger than it is to feel pain. Anger provides an increase of energy. It can decrease our sense of vulnerability and thus increase our sense of security. It is often a false security, but it is a kind of security nonetheless.

Anger Is a Signal

Anger is an emotion that God can use to get our attention and make us more aware of opportunities to learn, to grow, to deepen, to mature, and to make significant changes for the good. Anger, like love, is an emotion that has tremendous potential for both good and evil. That's why it is so important for us to understand it.

In her helpful book *The Dance of Anger* Harriet Lerner notes:

> Anger is a signal and one worth listening to. Our anger may be a message that we are being hurt, that our rights are being violated, that our needs or wants are not being adequately met, or simply that something isn't right. Our anger may tell us that we are not addressing an important emotional issue in our lives, or that too much of our self—our beliefs, values, desires or ambitions—is being compromised in a relationship. Our anger may be a signal that we are doing more and giving

more than we can comfortably do or give. Or our anger may warn us that others are doing too much for us, at the expense of our own competence and growth. Just as physical pain tells us to take our hand off the hot stove, the pain of our anger preserves the very integrity of our self. Our anger can motivate us to say no to the ways in which we are defined by others and "yes" to the dictates of our inner self.[5]

Anger is to our lives like a smoke detector is to a house, like a dash warning light is to a car, and like a flashing yellow light is to a driver. Each of those serve as a kind of warning or alarm to stop, look, and listen. They say, "Take caution, something might be wrong."

Anger Is a Powerful Emotion

Anger involves power. When you are angry you feel "charged up" and ready for action. Physiologically anger triggers an outpouring of adrenalin and other stress hormones to our central and peripheral nervous systems with noticeable physical consequences. Your voice changes to a higher pitch. The rate and depth of your breathing increases. Your perspiration increases. Your heart beats faster and harder. The muscles of your arms and legs may tighten up. The digestive process is slowed down. Many feel as if a war is being waged in their head and stomach.

In our experience when most people think about anger they associate it with the most painful and violent expression of anger they have seen or heard. Anger is often associated with (and confused with) hostility, rage, aggression, violence and destruction. And it's true that when anger gets out of control it can be expressed in horrible ways. But the problem isn't the anger. The problem is that people haven't learned how to understand and value their anger, how to listen to their anger, how to hear the warnings their anger provides them.

Anger Is the "Most Likely To Be Mislabeled" Emotion

In our counseling practice we've spent many hours with people who are confused, frustrated and stuck in their efforts to grow and live effectively. Much of this is due to their failure or inability to acknowledge, understand and constructively deal with anger. With the taboos on anger in many evangelical circles Christians can be particularly blind to the value of this powerful emotion. Instead of identifying the emotion and facing it squarely as a fact of life, they either try to shut out and silence their anger or they allow it to dominate and control their lives.

Anger can come packaged in many different shapes and sizes. It hides behind many different masks. Over our lifetime each one of us has developed our own unique style of dealing with anger.

> Of all the emotions anger is the one most likely to be labeled as something else. Of all the emotions anger is the one most likely to be identified as dangerous. What are some of the most common disguises anger can take? When we begrudge, scorn, insult, and disdain others or when we are annoyed, offended, bitter, fed up, repulsed, irritated, infuriated, incensed, mad, sarcastic, up tight, cross or when we experience frustration, indignation, exasperation, fury, wrath or rage, we are probably experiencing some form of anger. Anger can also manifest itself as criticism, silence, intimidation, hypochondria, numerous petty complaints, depression, gossip, sarcasm, blame, passive-aggressive behaviors such as stubbornness, half-hearted efforts, forgetfulness, and laziness. [6]

A person who is worried usually looks and acts worried. A person who is depressed usually looks and acts depressed. A person who is overcome by fear usually looks and acts afraid. But a person who is angry may or may not look and act angry. They may appear to be worried, depressed, afraid or there may not be any external indication of their anger.

Healthy Anger Has Tremendous Potential for Good

Anger is energy and we can choose whether we are going to spend it or invest it. While we may have minimal control over when we experience anger, we have almost total control over how we choose to express that anger. When we choose to harness and direct that energy in healthy, positive and constructive way and communicate it in biblically-consistent ways, we are able to solve problems and increase our trust and actually deepen our intimacy.

God has given us that choice. We can allow our anger to control us, or we can, with God's help, pursue "healthy" anger. Healthy anger involves open, honest and direct communication. It involves speaking the truth in love. It involves investing the energy God has given us to declare truth, to right wrongs, and to help ourselves and others "become conformed to the image of His Son" (Romans 8:29).

As we move on to the next section remember that anger is not necessarily or wholly negative. Anger involves physiological arousal, a state of readiness. When we are angry our body has increased energy that can be directed in whatever way choose. Anger is a natural and normal response to a variety of life's situations and stresses. Anger is a God-given emotion intended to protect and provide energy for developing solutions to life's inevitable problems. Anger, the ability to understand it and appropriately express it, is a sign of emotional and spiritual maturity.

What's Your Anger Style?

The first and easiest step in the change process is to identify your characteristic style of experiencing and expressing anger. When it comes to dealing with anger most people tend to fall into one of three reactive styles. What do we mean by reactive? A person who is reactive has an automatic and seemingly unconscious response to a situation. They may not always react in the exact same way but the majority of their responses fall into similar styles.

It's easy for people who don't identify and work on their anger style to get in an emotional rut and once there they are likely to stay there. They are vulnerable to becoming puppets of their past and slaves to their circumstances. While everyone is unique most people tend to fall into one of three characteristic styles of reacting to anger. As you read through them, think of which one might best describe your usual way of reacting. How do you see yourself? How do others see you? Where did you learn this style?

Cream-Puffs: Repressed

The main characteristic of the Cream-Puff is passivity. Cream-Puffs avoid making clear statements about what they think and feel, especially when their opinion might make someone else uncomfortable. Their energy is focused on protecting themselves or others, and maintaining harmonious relationships. Cream-Puffs avoid conflict like the plague.

Cream-Puffs often fail to share their own legitimate needs and concerns and thus those around them are unaware of their pain. Over time they become less and less aware of their own feelings, thoughts and needs. They can become so focused on hearing what everyone else has to say that they fail to hear what the Lord has to say. God's truths become real to everyone else but them.

Cream-Puffs characteristically avoid any direct experience or expression of anger. In situations that in healthy people would evoke appropriate expressions of anger and protest they are likely to remain silent. They are more likely to say "I'm sorry" rather than "I'm hurt," "I'm afraid," "I'm frustrated," or "I'm angry."

Do Cream-Puffs ever experience anger? Of course they do! However, when provoked they will usually say nothing. Most people think of anger as something hot such as in seething rage or an erupting volcano. But the Cream-Puff's anger is usually more subtle and cold. He or she is someone whose immediate and automatic response to even the slightest hint of anger is to suppress it.

What does it mean to suppress anger? Suppress means to hold in, to put down by force, to prevent the natural or normal expression, activity or development of an emotion. When I suppress my anger I'm aware of it but through a lot of practice I'm able to keep it down. Few people are even aware that I'm angry.

If over a period of time I continue to suppress my *anger it is likely that my anger will become repressed.* Repressed anger is kept from consciousness and I'm no longer even aware of it. People who have anger they're not aware of often express it in ways that are destructive to themselves and others. They are almost powerless to deal with it because they aren't really aware of it.

"The Cream-Puff is like a boat drifting aimlessly on the ocean with no motor, oars or sails. They are forced to go wherever the winds of circumstances blow them. The God-given emotion of anger can be a source of propulsion to move them out of their doldrums and help them move in healthy and constructive directions."[7]

Cream-Puff

■ anger	■ suppressed anger turned inward	■ apathetic	■ toxic shame
■ overcontrolled	■ passive reactor	■ guilt-prone	■ avoids problems
■ self-condemnation	■ denial	■ responsible for others	■ self-pity
■ conflict avoider	■ dependent		

Locomotives: Explosive

The exact opposite of the Cream-Puff is the Locomotive. In fact one of the fears that keeps many Cream-Puffs locked in their prison of passivity is the fear that if they ever let themselves get in touch with their anger, they will become like the Locomotive.

What is a locomotive? He doesn't have much time for the feelings or opinions of others. He has a sharp tongue and can be quick to criticize, put-down and humiliate others. On the outside he appears confident but inside he is riddled with fears and insecurities. Because he needs so much accept-ance it is difficult for him to compliment others. It gives them the attention that he believes he deserves and needs for himself. He needs to be right all of the time and when he errs it will be on the side of being tough and not tender.

While the Cream-Puff is a passive reactor the Locomotive is an aggressive reactor. While the passive reactor doesn't give adequate attention to legiti-mate personal needs, the aggressive reactor doesn't give adequate attention to the needs and rights of others. They are often so preoccupied with them-selves that they become insensitive to and unaware of the needs of others.

Whereas the anger of the Cream-Puff (passive reactor) is usually implo-sive the anger of the Locomotive (aggressive reactor) is most often explo-sive. When provoked the Locomotive, who already has a full head of steam, is likely to attack, label, put down, and humiliate others. They often communicate in ways that violate the dignity and rights of other people.

In Philippians 2:3 we are exhorted to regard one another as more important than ourselves. In I Peter 4:15 we read that "If you suffer, it must not be for murder, theft or sorcery, nor for infringing on the rights of oth-ers." The locomotive consistently ignores these biblical principles or twists them as a basis for blaming others for not esteeming them (the Locomotive) as most important.

What are some characteristics of the Locomotive?

When it comes to identifying their unhealthy anger style the majority of

Locomotive

▪ hostile	▪ rage –cruel teasing	▪ blatant sarcasm	
▪ anger against others	▪ over-concern for self	▪ loud –obnoxious	
▪ quick to blame	▪ critical	▪ underresponsible	▪ has all the answers
▪ shallow	▪ few intimate friends	▪ prone to violence	▪ suspicious
▪ punitive	▪ combative	▪ overcompetitive	▪ driven –power hungry

people would put themselves in the Cream-Puff or Locomotive category. However there is a third anger style that in some ways is more subtle and complicated than the first two but just as unhealthy.

Steel Magnolias: Passive Aggressive

The term passive aggressive was first coined during World War II to describe the behaviors of certain soldiers. We've already talked about this in chapter one but it is such a common response it deserves more attention. The military is highly structured for uniformity and compliance and individuality is not encouraged. Some soldiers thrived under this kind of environment. Others dealt with this enforced change by resisting, ignoring orders, withdrawing, or simply wanting out.

On the outside the Steel Magnolia appears very soft and tender. At times you will see the lovely and sweet-smelling magnolia blossom. But more than just a casual encounter will reveal hardened steel. She is a contradiction to herself and to others. She is the master of the "end-run." A part of you wants to trust her but the other part of you says that she can't be trusted.

You can trust the Cream-Puff to yield to the desires and expectations of others in order to gain approval. You can trust the Locomotive to ignore other peoples' desires and expectations. They are both fairly consistent. But you don't dare trust the Steel Magnolia. She can appear to be sensitive to the desires and expectations of others, but will often go ahead and do whatever she wants. She may appear to be passive but is actually quite aggressive.

On one hand she appears very soft and tender but more than just a casual encounter will reveal hardened steel. She may appear calm on the outside but there is a cauldron of bitterness and resentment boiling on the inside. The reality is that anger is frequently at the core of passive aggression, even when it is denied, suppressed, repressed or called something else. But however much she may try to disguise it, her anger will never be entirely hidden.

The Steel Magnolia is a contradiction to herself and to others. She looks like a cream-puff—she doesn't state her needs, she is indirect. Yet if you cross her or get in her way you are in serious trouble. On the outside she appears to be sensitive and tender but don't get too comfortable because the tough side is sneaking up behind you.

One of the most effective tools of the Steel Magnolia is sarcasm. Sarcasm is one way to express your anger while playing it safe. By pretending to be funny the anger is disguised and retaliation is discouraged. If you respond to the sarcasm you may be accused of being negative, assuming the worst, or of not having a sense of humor. "What's the matter—can't you take a joke?" may be the immediate response.

Sarcasm involves assault by misdirection, disguise, and sarcasm. It is a way of attacking while avoiding a clearly hostile intent. Over time they may even convince themselves that they don't have any aggressive feelings. They may come across as being shocked that anyone could misunderstand their pure motives and sincere intentions.

What are some characteristics of the Steel Magnolias?

Steel Magnolias

■ procrastination	■ subtle sarcasm	■ forgetfulness	■ stubbornness
■ fosters confusion	■ obstructionism	■ fear of intimacy	■ makes excuses
■ misunderstanding	■ silent treatment	■ sulking –lies	■ mixed messages
■ chronic lateness	■ inconsistency	■ ambiguity	
■ carelessness	■ resentful		

Are There Any Healthy Options?

One of the main reasons why the Cream-Puff, Locomotive and Steel Magnolias represent unhealthy anger styles is that they involve a denial of our real self. When we stuff, repress, suppress, deny, ignore or hurl our anger we are ignoring anger's potentially important message. We have lost touch with the primary emotion that triggered our anger.

All three of the anger styles we have discussed thus far involve unhealthy reactions. They are usually an automatic and unconscious reaction to some real or perceived threat to our sense of significance, safety or security. Each style is dysfunctional. Each one falls short of God's plan and purpose in giving us the gift of anger.

Reactors deny their real grief and pain. Resentment and rage keep them from dealing with legitimate fears and hurts and limit God's ability to bring recovery and restoration. If we refuse to allow God to help us face the real issues of our lives, how can we understand, how can we forgive ourselves, how can we forgive others, how can we grow?

The Mature and Assertive Responder

Fortunately God has given us a healthy option. God can help people trade in their unhealthy reactive style for a mature, healthy and biblically sound way of understanding and expressing their anger. There is a way of responding that allows us to "be angry and sin not." It is the assertive response.

The mature responder has a clear sense of who they are in Christ. Their emotions, mind and will work together and function in a balanced way. They can express their opinions but don't need to put others down. They delight in serving but aren't servile. They can be tough and tender. They aren't reactive, they are proactive. They have taken the time to look at, understand, and develop a healthy plan for dealing with their God-given emotion of anger.[8]

The mature response is a style of responding to anger without which this world of ours would be a much poorer place. What are some characteristics of a mature responder?

Mature Responder

■ responds	■ careful	■ indignation–trusting	
■ healthy shame	■ anger communicated	■ responsible–warm	
■ proactive	■ interdependent	■ motivated by love	■ unselfish–firm
■ I win/You win	■ direct communication	■ caring–listens	■ constructive

The mature responder is free to "speak the truth in love." When provoked the mature responder is less likely to immediately react without thinking but rather responds in a way that reflects some discipline and thought. She has learned the value of anger. She has learned to be aware of and choose her expressions of anger. She is more likely to have trained herself to think, act and feel more constructively. She expresses her thoughts, preferences and emotions directly to the other person in healthy ways that communicate a respect for the dignity and the rights of both herself and others. Her response is more likely to move her towards achieving both her personal goals and her relational goals.

Anger can be an invaluable tool in the hands of a responsible person. It is a force capable of being directed and used constructively. Aristotle acknowledged these positive aspects of anger when he said, "Those who do not show anger at things that ought to arouse anger are regarded as fools; so too if they do not show anger in the right way, at the right time or at the right person."

When Is the Best Time to Deal With Anger?

The best time to deal with anger is before one gets angry. That's right, *before* the anger. Why? Because one needs to learn how to seize opportunities to deal with discouraging, frustrating and painful situations *before* one reaches the boiling point. It is easier to be clear and objective when one plans ahead. Hence, with planning your client's perspective is less likely to be clouded by the intensity of his/her anger.

You might want to start counseling by asking, "Is your anger a problem for you or for others?" Just because one becomes angry once in awhile doesn't mean that one has an anger problem. Anger is a God-given emotion that is a normal part of everyday life. Healthy anger has tremendous potential for good. Anger only becomes a problem when we deny, suppress, repress, stuff and ignore it or when we don't listen to it understand it and allow it to serve its God-intended function.

Anger can become a problem when a client lets it get out of control and move into more destructive emotions such as hostility, rage and aggression. It becomes a problem when clients continue to allow themselves to be puppets of past patterns rather than using the resources that God has given to redirect the energy of this powerful emotion. It's a problem when clients haven't disciplined themselves to express it in healthy and constructive kinds of ways.

What Are the Benefits of Dealing With Anger?

Upon educating clients about their anger, some may be tempted to ask, "Working on this anger stuff is a lot more work than I had anticipated. Is it really worth it?" This is a query only the client can answer. Many people have found that one of the most helpful ways to answer that question is to remind themselves of the benefits of understanding and learning how to appropriately express their anger.

Over the years we've asked clients, "What have you found are the benefits of dealing with your anger?" Here are some of their answers:

- Understanding and dealing with my anger has improved my overall physical, emotional, mental and spiritual health.
- It gives me an increased source of energy to make the hard choices.

- It has improved the quality of my marriage.
- It has strengthened my relationships with the kids.
- It has alleviated my fear of someone else's anger.
- Now my children have a healthy model for this God-given emotion.
- It helps me keep things in perspective.
- The appropriate expression of my anger has helped others better understand me and what is important to me.
- It helps me clarify and protect personal boundaries.
- It helps me to protect myself physically and emotionally.
- It's given me the power and courage to remove myself from the victim role.

If one's desire is to become the person God wants him/her to be, one will make the time to learn how to make their anger work for them. Hebrews 12:15 says, "See to it that no one misses the grace of God and that no bitter root grows up to cause trouble and defile many." It is easy for a bitter root to grow up in the lives of clients. Some may think they are doing the right thing by not dealing with or dwelling on the past. There is a big difference between not dealing with the past and not dwelling on it!

What Are Some Constructive Steps for Dealing with Anger?

The first step in making a client's anger work for, rather than against, the client is to have the client decide in advance to invest his/her anger-energy and express it in a healthy way. This early decision is important because when anger is in control it can block one's ability to think clearly. Think back to the last time you, the counselor, experienced strong anger. How objective were you? How clearly were you thinking? It is important to develop a plan for dealing with anger before one becomes angry. Here are some simple steps to help clients make their anger work for them.

Step 1: Be Aware of It

One of the many myths regarding anger is that if a person doesn't look or appear on the outside to be angry, then they don't have a problem with anger, and they are clearly not an angry person. Someone may not appear to be an angry person on the outside but can be like a battlefield on the inside.

Therefore, do not assume, but ask clients: How often are you aware of being angry? What situations do you encounter that might make you more vulnerable to anger? How does your body respond to anger? What are your physical manifestations of anger?

Step 2: Put First Things First

As soon as one becomes aware of it, before doing anything else, one should ask oneself: What is meant by putting first things first? Take it to the Lord in prayer. In 2 Corinthians 10:5 Paul exhorts us to take every thought captive to the obedience of Christ. I don't think it does any injustice to the intent of that passage to suggest that we also need to get into the habit of taking every emotion to the obedience of Christ. This is especially true of the emotion of anger.

Before deciding what we are going to do, we need to set aside focused time to take all of our concerns, including our struggles with our emotions, to the Lord in prayer. In Psalm 42:4 David talks about pouring out his soul and in Psalm 68:8 David wrote, "Trust in Him at all times, O people; Pour out your heart before Him; God is a refuge for us." (NASB)

If a client is frustrated, hurt, discouraged and experiencing anger with someone, have the client talk to the Lord about it; first in silent prayer and then perhaps even out loud. Instruct the client to ask God for His help and His guidance. Have clients take advantage of the power of the Holy Spirit. In James 1:5 we are told that if we lack wisdom we only need to ask for it. In 1 Peter 5:7 we are told to cast all of our concerns on Him "because He cares for you." (NASB)

Many people have found the following simple prayer to be of help.

Dear Lord, Thank You for creating me in Your image with the ability to experience and express the emotion of anger. While sin has damaged and distorted anger in my life, I thank You that You have promised to be at work within me both to will and to work for Your good pleasure. I thank You that You can cause all things to work together for good and that I can do all things through You who strengthens me. I ask You to help me to change my anger patterns. Help me to experience and express this emotion in ways that are good and that bring honor and glory to You. Amen

Step 3: Accept Responsibility for Anger

One of the major effects of original sin is seen in our tendency to blame someone else for our problems. When God confronted Eve in the garden and asked her what happened she blamed the serpent. When God confronted Adam he first blamed Eve and then he blamed God. When clients are angry it is easy for them to say, "It's your fault, you made me angry." However, clients should be educated that they are responsible for how they choose to respond to their anger.

Step 4: Decide Who or What Is Going to Have Control

This is a critical step. When one experiences anger one is faced with a choice. One can either allow the anger to dominate and control, or with the help of the Holy Spirit one can choose to control the anger and invest the anger-energy in a healthy way. While a client can't always control when he/she will experience anger, with God's help one can choose how it is expressed. As your clients take their anger to God in prayer He will help them find creative and constructive ways to deal with it.

Step 5: Define It! Identify the Source and Cause of It

Anger is a secondary emotion that is experienced in response to a primary emotion such us hurt, frustration or fear.

Hurt is usually caused by something that has already happened ... something in the past. When we are hurt we feel vulnerable and open to more hurt. This is especially true of people who are very sensitive. For many people anger is an automatic defense mechanism to protect against hurt.

Frustration takes place in the present. We can become frustrated by blocked goals or desires or by unmet expectations. Frequently the things that lead to the greatest frustrations have one main characteristic ... they really aren't that important.

What kinds of situations cause your clients to become frustrated? Are there any specific individuals they find more frustrating than others? What situations frustrate your clients?

Fear is an emotion that tends to focus on things in the future. Many people associate fear with vulnerability and weakness. Some people, especially men, find it more comfortable to express anger than fear and so may respond to situations in which they are anxious or afraid by getting angry. If you suspect this, consider asking an angry client, "Is there something that you are afraid of that could be triggering your anger?"

Step 6: Choose Your Response: Spending and Investing Anger-Energy

When one becomes angry the first step is to identify the primary emotion. Then ask, "Is this really that important?" If it isn't, simply let it pass. If it is important then have the client ask him/herself, "How can I express my anger in a way that is biblically consistent and that will enhance the probability of resolution?"

Instruct your client to look at some of the key passages that deal with anger: Proverbs 15:18, 16:32, 29:11; Mark 3:5; Ephesians 4:26, 31; Colossians 3:8, 21. Have the client ask God to help; "speak the truth in love." Have the client take time to acknowledge the other persons' feelings, and remain open to an apology or an explanation. Facilitate a client to make the primary goal understanding, and then work toward a resolution.

Step 7: Evaluate It

Perhaps your client successfully navigates that emotional rapid. Or perhaps he/she was more successful than in the past but still needs to work on it. Whatever the result of the six steps was, the client is not quite finished yet. The last step in dealing with anger is to discover all one can from the experience. What went well? What was different than usual? Were there any positive surprises? What could one have done differently?

In order to complete the learning process it is important for the client to reflect on the question: "What have I learned from this experience?" One of the most encouraging aspects of being a Christian is that, whatever the experience, good or bad, with God's help we can learn from it. If you've been a Christian very long you have learned that Romans 8:28 is true. God carefully recorded the experiences of many men and women in the Bible. For over two thousand years God protected the record of those experiences. Why? So that we could learn from them.

Some Final Observations

For many Christians both the experience and expression of anger have become a habit. Habits can take some time to change. The good news is that with God's help we can change, we can grow, we can be more than conquerors. As we allow the Holy Spirit to fill us and apply promises in God's Word we can take the old unhealthy ways of responding and develop new, healthy and biblically consistent emotional responses.

In Daniel 1:8 we are told that Daniel "purposed in his heart" not to defile himself with the kings meat. And he didn't. We can purpose in our hearts not to allow our anger to control us but rather to put our anger as well as our other emotions under God's control. While we can't always control when or why we will experience anger we can with God's help control how we express that anger.

God has given us that choice. We can allow ourselves to be controlled by our anger or we can pursue "quality anger." Quality anger involves open, honest and direct communication. It involves speaking the truth in love. It involves investing the energy God has given us to declare truth, to right wrongs, and to help ourselves and others "become conformed to the image of His Son." (Romans 8:29)

As you help others develop creative ways to invest the God-given anger-energy, as you help them develop more effective anger management skills, as you learn how to approach anger from a biblical perspective, you will find one of the most powerful sources of motivation available to mankind. Martin Luther said, "When I am angry I can write, pray and preach well, for then my whole temperament is quickened, my understanding sharpened, and all mundane vexations and temptations are gone."

If you or your clients have struggled with unhealthy anger, we want to encourage and support you in your struggle. In our work with a wide range of people—university students here at John Brown University, couples in our marriage enrichment seminars across the country, corporate leaders—we have seen time and again that God can and will transform long-term unhealthy anger patterns into a healthy and constructive anger that strengthens individuals, marriages, families and work-teams.

ENDNOTES

1. S. Peck, Mission of madness, *Long Beach Telegram*, (18 December, 1997), A1, A6–7.
2. Gary R. Oliver and Oliver, Carrie, *Raising Sons and Loving It!* (Grand Rapids: Zondervan, 2004), 135.
3. Oliver and Oliver, *Raising Sons and Loving It!*, 134–136.
4. Gary R. Oliver, *Real men have feelings too* (Chicago: Moody Press, 1993).
5. Harriet Lerner, *The dance of anger* (New York: Harper & Row, 1985).
6. Gary R. Oliver, and Wright H. N., *A Woman's Forbidden Emotion* (Ventura, CA: Regal, 2005), 39–40.
7. Oliver and Wright, *A Woman's Forbidden Emotion*, 78.
8. R. Walters, *Anger: Yours & mine & what to do about it* (Grand Rapids, MI: Zondervan, 1981).

11

Personality Disorders

Henry A. Virkler

A personality disorder is more a [dysfunctional] way of life than an illness.

JAMES MORRISON

John was late for staff case consultation due to a crisis he had to intervene in, and came in to hear Jerry exclaim in exasperation and anger, "...she not only has her whole family 'walking on egg-shells,' she now has me on egg-shells as well!"

John knew exactly who Jerry was talking about with other clinical staff, and wondered whether he should have assigned her to a more experienced staff member. "What is Stella up to now?" he queried as he settled into supervisory role as Clinical Director of the Outpatient Mental Health Unit.

"She's threatening to kill herself again if I don't spend time with her on the phone over every alleged emergency!" Jerry was gesturing strongly and his anger was evident.

"Alleged emergencies....?" John let the question trail off, putting the issue squarely back in Jerry's lap.

"Yes, of course," Jerry asserted, "You know she is just trying to manipulate me...to control me in order to quell her raging fear that I'll abandon her…isn't that what all borderlines do?" Jerry shot back, more defiant than questioning.

"But what if she cuts herself again?" John queried, as he had seen Stella on the Unit three times over the past seven years, "or worse, finally kills herself in a drunken stupor…she has been hitting the bottle more seriously lately, hasn't she?"

"Yes she has…" Jerry sat back in resignation, "and I have to admit… (he paused and looked around at the staff as if to anticipate a shocked response) that at times I wish she would just go ahead and get it done!" His anger was rising again as he realized how seriously his statement reflected a lack of caring and positive emotional connection to his patient.

John knew that Jerry was a committed though still somewhat inexperienced clinician who was speaking more out of his anger and frustration, something he wanted his staff to be able to do without fearing retribution. He said to him, "Jerry we've all worked with borderline patients that, at times, we felt like strangling more than helping, and I know from experience that Stella will drive you right up the wall with her anger, threats, and demands. But it is important to maintain your boundaries, and follow through with a clear professional intervention here. It's likely that she will stabilize if you continue to work with her, but she must know that you still care and haven't given up on her. Can you do that, or should we consider transferring her case to some other staff?"

Jerry heard both the support and the challenge by John, and he resolved his moral and clinical dilemma the only way he knew how to grow further as a resilient clinician. He recommitted himself to stay with and reconnect with Stella, realizing all too well why borderline personality disorders were among the toughest kinds of cases to work with as a counselor.

An Entrenched, Long-term Pattern Disorder

A personality disorder is a long-term pattern of thinking, feeling, and behavior that differs significantly from the expected norms for one's culture. When a person has a personality disorder, he or she typically responds in the same way across a variety of interpersonal situations—the behavior is entrenched and repetitive, and is not simply a response to a particular person or situation. People with personality disorders tend to respond in similar ways to every situation, even when different responses would be more appropriate. Personality disorders usually appear in adolescence or early adulthood and tend to change little over time. They cause either stress or impairment in social, occupational or other areas of functioning.[1]

The Twelve Disorders of Personality

There are ten specific personality disorders identified in the main text of the DSM-IV—the psychiatric diagnostic system used by nearly all mental health professionals—and there are at least two experimental personality disorders that are likely to appear with some frequency in the counseling office. Brief descriptions of each of those twelve appear below.

Persons with *Dependent Personality Disorder* are typically overly submissive and have great fear of making decisions or being independent. They look for others who will lead and make decisions for them. People with Dependent Personality Disorder don't disagree with others for fear they will reject them, and seek an excessive amount of reassurance and advice from others. These people fit many of the characteristics of the literature on codependency, although some clinicians view codependency as a specific way of attempting to control others, whereas this concept is not included in the DSM-IV definition of Dependent Personality Disorder.

Persons with *Avoidant Personality Disorder* have the capacity and desire for intimacy, but are very shy and insecure, and are unwilling to reach out to people unless guaranteed acceptance. They typically feel socially inadequate and are overly sensitive to any signs of criticism or rejection. As a result, they are usually reluctant to take the risks necessary to develop new relationships, even though they sincerely would like to have them.

Persons with *Obsessive-Compulsive Personality Disorder* are overly concerned with doing things perfectly, and with ensuring that anything done by other people that reflects on them also be done perfectly. As a result they often manifest perfectionism that interferes with completion of their own tasks, and are over-controlling in their relationships to family members or work subordinates. Their concern with orderliness and perfectionism also affects them in the realm of morality and ethics, where they tend to be overly conscientious and inflexible.

Persons with *Histrionic Personality Disorder* tend to be lively and overly dramatic. They feel frustrated if they are not the center of attention. They frequently over-emphasize physical appearance and often engage in sexually provocative or seductive behavior. They tend to have a long history of brief romantic relationships that end as quickly as they start.

Persons with *Narcissistic Personality Disorder* have an exaggerated sense of self-importance. They expect to be recognized as superior without earning such recognition. They typically expect excessive admiration and believe they are entitled to favorable treatment and automatic compliance with their expectations. They tend to be exploitive and lack empathy and true concern for others. Other people often view them as arrogant and haughty.

Persons with *Antisocial Personality Disorder* have a pervasive pattern of disregard for and violation of the rights of others. They are typically impulsive, deceitful, and seem to lack remorse for the harm their behavior often causes. They enjoy the challenge of successfully "conning" other people. Some have good interpersonal skills and elicit trust (at least temporarily). From a Christian perspective, these would be people who grew up without a properly developed conscience code.

People with *Borderline Personality Disorder* have a very unstable sense of identity, and frequently feel empty inside. As a result they are constantly looking for someone stable with whom to form a relationship. When they find such a person they frequently become very demanding and jealous of any attention this person pays to anyone else. They constantly worry about being abandoned, and will engage in frantic efforts—including suicidal attempts or gestures—to avoid abandonment.

People with Borderline Personality Disorder are often impulsive in ways that are self-damaging, engaging in activities such as impulsive spending, promiscuous sex, substance abuse or reckless driving. They often express either adoration (when people are giving them the attention they want) or inappropriate, intense anger (when they believe they are being abandoned). They sometimes have episodes that look like mini-psychoses, especially when they feel lonely or afraid.

People with *Paranoid Personality Disorder* have a pervasive pattern of distrust and suspiciousness. They often believe others' motives are malevolent without any substantial reason for such a belief, and frequently read demeaning meanings into benign remarks or behavior. They typically bear grudges and are quick to react angrily.

People with *Schizoid Personality Disorder* are emotionally detached from those around them, but unlike the person with Avoidant Personality Disorder, they have no desire to develop close relationships. They usually have flattened affect. They rarely come to therapy because they are usually satisfied with their solitary existence, but sometimes come because family members (e.g., parents) want them to change, and those family members urge them to see a counselor.

Persons with *Schizotypal Personality Disorder* are also uncomfortable in close relationships, but in addition to their discomfort with intimacy, often have eccentric thinking and behavior. They often appear stiff in social settings, and their clothing is sometimes unkempt. They frequently have paranoid ideation. There is some evidence suggesting a relationship between Schizotypal Personality Disorder and the schizophrenias.

Passive-Aggressive Personality Disorder and *Depressive Personality Disorder* are two experimental personality disorders that may appear with some frequency in Christian counseling offices. Persons with Passive-Aggressive Personality Disorder may not indicate disagreement initially when asked to do something, but often resent demands or requests, and express these feelings indirectly by passively resisting social or occupational tasks. They are typically sullen, argumentative, envious and resentful of others. Some persons with this personality style will alternate between hostile defiance and contrition.[2]

Depressive Personality Disorder is different from Dysthymic Disorder, which is a chronic (at least two years) mild to moderate depression that seems to have significant somatic symptoms related to biological depression.[3] In contrast, Depressive Personality Disorder is a chronic lifestyle dominated by feelings of inadequacy and criticalness about self, pessimism about the world and the future, and negativism and criticalness toward others.[4] Thus it seems to be more likely to have a psychological etiology (a cognitive habit of always seeing the world from a dark, negative perspective) than a biological etiology (as Dysthymic Disorder seems to have).

It is estimated that 10 to 13% of the population—over 30 million people in the United States—have personality disorders.[5] Because of the distress or impairment personality disorders cause in relationships and in life functioning, they are likely to appear in counseling offices in higher percentages than they appear in the general population. Thus every counselor in general practice is likely to be faced with the prospect of treating people with personality disorders on a regular basis.

Up to the present time the general consensus has been that the prognosis for successful treatment of people with personality disorders was low, especially within the severe time constraints imposed by managed care. What this chapter will attempt to do is discuss a Christian cognitive-behavioral model for conceptualizing how the personality disorders develop, and how to treat personality disorders within a relatively short time frame (12 to 18 sessions). I will also suggest some ways to begin treatment, or to treat portions of a personality disorder if managed care or other financial considerations do not allow even that amount of counseling time.

How Personality Disorders Develop

This outline follows a cognitive-behavioral approach to personality development and builds on the work of Adler[6] and Young.[7] Alfred Adler believed that young children attempt to find ways to achieve significance and identity in their world. Assessing their own abilities, courage and confidence, they choose either to develop their identity through socially useful, constructive behavior, or they become discouraged at being able to achieve a unique identity in positive ways, and find their identity instead through unhealthy behavior.

The result of this choice is what Adler referred to as a "style of living" or a "life-style." In contemporary terminology we might say that all people have a personality style. We have no specific names for the healthy personalities of those who choose constructive life-styles—although the trend toward positive psychology and our dedication to redemptive living should challenge Christian counselors to construct such a taxonomy. Various kinds of Personality Disorders are the names we give to those who choose or live out unhealthy life-styles.

Each personality disorder can be identified with one or more of what Adler would call "mistaken beliefs." Psychologist-pastor Bill Backus calls these misbeliefs,[8] and Christian psychologist Chris Thurman[9] describes them as "the lies we believe." Adler believed that we often adopt beliefs about what is true, and then we act "as if" those things were true, whether or not they are.

For example, the mistaken belief that underlies Dependent Personality Disorder might go something like this: "I am not capable of making decisions or taking care of myself, and must find someone strong and wise who can do these things for me." The belief that underlies Avoidant Personality Disorder might be: "People would probably reject me if they truly knew me, so I must be careful what I allow them to see." A person with Obsessive-Compulsive Personality Disorder might be operating on the assumption that "I am only okay if I do things perfectly. If I let myself (or others whose behavior reflects on me) be satisfied with less than excellence, I will soon be overwhelmed with mediocrity and no one will respect me." The person with Histrionic Personality Disorder may be operating on the mistaken belief that "I am only okay if people are paying attention to me." The same kind of analysis could be done for each of the personality disorders.

Young[10] has extended this analysis further in his work with schemas (or core beliefs). He believes that, based on our early life experience, we all develop a set of core beliefs, or schemas, that encompass our view (1) of ourselves, (2) of the world (other people), and (3) of our relationship to the world. These core beliefs may be either healthy ones (adaptive schema), or unhealthy ones (maladaptive schema). Unhealthy core beliefs can result from trauma that occur anytime during the lifespan, but they most commonly develop during childhood. Young has identified 18 different *early* maladaptive schema (i.e., those that develop during the first five years of life). These early maladaptive schema lay the groundwork, without some sort of beneficent intervention, for various personality disorders.

Proposal for a Christian Taxonomy of Schema Development

From a Christian perspective, one could argue that core beliefs (the early, often unarticulated beliefs children develop based on their early experience in the world) should be expanded from these basic three *to at least eight categories*. These beliefs (either correct or mistaken), form the basis for our early views of ourselves, and determine whether we develop a socially-contributing lifestyle or an unhealthy one (a personality disorder). The eight types of core beliefs I would like to propose include the following:

1. *Beliefs about self* (e.g., Am I loveable or unlovable, worthwhile or not worthwhile?)
2. *Beliefs about others* (e.g., Are people trustworthy, untrustworthy, predictable or unpredictable?)
3. *Beliefs about the relationship between self and others* (e.g., Am I

optimistic that most of my needs will be met through my relationships with others, or am I pessimistic about this happening? Do I believe I have the power to exert a reasonable amount of influence on the world around me [self-efficacy], or do I see myself as relatively powerless in influencing what happens?). [Each of the following five kinds of core beliefs are not frequently mentioned by secular theorists.]

4. *Beliefs about God* (e.g., Does He exist? What is His nature? How much control does He have over what happens in the universe? Does He have a personal interest in human beings? Does God care?)

5. *Beliefs about God's feelings towards oneself* (Does God like me, dislike me, or is He indifferent to my existence? Do His feelings about me change when I make errors? When I sin? Does He reject me or punish me when I do wrong?).

6. *Beliefs about what one should and should not do* (Wolterstorff has called these "control beliefs").[11] This concept of moral direction has been typically avoided or pathologized in secular theorizing, yet it is evident that some sort of moral control beliefs are necessary, and failure to impart them to children has significant negative consequences.

7. *Beliefs about one's purpose in life* (What is the purpose in living? Is my most important purpose in life to minimize pain and maximize pleasure? Is it to achieve status, attention, wealth, or security? Is it to make a difference in the world by giving of myself to others?)

8. *Beliefs about expression of affection and sexuality* (e.g., What are appropriate ways of expressing love and affection? What are appropriate ways of expressing and receiving sexual love?)

Conceptualizing Human Personality Style

Knowledge about personality development is useful for understanding how personality disorders arise. A healthy personality style (and the dysfunctional personality disorders) can be conceptualized in terms of four activities:

- cognitive beliefs,
- cognitive processes,

- feelings, and
- resultant overt behavior.

In healthy people there is likely to be relative health in each of these four processes. In people with personality disorders there are likely to be a dysfunctioning mode of activity in one or more of these processes.

Cognitive Beliefs

Cognitive beliefs refer to *the content of what we believe.* Cognitive beliefs occur at three discernible levels—core beliefs, intermediate beliefs, and automatic thoughts.[12] Core beliefs are often formed by children based on their early observations about the way the world works. We usually are not aware of the fact that these core beliefs are assumptions or hypotheses about reality: unless someone draws our attention to this fact, we typically act "as if" they were true and base our responses to the world on these assumptions. As mentioned above, children and adolescents develop core beliefs in at least eight areas.

Intermediate beliefs are those rules, assumptions and expectations that people develop from their core beliefs. They also include expectancies (e.g., optimism or pessimism about how life in general and situations in particular are likely to turn out). They also include assumptions are how people are and rules about how people ought to behave.[13] Intermediate beliefs serve as the connection between core beliefs and automatic thoughts. For example, if a person developed the core belief in childhood, based on interactions with his family, that "I am inadequate," he might develop the intermediate beliefs (in this case a rule and an expectancy for himself that) "If I work very hard, I may be able to succeed, although there is a good likelihood that I won't." When faced with a problem in his daily life, the core belief and intermediate beliefs are likely to produce automatic thoughts such as "I'm probably going to mess up, and that will be terrible."

Automatic thoughts include the self-talk that people constantly give themselves. People with healthy personality styles tend to be more likely to give themselves healthy self-talk, whereas people with personality disorders are more likely to engage in *disabling* self-talk (e.g., Dependent Personality Disorder, Avoidant Personality Disorder, Depressive Personality Disorder, Obsessive-Compulsive Personality Disorder), *overly self-centered* self-talk (e.g., Histrionic Personality Disorder, Narcissistic Personality Disorder, Antisocial Personality Disorder), or *overly suspicious* self-talk (e.g., Paranoid Personality Disorder, Schizoid Personality Disorder, Schizotypal Personality Disorder).

Adler suggested that the word "unconscious" be used as an adjective rather than a noun—that these cognitions (core beliefs, intermediate beliefs, and automatic thoughts) sometimes affect us without us being fully consciously aware of their presence (they are to some extent operating outside of our conscious awareness). He broke with Freud, however, in terms of believing that there is an unconscious mind where these core beliefs reside which is ordinarily inaccessible to conscious thinking.

Cognitive Processes

Interacting with the cognitive beliefs that we hold are certain cognitive processes that keep data in or out of our awareness, and also determine the meaning we make of the data available to us. The three most important cognitive processes are selective attention, attributions, and cognitive avoidance processes.

Selective attention: According to Tor Norretrander,[14] a leading science writer in Denmark, conscious experience represents a miniscule portion of the stimuli we process. Norretrander asserts that our brains process approximately 11 million bits of information per second, but our consciousness processes only about 16 bits in that same time period. While some might argue with the exact figures Norretrander gives, even if he is off by several fold it is clear that our conscious mind cannot attend to all the internal and external data available to it. We have learned a variety of ways to selectively attend to the data that is most important to our survival, and find some way of not attending to that data that is less important or unimportant.

People with healthy personality styles tend to have cognitive selective attention processes that help them attain a relatively representative sample of the available data. They receive accurate data about the situations where they are doing well, and also receive accurate data about situations where they are doing less well and need to change. In contrast, people with personality disorders are likely to selectively attend to data in such a way that they receive a distorted view of reality and their performance.

People with certain of the personality disorders appear to have developed the cognitive habit of selectively attending to negative data about themselves and their performance (e.g., the Depressive, Dependent, Avoidant and Obsessive-Compulsive Personality Disorders). People with other personality disorders appear to have developed the cognitive habit of selectively attending to only the data that highlights their positives (e.g., Histrionic, Narcissistic, and Antisocial Personality Disorder). People with a third type of personality disorder appear to selectively focus on the data suggesting that others are not trustworthy and that one must always be on guard (e.g., the Paranoid, Schizoid and Schizotypal Personality Disorders).

Attributions: Attributions refer to the interpretations people make of their behavior and the behavior of others. People with normal personality styles tend to make relatively objective interpretations of events. People with personality disorders tend to make interpretations that are consistent with the core beliefs they hold. For example, if a person with Dependent Personality Disorder happens to make an independent decision that turns out well, they are likely to attribute this to "luck" rather than interpret it to mean that they can occasionally make good decisions on their own.

Similarly, if someone does something nice to someone who has Paranoid Personality Disorder, that person is likely to look for some "hidden agenda" rather than accept it as a genuinely caring behavior with no strings attached. Thus all people (those with and without personality disorders) tend to make interpretations that are consistent with the core beliefs they already hold and that allow them to keep their core beliefs intact.

Cognitive avoidance processes: One of the aspects of Freud's theory that most therapists have accepted as having some validity, whether or not they accept the validity of the rest of his constructs, is his theory of ego defense mechanisms. Ego defense mechanisms are mental processes that serve to keep overwhelming or anxiety-producing data out of conscious awareness, either temporarily, or if the data would be extremely overwhelming, out of conscious awareness for long periods of time. The DSM-IV has a very thorough and interesting description of the ego defenses, and organizes them from the more healthy to the less healthy.[15] Cognitive behavior therapists have recognized the value of having a way to incorporate these concepts into their theorizing, and have termed them "cognitive avoidance processes."

These four concepts—cognitive beliefs, selective attention, attributions, and cognitive avoidance processes—seem to exist in dynamic equilibrium. That is, once people have accepted a certain set of cognitive beliefs as true, they tend to selectively attend to data that confirms those beliefs, make consistent attributions about that data, and engage in cognitive avoidance processes that serve to reinforce those cognitive beliefs.

Normally it is only through some sort of significant event or intervention—a major life crisis, or conversion, or a significant breakthrough with God as a Christian, or therapy—that peoples' cognitive beliefs and cognitive processing style change significantly.

Emotions and Behavior

In a cognitive-behavioral model, emotions are considered to primarily be the result of the cognitions a person holds and the cognitive processes they engage in. Emotions are important for a number of reasons—they are an integral part of the total human experience, and it is important that a therapist recognize and respect them in order for a client to feel understood. From a therapeutic standpoint, they are a valuable entry point into understanding the cognitive content and cognitive processes that are producing them.

Whether or not thoughts and emotions are expressed in *overt behavior* depends on a number of things—how intense the emotions are, the client's appraisal of the benefits or risks of expressing those feelings in behavior, and the behavioral repertoire they possess. The combination of one's cognitive beliefs, cognitive processes, emotions, and behaviors produce their personality style, or in the case of unhealthy processes, their personality disorder.

Getting Oriented and Treating Personality Disorders

If the cognitive-behavioral model of understanding the personality disorders described above is valid, then it is possible to approach treatment of personality disorders by asking the following questions:

1. Is this person's difficulty caused by mistaken cognitive beliefs? If so, what are they?
2. Is this person's difficulty caused by faulty cognitive processes which they are using to assimilate the internal and external data

available to them? If so, how can they be helped to develop a
more balanced awareness of those data?

3. Is this person's difficulty caused because they have either (a)
    learned unhealthy behavioral responses or (b) failed to learn the
    behavioral skills they need in order to be successful? Or

4. Is this person's difficulty caused by problems in one or more of
    these areas?

Since emotions are considered, in a cognitive-behavioral model, to be
secondary to the cognitive content and processes people experience,
painful emotions are not treated directly. It is assumed that helping people
change their beliefs, their faulty cognitive processes, and their dysfunctional behavior will be the best way to help them change their maladaptive
emotions.

Identifying Mistaken Beliefs or Unhealthy Cognitions

Mistaken cognitive beliefs may be either mistaken core beliefs, intermediate beliefs, or automatic thoughts (i.e., self-talk). Therefore the therapist
may ask himself or herself the following questions (these questions do not
have to be asked to the client, but serve as a template as the counselor lis-
tens to the client). Is this client hampered by mistaken beliefs about:

1. Themselves and their own lovability or worthwhileness
2. The nature of other human beings
3. Their relationship to others
4. Their beliefs about God
5. Their moral standards (e.g., too strict, non-existent, inconsistent,
    etc.), and the value they place on living within their moral values
6. Their beliefs about God's feelings toward them
7. Their beliefs about how they will find purpose and meaning for
    their life, or
8. Their beliefs about how one should express affection and
    sexuality.

Since intermediate beliefs and automatic thoughts are related to (and generally outgrowths of one's core beliefs), the therapist can also be listening

for the intermediate beliefs and automatic thoughts that have developed from those core beliefs.

Identifying Cognitive Processes that Interfere with Healthy Living

Using the above model, one can also be listening for the presence of cognitive processes that contribute to the personality disorder by distorting the internal and external data the client is receiving. Three processes to listen for specifically include

1. Selective attention to internal or external data that reinforces the unhealthy personality style.
2. Misattributions (misinterpretations of that data), or
3. Unhealthy overuse of cognitive avoidance mechanisms (ego defenses).

Identifying Behaviors and Skill Deficits that Interfere with Healthy Living

The unhealthy behavioral responses in which clients with personality disorders engage may be a result of at least two very different sources. First, clients may have learned unhealthy behavioral responses through modeling unhealthy behavioral responses that need to be replaced with healthier ones. Secondly, they may fail to respond appropriately because they have never had an opportunity to learn the appropriate skill. Some of the skills that clients with personality disorders sometimes lack include:

1. Conversational skills
2. Knowledge of how to deepen friendships
3. Communication skills
4. Conflict-resolution skills
5. Assertiveness and anger management skills
6. Relaxation skills
7. Study skills
8. Decision-making skills
9. Knowledge of how to solve complex problems
10. Time-management skills
11. Money-management skills

12. Knowledge of how to move to a new developmental stage
13. Parenting skills for children without disabilities (normal parenting skills)
14. Parenting skills for children with specific disabilities (e.g., how to parent children with ADHD, developmental disabilities, chronic health problems, etc.)
15. Thus therapy in this area may include unlearning unhealthy responses, learning adaptive responses, or both.

Integration of the Above Three Areas

Since people are integrated functioning personalities, those who have a personality disorder may have things that could be changed in all three areas, i.e., in their cognitive content, in their cognitive processing, and in their behavioral responses. For example, with persons with Dependent Personality Disorder it may be helpful to help them (1) learn to change their core beliefs about their own abilities and identify and replace their disabling self-talk (cognitive content), (2) help them become aware of how they are selectively attending only to data that supports their feelings of inadequacy and ignoring data that shows they have strengths (cognitive processing), and (3) help them learn decision-making skills (a cognitive-behavioral skill).

Since people differ with regard to their openness to these various means of entry, therapists have the opportunity to choose the avenue that they believe a specific client will be most open to at a given point in time, whether it be looking a the historical roots from which they developed a certain core belief, learning to identify and dispute with the disabling self-talk in which they are presently engaging, or practicing and learning a new skill.

The fact that people are integrated bio-psycho-social-spiritual units also means that it may not be necessary to address every component of the personality disorder. For example, as clients learn to dispute their disabling automatic thoughts and learn new skills, the changes that happen as a result in their personal relationships may cause their intermediate thoughts and core beliefs (or their tendencies to selectively attend or misinterpret data) to change in healthy directions.

Thus by choosing (1) the part of the personality disorder that the person

is most willing to change and (2) the part which, if changed, would produce the most overall benefit, the therapist may be able to initiate a process
of change that can continue even after therapy is over. This is particularly
the case when the therapist *uses methods that teach clients cognitive and behavioral skills that they can use to continue to move toward healthiness without the
presence of the therapist.* When working under severe time constraints, as is
necessary in some managed care situations, the therapist may need to ask
which *single* change would produce the most benefit for the client, and simply focus on that.

The process may be likened to lumberjacks called to break up a logjam
on a crowded river. By careful assessment of which key "logs" are most
critical in preventing movement and focusing on them, a process of movement toward health may be started in which it is not necessary to personally attend to every log. A clear understanding of how cognitive beliefs,
cognitive processes, emotions and behavior are interconnected and which
ones are most critical in causing the present impasse can help therapists
determine where best to focus their attention.

Practical Aspects to Treating Clients with Personality Disorders

Ways of Changing Cognitive Content

This section (of the following three sections) is the one where Christian
therapy can differ most from secular therapy. One of the differences is that
Christian therapy recognizes the importance of core beliefs in the last five
areas mentioned above (beliefs about God, about moral control beliefs,
about God's feelings toward the person, about finding a meaningful purpose for one's life, and about the appropriate expression of affection and
sexuality). Since 81% of clients say that they would like their religious values integrated into counseling,[16] it seems that most clients realize that such
integration will in some way help them with the difficulties they are facing,
and hope that their counselors will help them do so.

Secular cognitive behavior therapy usually begins by helping a client
become aware of how their cognitive self-talk affects their emotions and
behavior, and then teaches them, via Socratic questioning and behavioral experiments, to develop data by which to dispute and eventually
replace the disabling self-talk in which they have been engaging. As

clients become adept at changing their automatic thoughts, emphasis gradually moves to doing a similar process with intermediate and core beliefs.[17]

Christian therapists can, and often do use this same process with Christian clients. But most Christian therapists can probably also attest to the fact that God is not limited to always working "from the top down." Through the process of conversion, personal devotions, Bible studies, worship, fellowship with other Christians, inner healing experiences, Christian journaling, etc., God sometimes changes intermediate and core beliefs much more rapidly than one would expect simply using the secular cognitive-behavioral methods.

As we help clients appropriate the promises found in God's Word, these promises can provide an antidote for much of the disabling self-talk with which clients often struggle. The following list (adapted from an unknown source) gives examples:

CLIENT SELF-TALK	GOD'S PROMISE
It's impossible.	With My help, all things are possible.
I'm exhausted. I can't go on.	I will strengthen you and will uphold you.
Nobody really loves me.	I love you, and nothing can ever separate you from My love.
I can't do it.	You can do all things with My strength.
I'm not able.	But I (God) am able.
It's not worth it.	It will be worth it.
I can't forgive myself.	I forgive you.
I can't manage.	I will supply all your needs.
I'm afraid.	Cast all your anxieties on Me, and I will give you My peace.
I'm not smart enough.	I will give you wisdom.
I feel all alone.	I will never leave you or forsake you.

Ways of Changing Cognitive Processes

The ways that Christian therapists can help clients change the dysfunctional processes that underlie personality disorders are similar to how secular therapists would work. Therapists can, through gentle, supportive questioning, help clients attend to a more balanced sample of the data available to them, and help them gradually assimilate that more accurate picture of themselves and the world into their core beliefs. They can also teach clients how to "check out" the interpretations they are making, and see whether there are other possible interpretations than the ones they are making. They can also support them as they examine data that they had previously been avoiding through use of their ego defense mechanisms.

But Christian therapists may also experience some advantages in the above process. Usually clients selectively attend, make misattributions, and overuse cognitive avoidance mechanisms out of fear of something. As counselors help clients know that, with God's help and support, they don't have to fear, these unhealthy cognitive processes can sometimes relax at a pace one would not expect if clients believe they are all alone in this battle with their fears.

Ways of Changing Behavioral Deficits

Some clients need to unlearn old behavioral habits before learning new ones. For others, it is simply a matter of learning cognitive or behavioral skills they never learned as they were growing up.

Not all clients need skills training. For some, they may have observed healthy role models and know how to do certain things, but have never done them because disabling self-talk held them back. For this group, simply teaching them how to dispute with their disabling self-talk and then encouraging them to apply what they already know in a gradual hierarchy of real-life situations may be all that is needed.

Even with clients who do not believe they know how to do a certain skill, it may not be necessary to go through explicit skills training. They can be assigned to think about how to do a certain thing, and/or to carefully observe how someone they respect does it, discuss a plan for trying out the new skill with their therapist, then go out and work their plan.

For those skills that are more complex there is value in each counselor knowing how to teach each of the 14 sets of skills listed in the previous section, or in having pamphlets, books, cassettes, or videos that can introduce the client to the needed skills. It may be helpful to roleplay the skills in a counseling session, giving clients feedback as they try them, and also identifying any self-talk that would interfere with using the skills in real life situations outside the counseling session.

Documenting Therapy for Clients with Personality Disorders

At least two forces point to the importance of ever-increasing specificity in treatment planning, not only for treatment of personality disorders, but for all therapy. One factor is the research indicating that, as therapists become more specific about identifying the treatment goals, identified problems, and treatment objectives, the efficiency of their interventions increases. To simply list "depression" or "anxiety" as an identified problem gives us little understanding of the causes of that specific client's depression or anxiety, nor does it lead to a meaningful or efficient treatment plan.

The second factor is that managed care providers and government agencies are demanding treatment plans that include identification of specific presenting problems and of interventions that follow logically from those problems.

The following is a suggested approach to writing more specific treatment plans. It involves identifying—for each problem the client is experiencing—treatment objectives, treatment plans (or interventions), and a way to measure whether each objective has been achieved. This model conforms to trends for treatment planning that are increasingly being required by the Joint Commission on Accreditation of Healthcare Organizations (JCAHO) and managed care systems. Some of the following points are from an article entitled "Basic Rules of Writing Treatment Goals and Objectives" found in *Practical Communications: Accreditation and Certification*, Vol. IV, No. 3, pp. 2–9.

Treatment Goals

Treatment goals are *general* statements that specify the results you hope to accomplish through therapy. They are general, abstract statements that will eventually be transformed into treatment *objectives*, which are observable and measurable.

Whenever possible, treatment goals should be stated positively (something the client accomplishes), rather than negatively (something the client eliminates or reduces). Examples of treatment goals might be "Client will be comfortable initiating and maintaining a variety of close friendships and work relationships as desired" (Avoidant Personality Disorder) or "Increase client's comfort in making decisions, initiating projects, assuming responsibility for personal life, and disagreeing with others when appropriate" (Dependent Personality Disorder).

The Identified Problem(s)

This step involves breaking the client's dysfunctionality down into component parts. For example, with each DSM-IV personality disorder, select those descriptors from the symptom list that are true for that specific client and are severe enough to be clinically significant in the person's life. (See examples in the tables that follow. The tables include illustrations using all the symptoms in the DSM-IV(TR). In real life situations choose only those symptoms that are important enough to be the focus of clinical attention, and that can realistically be addressed in the time insurance, or the client's financial resources, allow for treatment).

If the client is in a hospital setting for crisis stabilization, it may still be valuable to list all important problem areas, whether or not they will be dealt with during the hospital stay. Those identified problems not dealt with during the hospital stay will help give the outpatient therapist (or partial hospitalization program) direction for follow-up therapy.

Listing all important problems that are evident during the time of crisis is important for a second reason: After a crisis is partially stabilized and clients are discharged, they may sometimes be less willing to admit problems that need to be addressed in therapy. By having the problems already listed as part of the post-discharge treatment plan increases the likelihood that they will be addressed in follow-up therapy. A crucial ingredient in this step is to define the problems in ways that can be changed, either through therapy, medication, education, or some environmental intervention over which the client has some influence.

Sometimes the DSM-IV symptom lists contain criteria that are redundant from a treatment perspective. For example on the treatment planning sheet for Depressive Personality Disorder which follows, Symptoms 2, 3 and 6 are combined because they can all be treated using the same approach (review now).

Treatment Objectives

Each treatment objective should follow from the respective identified problem. Each treatment objective should be a specific, measurable behavior or cognitive goal. Objectives will usually be the "flip-side" of the identified problem. For example, if the identified problem (IP) is the absence of some necessary skill, the objective will be to learn that skill. If the IP is the presence of some dysfunctional behavior, the objective will be to decrease or eliminate the occurrence of that behavior and replace it with a more functional one. It may be helpful to identify Pre-discharge Treatment Objectives and objectives that, if the outpatient therapist is in agreement, would become Post-Discharge Treatment Objectives.

Treatment Plans (or Interventions)

This involves a succinct identification of the method you plan to use to accomplish the treatment objectives. The treatment plan chosen will vary depending on the theoretical orientation of the therapist, anticipated openness of the client to a specific approach, agency expectations and policies, insurance restrictions (some insurance companies restrict the types of interventions for which they will pay), and time available. In a time of managed care, the therapist should normally choose methods that have proven effectiveness in treating each specific identified problem, and will do so most efficiently.

Measure of Achievement and Target Date

This column lists the way you will measure whether or not you have achieved each objective and when. See following examples.

On the closing pages of this chapter are examples of treatment plans for two personality disorders—Avoidant Personality Disorder and Depressive Personality Disorder. The interventions are illustrative only, and not intended to be prescriptive—they represent *one possible way* a therapist could choose to treat each issue; and not the only way. It is hoped that they will spur further thinking and discussion about the treatment of persons with personality disorders.

Example of Treatment Planning Sheet: Avoidant Personality Disorder

Overall Goal: The client will be comfortable initiating and maintaining a variety of close friendships and work relationships as desired.

#	Identified Problem	Goal or Objective	Treatment Plan	Measure of Achievement and Target Date	Achieved Yes/No/ Provider/ Client Date
1	Views self as socially inept, personally unappealing, and inferior to others	Increase view of self as socially skillful, appealing, and equal to others in worth and lovability	Teach social skills. Teach how to dispute negative self-talk and how to engage in more positive self-talk about one's social acceptability	1. Teach social skills by [date]. 2. Use social skills twice per day by [date]. 3. Teach how to recognize negative self-talk and replace it with positive self-talk when it occurs by [date].	
2	Is mentally preoccupied with being criticized and rejected	Decrease cognitive preoccupation with being criticized and rejected by changing cognitive focus	Help client recognize how his preoccupation harms him and how to shift his focus from an emphasis on being criticized and rejected to an emphasis on accepting and caring for others	1. Help client recognize how his preoccupation harms him by [date]. 2. Teach client to recognize when focusing on being criticized or rejected, and how to shift focus to caring for others by [date]	
3+4	Client is unwilling to be involved with others unless certain of being liked.	Help client become willing to take social risks, even if acceptance by others is not guaranteed	Teach client to dispute with his catastrophizing self-talk, and shift his focus to those who respond positively to his initiatives	Client risk taking social initiatives twice per day and keep record of results starting on [date].	
5	Avoids vocational activities that involve significant interpersonal contact, thus hampering his career advancement	Help client overcome his vocational avoidance behavior	Assign small increases in vocational social interaction. Have client evaluate whether his negative expectations prove valid	Attempt at least one vocational social interaction per day by [date]. Evaluate results and use self-evaluation to improve next attempt.	
6	Client remembers a socially traumatic event, and expects future events will turn out similarly (not from DSM-IV symptom list).	Reduce impact of past trauma on present and future behavior	Help client recognize his over-generalization and use memory of positive events to combat that tendency.	Identify overgeneralizations by [date]. Develop ability to dispute with them using memories of positive events by [date].	

Example of Treatment Planning Sheet: Depressive Personality Disorder

Overall Goal(s): Help client develop a more balanced and positive set of attitudes toward self, others and the future (or the world)

#	Identified Problem	Goal or Objective	Treatment Plan	Measure of Achievement and Target Date	Achieved Yes/No Provider/ Client Date
1	IP$_1$ Usual mood is dominated by dejection, gloominess, cheerlessness, joylessness, unhappiness	TO$_1$ Increase correlation between mood and a realistic appraisal of the present	TP$_1$ (1) Help client recognize the relationship between cognitions and mood. (2) Help client learn to dispute with dysphoria-producing cognitions and replace them with more realistic ones.	1. Have client track relationship between cognitions and mood for 1 week starting [date]. 2. Have client start replacing negative cognitions with positive ones starting [date], and evaluate the results. 3. Have client become aware of cognitive processes (e.g., constant repetition of negatives) which produces brooding and reduce frequency by _ by [date]	
4	IP$_4$ Is brooding and given to worry	TO$_4$ Help client replace habitually negative cognitions with habitually positive ones.	TP$_4$ Help client become aware of the cognitions and cognitive processes that lead to brooding and worry, and replace them with more hope-inspiring ones.	Accomplish item 1 by [date]	
2	IP$_2$ Self-concept centers around beliefs of inadequacy, worthlessness, and low self-esteem	TO$_2$ and TO$_3$ Increase realistic view of one's strengths, ability to make contributions, and a realistic view of self.	TP$_2$ and TP$_3$ (1) Help client learn to affirm own strengths and realistically accept that everyone has growth areas. (2) Help client identify contributions he or she can make. (3) Develop healthy self-talk about one's self and contributions (or potential contributions)	Accomplish item 1 by [date] Accomplish item 2 by [date] Accomplish item 3 by [date]	
3	IP$_3$ Is critical, blaming, and derogatory toward self			Accomplish item 1 by [date]	
6	IP$_6$ Is prone to feeling guilty or remorseful	TO$_6$ Reduce unnecessary and inappropriate guilt feelings	TP$_6$ (1) Teach client to distinguish between true guilt and unnecessary guilt. (2) Teach client to distinguish between healthy guilt responses and unhealthy ones.	Accomplish item 1 by [date] Accomplish item 2 by [date]	
5	Is negativistic, critical, and judgmental toward others	Increase acceptance of others, despite their imperfections	(1) Help client become aware of the unhealthiness of the cognitions and cognitive processes that produce judgmentalism and negativism. (2) Help client change those cognitions and cognitive processes.	Accomplish item 1 by [date] Accomplish item 2 by [date]	

ENDNOTES

1. American Psychiatric Association, *Diagnostic and statistical manual of mental disorders*, fourth edition, text revision, (Washington, D.C.: American Psychiatric Association, 2000), 685–686.
2. American Psychiatric Association, 791.
3. American Psychiatric Association, 380.
4. American Psychiatric Association, 789.
5. American Psychiatric Association, *Diagnostic and statistical manual of mental disorders*, third edition (Washington, D.C.: American Psychiatric Association, 1980); American Psychiatric Association, *Diagnostic and statistical manual of mental disorders*, third edition, rev. (Washington, D.C.: American Psychiatric Association, 1987). American Psychiatric Association, *Diagnostic and statistical manual of mental disorders*, fourth edition, text revision (Washington, D.C.: American Psychiatric Association, 2000). M.M. Weissman, The epidemiology of personality disorders: A 1990 update, *Journal of Personality Disorders, Supplement, Spring,* (1993), 44–62.
6. Alfred Adler, *Understanding human nature* (New York: Premier Books, 1959); Alfred Adler, *The Practice and theory of individual psychology* (Patterson, NJ: Littlefield, 1963).
7. Jeffrey Young, *Cognitive therapy for personality disorders: A schema-focused approach,* 3rd ed. (Sarasota, FL: Professional Resource Press, 1999).
8. William Backus, *Telling each other the truth* (Minneapolis, MN: Bethany House, 1985).
9. Chris Thurman, *The lies we believe* (Nashville: Thomas Nelson, 1991).
10. Young, 1999.
11. Nicholas Wolterstorff, *Reason within the bounds of religion,* 2nd ed. (Grand Rapids, MI: Eerdmans, 1984).
12. Judith Beck, *Cognitive therapy: Basics and beyond* (New York: Guilford, 1995), 140.
13. D. H. Baucom, Epstein, N., Sayers, S., and Sher, T.G., The role of cognitions in marital relationships: Definitional, methodological, and conceptual issues, *Journal of Consulting and Clinical Psychology, 57,* (1989), 31–38.
14. Torr Norretrander, *The user illusion* (New York: Viking, 1998).
15. American Psychiatric Association, *Diagnostic and statistical manual of mental disorders*, fourth ed. (Washington, D.C.: American Psychiatric Association, 1994), 751–757. American Psychiatric Association, *Diagnostic and statistical manual of mental disorders*, fourth ed., text revision (Washington, D.C.: American Psychiatric Association, 2000), 807–813.
16. M. Bart, Spirituality in counseling finding believers, *Counseling Today* (Alexandria, VA: American Counseling Association, December 1998), 1, 6.
17. Judith Beck, *Cognitive therapy: Basics and beyond* (New York: Guilford, 1995).

Part 3

Addictions and Impulse Control Problems

12

Addictions

Mark R. Laaser, George Ohlschlager, and Tim Clinton

> ...addicts can't change their behaviors without help from God and wise
> counsel. None of us can find sufficient relief from pain without help. To
> expect something different from the...addict is to heap more shame on
> [him] and encourage Christians to respond to tough issues with simplistic
> solutions...We learn that we can make it if we just try harder and believe
> that those who haven't made it didn't try hard enough. But believing in
> ourselves and the fruit of our efforts works against the fact that we are
> sinful and can escape sinful behaviors only with God's help.
>
> HARRY SCHAUMBURG

Howard Hillman was an executive consultant living with his second wife
and her children in a tiny suburb on the north Chicago shore. He was also
an alcoholic who lived in denial of it due to his fairly competent functioning (which he grossly exaggerated).

His wholesome and successful veneer started to crack, however, after his
second DUI in which he lost his license and had to hire his stepson to chauf-
feur him around. He also had to engage in counseling in order to clear his
record and get his license back, and was required to take a routine medical
drug screen following his counseling intake. It was then that Howard's secret
addiction to OxyContin[r] was discovered, which he had taken two years previously due to a severe back sprain. During his group confrontation about
this, he also admitted his addiction to internet sexual pornography.

Now it all made sense to his wife. Howard had been cutting back on his
drinking—she knew that as they had been fighting about it—but she didn't
understand why he slept in a stuporous state so much, had so many

"minor" accidents around the house, and no longer seemed to be interested in having sex with her. He was mixing alcohol with narcotics and internet pornography.

Worst of all, Howard had become a very accomplished liar. He was lying to cover his lies and now it had all started to breakdown. He had been in a drunken car accident six months earlier, and had just paid cash to "persuade" the other party to get their car fixed and keep quiet. His finances weren't in good shape though, as he was buying his OxyContin[r] on the black market, paying huge credit card bills for internet sex, and his consulting business was starting to slip.

For weeks Howard vascillated between anger at being found out, fear of losing his marriage, and depression at facing reality. He was shedding both real and crocodile tears as he promised over and over to "get sober" and turn his life around. The addictions group he was part of would hear none of it, as they confronted his lies, denial, and avoidance of the truth for weeks.

His counselor knew he was finally ready to get serious about change when he came to group one night and admitted to everyone there that he couldn't change, that he really didn't want to, but that he knew he had to if he was going to live. After this session, things started turning for the better.

Addictions are a very common scourge, the desperate expression of life in a sin-sick world. When addictions are piled on top of one another, or are mixed with mental illness, the suffering is multiplied and the cure is complex, difficult to accurately assess and easily achieve. Medicating the pain and symptoms of psychopathology—whether done under a doctor's treatment or illicitly—is a primary pathway to addiction for many dual-disordered patients.

Dual disorders refer to someone who suffers both an addiction and a mental/emotional disorder of some kind. The prototypical sufferer is someone with depression or an anxiety disorder—some kind of felt dysphoria—who is also addicted to alcohol or other drugs that are usually used to medicate the pain of that dysphoric unpleasantness. And it is not unusual to encounter persons who live the process in reverse, as addictions will induce mental and physical suffering of various kinds, if carried on long and deep enough. Whether working with persons with an addiction, multiple addictions, or dual disorders, it is usually necessary to address the primary addiction first, and that is the focus of this chapter.

The following national data is from the 2003 National Survey on Drug Use and Health,[1] a project of the Substance Abuse and Mental Health Services Administration (SAMHSA) that interviews approximately 67,500 persons each year. It is the primary source of information on the use and abuse of alcohol and illicit drugs by people in the United States, aged 12 years and older.

Alcohol Use

An estimated 119 million Americans aged 12 or older were current drinkers of alcohol in 2003 (50.1%). About 54 million (22.6%) participated in binge drinking at least once in the 30 days prior to the survey, and 16.1 million (6.8%) were heavy drinkers. The highest prevalence of binge and heavy drinking was for young adults aged 18 to 25. The rate of binge drinking was 41.6% for this group and was highest (47.8%) at age 21. Heavy alcohol use was reported by 15.1% of this group, and by 18.7% of persons aged 21 (also highest). An estimated 13.6% of persons aged 12 or older (32.3 million) drove under the influence of alcohol at least once in the 12 months prior to the interview in 2003 (a decrease from 14.2% in 2002).

Illicit Drug Use

In 2003, an estimated 19.5 million Americans, (8.2%) were current illicit drug users, the same overall rate as in 2002. The rate of current illicit drug use among youths aged 12 to 17 dropped slightly between 2002 (11.6%) and 2003 (11.2%). Current marijuana use among youths was 8.2% in 2002 and 7.9% in 2003. There was a decline in lifetime marijuana use among youths, from 20.6% in 2002 to 19.6% in 2003. There were also decreases in rates of past year use of LSD (1.3 to 0.6%), Ecstasy (2.2 to 1.3%), and methamphetamine (0.9 to 0.7%).

Marijuana is the most commonly used illicit drug, with a rate of 6.2% (14.6 million) in 2003. 2.3 million persons (1.0%) were current cocaine users, 604,000 of whom used crack. Hallucinogens were used by 1.0 million persons, and there were 119,000 current heroin users. These 2003 figures are similar to the estimates for 2002. Ecstasy (MDMA) users decreased between 2002 and 2003, from 676,000 (0.3%) to 470,000 (0.2%). Although there were no significant changes in the past year use of other hallucinogens, there were significant declines in past year use of LSD (from 1 million to 558,000) and in past year overall hallucinogen use (from 4.7 million to 3.9 million), as well as in past year use of Ecstasy (from 3.2 million to 2.1 million).

6.3 million persons were current users of psychotherapeutic drugs taken nonmedically (2.7%). 4.7 million used pain relievers, 1.8 million used tranquilizers, 1.2 million used stimulants, and 0.3 million used sedatives. The 2003 estimates are all similar to 2002. A significant increase in lifetime nonmedical use of pain relievers between 2002 and 2003 was shown, from 29.6 million to 31.2 million. Specific pain relievers with statistically significant increases in lifetime use were Vicodin[r], Lortab[r], or Lorcet[r] (from 13.1 million to 15.7 million); Percocet[r], Percodan[r], or Tylox[r] (from 9.7 million to 10.8 million); Hydrocodone (from 4.5 million to 5.7 million); OxyContin[r] (from 1.9 million to 2.8 million); methadone (from 0.9 million to 1.2 million); and Tramadol (from 52,000 to 186,000).

There were 2.6 million new marijuana users in 2003, or an average of 7,000 new users each day. 69% of these new marijuana users were under age 18, and 53% were female. Decreases in initiation of both LSD (from 631,000 to 272,000) and Ecstasy (from 1.8 million to 1.1 million) were evident, and hallucinogen initiation dropped from 1.6 million to 1.1 million. However, in the past decade, pain reliever use increased from 573,000 initiates) to 2.5 million initiates annually.

Rates of current illicit drug use varied significantly among the major racial/ethnic groups in 2003. Rates were highest among American Indians or Alaska Natives (12.1%), persons reporting two or more races (12.0%), and Native Hawaiians or Other Pacific Islanders (11.1%). Rates were 8.7% for blacks, 8.3% for whites, and 8.0% for Hispanics. Asians had the lowest rate at 3.8%. An estimated 18.2% of unemployed adults were current illicit drug users, compared with 7.9% employed full time and 10.7% employed part time. However, of the 16.7 million illicit drug users in 2003, 12.4 million (74.3%) were employed either full or part time.

Substance Dependence or Abuse

Americans numbering 21.6 million in 2003 were substance dependent or abusers (9.1% of the population). Of these, 3.1 million were dependent on or abused both alcohol and illicit drugs, 3.8 million were dependent on or abused illicit drugs but not alcohol, and 14.8 million were dependent on or abused alcohol but not illicit drugs. Between 2002 and 2003, a slight drop was noted in the number of persons with substance dependence or abuse (22.0 million in 2002 and 21.6 million in 2003).

In 2003, 17.0% of unemployed adults were dependent or abusers, while 10.2% of full-time employed adults and 10.3% of part-time employed adults were classified as such. However, most adults with substance dependence or abuse were employed either full or part time. Of the 19.4 million adults with dependence or abuse, 14.9 million (76.8%) were employed.

Substance Abuse Treatment

3.3 million people aged 12 or older (1.4% of the population) received treatment related to the use of alcohol or illicit drugs in 2003. Of these, 1.2 million received treatment at a rehabilitation facility as an outpatient, 752,000 at a rehabilitation facility as an inpatient, 729,000 at a mental health center as an outpatient, 587,000 at a hospital as an inpatient, 377,000 at a private doctor's office, 251,000 at an emergency room, and 206,000 at a prison or jail. Between 2002 and 2003, there were decreases in the number of persons treated for a substance use problem at a hospital as an inpatient, at a rehabilitation facility as an inpatient, at a mental health center as an outpatient, and at an emergency room.

In 2003, 22.2 million people (9.3%) needed treatment for an alcohol or illicit drug problem, about the same as in 2002 (22.8 million). The number needing but not receiving treatment also did not change between 2002 (20.5 million) and 2003 (20.3 million). Of the 20.3 million people who needed but did not receive treatment, an estimated 1.0 million (5.1%) reported that they felt they needed treatment for their alcohol or drug problem. Of the 1.0 million persons who felt they needed treatment, 273,000 (26.3%) reported that they made an effort but were unable to get treatment and 764,000 (73.7%) reported making no effort to get treatment.

Among the 1.0 million people who needed but did not receive treatment and felt they needed treatment, the most often reported reasons for not receiving treatment were (1) they were not ready to stop using (41.2%), (2) cost or insurance barriers (33.2%), (3) reasons related to stigma (19.6%), and

(4) they did not feel the need for treatment (at the time), or they could handle the problem without treatment (17.2%).

Symptoms and Etiology of the Addict

The following list is, in our opinion, a good set of common symptomatic behaviors and characteristics—a universal diagnostic set—that could be generalized to all substance or behavioral addictions and compulsions.

1. A pattern of out-of-control substance usage or behavior for a year or more
2. Mood swings associated with usage or behavior
3. An increasing pattern of usage or behavior over time, this increase may be a constant elevation or marked by periods of abstinence alternating with elevation
4. The presence of major or milder forms of depression
5. The feeling of shame or self-worthlessness
6. The consistent need to be liked and find approval from others
7. Impulse control problems, especially with food, sex, drugs, or money/spending/gambling
8. Use of the substance or behavior to reward oneself or to reduce anxiety
9. Obsessing about the substance or behavior, and spending great amounts of time around it
10. Obtaining or doing the behavior becomes the central organizing principle of life
11. Failed efforts to control the addiction
12. Negative consequences due to the substance or behavior
13. Alternating pattern of out-of-control behavior with over-controlling behavior
14. A history of emotional, physical, sexual, or spiritual abuse
15. A family history of addiction, rigidity, divorce, or disengagement
16. Marked feelings of loneliness or abandonment
17. Arrested developmental issues

The addict represents someone who has become trapped in a web of deceit and dark forces too powerful to overcome without significant help from God and others. The Scriptures reveal the truth about it:

So I find this law at work: When I want to do good, evil is right there with me. For in my inner being I delight in God's law; but I see another law at work in the members of my body, waging war against the law of my mind and making me a prisoner of the law of sin at work within my members. What a wretched man I am! Who will rescue me from this body of death? Thanks be to God—through Jesus Christ our Lord! (Romans 7:21–25, NIV)

These words of the apostle Paul embody the spiritual journey of those struggling with addiction. The mind of an addict knows that he or she needs to stop using certain substances or doing certain behaviors, but seemingly can't. The addict knows that he or she must start doing positive behaviors, but will not. It is the great conflict that Bill Wilson, the co-founder of Alcoholics Anonymous, captured in step one: *"I admitted that I was powerless over alcohol and that my life had become unmanageable."*

Paul's self description also reflects the shameful nature an addict's self-perception when he says, "What a wretched man I am!" The feeling of being a bad and worthless person is common to all addicts. It is not only that addictive behavior produces shame; shame is a basic feeling that addicts have felt most of their lives. It is that addictive behavior perpetuates and inflames shame.

Addictive behaviors are problems per se, and they are also symptoms of deeper physical, emotional, and spiritual issues. Maintaining this dual awareness—as well as tolerating and appreciating the inherent tensions between these sometimes competing ideas—is important when working with addicts. Depending on the issues of therapeutic focus, the course of treatment, and the progress (or lack thereof) toward goal attainment, the addiction is best viewed as either symptomatic of the underlying mental disorder or as the primary problem itself.

Addicts by their very nature feel helpless and unworthy. They are desperately asking as Paul did, "Who will rescue me?" Addicts cycle through feelings of the high of addiction and the despair of worthlessness. They may be stubbornly resisting giving up the high because they feel it is the only solution to the despair.

Counseling addicts is often frustrating as they frequently sabotage the most basic answers, and tear down the most fragile progress. Competent Christian counseling must point them to the only lasting answer, a relationship with Jesus Christ. Treating persons with addiction and dual disorders assumes that competent Christian counselors will assess and understand the nature of what they are actually dealing with. The following are the classic factors that define addiction.

Mood Alteration

Understanding addiction must begin with what scientists are only beginning to understand about the human brain. Brain chemistry is at the heart of what creates and sustains addiction.[2] Addicts seek to either raise or lower their mood using complex (and sometimes criminal) rituals of self-medicating behavior. If they are depressed, sad, or lonely they seek to raise their mood. If they are anxious, frightened, or stressed they seek to lower their mood. In doing so, addicts will eventually train their brains to neurochemically "depend" on the substance or behavior.

We have long accepted that alcohol affects the chemistry of the brain. We can easily understand that other drugs such as marijuana, heroin, and cocaine (to name a few) change brain chemistry. Some scientists believe that nicotine might be the most addictive of all substances. Even caffeine can be considered as an addictive substance in its ability to raise mood as a facilitator or certain powerful brain chemicals, most notably dopamine, that elevate mood.

Addictive behavior and the brain. What has long been debated is whether or not certain behaviors can affect the chemistry of the brain. As scientists have increased their ability to scan and produce images of the brain (through MRI and PET studies, for example), research projects have begun to demonstrate that behaviors alone, without the use of substances, can also do this.

When a person looks at another person who he or she loves or has feelings of sexual attraction for, certain opiates (catecholamines) are produced more rapidly in the brain. These neurochemicals have a heroin-like quality in the pleasure centers of the brain. That is why some have suggested that we can become *Addicted to Love*.[3] At Vanderbilt University, researchers are showing the dramatic effects on the brain of looking at pornography.[4] Little doubt remains that all sexual thought and activity produce these same neurochemical effects.

Any behavior that causes a sense of fear or excitement can raise levels of norepinephrine, more commonly referred to as adrenalin, in the brain. Norepinephrine can elevate levels of dopamine and serotonin and, as such, has a mood elevating quality. Gambling, working hard to meet deadlines, shopping, sports, even mountain climbing can become addictive for some.

The need for constant stimulation that some addicts experience means that their brains need "rapid firing" to function properly. These persons are easily bored and distracted. They have problems thinking into the future and planning. As such, they may seem at times to be lazy or lacking discipline. In their academic careers they may have been labeled underachievers. Some addicts, then, may have neurological symptoms that reflect a level of attention deficit or hyperactivity disorder. Christian counselors will be careful to refer addicts for competent psychiatric and neuropsychological evaluation to evaluate these symptoms. Medications may be needed to balance an addict's brain, at least for a time.

Multiple addictions. As our case example noted, many addicts suffer from more than one addiction. It is not uncommon for them to use a variety of substances and behaviors to alter their mood. Carnes found, in a research project on addiction,[5] that half of all sex addicts suffer from chemical dependency. He also found that the more serious the wounds of childhood, the more likely there would be multiple addictions.

This dynamic has led to many speculating about "cross addictions," or the "comorbidity" of addictions. Carnes is currently proposing a new and broader diagnosis, "Multiple Addiction Disorder" (MAD—an appropriate acronym). Christian counselors need to evaluate a broad pattern of addiction and triage which of the addictions is the most immediately destructive.

The Tolerance Effect

God has made us "fearfully and wonderfully" (Ps. 139:14). One of the amazing qualities of the body is its ability to adapt. Whatever happens to the body, it will always seek to return to a normal state. Scientists and systems therapists call this homeostasis. A virus enters our body and the body works itself into a fever to expel it. If a person gets frightened, his heart and respiration rate increases to prepare the body to fight or flee. When the threat is gone, the body works to return it to the normal rate. What the body interprets as normal, however, can change if there is repeated challenge to the normal state of affairs. This is a powerful ability that God has created in all people, the power to adapt.

The first time an alcoholic drinks a beer, for example, he or she experiences the effects of that in the brain. Brain chemistry changes and feelings of intoxication begin. Eventually, the brain returns to normal and the person "sobers up." If the pattern is repeated over and over again, however, the state of what normal is will change. More and more alcohol will be needed to have the same effect. This is what scientists refer to as "tolerance."

The "tolerance effect" can be experienced with any neurochemical change. Whether it is a substance that is ingested or a behavior that produces the change, the brain and body will eventually adapt. More and more of the substance or of the behavior will be needed. Over time a pattern develops and the activity increases. Addiction specialists usually describe this as "escalation" or as "deterioration" because the pattern gets worse.

Counselors must evaluate this pattern over time. Some addicts can quit the substance for a time but will eventually come back to it, alternating between periods of usage and abstinence. Some alcoholics, for example, don't drink during the week, but binge on the weekend. They may convince themselves that they have control because they can occasionally or regularly stop.

An 86-year-old minister's wife presented with chemical dependency. She was addicted to alcohol and to prescription anxiety medicine. In her 20s she started having a glass of wine every few months. In her denomination, this was a major problem, so she kept doing it in secret. Over the next 60 years her pattern increased. She drank once a month, then once a week, then once a day. When I met her she was consuming a bottle of alcohol a day. Her drinking pattern was causing substance-induced anxiety and her doctor was medicating that. The pattern became a vicious cycle.

Unmanageability

Neurochemical tolerance is the reason addicts crave a substance or some repetitive behavior. These cravings are what can seem to the addict to be out-of-control. They intend to stop but find themselves "drawn" back in. Smokers quit smoking many times but feel the urge to start again, and dieters start their dieting over many times, for example. Cycles like these fuel the feelings of being out-of-control.

Addicts often believe that sobriety is merely an act of the will, and therefore often come to feel they have no willpower. As Christians, they assume that they should be able to stay "sober" without much effort, or if they were just a little bit stronger spiritually they could stick with a decision to quit. Sometimes these attempts at self-control are extreme. In my (Mark) first book about sexual addiction I described a case in which a man plucked out both of his eyes because Jesus said that "If your eye offends you, pluck it out," and he was addicted to pornography.[6]

Addicts pray fervently for help, even "deliverance" from their problems. They may try a variety of spiritual disciplines to stop. They pray, memorize Scripture, meditate, join new churches, and attend Christian 12-step groups galore. Eventually they become discouraged. They have a critical choice to make. Either there is something wrong with them or with God. Anger at self produces shame. Anger at God produces periods of despair and spiritual alienation. It is a terrible dilemma but it can also become the beginning of wisdom, *for self-effort in all its myriad disguises must die.*

Pride, fear, the need to be in control, and the unwillingness to completely surrender to God are also features of addiction and easily become inflamed at this stage.[7] Some addicts are afraid of giving something up that they think has been helping them cope with life for years. Some believe that they can quit when they really want to. Others are afraid that if they confess their problems they will be judged and condemned. Fear of their feelings and fear of rejection lead addicts to deny their problem and hold on to them. In the midst of this chaos, some just give up trying. It is important for Christian counselors to assess for the willingness to get well.

Need for Nurture

Many addicts feel lonely and abandoned. They long for love, affirmation, nurture, and touch. In many cases the substance or behavior is a substitute for true love and fellowship. This may take many forms. Alcoholics may find a friend in the bottle or in the community of other drinkers. Alcohol allows many to be less inhibited; while intoxicated, they may be friendlier and more outgoing. Food addicts may have certain comfort foods that they binge on. They remember that the act of eating may have been the only time they were being held as infants or gathered as a family. Sex addicts equate sex with love and assume that those who would be willing to be sexual with them, even prostitutes, offer them the only love, attention, and touch that they receive. Some sex addicts may even be more in need of the romance and love experienced in their fantasies or in their affairs.[8]

Feelings of loneliness and abandonment lead to feelings of anger and resentment. Addicts wonder why their needs haven't or aren't being met. These feelings may be very old going back into childhood. They can be mad at their spouses or others for not meeting their needs. The sense of anger produces a sense of entitlement, not unlike an angry child. Addicts think that they deserve to get their needs met and they deserve a reward. Loneliness drives anger and anger drives addicts past their own discipline and morals.

Assessment and Diagnosis

Most chemical addictions including alcoholism are defined by standard diagnostic codes (DSM-IV) as being Addiction or a lesser form of addiction, such as Substance Abuse. Behavioral addictions such as a gambling addiction, and sex addiction are being debated in the medical and psychological communities on how to accurately define and include these disorders in the diagnostic system.

The ICD model—the International Classification of Diseases—defines six clear criteria for diagnosing a Substance Abuse disorder, whereby three or more of the following must have been experienced or exhibited at some time during the previous year:

1. *Control problems:* Difficulties in controlling substance-taking behavior in terms of its onset, termination, or levels of use
2. *Compulsive use:* A strong desire or sense of compulsion—of being driven—to take the substance
3. *Increasing/exclusive focus:* Progressive neglect of alternative pleasures or interests plus the increased amount of time necessary to obtain or take the substance or to recover from its effects
4. *Continuing harm of denial:* Persisting with substance use despite clear evidence of overtly harmful consequences, depressive mood states consequent to heavy use, or drug related impairment of reasoning, judgment, and cognitive functionin

5. *Tolerance effect:* Evidence of tolerance—increased doses of the psychoactive substance or mixing in new drugs are required in order to achieve effects originally produced by lower doses

6. *Withdrawal symptoms:* A physiological withdrawal state when substance use has ceased or been reduced, as evidence by: the characteristic withdrawal syndrome for the substance; or use of the same (or a closely related) substance with the intention of relieving or avoiding withdrawal symptoms

Most addiction diagnostic codes provide similar lists and suggest that addiction is present if a constellation of similar and interrelated symptom indicators is present. The competent Christian counselor will always remember that he or she is looking for a pattern of behaviors and vulnerabilities. Each field of addiction has developed checklists, true and false tests, and other diagnostic guides to assist in the assessment of addiction.

Intuition and discernment. The spiritual discernment and experiential intuition of the counselor is also important in diagnosis, as the self-perception of the addict are often inaccurate. Addicts who have come to a point of helplessness and perceived unmanageability are on the verge of owning their addiction, yet may also fight and deny that reality. The competent Christian counselor will be able to discern this struggle and will also know when the addicted person has not come to this point, even when they claim they have. Some addicts will still be in some state of denial and delusion about their problems, and will often lie about their readiness for change.

Accurate self-reporting may not be possible. The report of others, such as the spouse or other family members will be important. An interesting form of assessment is to ask a potential addict how he or she theologically justifies acting out behavior. For example, how does an alcohol drinker justify drunken behavior, or how does a food addict justify the poor stewardship of being overweight, or how does a sex addict justify adultery, or how does a gambler justify chronic debt?

Multifaceted Addiction Treatment

The reasons for addiction are multi-faceted. The treatment of addiction, therefore, will also require a variety of approaches. Treatment must maintain a careful balance between confronting the addict's denial and minimization and supporting them when they do the painful and difficult work of honest disclosure and directed change. At times, direct and intense confrontation is necessary because of the tendency for denial and minimization, but also remember that it is quite a threatening and shame-filled experience for a person to openly discuss the secrets and sins and despairs of their addictions. Following are the five classic areas that must be addressed:

Physical Stabilization and Self-care

Addicts may have caused physical damage to their bodies. Alcoholics will have possible neurological, gastrointestinal, or liver complications. Food addicts may starve themselves to death or suffer the effects of chronic obesity. Sex addicts run the risk of sexually transmitted diseases or a variety of sexual dysfunctions. Any addict also runs the risk of stress resulting from chronic fear and anxiety, often due to the consequences of the addiction.

It is always wise for addicts to undergo a complete medical evaluation. Alcoholics and some drug addicts may need to be hospitalized in order to stabilize the detoxification effect of stopping use. Anorexics may also need to be stabilized in the hospital to prevent the effects of chronic malnutrition.

When stabilization has been achieved, it is also wise for an addict to undergo a thorough neuropsychiatric evaluation. Levels of depression must be determined. Assessment for the presence of a variety of forms of attention deficit disorder is also important. Some addicts will need pharmacological help for depression. Others will need different drugs that help manage the brains needs for constant stimulation. It is always wise to develop a relationship with a competent psychiatrist who can perform these kinds of evaluations and services.

Abstinence from the drug of choice will, over time, change the level of neurochemical tolerance the addict has developed over the years. With help and sure accountability, alcoholics and drug users are able to achieve total abstinence from a substance. Food addicts may be able to abstain from certain kinds of food.

Behavior addicts often have a harder time at abstaining, as secrecy is easier to maintain and accountability is so much more difficult. Some, like gamblers, can stop certain behaviors altogether. Sex addicts, however, can arouse themselves by fantasizing about sexual behavior. The protocol with sex addicts is to have them abstain from all forms of sexual activity for a period of time, even if married, in order to achieve a detoxification effect from sinful sexual activity.

Finally, addicts will need to learn adequate self-care. As opposed to Paul's teaching, they have been treating their body more like the city dump than the temple. Being tired or physically depleted makes any addict more vulnerable to acting out behavior.

Behavioral Change

Addicts have developed strong, highly programmed, even automatic behavior patterns in order to maintain their addiction. They will go to extraordinary lengths to deny, minimize, or rationalize this addictive behavior.

Focus honesty and behavior change. Therapist must maintain a strong initial focus on honesty and behavior change. When the addict seeks to divert discussion to family, emotional, or relationship concerns prematurely, the therapist must redirect attention to behavior. While effective treatment may eventually address these issues, the clinician must help the addict stop using them to escape dealing with his or her addictive behavior.

One way of doing this is to link the tangential topics the client raises with the central issue of their addiction. For example, a counselor might refocus a client's response toward the behavior in this way: "So how is the way you approach your anger toward your wife similar to the way you acted out your anger in your sex addiction?" "How is your tendency to denigrate yourself reflected in your addiction ritual?" The assumption here is that addiction has a life of its own and operates apart from other concerns. Unlike many other clinical issues, addiction is both symptom and disease.

Changing ritual behavior patterns. All addicts will need to change certain behavior patterns that lead them into their use. These behaviors are referred to in the addiction community as "rituals." The competent Christian counselor will help an addict assess the cycle of ritual behavior and how he or she acts out. Taking detailed histories of usage and behavioral patterns is essential. When this information has been sorted out, addicts must establish boundaries against those behaviors. Alcoholics will need to avoid certain friends, areas of towns, or stressful situations that lead them to drink. Food addicts may need to avoid going to the grocery store in the early days of recovery, or they may need to schedule meals at regular times and find help to eat at those times religiously. Sex addicts will need to avoid people and places that trigger them into their fantasies or "connecting" rituals. For example, those sex addicts who use the computer to connect will need to become accountable for every minute of access to it.

Can't do it alone. No addict can recover by him or herself. Yet, most feel that he or she should be strong enough to overcome this alone. Shame increases as the number of attempts to do so increases. The Bible teaches that we should never undertake a long journey or complicated project alone. In Nehemiah 2, for example, the king allows Nehemiah to go home to rebuild the wall of the city of Jerusalem, but he also sends the army officers and cavalry. Later in chapter 4 of Nehemiah, the strategy is that half the men build and half the men stand guard.

Accountability in recovery. The key to overcoming any addiction is accountability. All addicts need a number of people around them who help monitor and maintain behavior. These people will also provide support, encouragement, and affirmation. In the 12-step tradition of Alcoholics Anonymous, this is the power of the meeting and the people in it. Alcoholics have also learned they need a sponsor to help guide the process of accountability.

Addicts should not think that only one person can hold them accountable. They begin recovery believing that they are alone and abandoned. If they only have one person for accountability, they may fall into their abandonment routine if that one person is not available. Addicts will need an accountability group, at least four or five people who really know them and whom they can call any time, day or night. Remembering that loneliness is a major factor in addiction, finding the fellowship of a group will be extremely important.[9]

There are innumerable 12-step groups today for many different addictions. These phone numbers can usually be found in the local yellow pages. More and more, Christians are trying to set up Christ-centered support groups in local churches. In the field of sexual addiction, for example, several ministries are creating materials for such groups. Consult Web sites like *www.faithfulandtrueministries.com* for useful information. One Christian group, *Overcomers Outreach* (1994), has tried to create Christian materials for general addiction support groups.

The Nehemiah principle. Nehemiah, again in chapter 4, knew that the attack of the enemy could come at any time, and at the weakest place. He prepared for this. Addicts will need to prepare in their times of strength and resolve to change their thinking and behavior in times of weakness and attack. It is not enough to wait until the attack comes. Automatic and daily preparations should happen. For example, any addict should have daily phone calls from the accountability group and regular attendance at support groups even on those days when they don't feel like they need to. Following is a short list of accountability principles that should be followed by all addicts.

1. Never try to recover alone.
2. Fellowship is equal to freedom from addiction.
3. Prepare in times of strength and resolve for times of attack and weakness.
4. Be in intimate accountability with at least four people.

Emotional and Cognitive Restructuring

Addicts tend to come from families that have wounded them emotionally, physically, sexually, and/or spiritually.[10] They have deep sadness, feelings of shame, and loneliness.

Protect against emotional triggers. It is vitally important for these family and emotional issues to be addressed, once the behavior of addiction changes. Remember that *unhealed wounds raise painful feelings that often result in relapse.* Any stimulus that potentially triggers an addict into old, painful feelings can provoke the old answers and addictive activities that were used to medicate and change those feelings. These rationalizations and lies are referred to as *"stinkin' thinkin'"* in the AA vernacular. Cognitive restructuring involves identification, confrontation, and correction of this erroneous thinking and this requires a psychoeducational approach that should not be avoided. It is irresponsible to suggest that a person should just "forgive and forget." It is also irresponsible to suggest that a person who never let go of their anger so as not to get hurt again. Healing of life's hurt can be a lifetime journey but there are ways to get stuck in sadness and anger.

The competent Christian counselor will either be skilled in this kind of work or will know good cognitive therapists for referral. The process of healing requires several factors:

1. Understanding the nature of the harm that caused the woundedness
2. Providing support for the importance of dealing with it
3. Addressing any anger or bitterness that was part of the experience
4. Allowing the person to grieve the losses associated with the woundedness
5. Helping the person find meaning in the suffering of the experience
6. Guiding the person in the process of forgiveness of those who caused the harm
7. Adopting healthy new biblical thinking and self-talk

Thought-stopping interventions. Every addict starts his or her acting out behavior by obsessing or fantasizing about the substance or behavior. This very thought life is an attempt to alter mood, to relieve pain. Christian counselors will hear the fantasies of addicts and know that they are windows into the mind and heart of the addicted person. Substances and behaviors are often ways that addicts seek to heal wounds from the past. It is mostly useless to tell an addict to stop thinking about a substance or behavior. Seek understanding for what the thought life, the fantasies, mean. If healing can be achieved for the wound that the fantasy seeks to correct, the fantasy will eventually disappear.

Covert sensitization. Another approach is to directly intervene in an addict's fantasies. These fantasies are self-reinforcing because they are typically followed, in the case of a sex addict for example, by sexual arousal. In covert sensitization, the addict is instructed to articulate his or her preferred fantasy, and then to add to that fantasy an imagined aversive scene (such as the embarrassment of being caught and punished). Both exposing the secret fantasy and associating an aversive outcome reduces its attracting power. The goal is to reduce the reinforcement value of the fantasy by pairing it with an aversive consequence. Finally, the offender also adds a reward scene to the failed fantasy, emphasizing a positive outcome associated with successful control.

Relationship Repair

People who live with addicts know how painfully difficult it can be. Sometimes the spouses of addicts are referred to as "co-addicts" or "co-dependents."[11] The assumption of terms like these is that they somehow ignore, tolerate and even enable addiction. Competent counseling will need to assess the emotional and spiritual health of people living with addicts. It is safe to continue to live with them if they don't get help? Do co-addicts also suffer from their own wounds or addictions? It would not be uncommon for a spouse who lives with an alcoholic to also have drinking problems. My (Mark) research has shown that about one third of spouses who live with sex addicts are also sex addicts.[12]

Counselors should assess factors that brought spouses together. New theories are being developed which suggest that people find each other and seek to play out patterns of family of origin trauma with each other. Sex abuse survivors may, even unconsciously, find another sex abuse survivor to be in relationship. The theory is that addicts may be trying to replay old patterns, in order to find a different result. A corollary of this is that addicts will replay old family patterns, trying to be the one who controls the situation rather than the one who is victimized. The attempt to find healing from a relationship to a spouse for early life wounds is generally referred to as "trauma bonding."[13]

Counselors who deal with addicts and their spouses know that sometimes even the slightest of triggers can provoke rage, anxiety, or sadness. Deep healing work with both addict and spouse, together or individually, is vital to the restoration of marriage. Simple communication strategies or intimacy building exercises will not work in these situations. Work on the deep wounds with both partners is essential to helping these partners relate on the most basic of levels.

Suffer the little children. The children of addicts will be wounded by addiction. Counselors will do well if they are able to address these issues and be of support for the entire family. It is not easy to engage family members, even spouses, if there is the addict to blame for all problems. Gentle forms of education and support can be helpful. Helping family members to be in support groups for others with similar problems can help them see their own responsibilities for the dysfunctions of entire family systems. Support groups of many kinds exist for those who live in relationship with addicts.

The healing of relationships is an essential part of treatment for addicts. Couples counseling and family counseling are important. Addicts and those around them should be encouraged to be in networks of support. One of the best antidotes for addiction and co-addiction is fellowship with other growing Christians. Addicts have a profound longing for nurture. Christian counselors must be able to help them find it in true and lasting relationships.[14]

The potential for developing intimacy and self-honesty is crucial to addiction recovery. Addicts, in their shame, may feel that no one loves them and that if they talk about their most intimate feelings or reveal their worst acting out experiences, others will run from them. They will need to "practice" telling the truth to counselors and those in a support group, who are less emotionally threatening than lifetime loved ones (e.g. spouses). They will then be able to take greater risks by being honest with loved ones.

Victim empathy. Multifaceted addiction treatment encourages addicts to develop empathy for loved ones hurt by their addiction. The addict is taught to understand, and even experience the pain they cause their victims. By maximizing empathy for others, it becomes more likely that the addict will treat others as persons, rather than as objects to be used for their own gratification. As addicts develop victim empathy and consider the consequences of their actions, they may present with suicidal ideation, shame, and guilt. Jesus incarnated victim empathy, and a counselor's Christian background can aid in connecting the incongruence between client behavior and their spiritual worldviews.

The road to recovery in relationship is long and labor intensive, but the possibility of profound intimacy with others is well worth the task.

Spiritual Renewal

Addicts are spiritually immature by nature. They often search for child-like, black-and-white answers to their problems. If addicts have developmental issues it is easy to see that they will also have childish and adolescent beliefs about God.[15] They may have become angry with God for not "delivering" them of their cravings, longings, and lust. There are several spiritual challenges for addicts when working with Christian counselors, pastors, and lay helpers:

Addicts must address their own need to control. Many of them may have committed to Christ intellectually but not emotionally. They may be angry with God for not healing or delivering them. They have a hard time letting go of the high and the mood alteration of their addictive activities. Addicts have become accustomed to their ways. Being enslaved to addiction is what they know.

In the 13th and 14th chapters of Numbers, God is trying to prepare the people of Israel to go to the Promised Land. God has already done a mighty work in delivering them out of the land of Egypt. They are being led by one of the greatest religious leaders of all time, Moses. Spies who have been sent to survey the new land give a negative report of how difficult it will be to go there because of "giants" in the land. In the opening of the 14th chapter, the people cry out for a new leader and declare that it would be better to go back to Egypt and die as slaves than to go to a place they don't know.

This is how addicts often react. They don't know a new place or a better way. They will want to hang on to the familiar. They are unable to trust God to see them through unknown and frightening future events. It is an issue of trust and total surrender. They will need to be guided to totally turn their lives over to God and face their own fears and need to control. In John 5, Jesus (our master psychologist) asks the paralyzed man at the pool of Bethesda, "Do you want to get well?" It seems like a silly question for a man who has been lying by this healing water for 38 years. The man, however, doesn't answer affirmatively but instead gives excuses for why he hasn't been able to get into the pool.

Christian counselors will also have to ask this hard question, "Do you want to get well and are you willing to take the risks, make the surrender, and do the hard work that will be necessary?" In Numbers 14, it is Joshua who says to the stubborn people, "We can do this with God's help."

Much of what has motivated addicts historically is fear and anxiety. They have sought to avoid consequences and trouble. They have been selfish in their pursuits. In recovery they will need to learn to be motivated for others. In Nehemiah 4, Nehemiah offers a great battle cry to the people. He tells them to fight for the brothers, sons and daughters, wives, and their homes. This is better motivation for addicts. I have never known an addict who has recovered and found sobriety just for him or herself. The 12th step of Alcoholics Anonymous says that having had a spiritual awakening; addicts should carry the message to others. Service to others is an important part of maturing spiritually, and is vital to getting well.

In Ephesians 5:1–3, Paul tells us that we should be "imitators of God, just as dearly loved children," and that we should "lead a life of sacrifice, just as Christ loved the church." Addicts must learn to lead a life of sacrifice, giving over their lusts and cravings. Addiction is selfish; recovery is selfless.

Addicts don't know a better life. In most cases addicts don't know true love and intimacy—they don't know a true relationship with God. Addictions are embraced as the perverse substitutes—false love and false intimacy.[16] Christian counselors must be able to model to them what these things are like. An addict needs a true spiritual vision. One of the great challenges in working with addicts is in helping them exchange the short-term highs for long-term truth. Intimacy with God and others is so much more satisfying than the high of any addiction.

When the Jewish people wanted to return to Egypt and live as slaves rather than go to the Promised Land, it was Joshua who reminded them to depend on God. Christian counselors will need to be like Joshua. Leaders like Joshua can also be found in those recovering people who have achieved a number of years of sobriety. These recovering people have assembled a more serene life and testimony of God's ongoing work in their lives. Networking newly assessed and willing to recover addicts with these "old timers" is often one of the joys of Christian counseling.

Christian counselors are able to place more emphasis on spirituality in an appropriate clinical manner as the cornerstone of treatment. It is likely that addicts seeking Christian counselors have done so on purpose, and this can be a powerful beginning to recovery, as well as prognosis for continued alliance, rapport, and investment in treatment. Attitudes toward religion can also provide diagnostic clues. "By examining the patient's religious views in the context of his or her personality dysfunctions, the clinician can differentiate between valid expression of spirituality and defensive religiosity."[17]

Putting It All Together

Nearly three decades of scientific research have yielded 13 fundamental principles that characterize effective drug abuse treatment. These principles are detailed in *NIDA's Principles of Drug Addiction Treatment: A Research-Based Guide,*[18] from the National Institute of Drug Abuse.

1. No single treatment is appropriate for all individuals. Matching treatment settings, interventions, and services to each patient's problems and needs is critical.

2. Treatment needs to be readily available. Treatment applicants can be lost if treatment is not immediately available or readily accessible.

3. Effective treatment attends to multiple needs of the individual, not just his or her drug use. Treatment must address the individual's drug use and associated medical, psychological, social, vocational, and legal problems.

4. At different times during treatment, a patient may develop a need for medical services, family therapy, vocational rehabilitation, and social and legal services.

5. Remaining in treatment for an adequate period of time is critical for treatment effectiveness. The time depends on an individual's needs. For most patients, the threshold of significant improvement is reached at about 3 months in treatment. Additional treatment can produce further progress. Programs should include strategies to prevent patients from leaving treatment prematurely.

6. Individual and/or group counseling and other behavioral therapies are critical components of effective treatment for addiction. In therapy, patients address motivation, build skills to resist drug use, replace drug-using activities with constructive and rewarding non-drug-using activities, and improve problem-solving abilities. Behavioral therapy also facilitates interpersonal relationships.

7. Medications are an important element of treatment for many patients, especially when combined with counseling and other behavioral therapies. Methadone and levo-alpha-acetylmethodol (LAAM) help persons addicted to opiates stabilize their lives and reduce their drug use. Naltrexone is effective for some opiate addicts and some patients with co-occurring alcohol dependence. Nicotine patches or gum, or an oral medication, such as buproprion, can help persons addicted to nicotine.

8. Addicted or drug-abusing individuals with coexisting mental disorders should have both disorders treated in an integrated way.

9. Medical detoxification is only the first stage of addiction treatment and by itself does little to change long-term drug use. Medical

detoxification manages the acute physical symptoms of withdrawal. For some individuals it is a precursor to effective drug addiction treatment.

10. Treatment does not need to be voluntary to be effective. Sanctions or enticements in the family, employment setting, or criminal justice system can significantly increase treatment entry, retention, and success.

11. Possible drug use during treatment must be monitored continuously. Monitoring a patient's drug and alcohol use during treatment, such as through urinalysis, can help the patient withstand urges to use drugs. Such monitoring also can provide early evidence of drug use so that treatment can be adjusted.

12. Treatment programs should provide assessment for HIV/AIDS, hepatitis B and C, tuberculosis and other infectious diseases, and counseling to help patients modify or change behaviors that place them or others at risk of infection. Counseling can help patients avoid high-risk behavior and help people who are already infected manage their illness.

13. Recovery from drug addiction can be a long-term process and frequently requires multiple episodes of treatment. As with other chronic illnesses, relapses to drug use can occur during or after successful treatment episodes. Participation in self-help support programs during and following treatment often helps maintain abstinence.

Restoration and Relapse

In aftercare treatment planning, one must include a clear plan of restoration. This plan must include a great deal of accountability and ongoing oversight. Relapse and recidivism rates for addicts still remain relatively high after completion of treatment. One must be on guard to discern the role of spiritual transformation in the life of the addict. Addicts will say—and genuinely believe, along with many others supporting the addict—that they have committed or recommitted their lives to Christ, that God has forgiven their sin, and they have been healed from their addictive desires.

The implication here involves an odd paradox—that if the therapist continues to insist on strong accountability or a need for continued treatment, they are doubting the power of God to change lives. This is a very difficult bind for Christian counselors. On one hand we must seriously believe in the power of God to heal and change lives, while also being aware that healing is almost always a gradual process. Furthermore, the Christian counselor knows as well as anyone the subtle power of sin and the ways of the world to tempt the addict to use again. Even in the midst of the healing process, offenders can and do experience relapse—some relapse numerous times—before eventually getting control over the problem.

We must balance the need to affirm healing in the offender with appropriate concern for the reality of relapse and renewed addiction. The church, as a community of grace and healing, looks to the hope of the gospel for the power to change the behavior of addicted persons, to heal the wounds of their victims, and to provide reconciliation with the body of Christ.

Conclusion

Working with addicts is usually both challenging and frustrating. A competent Christian counselor will often direct and guide an addict through a variety of resources and network of people. Sometimes the counselor will be like a team leader, shepherding counselors and others who are working with the addict, his or her spouse and children, and addressing other aspects of the problem.

Beware of those who don't have willingness. One sign of an addict willing to recover is a felt sense of brokenness and humility. If you continue to encounter denial, selfishness, or stubbornness, don't think that you have to be the one to make the final breakthrough. Establish your own boundaries of whom you are willing to work with. Even Jesus let some walk away. I often wonder how successful He must have felt as He hung on the cross and looked at the lack of faith in those around Him.

When you are thanked by those who have been broken, felt powerless, and who are working hard, you will see a growing life of peace and serenity, major life changes, and restored relationships. The personal, familial, and intergenerational cycle of addiction can be broken. This is what makes what we do so worthwhile.

ENDNOTES

1.   2003 National survey on drug use and health, available from, <http://oas.samhsa.gov/nhsda.htm>.

2. See Daniel Amen, *Change your brain change your life* (New York: Random House, 1998); and H. Milkman, and Sunderwirth, S., *Craving for ecstasy: The consciousness and chemistry of escape* (Lexington, MA: Lexington Books, 1987).

3. Steven Arterburn, *Addicted to love* (United Kingdom: Vine Books, 2003).

4. Patrick Carnes, *Don't call it love* (New York: Bantam Books, 1991).

5. Ibid.

6. Mark Laaser, *Faithful and true,* (Grand Rapids, MI: Zondervan, 1996).

7. E. Kurtz, *Not God: A history of alcoholics anonymous* (Center City, MN: Hazelden, 1979).

8. B. Schaeffer, *Is it love or is it addiction* (Center City, MN: Hazelden, 2000).

9. *The twelve steps: A spiritual journey* (San Diego: Recovery Publications, 1988).

10. Patrick Carnes, *The betrayal bond* (Deerfield Beach, FL: Health Communications, Inc., 1997).

11. Melody Beattie, *Codependent no more* (New York: Harper/Hazelden, 1987).

12. These results are as yet unpublished but were discussed at the First Annual Vanderbilt Symposium On Sexual Addiction/Compulsivity in March, 2001.

13. Patrick Carnes, *The betrayal bond* (Deerfield Beach, FL: Health Communications, Inc., 1997).

14. Patrick Carnes, Laaser, D., and Laaser, M., *Open hearts* (Wickensburg, AZ: Gentle Path Press, 2000).

15. Gerald May, *Addiction and grace* (San Francisco: Harper and Row, 1988); and J. Miller, *Sin: Overcoming the ultimate deadly addiction* (San Francisco: Harper and Row, 1987).

16. Harry Schaumburg, *False intimacy: Understanding the struggle of sexual addiction* (Colorado Springs: NavPress, 1992).

17. R. H. Earle, Earle, M. R., and Osborn, K., *Sex addiction: Case studies and management* (New York: Brunner/Mazel, Inc., 1995).

18. NIDA's Principles of Drug Addiction Treatment: A Research-Based Guide, available at<http://www.nida.nih.gov/PODAT/PODATIndex.html>.

13

Sexual Addiction

Mark R. Laaser

In our current sexually absorbed culture, working with sex addicts is a growth industry.

RECENT STATEMENT OF A COLLEAGUE OF MINE.

"Warren" was a pillar of his church. He was always seen as a great family man. He attended church all the time and often taught Bible classes. His wife and family seemed happy and content. As a Christian counselor at this church, you were surprised when he came in one day because he had been fired from his job for looking at internet pornography.

In the late 1970s, in three separate parts of the country, groups of men started gathering to use the 12 steps of Alcoholics Anonymous to try to get free of their sexual sins.[1] Many of them were recovering alcoholics at first and knew that these principles had helped them get sober. It was the first time that the word addiction came to be applied to sex and the term sex addiction was born.

In 1981, Dr. Patrick Carnes, a clinical psychologist, wrote the first book on the subject, *Out of the Shadows*.[2] Today there is still a clinical debate in the medical and psychological communities as to whether or not sex can truly be addictive. Thousands of recovering sex addicts would attest that using this diagnosis is helpful in knowing how to find freedom.

I write myself from the perspective of being a recovering sex addict. I began looking at pornography at age 11 and progressed into daily acts of masturbation. I started to visit massage parlors while in graduate school. In my early professional life I began having sexual encounters with a variety of women even to the point of being sexual with some women I counseled.

In 1987 I was intervened on and fired from every job I was doing. Fortunately a recovering alcoholic was a part of that intervention and knew that there was a treatment center directed by Dr. Carnes in Minneapolis where I went for in-patient treatment. I have been sober since that time and God has been gracious to me (Phil. 1:6) and allowed me to have a worldwide ministry trying to bring hope to others that they can be free.

My wife, Deb, stayed with me and has been a faithful companion in the journey of healing. From 1988 through 1992 I trained and worked with Dr. Carnes at the same hospital where I was treated. In 1992, I published the first book in the Christian community to address sexual addiction. This book has recently been revised.[3]

There have been other wise counselors who have written helpful books in this field: Harry Schaumberg[4], Ralph Earle[5], Pat Means[6], Russ Willingham[7], Earl Wilson,[8] and Steve Arteburn and Fred Stoeker.[9] We now know much more about how to identify sexual addiction and how to treat it. This is of paramount importance in our current culture. Cases like Warren's are becoming more and more common.

To realize how sexually saturated our culture is, simply remember what the availability of pornography was in the 1950s when Hugh Hefner published the first issue of *Playboy* and what it is today given the availability of it on the Internet. Now take note of every sexual stimulus that hits you on a daily basis as you watch TV, read a magazine, listen to the radio, go to a movie, or visit a shopping mall. You might even think about it when you go to church and notice what even the girls in the youth groups are wearing.

At a recent conference of the Coalition of Christian Colleges, one president told me that in one recent study 50% of his students lost their virginity while at school. Even in an attempt to stay "virgins" our youth are turning to all kinds of practices short of intercourse, most notably oral sex. Kids today are "hooking up" and having "friends with benefits." Sex has become part of even casual friendships.

Christianity Today magazine through its *Leadership Journal* discovered in a survey of pastors that 40% of evangelical pastors admitted to looking at

Internet pornography.[10] One third of those said they had looked at it in the last year. There is a moral crisis in Christian leadership and rarely a day goes by when we don't hear of some pastor or leader who has fallen. Satan has been attacking great church leaders since the beginning of time. Think of Samson who visited a prostitute in Gaza and had perhaps a love addiction with Delilah. Then there was King David who had an affair with Bathsheba and committed murder to cover it up. What of Solomon whose 700 wives and 300 hundred concubines turned him away from the true worship of God.

While there has not been pure empirical research on the prevalence of sexual addiction in the general population, conservative estimates in the field would place it as around 10%. Some also speculate that the incidence amongst Christians might be higher. In informal and unpublished research it has been found that the use of in-room pornography increases at hotels hosting Christian conferences. The Leadership study cited above would also cause us to wonder. Promise Keepers did a study several years ago and found that as many as 60% of the attendees at its conferences said they struggled with pornography.

If ever there was time to understand how sexual sin can become addictive, it is now. Paul's time was not much different when he said in Romans 12:2, "Don't be conformed to the ways of the world." Roman culture was also saturated with sex. What is even more frightening today is how available sex is electronically on the Internet. Pornography is the number one selling product on the Internet. People who might have been otherwise inhibited are using the relative privacy of the Internet to see levels of pornography that used to be available only in the darkest of places. Prostitutes now have their own web sites. Matching services can find you a sexual partner, willing to do all manner of sexual practices, in less than 24 hours.

What we are seeing is a dramatic rise in the number of cases of sexual addiction. Our churches are being attacked by the moral failure of the members and leaders. It is time for Christian counselors to get the knowledge they need to be able to identify and treat this terrible disease.

Definition of Sexual Addiction

There are five classic criteria that define sexual addiction:

Unmanageability. A sex addict believes that his problems with sex are out of control and that he or she is powerless. They have tried to stop and can't. They have prayed and beseeched God to remove their lust. Many have sought salvation in different churches and denominations. What is really true is that sex addicts hang on to wanting to control their own lives. They are participants in original sin, the inability to trust God. Sex addicts are "double-minded" (James 1:8). A part of them wants to get well and a part of them doesn't. Sex has been the way they seek love and nurture most of their lives. They may be Christians, but they want God to magically cure them without them doing any work. What is unmanageable is that they haven't totally surrendered to God.

Carnes was the first to describe that unmanageability leads to a cycle of addiction.[11] It starts with fantasy or preoccupation with sexual thoughts at the top of the cycle. It then progresses to rituals, which lead to acting out at the bottom of the cycle. Acting out brings despair. Most sex addicts experience depression at some level and many have even thought of suicide. Despair is a feeling that sex addicts cope with by turning back to fantasies and the whole cycle repeats endlessly.

Neurochemical Tolerance. For anything to be addictive, according to modern psychiatry, it must produce a chemical tolerance in the brain. This means that the brain will literally crave more and more of the same substance or activity to achieve the same effect. This is because receptor sites on nerve endings become desensitized to the chemicals that the addiction creates in the brain.

For an activity like sex to create this chemical tolerance it must be capable of producing powerful neurochemicals. Such effects have been well discussed by researchers like Milkman and Sunderwirth among others.[12] Depending on what kind of sex, love, or romance a person is thinking about or doing, he or she can elevate adrenaline, serotonin, dopamine, and the powerful heroin-like catecholamines.

Progression. Because of the tolerance effect sex addiction will progress over time. It will get worse. This does not mean necessarily that an addict will progress from basic sexual activities like pornography or masturbation, but it always will mean that more and more activity will be needed. Over the life of an addict there will be a steady progression. This may take weeks, especially with Internet types of addiction, or years to develop. An addict may go through periods of time when he or she controls the addiction, sometimes referred to as "white knuckling." Eventually, the addiction will progress. In taking a sexual history of an addict a counselor will see how the level of sexual activity has increased over time.

Feeling Avoidance. Addicts are lonely, angry, and anxious. They need to deal with these "negative" feelings by ignoring them or by changing them. The neurochemistry of sex addiction can either elevate their mood (through adrenaline, serotonin, or dopamine) or if they are stressed it can moderate their mood (through the catecholamines). Sex addicts are literally "pharmacologists of their own brains." It is really true to say that they are drug addicts.

Consequences. Immoral sexual activity will always lead to negative consequences. These can be spiritual as in estrangement from God, emotional as in greater loneliness and stress, financial, legal, physical, vocational, and social. Addicts can be arrested, lose their jobs, spends hundreds of thousands of dollars, get AIDS or STDs, or wind up divorced. Part of the unmanageability is that the fear of consequences is not enough to stop them from their sexual sins.

Sex addiction can be expressed in any sexual behavior. At one end of the spectrum are those who simply fantasize and masturbate. On the other end are those who commit sexual crimes. Even marital sexuality can be addictive if an addict is engaging in it simply for the purposes of avoiding, and not expressing, intimacy. Do not equate sexual sin with sexual addiction. There are many who sexually sin but who do not become involved in repetitive, progressive, and unmanageable behaviors. To have an affair, look at pornography, or even commit a sexual crime is not automatically addictive. Applying the criteria is always the answer.

There are no diagnostic codes for sexual addiction in the Diagnostic and Statistical Manual (DSM) of the American Psychiatric Association. We hope that one day this will change. In the meantime, we often use comorbid mental health diagnoses such as Depression, Anxiety, Post-Traumatic Stress Disorder, and Adjustment Disorder. Some forms of sexual acting out fit into existing categories such as the paraphilias, voyeurism, or exhibitionism.

More and more we believe that women suffer from sexual addiction just as frequently as men do. With women, sex addiction is more often experienced with romance or love addiction. Young women, however, are being trained through culture to be more visually stimulated by pornography and to be more sexually aggressive than originally thought. According to one pioneer in the field, Marnie Ferree, women also experience a harder time asking for help and submitting to treatment as the stigma for women is often greater.[13] While a man may be seen as a "stud," a woman may be seen as a "slut" or "whore."

Etiology

Causative factors can be understood in five categories:

Emotional. Sex addicts are emotionally wounded. In a classic study Carnes found that 81% of them were sexually abused; 74% were physically abused; and 97% were emotionally abused.[14] More study is needed to see if the same kind of abuse statistics apply to the legions of men and women who are getting addicted to the Internet. My own experience would suggest that they are lower and that it is more the factor of cultural enticement that seduces the average Internet addict. Abuse can take two forms: invasive types (such as being sexually molested, physically hit, or emotionally yelled at) and abandonment types (sometimes called neglect). I, personally, have never known a sex addict that was not abandoned in some way. These two types of abuse leave an addict starving for love and nurture but not feeling that he or she deserves it.

Abuse leaves addicts lonely, angry, frightened, and confused. They develop core beliefs: I am a bad and worthless person. No one will love me as I am. No one will take care of me but me. Sex is my most important need. At some time in the life of an addict sex becomes a solution to the feelings. When it does it gets "cemented" in the brain as the way out or escape from the feelings. This is referred to in our field as the "arousal template." It could happen at any time in the life cycle. Whatever age the addict is, he or she will get developmentally arrested, or stuck, at that age. This leaves most at very immature levels.

The arousal template may also determine what kinds of sex a person will get addicted to later on. For example, his mother profoundly emotionally abused Larry when he was a boy. He thought she hated him. There was a family down the street that had four girls in it that were roughly his age. This was in the 1950s. They would play together. The girls would always be dressed in dresses with frilly white socks and patent leather shoes. Play would sometimes involve the old "I'll show you mine, if you show me yours" games. When he was married, Larry longed for his wife to dress up in fancy dresses with white frilly socks and patent leather shoes. He said that he couldn't get aroused if she didn't do this.

For some addicts it may simply be that looking at pornography or masturbating brought the pleasurable feelings that were a way out of the lonely and negative ones. Later in life, when they find themselves compulsively looking at the Internet, it is really one of the oldest solutions they know to deal with their feelings.

Relational. Abuse can lead to relationship and intimacy difficulties. If a child does not learn healthy connections, how will he or she know about them as adults? Lately, attachment theory has begun to explain how devastating this can be.[15] Addicts suffer from intimacy disorder. They feel that if they were really known, people would hate them and leave them. This predisposes them to lying and avoiding the truth. They long for approval and usually develop approval disorders which many have called "co-dependency." This is at a deep level of their soul.

Addicts hope that their relationships, especially their marriages will solve all these attachment and intimacy issues. When they don't seem to, at least in the magical way addicts would like, they get angry with themselves and others. They may think that they have found the wrong spouses or friends. As they take this feeling further, it may lead them to think that they need, and even deserve, to find better relationships. This can obviously lead to affairs and other unhealthy relationships. Their co-dependency can keep them locked into these relationship and they wind up feeling trapped.

The bottom line etiologically is that sex addicts may feel that the only way they get their needs for love and nurture met is through sex and/or infatuated romance.

Physical. I have already described that one of the main features of addiction is that addicts become neurochemically tolerant to the chemicals that sex, love, and romance produce. They are literally physically dependent. When sex is combined with excitement and danger, adrenaline can be dependently involved. It is very common for sex addicts to be addicted to other substances or activities that produce these same chemicals. Addicts can be addicted to one or the other and, sometimes, trade them off against each other. This is referred to as "Addiction Interaction Disorder." For example, Carnes found that roughly 50% of all sex addicts are also alcoholics.[16] In the same study Carnes also found that the more severe the abuse was to the addict as a child, the more likely he/she will have multiple addictions.

Mike realized that he was an alcoholic in his early 20s. It took him several years to finally go to AA, but eventually he achieved sobriety. Over the next years he discovered that smoking, eating, and his sexual activity (mainly pornography and masturbation) gradually increased. He was bewildered by the ongoing difficulties he had. Finally, someone introduced him to a program for sex addiction and he found recovery in this area of his life too. Today he knows that recovering from sex addiction was even harder than his alcohol recovery because he didn't need to go to a bar, just his head, to get his supply.

Addicts like Mike realize that recovering from food or sex is more difficult than recovering from a substance because with food and sex they can't totally stop. These are normal, natural, and necessary desires of the body.

Many researchers now believe that there is a correlation between Attention Deficit Disorder (ADD or ADHD) and addiction. One belief is that untreated ADD will "metastasize" to addiction. Suffering from ADD can mean that a person is bored and craves stimulation in whatever way they can get it. He or she may also be distracted more easily by the stimuli of sex so prevalent in the world.

In one study, conducted by me and my colleague Richard Blankenship, we found that in a population of positively diagnosed sex addicts, roughly 70% tested as possibly having ADD and roughly 50% tested as highly probable for ADD. I have become very impressed with the work of Dr. Daniel Amen who does SPEC brain scans.[17] He is doing pioneering work in distinguishing types of ADD. We are working together to research what correlations there are between these types and sex addiction.

Cognitive and Behavioral. Sex addicts, like alcoholics and other addicts, suffer from "stinking thinking." We might call this "distorted cognitive beliefs." They have lost touch with who they really are in Christ and believe themselves to be worthless. They suffer from the core beliefs listed above. They have unrealistic expectations of themselves and others. This kind of thinking can lead them to totally irrational justifications for why it is OK for them to sexually sin.

Gary didn't think much of himself. He had prayed for God to help him but had come to the conclusion that God either didn't really care about his sexual sin or that God didn't really care for him. "Why not go for it," he would say as he deluded himself into thinking that he wouldn't suffer any consequences of his acting out.

Because of their beliefs and relational issues, sex addicts don't connect with others. It is hard for them to participate in community. They become or remain isolated or alone. No one knows the truth about them and they lead a "double life." Since no one really knows them they are accountable to no one. They may think they have accountability partners, but if one of them would ask if they were OK, they would always reply, "Sure, I'm fine." They wouldn't want their accountability partners to really know them for fear that they would be judged and left alone.

Spiritual. Sexual addiction is, at its deepest core, a spiritual act of rebellion against God. Sex becomes the false idol. Sex addicts are spiritually immature and often into black and white thinking. They may be angry at God for not giving them the magic answer. They have not truly surrendered to God and continue to be self-centered and selfish, which in its more profound form is narcissism. Sex addicts have fantasies of an imagined answer that they think will solve all their problems. They don't have a vision of God's true calling in their lives.

Assessment

A diagnosis of sex addiction can be made mainly and most reliably through a psychosocial interview. The entire life of the person must be understood including a very rigorous sexual history. Develop your skills at asking probing questions and help the addict feel safe to answer them. You can do this by being non-judgmental of them as people. Never ask for graphic specifics. That can get verbally exhibitionistic or voyeuristic.

Nevertheless, be direct. For example, you might not want to ask, "Were you ever sexually abused?" Rather, ask, "When was your first sexual experience?" An addict might not interpret early sexual activity as abusive. You need to know the history and development of sexual activity. When you believe that the five criteria listed above are met, you are dealing with a sex addict.

There is also a very commonly used test that is available without copyright infringement. It is called the Sexual Addiction Screening Test (SAST) and consists of 25 true and false questions. It first appeared in Carnes' book, *Contrary to Love.*[18] Answering 13 or more "yes" connotes a diagnosis of sex addiction. This test has been modified for female sex addicts by some authorities in the field of female sex addiction, such as Marnie Ferree.[19]

Treatment

Treatment for sex addiction, whether in a counseling office or treatment center can be understood in the same five categories described in the section on etiology:

Emotional. Since sex addicts are so profoundly abused, treating trauma wounds will be one major goal of treatment. The treatment of trauma usually consists of using various counseling methods to identify the history of trauma and allowing the person to express and understand feelings about this history. Next, learning how people have coped with trauma is vital. Carnes, for example, has identified 8 ways that people cope.[20] Using sex as a coping strategy is one of the ways, according to him, that we "numb" trauma. Sex may also be a way we repeat the trauma hoping for a different result (the old definition of insanity).

Shame is the by-product of trauma and spiritual truth is an essential part of the treatment of trauma. Reminding addicts that they are "fearfully and wonderfully made" (Psalm 139) and that Christ died for them is vital. Grieving the loss of so much love and nurture is often a part of the process of healing from trauma.

I have found that the only way to truly heal trauma is to help addicts find meaning in it. Addicts can spend lots of time being victims and feeling sorry for themselves; or they can ask, "What meaning can I make of this?" It is true that God can "work for good" in any situation (Rom. 8:28). God can use our experience of trauma to make us stronger and more sensitive to others. It can also be true that when we experience the pain of our trauma, we are experiencing the pain of all humanity.

Addicts can learn that they grow together in community when they share their pain with others who also have pain. I believe that is what Jesus asks us to do when He says in Matthew 11:28–30 that we can find comfort in our weariness when we take upon ourselves His yoke. When we know that Jesus shares our pain through the cross and that He thereby takes it upon Himself, it becomes a whole lot lighter and easier burden to bear.

Ultimately, the final act of healing from trauma is to forgive those who "persecuted us." That is clearly our spiritual calling. Addicts know that when they carry the burden of anger and resentment, it leads to despair. When they decide to forgive they will start acting like they do and will feel like it later.

Finally, most treatment for addiction would seek to help addicts stop fantasizing about sex. Some would have them "take every thought captive" by just avoiding the thoughts or by guarding the mind against them. Some would say that we have 3 seconds to stop thinking about the fantasy. Finally, some very popular but misguided therapy would have addicts do painful things to themselves when they fantasize, such as using rubber bands about the wrist and popping them when they think sexual thoughts. These strategies may work for a time during the early days of treatment but, ultimately they serve to recreate the trauma that the addicts experienced in the first place and thereby re-injure the brain.

I have found that it is better to ask what the fantasies are trying to teach us about pain. I believe that every fantasy is an attempt to heal a wound from the past. In the fantasy a person will create ways to stop the memory of harm or ways to get the love and nurture that was missed. To turn off a fantasy will miss the message in it. If addicts will ask themselves what the fantasy means about their past, and if they will seek healing from the wounds it seeks to deal with, the fantasy will go away. The addict doesn't need it anymore to bring the message.[21] Ralph Earle and I describe how therapists can help addicts interpret their fantasies in our book *The Pornography Trap*.

Relational. Sex addicts will need to learn how to connect intimately. That is why the honesty of support groups can be a vital part of treatment. Just as others may not trust addicts, addicts don't trust that they can be honest with others. They will need to learn in a healthy and safe community that there are trustworthy people. I have never known a sex addict who has recovered alone.

In order to build trust, addicts will need to be completely sober and to become completely honest about their thoughts and behaviors. That is why I believe it is vital for an addict to disclose his or her story to spouses, children, and close friends and family. This can be daunting. The actual specifics of the story are not as important as the exact nature of the activity. It is morally imperative to do so particularly if the addict has put others in physical danger (such as exposure to disease). Others, like spouses, will need to know why they want to know specifics of acting out behaviors. Do they want to connect intimately or do they want to punish or become better private eyes?

My wife, Debbie, and I believe that there are three acts of surrender for couples to recover from sexual addiction. First, each spouse must be surrendered to Christ. Second, each spouse must surrender each other to Christ knowing that they can't control each other. Third, the couple must surrender their marriage to Christ. Only in this act of "one flesh union" can couples build a better relationship.

Carnes found that the spouses of addicts are equally wounded in their childhoods.[22] This means that they will need to honestly heal from their trauma and not blame the addict for all of their pain. Couples who are equally wounded might be what Carnes called "trauma bonded." They have found each other in the pain. This can seem like all the wrong reasons for being married. We have found, however, that this can be part of God's design. We are called together and may well trigger each other into the deepest places of pain, but this is God's way of helping us grow and be each other's healer. When we know this, we can become companions and soul mates in the journey of growth.

Couples therapy for sex addiction will involve three equal pieces of work: the addict, the spouse, and the couple. Couples' counseling, from day one, is vital in facilitating growth. Today, there are workbooks to help couples on the journey.[23]

Physical. Because sex addicts have become neurochemically tolerant to sex, they will need to go through a period of total abstinence from sexual expression in any form. They should sign a contract not to be "sexual with themselves or others." This would include spouses. It is important to help spouses understand the need for this and to agree with it. Paul said in 1 Corinthians 7 that couples "should not deprive each other except by mutual consent and for a time so that they may devote themselves to prayer." (v. 5) When addicts do this, they will detoxify their brains and may go to similar, albeit less severe, symptoms as an alcoholic would. It is important during this time to find them support.

After about 7–14 days of abstinence, addicts will notice that it becomes easier to stay free of sexual acting out. My experience would suggest that it is easier to be completely abstinent than to be regularly sexual with a spouse. This is a neurochemical phenomenon. Single people, therefore, may have an easier time being sober than married people. For an addict, at least, there is no amount of sex that is ever enough to satisfy biological desire. They will always want more. I have found that the only way to satisfy sexual desire ultimately is in the spiritual intimacy of marriage.

Addicts may need to have physical evaluation of the possibility of any STDs. They may also need help with any sexual dysfunctions that have developed. Getting competent Christian sex therapy could be important. Physical self-care is also vital. Lack of exercise, proper nutrition, and rest could make addicts more vulnerable to temptation.

Finally, psychiatric treatment for any imbalances of neurochemistry is incredibly important. Since ADD/HD may be a comorbid condition, treatment for it could often be the missing link in staying sober. In my personal experience, brain scan imaging (such as Daniel Amen's work) can be indicated especially in those cases where traditional psychiatry does not seem to be able to adequately diagnose the problem.

Cognitive/Behavioral. Talk therapy and spiritual direction will be essential parts of a treatment plan. Helping addicts understand their own wounded core beliefs and the truth of the gospel will be a life journey of healing.

Helping addicts find and maintain accountability is a critical part of treatment, especially in the early months. I have found that the book of Nehemiah is a virtual blueprint of how to do this. In two separate books I have completely outlined an 18-principle approach to accountability based on this book.[24] To highlight several of these principles:

- Accountability begins with willingness and with brokenness.
- Accountability begins with confession and a spirit of repentance. (Neh. 1)
- Accountability is maintained in groups of men or of women dedicated to sexual purity. These are the "warriors" of an addict's life. (Neh. 2:9)
- Addicts must get rid of all "dung" in their lives (Neh. 3:14). Pornography, affairs, secret phone numbers, and irrational thinking are examples of this.
- Addicts must identify the enemy. This is to discover how they become vulnerable in their rituals.
- Addicts must prepare when they are strong for the temptations that will come. They must not wait until it happens for that is part of the temptation.
- Addicts must be accountable to do positive actions and defend against negative ones.

- Addicts must find a higher calling and purpose for which to recover, like fighting for their families and their homes. (Neh. 4:14)

Addicts will learn how to define their sobriety and the rituals that lead them into this acting out. For most Christian addicts sobriety will mean no acting out with self (masturbation) and others outside of marriage. Masturbation has sometimes been controversial in the Christian community especially with singles. My experience is that masturbation is never possible in that it conditions a person emotionally and physically to be dissatisfied with marital and genital intercourse.

Finding sobriety from sex addiction is in some ways more like an eating disorder than it is like alcoholism. Both sex and eating are natural desires of the body. Just as eating can't be totally abstained from, so sex (for those married) can't be given up either. Learning how to be sexual or to eat for the healthy purposes of it is vital to the journey of accountability.

Spiritual. Sex addicts will need to answer three spiritual questions in order to begin the journey of healing. First, "Do you want to get well?" This is the question that Jesus asks the paralyzed man in John 5:6. Had this man adopted the attitude of being paralyzed? Addicts do. They must be willing to change and give up their own control and give it to God.

Second, "What are you thirsty for?" In the story of the Samaritan woman in John 4, Jesus tells her that earthly water does not satisfy thirst and that only "living water" does. Recovering sex addicts know that they have been thirsty for sexual solutions and that now they must be thirsty for Christ.

Third, "Are you willing to die to yourself?" In John 11 when Jesus heals Lazarus, He is demonstrating that He will let someone die in order for them to experience the resurrecting power of a relationship with Him. Addicts are often like Lazarus's two sisters, Mary and Martha, and think that if Jesus would only have come, they wouldn't have died. Only addicts who stop looking for the magic answer and who are willing to die to their own control and power, will find true healing.

Ultimately, addicts must have a vision of God's calling in their lives. They have created fantasies of their solutions and must now find God's. Addicts without a vision will perish. A vision is the motivation to follow God and not the self. Fantasy is a magic answer; vision is God's. Vision directs all we do and gives us an appetite and thirst for "things above" and not "things below." When addicts start a cycle of vision it will lead to healthy discipline, healthy behavior, and joy. This is opposed to the addict's historical cycle of fantasy, ritual, acting out, and despair.

Conclusion

As one of my colleagues recently put it, a statement I penned for the epigraph of this chapter, "In our current sexually absorbed culture, working with sex addicts is a growth industry." There is no shortage of work to go around. I encourage you to be involved if you feel capable. There are plenty of ways to acquire further training and to even get certification. AACC conferences and video series are great sources.

There is one last word of caution. Working with sex addicts will challenge a counselor's own sexuality. Listening to the stories can be troubling at some times and sexually provocative at others. If a counselor's own sexual health is not in good order, working with addicts can be dangerous. When in doubt, refer to a competent therapist in your area.

When successful work with sex addicts and their spouses is accomplished, however, transformation of lives and marriages is a very fulfilling result.

ENDNOTES

1. These groups are: Sex Addicts Anonymous, Sexaholics Anonymous, and Sex and Love Addicts Anonymous. Phone numbers and contact information are listed in the resource section.
2. Patrick Carnes, *Out of the shadows* (Center City, MN: Hazelden Books, 1984).
3. Mark R. Laaser, *Healing the wounds of sexual addiction* (Grand Rapids, MI: Zondervan, 2004).
4. Harry Schaumberg, *False intimacy* (Downers Grove, IL: InterVarsity, 1992).
5. Ralph Earle, Earle M., and Osborn, K., *Sex addiction: Case studies and management* (New York: Brunner/Mazel, 1995). and Ralph Earle and Crow, G., *Lonely all the time* (New York: Pocket, 1989).
6. Pat Means, *Men's secret wars* (Grand Rapids, MI: Revell, 1996).
7. Russ Willingham, *Breaking free* (Downers Grove, IL: InterVarsity, 1999).
8. Earl Wilson, *Steering clear* (Downers Grove, IL: InterVarsity, 2002).
9. Steve Arteburn and Stoeker, F., *Every man's battle* (Colorado Springs, CO.: WaterBrook Press, 2000).
10. The Leadership survey on pastors and internet pornography, *Leadership Journal* 2001:001
11. Carnes, 1984.

12. Harvey Milkman, and Sunderwirth, S., *Craving for ecstasy: The consciousness and chemistry of escape* (Lexington, MA: Lexington Books, 1987).

13. Marnie Ferree, *No stones: Women redeemed from sexual shame* (Fairfax, VA: Xulon, 2002).

14. Pat Carnes, *Don't call it love* (New York: Bantam Books, 1991).

15. Tim Clinton and Sibcy, G., *Attachments,* (Brentwood, TN: Integrity, 2002).

16. Carnes, 1991.

17. Daniel Amen, *Change your brain change your life* (New York: Random House, 1998).

18. Pat Carnes, *Contrary to love* (Minneapolis: CompCare 1989).

19. Marnie Ferree, 2002.

20. Pat Carnes, *The betrayal bond* (Deerfield Beach, FL: Health Communications, Inc., 1997).

21. Mark Laaser and Earle, R., *The pornography trap* (Kansas City, KS: Beacon Hill Press, 2002).

22. Carnes, 1997.

23. Patrick Carnes, Laaser, D., and Laaser, M., *Open hearts* (Wickensburg, AZ: Gentle Path Press, 2000).

24. Laaser and Earle, 2002. and Mark Laaser, *A L.I.F.E. guide: Men living in freedom everyday* (Fairfax, VA.: Xulon, 2002).

14

Gambling, Spending, and Credit Abuse

Gregory L. Jantz

Many individuals with Pathological Gambling believe that money is both the cause of and the solution to all their problems.

DSM-IV[1]

For the love of money is a root of all kinds of evil.

1 TIMOTHY 6:10A

Jerry and Susan came in for counseling. Married eleven years, with two boys, they found themselves growing apart. Jerry described sexual difficulties. Susan complained of financial struggles and a general feeling of estrangement. Both were cautiously willing to enter into therapy, each convinced the other was mostly at fault.

Deep down, Susan expressed a fear that Jerry was having an affair. He came home later and later from work. Money was missing from the checking account and Jerry became angry when she asked about it. One time, she said, she'd called him at work, a rare occurrence, only to find he'd "gone home sick." When she'd driven home to check on him during her lunch break, he wasn't there. His explanation of where he'd actually gone just didn't sound plausible. It seemed to Susan that Jerry was becoming more irritable with her and the boys, as if he resented them. His beer on the weekends was turning into a nightly routine. Susan felt afraid and angry.

Jerry was frustrated in his marriage. He said Susan didn't respond sexually the way he wanted and that she put more time into the boys than him. The stress of providing for a family, especially in a tight job market, was taking its toll and Jerry didn't like having to answer to Susan every time he was late getting home. He felt he had to schedule his entire day in order to get everything done. All the things he did to help handle the stress seemed to cause strife and irritation in Susan. Jerry felt confined and stressed.

Susan came into counseling expecting to be told that Jerry was in love with another woman. Jerry came into counseling expecting Susan to be told to be a more understanding wife. The key to resolving their difficulties lay in a completely different direction, one that did not surface immediately. Pressed by the demands of family responsibilities, Jerry had indeed sought out an alternative relationship, one that was exciting, energizing. Not with another woman, as Susan feared, but with an activity. Jerry had fallen in love with the thrill and promise of gambling.

Dinner with a friend at a local restaurant and casino, while Susan and the kids were out of town, led to a night of slots and blackjack. More than a year later, Jerry still continued to gamble. Even when confronted with the negative consequences, he tried to downplay them and insisted there was nothing wrong with his newfound recreation.

What started out as marital difficulties to Susan and a necessary outlet for Jerry was fast approaching a DSM-IV classification of 312.31.

Pathological Gambling

Pathological gambling, in the DSM-IV, 4th Edition, "is characterized by recurrent and persistent maladaptive gambling behavior that disrupts personal, family, or vocational pursuits." What it meant in Jerry and Susan's life was financial stress, deterioration of personal credit, loss of affection and heightened anxiety. The following is taken from the DSM-IV Diagnostic Criteria for 312.31 Pathological Gambling:

A. Persistent and recurrent maladaptive gambling behavior is indicated by five (or more) of the following criteria:

1. is preoccupied with gambling (e.g., preoccupied with reliving past gambling experiences, handicapping or planning the next venture, or thinking of ways to get money with which to gamble)

2. needs to gamble with increasing amounts of money in order to achieve the desired excitement

3. has repeated unsuccessful efforts to control, cut back, or stop gambling

4. is restless or irritable when attempting to cut down or stop gambling

5. gambles as a way of escaping from problems or of relieving a dysphoric mood (e.g., feelings of helplessness, guilt, anxiety, depression)

6. after losing money gambling, often returns another day to get even ("chasing" one's losses)

7. lies to family members, therapist, or others to conceal the extent of involvement with gambling

8. has committed illegal acts such as forgery, fraud, theft, or embezzlement to finance gambling

9. has jeopardized or lost a significant relationship, job, or educational or career opportunity because of gambling

10. relies on others to provide money to relieve a desperate financial situation caused by gambling

B. A diagnosis is not made if the gambling behavior can be associated with a Manic Episode.

New Twist to an Ancient Malady

Prior to 1980, there wasn't even a diagnostic code for pathological gambling. Since that time, gambling has moved in and made itself accessible. It used to be if you wanted to gamble, you had to go to Las Vegas or Atlantic City. Now, you need go no further than the blackjack room down the block or the tribal casino out on the interstate. With the rise of internet gambling, you need go no further than your den or bedroom.

Accessibility can prove problematic to those with an impulse-control disorder, such as pathological gambling. The more communities welcome gambling, the higher the likelihood you will see gambling-related issues coming in the front door of your counseling practice or ministry. The greater the types of gambling allowed, the higher the lifetime rates of pathological and problem gamblers (Volberg, 1994).

It has generally been my experience that gambling does not surface immediately as a primary reason for a person or a family to seek counseling. More often, I've seen the Jerry-Susan scenario, with gambling interwoven around other issues. One of the most common companions to pathological gambling is alcohol abuse and a current study suggests that those with problematic gambling behaviors should undergo a chemical dependency screening.[2]

Gambling Gaining Ground

Most Americans gamble. A study for Arizona's state-run lottery reported that "the majority of adults in the United States have gambled at some time in their lives. Nationally, the proportion of the population that has ever gambled ranges from 81% in the Southern states to 89% in the Northeast."[3] In Arizona, 7 in 10 adults gambled within the past year and 23% gambled within the past month. Ten percent gambled within the past week, with the majority of gambling occurring through visiting a casino or playing the lottery.

According to information put out by the National Council on Problem Gambling, an average of 3 million adults meet the criteria for pathological gambling each year. They are more likely to have problems with alcohol, drugs, smoking, and depression. Serious gambling problems can lead to suicide. While the poor appear to be an at-risk population for pathological gambling (Ladd, Petry, 2002), in the Arizona study, 60% of those identified as problem gamblers worked full-time, with only 10% disabled or unemployed, a rate half of that of non-problem gamblers (20%).

Gamblers now come in both genders, across age groups and in all colors. Three million of our fellow Americans. At-risk populations appear to be the elderly, the young, minorities and the poor. Because of this, "the National Council on Problem Gambling has advocated a public health perspective, pointing out that pathological gambling is more prevalent where gambling is more available, and advocating a national gambling policy to restrict the availability of gambling (National Council on Problem Gambling, 1993)."[4]

Thirty years ago, this issue wasn't even on the horizon. "Since the mid-1970s, America has evolved from a country in which gambling was a relatively rare activity—casinos operating only in the distant Nevada desert, a few states operating lotteries, and pari-mutuel gambling relatively small scale and sedate—into a nation in which legalized gambling, in one form or another, is permitted in 47 states and the District of Columbia."[5] Over time, and with the continued increase in gambling, attitudes have incrementally changed. According to research by the Barna Group, "Of the ten moral behaviors evaluated, a majority of Americans believed that each of three activities were "morally acceptable." Those included gambling (61%), cohabitation (60%), and sexual fantasies (59%)."[6] Moral acceptability of gambling is currently directly related to age, according to Barna. For the oldest Americans, half find gambling acceptable, while the number jumps to 3 in 4 for those just graduating from high school. This culture increasingly finds gambling an acceptable behavior. The more who engage in it, the more who will become trapped.

The Downward Spiral

Looking back over the past five years, I realized I lost a good portion of my life. I remember the pain and the continuous deception as I awoke each and every morning. I lied to my wife and I lied to my friends. I cannot believe how my personality changed as I became more and more manipulative over time. I knew I had a problem. I did not know how to face it when I lost all of my money, maxed out my credit cards and kept this secret from my wife and kids. I was a good husband and I was a good person but life all changed as I became more and more involved with gambling. My wife found out since bills were mounting. I sat down and told her what I had done. She was in shock and disbelief. She told me either to get help or get out.[7]

Even with other issues present, it is imperative that gambling be addressed, because of the destructive and progressive nature of the disorder. What starts as a preoccupation with thinking about gambling can lead to criminal activity to obtain funds to gamble, the loss of family relationships, financial resources, and employment. Simply stated, pathological gambling wrecks lives and ruins families.

There are three distinct phases in the progression leading to pathological gambling. Counseling may be sought during any of these phases, although the financial, personal, and peer pressure to confront gambling consequences may increase in the later stages and motivate a person to seek help.

The initial phase is known as the *winning phase*. It is during this phase that the gambler does not perceive any negative consequences to the gambling behavior. On the contrary, this phase is characterized by a sense of excitement and even euphoria. (For this reason, a manic episode involving excessive gambling and loss of judgment can sometimes appear to be pathological gambling. It is important to differentiate whether or not the manic characteristics are sustained outside of the gambling behavior, hence item B in the DSM-IV criteria.) About half those identified as compulsive gamblers begin with a big win early on. This early win is identified as pleasurable by the gambler, who then seeks to replicate the feeling. Even if there is not an initial win, the sheer excitement of the act of gambling is interpreted as pleasurable, enticing the person to continue the behavior.

The more the person gambles to replicate the pleasure, the higher the odds s/he will lose. In the *losing phase*, the person starts to increase the amount of gambling in order to recoup losses (known as "chasing" losses) to recapture that initial feeling of excitement. The magnitude of the bets and/or the frequency of the activity increases to produce the same level of thrill or financial windfall. It is at this stage that the gambler will begin to alienate family and friends, jeopardize employment, and borrow money. Sometimes, the gambler will experience a win during this phase or be enabled by family and friends to continue. These events merely forestall the inevitable. The heavier reliance on gambling, however, does not produce the desired results long-term and the gambler sinks into the final phase.

As the person continues to gamble, s/he enters the *desperation phase*. Gambling has now taken precedence over other, important considerations such as family, friends, work, finances. In a desperate attempt to gain funds to maintain or even increase the amount of gambling, the person may resort to unethical or criminal behavior. Family members or friends may be lied to about the true reason for needing money. The person may cheat or steal from employers. Gamblers have been known to embezzle funds entrusted to them. (One sad example in my home state of Washington involved a high-school band director who gambled away $4,000 raised by students and parents through a bake sale, car washes, and other fundraising events for a trip.) It is during the desperation phase that pathological gamblers will have increased incidences of suicidal ideation as a way out of their difficulties brought by gambling.

At War, At-Risk

Those who provide gaming resources, services and equipment are adept at developing gambling venues that are most effective. Internet gambling combines immediacy, convenience and anonymity. This potent combination can prove overpowering to someone on the edge of pathological gambling behaviors.

In addition, there is another form of gambling that is proving to be highly addictive—machine gambling, including slots and video poker. Called the "crack cocaine" of gambling, this "analogy implies that machines are more addictive than other, more "traditional" forms of gambling, such as horse-racing and card games."[8]

It is in the financial interest of gaming business, even state governments that rely on gambling revenues, to become even "better" marketers of gambling venues and products. Their efficiency, however, easily translates into higher rates of pathological gambling. Gambling has become another skirmish in the ongoing culture war, with pathological gamblers and their families caught in the crosshairs.

Warning Signs

In some instances, a pathological gambler, realizing the devastation his or her compulsion is causing, will come in for counseling specifically on this issue. However, pathological gamblers are not always forthcoming about their gambling behaviors, so there are specific signs to watch for during counseling on other issues that may point to the existence of a gambling addiction:

- Unexplained withdrawal of personal or family funds
- Unexplained time away from school, work, or home
- Heightened irritability and hostility over financial matters
- Increased signs of depression and/or anxiety
- Increased isolation from family members
- Withdrawal from previously enjoyed social activities
- Unexplained mood swings
- Selling personal possessions
- Unexplained gifts or excessive generosity

- Borrowing from family and friends
- Unexplained indebtedness to credit cards
- Associated disorders

There are a variety of diagnostic tools available to help assess the presence of pathological gambling. The least "clinical" in my view can be obtained through the National Council on Problem Gambling (www.ncpgambling.org), which presents the person with ten statements about his or her gambling behavior. They are:

1. You have often gambled longer than you had planned.
2. You have often gambled until your last dollar was gone.
3. Thoughts of gambling have caused you to lose sleep.
4. You have used your income or savings to gamble while letting bills go unpaid.
5. You have made repeated, unsuccessful attempts to stop gambling.
6. You have broken the law or considered breaking the law to finance your gambling.
7. You have borrowed money to finance your gambling.
8. You have felt depressed or suicidal because of your gambling losses.
9. You have been remorseful after gambling.
10. You have gambled to get money to meet your financial obligations.
11. According to the "Problem Gambling Resource & Fact Sheet" put out by the NCPG, if the person answers "yes" to any of these, he or she should consider help from a professional.

Twenty Questions. Gamblers Anonymous was started by two compulsive gamblers in 1957 in Los Angeles, California. It was decidedly ahead of its time, and has a checklist of twenty questions that are still valuable diagnostic tools:

1. Did you ever lose time from work or school due to gambling?
2. Has gambling ever made your home life unhappy?
3. Did gambling affect your reputation?
4. Have you ever felt remorse after gambling?

5. Did you ever gamble to get money with which to pay debts or otherwise solve financial difficulties?
6. Did gambling cause a decrease in your ambition or efficiency?
7. After losing did you feel you must return as soon as possible and win back your losses?
8. After a win did you have a strong urge to return and win more?
9. Did you often gamble until your last dollar was gone?
10. Did you ever borrow to finance your gambling?
11. Have you ever sold anything to finance gambling?
12. Were you reluctant to use "gambling money" for normal expenditures?
13. Did gambling make you careless of the welfare of yourself or your family?
14. Did you ever gamble longer than you had planned?
15. Have you ever gambled to escape worry or trouble?
16. Have you ever committed, or considered committing, an illegal act to finance gambling?
17. Did gambling cause you to have difficulty in sleeping?
18. Do arguments, disappointments or frustrations create within you an urge to gamble?
19. Did you ever have an urge to celebrate any good fortune by a few hours of gambling?
20. Have you ever considered self-destruction or suicide as a result of your gambling?

According to Gamblers Anonymous, most compulsive gamblers will answer yes to at least seven of those questions.[9]

The National Council on Problem Gambling has a "Problem Gambling Self Test" on-line that can be found at http://www.ncpgambling.org/about_problem/about_problem_test.asp.

There are other diagnostic screening tools that can be utilized. Two are the South Oaks Gambling Screen (SOGS)[10] and the NORC (National Opinion Research Center) DSM-IV Screen for Gambling Problems[11], both of which were used in the Arizona study. The SOGS was used in the 1999 report to the Washington State Lottery on my state's gambling and problem gambling behaviors.

Associated Disorders

In my research, I believe that people become trapped in gambling behaviors for the same reasons that any addict uses whatever their "drug of choice" may be: out of a desire to obtain a euphoric thrill, to gain control over their lives through money, or to provide an escape from uncomfortable feelings and/or situations. Where one disorder takes hold, another can follow.

A link appears to exist between gambling behaviors and substance abuse through alcohol or drugs. These are not the only companions to gambling. The DSM-IV identifies "Mood Disorders, Attention-Deficit/Hyperactivity Disorder, Substance Abuse or Dependence, other Impulse-Control Disorders, and Antisocial, Narcissistic, and Borderline Personality Disorders"[12] as being linked to Pathological Gambling. In some cases, these associated disorders precede and intensify the gambling behaviors, making it difficult to identify which came first. At some point, the only effective treatment is to recognize all of the associated disorders and factor them into a comprehensive treatment plan. In the case of Substance Abuse or Dependence, this would require treating the person under a dual diagnosis of mental health and chemical dependency.

Treating the Whole Person

It is my belief that recovery from pathological gambling is possible and best achieved through a whole-person treatment model. By whole-person, I mean addressing the emotional, relational, physical, and spiritual components contributing to the person's compulsion to gamble. The Jerry-Susan scenario provides an example of how the whole-person treatment model functions.

Jerry's sense of dissatisfaction with his life and marriage preceded his gambling experience. Emotionally, Jerry felt anxious and overwhelmed by the pressures of providing for his family financially. He also resented the increasing amounts of time necessary to fulfill his family and employment responsibilities. He felt squeezed out and marginalized by his family. Jerry was able to articulate how he felt but it took longer to identify why he felt that way and where the thoughts supporting those feelings originated.

When Jerry was growing up, his father was the sole support for the family. As such, he was exempted from household chores, which were accomplished by Jerry's mother, Jerry and siblings. Jerry perceived that if you worked and brought income into the home, this activity exempted you from the mundane tasks of the family. It also seemed to Jerry that he and his younger sister were burdened with the worse jobs around the house and yard, while his older brother was increasingly excused from chores. Jerry grew up feeling deep resentment over this family inequity. He determined that being an adult and bread-winner, he would be relieved of these types of responsibilities. Adulthood, to Jerry, meant getting to do more of what you wanted to, of having more control of your life.

At a time when Jerry was experiencing increased stress in his work and family, the gambling opportunity arose. It was exciting, self-focused, more of what he always thought being an adult should bring. It was, after all, his money and his time and he should have the freedom to spend it on whatever he wanted, not have to explain every penny to Susan. He was tired of handing over each paycheck and finding out how little was left at the end of each month, after everyone else's items were paid for. Jerry began to fantasize on how much better his life would be if he could just win some extra money so the pressure would be off. He thought if he could just bring home enough money, his life would be eased and he'd be able to gain more control over his time.

As Jerry sought to incorporate his hidden gambling into an already busy schedule, however, his stress increased. He began to lose sleep. His consumption of alcohol, caffeine, and tobacco increased. His eating habits deteriorated and he developed headaches, which made him even more irritable around his family and coworkers. Productivity at work fell, causing additional stress about the permanency of his position. The less sure his job became, the greater the desire to hedge his bets through anticipated winnings.

The more Jerry turned to gambling and alcohol to numb his problems, the less he became available to Susan and his children. As his isolation increased, Jerry began to lose touch with his identity as a husband and father, substituting his identity as gambler. This precipitated a spiritual crisis: Jerry began to question his purpose in life.

Created as complex beings of mind, body, and spirit, recovery and wholeness are best achieved when these factors are integrated into treatment. Through therapy Jerry examined the source of his feelings of discontent and learned skills to help make intentional choices to redirect his negative thoughts. He identified unrecognized family-of-origin patterns affecting his current family relationships. Working with a medical professional, Jerry cut down on his consumption of alcohol, caffeine, and tobacco. He also began a regular exercise routine in order to provide physical release for feelings of restlessness or anxiety. His church was able to provide Jerry with pastoral counseling regarding his faith questions and Jerry and Susan began work with a financial planner to reconstruct their finances.

Susan, working with her own therapist, examined how her relationship with Jerry was altered by the birth of their sons, especially her sexual response to Jerry. They worked as a couple on relationship issues. Jerry and Susan learned how to manage conflicts and effectively communicate needs. They spent time together alone and placed renewed emphasis on their own identity as a couple.

Jerry, of course, had to stop gambling. He began attending a local Gamblers Anonymous meeting to provide support for his gambling abstinence. Approaching every person whom he owed money, both family members and friends, he explained his gambling addiction and obtained a promise from them that they would not loan him any more money, no matter the reason. He also made arrangements to pay each of them back the money he'd borrowed for his gambling. At his church, Jerry was open about his need for prayer and support in his desire to stop gambling. Several men in the congregation pledged to form an accountability group with Jerry and meet on a regular basis with him.

Community Resources

Recovery from pathological gambling requires a concerted effort not only by the individual but also by the community surrounding that individual. As a counselor, you can provide an important piece of understanding and clarity of the true nature of the disorder. You can assist the person to make positive behavioral changes. You can provide motivation for the person to assemble outside resources from family, friends, support groups, financial counseling, and churches.

As the course of recovery progresses, the more additional resources the person has, the greater the success in overcoming an inevitable relapse. As a counselor, you will not be available to this person 24 hours a day and a relapse could occur during non-business hours. The more community support available to the individual, the better.

As a counselor, you recognize the need to be creative and flexible when dealing with individual situations of gambling. The following is presented as examples for potential auxiliary recommendations:

- If the person lives near a gambling establishment, map out a route to work or home that avoids the area.
- Have a family member or friend go with the recovering gambler to every gambling establishment that will allow him or her to "self-exclude" from that business. (Self-exclusion has been an option for Washington state gamblers since 1999. Under a self-banning agreement, a gambling establishment has the authority to call the police and charge the person with criminal trespass. However, some local police departments have refused to become involved and make an arrest.)
- Have the person cut up all credit cards and deal only from a cash or check basis.
- Determine if there was a specific day/time element to the gambling behavior (for example, Friday nights after work) and assist the person to substitute an appropriate activity into that time slot.
- If the person is going to be apart from his or her support structure, such as on a business trip out of town, have them arrange to check in with and be accountable to others during their time away.
- Go on-line and locate a Gamblers Anonymous support group, if possible, in the destination city.
- If they have participated in gambling activities with any family members or friends, have them contact that person and explain that they will not be able to continue gambling together and suggest they find alternate ways to maintain the relationship. If any of them refuses to respect the person's desire not to continue to gamble, assist the person in finding a way to terminate the relationship until that changes.
- If the person engages in Internet gambling, engage a protection program to restrict access to the Internet during vulnerable hours.

Family Support

It is an unhappy reality that some pathological gamblers will choose not to stop. Even when presented with the truth of the damage they are causing to themselves and others, the lure of the disorder will exert too strong a pull. As a counselor, you may be left with the task of working to shore up a family torn apart by the person's behavior. In some situations, the person left in your office will not be the gambler, but the spouse, the parent, or the child. Again, your assistance in identifying, creating, and maintaining a community support structure will be crucial. That left-behind person or family will benefit from the resources of the community—the love of extended family and friends, financial council, legal options, and support from their family of faith. If the person cannot be redeemed from gambling, the family still can.

Unfortunately, resources on the issue of pathological and problem gambling are slim. Gamblers Anonymous (www.gamblersanonymous.org) and the National Council on Problem Gambling (www.ncpgambling.org) have a national reach. From the National Council on Problem Gambling website, you can find state affiliates (www.ncpgambling.org/state_affiliates/), however only about half the states have this resource available. One of the greatest sources of biblically based information is Focus on the Family (www.family.org). Just type in "Gambling" in the Search field on their homepage. This organization has a research document on problem and pathological gambling by Ronald A. Reno, as well as a policy statement by Dr. James Dobson, an informational video, and information on gambling activities by state.

For a more clinical approach, Nancy M. Petry, Ph.D., cited under References, has a book available entitled, *Pathological Gambling: Etiology, Comorbidity, and Treatment* (2004, APA Books). Petry takes a three-pronged approach in this book, going over the most common treatment modalities in use for pathological gambling, non-professional intervention and self-help through groups such as Gamblers Anonymous and a cognitive-behavioral approach she uses. This book is written for an audience of mostly researchers and clinicians.

Especially for pastors or church or ministry leaders I recommend my book, *Turning the Tables on Gambling* (Waterbrook Press, 2001), available through my website at www.aplaceofhope.com. Written from a whole-person approach, it provides information and insight from a biblical perspective. Its commonsense presentation makes it accessible to the lay counselor or ministry leader, as well as valuable for the professional.

Spending and Credit Abuse

The rich rule over the poor, and the borrower is servant to the lender.
Proverbs 22:7

There are no diagnostic criteria for spending too much or ringing up high credit card balances while binge shopping. If there were, many of us would probably fall into that category. While an official "disorder" has not been named, some are already calling this "compulsive shopping disorder" or "shopaholism" and it has attracted the eye of big business.

Pharmaceutical companies have taken note and are interested in providing relief to problem shoppers in a pill. According to a May 23, 2000, article in *Mother Jones* by Chris Berdik entitled, "Selling the Cure for Shopaholism," Stanford University researchers are looking into a pharmaceutical answer for overspending.[13] Relief, however, is unlikely to arrive in a small brown bottle.

No matter how you characterize it, as a society we are overburdened with debt. While you may not experience this on a personal level, my guess is you've seen it first-hand in your counseling practice. I'd also venture to guess that several people, who should have continued working with you on other issues, found they were unable to continue counseling due to their high debt load and payments. They needed to see you because of their spending, but couldn't afford to because of their debt.

The burden of debt creates an atmosphere of oppression and hopelessness. As such, debt becomes a breeding ground for depression, anxiety, marital stress, and avoidance behaviors such as substance abuse. Debt can be caused by a variety of factors. In my practice, I have seen spending and credit abuse due to ignorance, lack of impulse control, and tied to obsessive-compulsive behaviors.

Sometimes, young adults will come in to work on relationship issues and one partner will express distress over the spending and charging habits of the other. In this case, often resolution can be achieved through an understanding of family-of-origin issues concerning the handling of money, as well as a recommendation to seek a financial counselor to establish goals and a budget. Ideally, the whole concept of family budgeting and fiscal responsibility should be addressed within the umbrella of premarital counseling. Disagreements over financial matters consistently rank high on marital stressor lists.

Lack of impulse control can also lie at the root of a problem with spending and credit abuse. This is exacerbated by the sheer volume of credit card invitations the average person receives in the mail each week. The first one might be resisted, while the tenth accepted. Even without a specific diagnosis code, there is still a great deal of help counselors can provide to those challenged by an overwhelming desire to spend beyond their means. By utilizing a whole-person approach, the origins of the desire to spend can be identified and addressed.

Many times, spending contains a highly emotional component. I have had people sit in my office and explain how buying even unneeded items made them feel better. If they felt upset or sad, spending was their chosen method of providing comfort. Buying something enabled them to feel empowered and special. The greater the worth of the item bought, the higher their feelings of personal value. Some have explained that they viewed spending as a reward and whenever they felt unappreciated or undervalued by others, they would counter those feelings by rewarding themselves through shopping.

Almost universally, spending and credit abuse behavior can be linked to family-of-origin issues. The family is the first schoolhouse for how and why to spend money and children are quite perceptive to links made between personal worth and monetary value. Often, I've found the reason given for extravagant spending is to make up for a perceived lack of care by parents growing up. Adults attempt to compensate for a sense of deprivation as a child by spending to fill the void as an adult.

Purchasing an item, whether with cash, check, or credit, can be an emotional action with a physical component. Feelings of sadness and depression can be given as a reason for spending money on an unneeded or extravagant item. In some ways, finding just the right item to purchase can be similar to the type of physical response produced by gambling behavior, triggering activity in the pleasure-center of the brain. When people tell me it feels good to shop and spend, this isn't just hyperbole—it actually does produce a physical pleasure response. As such, people can become dependent upon this physical response and seek to replicate it through spending or shopping, regardless of the financial cost.

Often, an important component of a desire to spend is a spiritual one. A person has prayed for something. God has answered "no" or "not now." The person then decides to take it upon him or herself to go ahead and obtain the item or a substitute anyway. The tension of not having creates an impetus, not for more prayer, but for gratification.

Often, God delays the presentation of something we want in order to teach us patience. Patience is never gained instantly. Rather, patience is perfected only through the passage of time and the sure knowledge that God will provide what we need.

The difference between needs and wants can also be a spiritual issue. Jesus expressed this concept so eloquently during the Sermon on the Mount when He said, "So do not worry, saying 'What shall we eat?' or 'What shall we drink?' or 'What shall we wear?' For the pagans run after all these things, and your heavenly Father knows that you need them. But seek first His kingdom and His righteousness, and all these things will be given to you as well." (Matt. 6:31–33) As a counselor, you can assist people in determining whether psychological factors have obscured their ability to accurately distinguish between a need and a want, and how to regain emotional equilibrium.

God has made it clear in Scripture of the value of delayed gratification. Society says now, today. God explains that a day could be a thousand years. That's not necessarily a lesson we want to learn. And the only delay a credit card company considers gratifying is a delay in you actually paying off your principle so they can continue to charge you interest, on the interest.

I believe it is possible to work with people to help develop and strengthen their internal controls over spending. At some point, it might be helpful for the person to work with you on the reasons why they spend and work with a financial counselor to determine how and when they will spend. Your primary role is to assist them in understanding what needs they are attempting to fill through their spending and credit abuse, and to develop the ability to be objective about whether their desires are needs or wants. Again, creative suggestions to individual situations can provide real-life answers to those seeking help:

- For those struggling with spending and, specifically, credit abuse, the number one suggestion from financial counselors is to cut up all credit cards. Learning to live on available resources is vital.

- Some people have found value in working with a financial consultant to whom they give over control of their finances, to increase accountability and provide an established system for accomplishing larger purchases beyond life's necessities. The process often can provide the brakes needed to slow down an impulsive drive to spend.
- Because the impulse to shop can really be a cry for pleasure, or relief from sadness or boredom, the person can be assisted in determining other activities that can be replaced and still achieve the desired effect. If a person finds they shop to relieve boredom and they have a great deal of free time on their hands, they could, for example, be motivated to identify a local volunteer opportunity that would provide contact with other people, connection to a worthwhile goal or purpose, and be mentally engaging.
- As in the case of someone whose finances are devastated by a gambling addiction, out-of-control spending and credit abuse can also destroy personal finances. In this case, the person would most probably benefit from financial counseling. In most major cities, there are consumer credit counseling bureaus that work with individuals and families to create repayment plans with creditors and reestablish a healthy income-debt ratio. Of course, after a person comes to understand the reason for their debt, they still are in debt. And while they seek to not incur more debt, they may need real help in working their way out of debt. Just knowing there is a plan in place can help give people hope as they make the sacrifices necessary to reduce or eliminate their debt.

Sometimes, when working with an individual on spending or credit abuse issues, it can take persistence and patience to uncover the root of the behavior. Just as eating disorders often mask histories of abuse and neglect, these spending behaviors may have been developed by the person to compensate for deep-seated psychological trauma. As such, no amount of financial counseling or creative action steps will significantly alter the behavior in the long-term.

A successful outcome can only be gained by detaching the behavior from the causal event or situation, sometimes a process requiring great patience and perseverance. A person may start out masking their pain through one compulsive behavior and transfer it on to another and then another. This is similar to people giving up smoking only to find they've begun to compulsively overeat. This shell game does little to truly alleviate the root cause. However, by continuing to work through each behavior, it is possible to peel back the layers and uncover the heart of the behavior.

The True Value of Money

For good or ill, money means power and control in our society. As such, how and why we use it will continue to be an issue for people. Some of those people will wind up in our offices and homes, seeking help. From a psychological standpoint, we have ways to assess whether a disorder exists and ways to treat it. From a spiritual standpoint, we have a wealth of scriptural teaching on money, value, and worth.

Therapeutically, each individual will need a slightly different mix of psychological intervention, common sense, and spiritual help. As Christian counselors and ministers, we are blessed to have all of those palettes in our paint box, unlike purely secular counselors who reject the efficacy, or even existence, of the power of the Spirit of God.

Jesus notes also in the Sermon on the Mount, "no one can serve two masters. Either he will hate the one and love the other, or he will be devoted to the one and despise the other. You cannot serve both God and Money." (Matt. 6:24) It is significant to note that the lure of money is powerful enough to replace God as master in our lives. It was true 2,000 years ago and it's still true today. Our ultimate goal as Christian counselors is to help those suffering from whatever compulsion—gambling, spending, or credit abuse—to return God to His rightful place. As we labor in this task, with those entrusted to us, it is comforting to realize we are not alone. We are in complete agreement with the will of God in the lives of those we seek to help.

ENDNOTES

1.   American Psychiatric Association, *Diagnostic and statistical manual of mental disorders* 4th ed. (Washington, DC: APA, 1994), 672.
2.   J. E. Grant, Kushner, M.G., and Kim, S.W., Pathological gambling and alcohol use disorder, *Alcohol Research & Health*, 26, (2002),143–150.
3.   R. A.Volberg, *Gambling and problem gambling in Arizona: Report to the Arizona*

lottery, (2003), available from <http://www.problemgambling.az.gov/preva-lencestudy.pdf.

4. J. W. Welte, Wieczorek, W. F., Barnes, G. M, Tidwell, M. C., and Hoffman, J. H.,
    The relationship of ecological and geographic factors to gambling behavior and pathology,
    (2003), 4.

5. National Gambling Impact Commission, *National Gambling Impact Study Commis-sion final report* (Washington, DC, 1999), 1.

6. Barna Group, Morality continues to decay, *The Barna Update* (3 November, 2003),
    available from <http://www.barna.org/FlexPage.aspx?Page=BarnaUpdate&Bar-naUpdateID=152>.

7. <http://www.istoppedgambling.com/view1gambler.htm>.

8. R.B. Breen, and Zimmerman, M., Rapid onset of pathological gambling in
    machine gamblers, *Department of Psychiatry and Human Behavior, Brown University
    School of Medicine,* (2000), 1.

9. <http://www.gamblersanonymous.org/20questions.html>.

10. <http://www.gamblinghelper.com/staticpages/index.php?page=south-oaks

11. <http://www.npgaw.org/pdfs/PDF4.pdf>.

12. American Psychiatric Association, *Diagnostic and statistical manual of mental disor-ders* 4th ed. (Washington, DC: APA, 1994), 672.

13. <http://www.motherjones.com/news/feature/2000/05/shopaholic.html>.

15

Eating Disorders

Linda S. Mintle

Whatever you eat or drink, or whatever you do, do it all to the glory of God.

1 CORINTHIANS 10:31

One of the guiding lights of modern life is that "you can't be too thin or too rich." Whether or not you agree with the cultural values expressed in this phrase, it is undeniable that a vulnerable sub-population of America lives literally by these words. We pass on the greedy and money-obsessed herein to concentrate on the other group of focus: those whose lives are controlled by how and what and when and why they eat.

Millions of Americans live on a permanent cycle of dieting—now a multibillion dollar industry.[1] America is increasingly obsessed with physical culture, with looking good, good health, being thin, being fit, being and functioning at all times at peak levels. This growing obsessiveness drives millions to shape their daily lives around time-consuming regimens of dieting, exercise, muscle toning, cosmetics, plastic surgery, sports competition, and sweat-producing activity of every kind imaginable.

At the same time, tens of millions of Americans are so fat that obesity has recently been tagged a national health problem, affecting one-third of the children, youth, adults, and elderly of the nation—nearly 100 million people![2] We are a nation that has embraced self-indulgence over self-discipline, and now eat for taste and pleasure rather than for sustenance and health. A multibillion dollar culture of fast food, fried food, and junk food has created millions of "couch potatoes" who neither exercise nor control their eating habits in any meaningful way.

While a case may be made that these many millions are beset with eating disorders of myriad types and styles, embedded within this large mass of humanity is our target group of concern—those with truly life-threatening eating disorders. The anorexic, the bulimic, and the severely obese persons suffer uniquely, with psychological, spiritual, familial, and medical problems all converging in a potentially deadly mix of issues that requires a concerted wisdom to help untangle and resolve.

Identifying the Eating Disorders

The psychiatric eating disorders are considered a major public health problem and have the highest morbidity and mortality rates among the psychiatric disorders. Contrary to popular opinion, eating disorder clients are not helped by messages to "just eat" or "get control." Their disorders are serious, even life-threatening, but they are treatable and require careful intervention.

The three types of classified eating disorders from the DSM-IV include anorexia nervosa, bulimia nervosa, and eating disorders not otherwise specified (ED-NOS).[3] The DSM-IV criteria for diagnosing each disorder are indicated in tables 15.1 and 15.2.

Clients diagnosed with anorexia self-starve and may reduce their weight through purging. Purging by vomiting, excessively exercising, using laxatives, diuretics, enemas, or other weight control methods creates more physical damage to the emaciated body than food restricting alone.

An anorexic client may wear baggy clothes to cover her body form. Food may be cut up and moved around the plate to give an illusion of eating. Eating in front of others is often avoided. Food choices are limited, with food categorized as "good" or "bad." Repeated daily weigh-ins are common. The fear of weight gain is beyond reasonable and motivates one to dangerously low weights.

Medical complications often include but are not limited to primary or

TABLE 15.1:
ANOREXIA NERVOSA (307.1)

A. Refusal to maintain body weight at or above a minimally normal weight for age and height (e.g., weight loss leading to maintenance of body weight less than 85% of that expected; or failure to make expected weight gain during period of growth, leading to body weight less than 85% of that expected.

B. Intense fear of gaining weight or becoming fat, even though underweight.

C. Disturbance in the way in which one's body weight or shape is experienced, undue influence of body weight or shape on self-evaluation, or denial of the seriousness of the current low body weight.

D. In postmenarcheal females, amenorrhea, or the absence of at least three consecutive menstrual cycles. (A woman is considered to have amenorrhea if her periods occur only following hormone, e.g., estrogen administration.)

Specify subtype:

Restrictive Type: during the current episode of Anorexia Nervosa, the person has not regularly engaged in binge-eating or purging behavior (i.e., self-induced vomiting or the misuse of laxatives, diuretics, or enemas).

Binge-Eating /Purging Type: during the current episode of Anorexia Nervosa, the person has regularly engaged in binge-eating or purging behavior (i.e., self-induced vomiting or the misuse of laxatives, diuretics, or enemas).

secondary amenorrhea, sexual disinterest or dysfunction, failure of normal breast development in prepubertal females, fetal risk for lower birth rate with active anorexia in pregnancy, dehydration, possible fertility problems even after weight is restored, osteoporosis, GI complications, constipation, abdominal pain, EEG abnormalities, sinus bradycardia, electrolyte disturbances, decrease in muscle mass, MVP, congestive heart failure in aggressive refeeding, cardiac causes of sudden death, anemia, leukopenia and thrombocytopenia, lanugo, and hand calluses from vomiting.

Bulimia usually begins in adolescence and is related to intense feelings of being out of control. While food is the substance used to numb out emotional pain and difficulty, underlying issues must be faced. Food is often

---

TABLE 15.2

BULIMIA NERVOSA (307.51)

A. Recurrent episodes of binge eating. An episode of binge eating is characterized by both of the following:

    (1) eating, in a discrete period of time (e.g., within any 2-hour period), an amount of food that is definitely larger than most people would eat during a similar period of time and under similar circumstances

    (2) a sense of lack of control over eating during the episode (e.g., a feeling that one cannot stop eating or control what or how much one is eating)

B. Recurrent inappropriate compensatory behavior in order to prevent weight gain, such as self-induced vomiting; misuse of laxatives, diuretics, enemas, or other medications; fasting; or excessive exercise

C. The binge eating and inappropriate compensatory behaviors both occur, on average, at least twice a week for 3 months

D. Self-evaluation is unduly influenced by body shape and weight.

E. The disturbance does not occur exclusively during episodes of Anorexia Nervosa.

Specify **type:**

Purging type: during the current episode of Bulimia Nervosa, the person has regularly engaged in self-induced vomiting or the misuse of laxatives, diuretics, or enemas.

Nonpurging type: during the current episode of Bulimia Nervosa, the person has used other inappropriate compensatory behaviors, such as fasting or excessive exercise, but has not regularly engaged in self-induced vomiting or the misuse of laxatives, diuretics, or enemas.

---

used as the coping mechanism for anger, anxiety, depression, and stress related to many areas of life. The shame and guilt that accompanies bingeing is relieved through the act of purging. This cycle of shame then relief lends itself to secrecy. It is not uncommon for family members or spouses to be unaware that the client is engaging in bulimic behavior.

Bulimia is not always observable. Weight can be normal because of the compensatory mechanism of purging that stabilizes possible weight gain from bingeing. Weight gain is feared and body dissatisfaction is high.

Medical complications can include but are not limited to: dehydration, hypochloremia, hyperkalemia, pulmonary symptoms associated with vomiting, erosion of dental enamel, salivary gland hypotrophy, pancreatitus, esophagitis and perforation, gastric dilatation, reflex constipation, idiopathic edema, EKG abnormalities, MVP, dry skin, finger and hand abrasions, abnormal EEG, endocrine and metabolic abnormalities.

Eating Disorder Not Otherwise Specified (307.50)

According to the DSM-IV, this category is reserved for "disorders of eating that do not meet the criteria for any specific Eating Disorder."[4] Six examples are given and include clients who

1.   have anorexic symptoms but are menstruating,
2.   self-starvers with a weight loss less than 15% of ideal body weight,
3.   binge eaters who binge less often than the determined criteria,
4.   those who purge after eating small amounts of food,
5.   not swallowing but chewing and spitting out food, and
6.   those who binge eat but do not purge.

Binge eating disorder. It is this last subclinical category—binge eating disorder—that accounts for a large proportion of clients who enter treatment. Research criteria for this disorder are found on p. 731 of the DSM-IV.

The major difference with bulimia nervosa is that these clients do not purge their bodies of excess calories by vomiting, laxative abuse, diuretics, etc. They gain weight and basically engage in a form of compulsive eating.

Binge eaters present with more depression, anxiety and other psychological disturbances when compared to people with similar weight problems. It is estimated that 30% of people who participate in hospital-based weight programs; 10–15% of participants in nonmedical diet programs; 4% of college students; and 2% of people in the general population may be defined as binge eaters.[5]

Binge eating has serious emotional and physical side effects. The constant battle with feeling out-of-control often leads to feelings of self-disgust, low self-worth and self-esteem. Overweight or obesity can bring social bias, discrimination and prejudice, as well as body image problems. Dieting leads to a yo-yo cycle of weight loss and gain that takes a physical toll on the body.

Binge eaters may suffer medical risk similar to obesity—diabetes (Type II, or adult onset), hypertension, stroke, dyslipidemia, cardiovascular disease, gallbladder disease, respiratory disease, cancer, arthritis and gout.

Etiology of Eating Disorders

Eating is a behavior of complex influence. Researchers continue to study why some people move from occasional struggles with food and weight to preoccupation and obsession. What causes a 16-year-old to jeopardize her health by repeated laxative abuse? What makes an honor student starve herself to the point of serious metabolic imbalance? What motivates a young adult to think only of her next binge?

Eating disorders are primarily of psychological and spiritual origin even though they have physical complications and may be influenced by genetic/biological factors. There is no one single cause but rather a host of variables that may contribute to onset. The combination of multiple influences and vulnerability to those influences over time, can lead to development of a disorder.

Clinical presentation involves abnormal eating patterns that include self-starvation, compulsive eating, or compulsive eating and self-induced purging. While dieting and weight focus may be an obvious entrée to an eating disorder, there is more to consider. All three patterns share in common certain symptoms: intense fear of gaining weight, excessive preoccupation with food and eating, chronic dieting, poor body image, depression and the need for approval by others.

Age, Gender, Race and Ethnicity

Development of eating disorders favors females more so than males. The ratio for anorexia and bulimia is approximately one male to ten females in community based epidemiology studies. This ratio also holds true in larger clinical-based studies. Binge eating disorder claims a higher percentage (35%) of males, with the overall rate of eating disorders increasing in males.[6]

Males who develop eating disorders are influenced by a culture that promotes a fit and buffed body as a sign of masculinity and success. Body shape versus weight is more the concern of men. Exercise, as opposed to dieting, is often the entrée into symptom development. Dieting plays a role related to playing sports, past obesity, gender identity conflicts, and avoidance of feared medical illness.

Anorexia is estimated to affect 0.5% to 3.7% of females in their lifetime; bulimia will affect 1.1% to 4.2% of females;[7] and binge eating in a six-month period will be experienced by 2–5% of both genders.[8] Approximately half of all Americans are overweight, with one-third falling into the category of obese (usually measured by at least 20% over ideal body weight).[9]

In the past, eating disorders were most prevalent among higher socioeconomic Caucasian groups. Now they cut across all classes, races and ethnicities. No longer relegated to the Western world, eating disorders have appeared in remote places like the Fiji Islands. What was once only a concern of the Western world has taken on global significance.

No other psychiatric disorder has higher morbidity or mortality rates. The mortality rate for people with anorexia is 0.56% per year. This rate is 12 times higher than the annual death rate due to all causes of death among females ages 15–24 in the general population.[10] Generally, about one-third of eating disorders fully recover; one third recovers with periodic problems; and one-third remains chronically ill.[11]

Family and Life Cycle Development

The clinician should identify the client's life and family developmental stage. Typically, these disorders emerge at transition to puberty and launching from the family home. Adolescence is also a developmental hot bed for onset because it is a time of identity formation and definition. Anorexia not only keeps a client childlike in physical appearance but also retards the normal development of separation and individuation.[12]

Dating, sexuality, gender identity and assertion of the forming self are put on hold for pursuit of a false identity that becomes enslaving, but protective. Progressive growth toward independence is expected but frightening given the challenges faced by the culture, family, interpersonal relationships and self-expectations. Anorexic symptoms may represent a failed attempt to separate and individuate.

Bulimia usually develops later in adolescence and young adulthood related to similar developmental transitions. A crisis time for many is the launching phase from family to independent functioning outside the family system. Bulimia can signify difficulty making this transition. Bulimics tend to approach life from an all or nothing mind set, thus mimicking the binge-purge cycle of their symptoms.

It should be noted that failure to discover a spiritual identity in Christ is also lacking with these clients. Often they have distorted views of God the Father and are unaware of accurate biblical descriptions of who they are in relationship to God and others.

Cultural Influences

Cultural influences, particularly attitudes about weight and the feminine ideal, play a role in the development of eating disorders. Women are expected to be thin and attractive, men to be buffed and in shape. Media vilify overweight people and convince girls early on that they need to be thin to be successful or accepted.

Other cultural influencers include the food, diet, fashion, beauty and health industries. All dangle the "thin" carrot promising a life of happiness and love through attainment of the perfect body. This message stands in stark contrast to the words of Jesus. He looks on the heart, prioritizing the building of inner character conformed to His image. To be like Him is often counter to the message promulgated by our culture.

Personality Factors

Those who develop eating disorders often have difficulty coping with stress. Other problem areas include dealing with conflict, appropriately asserting the self, negative thinking and holding unrealistic expectations.

Studies link avoidant personalities with anorexia, citing the tendency towards perfectionism and emotional and sexual inhibition as characteristic. Other studies on bulimia have found connections between borderline and narcissistic personalities, hallmarked by impulsivity, unstable mood, thoughts, behavior and self-image. Chaos is a chronic state. Hypersensitivity to criticism along with an inability to sooth the self or empathize with others describes many bulimics.[13]

Comorbid Disorders

In many cases, eating disorders coexist with other psychiatric disorders. Most frequently noted are depression, anxiety, obsessive-compulsive disorder, post-traumatic stress disorder, personality disorders (as noted above) and occasionally psychotic disorders. Eating disorders also correlate highly with sexual abuse and bulimics have high rates of substance abuse.[14]

Mood, thinking, concentration and behavior are all affected by starvation and should be assessed as they relate to the eating disorder. The same is true for other medical conditions that may mimic eating disorder symptoms.

Assessment of Eating Disorders

Assessment—which is, in fact, the beginning of intervention—includes a structured interview with the client and the family; a complete physical to rule out medical causes and assess the client's physiological state related to the disorder; and nutritional work-up to determine eating habits, calorie intake, refeeding strategy and food choices. In addition, self-report measures may be used to help assess severity of the disorder and treatment progress. Commonly used surveys are the EAT,[15] the EDI—2[16], and the BULIT—R,[17] a reliable measure of the severity of bulimia nervosa.

The eating disorder evaluation should cover presenting problem, history of presenting problem, height, weight, dieting efforts, weight history, frequency and type of binges and purges, substance abuse or use, exercise behavior, weight phobia, past psychiatric history, mental status, medical complaints and history (including amenhorrea), and family history of functioning and psychiatric disorders, losses, changes, and stressors. During evaluation, particular attention should be paid to the psychosocial barriers to treatment, with reducing them an implicit goal even at this stage. Diagnosis of co-morbid conditions also should be made at this time.

Assess Family and Interpersonal Influences

Negative family patterns influence the development and/or maintenance of eating symptoms. Parental and sibling behavior and attitudes towards dieting and appearance are frequently mentioned as negative. The level of enmeshment or detachment among family members plays a role and should be evaluated. Marital distress, substance abuse and sexual abuse should be areas of investigation.

Anorexic families tend to be more rigid and have less clear interpersonal boundaries. Disagreement between members rarely surfaces because of the premium placed on family consensus. In an attempt to appear adequate and respectable, families often hide their indirect communication, chronic unhappiness, fear of their daughters' emerging sexuality, and preoccupation with their own looks and dieting. The family typically tries to please the therapist and appear socially desirable. An ideal view of family life is often purported. Under the surface may lurk parental conflict, need, anger and stress.

Bulimic families tend to be more unstable in their organization. It often appears that parents are somewhat neglectful or hostile in parenting, with the bulimic daughter angrily submitting to their authority. Mothers of bulimic daughters are commonly described as "neglectful" and fathers as "affectionless." Criticism toward the child is higher than in anorexic families.[18]

In both family systems, joint parental authority is questionable. Parents often struggle with giving their child age-appropriate autonomy or reasonable control. Child-rearing differences may be a function of lack of agreement or distress in the marital subsystem.

Do Genetics and Biology Play a Role?

At present, researchers are investigating the role genetics and biology play in the transmission of eating disorders. Eating disorders run in families with anorexics having an eight times higher chance of developing the disorder if a relative has it.[19]

Peg a Target Weight

Important to the initial evaluation is establishing an ideal and target weight to be used throughout treatment. *Ideal weight* is usually determined by locating numbers on the most recent insurance charts that provide weight ranges by height and body frame. Body mass index (BMI) is a more accurate measure of body fatness but few clinicians can work easily with this index.

A *target weight* (the lowest safe weight acceptable for treatment) is calculated by taking 90% of the midpoint of the ideal range. It is best to have agreement on the target weight with the physician and dietitian because clients regularly try to negotiate this number. Calculate the target weight, talk to the client and team and make the number nonnegotiable.

To estimate the client's percentage of weight below ideal, divide the client's current weight by the ideal midpoint (It helps to have a doctor's scale or access to one in order to weigh the client.). For example, a client is 5'6" tall, weighs 110 pounds. According to the insurance table, her ideal range is 128–143. The midpoint of that number is 135.5.

Divide her current weight (110) by the midpoint (135) to obtain a percentage of her weight against her ideal. In this example, the percentage is 81. Then subtract that percentage from 100 and you have the percent below ideal weight to use for diagnosis (DSM-IV criteria for anorexia is 15% or more below expected body weight). This client is 19% below ideal and meets clinical criteria.

Define the Level of Care

Two important questions should be asked prior to determining level of care:

1. How chronic are the symptoms? Generally, the longer an eating disorder is untreated, the more difficult it is to remit.
2. How severe are the symptoms? Hospitalization or residential services should be seriously considered when clients are suicidal or psychotic, have very low weight, refeeding must be supervised, purging is excessive, there is repeated outpatient failure and/or immediate medical danger (e.g., severe electrolyte imbalance).

Reduce Barriers to Treatment

This population is especially difficult to treat because of numerous psychological and physical barriers. Barriers to successful treatment that should be assessed include:

1. Labeling these disorders as acts of will and self-control. Clients and family members often believe they should be able to *will* themselves out of these disorders and take control. Usually there is little to no understanding of the emotional, spiritual and interpersonal complexities involved in healing.
2. Denial. Clients usually have distorted body images. They often deny the level of self-harm they inflict. A low weight anorexic

truly sees herself as fat no matter what people say to her. This deception allows her to continue self-harm. Spiritually, denial and deception are married in an unholy union that leaves the client paralyzed to move out of this bondage. Past hurts and woundings are gateways for deceptive thinking to enter the mind. Denial serves a secondary gain function to push away painful feelings and experiences. Pain is redirected to the body through false control of food.

3. Idols in the form of food and restraint. Food is less about sustenance and more about preoccupation and obsession. When a client loses weight, she is often complimented. After significant weight loss, worry replaces compliments. The client begins to idolize the pursuit of thinness. Food restriction feels self-righteous and is often described as a desired "high." Food claims the client's loyalty. What began as a method of control, ends as idol worship. "The thinner I am, the better I am. Denial of the self brings suffering that elevates me above others."

4. Minimizing the problem. Many clients delay treatment because they hope the eating disorder will resolve itself with time. The eating disorder may be reframed as "a phase," "a fad" or "experimentation."

5. Shame and guilt. It is very unpleasant to admit to bingeing and then vomiting. Secrecy and shame surround these disorders and often block cries for help.

6. Pride. It is difficult to admit to a therapist and to God that you are out-of-control and need outside help. Pride prevents clients from laying down the self-sufficiency gauntlet and depending on God.

7. Lack of faith. To trust someone to help you requires an act of faith. When a client is bound by an eating disorder there is no evidence of eating returning to normal. Preoccupation and obsession take hold. Freedom is unseen but hoped for. Faith requires a client to say, "I see no way out of my bondage, but I will trust the therapist, and more importantly God, to help me be free."

8. Fear of treatment. Freedom means giving up a false identity and doing the hard work to create whom you were intended to be. It means facing pain, emptiness and hurt. It means discomfort, struggle and reorganization.

9. Financial barriers. Unfortunately, eating disorders treatment can be expensive. Lack of health insurance coverage, high hospital and program costs prevent many from accessing or continuing care.

10. Access: Available programs and specialty therapists. There may be few to no eating disorder programs or therapists available in a community. Shorter hospital stays, combined with rigid admission criteria, may prevent many from getting needed services. In addition, managed care policies limit visits, services, and choice of providers. Treatment options may be limited to availability of affordable services.

Treatment: A Multidisciplinary and Multifaceted Approach

The therapist assesses a client's clinical picture and knows when to act. Care giving for this population requires participation with a multidisciplinary team of professionals, all playing an important role in the transformation and healing of the client.

Assembling the Multidisciplinary Team

The multidisciplinary team should include the following:

1. A psychiatrist (MD). A complete physical is highly recommended for all clients entering treatment and becomes part of the three-pronged assessment process (see Assessment). The use of medication is a treatment decision made collaboratively by the therapist, the psychiatrist and the client. Not all eating disorder clients need medication. And in many cases, medications may be counter indicated. However, when appropriate, particularly when comorbid conditions exist, a psychiatrist or knowledgeable physician prescribes these medications as therapy adjuncts.

2. Other medical doctors (MD). A working relationship with an internist, endocrinologist, family practitioner, or in the case of younger children, a pediatrician is essential. The MD follows the client's physical condition and offers baseline and ongoing monitoring of physical status (e.g., electrolyte imbalance, weight gain, gastric distress, amenhorrea, etc.). It is important to find a

physician who is empathetic to eating disorder clients and understands his/her role on the team.

3. An individual therapist. This person should be trained in the specialty practice of eating disorders so that cognitive and behavioral connections with eating and weight issues can be directly linked to underlying problems. The individual therapist works with the client to address those personal issues leading to symptomatic eating behavior and monitors progress towards healing.

4. A family therapist. The family therapist works with the individual in the context of his/her intimate relationships and family. Families influence the development and maintenance of eating disorders and are an integral part of treatment. Generally, the younger the client, the more essential it is to have the family directly participate in treatment.

5. A group therapist. Eating disorder clients can benefit from group work whether it is supportive, psychoeducational or interpersonally focused. Group needs to be a safe place to share struggles with fellow sojourners. It can be an adjunct to therapy or a hot bed for dealing with dynamics in interpersonal functioning. Group work is particularly meaningful for college students and young adults living away from their families because it provides a therapeutic arena for interpersonal work.

6. A registered dietitian (RD). The RD completes an evaluation of eating habits, food choices and caloric intake. He/she then works with the client to develop healthy eating patterns and food choices. Often this requires the client to keep a food journal. If weight gain is needed, the RD, along with the physician, directs that path. If weight loss is an appropriate goal, the RD sets a sensible course based on healthy eating. The client's frequency of RD visits depends on treatment goals, weight and/or the client's need for on-going food supervision and accountability.

7. An exercise physiologist. This person provides input regarding exercise. Very low weight patients may need to stop exercise and temporarily be placed on bed rest during refeeding. An exercise physiologist can instruct the client how to safely add exercise into a daily living plan. Since exercise is often an area of obsession and excess, regulating the amount and intensity may be a treatment goal.

8. Supervision and peer consultation. The seriousness of symptoms, the power of denial and resistance, a therapist's own biases and tendency to be inducted into the family system are all reasons to have access to supervision and peer consultation.

Treatment Planning

Post evaluation, you should develop a working plan with the client and establish a workable treatment plan. The plan should include recommendations for intervention from the physician and dietitian, input from the exercise physiologist, psychiatric follow up for medication if needed, a target and ideal weight goal, level of care (inpatient, outpatient, day treatment, etc.), modalities of treatment (individual, family and/or group therapy, adjunctive therapies and supports), collaborative goals, and estimated length and frequency of treatment.

Treatment Goals

Treatment goals would include but should not be limited to:

1. attaining and maintaining a healthy weight
2. restoration/establishment of healthy eating habits
3. treatment and stabilization of comorbid conditions
4. behavioral and cognitive changes regarding eating, food and weight
5. affect regulation—maintaining a stable mood and learning how to regulate mood without resort to destructive behaviors
6. increased acceptance of self and body
7. reducing drives toward perfectionism, control, and distorted (fat) perceptions of self and body
8. clearer sense of identity—especially attaining a new and deeper sense of one's identity in Christ
9. family changes that support separation-individuation, launching and independent functioning
10. relapse prevention (and what to do if one relapses)
11. reintegration into family, school, and peer groups

The Role of Individual Therapy

The individual therapist is usually the point of contact for the client. The individual therapist manages the patient's care like a quarterback leads the team. It is important for him/her to understand the life-threatening nature of these disorders. Treatment is usually intense and prolonged. The therapist must be able to manage his/her countertransference and be genuinely caring and empathetic.

The therapist should be knowledgeable concerning the connection of eating with psychological issues, be truthful about treatment plans and tolerate hopelessness from the client. An ability to be firm, yet loving, consistent and challenging, and have a sense of humor helps. The work is often slow but rewarding.

It is helpful for the therapist to be at a healthy weight and have resolved any issues concerning his/her weight and body image. A vibrant Christian life and spiritual passion fuels the work as well. Emotional, spiritual and interpersonal issues are played out through the arena of food and weight preoccupation. The most effective models of individual therapy use a cognitive-behavioral or interpersonal therapy approach.[20]

Challenges to identity, denial, and faith. Individual therapy challenges the client to relinquish the false identity of the eating disorder. Preoccupation and obsession with food and weight distracts from individual development. Letting go of symptoms may be desired, but frightening. The client must face what feels like an overwhelming world without her false sense of security. This is why change is so powerfully resisted.

Individual therapy must also address eating symptoms, i.e., decreasing the binge/purge cycle and food restriction. Denial of the severity and power of symptoms creates resistance. Surrender requires an act of faith. The client must choose to uncover underlying symptoms and have the courage to make change. Trust in the therapist is needed. Since other people are perceived as a mistrustful, trust is not quickly established. It is an act of faith to relinquish control and trust.

Repentance is also required in that the client, through spiritual pride, has concluded, "I must handle life on my own. I cannot trust God nor will I be dependent on Him. I must take control." This position, born out of pain, confronts the reality that control is elusive. A cycle ensues—pain and failure followed by attempts to seize control (through the food), followed by loss of control that leads to pain and failure.

The client must understand that to be whole and function with a sound mind is not accomplished by perfection or success, but by allowing God to work through her for His glory. He will direct her path if she is willing to be led. He unconditionally accepts her. Walking down this unseen and unfamiliar path requires faith.

The eating disordered person lives by some powerful lies about God and self. These must be exposed and the truth learned and recited and practiced on a daily, even hourly basis. Dependence on God is not weakness. God, unlike people, does not disappoint. Belief in self-sufficiency ends in continual striving. Anorexia is a misguided attempt to be self-sufficient; bulimia utilizes self-striving in an effort to gain control.

Symptom Tracking

The therapist helps the client connect eating symptoms with underlying psychological issues and directs her towards health. Underlying issues have to do with separation/individuation from family of origin, facing developmental tasks such as dating, budding sexuality, and launching from the home, finding identity through Christ, correcting distorted views of self, identifying and appropriately expressing emotion, working though personal experiences such as sexual abuse, substance abuse or other losses and trauma, tackling perfectionism and dichotomous thinking, learning to be less hypersensitive to criticism, identifying fears of intimacy and closeness, confronting conflict, learning to problem-solve and becoming appropriately assertive. Overall, the therapist helps empower the client to discover and be her authentic self.

A simple tracking chart can be used to help clients connect symptoms to situations, emotions and thoughts. Consider using the Dysfunctional Thought Record (DTR) to track key behavior, emotions, and thinking.[21]

Once the client begins tracking her eating behavior, she can identify patterns with situations, emotions or thoughts that trigger symptomatic behavior. Intervention can focus on changing the situation (antecedent or consequence), working through the emotion and developing better coping skills. The DTR is useful not only for correcting dysfunctional thoughts in the process of renewing the mind, but for finding positive thoughts and situations that can be reinforced and encouraged (such as the last interaction noted above).

DYSFUNCTIONAL THOUGHT RECORD

Basically, the client keeps a record under three columns—Situation (a brief description of what was happening when the eating behavior occurred), Emotion(s) (What did the client feel? On a scale from 0–100, how strong was the feeling?), Automatic Thought(s) (What was the thought that ran through the client's head? On a scale from 0–100, how strongly did the client believe the thought?). Adding a fourth column entitled "Behavior" is used to record a binge, purge or food restriction. The client lists the eating behavior under the first column "Behavior", then the "Situation" under which it occurred, next the felt "Emotion" and it's intensity, and finally the "Automatic Thought" that ran through his/her mind, rating how strongly he/she believed it. For example:

Behavior	Situation	Emotion	Automatic Thought
Binged/purged	Break up with boyfriend	Hurt 90%	I am unlovable (80%)
Food restricted	Mom telling me to eat	Angry (40%)	I am not a child (90%)
Looking at self in mirror	Morning habit	Discouraged (70%)	Still too fat (90%)
Flirting w/ boyfriend	After school	Pleased/confused	He's wrong—I can't look that good (70%)

Identity in Christ

Central to the work of healing is developing a strong identity based in Christ. While family, peers and culture influence who we become, it is through an understanding and experience of the one true Christ that a client is empowered to be who God intended him/her to be.

A Christ-based identity is not easily shaken and is a point of reference when facing turmoil from the stresses of life. The client must understand that God cares more about his/her character and conformity to Him than his/her outward appearance and accomplishments. Perfection is unachievable and works do not warrant God's grace.

As respected apologist Os Guinness notes, "A life lived listening to the decisive call of God is a life lived before one audience that trumps all others—the Audience of One." Twenty Scripture references such as Ephesians 1:4, Psalm 139:2 & 14, Hebrews 13:5 lay the foundation for discovery of true identity and pleasing only the "Audience of One."[22]

Thinking is often distorted leading to a negative view of the self and others. A renewing of the mind is also essential to healing. Distorted thoughts should be challenged in therapy and the client asked to generate more rational thoughts based on biblical knowledge and an enlightened view of self.

For example, the thought, "I am no good because I am not thin enough" can be challenged by asking the client to defend that position biblically and uncover fears of inadequacy. "Thin enough" is an attempt to achieve "goodness." It is a failed solution. We can never be "good enough" for God's grace. His Holy Spirit can help us accept our "good enough" status as God's creation and beloved.

Family Therapy

Family therapy is especially needed when working with younger clients. However, it is highly recommended for treatment of all eating disorders. Typically the eating disorder client has been the caretaker of others in the family. This role preempts focus on critical self needs and development.

In general, fathers tend to be emotionally unavailable and mothers over- or under-involved. Siblings do not form a cohesive subsystem. Communication is often indirect and conflict is poorly managed. Eating and weight issues are symptomatic of these struggles.

Marital tension is usually present but unresolved. The client is often the peacemaker or apex of a marital triangle. One or both parents may confide their unhappiness, burdening the client who has no way to make repair. Client needs are usually sacrificed for family needs.

In the case of anorexic families, emotions are constricted as the family strives to give the impression of happiness and perfection. In bulimic families, problems are more clearly identified but not resolved. The eating disorder is an attempt to bring order to a chaotic system. The "identified patient" requires the family to rally around the problem, thus bringing order and solution to an out-of-order system.

Parenting is often characterized by extremes—either enmeshed and overprotective or under-involved and disconnected. Symptoms serve to help the client separate but still be cared for and nurtured.

The work of the family is to free the eating disorder client from her assumed role of solving family problems or reorganizing relationships through illness. The eating disorder is reframed as a system problem with the client responsible for symptom reduction. Stopping food restriction or bingeing and purging are reframed as responses to interpersonal and intrapersonal pain and emptiness. New responses are possible and more adaptive. The family has the choice to grow and learn new ways of nurturing each other and deal with their pain. This family context must be addressed directly with the family system or indirectly in individual therapy with a systemic therapist.

Transformation, Not Just Recovery

As noted, about one-third of all clients with eating disorders recover. This statistic is disheartening when you consider two-thirds remain ill or chronically trying to cope. From a faith perspective, healing, through the grace and mercy of our sovereign God, is always possible. Therefore, the Christian seeks more than recovery. The desired outcome is personal transformation through the power of Jesus Christ. Everything old becomes new when surrendered to Christ.

The power of the Holy Spirit can heal and transform in ways unknown to our limited understanding. While we use all the training and knowledge extracted from research and clinical practice, we recognize the supernatural realm as greater than our comprehension. Both therapists and clients should depend on the work of the Holy Spirit to give wisdom and intervene to change lives.

There is hope for even the most desperate case because of Christ. Because of the abiding presence of God, the hope and future promised in Him, promised freedom from bondage and enslavement, and the radical message that, in Christ, past is not prologue to future, we can be transformed and set free.

"Therefore, if anyone is in Christ, he is a new creation; old things have past away; behold all things have become new." (2 Cor. 5:17)

ENDNOTES

1.   Statistics: *How many people have eating and exercise disorders?* Available from <http://www.anred.com.

2.   Statistics,<http://www.anred.com.

3.   American Psychiatric Association, *Diagnostic and statistical manual of mental disor-*

ders, fourth ed. (Washington, D.C.: American Psychiatric Association, 1994).

4. American Psychiatric Association, 550.

5. J. E. Brody, Study defines "Binge Eating Disorder": Report from Dr. Robert L. Spitzer at the Annual Scientific Meeting of the Society of Behavioral Medicine, *New York Times,* (March 27, 1992), A16.

6. A. Anderson, Eating disorders in males, in K.D. Brownell, and Fairburn, C.G. (eds.), *Eating disorders and obesity: A comprehensive handbook* (New York: The Guilford Press, 1995).

7. American Psychiatric Association Work Group on Eating Disorders, Practical guidelines for the treatment of patients with eating disorders (rev.), *American Journal of Psychiatry* 157 (1 Suppl), (2000), 1–39.

8. Robert Spitzer, Yanovski, S., Wadden, T., Wing, R., Marcus, M. D., Stunkard, A., Devlin, M., Mitchell, J., Hasin, D., and Horne, R. L., Binge eating disorder: Its further validation in a multisite study, *International Journal of Eating Disorders* 12, (1992), 137–53.

9. Statistics,<http://www.anred.com.

10. P. F.Sullivan, Mortality in anorexia nervosa, *American Journal of Psychiatry* 152(7), (1995), 1073–1074.

11. M. Maine, AAMFT clinical update: Eating disorders, *A supplement to the Family Therapy News* 1 (6), (November 1999), 1.

12. W. Vandereycken, The families of patients with an eating disorder, in K.D. Brownell, and Fairburn, C.G. (eds.), *Eating disorders and obesity: A comprehensive handbook* (New York: The Guilford Press, 1995).

13. WebMD Health On-line, what are eating disorders?, Available from <http://www.webmd.com.

14. Maine, 1999

15. D. M. Garner, Garfinkle, P.E., Olmstead, M.P., and Bohr, Y., The eating attitudes test: Psychometric features and clinical correlations, *Psychological Medicine* 12, (1982), 871–878.

16. D. M. Garner, *Eating disorders inventory—2* (Odessa, FL: Psychological Assessment Resources, 1991).

17. M. H. Thelen, Farmer, J., Wonderlich, S., and Smith, M., A revision of the bulimic test: The BULIT-R. psychological assessment, *Journal of Consulting and Clinical Psychology,* 3, (1991), 119–124.

18. Vandereycken, 1995.

19. WebMD Health Online.

20. National Institute of Mental Health, *NIMH eating disorders: Facts about eating disorders and the search for solutions* (NIH Publication No. 01–4901, 2001).

21. A. T. Beck, Rush, A.J., Shaw, B.F., & Emery, G., *Cognitive therapy of depression* (New York: Guilford Press, 1979).

22. Os Guinness, *The call* (Nashville: Word, 1998).

16

Suicide Intervention

*George Ohlschlager, Mark Shadoan, and Gary Stewart**

> Suicide is not abominable because God prohibits it; God prohibits it
> because it is abominable.
>
> IMMANUEL KANT

The room was packed. It was full of experienced helpers—really, of shell-shocked and tough-minded New York counselors, pastors, and emergency workers who had been living with 9–11 and its aftermath for over a month. In 40 days they had seen, smelled, tasted, and soaked in more death than most of us will in a 40-year career. We at AACC had collected some of our best therapists and academics, grief workers, crisis interventionists, and pastors from all over the country to join us in New York City in late October 2001 and intensively train nearly 1,500 Christian leaders who were helping people deal with the death and trauma.

As I surveyed the audience I could already see the exhaustion, the beginnings of a long-term vicarious trauma in too many faces—the impact

---

* This chapter adapts and updates the first author's chapter on suicide from his coauthored book on *Law for the Christian Counselor* (Word Books, 1992). Additional material, on treatment process and on the attributes and orientation to God of the suicidal person, was graciously contributed by the 2nd and 3rd authors.

of 9–11 was thick and heavy among the group. Yet, at the historic Calvary Baptist Church in mid-town Manhattan, they were ready to hear me speak about "Suicidal Distress." I was going to pile death to come upon the mass death that already existed. I prayed silently for divine guidance, took a deep breath, and dove right in:

Increased suicide and suicidal thinking is one perverse outcome—one that is fairly predictable—of the terrorist trauma of September 11 and the crisis of post-traumatic stress that is growing in New York City. This great city will likely experience a level of suicidal distress—which will include many suicidal attempts and far too many successful attempts—over the next few years unlike anything previous in its spiritual and mental health history. We can expect a rise of suicidal distress—and should target our precious intervention resource—among three groups:

- *those directly affected—people injured and families who have lost loved ones,*
- *the heroes of 9–11—police, firemen, rescue workers, and other emergency personnel, and*
- *those vicariously affected by the September 11 terror strike who already live on a fragile edge.*

That's the bad news. And the worst of this bad news is that the pool of at-risk people likely numbers in the tens of thousands, maybe over a hundred thousand people. The possibility of overwhelming the care and response systems of this city is significant.

The good news is that you—the Christian counselor armed with this foreknowledge—can be available to help pre-empt and cut-off some (and we mean just some) of this horrible and further death before it strikes those survivors who will lose hope of living. And among those who succeed in the terrible tragedy of self-murder, you will be prepared to give succor and solace to the grieving ones who loved the suicide victim.

The seeds of lost hope are contained in many of the stories now being told by the families who lost a loved one on that black day in New York. At the funeral of her 45 year-old son, one widowed woman carried on with her friend about how her son's coffin contained just a picture and a rock-n-roll CD he particularly enjoyed. At the end of the service, she cried and exclaimed to whoever would listen, "This can't be for my son . . . I don't even have a body! This isn't a death. It's a disintegration, an abolishment."[1]

Powerful words that are now spoken in shock and anger, in a state of surreal confusion. In the months and years to come, however, these same words may just as easily be spoken in despair and hopelessness, by an old woman now alone in the world and longing for death in a brutal and horrible world. This first winter after the terror there will be hundreds of fragile victims who, overcome by the evil of this mass murder, the craziness of it, the horror of it, will look upon death—will embrace a hoped-for painless suicide—as sweet release from a life that has turned ugly, painful, bitter, and meaningless. When all the help and hoopla are gone, things may even be worse.

If this sounds bad, it is because it is bad. There are literally tens of thousands of traumatized, struggling people who have suffered through the hardest winters of their lives over the last few years. All the more reason to pray for and call down a spiritual revival of enormous proportions. God alone can transform the evil, can make straight the crooked way, can bring life out of death and ashes and despair.

The Data and Dynamics of Suicide

Facing a suicidal client or parishioner is one of the most stressful—and most fearful—times in the life of a counselor or pastor. Suicide is surely one of counseling's most difficult "occupational hazards." A client or parishioner who kills themselves not only devastates family and friends, but also adversely impacts the counselor long after the event.[2] We explore this tragedy and the moral, clinical and pastoral aspects of suicide assessment and intervention in this chapter.

Friedrich Nietzsche, the famous 19th-century German philosopher, asserted in *Beyond Good and Evil* that "The thought of suicide is a great consolation; with the help of it one gets successfully through many a bad night." This statement reveals a number of reasons why suicide is such a paradox; why it has a complex and controversial history in America and Western culture. Suicidal thinking in time of crisis is fairly common, even attractive to the desperate, yet there exists great fear and a seemingly cultural taboo that bars open acknowledgment of its attraction and familiarity.

This strange attraction, the tragic choice of death over life, is what so greatly confounds us and strikes us with fear. It makes no sense to the well-living how suicide could be such "great consolation." To the person who has lost all hope of relieving intense and unending pain, whether physical or psychological, suicide can easily become an obsessive consolation, a final solution when nothing else beckons.

In the distorted and pain-dominated judgment of the sufferer, suicide may be the most logical and effective choice to resolve what is perceived as an impossible problem. And for family and friends left behind, it is a shocking trauma that leaves scars that can take a lifetime to heal. The gripping story of her son's suicide by Corrine Chilstrom, a pastoral consultant in the Evangelical Lutheran Church of America, reveals the unique tragedy of suicide.

> As a pastor and mother, I have witnessed the tragic death of my youngest son by suicide... Eighteen, a freshman in college, [Andrew] was home for the weekend when he died of a self-inflicted wound to his head...It happened about 3 A.M...Sleeping in our bedroom, buffered from the sound...we slept through the shot which would forever change our lives.
>
> It was our Sunday off. We had planned a leisurely breakfast, worship with Andrew, brunch at a restaurant...Those well-made plans suddenly turned into chaos, finding his room empty, lights and TV on, and his note by the phone...his words grabbed us with panic. We rushed to the basement...
>
> Herb was first to the landing. As if he had been grabbed, he stopped short, gasping, "Oh, my God!" White as a sheet, he held me back, saying, "Don't look." All I saw was Andrew's legs. Favorite old khaki pants and black high top canvas shoes.
>
> There are no words to describe the fright of finding him. Or the stumbling up the stairs. Or the frenzy to make those first calls for help. Or what followed. Police. Coroner. Sisters and friends coming on the run. Getting our children home. Crying with his friends. Choosing a casket. Facing the fact of family suicide. Missing him. Wanting him. Becoming suicide survivors.[3]

We must pull back, however, and not let an empathy that helps us understand the suicidal mind push us to accept suicide as a right to be exercised by all those wishing it. Ideas have consequences; good ones have good consequences and bad ones have bad consequences. One bad idea, increasingly prevalent in our day, is that suicide is acceptable in all its forms (self-murder, euthanasia, physician-assisted). The euthanasia movement that asserts a "right to die" and to assist those wanting to die is a growing and powerful assault against our moral and legal prohibition that forbids suicide assistance.

Suicide has pushed its way into the eighth leading cause of death in the United States—tragically, it is the third leading cause of death among teenagers. Approximately 3/4 million suicide attempts take place in America every year—over 2,000 people attempt to kill themselves every day, and 85 of these succeed; 31,000 die every year, or about 4% of those who make attempts.[4] Roughly 40% of these deaths are by persons over 65 years of age, most suffering in pain from terminal and debilitating disease. A quarter of all suicides are by young people between the age of 15 and 24, a three-fold increase in the rate of suicide within this age group in a quarter-century.

The dynamics of suicide are highly complex; simplistic reasons to explain it and easy solutions to prevent it are nonexistent. It is not just a matter of acute and severe depression, although the National Institute of Mental Health considers depression the leading cause. It requires more than restraining or avoiding lethal behavior, although individuals must act aggressively to kill themselves. Though options always exist, the suicidal person is overcome by constricting choices, sabotaged by a perverse tunnel-vision that survivors often express as, "It became *the only thing left* to do."

Finally, it is not just a problem of meaningless and existential despair, although Aaron Beck and his colleagues[5] have shown that hopelessness is even more influential than depression in completed suicides. A pastor and Christian psychologist cogently argue that "suicide is primarily, although not entirely, a spiritual problem. Persons who are suicidal are asking, either explicitly or implicitly, such critical existential questions as: Does my life have meaning or purpose? Do I have any worth? Is forgiveness possible? Is there any hope for a new life beyond this current mess?"[6]

We Are All Vulnerable

Under certain circumstances, most of us can be tempted to opt for "deadly peace" at the expense of life itself. Whether we are speaking of self-execution in our formidable years or assisted suicide because of the ravages of disease at the end of our life, it is essential that each of us realize our own vulnerability to suicide when the pressures of persistent physical, intellectual, emotional and, yes, even spiritual weakness mount and threaten us.

We would do well to heed the warning of the apostle Peter, "Be of sober spirit, be on the alert. Your adversary, the devil, prowls about like a roaring lion, seeking someone to devour. But resist him, firm in your faith, . . ." (1 Pet. 5:8–9a). However we struggle with the adversary's destructive efforts against us, or our family, our church and community, each of us must keep vigil over our lives to ensure that the normal chaos and assaults we all face are consistently and regularly resolved. Normal pressures that go unresolved gradually mount, one upon the other, eventually threatening potentially lethal responses.

Sometimes difficulties come so rapidly or require such long-term attention, that immediate or timely resolve is impossible. In these circumstances, we can become so mentally and emotionally burdened that our vulnerability to self-diminishing and destructive thoughts is considerably heightened. We can entertain risks that under normal circumstances would never cross our minds. In a sense, we are exactly where our adversary wants us—where our sinful disposition must not remain. So the struggle against suicide in our society must begin with the safeguarding of our own soul.

Embracing a Biblical Worldview: The Culture of Life

Everyone has a worldview—Christian and non-Christian alike. Christianity proclaims the certainty of truth, the sufficiency of Scripture, and the sacredness of life. The Christian worldview applies just as much to our emotional trials in life as to our intellectual ones, asserts the truth in the public sphere as well as sacredness in our private lives. It touches every area of life. In *The Universe Next Door*, James Sire reminds us that our theistic Christian worldview encompasses much more than intellectual assent.

To accept Christian theism only as an intellectual construct is not to accept it fully. There is a deeply personal dimension involved with grasping and living within this worldview, for it involves acknowledging our own individual dependence on God as His creatures, our own individual rebellion against God and our own individual reliance on God for restoration to fellowship with Him. And it means accepting Christ as both our Liberator from bondage and Lord of our future. To be a Christian theist is not just to have an intellectual worldview; it is to be personally committed to the infinite-personal Lord of the Universe. And it leads to an examined life that is well worth living.[7]

For the Christian it is not enough, in this encroaching 21st-century culture of death, to rest upon the security of a Christian worldview. The Christian must also apply one's worldview and cling to it during the crises of life. Through God's grace, the application of Scripture, and fervent prayer, the worldview of the Christian gives indispensable direction and protects individuals from deadly, detrimental and debilitating thoughts and emotions.

It is a constant challenge to maintain a biblical worldview in a contemporary society slipping from the moorings of truth and the God of the Bible, adrift in an ocean of God-rejecting relativism and self-indulgence. In the free-fall of chaotic emotions that push suicidal ideation, one's worldview is a critical safety net. Our belief system provides not only theological and philosophical security, but psychological safety as well. Our worldview affects how we think about life and death, and what we do about it. A Christian worldview, biblically grounded and consistently applied, will generate valid theological conclusions and assist personal resolution to these issues.

The relevance of Christianity to every area of life cannot be discarded. When faith and religious principles are abandoned, we should not be surprised that Dr. Jack Kevorkian advocates the goodness of "planned death."[8] He understands that in order for this to be accepted in "our modern world, medicine and religion should be completely divorced from one another."[9] Our present culture is coming to a radically different view of humanity. Having jettisoned God, the biblical perspective of humanity as created and sacred is now also being cast away. As Robert Bork ominously noted, "Convenience is becoming the theme of our culture. Humans tend to be inconvenient at both ends of their lives."[10]

Suicide and a Biblical Worldview

A consistent biblical worldview is relevant to every aspect of suicide in our present culture. Only when we fully embrace the biblical worldview, with all of its ramifications, will we be able to adequately respond to the personal, social, and cultural crises of our time. Even for those who are old and dying, for the infirm, or those who feel worthless and helpless, there must still be the conviction of human dignity. Every living person is significant and worthwhile, even if all circumstances suggest the opposite.

Ultimately only a biblical perspective can accomplish and sustain this truth with any certainty or permanence. Writing of his experiences at Auschwitz, Dachau, and other Nazi death camps, physician Viktor Frankl commented frequently on suicide and its rejection even in the midst of unspeakable personal horror. He tells of talking to fellow prisoners on one occasion after food had been taken away from them.[11]

> Then I spoke of the many opportunities of giving life a meaning. I told my comrades (who lay motionless, although occasionally a sigh could be heard) that human life, under any circumstances, never ceases to have a meaning, and that this infinite meaning of life includes suffering and dying, privation and death. I asked the poor creatures who listened to me attentively in the darkness of the hut to face up to the seriousness of our situation. They must not lose hope but keep their courage in the certainty that the hopelessness of our struggle did not detract from its dignity and its meaning.

For the Christian, then, the creation of humanity in the image of God has far-reaching personal, theological, and cultural ramifications that must be considered; among them, the rejection of suicide in all of its manifestations. As we daily face the issues of suicide in our personal, professional and public lives, we must move beyond the rhetoric, slogans, and euphemisms. In a culture of convenience and bumper-sticker ethics, we must adhere to sound doctrine and biblical perspectives.

A nominal Christian worldview—one that gives only casual attention to God and to the knowledge of "the Holy"—is weak and inconsistent. Therefore, it may not forestall a personal or cultural slide into the acceptance of suicide, and of physician-assisted suicide.

Christians must hold firmly to God and apply central doctrines to their faith. In part, it is through a love and understanding of God the Father, acceptance and devotion to the person and work of God the Son, and application and appreciation of the life of God the Holy Spirit that the option of suicide is diminished and discarded. Knowing who it is that brings us out of the depths of despair can instill immeasurable comfort and consolation when those depths drown us.

The Immanent/Transcendent God

David Wells believes that modern evangelicalism has lost sight of God's transcendent nature in favor of his immanent qualities.[12] He observed that when a society overemphasizes transcendence, there emerges

> ... a deism with a remote God, cool rationalism, and complete loss of Christological interest. On the other side [a focus on immanence], there emerged modern evangelicalism, which looked to a God "invested with all the gospel's transformative passion" but with a greatly diminished aura of transcendence—the God "below," warmer, closer, more engaging, and more susceptible to be translated into a purely private deity. In other words, evangelicals tended to dispense with God's otherness in the interests of promoting his relatedness through Christ and gospel faith.[13]

To live the Christian life effectively—including the suicide-inducing struggle with pain and suffering—we must strike a balance between the God who loves us and the God who will forever be outside our complete understanding, to whom we are ever subject. To miss or ignore this balance is to impinge upon life an unstable pride in one's spirituality or, to the other extreme, in one's humility. An overemphasis of immanence means that God is too much "for us" (we become too self-centered and, therefore, overconfident in our willingness to speak for God or discouraged when it appears that God is not "meeting our needs" the way we think He should). An overemphasis of transcendence means that God is too much "from us" (we become legalists or skeptics, doubting that a holy and incomprehensible God would be involved in our personal problems, and thinking that God is undaunted by human tragedy).

Erroneous thoughts and decisions rooted in these unbalanced misbeliefs about God in the area of suicide and physician-assisted suicide include:

- "I'll be better off with the Lord."
- "God wouldn't want me to go through this kind of suffering."

- "He'll understand our decision—God is so much more compassionate than we are."
- "The Lord wouldn't want anyone to sacrifice financial security to prolong a life unnecessarily."
- "If God was so concerned about my life, He would not cause me so much difficulty."
- "I'll never be what God wants me to be; life's just too hard for some of us."
- "God doesn't have time for a mess-up like me."

Because God is immanent, He is keenly interested in the way we live our lives and the way we care for the lives of others. Because He is transcendent, His greatness, power, knowledge, compassion, goodness and purity establish a standard that is above and not subject to human experience. He is who He is and *not* what we make or want Him to be (Isa. 55:8–9). Consequently, human value is divinely established and, therefore, not subject to the elastic judgments of human wisdom.

There is something that gives value to man from above. The value of man is not that he is the highest of the evolutionary process thus far, but that the Supreme Eternal Being made man in His own image. It is not man's estimation of himself, but the judgment of the holy God that gives man value.[14]

Human life cannot be qualified by degree of function (healthiness vs. disability), age, race, net worth, or any of the many ways the world judges human worth. Life, in and of itself, is valuable because it comes from God—to live is to be valued. And since both the suffering and the dying have life, their value is equal to anyone else's. All decisions that involve the termination of life must be made in the context of God's view of life. As long as an individual has life, there remains purpose to that life.

Even the life and death decisions regarding a non-cognitive terminally ill patient are filled with theological implications for those who must decide when to acquiesce to the disease.[15] The decision to kill oneself or to allow oneself to be killed *circumvents the divine purpose of one's life*, which is an open book, with a finite understanding of one's present experience, which is but one of many chapters. We must always remember that our story is comprised of more than one character, and therefore, the purpose of our life intertwines with that of others (cf. Phil. 2:3–4).

The Incarnate God

The most visible expression of God's immanence and transcendence is seen in the Incarnation of God's Son, the Lord Jesus Christ. He who was "equal with God" became one of us, even "to the point of death." How does the truth of the Incarnation impact the way we view suffering and the way we die? From the heavens God entered His creation as a human being, as the perfect image of God, not to help us escape physical death, but to give us abundant and eternal life before and after death.

Without the earthly existence of the God-Man, we would not have a perfect reflection of the image of God or a living example of God's commitment to the redemption of humanity. We would be subjects of a King who would seem distant or uninvolved (transcendent) and whose understanding of our human weakness would, therefore, be suspect. We would have no sacrifice for our sin which would leave us without hope, victims of our incessant guilt or our seared and unfeeling consciences. Without the Incarnation, suffering would be meaningless and death would be a welcome relief.

How we live and die is inextricably linked to our understanding and commitment to the incarnate God. Our joys and our sufferings have purpose, just as our Savior's did. The work that Jesus loved was devoted to providing insight, through instruction and personal example, into the value of living life in communion with God and others. However, even the unrelenting accusations of an ungrateful and blind hierarchy and the incomparable agony in the Garden of Gethsemane delineate purpose and direction to the difficulties that confronted our Savior (cf. Heb. 12:3–4).

The incarnate God impacts every aspect of our lives. Jesus Christ teaches us about the will and character of God. He provides a path to fellowship with God, and instructs us in our dealings with the world. He encourages us to struggle through the trials that threaten to undo us, and guarantees purpose of effort and an eventual end to all manner of suffering. He grounds our hope beyond our present experience. The incarnation is truly the central fact around which all human history revolves.

To align oneself with the Incarnate God is to become a prophet in favor of healing, not a proponent or actor of premature death. It is to be an advocate for sure intervention and palliative care, not an adversary of suffering. It is to be an acquirer of solutions, not an acquiescer to the final solution.

The fruits of the Spirit of God that describe the life of the Incarnate Christ are incompatible with the depressive and hopeless characteristics of a person considering self-termination. They are also uncharacteristic of a human being who looks at suffering terminal patients as individuals who have lost their value as human beings simply because their quality of life does not meet a subjective societal standard.

Suffering is a difficult experience to endure, but we must not be too quick to eliminate it, for even the Lord "who for the joy that was set before him endured the cross, despising the shame, . . . " (Heb. 12:2). It was an act of obedience that provided hope to the entire human race. Suffering is the product of physical, intellectual, or spiritual conflict. It is neither moral nor immoral, and it is not something to be stoically endured for the sake of character or higher purpose.

Suffering is an experience that demands serious attention, and demands serious treatment when it becomes chronic and severe. It is surely an event that changes the lives of those who pass through it. Its greatest purpose is to bring us face to face with our finite humanity so that we might more clearly see the face of the divine (1 Pet. 1:6–12). Like the suffering of the blind man, our suffering can become a testimony to the glory of God (John 9:1–5). And like the suffering of the Incarnate God, our suffering can reflect His effect on our lives and possibly lead some, who are ignorant of His grace, into the presence of the Father.

The Resurrected God

The solution to the complexities of the world is the simplicity of the gospel and its attending consequences. The simplicity of the gospel rests on the message of the resurrection of the Son of God. Paul's words in 1 Corinthians 15 emphasize the importance of the resurrection for the Christian faith: "And if Christ has not been raised, your faith is worthless; you are still in your sins" (15:17). With Christ there is hope, without Christ there is no hope.

Helpless, hopeless, and *worthless* are three words frequently used to describe the feelings of those who are suicidal. Such feelings are not restricted solely to non-Christians—suicide claims believers as well. Yet, an understanding of, appreciation of, and daily application of the reality of the resurrection of Jesus Christ provides daily hope for the believer that reaches into the depths of the human heart.

The resurrection of Christ offers not only hope for the next life: it offers hope in this life. Pain, fear, frustration, uncertainty, loneliness, discouragement are all real and debilitating physical and emotional experiences. The reality of the resurrection of Jesus Christ, through which we have present and eternal hope, is equally real but in no way debilitating. Because of the resurrection we are not *helpless*, for we have a risen Priest; we are not *hopeless* for we hear the risen Prophet; and we are not *worthless*, for we serve the risen King. Because Jesus rose from the dead, the Christian has "a living hope" (cf. Titus 2:13). The Resurrected God offers to all who respond a hope for living—a hope beyond suffering, pain, and despair.

The Loving God

"We have come to know and have believed the love which God has for us. God is love, and the one who abides in love abides in God, and God abides in him" (1 John 4:26). The apostle John's words proclaim that relying on the love of God is an integral part of the Christian life. Knowing and understanding God's love for humanity, and for us as individuals, has enormous consequence. *The human need for acceptance is finally and fully realized in the character of God when there is a proper relationship with Him.*

Describing God's attribute of love, J. I. Packer writes, "God's love is an exercise of his goodness toward individual sinners whereby, having identified himself with their welfare, he has given his Son to be their Savior, and now brings them to know and enjoy him in a covenant relation."[16] God's love toward humanity is observed in four dimensions: benevolence, grace, mercy, and persistence.[17] God's benevolence is expressed through the attention He pays to those He loves. It is His unselfish interest in each of us for our own sake. Intrinsic to His love is a concern for every aspect of our life which is expressed indirectly (Matt. 5:45; Acts 14:17) and directly, the most obvious expression evidenced by the sending of His Son to redeem those who would believe (Rom. 5:6–10; 1 John 4:10).

It is through God's grace that He deals with us, not on the basis of our merit but according to our need, requiring nothing from us in return (Eph. 1:5–8; 2:8–9). To speak of God's mercy is to address the tenderhearted compassion He has for His people. Erickson notes, "It is his tenderness of heart toward the needy. If grace contemplates man as sinful, guilty, and condemned, mercy sees him as miserable and needy." (1983, p. 295) It is in this dimension of God's love that he responds to our spiritual and physical infirmities, frailties, and fears (cf. Exod. 3:7; Matt. 34:14; Mark 1:41). The persistence of God reveals His love in that He is patient in withholding judgement (2 Pet. 3:9).

Each of these dimensions touches on suicide and the suicidal person in that they help us to see the *depth* of God's care and concern for us. The intense introspection of the suicidal individual and the anthropocentric focus of those who would assist in suicide ignore the active love and concern of God. The difficulties we face in life are very real, but so also is the loving God to whom we can take them. An inadequate view of God will always lead to an inadequate view of humanity. When the former is diminished the latter is exalted with the inevitable result, not of "Thy will be done," but, "my will be done." Such an end leads to suicidal thoughts and other related inhumane acts in individuals and cultures that abandon the infinite and selfless love of God for finite and self-serving human reason.

Suicide Assessment and Intervention

Guidelines for assessment and intervention with the suicidal person are made with both the counseling professional and pastor in mind. It is assumed that pastors and churches will adapt policies from these recommendations that incorporate some, if not all the suggestions offered. This analysis further assumes the historic duty of the care-giver to intervene for the purpose of saving and prolonging life.

1. General Policy Guidelines

A. *Work from a written policy.* Develop and follow clear step-by-step procedures for yourself and your staff that will guide decision-making throughout a suicidal crisis. Clearly written policies help guide you through moral and ethical dilemmas and provide a reference or "common language" for consultation and referral. A well-written policy also communicates favorably to courts and lawyers that you are a thoughtful and serious professional, not one prone to negligence, foolishness or exaggeration in your decision-making about people in your care. This evidence will carry great weight in the event you are sued or have to defend yourself in any forum.

B. *Set clear limits on yourself, then consult and refer.* Every clinician and pastor must be able to define clear limits of competence and the level of intervention beyond which you will not work. *Working within your competence is the first line of malpractice defense, a "safety zone" within which the court will not intrude to find you liable if you stay inside its shelter.* When events push beyond the limits of your competence, then consult and refer. Sullender and Malony strongly challenge clergy—a challenge appropriate to all Christian counselors—to "not work in isolation."[18] There will be trouble for those who don't respect this key requirement of risk-avoidant ministry.

The clergyperson's own needs and self-deceptions are common barriers to effective referrals. Clergy must be mature enough and professional enough to know their limits when it comes to counseling troubled persons. These limits may involve training, available time, conflict of interest, or just available energy. They must not feel obligated to "save" everyone who enters the door seeking help. Unfortunately, not all clergypersons are that mature or that professional. Some have messiah complexes that get in the way of effectively using referrals.[19]

C. *Consult first, then refer.* The clinical professional and committed pastoral counselor should first consult with a respected and knowledgeable colleague when dealing with suicidal crises. Referral may not be necessary with close consultation to confirm and add to clinical decision-making on behalf of the person in crisis. This not only improves and advances the professional's clinical skills, it also serves the client who may be confused and mistrusting by having to face referral to a probable stranger. If referral is indicated, however, by all means do it. It is far better to refer to an expert stranger than to carry on a case that may lead to suicide.

D. *Work with your own "flock."* We agree with Sullender and Malony that pastors and churches should not counsel with those outside their own "flock." The inherent moral and legal protection of the clergy-congregant relationship is lost to a pastor counseling someone outside his church. Other than in short-term crisis situations that would lead to early referral, pastors should limit their counseling help to their own parishioners. Beyond the time and energy that such work demands in lieu of service to one's own church, there are simply too many legal, ethical and moral risks to the counseling pastor in working with persons outside the local church or parish.

2. Suicide Assessment

Assessment of suicidal risk involves gathering information from multiple sources across a number of key variables. The essential two-part question of suicide assessment is:

- Is this person at risk for committing suicide, and
- If so, how serious is the risk?

The competent counselor will assess this risk according to history, trait, mood, personality, and situational factors.

E. *Begin counseling with assessment of suicide risk.* The easiest way to get information about suicide risk is to ask questions at the beginning of counseling. We incorporate questions about suicide (and homicidal and assaultive behavior) in our clinical intake forms. This gives us direct access to these issues at the start of professional relations and allows us to intervene early in cases where these issues are pressing. Structuring assessment this way and addressing these questions on initial interview puts clients more at ease as they see it as part of the routine we follow with all new clients. Evaluate suicide risk across the seven key variables that follow. Risk for suicide increases according to:

1. *Past suicide attempts and their seriousness.* Clinically and empirically, past behavior is the best predictor of future behavior. Careful assessment of both the incidence and seriousness of past suicide attempts is a significant factor in assessing current risk. Also, assessment of the seriousness—the degree of lethality of past attempts—can give important clues distinguishing whether one has an intent to die or whether one is using suicide to manipulate others. Superficial wrist slashing or "overdosing" on aspirin may yield a different hypothesis about client intent compared to the person hospitalized in intensive care following a failed gunshot wound or massive overdose on sleeping or pain medications. Suicide is also a higher risk for those who have a family history of suicide, especially suicide by the same-sex parent.

2. *Communication of intent / denial of intent.* A second factor, estimated in 75–80% of all suicides (Maris, 1992), is a client who communicates or gives other clues to suicidal intent or, following a serious attempt, denies any intent to further harm themself. This information is rarely offered by the person at risk. You must ask directly and matter-of-factly about suicidal

thoughts and intent. Incorporating these questions into your intake will serve this interest well.

3. *Assessing the violent-angry-impulsive person.* Clinical researchers have identified two major constellations of behavior and mood that correlate strongly with suicide risk.[20] One is the impulsive person revealing a history of violence and unmanaged anger, which empowers suicidal and, sometimes, murderous action as well. Suicide by this kind of person has, in fact, been deemed to be "murder in the 180th degree".[21] The second type (below) shows a history of depression and hopelessness without violence. The violent-angry-impulsive person will:

a. show a history of violent and assaultive behavior—assault, hitting and injuring others, destroying or damaging property, and injury to self for such action;

b. reveal impulsive anger or rage that is explosively triggered by various people or events—the person quickly gets out-of-control and becomes destructive to things or people and relationships;

c. show a tendency to hurt others and vengefully react when angry—using cutting, harmful words or hiding or destroying things special to the person who is the focus of one's anger;

d. project blame onto others—is critical and condemning of others while being unable to receive and react against any criticism from others;

e. justify anger and harmful expression, unable to forgive, tending to hold grudges and resentments over a long period of time;

f. suppress anger—deny anger in the face of obvious evidence—flushed face, clenched teeth and muscles, harsh and loud tone of voice, threatening posture;

g. repress anger—deny anger problems (contrary to history) without obvious anger signals—passive-aggressive, aloof, sarcasm-cynicism, conflict-avoidant;

h. show associated physical complaints and symptoms—gastric-intestinal distress, ulcers, spastic colon, headache, hypertension, and cardiac irregularities.

4. *Assessing the nonviolent-depressed-hopeless person.* The other key pattern in assessment of suicide risk is the person showing depression with little or

no history of violence, but who exhibits much hopelessness and a very pessimistic cognitive style.[22] Clinical depression with a strong streak of hopelessness is implicated in over 75% of all suicides.[23] Of critical concern with
the depressed person is the "rebound suicide" where the person is empowered to act destructively as the depression lifts. Depression of this nature is
much more than a bad case of "the blues;" a variety of clinical and medical
indicators exist for suicide risk, including:

a.   recurrent, hard-to-control, sometimes obsessive thoughts of
     worthlessness, hopelessness, helplessness, death or suicide;
b.   problems in mental function: inability to concentrate, short-term
     memory lapses, and difficulty with reasoning, decision-making
     and problem-solving abilities;
c.   mood disorders: sad, flat, "numb" feelings, or strong anxiety, agi-
     tation or quick-tempered irritability, or swings between these
     moods;
d.   crying easily and frequently or an inability to cry at all;
e.   sleep disturbance: sleeping too much but not feeling rested, or not
     getting enough sleep, awakening often in the night and sleeping
     fitfully;
f.   appetite disturbance: overeating and weight gain or undereating
     with resultant weight loss;
g.   disinterest in people and self: increased social withdrawal and iso-
     lation, poor diet, and/or increased neglect of personal appearance
     and hygiene;
h.   loss of interest in sex, hobbies and things that have been pleasurable;
i.   various physical complaints: chronically fatigued and tired,
     headaches, floating aches and pains, gastric distress, constipation,
     fast heartbeat in some.

   5. *Other marked changes in personality and behavior.* Other cumulative or
sudden changes in personality and behavior changes that correlate with
suicidal risk include:

a.   increased alcohol and drug abuse: combining drugs with depres-
     sion and suicidal threats is serious as the last internal barriers to
     suicidal action may be relaxed by the drug;

b.   recently filling out a new will or purchasing life insurance;

c.   a recent injury or illness or loss of ability that leaves the individual with a handicapping condition or in significant or chronic pain;

d.   quitting work or leaving school for no good or apparent reason;

e.   giving away favorite or treasured possessions and "putting one's affairs in order" may precede deadly action that has been secretly decided upon by the person;

f.   failed or declining performance: school grades plunge or work performance falters and high level of absenteeism may precede an attempt;

g.   trivial things become important and important things are trivialized.

6. *Environmental stressors.* A key correlate with suicide is the sudden, massive experience of recent loss. The tragic death of a spouse, child or best friend may precipitate suicidal crisis, especially if one is left living alone after such death. A conflictual divorce, coupled with loss of child custody is all too common these days in headlines about murder-suicides. Loss of physical or mental ability following an accident or medical crisis is a risk, especially if one is left with chronic, intractable pain. Major financial or job loss can also be critical, especially if criminal behavior is involved. Acute suicide risk begins to decline, however, after two or three months following such loss.

7. *Demographic factors.* Seventy percent of all suicides are white males (which also reflects the no-turning-back lethality of shooting oneself in the head). Of the remaining 30% of all suicides, 22% are white females (although women attempt suicide at over twice the male rate), and just 8% are people of color of either gender.[24] Increased risk of suicide is also indicated for:

- non-believers over religious believers,
- Protestants over Catholics and Jews,
- higher incomes over lower incomes,
- homosexuals over heterosexuals,
- men between the ages of fifteen to thirty-five, and
- women between the ages of twenty-five to seventy-five,
- singles, who commit suicide at twice the rate of married persons, and

- divorced and widowed persons, who commit suicide at a rate four to five times that of the married.

3. Suicide Intervention

F. *Discuss suicide openly and matter-of-factly.* Contrary to seemingly popular opinion, talking about suicide doesn't make it happen. Keeping it secret and not hearing the cry for help are far more likely to facilitate a tragic death. Getting the issue out in the open robs it of some of its mystique and power, including Satan's power to tempt the at-risk person with deadly thoughts. Questioning about suicide openly and discussing it in a matter-of-fact tone helps the one in crisis see it more normally and easily. Communicating that suicidal thinking and feelings are common in crisis also helps people evaluate themselves more soberly and realistically. They are much more able to conclude they aren't "going crazy" even though they're struggling with or attracted to suicidal ideas.

G. *Expand alternate thinking and options to suicide.* The suicidal person's thinking often "tunnels" and fixates on suicide to the exclusion of alternate ways to deal with the crisis. Explore, reinforce, and gain client commitment to alternate courses of action. Often, they will protest that they've tried your suggestions or are convinced that nothing will work. Help the client focus the least offensive option or refocus something they've tried in the past that was partially successful. Assist the client to develop and work simple behavior plans, reporting frequently to you about progress and revision of the plan.

This part of suicidal intervention is crucial to your ongoing assessment of continued risk. A client who will explore and work options to suicide is resolving his or her suicidal crisis. The client who does not engage this part of your intervention—or who engages you without any real motivation or seriousness—is displaying continued risk and may need further or more comprehensive intervention to live.

H. *Respect and use the fears that block suicide.* Discuss and constructively use the things that block the person from further suicidal thinking or action. Many things stop people from suicide: fear of death and going to hell (believing there is no chance to repent), failing to die and being left an invalid, the pain of dying, being found by spouse or family, leaving children to be raised by spouse or parents, or leaving children a suicidal legacy. These things are important internal boundaries that are better nurtured than challenged when suicide is at issue.

I. *Increase clinical or counseling intervention.* Keys to increase and intensify the level of intervention to increase protection against suicidal risk include:

1. *Increase frequency of sessions.* Meeting more frequently should always be considered in suicidal crisis, with daily contact justifiable in high risk cases. Setting limits here and respecting referral needs is critical, especially if the person is manipulative or overly dependent.
2. *Use the telephone wisely.* Meeting more frequently without major schedule disruptions or excessive use of time can be facilitated by brief telephone contacts. Daily five-to-ten minute calls may be far more helpful and protective than the weekly one-hour session. Again, some can abuse the phone and clear limits need to be set here as well.
3. *Get friends and family involved.* With consent from your client or congregant, disclose the risk to family or friends who can make a commitment to assist the person through the crisis. Surrounding the suicidal person with caring, praying, supportive, non-judgmental and available people can greatly reduce the risk of isolated, deadly action. Temporary helping networks can be powerful channels through which God's power can flow mightily to the needy person. We frequently rely on this means of suicide intervention because it is so effective.

J. *Act assertively to protect in crisis situations.* In a serious suicidal crisis, referral should be made to a hospital emergency center, acute psychiatric care facility, suicide prevention center or even the police. Connect the person in crisis with resources able to handle emergencies and act quickly to intervene to protect life. Less serious or acute crises widen the range of potential referral sources. Sending the suicidal parishioner to a trusted Christian mental health professional is a valuable resource for the busy pastor. If none exist, make referral to an honorable professional who respects and will not denigrate Christian values. Also important is referral to a psychiatrist or competent family physician who can evaluate depression and respond medically, either to facilitate hospitalization or to prescribe antidepressant medications.

K. *Make good referrals to people you know and trust.* Know and trust the person to whom you refer—your client will want to know these things and will carry your trust to another person when they are in crisis. If you are new in an area, ask your colleagues to list their referral sources and develop a list of trusted people as one of your first professional tasks. Make an effort to meet and discuss referral situations with community professionals if you do not have a good referral network. Maintain contact with these referral sources during the crisis and afterwards for a time until the client or parishioner is resettled into a normal life routine.

L. *Remove access to lethal weapons and means of death.* Having the client or family remove or reduce easy access to the means of death can be critical to suicide prevention. Help the client agree to give up or lock away guns or ammunition, allowing a third-party to control access to guns and lethal instruments. This can also be necessary for drugs, prescription medications, and car keys as well. Increasing the difficulty of killing oneself can be a crucial factor at the height of a crisis when, if easy means were available, tragedy might well occur.

M. *Contract for "no suicide" and community care.* When non-acute risk exists, negotiate and contract with your client or congregant against suicide. Help them agree with you not to take suicidal action for a time-limited period that is as long as possible—months preferably, session to session at the very least. Let them know you realize they can kill themselves if they choose, but that if they contract with you they will be counted on to maintain their agreement with integrity. If possible, get them to agree to call you or someone else before they take deadly action. Formalize the agreement and reinforce its power by putting it in writing and having both of you sign and date it.

Recent research has called into question the reliability of no-suicide contracts—showing that 41% of psychiatrists who used them had patients go on to kill themselves or make a serious attempt.[25] We have found that the most useful contracts are those that incorporate and gain commitment from many people to work in the prevention circle (as in I.3. above).

When a group of caring people covenant to stay close to, pray for, call on and visit an at-risk person, that kind of community support is a major aid to prevention. Contracting against suicide in this manner is an effective and flexible procedure that increases protection and aids the clinical process through the crisis period. This helps clients realize they have caring people surrounding them, and more control than they often perceive they have when in crisis. It can also serve to distract the one whose obsession with suicide is so isolated, creating a clearer mental picture of how suicide would take place.

4. Case Management

N. *Help hospitalize the suicidal person.* Again, hospitalizing a suicidal person may be necessary to save his or her life. Seek agreement to admit themselves to a hospital voluntarily and refer them, even take them to the nearest Christian or other inpatient facility. If they will not agree to admit voluntarily, seek involuntary admission for crisis assessment and intervention. If admission criteria is met—serious mental illness and danger to self—most states allow a person to be held for 48 to 72 hours initially. If the risk is serious and protracted, a hearing will be held to prove the need for longer detention, which may last for a number of weeks. This often is all that is necessary to help a person get beyond the acute and deadly phase of a suicidal crisis.

O. *Monitor your client closely.* Staying with your client or congregant is essential through a suicidal crisis. Even if you refer, they will likely return to you, so your legal duty does not end with referral. It is usually necessary to walk a "second mile" with them, sacrificing some time and energy to insure their safe passage through "the valley of the shadow of death." Since suicidal risk is transient and the great majority of people live through the crisis, you will gain significant influence in their lives if you have walked with them. Your ability to assist them to grow in Christ and to maturity may be keyed to your crisis commitment to the person.

5. When Suicide Intervention Fails

The suicide of a 12-year-old male client nearly drove me (George) out of counseling months after beginning my full-time clinical career in community mental health practice. Living with his grandmother and rebounding from the deep anger and depression of his father's drug overdose death and mother's subsequent suicide, I was convinced we were past the worst of his own suicidal threats. The lifting of his depression merely empowered him to fulfill his threat as his grandmother came home one day and found him hanging by his belt in his bedroom closet.

P. *Take time off and get counseling yourself.* Client suicide touches all kinds of emotions and triggers all kinds of thoughts in a counselor—many of them that are not good. Time off or reduced time in your clinical practice to debrief, reflect, and renew-review your basic values and commitments is a wise policy. Talk through your own issues and questions with a trusted colleague or counselor with some real experience with the tragedy of life. Above all, don't deny the impact of client suicide and try to go it alone.

Q. *Help the victim's family get counseling or debriefing.* The family of the suicide victim is going through its own turmoil and trauma, multiplied by the family interactional patterns. If possible, assist them to find a resource for counseling and debriefing. If you have worked with them, you might be the best resources for this, but if there is tension, or mistrust, or rumors of lawsuit, refer them to someone else.

A Note on Legal Liability in Suicide Intervention

The Christian counselor owes a broad duty to intervene in the life of the suicidal person to give that person a fair chance to live. Professional clinicians are increasingly at legal risk for the suicide of their clients and patients. Indeed, the clinician working in an inpatient or restrictive treatment setting has a strong duty to intervene in the life of someone judged to be a substantial risk for suicide. In contrast, a pastor in a church setting may be ethically and morally, but not legally bound to a duty of suicide intervention.

There is no pure legal duty to prevent suicide—the duty is to intervene appropriately—the law recognizes limits in the ability to stop a determined person from killing themselves. The duty to intervene is judged according to the degree of suicidal risk exhibited by a client and the counselor's ability to accurately assess and control that risk. The counselor's liability increases as the risk of suicide increases and the counselor is able to foresee and control the client's actions. Since the clinician in an inpatient facility can control the patient's behavior far more than in an outpatient setting, liability is greater when suicide occurs in a hospital, day treatment, or residential care facility.

Lawsuits following suicide have risen dramatically over the past quarter-century. Among the litigation fears of psychiatrists, Messinger and Taubnoted suicide risk at the top of their list of clinical problems of concern.[26] In the first comprehensive APA Insurance Trust study, client death, predominantly from suicide, made up 10% of the cases against psychologists.[27] Lawsuits have increased here not so much because the law itself is changing—but because of the seriousness of the harm—the unexpected death of a client that shocks the family—that is driving suit in this field. One commentator revealed this connection between emotions and lawsuit very well:

> Wrongful death (to compensate survivors for monetary loss) and malpractice suits for the suicide of a patient are more frequent than other causes of death for two reasons that are peculiar to suicide. Unlike other types of serious illness, there is usually no expectation that mental illness will be terminal. It is assumed that given proper medical care the patient will survive. Premature death, the likely outcome of some maladies, is felt to be preventable for the depressed patient. Hence, the outcome of suicide is per se unreasonable, bizarre, unexpected, and often irrational.

Prior to the suicide, the relationships between the deceased and close family members are bound to be emotionally charged and at the same time ambivalent. Typically, relatives who love him and have his best interests at heart become angered and frustrated by his helpless and despondent behavior. His suicide may be perceived as a personal attack, for it "represents the ultimate in undiluted hostility." Family members are plunged into a morass of contradictory feelings: sadness, shame, guilt, shock, bewilderment, and hostility toward the deceased. They alternately blame themselves and the deceased. To resolve this apparent contradiction, the bereaved may displace their hostility on to the treating psychiatrist or psychologist. The resulting malpractice suit absolves the family of both guilt and helplessness and gives them a reasonable outlet for their anger by blaming the psychotherapist for the suicide.[28]

The Legal Dilemma for the Church

There is no legal duty for pastors, churches, or counselors working under church supervision to assess and intervene effectively to prevent suicide. The famous California case of *Nally v. Grace Community Church* (1988) reaffirmed historic common law protection of clergy against liability for parishioner suicide. But in practice, churches should disregard this apparent protection and act as if liability does exist, because they may be sued anyway. The church, then, must intervene effectively with the suicidal person, not so much because of legal duty, but rather to fulfill the call of love and to avoid the massive costs of legal defense.

Should clergy counsel the suicidal? Following the *Nally* case, there has been increasing debate as to whether clergy should even counsel suicidal persons.[29] The arguments against such clergy counseling assert growing legal liability, the lack of effective training, the demands of a suicidal crisis, the lack of time and energy to address it, and the failure of many pastoral counselors to recognize and respect these limitations. Those making these arguments assert that clergy not engage in this counseling, but instead refer the suicidal person on to psychiatrists or other professional helpers.

On the other side of this argument is the thoughtful analysis of Sullender and Malony, who support the role of the clergy counselor in work with suicidal persons.[30]

To treat suicide or suicidal depression as just a psychiatric problem—a problem to be treated primarily through medication or hospitalization—is to miss the complexity of the dynamics and do sufferers a disservice. And to argue from the false premise that pastors should never work with suicidal persons and always refer them elsewhere for "real" professional help is to belittle the expertise of clergy and the contribution that the religious community can make to the healing of persons. There are clear religious and spiritual dimensions to most if not all suicidal dynamics, and therefore religious professionals have a definite and significant contribution to make in the overall treatment of depressed and suicidal persons.[31]

These writers, while cautioning against attempts to "save" everyone who comes in crisis, assert that "suicidal persons really need to hear and experience anew . . . the 'good news' of God's forgiveness and new life."[32] To experience this life afresh requires pastoral intervention for many. "Often, the average parishioner perceives a pastor to be more available and more trustworthy than most mental health professionals. Furthermore, many people see their problems primarily as spiritual and moral in nature and specifically want the counsel of their pastor regarding their troubling situation."[33] The question, then, needs to be reframed—not should clergy counsel the suicidal, but how best to do it, a question we have sought to answer in this chapter.

Conclusion

My conclusion in *Law for the Christian Counselor* still holds true today: If Nietzsche is right and suicide is "great consolation," it could only be so to a very pained and desperate few. For most, especially for those who loved the deceased, it is much more a tragedy and painful heartache carried throughout life. Even though never fully washed away, the grief of suicide can be redeemed by the Crucified and Risen Savior, the "man of sorrows" who was and is "well acquainted with grief." Counselors who lose a client or congregant to suicide are sometimes devastated, but must still go on in the work of ministry. To go on without great sorrow, or fear that it will happen again, or without anger and repressed hostility toward the deceased requires great faith in response to unyielding grace from God.

ENDNOTES

1. In order to protect the privacy of individual identities, this story is a compilation of reports from recent newspapers and personal stories told to the first author during the AACC Trauma Response and Intervention Project in New York City, October 23–24, 2001.

2. C. Chemtob, Bauer, G., Hamada, R., S. Pelowski, S., and Muraoka, M., Patient suicide: Occupational hazard for psychologists and psychiatrists, *Professional Psychology:Research and Practice, 20* (5), (1989), 294–300.

3. C. Chilstrom, Suicide and pastoral care, *The Journal of Pastoral Care, 43*(3), (1989), 199–208.

4. Centers for Disease Control and Prevention, *Suicide injury fact book*, <http://www.cdc.gov/ncipc/fact_book/26_Suicide.htm>: Author.

5. Aaron Beck, Brown, G., Berchick, R., Stewart, B., and Steer, R., Relationship between hopelessness and ultimate suicide: A replication with psychiatric outpatients, *American Journal of Psychiatry, 147*(2), (1990), 190–195.; Aaron Beck, Resnik, H., and Lettieri, D. (eds.), *The prediction of suicide* (Bowie, MD: Charles Press, 1974); M. Weishaar, and Beck, A., Clinical and cognitive predictors of suicide, in R. Maris, Berman A., Maltsberger, J. and Yufit R. (eds), *Assessment and prediction of suicide* (New York: Guilford Press, 1992).

6. R. S. Sullender, and Malony, H.N., Should clergy counsel suicidal persons? *The Journal of Pastoral Care, 44* (3), 203–211, (1990), 204.

7. J. Sire, *The universe next door: A basic worldview catalog*, 3rd ed. (Downers Grove, IL: InterVarsity Press, 1997).

8. We recognize that the boundary between life and death, between passive and active forms of euthanasia can be very narrow, and will address "end-of-life" issues and ethics more fully in volume 3 of this series.

9. J. Kevorkian, *Prescription—medicine:The goodness of planned death* (Buffalo: Prometheus Books, 1991).

10. Robert Bork, Inconvenient lives, *First Things 68*, (1996), 13.

11. Victor Frankl, *Man's search for meaning*, rev. ed. (New York: Pocket Books, 1984).

12. David Wells, *God in the wasteland: The reality of truth in a world of fading dreams* (Grand Rapids, MI: Eerdmans, 1994).

13. David Wells, *God in the Wasteland*, 129.

14. Millard Erickson, *Christian theology* (Grand Rapids, MI: Baker, 1983).

15. J. E. Tada, Decision-making and dad, in G. Stewart and Demy T. (eds.), *Suicide: A Christian response, crucial considerations for choosing life* (Grand Rapids, MI: Kregel, 1997), 471–475; T. Oden, *Should treatment be terminated?* (New York: Harper and Row, 1976).

16. J. I. Packer, *Knowing God*, rev. ed. (Downers Grove, IL: InterVarsity Press, 1993), 116–117.

17. Erickson, *Christian theology*, 292.

18. Sullender and Malony (1990), 206.

19. Sullender and Malony (1990), 206.

20. A. Apter, Kotler, M., Levy, S., Plutchik, R., Brown, S., Foster, H., Hillbrand, M., Korn, M., and van Praag, H., Correlates of risk of suicide in violent and nonviolent psychiatric patients, *American Journal of Psychiatry, 148* (7), (1991), 883–887; M. Weishaar, and A. Beck, 1992; J. Motto, An integrated approach to estimating suicide risk, in R. Maris, Berman, A., Maltsberger, J., and Yufit, R. (eds). *Assessment and prediction of suicide* (New York: Guilford Press, 1992).

21. K. Menninger, *Man against himself* (New York: Harcourt, Brace, and World, 1938).

22. Beck, et al, (1990), 190–195; Beck, et al, (1974).

23. D. Black, and Winokur, G., Prospective studies of suicide and mortality in psychiatric patients, *Annals of the New York Academy of Sciences, 487*, (1986), 106–113.

24. R. Maris, Overview of the study of suicide assessment and prediction, in R. Maris, Berman, A., Maltsberger, J. and Yufit, R. (eds), *Assessment and prediction of suicide* (New York: Guilford, 1992).

25. J. Kroll, No-suicide contracts, *American Journal of Psychiatry*, (2000).

26. Messinger, Malpractice suits—the psychiatrist's turn, *Journal of Legal Medicine* 3, (1975), 21; Taub, Psychiatric malpractice in the 1980's: A look at some areas of concern, *Law, Medicine and Health Care* (1983), 97.

27. S. Fulero, Insurance trust releases malpractice statistics, *State Psychological Association Affairs 19*(1), (1987), 4–5.

28. Swenson, *Margin: Restoring emotional, physical, financial, and time reserves to overloaded lives* (Colorado Springs, CO: NavPress, 1992), 411–412.

29. Sullender and Malony (1990).

30. Ibid.

31. Sullender and Malony (1990), 205.

32. Sullender and Malony (1990).

33. Sullender and Malony (1990), 204.

Part 4

Counseling for Grief and Trauma

17

Loss and Grief Work

Sharon Hart May

Death is about life, as birth is.

The death of a family member or close friend *is a grievous event*—one of the most difficult of all challenges confronting individuals and families.[1] Expert researcher John Bowlby states clearly, "Family doctors, priests, and perceptive laymen have long been aware that there are few blows to the human spirit so great as the loss of someone near and dear."[2]

The death of a loved one deeply impacts the souls of individuals bereaved, and can shake the foundation of one's family system. Counselors seeking to help sufferers of such loss should understand the current theories of bereavement that focus on the *individual's* intrapsychic (within/personal) experience and the *family system's* interpsychic (between/relational) impact from loss.[3]

A More Comprehensive Model

This chapter challenges the Christian counselor to broaden their understanding of bereavement counseling by placing the bereaved in a holistic context that emphasizes *the systemic nature of attachment.*

Although the death of a loved one impacts the attachment bond between the living and the deceased, the effect of death is not confined to that dyadic relationship. Furthermore, according to systems theory, even with death the relationship is not "removed from the system in which it is embedded—most particularly the family system."[4]

Usually presented alone, attachment theory and systems theory need not be exclusive and together provide a comprehensive model of bereavement, one that broadly informs the Christian counseling treatment plan when working with grieving individuals and families.

An Attachment Perspective on Loss

Bereavement is different from the other necessary losses we experience in our lives, such as leaving home, changing jobs, aging, and living an imperfect life. With most, the connection we have with others is deeper and more profound than the ties we have with our possessions, purses, or positions. Bowlby described relationships between two people (such as between child and parent, husband and wife, or siblings) as close emotional attachments or bonds.

In the shelter of these close relationships, we develop as infants, grow as children, and continue to flourish as adults. We turn to these relationships for comfort and support and from these relationships we venture out into life. When children, or adults, perceive their loved one to be available, accessible and responsive, they experience a felt security. When these close bonds are threatened, or if the attachment figure is inaccessible or unresponsive, then an innate set of behaviors (attachment system) are triggered, designed to maintain proximity and restore the disrupted bond.

According to attachment theory, when a loved one dies, the attachment system is triggered. The response is similar to the response children exhibit when they experience their mother to not be there for them. The distressed child, or the bereaved, attempts to restore the bond by first protesting, then clinging, then becoming angry. If the bond is not restored, the anger gives way to sadness and despair, and finally to resignation and defensive detachment.

Freud originally believed that a person mourning the loss of their loved one eventually "detaches" or "decathects" him or herself from the loved one.[5] Freud suggested that "mourning has a quite precise psychical task to perform: its function is to detach the survivor's memories and hopes from the dead."[6] Based on this, psychoanalytic clinicians aimed at moving a person through a process of "detaching." The mourning reactions were seen as immature and pathological, and clinicians tended to hurry the grieving process, in an attempt to get the griever to "let go" and "get on with life."

Bowlby reacted to the orthodox psychoanalytic thinking and viewed the mourning reactions of grievers as natural components of the attachment system. Rather than viewing the grieving process as detachment or the severing of the emotional bond, Bowbly viewed grief as the process of readjusting the attachment bond and reorganizing life in light of the loss. Continuing a bond with the deceased loved one is "a natural result of the dynamics of the attachment system designed to ensure proximity" with the loved one whether or not the loved one is available.[7] In a nutshell, attachment theory, as opposed to psychoanalytic thought, views loss and its resultant grief not as something primarily to "get over" but as a natural part of life that requires adjustment to a new reality.

Fraley and Shaver outline the importance for the bereaved to find a way "to maintain a secure bond with the attachment figure while simultaneously acknowledging that the person is not physically available to provide comfort and care."[8] This "comfort and care" is then derived from personal faith, prayer, and a sense that the loved one is still there. Studies show that the ability for children and adults to alter and then continue their relationship with their deceased loved one was both comforting and productive. The assurance of the continued bond allowed the bereaved to cope with the loss and make necessary changes in light of it.[9]

A Systems Perspective on Loss

A social system is a bounded set of people, such as a family or a neighborhood, and "the relationships between them, and the relationships between the attributes or characteristics of the elements."[10] Systems theory aims at understanding the relationships within a family and the interactional patterns between the members. As with attachment theory, it does not view causality as linear but rather as a more circular, repetitive, and shared experience between members of the system. In the context of a relationship, each person influences the other and "both are equally cause and effect of each other's behavior."[11] The grieving process of the bereaved takes place not in isolation, but within the greater context of family relationships. The emotions experienced by the bereaved during grief include the grief over the lost loved one, as well as the emotional responses to the family system's reactions.[12]

The family life cycle model of McGoldrick and her colleagues offers a systemic framework for understanding the "reciprocal influences of several generations as they move forward over time and as they approach and respond to loss."[13] Walsh & McGoldrick identify two major family tasks that need to be continually addressed for the long-term well-being of the family. First, the family needs to share in acknowledging the reality of the death and share the experience of the loss. The family comes to accept the reality of the death and the subsequent impact on the family unit. Rituals such as visiting the grave help families share the experience of the loss.

Second, the family system needs to reorganize and reinvest in other relationships and life pursuits. The task of the family is to redefine their identity and purpose as well as reorganize themselves around the loss. This will need to occur over the life cycle of the family and across the developmental stages of each individual family member. The research and clinical experience of Carter and McGoldrick concludes that if the family is not able to adapt to the changes, then the risk of family difficulties and dissolution greatly increases.

The Main Task of Grief

The main task of grief, according to a systemic approach of attachment theory, then, is to help the bereaved reorganize their inner and outer worlds in accordance with the loss, while negotiating the impact of the family system upon their bereavement, and in turn, their bereavement upon the family. The grieving process is a natural, innate, God-given means for humans to accept, adjust to, and live on in light of the death of loved ones. This means that both the (a) family as a unit, as well as (b) each member of the family needs to:

1.   mourn the loss of the bond in its previous form (not physically here anymore)
2.   readjust, thus allowing a more appropriate continuing bond with the lost loved one

3.   reorganize themselves, their relationships, and their life pursuits
     in light of the loss.

In light of the close, emotional bonds and reciprocal connections between family members, what does the grieving process look like for the
individual and the family? What factors foster the natural grieving process?
And how can the counselor be part of their healing process?

It is important to view the grieving process as a natural and productive
process of restructuring a bond and a new life in light of the death of a
loved one. Therefore, understanding the different facets of mourning will
guide you (the counselor) through the bereaved person's grief experience.
It will alert you to when the grieving process is stuck or compounded, and
it will direct you to the possible needs of your client. Use these analytical
tools as guidelines, but don't hold fast and firm to them (or any set of
stages) as no person or family will follow them neatly.

The Five Stages of Grief Process

The classic process outline of grief was conceptualized by physician Elizabeth Kubler-Ross, in her now-famous work *On Death and Dying*.[14] She
defines five stages through which the grieving live and resolve their loss,
including:

1.   *Denial:* a dazed numbness that is much like the shock reaction of
     physical trauma; a refusal to accept the loss. In this stage, most
     people try to return to normal routine and intellectualize loss.
2.   *Anger:* normal and unavoidable reality sets in that often creates
     much somatic distress. Too many people internalize anger and
     block the grief process, ending up with guilt, depression, and
     long-term physical problems. Many people will exhibit avoidance
     and blame others for the loss, in this stage.
3.   *Bargaining:* people try to recover the lost person by bargaining
     with God. In addition, the grieved is often obsessed with meta-
     questions such as "Why?" "How could You let this happen,
     God?!" and "Why me?" Sufferers may also get trapped in "If only
     . . ." thinking: "*If only* they had done this that day . . . *If only* I had
     said [something different]."

4. *Depression*: depression is often mixed with guilt, and sometimes anger, during this stage for the bereaved will blame themselves for not doing what they "should have done." Give permission for one to feel the pain of the loss and allow them to grieve. It is important for the church family to allow people the "luxury" of being depressed as they face the loss of a unique person or opportunity.

5. *Acceptance:* resolving the loss by accepting the hurt and the memories; moving on with a focus for what is yet to come.

The process of grief is just that—a process. Visualize the grieving process, not as linear stages to grow through, but rather as layers of an onion unfolding, or as a spiral, or roller-coaster. Few experience the process in the linear way presented here. Many will report living one or more stages at the same time, or rolling through parts of the process again and again.

Allow the bereaved to inform you of where they are and what they need. Although grief is universally similar, it is also very personal. It is continually impacted by individual as well as systemic dynamics. The entire grief process normally takes from 1 to 3 years to resolve, and must be respected as part of living.

How Grief Is Experienced by the Individual

When grief is like shock and numbness. Each of us who have lost a loved one can recall the sharp words confirming the finality of death. The initial reaction is one of shock, numbness, and disbelief which usually lasts a few hours or even a few weeks. It is interjected with intense sadness or anger, and even laughter and acting like nothing has happened.

> Mr. Wolterstorff, Eric is dead. For three seconds I felt the peace of resignation: arms extended, limp son in hand, peacefully offering him to someone—Someone. Then the pain—cold burning pain. [15]

For some the news of death ends a long period of illness. Therefore, initial emotions may include relief, followed by guilt, anger and sadness. For others the news comes out of the blue, shocking and numbing and disorienting. At first, the news and reality of the death just does not seem real. The mind, emotion, and soul pause to register the reality of loss. It is similar to a car having to come to a full stop before being able to be put into another gear. It is in the moment of pause that the gears are shifted, heading the car in a new direction.

It is important for the family to share in this experience together, openly and honestly. Children should not be isolated from the news, and they should also be included in the rituals that confirm the reality of the death. Since each family is tending to their own shock, it would be important for extended family and friends to be there, providing a sense of stability and continuity to such necessities as meals, care of children and house.

Glen Davidson followed 1,200 adult mourners for 2 years after the death of their loved ones.[16] From their experiences, he found that the phase of shock and numbness peaks during the first two weeks after the death of a loved one. Mourners also reported experiencing a sense of disbelief again after one year. At this time the bereaved reviews from whence they have come and says "oh my goodness, has this really happened? It is hard to believe it!"

When grief is like yearning, searching, and anger. As the reality of the death begins to register, pangs of intense pain, sadness, restlessness, anger, guilt, and deep sorrow are felt.

> For that grief, what consolation can there be other than having him (his deceased son) back. [17]

There is also great restlessness, sleep and eating difficulties. Mourners express an inability to relax, and often are unable to concentrate or keep a flow of thought. Sometimes mourners fear they will go crazy, and hold in emotions lest they become out of control. Also, they may worry their intense emotions will burden family and friends, furthering the urge to suppress their grief while in the company of others. Often if the bereaved does not feel they can suitably hide their brokenness, they will isolate themselves from social contact.

Anger arises that is often directed toward the deceased, the comforters, and those who may be remotely responsible for the death of the loved one. When this anger is turned inward the bereaved experiences a sense of guilt, blaming him or herself for not having done more, having done the wrong thing, or having done too little. Many, especially children, fear that their indifference, angry feelings, or wishful prayers played a part in the death. It is important for the family system to allow the expression and experience of grief by each family member. Mourners need to express their guilt in a safe and supportive environment to sort out what they realistically are, and are not, responsible for.

During the first year after a death, there is a preoccupation with thoughts of the loved one that includes attempts to find pieces of the loved one in everyday activity. The longitudinal research of Balk suggests that rather than letting go, the bereaved "seemed to be continuing the relationship" with the deceased. Balk found that the bereaved, in the process of healing, were "altering and then continuing their relationship to the lost or dead person."[18] It was found progress toward recovery is enhanced by one's continued sense of attachment with their lost loved one. Stated, the "abiding sense of the lost person's continuing and benevolent presence" helps a person heal, and "reorganize their lives along lines they find meaningful."[19]

When grief looks like disorganization and despair. Between the 5th and 9th month after the death of a loved one, the bereaved may find oneself disorientated, though it is still not until one year that the pain of grief tends to peak.

> Loss can also be transformative if we set a new course for our lives. (Our) loneliness and isolation force (us) to see life from another point of view.[20]

This season is also marked by depression, guilt, fluctuation of weight, and an awareness of the reality of the death. There is a loss of joy and meaning in life, and getting through the day requires much effort. Common experiences of confusion, loss of memory, and impairment of fine motor skills can leave the bereaved feeling concerned that they are "losing it." Often, physical complaints and ailments arise, and the bereaved find themselves worried that they may have some serious illness.

This season, if used productively, becomes a season of reexamining personal values and philosophies of life. In this time the bereaved can come to gradually accepting the loss and realize life must be "shaped anew." Life is reassessed and new priorities emerge.[21]

Although life will never be the same, mourners adapt to the changes forced on them by the loss. This becomes a season of "relearning the world." It involves "finding our bearings in the world and give direction to, and seek a sense of purpose in, our ongoing living."[22] The task of the bereaved, and the family, is to find their way by learning how to be and act in the world differently. Habits, motivations, and behaviors are impacted, as well as the connections and interactions with others. The world is relearned, and this way life becomes anew.

When grief looks like reorganization. This phase is marked by a sense of release and it is experienced around one to two years after the death, depending on the nature of the loss. Some widows and widowers, report this phase only after 3 years.

> Eventually I had to decide, however, to become a contributing member of the community once again, not only willing to receive but also to give love.[23]

During this time, the bereaved begins to give more focus to the challenges and opportunities for living. New rituals begin to form, bringing meaning and renewed enthusiasm and interest for life. The bereaved begins to reinvest emotional energy into life, in light of their loss.

The bereaved will need to learn new skills and take on added responsibilities and what will impact the reorganization phase is the bereaved's ability to successfully master and adapt to these new roles. This is impacted by the response of the bereaved's community to their reorganization of life. The bereaved's community system will need to be flexible and accepting to allow the bereaved to master the new roles, foster new relationships, establish new rituals, and seek lifestyle changes.

It is at this phase that the bereaved, and family, can visualize themselves living beyond the pain and making a life for themselves. As they look into the future, they can see life blossoming up around them. And they want to be part of it.

How Grief Is Experienced by the Family

The impact and meaning of the death on the family unit should be carefully considered, even if you only see one member of the family. As previously shown, the bereavement process is not experienced alone, but rather in the context of the individual's family system. Since the counselor will effectively have only one or two hours with the client a week, it will be important to focus on integrating the client back into their family system for emotional and social support during the grieving process. Therefore, the greater context of the individual should be assessed and taken into consideration when outlining therapeutic interventions. This context should also include the wider cultural and ethnic influences upon the family's beliefs. According to Walsh & McGoldrick, coming to terms with the loss and adjusting to its implications is a task revisited throughout the life cycle.

The timing and type of loss. The timing of the death has an impact on the family. Sudden deaths impact families differently than long-term illnesses. The unexpected deaths don't allow for good-byes or preparation for the loss. Many family members are left with regrets, guilt and unfinished business. In contrast, prolonged illnesses have the potential to place strain on the family system as well as on the finances, time, energy, and emotional availability of family members.

The farther along in the natural life cycle the death occurs, the less distress on the family. Death of an elderly grandparent is viewed as much more natural than the death of a thirty-six year old husband or, especially, a young child.

The death of a child is likely the most tragic of griefs as it appears so unnatural to the life cycle. The impact of a child's long-term illness and death has profound impact on the marital relationship. Studies found that in cases where the children were hospitalized, 70 to 90% of those marriages resulted in separation or divorce.[24] Hospice studies found that families who were able to care for their dying children at home, had fewer marital problems and a greater sense of power and control. Unusual circumstances surrounding the loss, such as traumatic accidents, violence, suicide, abortion, or other complications increase the family distress and compound the grieving process.

Nature of the relationship. If there are unsettled feelings toward the deceased or if the relationship was cut-off, the grieving process will be complicated. Also, if the bereaved's sense of well-being is significantly tied to the deceased, the grieving process will be prolonged and complicated.

Death does not change the nature of the relationship. One's mother, whether dead or alive, will always be one's mother. Whenever a deceased loved one is remembered, the memories can trigger emotions causing the bereaved to sigh, yearn, or even have a good cry.

Family structure. The more securely attached (rather than clingy or disengaged) a family is the more able they are to adapt to the loss. Flexible, rather than chaotic or rigid boundaries enable a family to accept the changes ahead. A family needs to be a haven of safety where each individual's process of mourning is supported. It is important for the family to openly talk about the pain of the loss as well as the restructuring of the family.

A family came into my counseling room where the mother had lost both her parents tragically just several months earlier. The family was rigid and did not allow one another to cry, mourn, or talk openly about the grandparents' death. Consequently, the mother longed to express her sadness, but could only find rage. With counseling, rather than attempting to keep things the way they were, the family learned to mourn together and reorganize themselves around the loss.

Family connections to social networks. The experience of loss is buffered by the family's ability to draw upon emotional and practical resources from extended family, friends, and other communities such as the church. The lack of connection to these communities leaves the family without a sense of support and structure. It would be of great benefit for you, the counselor, to encourage the bereaved's reaching out and participation in a greater community. For example, after the tragic death of his 36-year old son, a father reconciled with his 85-year old mother after years of hurt and disconnection. This provided added support and family cohesion.

Concurrent losses or life cycle changes. Often the death of a loved one is compounded by concurrent loss or life cycle changes. When one loss is stacked upon another, the original loss is compounded. Each loss needs to be separated and mourned appropriately.

Developmental markers such as graduations and weddings add to the distress of grief. Even though they should be times of great joy and celebration, they become reminders of the absence of the loved one. Each life event without the loved one will need to be both mourned and celebrated.

Counseling the Bereaved

The mourning process lasts longer than most expect. Bowlby emphasized that many clinicians sometimes have "unrealistic expectations of the speed and completeness with which someone is expected to get over a major bereavement"[25] Healing and reorganizing one's life without the physical presence of the lost loved one takes time, approximately 1 to 3 years, or longer. For some, the mourning process is delayed, or it gets stuck, so the process is revisited numerous times over many years.

Furthermore, just having time pass does not necessarily heal the soul. It is what a person chooses to do during their healing time that determines the new meaning life takes on. Remember, each family member will have their own timeline of mourning. It is possible that when one member is at one phase, the other members are at other phases.

Children and Grief

As you are working with bereaved children, the emotions of grief don't seem all consuming for children as they are for adults. However, children still experience the same range of emotions as adults.[26] Features of child bereavement are diverse, ranging from regression, fear of separation, clinginess, aggressive behavior and discipline problems. Children need time and a haven of safety to reorganize their inner and outer worlds in light of the loss.

The adolescent years are already filled with turmoil as teenagers face new tasks and responsibilities of growing up. Similar to adults, a teenager's response to the death of a loved one will often include anger, guilt, sadness, confusion, depression as well as physical symptoms such as aches, pains, eating and sleep disturbances. Unique to adolescents is that they commonly try to control their emotions, but also act out, in an attempt to make sense of the loss. This usually places added distress onto the family and complicates the adolescent's developmental task.

Physical Well-being and Medication

It is of great importance to consider the medical and physical well-being of the bereaved, for there is a high correlation between physical ailments or illness, and the loss of a loved one. Mourning is as much a physical process as it is an emotional one; it can be physically draining, is linked to a weaker immune system, and brings with it medical conditions of many sorts. Adequate exercise, enough sleep, small frequent meals, and keeping hydrated will help fortify one's grieving body.

During the months and years of mourning, the bereaved can become physically and emotionally exhausted and anxious. Reaching for sleeping pills, alcohol, antidepressants, antianxiety medications, or other substances should be done with wisdom and caution. A study found that 87% of physicians in Illinois "assumed a standard care that called for prescribing either a barbiturate or tranquilizer for mourners at the time of the loss."[27]

There are times that medications are necessary to assist in a good night's sleep, or enable the bereaved to function in everyday living. Yet, there are other times when the numbing of the grief experience can complicate the healing process. As you are working with the bereaved, help them explore more natural and holistic methods to aid in stress reduction and sleep disturbances such as relaxation techniques and soothing rituals before bedtime, like taking a bath or listening to music.

Expression of Emotions

It is of value to help family members express their emotions in a manner that is consistent with who they are. Some mourners view expression of emotions as humiliating, or even as inviting criticism and contempt. Sometimes the unspoken messages from family members and friends include "get on with your life," "snap out of it," or "pull yourself together"—which further increases the need to work through emotions in the counseling session.

Stifling emotions does not help the mourning process. Yet, not everyone will express emotions the same way. Respect the quiet, gentle grievers. It is more so those who long to give their grief a bolder voice—but for some reason can't—who potentially complicate their mourning process.[28]

Real Loss and Imagined Loss

Concrete losses are tangible losses, such as the actual person who has died, loss of marital status, loss of income. Abstract or intangible losses are those such as loss of hope in the future, or loss of ambition. Imagined losses are not based in actual reality, yet are powerful influences on the grieving process. These losses are only in our minds and emotions, and their meanings need to be understood and put into perspective.

There are also losses I call "feared" or anticipated losses, such as the fear of never loving again, or never having a happy life. Threatened losses are those lurking in the wings, threatening to become real. These include the possible loss of income resulting in the possible loss of the family house.

Whether the loss is real, imagined, feared, or anticipated, each loss triggers a deep emotional response. It is important to help the bereaved separate out actual losses from the imagined or feared losses, while avoiding being dismissive or underplaying the importance of the feared/imagined losses.

Making Sense of God

It will be important to allow the bereaved to make sense of why God allowed the death, and why He did not intervene. We think that we are protected from the deeper hurts of living because we are Christians. But all human beings have been given only a finite number of years to live here on earth. And that reality is sometimes too hard to understand or too difficult to trust God for the outcome.

At one stage or another, all who have lost loved ones wrestle with God. Sittser describes how "We move toward God, then away from Him. We wrestle in our souls to believe. Finally we choose God ... we decide to be in relationship with Him"[29] As counselors, we should allow our clients to actively wrestle with God, and in doing so move them toward understanding and walking close with Him.

Developing the Treatment Plan

A good treatment plan is helpful for the counselor as it outlines what will be done during the counseling sessions. The theoretical framework outlined in this chapter serves as a foundation on which the counselor can build a treatment plan. An effective treatment plan will include therapeutic parameters, assessment, diagnosis, and interventions.

A. Therapeutic Parameters

1. Who will be the client? The individual, couple, or family?
2. Would they benefit from other therapies such as a grief group,

family or individual therapy? Do they need to be referred to a medical doctor as well?

3. How many sessions will you see them? Adjust your interventions to fit your time frame.

4. Will the counseling be supportive counseling (walking the bereaved through the grief process) or more in-depth grief counseling (complicated or compounded grief)?

B. Assessment and Diagnostic Considerations

1. Gather the story around the death including: who died, how, where, and when?

2. How would the relationship between the client, the family, and the deceased be described?

3. What role did the deceased play in the life of the bereaved and greater family context? What roles or responsibilities will the client need to learn and take over in light of the loss?

4. Consider the developmental stage of the client and each family member. Also assess the family life cycle stage. In light of this, keep in mind what tasks and adjustments the bereaved and the family will be facing. Be aware of coming life markers—births, graduations, and weddings.

5. Consider cultural, ethnic, gender, and economic factors that may impact the bereaved and family.

6. What previous loss has the client and family faced, and how was it dealt with?

7. How do the client and family express emotional pain?

8. What cultural, gender, ethnic, and spiritual beliefs need to be considered?

9. Assess for suicidal thoughts, and a sense of hopelessness, or worthlessness.

10. What support system is the client and family a part of? Are they able to ask for needs to be met and utilize the support?

11. Refer back to the previously listed concerns and phases of mourning and ask questions that will give you a broader picture of the client, their experience, and the system in which they live.

C. Treatment Strategies

1. If the grieving event is anticipated, such as with a terminal illness, talk openly about it with the dying and their family members. Make sure that preparations for the death are in order.
2. Give accurate information about the grieving process, especially the possible range and intensity of emotions, and time it will take to heal, so that any false expectations or beliefs may be discussed and corrected.
3. Encourage decision-making and follow through on the little things that keep day-to-day life functioning in at least a minimally healthy way. Help out and make sure the grieving person is eating properly, maintaining personal hygiene, keeping bills paid, and basic appointments kept. Discourage major decisions and action on big changes until the crisis event has subsided and some time for perspective is gained.
4. Challenge any hostile, irrational, or slanderous judgments, and reframe any inaccurate expressions about the one lost, communicating your commitment to honesty and truth and how important that is to the healing process.
5. Encourage discussions about and assist planning regarding the future, including how to go about finishing any "unfinished" business that may be expressed.

Assessment and Diagnosis

To develop well-informed interventions, it would be in the client's best interest to understand whether your client is going through the normal bereavement process, or if there are other compounding factors that need to be addressed. Diagnosis is valuable for helping you rule out more serious conditions. It would be of value to read the DSM-IV diagnosis of conditions similar to bereavement. It is important to note that the three main symptoms distinguishing bereavement from major depression is suicidation, hopelessness, and unworthiness continuing for more than 2 weeks. If trauma surrounds the death, such as violence, murder, a car accident, a child's discovery of the deceased, then it is important to rule out post traumatic stress disorder (PTSD). If you discover that your client is going through more than just the normal bereavement process, it would be wise to get supervision, further training, or refer your client to a trained professional.

Axis I:	296.2x	Major Depressive Disorder, Single Episode
	296.3x	Major Depressive Disorder, Recurrent
	V62.82	Bereavement
	309.0	Adjustment Disorder with Depressed Mood
	309.3	Adjustment Disorder with Disturbance of Conduct
	309.04	Dysthymic Disorder

Interventions

Be there and listen. Most people come to counseling to make sense of the intense and confusing emotions they experience. Research and experience has found that most people are able to adapt to their loss. Key to their healing is an adequate and stable support system. Your ability to listen and enabling them to give their grief a voice will be very healing.

Listen actively and respond reflectively. During the crisis, grieving persons are not so desirous (or ready) to hear complex answers to the questions about tragedy and suffering, even though these things come up from time to time. Allowing them the opportunity to talk out their concerns, confusions, and affirmations is important. Listening and reflecting back their communications is often more helpful than engaging in long treatises about God's purposes in these things.

Normalize their experience. The emotional experience of bereavement is very painful and often disturbing to the bereaved if they have never experienced it before. It would be good to begin by normalizing the experience, and helping the client understand the experience of bereavement and what to expect. Give permission to talk about the lost person or object, to express fears and emotions, but don't push it. Don't be surprised if strong feelings and displays go on. If you are able, cry when others cry, and laugh when they laugh.

Encourage and participate in grieving rituals. Funerals, wakes, family gatherings, memorials, sorting through photos, and watching videos are usually healthy and necessary events that both recall the best times and assist in mourning the loss. The rituals around the death repeatedly confirm that the loved one is not returning. The funeral, memorial service, and visiting the grave-site are rituals that your client and their family can do together. They are healthy aspects of mourning, and it is important to participate in these events.

Explore and expand the dynamics of the family system. A broader picture of the client's family system can be drawn through a genogram, as well as a time line of family life events. Allow the client to tell the history of the family through stories, pictures and memorabilia.

Rituals for staying connected as a family are important. Explore with your client other rituals of remembrance they can do to help them stay connected to their loved one. A 10 year old boy asked me whether or not he should continue to keep his deceased father in his prayers. Together we came up with a prayer that thanked God for allowing him to have his father, even though it was only for 10 years. Still being able to pray for his dad kept him in a continued bond with his father. One woman placed a single flower in a vase on her mantel every Friday in honor of her deceased mother. It was one way she continued to feel the beauty of her mother's countenance.

Explore and expand the life story of the lost loved one. Old documents, scrap books, high school yearbooks, newspaper articles, pieces of clothing and hobby tools can be gathered to help tell the story of the loved one.

Exploring and expanding the feelings and experiences of the client. As clinicians, it is easy to get caught up in the content, or story of the client and be fogged in regarding the process. To help expand the feelings and experience of the client consider the following:

1. Allow the expression of emotions, remembering to help and encourage the client to identify and label the feelings.
2. Help the client understand the link between their behavior and their emotions. This enables them to realize that there is more going on than just what is on the surface. For example, you might say, "When you feel sad you are unable to share your sadness with your family. So, instead you get angry and yell because being mad is more acceptable than being sad. Being sad is more painful than being mad."
3. Provide corrective emotional experiences. That is when you

respond with understanding and acceptance of emotions and behavior that your client anticipates rejection and criticism. A corrective emotional experience is when your client expresses a negative emotion and receives understanding and acceptance rather than the anticipated punishment or rejection.

4. Help the client lean on God. The Bible is a treasure-store of comfort and consolation in the face of grief. The grieving experience is a time to know the grieving heart and tender heart of God in a way that no other experience allows.

Isaiah 53 presents one of the most powerful pictures of Christ in the Scriptures—a picture of the "man of sorrows," well "acquainted with bitterest grief." (v. 3). Wounded and abused for our sins, "He was beaten that we might have peace. He was whipped, and we are healed." (v. 5). Those who allow the Suffering Servant, Jesus Christ, to minister to them in their sorrow come to know a beautiful Savior, a Wonderful Counselor to whom their devotion can soar.

Psalm 23 has been a favorite verse to grieving hearts throughout history, for it invites God to come alongside and walk with us "through the dark valley of death." (v. 4) God never abandons us. He never fails us, even in the worst hours.

No one is able to carry the wounds of loss alone without eventually being overcome. By letting God, and God's people help us, we are able to bear our slow healing wounds of grief.

Other Considerations

There is more to therapy than one-on-one dialogue. Techniques such as sand tray, play therapy, art therapy, journaling, telling stories, creating a memory book, and letter writing are other ways that allow the client to make sense of their feelings and experience. Often more emotions and behaviors come out in these modes of therapy than in just plain talking. Again, allow your client to lead you in what best fits for them.

Counseling with children. Cook and Dworkin identified six common topics that can be discussed and explored. It will be necessary to adjust the discussion according to the age of each child.[30]

FROM SUFFERING TO SURRENDER,
BY TIM CLINTON AND GEORGE OHLSCHLAGER

When we suffer [in our grief], it is not uncommon to believe that God has forsaken us and broken our trust in Him. When others tell us to 'trust in God' during this time, the words suddenly make no sense. They sometimes sound absurd, like a huge cosmic joke.

How can we trust God when our hopes and dreams with our loved one have been unexpectedly shattered? How can we trust the One who took our loved one away? How do we trust Someone with the very power of life and death in their hands? These are common questions—questions we must take to God and wait for Him to answer. At some point we will realize that God wants us to trust Him even when we don't understand why. Since God is the only One who can fix the problem, He often becomes the focus of our anger. The more intimate our relationship with God, the more betrayed we feel by the One who was supposed to intervene in our hour of need.

Lazarus' sister Mary is an excellent example. She was angry at Jesus when He failed to prevent her brother's death. "If You had been here," she admonished Him, "my brother would not have died!" We assume that Mary's trust in Jesus had definitely diminished.

Trust is one of two aspects of faith. Faith is comprised of trusting God and believing what He has said. With this in mind, we need to remind ourselves that our understanding is limited to an earthly perspective. Death makes us feel small, vulnerable, insecure—we come face-to-face with the fact of our own mortality—that death may just as easily (and soon) take us as well.

Grieving the death of a loved one challenges us—to our very core—to believe and trust that God's eternal perspective is better, even far superior to our own. We wrestle with the holes in our knowledge of the future—will God take care of me, will I eventually be privy to His plan? We wrestle with faith in God's goodness—uncomfortable in the awareness that our faith is so weak in the face of such tragedy. Psalm 130:5 tells us; "I wait for the Lord, my soul waits, and in His Word I put my hope."

As the intensity of our emotions levels out and we begin to live with the reality of this death, it is not uncommon for family and friends to suggest disposing of personal items in order to "get over" the loss. While they may have your best interest in mind, do not get rid of anything until you are ready to. (When you do discard some things, it can be difficult to decide which ones to throw away and which ones to keep. Separate those that hold significant meaning and those that don't. For example, disposable items may include deodorant, toothbrushes, razors, etc. More personal items may include family pictures, heirlooms, and other items that hold memories for family and friends.)

It is hard to trust and believe in God, to take His Word as His sure promise. Trying to will ourselves to believe doesn't work—we see it for the weak, self-centered, will-powered sham that it is. We recognize the absurdity of our dilemma—I must go to the One I don't trust to find the trust to trust in Him once again. Sometimes if we don't laugh at the situation, we will do nothing else but cry and lament.

One of Shakespeare's famous characters, Macbeth, said, "Give sorrow words; the grief that does not speak knits up the o'er wrought heart and bids it break."

Grief forces us to face this grand paradox—I am going to get better or become bitter. Too many get embittered. A long-term study indicated that the death rate of widows and widowers is from two to seventeen times higher during the first year following the death of a spouse. Dr. Glen Davidson has discovered that about 25% of those who mourn experience a dramatic decrease in the body's immune system six to nine months after their loss. This is one of the reasons why grieving people are more susceptible to illness.

However if the grieving process is handled in a healthy manner—if the bereaved one pursues God's design to get better—this immune deficiency is avoidable. And in order to believe Him, to put our faith in His Word, we are driven to search Him out in prayer, in the Bible, in the hands and faces of others—compelled to seek Him in order that He may reveal Himself even more—more than ever before.

While you may be ready to accept that God is not your enemy because of your loved one's death, you still may not understand why He chose to take them. As mentioned earlier, our questions may not find full answers while we are here on earth. But we have chosen to walk by faith, believing that God was, is, and will be with us on earth and in heaven. And though grief is an inescapable part of the human condition, He demonstrates His love for us through His loving compassion (Lamentations, ch. 3).

At some point we will arrive at a partial understanding of this process called grief: to grapple with overwhelming loss and eventually adapt to it. During this time, necessary changes must be made so that we can live with our loss in a healthy way. This occurs when our questions change from, "Why did this happen to me?" to "What can I learn from this and how can I best proceed with my life?"

Even as we move—as we begin to grow—through the grieving process we will experience days that are more difficult than others. Tears, fears, anger and confusion are still ahead, but God gives them to us to help release our feelings. We slowly begin to understand, to accept this death.

We also realize that grieving is a two-part process: the loss of a loved one, and the recovery of our spirit. It is natural to want to return to the life we knew before this traumatic event occurred, but it's imperative we create a new "game plan." We do this by refusing to be locked away in a tomb of agony for the remainder of our lives, and instead, come to a place of surrender.

God promises to deliver those who seek Him. Surrender comes when we finally accept that we could not have changed the events that led up to our loved one's death. We accept that we are unable to turn back the hands of time—we cannot bring them back, nor are they coming back. No matter how much we would like to, we cannot change the circumstances.

But we have a choice, and this choice is critical to our healing, to getting better or becoming bitter. We can remain angry at God, blaming Him for everything. Tragically, far too many people get stuck in exactly that. I'm sure you know some, still angry over events that transpired decades ago! On the other hand, we can surrender to God and seek His comfort, healing, and direction. In the midst of grief's pain neither choice seems attractive or acceptable. However, it is inevitable that we choose one or the other.

Most believers, at some point, surrender their grieving to the Lord. In so doing, He comes to our side and answers our cries. God comes to our rescue. Surrender occurs when the bereaved acknowledges the loss of their loved one, readjusts their bond with this person on a more spiritual level, and eventually reorganizes their life following this loss. Death is a life-changing event—one that alters our nature, our view of life, our priorities, our spiritual perception of God and His goodness, and every other aspect of our life. It is inevitable that change will affect every area of our life because loss is not singular.

Resolving our loss and surrendering it occurs when we accept the hurt and the memories but we can move on with a focus when we accept God's promise:

"I tell you the truth, you will weep and mourn while the world rejoices. You will grieve, but your grief will turn to joy." —John 16:20

1. Have the child describe the loved one who died, how they died and how they heard about the death. This can be done verbally, through art, writing of a play, or putting together a scrapbook.

2. Examine thoughts and feelings about the funeral and other rituals that the family shared to confirm the death of the loved one.

3. Discuss changes that have occurred in the family since the death, and how the changes feel. As you listen to the child, assess for coping strategies, family support of their experience, and how the child is making sense of life without the loved one.

4. Discuss the future and what it will look like without the loved one.

5. Find ways that the child can still feel connected with the loved one. Through the enjoyment of memories and the review of hopes the loved one had for them, the child can sense the loved one's continued security and comfort. This can be done through the writing of notes, putting together a scrapbook, or recalling how the loved one valued them and hoped they would do well in life.

6. Again, be creative and allow the child to lead you. Begin each session with play therapy, art work, story writing, or some form of activity that allows the child to express himself creatively.

Counselor Self-care

Like vicarious or secondary trauma, counselors working with the bereaved are susceptible to carrying too much of their client's grief within themselves. It is important to be able to distinguish between empathic grieving—burden-bearing within proper and manageable limits—and being overladen with sorrow. Unfortunately, this boundary is rarely clear, so counselors need to engage in ongoing self-assessment of the impact of grief work. So then:

1. Do your own grief work. What losses have you faced, or are you facing?
2. Be aware of your limitations. Be aware when the story of your client is affecting you and you can't seem to leave it behind at the office. Also, be honest when you need further training or need to refer your client to someone with more experience. Growing your skills as a counselor will make you more effective.
3. Find your own support system where you can share your concerns, emotions and experiences.
4. Always check your stance in the room. Don't be condescending. Your client is the expert of their own experience; respect that. No matter how many degrees you do or don't have, remember that it is the Holy Spirit at work in your client, not you. You are about the work of the Lord, so allow God to use your expertise to do His work. Bless you. Sitting with the pain of the bereaved is not always easy.

Conclusion

The death of a loved one is painful and difficult for both individuals and the families in which they live. Gerald Sittser, after an accident that took the lives of his wife, mother and one of his daughters wrote, "I believe that "recovery" from such loss is an unrealistic and even harmful expectation, if by recovery we mean resuming the way we lived and felt prior to the loss."[31]

Life does not get back to normal, life is reorganized and a new "normal" must be created. Our clients are not the same after a loss, nor do they return back to how things were. They are changed, and a new routine, a new normal becomes familiar. Kate Convissor, with five children and five years after the death of her husband explained it this way, "Still the effect of Richard's death lingers. Whatever effort I expend, "normal" will never be as I remember it. To continue living I must accept, adapt, and create something new."[32]

As counselors, our task is to come alongside the bereaved and create a safe place where they can accept, adapt, and reorganize life in light of their loss. As outlined in this chapter, attachment and systems theory together adequately expand the understanding of bereavement by appropriately placing the bereaved within their natural context of the family. Bereavement, then, is seen as a natural healing process that is reciprocally influenced by the bereaved and their family.

Even though the family of the bereaved may never enter your counseling room, when the bereaved leaves your office after one hour, he or she will return back into their family system. Therefore, it would benefit both the bereaved and the family for the counselor to consider both intrapsychic and interpsychic levels of the grieving process. In this way, the Christian counselor is better equipped to formulate a holistic and effective treatment plan fostering healing and wholeness within the souls of those who lost a loved one.

ENDNOTES

1.   F. Walsh, and McGoldrick, M., A family systems perspective on loss, recovery and resilience, in P. Sutcliffe, Tufnell, G. and Cornish, U., *Working with the dying and bereaved* (New York: Routledge, 1998); John Bowlby, *The Making and breaking of affectional bond* (New York: Routledge, 1979); R. C. Fraley, and Shaver, P. R., Loss and bereavement: Attachment theory and recent controversies concerning "grief work" and the nature of detachment, in J. Cassidy and Shaver P.R.(eds.), *Handbook of attachment: Theory, research, and clinical applications* (New York: Guilford, 1999).

2.   John Bowlby (1979), 67.

3.   John Bowlby, *Attachment and loss: Vol. 3. Loss: Sadness and depression* (New York: Basic Books, 1980); F. Walsh, and McGoldrick, M., A family systems perspective on loss, recovery and resilience, in P. Sutcliffe, Tufnell, G. and Cornish, U., *Working with the dying and bereaved* (New York: Routledge, 1998).

4.   P. Sutcliffe, Tufnell, G., and Cornish, U. (eds.), *Working with the dying and bereaved* (New York: Routledge, 1998), X.

5.   Sigmund Freud, *Mourning and melancholia*, SE, 14, (1917), 243–58; Fraley & Shaver (1999).

6.   John Bowlby (1980), 100.

7.   John Bowlby (1980), 19–21, 93–100.

8. Fraley and Shaver (1999), 754.

9. D. Klass, Silverman, P.R., and Nickman, S. L. (eds.), *Continuing bonds: New understandings of grief* (Washington, DC: Taylor and Francis, 1996); N. Hogan, and DeSantis, L., Adolescent sibling bereavement: An ongoing attachment, *Qualitative Health Research*, 2, (1992), 159–177; P. R. Silverman, Nickman, S., and Worden, J. W., Detachment revisited: The child's reconstruction of a dead parent, *American Journal of Orthopsychiatry*, 62, (1992), 494–503; K. Tyson-Rawson, Relationship and heritage: Manifestations of ongoing attachment following father death, in D. Klass, Silverman, P.R. and Nickman S. L. (eds.), *Continuing bonds: New understandings of grief* (Washington DC: Taylor and Francis, 1996), 125–145.

10. N. Frude, *Understanding family problems*, (Chichester: J. Wiley and Sons, 1990), chapter 10.

11. D. Becvar, and Becvar, R., *Family therapy: A systemic integration* (Boston: Allyn and Bacon, 1993), 9.

12. Walsh and McGoldrick (1998).

13. Walsh and McGoldrick (1998), 6; B. Carter, and McGoldrick, M., *The changing family life cycle* (Boston: Allyn and Bacon, 1989).

14. Elizabeth Kubler-Ross, *On death and dying* (New York: MacMillan, 1969).

15. N. Wolterstorff (1987). *Lament for a son* (Grand Rapids, MI: Eerdmans, 1987), 9.

16. Glen Davidson, *Understanding mourning: A guide for those who grieve* (Minneapolis: Augsburg, 1984).

17. Wolterstorff (1987), 31.

18. D. E. Balk, Attachment and the reactions of bereaved college students: A longitudinal study, in D. Klass, Silverman, P. R., and Nickman, S. L. (eds.), *Continuing bonds: New understandings of grief* (Washington, DC: Taylor and Francis, 1996), xvii, 311–328.

19. John Bowlby (1980), 243, 98.

20. Gerald L. Sittser, *A grace disguised* (Grand Rapids, MI: Zondervan, 1996), 91.

21. John Bowlby (1980), 94.

22. T. Attig, *How we grieve: Relearning the world* (New York: Oxford University Press, 1996), 107.

23. Gerald. L. Sittser (1996), 164.

24. Carter and McGoldrick (1989).

25. Bowlby (1980), 101.

26. S. A. Cook, and Dworkin, D. S., *Helping the bereaved* (New York: Basic Books, 1992).

27. G. W. Davidson, *Understanding mourning: A guide for those who grieve* (Minneapolis: Augsburg, 1984), 22.

28. John Bowlby (1980); R.C. Fraley, and Shaver, P. R., Loss and bereavement: Attachment theory and recent controversies concerning "grief work" and the nature of detachment, in J. Cassidy and Shaver, P.R. (eds.), *Handbook of attachment: Theory, research, and clinical applications* (New York: Guilford, 1999).

29. Gerald L. Sittser (1996), 144.

30. Cook and Dworkin (1992).

31. Gerald L. Sittser (1996), 9–10.

32. Kate Convissor, *Young widow: Learning to live again* (Grand Rapids, MI: Zondervan, 1992), 161.

18

Trauma and PTSD: A Clinical Overview

Michael Lyles, Tim Clinton, and Anthony J. Centore

The increasing stress of living in the 21st century, on both a global and personal level, has been sufficient to considerably elevate the numbers of people who suffer from PTSD.

FROM HEALTHYPLACE.COM

The headline said it all: "Low-flying Plane Spooks New Yorkers."

A 777 airliner bringing troops back from Iraq was given permission by the FAA to fly low near the Statue of Liberty and over Manhattan as a special welcome-home gift. The sight of the low flying jet triggered hundreds of calls by frightened New Yorkers, presumably post-traumatic stress sufferers reliving the trauma of 9–11.

Whether one is directly involved or a witness, situations concerning the threat of serious injury, or death, in which one feels intense fear or helplessness, is experiential trauma and places one at risk of Post-Traumatic Stress Disorder (PTSD). During the terrorist attacks of 9–11 thousands of Americans felt the threat of harm, and a PTSD epidemic began.[1]

A Common Disorder

PTSD is extremely common—the 5th most prevalent psychiatric illness behind anxiety, depression, phobias, and substance abuse. Currently, 5.2

million Americans ages 18–54 are diagnosed with PTSD and statistics show that in any one year 5.6% of the U.S. population will suffer from PTSD, with females at about twice the rate of males.[2]

In addition, some studies suggest rates of PTSD to be even higher. A general population sample of 1007 Detroit residents ages 21–30 presented a 9% occurrence of persons who met the DSM-IV criteria for PTSD. In another study, researchers randomly selected 4,008 females and found life-time prevalence of PTSD to be 12.3%. According to the American Psychiatric Association, 10% of the U.S. population at some point presents clinically diagnosable PTSD, and higher numbers show symptoms of the disorder.[3]

Risk Factors

It is said over 75% of people will experience some type of severe trauma in their lifetime, and 20% of those will develop PTSD. In review of this discrepancy, much research has taken place to investigate the question of why some people experience PTSD in response to trauma, while others do not. Results suggest several major risk factors.

Trauma type. The probability of one developing PTSD varies strongly depending on the type of traumatic event experienced. For example, traumas that are not of human design including natural disasters (e.g. a hurricane, earthquake), technological disasters (e.g. a train wreck, nuclear power-plant meltdown), or human mistakes (e.g. motor vehicle accidents, pilot error) tend to be less often catalysts for PTSD. On the other hand, trauma of human design is much more powerful in promoting PTSD as a result.[4]

In specific to trauma of human design, though statistics vary, soldiers held captive or tortured have the highest incidence for male PTSD, one study showing World War II prisoners experiencing PTSD in 50% of cases.[5] For women, rape (or sexual molestation) is the number one cause, at 49%.[6] Crime victims in general have a PTSD prevalence of 25.8%, while research shows 38.5% of females exposed to a physical assault will develop PTSD.[7]

Duration and severity. Apart from trauma *type*, increased duration and severity of trauma are positively correlated with PTSD onset. One's resiliency is depleted with repeated stressors, and it is said trauma and PTSD have a dose-response relationship—the more trauma one endures the more post-traumatic stress one experiences.[8] In confirmation of this, a study investigating posttraumatic stress in *twin* Vietnam Veterans shows decisively that increased trauma exposure leads to increased PTSD symptoms.[9]

Reviewing the 9–11 attack, the actual event was relatively short. However, graphic video footage that aired for several weeks promoted a continuous traumatic experience that may have increased the psychological damage to the nationwide witnesses of the event.[10] Of course, local New York residents experienced the most sustained trauma, having repercussions long after the attack (and long after media focused on newer headlines). This may explain that though the trauma of 9–11 was felt nationwide, 8% of Manhattan residents living below 110th street (approximately 67,000 people) have PTSD related to 9–11, as compared to 2–4% of the coast-to-coast population.

Early childhood experiences. Often described as "family history," early childhood experiences can be either a defense against, or risk factor for, developing both PTSD and Complex PTSD (CP, discussed later). Expert John Briere, addressing risk factors, categorizes child trauma as either abuse by omission or commission.[11]

Omission. According to Briere, omission involves the neglect of a child through parent unresponsiveness, and psychological or physical unavailability. Described as "the great unrecognized trauma," with omission a child does not receive normal social stimulation, soothing, or support from a parent—and lacks the opportunity to learn how to regulate emotions (decreasing the child's ability to cope with stressors).[12] Also with omission, there are no parent-child interactions that promote self-awareness, security, and positive views of others. Lastly, research by attachment expert John Bowlby shows that neglect is a severe traumatic experience, depriving a child of its innate needs for nurturance and love.[13]

The essence of attachment is displayed when children remain in close proximity to their parents. This is a God-given safeguard, since they are dependant on their guardians for survival and protection. Hence, when physically separated from parents, children may experience severe trauma.[14] The following vignette shows an adaptive response to temporary omission.

A little girl skips down the isle of a department store. She feels safe, knowing her mother is following right behind. Things are going just fine for the young girl until she looks back and notices that her mother is gone! At that moment the little girl's knees buckle. She crumbles to the floor, letting out at the same time an ear piercing scream. People from every direction come to her aid and her mother one aisle over, runs back to her immediately.

In this vignette, the child experiences trauma for a brief moment. However, her God-given survival mechanisms (being unable to stand, screaming) worked to quickly reunite her with her mother, and assuage her stress. With the abuse of omission, children remain in a persistent state of neglect, and experience similar trauma constantly.

Commission. The sibling of abuse by omission, act of commission, is abusive behavior—psychological, physical, or sexual—directed toward the child. Such abuse is the single most powerful risk factor for developing a mental disorder of any kind for it creates longstanding attachment issues that distort one's core perceptions of self, others, and the world.[15]

Brain Development. Whether it is commission or omission, early childhood trauma is many times more powerful than that experienced as an adult for it not only generates extreme stress, it disrupts one's development of mental and emotional abilities to cope with interpersonal challenges.[16] In place of healthy regulation, sufferers of early trauma develop maladaptive conditioned emotional responses (CERs) to interpersonal and external stimuli.

As the brain develops, it does so from the bottom up—beginning with the limbic system, a non-verbal section of the brain that controls the formation of one's memories and emotions. For a child who has experienced abuse, negative schemas are rooted in this part of the mind. For example, a child abused by his/her caregivers may infer that he/she is unacceptable, bad, worthy of punishment, and that he/she is weak, inadequate, not deserving of love, and helpless. At the same time the world becomes to that child dangerous, rejecting, and uncaring.

Later, a neocortex develops above the limbic part of the brain, providing a person with verbal, rational, higher level thought processes. With normal development, one can regulate his/her emotions by rationally considering the safety of his/her present environment. However, for those with negative perceptions deeply rooted in the (non-verbal) limbic system, rational thought is not sufficient for affect regulation, and one may constantly experience stress due to negative CERs. Consider the following vignette:

Growing up, Ryan's parents were rarely ever home. When they were, they would tell Ryan, "I wish you were never born," or "You were an accident!" Now, at 26, Ryan lives alone and experiences extreme stress anytime he receives the slightest social rejection. For example, today one of Ryan's friends "took a rain check" for dinner because she had to work. Though Ryan rationally tells himself that his friend cares about him, and is not rejecting him, he feels extreme rejection. Memories of Ryan's childhood flash in his mind, and he quickly pushes them away.

Ryan's schema is such that he believes he is unacceptable, and that people do not want to be with him. Therefore, his CER is a pervasive feeling of rejection, even when he knows rationally that he has not been rejected. Though discussed later, it should be mentioned that since the limbic brain can be both incongruent and autonomous from one's rational thought, treatment must involve in large part experiential learning.

Here is a quick summary of symptoms that may become present in direct relation to early childhood trauma.

- Preverbal negative beliefs about one's self
- Preverbal negative beliefs about the world and others
- Negative conditioned emotional responses (CERs)
- Poor emotion/affect regulation
- Inadequate ability to gain or accept social support

Genetics. When assessing whether one is genetically disposed to PTSD, a practitioner should remember that genes are not closed symptoms. Hence, genetics will never exclusively determine whether one will develop PTSD—one must encounter trauma.

However, some persons are genetically "wired" in ways that make them more attuned to stress. Recalling principles of survival, our God-given reactions to stress are extremely powerful, and in the wild, one's stress response provides a quick reflex to run from or fight predators. When humans transitioned from the wilderness to modern society, our biological systems did not adapt perfectly, and some of us present similar responses to more benign stresses—memories of trauma, for instance.

Medication may be a wise choice to assist the biological regulation of such trauma survivors (described further below).

Personality. Though PTSD is not evidence of personal weakness, individual personality uniqueness plays a role in susceptibility. Reportedly, someone who has a tendency toward fear, worry or anxiety is more at risk than his or her less anxious counterparts. This is because trauma is in fact a subjective experience of objective events, and what is traumatic for one may not be traumatic for another.

Trauma expert Jon Allen tells of a drug dealer placed into a trauma support group because he had witnessed multiple homicides. However, the drug dealer, having an anti-social bent, was not traumatized and instead felt invulnerable and excited by the events.[17] Also showing the subjectivity of trauma, one study found that the post-traumatic stress of burn patients was often not due to the severity of burns, but instead to individual subjective experiences.[18]

Due to their personal vulnerabilities, some clients may feel inferior because they are unable to fully cope with their traumatic experience, while others seem to have experienced similar trauma unscathed. A counselor should always reiterate to clients, they are trauma *survivors*, as opposed to victims of PTSD.

Comorbidity. Comorbid psychiatric disorders may exacerbate the symptoms of PTSD,[19] or make one more prone to developing PTSD after a trauma. Counselors be aware that preexisting disorders may make PTSD difficult to identify, for past sufferers of depression or panic disorder often confuse PTSD with a relapse. A client may ask, "Is my depression returning?" when PTSD is the root cause of discomfort.

Onset

Though many persons immediately following a trauma endure a reaction that meets the criteria for Acute Stress Disorder, symptoms of PTSD usually surface within the first three months after a trauma. The following vignette elaborates:

> Ronald, a family man, while driving is sideswiped by a pickup truck running a stop sign. In the wreckage, his wife dies while he is severely injured. Ron is hospitalized for a time, then immediately returns to work so to financially support his children. After several months, when things "settle down" he begins reexperiencing the trauma of his wife's death, along with sleeplessness, social withdrawal, and other post-traumatic symptoms.

In contrast, onset may be delayed for decades.[20] For example:

Susan experienced neglect and physical abuse at the hand of her parents. She left home at 17 and never looked back. While attending college she managed to build healthy relationships, despite her past trauma, and she moved on with her life to get married, raise children, and sustain a career. At 45 years old, minor stressors begin to pile up: marital conflict, financial problems, a friend's death, and in her state of heightened stress she begins to reexperience—and avoid—painful childhood memories.

Symptoms and Patterns

The modern understanding of PTSD has a long history with combat-related trauma. After World War I, "shell shock," was the designated title for supposed brain damage related to soldiers' exposure to explosions. During World War II, the term "combat fatigue syndrome" was popularized. It was not until 1980 that the diagnostic term PTSD was adopted after extensive research and treatment of Vietnam veterans.[21] Whatever the term, it is said persons with PTSD are nearly "walking around in a constant state of shock."

Reexperiencing the Trauma

With PTSD, a traumatic event is persistently reexperienced by the sufferer in three possible ways—memory, dreams, and flashbacks.[22] In powerful form memories are distressing and intrusive, dreams become night terrors, and flashbacks are vivid hallucinations specific to the trauma. In extreme cases—most common with sexual abuse—persons with PTSD experience dissociation and numbing during the recall of traumatic memories.

When reexperiencing trauma, perceptual and emotional reverberations cause intense psychological or physiological distress, sometimes in response to a triggering cue and at other times with no identifiable catalyst. Cues (when identified) may be related to the trauma: in the instance of someone reexperiencing the 9–11 attack in response to seeing a low flying plane. Cues can be unrelated as well. For example, a woman out of breath from exercising recalls being smothered by a perpetrator.

Pervasive Avoidance

Recalling trauma, though uncomfortable, is a therapeutic opportunity for the mind to process an upsetting past; and reexperiencing alone is not sufficient for a PTSD diagnosis. However, diagnosis is justified when the intensity of memories is severe to a degree that sufferers avoid thoughts, feelings, people, places, situations, or conversations connected to the trauma. Those with PTSD often forget or repress significant aspects of stressful events. They lose interest in previously enjoyable activities, and they detach from others—often becoming isolated and emotionally restricted.[23] In addition, such persons often avoid counseling because it involves recalling and discussing stressful memories.

Hyperarousal

PTSD sufferers are very nervous with no present cause, for post-traumatic stress makes an event from the past seem evasively present in one's day-to-day functioning. The stress of this evasive presence produces symptoms of constant arousal—one cannot sleep, presents anger and irritable affect, has difficulty concentrating, hypervigilance, and may become very short with spouse and children.[24] One in a state of hyperarousal is said to be "on pins and needles," suffers from exaggerated anxiety, and physiologically has increased adrenaline and sympathetic nervous system activity.

Somatic Symptoms

It is now accepted that psychological trauma effects biological homeostasis and can cause both short- and long-term disruptions in organs and systems of the body. Persons with PTSD are frequently ill with psychosomatic symptoms that may appear to be exclusively biological. Common physical complaints include stomach pain, chest discomfort, irregular heart rhythms/palpitations, shortness of breath, back and joint pain, and headaches. Moreover, the inability of a physician to identify a biological cause of these problems can further increase frustration and anxiety in a PTSD sufferer.

The physical symptoms of PTSD are not anecdotal. In fact, people with PTSD present many health problems and utilize more health services than sufferers of any other psychiatric disorder. In addition, sufferers frequently become functionally impaired, they are often unable to fill the role of spouse or parent, and suffer in vocational performance.[25]

Spiritual Issues

Research shows that persons with PTSD often develop spiritual problems. Avoidance of church, prayer and Christian fellowship are common, as are pervasive doubt and crises of faith. Sufferers display strong anger toward God, and suffer the same detachment from God that they do from other social interactions.

However, very recent studies find that traumatic experiences can lead to a deepening of religiousness and spirituality, and that religion and spirituality are usually beneficial in the recovery of those dealing with trauma's aftermath. One study shows that when writing about their traumatic experiences, 80% of participants wrote narratives with religious themes, with some participants detailing their use of specific religious behaviors, such as prayer.[26]

Traumatic Guilt

Guilt and shame are common for PTSD sufferers. Sometimes justified, one study shows guilt among reckless drivers with PTSD and another among a group of Veterans with PTSD who committed atrocities at war.[27]

However, often guilt is not justified. For example, some have shame over their perceived undeserved fortune to survive a traumatic event.[28] Others display backwards thinking, a type of traumatic guilt where the client thinks "I should have been able to stop this!" This magical thought provides a sense that one can control the world; they just weren't ready at the time of the trauma.

A counselor's role when presented traumatic guilt is to reiterate the truth that the earth is a fallen place, where at times bad things happen that are outside the client's control. For those with justified guilt, clients— through confession—can begin the journey toward repentance and healing.

Suicidal Thinking

Approximately 20% of people with PTSD attempt suicide, compared to only 15% of people with untreated clinical depression. Hence, the suicide rate in people with PTSD (without intervention) is nothing less than tragic.[29]

Suicide is a crucial topic when addressing the church, for many Christians with suicidal thoughts will not seek help due to shame, assumptions that they will be blamed, or even considered sinful for struggling with suicide. This dynamic must be reformed if the church wishes to minister to its suffering congregants. Thankfully, when one forfeits the secrecy of suicide, it loses much of its power and the probability of a completed suicide decreases.

Comorbidity

PTSD often brings on other problems. It increases the risk of developing depression, alcohol or drug abuse (self-medicating), social phobias, and other anxiety disorders. Roughly 79% of women and 88% of men will develop at least one more psychiatric problem besides PTSD, and 40% of women and 59% of men will develop at least three other psychiatric problems.

Though some researchers are dogmatic that technically for two disorders to be truly comorbid they must be independent of one another, not overlapping in symptomatology or increasing the risk of having the other,[30] the following disorders have been traditionally considered often comorbid with PTSD.

Depression. Depression affects 20% of the U.S. population at any time, and women twice as much as men. While alone depression can be incapacitating, when occurring with PTSD it is significantly worse.[31]

Panic Anxiety. In the DSM-IV, PTSD is categorized as an anxiety disorder. Hence, it presents an increased risk of developing symptoms from other anxiety diseases. In reverse, a past history of anxiety disorders also increases one's susceptibility to PTSD.

A panic attack is not an uncommon occurrence for those with PTSD. Described as 3–30 minutes of extreme emotional and physical stress, one may experience increased heart rate, sweating, shortness of breath, nausea, dizziness, asphyxiation, and chest pains (to name a few). Panic anxiety severely exacerbates PTSD because trauma survivors will have increased avoidance to stress provoking thoughts and situations.

Obsessive-compulsive disorder (OCD). OCD is very similar to PTSD in that those with OCD are remarkably afraid of their thoughts, and have difficulty distinguishing their thoughts from the present environment. One may exhibit obsessive-compulsive behavior as a way to manage the painful symptoms of PTSD; participating in compulsive rituals (washing hands, checking locks, meticulously folding clothes, counting) to assuage obsessive thoughts.

Sleep disorders. One of the major problems for PTSD sufferers is decreased sleep.[32] Having immediate consequences, one becomes fatigued, sore, irritable, lacks concentration, creativity, and work performance. In addition, insomnia increases the risk of one developing PTSD. During sleep, brain activity decreases while neurotransmitters are replenished. Necessary for normal brain functioning, sufficient sleep increases one's resilience to stressors, including those that facilitate PTSD.

Complex PTSD

Previously known as complicated PTSD, the first requirement for the diagnosis of complex PTSD (CP) is that an individual has experienced a prolonged period—months to years—of total control by a perpetrator, or perpetrators.[33] Victims of CP are generally held in a state of captivity such as with a POW or concentration camp, sex-trafficking ring, incest victimization, or long-term domestic violence situations,[34] and are exposed to extreme personal stress.

The result of such victimization is the destruction of one's psychological integrity, or "mental death." In detail, it is the loss of a victim's pre-trauma identity, and incorporates a sense of being permanently damaged.[35] Those suffering from CP present a combination of the following symptoms:

1. *Diminished Regulation of Affect*
   The inability to control emotions or CERs; may include emotional outbursts, suicidal thoughts, catatonic states, and risk taking behaviors.
2. *Distorted Attention or Consciousness*
   This may involve amnesia, repression or suppression of traumatic events, as well as numbing or dissociation.
3. *Distorted Self-Perception*
   Includes shame, guilt, perceived helplessness or weakness, or a sense of being permanently damaged.

4. *Distorted Perception of the Perpetrator*
   Victims may attribute god-like power to, or idealize, the victim-izer. Victims may also evince a preoccupation with revenge.

5. *Damaged Relationships with Others*
   A diminished ability to trust, social isolation, victimizing others, feelings of interpersonal rejection, and the repeated search for a rescuer are common.

6. *Somatic Symptoms*
   Physical manifestations of CP include digestive problems, chronic pain, cardiopulmonary symptoms, and sexual dysfunction.

7. *Loss of Value or Belief Systems*
   Hopelessness, despair, spiritual crisis, and a loss of religious faith are common occurences.

The assemblage of possible symptoms under the CP nomenclature is consistent with developmental models regarding the long-term impact of victimization. For example, health problems without known etiology, dissociation, self destructive behavior, and maladaptive affective and cognitive constructions of one's self, world, or others have been noted among incest survivors. In addition, developmental research reveals that many brain chemical and hormonal changes may occur as a result of early prolonged trauma, and these changes contribute to difficulties with memory and learning.[36]

As adults, victims of CP are often diagnosed with depressive disorders, personality disorders, or dissociative disorders. Treatment often takes much longer than with regular PTSD—progressing at a much slower rate—and requires a sensitive and structured treatment program delivered by a trauma specialist.

PTSD Treatment

At the core of PTSD is the issue of affect deregulation and at the root of treatment is the development of emotional regulation skills. Very basically, since one who possesses PTSD is impaired in his/her ability to cope with traumatic memories, treatment must involve equipping a client such that he/she no longer relies on avoidant strategies (i.e. dissociation, numbing, self-medication, or tension reducing behaviors (TRBs) such as cutting, sexual acting out, etc.).

Coping involves both mentally and viscerally dividing the past from the present and gaining control over both painful memories and emotions, and the avoidant defenses erected against them. Moreover, a therapist must attempt to instill in a client new relational and behavioral schemas that will lead to more benign and adaptive CERs.

Education and Orientation

A good PTSD treatment plan covers medical, psychosocial, spiritual, familial, and even vocational factors. PTSD-specific treatment is begun only after the survivor has been safely removed from a crisis situation.[37] If a survivor is still being exposed to trauma (such as ongoing domestic violence, abuse, or homelessness), is severely depressed or suicidal, is experiencing panic or disorganized thinking, or is in need of drug or alcohol detoxification, it is important to address these crisis problems as part of the first phase of treatment.

It is important that the first phase of treatment includes educating trauma survivors and their families about how persons develop PTSD, how PTSD affects survivors and their loved ones, and other problems that commonly accompany PTSD symptoms.[38] The client's understanding that PTSD is a medically recognized disorder that occurs in normal individuals under extremely stressful conditions is essential for effective treatment.

One aspect of the first treatment phase is to have the client examine and resolve strong feelings such as anger, shame or guilt, which are common among survivors of trauma.

Another step is to teach the client strategies to cope with post-traumatic memories, reminders, reactions and feelings without becoming overwhelmed or emotionally numb. Trauma memories usually do not go away entirely as a result of therapy; instead they become manageable with the mastery of new coping skills.

Pace of Therapy

Due to shame or guilt that is often co-present, there can be reluctance on behalf of the client to disclose meaningfully. In addition, since avoidant behaviors are seen as necessary to survival, overzealous attempts by a counselor to remove either denial or dissociative symptoms can overwhelm a client and facilitate use of such defenses in therapy.

A counselor may need to wait for a client to take the initiative to disclose, and will need to operate within what is called the "therapeutic window." Interventions operating within the therapeutic window challenge, but do not overwhelm the emotional or cognitive processes of a client.[39] A counselor must have his/her finger on the pulse of the counseling relationship at all times, for disclosure will be tightly correlated to a client's level of trust, and perception of safety in the counseling environment.

Relationships as the Antidote for PTSD

Affect Regulation. Mentioned earlier, those who suffer early childhood trauma are deprived of growth-promoting opportunities, and instead develop destructive schemas. This can be thought of as a developmental retardation, one which—over time—can be reversed with the integration of healthy relationships. One author states about persons traumatized:

> But sooner or later, many persons *are* able to leave traumatic environments. They *can* find environments conducive to putting their development back on course. Even if you have undergone prolonged trauma, you can potentially choose and construct a healthier environment for yourself. The new environment will foster new learning: The world is dangerous; people are dangerous, but not *that* dangerous. The world can be relatively safe, and many people can be trusted.[40]

It is said that learning to trust one person enables one to trust others, and as persons consistently prove themselves trustworthy, one's capacity to trust society in general will increase (and when the world is perceived as safe, PTSD has much less of a stronghold).

Social Support. In addition, social support helps with the coping of new traumas. Take for example the following vignette of two women who experienced the same traumatic situation:

> Two separate woman, each alone, are nearly attacked in a parking garage but escape without physical harm. One woman arrives home upset and is immediately encountered by her husband who is emotion-

ally supportive, reassuring, calls local authorities, and who asks her to talk about the experience. After several minutes the woman calms and begins to feel relief from the stress. A few minutes later her children arrive home from school smiling and calling "Mommy, Mommy!" further confirming that the world is generally safe and good.

In contrast, the second woman arrives home to an empty apartment—she does not talk about the encounter, and instead rethinks the event many times without resolve before she begins to try and distract herself from the memory. She feels nervous, on edge, and she double checks the locks on her doors before retreating to her bedroom for the first of many sleepless nights.

Because relationships are healing, empowering one to establish secure attachment is a cornerstone of PTSD treatment.[41]

Group Therapy

Group treatment is often an ideal therapeutic setting because trauma survivors are able to share experiences within the safety, cohesion, and empathy of other survivors. As group members achieve greater understanding of their trauma, they often feel more confident in the integrity of themselves and others. As they share trauma-related shame, guilt, rage, fear, doubt, and self-condemnation, they focus themselves on the present rather than the past.[42] Telling one's story—known as the "trauma narrative"—and directly facing the grief and anxiety related to trauma, enables many survivors to cope with their symptoms, memories, and other aspects of their lives.

Therapeutic Relationship

Also utilizing the power of relationship, brief psychodynamic psychotherapy focuses on the emotional conflicts caused by the traumatic event, particularly as it relates to early life experiences. Client centered therapies promote the retelling of the traumatic event to a calm, empathic, compassionate, and nonjudgmental therapist. With either relationship, the trauma survivor achieves a greater sense of self-esteem, develops effective ways of thinking and coping, and learns to deal more successfully with intense emotions.

Medication

Due to the stress and anxiety involved with severe PTSD, chemical imbalances (serotonin disturbances for example) are not uncommon. Therefore, for some there is a need of medication as a means of chemical regulation—to correct serious neurological problems facilitated by the trauma.

Medication can reduce the anxiety, depression, and insomnia often experienced with PTSD; and in some cases it may help relieve the distress and emotional numbness caused by trauma memories.[43] Several kinds of antidepressant drugs have contributed to patient improvement in clinical trials, and some other classes of drugs have also shown promise. At this time, no particular drug has emerged as a definitive treatment for PTSD, but serotonin enhancing antidepressants appear to hold the most promise. However, medication is clearly useful for symptom relief, which makes it possible for survivors to participate in psychotherapy.

Christian counselors should have a working relationship with physicians—general practitioners and psychiatrists—in their local community. Antidepressants used to treat PTSD are not addictive, and they do not produce a "high." On the contrary, they require 2 to 3 weeks (and sometimes as long as six weeks) to deliver therapeutic effects. On average, clients will need to take medicine for about 6 to 12 months before experiencing the most therapeutic effects.

Cognitive Behavioral Approaches

Cognitive-behavioral therapy (CBT) involves addressing disruptive cognitions as a means to change one's emotions and behaviors. Cognitive-behavioral techniques are important in PTSD treatment because they help to challenge the distorted thoughts and exaggerated fears present with the disorder. However, due to CERs based in the non-verbal brain, a practitioner will find PTSD treatment similar to phobia treatment, in that rationalization does not produce a cure.

Exposure therapy. Exposure therapy is one form of CBT unique to trauma treatment. It uses careful, repeated, detailed exposure of the trauma in a safe, controlled context to help the survivor face and gain control of overwhelming fear and distress.[44] Though in some cases trauma memories can be confronted all at once with "flooding,"[45] with PTSD it is preferable to use "systematic desensitization" and increase exposure anxiety gradually by using relaxation techniques, and by exploring traumatic memories "one piece at a time."

EMDR. Eye Movement Desensitization and Reprocessing (EMDR) is a treatment that attempts to move memories from the limbic brain to the cerebral cortex with therapy that includes top-down (cognitive) and bottom-up (affect/body) processing. In brief, a client is asked to recall traumatic memories while grounded in the present by incorporating eye movements, hand taps, or sounds. While research is still evolving, a recent study investigating EMDR efficacy in treating PTSD found it to be helpful but less effective than systematic desensitization. The most therapeutic aspect of EMDR seems to be the telling of the narrative, with the grounding aspects often seen as more ancillary.[46]

How Long Does PTSD Treatment Take?

Treatment outcome and duration will depend on several factors, including the length of time between the PTSD symptom onset and the start of treatment. Someone who solicits help very soon after developing symptoms might experience relief in a matter of weeks, or a few months. However, 50% of those with PTSD develop chronic problems and do not seek treatment for months or years after experiencing the disorder. Unfortunately, the longer one has existed without care, the longer treatment will take. It cannot be overstated that, with any instance of PTSD, early intervention is extremely important.

Lastly, issues of disorder severity, CP, and comorbidity will influence the length of PTSD treatment.

Conclusion

Trauma and PTSD are becoming an all too common experience in modern life—one that will be exaggerated and exploited by a culture bent on victimhood and dependency, but one that should never be minimized in those suffering its ill effects. Christian counselors are poised to become compassionate advocates and effective interveners for trauma sufferers and should do everything possible to prepare—from the first of graduate courses to continuing education—to be the best helpers possible.

The apostle Paul's life was replete with trauma: "...five times I received forty stripes minus one. Three times I was beaten with rods; once I was stoned; three times I was shipwrecked...in perils...in perils...in perils..." (2 Cor. 11:24–27). Furthermore, he was given "a thorn in the flesh" which caused him to plead with God over and over again that it be removed from his life. But these troubles were not removed (2 Cor. 12:7–8). Instead, God told Paul that "My grace is sufficient for you, for My strength is made perfect in your weakness" (2 Cor. 12:9a) and in response Paul learned the deep mystery of power and perseverance in the face of trauma, "...I will rather boast in infirmities, that the power of Christ may rest on me. Therefore I take pleasure in infirmities, in reproaches, in needs, in persecutions, in distresses, for Christ's sake. For when I am weak, then I am strong" (2 Cor. 12:9b–10).

Paul beat the onset of PTSD by embracing trauma that could not be avoided, by seeing God's hand at work in the further training of His disciple, for the glory of God and the building up of the new church in a hostile world; "I will very gladly spend and be spent for your souls..." he told the young Corinthian church (2 Cor. 12:15). So then, let us not look for and revel in trauma—we are not called to be foolish masochists. But when trauma comes unavoidably, let's embrace it and ask God to work His will in and through it for His glory and our growth. Then let it be gone!

ENDNOTES

1. Nikki N. Jordan, Hoge, C. W., Tobler, S. K., Wells, J., Dydek, G. J., and Egerton, W. E., Mental health impact of 9/11 Pentagon attack: Validation of a rapid assessment tool, *American Journal of Preventive Medicine*, 26(4) (April 2004), 284–294.
2. National Institute of Mental Health, *Reliving trauma: Post-traumatic stress disorder: A brief overview of the symptoms, treatments, and research findings* (2001); O Frans, Rimmö, P.A., Åberg, L., and Fredrikson, M., Trauma exposure and post-traumatic stress disorder in the general population, *Acta Psychiatrica Scandinavica*, 111(4) (April 2005), 291–293.
3. N. Breslau, and Davis, G.C., Post-traumatic stress disorder in an urban population of young adults: Risk factors for chronicity, *American Journal of Psychiatry*, 149 (1992), 671–675; Heidi S Resnick, Kilpatrick, D.G., Dansky, B.S., Saunders, B.E. et al, Prevalence of civilian trauma and post-traumatic stress disorder in a representative national sample of women, *Journal of Consulting & Clinical Psychology*, 61(6) (December 1993), 984–991; American Psychiatric Association, *Let's talk facts about post-traumatic stress disorder* (Accessed June 20, 2005 from <http://www.psych.org/public_info/ptsd.cfm: Author, 1999).
4. Jon G. Allen, *Coping with trauma: A guide to self-understanding* (American Psychiatric Press Inc, 1999); D.J. Gelinas, Relational patterns in incestuous families, malevolent variations, and specific interventions with the adult survivor, in P.L.

Paddison (ed.), *Treatment of adult survivors of incest* (Washington, D.C., American Psychiatric Press, 1993), 1–34.

5. Kathleen McCullough-Zander, and Larson, S., The fear is still in me: Caring for survivors of torture, *American Journal of Nursing, 104*(10), (October 2004), 54–65; Allen S. Keller, Rosenfeld, B., Trinh-Shevrin, C., Meserve, C., Sachs, E., Leviss, J. A., Singer, E., Smith, H., Wilkinson, J., Kim, G., Allden, K., and Ford, D., Mental health of detained asylum seekers, *Lancet, 362*(9397), (November 2003), 1721–1724; A.S. Blank Jr., The longitudinal course of post-traumatic stress disorder, in *Post-traumatic stress disorder: DSM IV and beyond* (Washington DC: American Psychiatric Press, 1993).

6. Steven Cufee, Addy, C., Garrison, C., Waller, J., Jackson, K., Mckeown, R., and Chilappagari, S., Prevalence of PTSD in a community sample of older adolescents, *Journal of the American Academy of Child & Adolescent Psychiatry, 37*(2), (February 1998), 147–154.; R.C. Kessler, Sonnega, A., Bromet, E., Hughes, M., and Nelson, C.B., Post-traumatic stress disorder in the national comorbidity survey, *Archives of General Psychiatry, 52*(12) (December 1995), 1048–1060.

7. Heidi S Resnick, Kilpatrick, D.G., Dansky, B.S., Saunders, B.E. et al, Prevalence of civilian trauma and post-traumatic stress disorder in a representative national sample of women, *Journal of Consulting & Clinical Psychology, 61*(6) (December 1993), 984–991.

8. Catlina M. Arata, Sexual revictimization and PTSD: An exploratory study, *Journal of Child Sexual Abuse, 8*(1), (1999), 49–66; O Frans, Rimmö, P.A., Åberg, L., and Fredrikson, M., Trauma exposure and post-traumatic stress disorder in the general population," *Acta Psychiatrica Scandinavica, 111*(4) (April 2005), 291–293.

9. W. R. True, Rice, J., Eisen, S. A., Heath, A. C., Goldberg, J., Lyons M. J., and Nowak, J., A twin study of genetic and environmental contributions to liability for post-traumatic stress symptoms, *JAMA & Archives, Archives of General Psychiatry*, accessed June 20, 2005 from http://archpsyc.amaassn.org/cgi/content/abstract/50/4/257.

10. Jennifer Ahern, Galea, S., Resnick, H., Kilpatrick, D., Bucuvalas, M., Gold, J., and Vlahov, D., Television images and psychological symptoms after the September 11 terrorist attacks, *Psychiatry:Interpersonal & Biological Processes, 65*(4), (Winter 2002), 289–301; O Frans, Rimmö, P.A., Åberg, L., and Fredrikson, M., Trauma exposure and post-traumatic stress disorder in the general population, *Acta Psychiatrica Scandinavica, 111*(4) (April 2005), 291–293.

11. Atia Daud, Skoglund, E., and Rydelius, P., Children in families of torture victims: Transgenerational transmission of parents' traumatic experiences to their children, *International Journal of Social Welfare, 14*(1), (January 2005), 23–33; John Briere, Treating adult survivors of severe childhood abuse and neglect: Further development of an integrative model, in *The APSAC handbook on child maltreatment, 2nd Edition* (Newbury Park, CA: Sage Publications, 1996).

12. Gary Sibcy, Lecture: Advanced psychopathology, *Liberty University*, (June 2005); John Briere, Treating adult survivors of severe childhood abuse and neglect: Further development of an integrative model, in *The APSAC handbook on child maltreatment, 2nd Edition* (Newbury Park, CA: Sage Publications, 1996).

13. John Bowlby, *A secure base: Parent-child attachment and healthy human development* (New York: Basic Books, 1988).

14. C. Dissanayake, and Crossley, S. A., Proximity and sociable behaviours in autism: Evidence for attachment, *Journal of Child Psychol Psychiatry. 37*(2), (February 1996), 149–156; Mary Ainsworth, Blehar, M. C., Waters, E., Wall, S., *Patterns of attachment: A psychological study of the strange situation* (Hillsdale, NJ: Erlbaum, 1978).

15. John Briere, Treating adult survivors of severe childhood abuse and neglect: Further development of an integrative model, in *The APSAC handbook on child maltreatment, 2nd Edition* (Newbury Park, CA: Sage Publications, 1996); John Bowlby, *A secure base.*

16. P. Fonagy, *Pathological attachments and therapeutic action* (Paper Presented at the Annual Meeting of the California Branch of the American Academy of Child and Adolescent Psychiatry, Yosemite Valley, CA., 1999).

17. Jon G. Allen, *Coping with trauma: A guide to self-understanding* (American Psychiatric Press Inc., 1999), 6.

18. Michael G. Madianos, Papaghelis, M., Ioannovich, J., Dafni, R., Psychiatric disorders in burn patients: A follow-up study, *Psychotherapy and Psychosomatics, 70,* (2001), 30–37.

19. Maria Oquendo, Brent, D. A., Birmaher, B., Greenhill, L, Kolko, D., Stanley, B., Zelazny, J., Burke, A. K., Firinciogullari, S., Ellis, S. P., and Mann, J. J., Post-traumatic stress disorder comorbid with major depression: Factors mediating the association with suicidal behavior, *American Journal of Psychiatry, 162*(3), (March 2005), 560–567; Ill Holtzheimer, Russo, P. E., Zatzick, J., Bundy, D., Roy-Byrne, C., and Peter P., The impact of comorbid post-traumatic stress disorder on short-term clinical outcome in hospitalized patients with depression, *American Journal of Psychiatry, 162*(5), (May 2005), 970–977; Sandra Anton, and Mrdenovi_, S., Working ability of patients with post-traumatic stress disorder (demographic and social features): Comparative study, *Journal of Loss & Trauma, 10*(2), (March/April 2005), 155–162.

20. Cynthia Lindman Port, Engdahl, B., and Frazier, P., A longitudinal and retrospective study of PTSD among older prisoners of war, *American Journal of Psychiatry, 158*(9), (September 2001), 1474–1480.

21. American Psychiatric Association, *Let's talk facts about post-traumatic stress disorder* (accessed June 20, 2005 from <http://www.psych.org/public_info/ptsd.cfm: Author, 1999); Jon G. Allen, *Coping with trauma: A guide to self-understanding* (American Psychiatric Press Inc., 1999).

22. Nancy Fagan, and Freme, K., Confronting post-traumatic stress disorder, *Nursing, 34*(2), (February 2004), 52–54; National Institute of Mental Health, *Reliving trauma: Post-traumatic stress disorder: A brief overview of the symptoms, treatments, and research findings* (2001).

23. Hans Peter Söndergaard, Ekblad, S., and Theorell, T., Screening for post-traumatic stress disorder among refugees in Stockholm, *Nordic Journal of Psychiatry, 57*(3), (May 2003), 185–190.

24. Eldra P. Solomon, and Heide, K. M., The biology of trauma, *Journal of Interpersonal Violence, 20*(1), (January 2005), 51–61; Thomas A. Mellman, and David, D., Sleep disturbance and its relationship to psychiatric morbidity after Hurricane Andrew, *American Journal of Psychiatry, 152*(11), (November 1995), 1659–1664; Jean M. Thomas, Traumatic stress disorder presents as hyperactivity and disruptive behavior: Case presentation, diagnoses, and treatment, *Infant Mental Health Journal, 16*(4), (Winter 1995), 306–318; Kathy A. Pearce, Schauer, A. H., Garfield, N. J., Ohlde, C. O., and Patterson, T.W., A study of post-traumatic stress disorder in Vietnam veterans, *Journal of Clinical Psychology, 41*(1), (January 1985), 9–15.

25. Dorcas Dobie, Kivlahan, D. R., Maynard, C., Bush, K. R., Davis, T.M., and Bradley, K.A., Post-traumatic stress disorder in female veterans: Association with self-reported health problems and functional impairment" *Archives of Internal*

Medicine, 164(4), (February 2004), 394–401; P. Niels Christensen, Cohan, S. L., and Stein, M. B., The relationship between interpersonal perception and post-traumatic stress disorder-related functional impairment: A social relations model analysis, *Cognitive Behaviour Therapy, 33*(3), (2004), 151–161.

26. Annick Shaw, Joseph, S., and Linley, A. P., Religion, spirituality, and post-traumatic growth: A systematic review, *Mental Health, Religion & Culture, 8*(1), (March 2005), 1–11; Julie J. Exline, Smyth, J.M., Gregory, J., Hockemeyer, J., and Tulloch, H., Religious framing by individuals with PTSD when writing about traumatic experiences, *International Journal for the Psychology of Religion, 15*(1), (2005), 17–34.

27. Tamar Lowinger, and Solomon, T. Z., PTSD, guilt, and shame among reckless drivers," *Journal of Loss & Trauma, 9*(4), (October-December 2004), 327–345; Mel Singer, Shame, guilt, self-hatred and remorse in the psychotherapy of Vietnam combat veterans who committed atrocities, *American Journal of Psychotherapy, 58*(4), (2004), 377–386.

28. Jennie Leskela, Dieperink, M., Thuras, P., Shame and post-traumatic stress disorder, *Journal of Traumatic Stress, 15*(3), (June 2002), 223–227.

29. Marcelle Ferrada-Noli, Asberg, M., Ormstad, K., Lundin, T., and Sundbom, E., Suicidal behavior after severe trauma. Part 1: PTSD diagnoses, psychiatric co-morbidity, and assessments of suicidal behavior, *Journal of Traumatic Stress, 11*(1), (January 1998), 103–113; Rani A Desai, Dausey, D. J., and Rosenheck, R., Mental health service delivery and suicide risk: The role of individual patient and facility factors, *American Journal of Psychiatry, 162*(2) (February 2005), 311–319.

30. R. D. Alacorn, Glover, S.G., and Deering, C.G., The cascade model: An alternative to comorbidity in the pathogenesis of post-traumatic stress disorder, *Psychiatry, 62* (1999), 114–124.

31. Archibald Hart, and Weber, C.H., *Unveiling depression in women: A practical guide to understanding and overcoming depression* (Grand Rapids, MI: Fleming H. Revell, 2002), 20; Reginald D.V. Nixon, Resick, P. A., and Nishith, P., An exploration of co-morbid depression among female victims of intimate partner violence with post-traumatic stress disorder, *Journal of Affective Disorders, 82*(2), (October 2004), 315–321.

32. Johnathan D. Huppert, Moser, J. S., Gershuny, B. S., Riggs, D. S., Spokas, M., Filip, J., Hajcak, G., Parker, H. A., Baer, L., and Foa, E. B., The relationship between obsessive-compulsive and post-traumatic stress symptoms in clinical and non-clinical samples, *Journal of Anxiety Disorders, 19*(1), (January 2005), 127–137; Anne Germain, Hall, M., Krakow, B., Shear, M. K., and Buysse, D. J., A brief sleep scale for post-traumatic stress disorder: Pittsburgh Sleep Quality Index addendum for PTSD, *Journal of Anxiety Disorders, 19*(2), (March 2005), 233–245.; Pallavi Nishith, Resick, P. A., and Mueser, K. T., Sleep difficulties and alcohol use motives in female rape victims with post-traumatic stress disorder, *Journal of Traumatic Stress, 14*(3), (July 2001), 469–480.; Javaid I. Sheikh, Woodward, S. H., and Leskin, G. A., Sleep in post-traumatic stress disorder and panic: Convergence and divergence, *Depression & Anxiety, 18*(4), (2003), 187–198.

33. S. Roth, Newman, E., Pelcovitz, D., Van der Kolk, B., and Mandel, F. S., Complex PTSD in victims exposed to sexual and physical abuse: Results from the DSM-IV field trial for post-traumatic stress disorder, *Journal of Traumatic Stress, 10*, (1997), 539–555.

34. Julia M. Whealin, *Complex PTSD a national center for PTSD fact sheet* (accessed on June 20, 2005 from <http://www.ncptsd.va.gov/facts/specific/

fs_complex_ptsd.html>: Department of Veterans Affairs).

35. Angela Ebert, and Dyck, M. J., The experience of mental death: The core feature of complex post-traumatic stress disorder, *Clinical Psychology Review*, 24(6), (October 2004), 617–36.

36. Martin H. Teicher, Andersen, S. L., Polcari, A., Anderson, C. M., Navalta, C. P., and Kim, D. M., The neurobiological consequences of early stress and childhood maltreatment, *Neuroscience & Biobehavioral Reviews*, 27(1/2), (January 2003), 33–45.; Michael D. De Bellis, Keshavan, M.S., Shifflett, H., Iyengar, S., Beers, S.R., Hall, J., and Moritz, G., Brain structures in pediatric maltreatment-related post-traumatic stress disorder: A sociodemographically matched study, *Biological Psychiatry*, 52(11), (December 2002), 1066–1079.

37. Jonathan I. Bisson, McFarlane, A. C., and Rose, S., *Psychological debriefing, effective treatments for PTSD* (New York: Guilford Press, 2000), 41.

38. Matt J. Gray, Elhai, J. D., and Frueh, C. B., Enhancing patient satisfaction and increasing treatment compliance: Patient education as a fundamental component of PTSD treatment, *Psychiatric Quarterly*, 75(4) (December 2004), 321–333.

39. John Briere, Treating adult survivors of severe childhood abuse and neglect: Further development of an integrative model, in *The APSAC handbook on child maltreatment, 2nd Edition*, (Newbury Park, CA: Sage Publications, 1996).

40. Jon G. Allen, *Coping with trauma: A guide to self-understanding* (American Psychiatric Press Inc., 1999).

41. Tim Clinton, and Sibcy, G., *Attachments: Why you love, feel and act the way you do* (Brentwood, TN: Integrity, 2002).

42. American Psychiatric Association, *Let's talk facts about post-traumatic stress disorder* (accessed June 20, 2005 from <http://www.psych.org/public_info/ptsd.cfm>: Author, 1999); Irvin D. Yalom, *The theory and practice of group psychotherapy* (New York: Basic Books, 1995).

43. Ulrich Frommberger, Stieglitz, R., Nyberg, E., Richter, H., Novelli-Fischer, U., Angenendt, J., Zaninelli, R., and Berger, M., Comparison between paroxetine and behaviour therapy in patients with post-traumatic stress disorder (PTSD): A pilot study, *International Journal of Psychiatry in Clinical Practice*, 8(1), (March 2004), 19–24.

44. Jaye Wald, and Taylor, S., Interoceptive exposure therapy combined with trauma-related exposure therapy for post-traumatic stress disorder: A case report, *Cognitive Behaviour Therapy*, 34(1), (2005), 34–41.

45. Philip A. Saigh, In vitro flooding of an adolescent's post-traumatic stress disorder, *Journal of Clinical Child Psychology*, 16(2), (June 1987), 147–151.

46. Eldra P. Solomon, and Heide, K. M. The biology of trauma, *Journal of Interpersonal Violence*, 20(1), (January 2005), 51–61; Steven Taylor, Thordarson, D. S., Fedoroff, I.C., Maxfield, L., and Ogrodniczuk, J., Comparative efficacy, speed, and adverse effects of three PTSD treatments: exposure therapy, EMDR, and relaxation training, *Journal of Consulting & Clinical Psychology*, 71(2), (April 2003), 330–339; Gary Sibcy, Lecture: Advanced Psychopathology, *Liberty University* (June 2005).

19

Adult Survivors of Sexual Abuse:
Trauma, Treatment, and Living in the Truth

Diane Langberg

> Rarely in human history . . . has there been this degree of wanton . . . violence [done against] helpless victims, ranging from child abuse to state-sanctioned torture. Although a historical perspective will not directly help the victims of child sexual and physical abuse . . . it undergirds the observation that the trauma done to humans by other humans is considerably more damaging and enduring in its . . . effects than trauma done by floods, earthquakes [and other natural disasters]. It is not that natural traumas are trivial, but rather that there is something about being hurt intentionally and gratuitously by other human beings . . . that is particularly gripping in its destructiveness and demoralization.
>
> JEROME KROLL[1]

"My father raped me."

It has been thirty years since I first heard the words. I had just finished a Master's degree in psychology and was entering a doctoral program. Nothing in my personal life or in my training to that point had prepared me for such a statement. But I did what all good students do when they hit a wall—I went to talk to my supervisor. The response I got was that women sometimes tell these hysterical stories and your job is to not get hooked by them. They are essentially looking for attention and if you give it to them you will contribute to their pathology.

As time passed I began to hear more stories of sexual abuse from other women. I decided to listen. I basically told my clients that I knew nothing about such things, nor did I know anyone to ask. I wanted to help and was willing to learn if they would teach me what they knew while I struggled to find what would be helpful for them. They, probably out of desperation, agreed and thus began an aspect of my professional life that has changed me irrevocably, challenged me constantly, and continues to teach me to this day.

To give you a full presentation on the treatment of sexual abuse in one chapter is, of course, impossible. My fuller thinking about treatment is in a book entitled *Counseling Survivors of Sexual Abuse.*[2] So rather than simply give you what you can go read I have chosen to present an overview of treatment as a backdrop for specific consideration of the spiritual impact on the survivor and the resultant struggles you will face as a counselor.

Human beings, as you know, commit atrocious acts against other human beings. One of the most horrible of these is the sexual abuse of a child. Most of the men and women I have worked with are survivors of chronic and often violent sexual abuse. I acknowledge without question that all sexual abuse is not traumatic. However, for most victims it is traumatic beyond words and because of my experience, and for the purpose of this chapter, I will treat abuse as trauma.

A child is by definition developing or in process. The sexual abuse of a child shatters and violates every aspect of their being—their world, their self, their faith and their future. Such violation forces the child to adapt in ways that are often maladaptive in the larger world. Such violation causes the child to develop a view of himself and his world that is based on repeated and destructive lies. Obviously an understanding of this must inform treatment or we will be ineffective.

These are the stories I listen to in my practice. When I first began to hear them, there were no books on the subject, no articles, no TV shows, no workshops. I learned from my clients. Those women taught me what it felt like to be molested as children, what it felt like to be adults with such memories, and what they needed to start on the road to healing. I made many mistakes. I missed a lot of clues. I'm sure they suffered needlessly as a result. But they grew, and I grew with them. I owe them, as do my later clients, a great debt. Now I hope to pass on to you some of what I have learned.

Prevalence: Prying Open a Secret World

A therapist tells the story that during an initial therapy session with a senior citizen, she asked a routine interview question: "Have you ever been sexually abused?" The older woman paused, then nodded slowly. Although she had been in therapy most of her adult life, there was no

A CASE-BASED VIEW OF CHILD SEXUAL ABUSE

I would like to define sexual abuse for you—not a technical one (we will do that next) but a graphic one—seeing abuse through the eyes of the victim. Think about a little girl, around 6 years old, who is ready for bed. What images come to mind? Clean, safe, protected, stories, trust, closeness. I am sure many of you reading this have lived this image out with your own daughters and know there is something very special and tender about tucking your child in bed at night.

The reality of sexual abuse shatters that image. The little girl lies in bed in paralyzing fear. She is listening for footsteps, for the sound of her door opening. She wraps her covers around her in a mummy-like fashion—a desperate attempt to provide safety for herself. But she is little and he is big, and she has no place to go. He confuses and frightens her. He touches and hurts her and tells her it's their secret. She's not to tell anyone, or she will lose her daddy forever—and it will be her fault.

His fondling intensifies and he starts doing other things, things she doesn't understand. It hurts so badly and she wants it to stop. She tells him, but he says this is what father's do for their daughters and it's for her good. He also says it's her fault for leading him on. What does that mean? All she did was get in bed to go to sleep.

It's especially confusing because in the morning everything goes back to normal. He greets her at breakfast like nothing happened and she goes off to school. Then he begins doing some of the same things in the daytime if they are alone. She dreads the times when her mother leaves the house. She tries to go to her friend's house after school as much as possible. One night she tried sleeping in her closet—but he always finds her. Nothing works.

She thinks about telling her Mom, but is afraid. Mom encourages her to be with Dad. Maybe she knows and thinks it's okay. Maybe she would be angry and say it was all her fault. She is very confused about all this. One time Mom caught Dad in her room, but he said she'd had a bad dream and he was calming her down. Mom believed him.

Sometimes when it's happening she pretends she's real little and can hide under the flowers in her wallpaper. It's funny, because she feels like she's watching herself from faraway. She digs her fingernails into her palms and sometimes pulls on her hair so hard it comes out. The pain from those things distracts her. She thinks often about running away. Just wait till she's older.

In the meantime, his pursuit is relentless, and his anger toward her increases. He calls her terrible names and tells her how bad she is for making him do this. Doesn't he understand that she doesn't want to do this? What could she possibly be doing to make him do these things? Then, after she does just what he wants so he won't get mad, he gets mad anyway. It just doesn't make any sense. *Nothing she can think of is successful in stopping it . . .* Maybe it would stop if she were dead . . .

record of sexual victimization in her overflowing patient file. Her stark response, "No one ever asked."[3]

Too often, we do not ask. We survey clients on alcohol use, drug use, suicidality, depression, physical abuse, and sometimes consensual sexual contact. But we fail to ask about sexual victimization. The nature of the crime constituting child sexual abuse is enmeshed in victim secrecy. Research began exposing sexual abuse as a problem of sizable proportions in the late 1960s and early 1970s. One theme remains consistent: sexual abuse is extensively undisclosed and underreported.[4]

There are many factors relating to the dynamics of the insufferable crime that may impact victim failure to disclose. Abuse victims frequently experience feelings of shame, guilt, isolation, powerlessness, embarrassment, and inadequacy. They may even accept responsibility for the abuse by blaming themselves. Victims often feel that "something is wrong with me," or that the abuse is their fault.[5]

Research on Victims

David Finkelhor and his colleagues [6] conducted the first national telephone survey of men and women victims of abuse. Of the 2,626 Americans questioned regarding prior sexual abuse, victimization was reported by 27% of the women and 16% of the men. One of the major findings was that many victims never disclosed the experiences to anyone. Of those participants who confirmed sexual abuse, 42% of the women and 33% of the men acknowledged never having disclosed.

Based on his extensive research on sexual abuse, Bagley affirmed that child sexual abuse is much more frequent than previously assumed. He reported 32% of the sampled adult females in his community study responded they experienced child sexual abuse, with sexual abuse greater for women born after 1960 than before.[7] These figures coincide with best estimates that range from 1 in 4 to 40% of the female population as having had an experience of sexual abuse at sometime in their childhood. Estimates for males usually are around 1 in 6.

Most child sexual abuse is perpetrated either by a family member or someone known to the child. The majority of abusers of both male and female victims are male, however, some unknown percentage of abusers are female. The ultimate irony is that abuse may be the biggest cause and effect of abuse... among abusing parents 30 to 60% say that they were abused as children.[8]

Child sexual abuse usually begins between ages 6 and 12, but for many children it begins at a much younger age. Abuse that occurs at a very young age and is forceful and repeated is most likely to be forgotten or repressed by the child. This is because children do not have sophisticated defense mechanisms in their repertoire, so they are limited to dealing with trauma in relatively primitive ways.

Most sexual abuse does not involve force, but rather involves some sort of manipulation and misrepresentation to the child. However, it is important to note that even when abuse in non-forceful, it is violative, and therefore is a form of violence. In other cases, physical force, violence, threats and coercion are used. Children may be frightened into participation by an abuser who threatens harm, abandonment and rejection.

Definitions of Abuse

Let's move on to a technical definition for sexual abuse and then describe its effects. Then we will consider the treatment process, with an emphasis on what therapy needs to include. Later, we will discuss the dangers inherent for the therapist in doing this kind of work, as well as some of the lessons I have learned that have not only been helpful, but necessary, in maintaining my sanity, my compassion, and my endurance.

I am going to focus on adult female survivors because I do not work with children—my expertise is with adults and, for the most part, victims tend to be female and perpetrators male.[9] Most of the work and research that has been done concerns this particular dyad. However, I would like to add that in recent years I find myself seeing more and more men who have been sexually abused and who have entered therapy for the express purpose of dealing with it.

Sexual abuse is defined in *Renewal: Hope for Victims of Sexual Abuse* as "any sexual activity, verbal, visual or physical, engaged in without consent, which may be emotionally or physically harmful and which exploits a person in order to meet another person's sexual or emotional needs. The person does not consent if he or she cannot reasonably choose to consent or refuse because of age, circumstances, level of understanding and dependency or relationship to the offender."[10]

Verbal sexual abuse includes things like sexual threats, innuendoes, comments about a person's body, harassment, sexual and pornographic jokes, coarse jesting, etc.

Visual sexual abuse includes voyeurism, exhibitionism, viewing of pornographic material, genitals, or of any sexual activity, and displaying pornography in public or the workplace.

Physical sexual abuse can range from intercourse with seeming "consent," to intercourse by force, and attempted intercourse, primarily fondling of breasts and genitals.

As can be seen from the above, sexual abuse involves a wide range of behaviors, alone or in combination with other behaviors.

The Effects of Sexual Abuse

First and foremost, we must keep in mind that sexual abuse is traumatic. Trauma involves "intense fear, helplessness, loss of control, and threat of annihilation."[11] *These are natural emotions and behaviors in response to catastrophe*, its immediate aftermath, and the memories of it. Judith Herman, in her book *Trauma and Recovery* says, "Traumatic events are extraordinary, not because they occur rarely, but rather because they overwhelm the ordinary human adaptations to life."[12]

We know from experience and from the literature that trauma results in silence, isolation, and helplessness.[13] Silence because words are inadequate for communicating the unspeakable. Isolation because no one knows, no one comes to help, no one enters in. Helplessness because every attempt to stop the abuse is ineffective, and indeed often exacerbates the abuse.

Finkelhor and Browne acknowledged that the effects of childhood molestation may be delayed into adulthood. Long-term effects that are frequently reported and associated with sexual abuse include depression, self-destructive behavior, anxiety, feelings of isolation and stigma, poor self-esteem, difficulty in trusting others, tendency toward revictimization, substance abuse, and sexual maladjustment.[14]

Arrested development. There are three other things to keep in mind about sexual abuse trauma—three effects of the arrested development of abuse. The first is that much of a survivor's thinking is "frozen" in time. A woman who was chronically abused by her father for fifteen years, thinks about her self, her life and her relationships through the grid of the abuse. She may have encountered situations where people proved trustworthy, but she does not trust. She may have heard thousands of words about how God loves her, but she believes she is trash, an exception to the rule. Trauma stops growth because it shuts everything down. Abuse trauma brings death. The input from many other experiences, relationally and spiritually, does not usually impact the thinking that originated within the context of the abuse.

Second, the abuse occurred to a child, not an adult. Children think concretely, not abstractly. Children learn about abstract concepts like trust, truth, and love from the concrete experiences they have with significant others in their lives. They learn what love is by how mommy and daddy treat them. They learn about trust by the trustworthiness (or lack of trust) of mommy and daddy. In essence, they learn about intangible things, ideas, values, through the tangible. If those who teach them are repeatedly untrustworthy, cruel, hurtful, and lying, then to grasp and live out concepts like trustworthy, safe, loving and truthful seems like an exercise in the ridiculous.

Third, not only do children think concretely, and learn about the abstract by way of the concrete, I believe that as adults, we continue to be taught about the unseen through the seen. We are of the earth, earthy. God teaches us eternal truths through things in the natural world. We grasp a bit of eternity by looking at the sea. We get a glimmer of infinity by staring into space. We learn about the shortness of time by the quick disappearance of a vapor.

Jesus taught us eternal truths the same way. He said He was the Bread, the Light, the Living Water, the Vine. We look at the seen and learn about the unseen. Consider the sacraments—water, bread, and wine. We are taught about the holiest of all things through the diet of a peasant. This method is used all the way through understanding the character of God Himself. God in the flesh, God with skin on. God explains Himself to us through the natural and the temporal.

If we consider the combined impact of these factors, we see that many survivors exhibit this quality of thinking, frozen in time, in that they learned repeatedly through the concrete how to think about the abstract, and they learned repeatedly through the seen what to believe about the unseen.

These reactions can occur anytime after the trauma, even decades later. The reactions can be acute, which is the immediate response to the stressor;

chronic effects that persist over time; or delayed, obviously symptoms which develop later. Some women react in all three ways. Post-traumatic stress reactions include three major sets of symptoms.

1. Numbing of emotional responsiveness.
2. Increased arousal and vigilant reactiveness to anything reminiscent of the event—often referred to as the "fight-or-flight" syndrome.
3. Avoidance, even the running away from of anything that reminds one of the event—the "flight" side of the syndrome.

Some of the common characteristics in women experiencing post-traumatic stress are:

- sleep and dream disturbances,
- irritability and an increased startle response,
- explosive anger (toward self or others),
- reduced ability to function,
- prone to drug, alcohol, gambling, shopping, sexual, and food/diet addictions,
- increased fantasy, helplessness, and inability to differentiate between emotions,
- trouble forming attachments and being satisfied in relationships,
- repeating traumatic relationships, including poor marital and sexual relations,
- self-blame and self-hatred.[15]

Severity of effects. The severity of an individual woman's reaction to sexual abuse depends on many factors. Abuse that occurs more frequently and is of longer duration is potentially more harmful. Sexual abuse involving penetration of any sort is typically more harmful. The more closely related the victim and the perpetrator and the wider the age difference, the greater the damage. Women who responded to the abuse passively or willingly, tend to engage in more self-blame. Disclosed abuse that receives no help has more potential for damage, as does either negative parental reactions or ineffective or stigmatizing institutional responses (the death of hope).

Duration of effects. Long-term effects of child sexual abuse can be quite extensive. It is important to recognize that the following list consists of indicators, they are not proof that sexual abuse has occurred. Adult survivors often have very distorted images of self, are unable to trust others, need to be in control to feel safe, and deny feelings and needs or do not even recognize them. Because they were betrayed and used by people who should have protected them, they end up fearing and mistrusting others.

Psycho-sexual effects. Abuse victims often feel vulnerable and fear danger, rather than feeling comfortable when they get too close to others. Relationships may be fraught with difficulty, and intimacy and parenting may be especially threatening. Survivors commonly feel isolated, and different from others, and may attempt to gain approval by either taking care of others or by being excessively dependent or some combination of these. Some try to cope with their fears by being controlling or extremely rigid.

Child sexual abuse often results in psychological problems including chronic depression, phobias, shame, physical problems, emotional numbness, dissociation, eating disorders, self-mutilation and suicide attempts. Victim relations and revictimizations such as battering relationships are far too common, as are addictions and compulsions.

Sexual dysfunctions can sometimes be traced to child sexual abuse, such as: sexual aversion, pain, desire disorder, arousal problems and orgasmic difficulties. Survivors may be confused about their sexual orientation. It is not uncommon, when the perpetrator was male, to be so fearful of or "turned off" by men that a woman feels unsure of her sexual identity. Sexual abuse and homosexual behavior have some strong correlations.[16]

Effects on father-image and self-image. In the movie *"Forrest Gump,"* Jenny kneels down in a cornfield, asking God to please make her a bird so she can fly away. While she is praying her drunken, sexually abusive father comes in pursuit. God does not make her into a bird and she is left to her father. A child is told to get down on her knees nightly by her bed and pray with her father. As he tucks her in, he molests her, saying, "Why are you such a whore that you make me do this after we have prayed?"

What does incest teach about fathers? That they are untrustworthy. They have a great deal of power. They are unpredictable. They inflict pain on those they are supposed to care for. They betray, they abandon, deceive, use, and rip apart. They speak love and reassuring words and then suddenly abuse. Rest and peace is out of the question.

What does abuse teach the survivor about herself? That she is unworthy, trash. She is not loved and probably never will be. That her prayers are useless.

That she brings evil to people or makes them do evil things. That no effort on her part brings change or relief.

What does the survivor learn about things like trust, faith? Those are things you never do unless you are an idiot. Love? Love is a word you use when you want to make someone do something they do not want to do. Hope? Hope is a set-up. Nothing ever changes anyway.

It is important to remember, however, that abuse does not automatically cause sexual dysfunction, nor does a dysfunction in this area automatically prove the existence of sexual abuse.

Spiritual Impact of Trauma

Finally, abuse profoundly impacts the spiritual realm. What does it teach about God? That He is cruel, impotent or uncaring. He does not hear or if He hears, He does not answer. He thinks children are expendable. He does not keep His word. He is not who He says He is. Who God is and what He thinks about the survivor, is understood based on who daddy was, or grandfather, or youth pastor or whoever. They have learned about love, trust, hope, faith, through the experience of sexual abuse.

They have also learned about the unseen through the seen. The ins and outs of ordinary life have taught them many lessons about who God is. The sexual violation of a child can have many spiritual effects—a distorted image of God, coupled with a distorted image of self, creates multiple barriers to experiencing God's love and grace. God is often seen as punitive, an impossible taskmaster, capricious or dead, nonexistent. Sometimes children are even abused in God's name, being told it is God's will for them to submit to the abuse in order to "obey their parents." (Example: abuse followed by bedtime prayers.)

That is why a therapist or pastor may have the experience of speaking the truths of Scripture to a survivor, truths desperately needed, and yet finding that they seem to have no impact. *They don't go in*. Many times I find that survivors can speak eloquently to me of the truths of Scripture, but on an experiential level their lives are lived out in the context of what the abuse taught them, rather than the truths of the Word of God. Intellectually, truth is rooted in the Word of God. Experientially, or personally applied, the truth is rooted in the lessons of abuse.

Sometimes, of course, we find an exception to that. God is certainly still capable of the miraculous. They are few and far between however. There are also those who seem to experientially know the truths of Scripture and apply them to themselves, but on closer look are found able to do so because they have yet to face the truth of the abuse they endured.

Self-deceit to believe in God. Oftentimes I find that survivors can hold on to their belief in God because they are living in self-deceit. "It was not really abuse." "It wasn't that bad." "He didn't mean it." In other words, "I can believe God is really alive, or truly loves me, because I have in essence 'gone to a nearby room' away from the abuse, so I can think God is still alive."

Elie Wiesel, one of the foremost writers of the Holocaust, states the problem eloquently. Throughout his books he tells the reader not to assume the consolation of believing that God is alive. Rather than being the solution, saying "God is alive" simply reinforces the problem. He struggles again and again with two irreconcilable realities—the reality of God and the reality of Auschwitz. Each seems to cancel out the other, yet neither will disappear. Either alone could be managed—Auschwitz and no God, or God and no Auschwitz. But together? Auschwitz *and* God? How is that possible?[17]

For many survivors of sexual abuse, the same two irreconcilable realities exist: the reality of a God who says He is loving and a refuge for the weak, and the reality of the ongoing sexual violation of a child. Each seems to cancel out the other, yet both exist. Again, the human mind can manage either alternative—the sexual abuse of a child and no God, or God and protection from sexual abuse.

What is one to do with the rape of a child *and* the reality of God? Most survivors will come down on one side or the other. They have faced the rape and God is not to be trusted. Or they hang on tightly to God and the rape is a blur, a fantasy, a blip on the screen. Believe me, the dilemma is not easily resolved. For some, in fact, it is never resolved.

Many survivors do not struggle with these issues so articulately. I use them because they clearly demonstrate the grappling that goes on and carefully delineate between the lies and the truth (a process that is often very muddy for survivors). This woman has allowed me to not only show these today, but has also given me permission to use them with other survivors. I have found them extremely helpful with adults for two reasons. One, they respond to their thinking. Their questions and thinking are

SEXUAL ABUSE AND THE
TWISTED KNOWLEDGE OF GOD

Before we go on I want to make sure that we grasp the profound impact of ongoing abuse to a child's understanding of God. Let us consider some specific examples.

Sarah is five. Her parents drop her off at Sunday school every week. She has learned to sing "Jesus loves me, this I know, for the Bible tells me so. Little ones to Him belong. They are weak, but He is strong." Sarah's daddy rapes her several times a week. Sometimes she gets a break because he rapes her eight-year-old sister instead. The song says that Jesus loves her. It says that He is strong. So she asks Jesus to stop her daddy from hurting her and her sister. Nothing happens. Maybe Jesus isn't so strong after all. Or at least not as strong as daddy. Nothing, not even Jesus, can stop daddy. The people who wrote the Bible must not have known about her daddy.

Mary is seven. She lives in a house where she is taught about God. God seems to have a lot of rules. God says children have to do whatever their parents tell them to do. Mary tries very hard to do what her mommy and daddy say. When she doesn't obey then daddy hurts her and says this is how God told daddies to teach their little girls. Mommy sends her to daddy when she is angry with Mary and daddy hurts her then too. She guesses that if you don't do what God says then He will hurt you too. She will try very hard to be good.

Stan is a young boy whose father abandoned them. Many nights his mother requires him to get in bed with her. She tells him that God gave him to her to take care of her since his dad left. She says God knew she couldn't live without him. Stan feels angry with God and wonders why He demands such confusing and repulsive behavior. He is full of shame because he also finds pleasure in it. God seems an enigma, at best, or at worst, cruel.

A young woman in her twenties was sexually abused by her father and others for all of her childhood. She wrote about what it means to be raped by the man you call daddy. She has struggled long and hard, and continues to do so, with why God did not stop it. What was God thinking and feeling while my daddy raped me? She wrestles with both the lies she learned from her father and the truths of the Word of God. She has written four exceptional little books on the struggle to apply the truth of the Word of God to herself and the lies she learned as a result of the abuse.

1. Mister Jesus Cried
2. Mister Jesus Knows All About That
3. Mister Jesus Knows That It's Not Your Fault
4. Mister Jesus Wants You

frozen in these areas. These adults still talk and think and reason like a child about God. Also, these books keep the work of Christ on the cross central. That truth, and that alone, is the sufficient answer to the thinking, questions, and struggles that the abuse causes. We will focus on that now in treatment considerations.

Treatment and Healing

You have an appointment with a woman in her 30s who complains of depression. In some fashion—perhaps with shame and a quiet voice and dropped head, perhaps glibly and with the wave of a hand on the first visit, maybe six months later after weeks of you both feeling stuck—she tells you: "My father used to do weird things to me," or "My father would touch me."

"Ah-ah!" you think, "no wonder we're stuck. But now what?"

Stay focused. Keep in mind that the motivation for entering therapy is related to presenting symptoms, not the sexual abuse. Often a crisis has developed due to delayed after-effects of the original trauma, a re-experiencing of the trauma in some form or exposure to events that trigger symptoms. Please note that all of these meet DSM-IV diagnostic criteria for Post-Traumatic Stress Disorder (PTSD). Anyone who is going to work with abuse survivors needs a good understanding of this diagnosis. If/when these symptoms are stabilized, you then have the opportunity to focus on abuse treatment.

The model that I use for treating survivors of sexual abuse has three phases. The initial phase of treatment involves: safety, symptom relief, and memory work. Safety is an unknown to those who have been chronically abused. Many patients respond to the question, "Couldn't you get to a safe place?" with incredulity. Often they tried to create one only to have it discovered and then destroyed. Others had safe places that were not physical in nature, but rather a place they created within their own minds. Safety then, is often defined as the absence of people.

Any of you who have worked with survivors of chronic abuse know the intense need for safety and the ongoing disbelief that it is real. Survivors always want to know where the door is. They want an explanation for every sound. Your movements are watched and anything sudden or not explained results in fear and defensiveness. Most prefer to follow me down the hall to my office rather than have me behind them. Many stand for their sessions in close proximity to the door. It is crucial that I do not sit between them and the exit.

Intake and Assessment

Whatever the mode of presentation, a therapist should ask about childhood sexual experience with adults as part of routine intake procedures. The best approach is a straightforward one, such as: "Did you have any sexual experiences with adults in childhood or adolescence? Words like incest, sexual abuse, or victim are so loaded today, that I would suggest not introducing them initially unless the client herself does.

A disclosure of incest is not always uncomfortable for the client, and a therapist should not assume that it is. You should proceed with caution and sensitivity, demonstrating approachability, understanding and responsiveness. You will assist your client in making fuller disclosures by avoiding such responses as rage toward the perpetrator, minimizing the abuse or its effects, showing excessive interest in sexual details, ignoring the disclosure or pushing the client to say more.

Many clients hold certain beliefs about what will happen if they tell. It is important for you to learn what disclosure means to your client. Respond with belief, a confirmation of her safety with you, and let her know that you will not rush her nor try to force her to deal with more than she is able or chooses. Make it clear to her, however, that disclosure does not equal resolution.

Many women often feel such relief at telling that they eagerly assume they are now "all better." It is important that you communicate that disclosure is the first step in the working-through process. Reassure the client of your willingness and commitment to see her through that process, being careful not to coerce nor frighten her into continuing. Choice-making in therapy is crucial with incest survivors because one of the key components of sexual abuse is the inability to refuse. It is vital that dynamic not be reenacted in therapy.

Adults coping as children. Not only the inability to refuse, but most coping that the adult attempts shadows the ways (and failures) of coping learned during the abuse. Each child who undergoes sexual abuse develops certain coping strategies in order to survive the trauma and its concomitant feelings. When out of the context of abuse, coping strategies sometimes seem strange.

This was made very clear to me many years ago when I was visiting in the home of a holocaust survivor. Every time a police or ambulance siren sounded this woman became terrified and ran and hid in a closet, under a bed, any place she could find. To put yourself in a closet at the sound of a far off siren is strange behavior indeed—out of the context of the specter of being sent to a death camp. Within that context it made perfect sense.

Coping strategies are numerous and diverse. Some are highly individualized. Others are more universal. Let's consider a few:

1. *Denial and distortion of self.* Many children deny what is happening to them, as well as deny the feelings they have about it. They hide who they really are (a child who is being neglected and abused) to maintain approval within the family. As reality is denied and distorted, the true self is denied. A "false self" develops that is dependent on others for self esteem. The "true self" is hidden and seen as not trustworthy for it threatens her ability to cope. As time goes by this affects her ability to delineate the true from the false.

2. *Dissociation and splitting.* This occurs when the survivor alters her identity, consciousness and memory. She copes by splitting off conflicting aspects of consciousness, memory and identity. One way to do this is via amnesia or blocking out memory. Another way is to psychologically separate from the abuse. Survivors talk about spacing out, leaving the body, or making themselves disappear into the wallpaper. It is a way of removing the "me."
We have all had the experience of something that feels so bad we find ourselves thinking, "This can't be happening to me." This can become so automatic that it is done in response to any stressor in the survivor's life, not just sexual abuse. The most extreme from of dissociation is, of course, Dissociative Identity Disorder (DID, or more commonly known as multiple personality disorder), where the split truly becomes other than "me" and entirely distinct personalities come into play (see chapter 20).

3. *Rationalizing and minimizing.* Many victims engage in this to cope: "He was lonely, drunk, etc." or "It wasn't so bad. At least he didn't..."

4. *Addictions and other physical mechanisms.* Self-mutilation, suicide attempts, compulsive behaviors and addictions, such as: drugs, alcohol, spending, sex, food, chaos, danger and crises.

5. *Deviant behaviors.* Some live out the "bad-girl" persona that the perpetrator foisted on them: lying, manipulation, violence, prostitution.

6. *Relational coping mechanisms.* Over involvement and codependent attachments, withdrawal, repeating the abuse, abusing others, being abandoned, abandoning others.

7. *Magical spirituality.* Commenting on the movie *"Forest Gump"* again, there is that one small but incredible scene of what effect abuse can have spiritually. When Jenny is running from her drunken father and hides in the cornfield, getting down on her knees and asking God to turn her into a bird so she can fly away—this is an excellent example of the magical spirituality that is carried into adulthood.

It is crucial in working with a survivor of any trauma to keep in mind that these coping mechanisms make sense or are reasonable in the context of the trauma. Another illustration is from a Holocaust survivor—standing on an airfield on a brilliant summer day watching a fun-filled, daredevil air show. This woman standing next to a friend screams, clutches her friend's arm, and buries her face in her shoulder. Reasonable in the present context? No—but when she was young, growing up in Europe, the sound of airplanes close by meant chaos and death.

Beginning Treatment: Safety and Symptom Relief

Most clients come initially in need of symptom relief. The beginning phase of therapy involves both the building of a trust relationship with the therapist and the facilitation of symptom relief. The symptoms are often debilitating and they generally are what brought the client into therapy.

I find it very helpful to begin by normalizing my clients' symptoms. They are usually terrified that they are "losing it," "going crazy," are "weird," etc. As I educate them regarding how their symptoms are reactions to severe trauma it enables them to relax somewhat, thus providing some immediate relief. Just as a holocaust survivor's response to sirens was normal in World War II, so the incest survivor's reactions are normal in the context of sexual abuse.

It is important to do this even with the more severe symptoms, such as self-mutilation. You can normalize without condoning by showing how such a reaction makes sense in context, yet saying that the point of working together is to find healthy ways of expressing feelings and needs. You will find frequent repetition necessary in this area. Ongoing reassurance that your client is not crazy and that her symptoms are normal within the context of abuse is vital.

Presenting symptoms need not only to be normalized, but new ways of coping need to be found. This stage usually involves work with anxieties, phobias, depression and addictive behaviors. Often a medical examination is warranted (e.g. in the case of ongoing headaches or intestinal problems). Stabilizing the client and making certain she is safe is crucial before proceeding with any memory work. If, for example, your client is an alcoholic, it is necessary to get her into treatment for that before considering the trauma. If you do not, looking at the trauma will simply increase her drinking.

It is also important to find out about suicidal ideation or any other destructive or life-threatening behaviors. To proceed to consider the history of a survivor with the tremendous emotional upheaval that usually produces without first helping a client learn some ways to feel safe, find some measure of safety with you as the therapist and learn how to monitor self-destructive behaviors so her life is not at risk, is irresponsible therapy indeed.

This phase of therapy involves trust-building, safety education, symptom relief, and giving comfort. Normalizing your client's reactions to the sexual abuse is part of the educational process. Comforting her, reassuring her, affirming her courage in surviving and now in dealing with the trauma will all enable her to squarely face the truth about her life and form a strong alliance with you. Establishing safety lays the foundation for trust to develop and is also how you prevent the therapeutic process from re-traumatizing your client. It also prepares you both for the plunge into memory work.

Healing of memories. Memory work, the third component of phase one must be done with great care. It is essentially a search for truth. The memory of something does not guarantee its truth. But it is also true that the fact that a memory was "lost" for years and later recovered does not mean it is untrue. When something terrible happens to us we often do not want to remember because of the pain involved in that memory.

At the same time, we do not want to forget because of the significance of the memory. It is a place of great ambivalence and fear. A client recently said to me that she desperately wanted her memories to be false. She did not want such things to be true about her life. After a brief moment of silence she realized with horror that it would be equally terrifying to learn that the things her mind was throwing at her were false. There was no good answer.

The purpose of memory work is not simply to retrieve memories. The act of remembering something is not, in and of itself, healing. God has called us to truth. He is truth. He reveals truth. Two very important things begin to occur during the process of memory work. One is that the survivor is afforded a safe relationship where she can give voice to the truth of her life and her response to it. As she does this, healing begins to occur to her damaged person. She is heard. She is cared for. She matters.

Second, as the events of abuse are exposed so are their accompanying lies. There are lies told by the actions of abuse. There are lies told by the abuser. There are lies the survivor told herself. As that which was carried out in darkness is exposed, the lies too are revealed for what they are. This becomes very important when we begin to look at the spiritual issues with which the survivor grapples.

Memories and emotions. As memories surface they produce powerful emotional reactions. Your response is critical, because it is what will, in large measure, determine the trust relationship that develops. These memories afford you the opportunity to respond differently from those people who surrounded your client when the abuse was actually occurring.

This memory retrieval is necessary. What was hidden needs to be exposed, what has been in the dark needs to be brought to the light. One of the reasons for this is that memories are stored with their concomitant distortions, lies, accompanying emotions and interpretations. As they come to the light, your job will be to help your client to separate the truth from the lies.

This process can be quite difficult, for both client and therapist. For the client two things can happen. First, her own reactions to the events that occurred are stirred up as she recalls them. She will feel rage, hate, terror, loss of control. Sometimes she will feel in her body the pain she felt when the abuse was actually occurring. These are all feelings that she has worked hard not to experience. You will find her resistant to them again.

Second, for some the horrors remembered become a new traumatizing event. The thought of the upcoming therapy hour can produce fear and flight reactions. The client may respond by becoming severely depressed, or acting out in some way, such as self-mutilation or suicidal gestures. Therapy must proceed at a pace that the client can tolerate. You will have to be vigilant, and if things get too intense or your client is too self-destructive, then the memory work needs to be temporarily shelved. As her trust in you and attachment to you grows, she will be able to pursue it again. Often extra contact via phone, or emergency sessions are necessary during this time.

This is a critical time, for your own reactions to her traumatic memories and your need to distance from them, could easily cause you to emotionally remove yourself in some way. However slight, this distancing will be traumatic for your client. An awareness of your own responses, your ability to cope and what you are communicating to your client are essential.

The goal of memory work. As her therapist, where do you want to help her move on to? Once she has recognized what was done to her by the perpetrator as well as by the non-protecting family members and her presenting symptoms have begun to abate, the focus shifts to helping her see herself, not as traumatized child-victim, but as responsible adult.

I find that many therapists do not understand this shift, nor do they know how to help their clients make it. Many clients, and their therapists with them, end up stuck in the victim stage. More writing is being done about what is often referred to as a "victim mentality," which many rightly see as being far too prevalent in our society. One only has to look at the ridiculous litigation today to see this.

However, those who are troubled by this mentality are frequently in danger of forgetting that there are true victims. Scripture not only makes it clear that humans put other humans in the position of being victimized or oppressed, but that those of us who know Christ are to tenderly reach out and assist such people. Any man or woman who has been sexually abused or raped is a victim.

At the same time, part of our assistance to those who are indeed victims is to appropriately, and in a timely fashion, help them grow beyond that place. That is not to say that the issues of sexual abuse will cease to exist or be a struggle for them. The grave sins of others against us often reverberate through our lives for years and we do not want to be naive about this. But neither do we want to fail to empower people to grow beyond the evil that has been done to them.

The Middle Phase of Treatment

The middle phase of treatment is a turning point. Up to this point the therapist has assumed the role of educator, comforter, listener. These roles are not abandoned by any means; however, as we move into the middle phase more active and directive responses are called for. The more a survivor deals with her history and the lies embedded there, the more she will find she has choice. She has learned to speak. How will she use her voice? She has learned something about relationship. How will she use her ability to relate? She has learned that she has impact. How will she use her power to affect others?

It is during this middle phase that the lies are articulated more fully, that they are renounced, and the work is done to put truth in their place. Many lies will be found to be deeply embedded in the survivor's mind and heart: "Abuse occurred because I was bad." "I was not worth protecting." "It is always bad to be weak." "No one is trustworthy." "Safety only comes in isolation." "I am unforgivable." It is not hard to see how misconceptions about God and how He thinks about us are very closely intertwined with such lies.

Client empowerment to overcome these lies is what the middle phase of therapy is all about. It will prove to be a crisis and a turning point for both the therapist and survivor. I believe the challenge of turning as a therapist is a key reason it does not occur. It requires the therapist to assume a more directive and active stance toward a person whom they are comfortable nurturing and comforting. These behaviors should not cease, but if they continue without more directive approaches being added, the client will stalemate. However much courage is required to face the terror of incest and its aftereffects, this is not a sufficient condition for change. The therapist now needs to carefully begin to treat the survivor like an adult who has power and can make choices, characteristics which the abuse crushed.

One of the reasons treatment can get stuck here is that the survivor will usually put up a good deal of resistance. The major fear in her life, up to this time, has been facing the incest. She has done that and lived to tell the tale, and wants to settle in to enjoy that fact. It is a far more comfortable place than she has experienced previously, and it looks like a good place to live. The therapist can help her verbalize this, and show understanding for those feelings, but must also gently nudge her along.

Part of that is to help the client see that to stay in such a place is to basically stay crippled—and in some sense her abuser will have won. Part of God's work in our life is to bring us into truth. One of the pieces of that is facing the truth of the past. However, it doesn't stop there. Not only is another piece of truth that your client is now an adult, but also the fact that a second aspect of God's work in our lives is growth. God does not produce "stuckness" in our lives, but change—a constant growing up into Him.

Difficult work also surrounds the issues of grief, confrontation and forgiveness. To face abuse means to confront loss. She never got to be a child. She never really had a daddy. She never had a sense of moral integrity. She may have lost children. Such grieving is a dark and painful process. God is seen as impotent, absent or cruel. Those whose faith remained strong during memory work are often rocked hard during this time.

The End Phase

The final phase of treatment is in many ways a time of joy and hope. Therapist and client have formed a strong alliance. The client has faced memories and feelings she thought would destroy her. She has exchanged many destructive coping skills for healthy ones. She has established relationships outside the therapy room that are supportive and safe. She has grieved (though of course such grief is never done). She has dealt with her family and her abuser in ways she decided were both safe and wise. What remains is far more present and future oriented.

What happens in the final phase of therapy? Once the family of origin issues have been handled and relational skills built up, the client feels stronger and individuated. It is this that sets the stage for separation from the therapist. This stage continues to include marriage counseling if the survivor is in a marriage. Most of the work that is done is in the present tense. The survivor feels much less encumbered by her past and more capable of handling issues that exist in her marriage. As that relationship (or in the case of a single woman, a network of relationships) becomes more solidified and healthy, the thought that perhaps the therapist is not so necessary anymore begins to surface.

It is initially a frightening thought and requires a response of reassurance, as well as a statement that indicates that termination is the client's choice, not something that will be forced by the therapist. I usually proceed at a careful rate of digression, reducing sessions to every two weeks, then once a month, every other month, in three months, in six months, and finally a year later. Each step is held until the client signals readiness to move on. Some will want to proceed too quickly due to fears of saying good-bye. I suggest being firm in suggesting a more cautious approach and explaining why. Some will get stuck at a particular point and fear moving on. In that case, you need to back up and deal with the underlying anxieties.

This phase will include more extensive work in the area of relationships. I work hard with my clients to help and encourage them to develop a strong and healthy support network. The friendships they have, the churches they attend, all will be the places they will continue to grow in long after they have left me behind. This phase usually includes marriage counseling. Working with the marriage of the survivor is inevitable, in part because the person who started in treatment with you is not the one who ends—spouses tend to not know what to do with the changes. In fact, they don't always like all the changes! This phase also involves increased focus and strengthening of the survivor's relationship with God.

Another area that gets attention during this phase is the body. Learning how to live on friendly terms with a body that has been viewed as the enemy for all of one's life is no small task. How to care for a body rather than ignore or destroy it requires hard work and much repetition. Learning to be connected rather than dissociated is frightening. The possibility of some level of control over one's feelings and one's physical body is an astounding discovery.

The final pieces of the last phase involve the desire of the survivor to give to others in some fashion what has been given to her. Anyone who has experienced some measure of redemption in their own life knows that an eagerness to give naturally flows out of that. There is great joy in seeing someone who came to you simply trying to survive, now leave with a desire and readiness to serve others. I would just like to make a few comments about confronting the perpetrator and family-of-origin issues (since it is currently such a hot topic).

This work will bump hard into many spiritual issues if your client is a Christian. One of the main issues will be that of forgiveness. Again I think we tend to fall off on one of two sides of the horse. One side is that of cheap and hasty forgiveness. The two words, "I'm sorry," immediately are to eradicate years of suffering, lying and abuse. Repentance is verbal, certainly, but it is far more than verbal—it is transformation from the inside out, demonstrated over time.

Many Christians also abuse Paul's words regarding forgetting what is behind, superficially stating "Just put it behind you. Forgive and forget. Forgive and move on." Such an approach is ludicrous. We know from research that the mind doesn't forget anything, it is recall that is the problem. To tell a holocaust survivor to forget is nonsensical. It is equally ridiculous to tell that to an incest survivor, as well as a complete misreading of the New Testament text.

Scripture takes sin seriously, not lightly. Repentance from sin is seen as change in words yes, but also in attitude and behavior, indeed in the whole person. For us to do less is to cheapen what God has named radically expensive. If the perpetrator or silent parent says, "I'm sorry," a response might be, "I am so glad to hear you say that to your daughter. Now let's talk about how you would like to demonstrate it to her."

On the other hand, much of the secular literature states that forgiveness is not a necessary part of healing for the survivor. I disagree. As a believer, that would mean asserting the antithesis to Jesus' words. God says it is not okay to remain bitter and unforgiving. He makes no exceptions for certain sins. Scripture gives a radical picture of forgiveness. It is costly, sacrificial and repetitive. Repentance is significant and sustained change—it unfolds and is evident over time.

God's children are called to forgive. Both repentance and forgiveness are the work of the Spirit of God, not man, and yet they require tremendous, ongoing work on our part. We are to hold our clients (and ourselves) to the highest before God, yet acknowledge that it is God who brings about such mysterious and awesome changes in the human heart.

Again, obviously much more could be said about these issues and this phase of therapy. The topic warrants extensive handling and I am keenly aware that I am referring to serious subject matter. I am hoping that you

CONFRONTING THE PERPETRATOR

I have found with many of my clients that there often arises a need/desire to confront their family of origin. It is also strongly resisted and feared. It is important to note that I have said that the need/desire arises from the client, NOT the therapist! Example: A counselor who is working with a survivor is insisting that she confront her mother and her grandmother regarding the sexual abuse she experienced from her grandfather. Now she may indeed need to do so at some point. But he is insisting, telling her nothing more can be done unless she does what he tells her, etc.

My question is, Who is it here who has unresolved family issues? Such a confrontation is not to be based on my need nor do I insist that it happens. I do not make a rule that all survivors have to do this. I think for some it is a necessary and helpful part of growth. To maintain silence continues the feeling that the incest is somehow unreal or "made up." It is to actively support a lie, to pretend as if something horrific is not there. I discuss all of this with my client, the topic almost always being initiated by her.

If this confrontation is to take place, much work must be done. It should never be handled quickly or superficially. The client's choices should be respected at all points. If at some point she chooses to back down, honor that choice. A good many of the false memory accusations seem to have risen out of hasty and even coerced confrontations, with the therapist often being the one who insists it had to occur.

You must also keep in mind that a confrontation involves two sides and your goal here is not to destroy a family or verbally beat up on a perpetrator. You need to be keenly aware of your own reactions and motives throughout. You are there for your client. She is your primary focus. But you are also responsible for how you treat the family. God's standard for all communications is that we speak the truth in love and this kind of confrontation is no exception to that.

It is extremely difficult to speak the truth of incest. No one wants to hear it, least of all the family in which it occurred. To name it is to crash through an almost impenetrable barrier that family members have colluded to erect. However, to confront evil and abuse in a manner that reflects the love of God in Christ is no less difficult. The inner work you will need to do as a therapist is no less massive than that of your client.

Preparing your client for this very difficult part of her therapy requires several things: establishing realistic goals, confronting her fairy-tale endings and expectations, deciding how to contact the family and how to conduct the sessions. Role-playing is often a very helpful tool at this juncture. Part of the therapist's responsibility is to assess the level of danger or acting out with respect to family members. Ongoing substance abuse, a history of violence or a history of suicidal or homicidal threats are all serious contraindications to a family confrontation.

Especially when violence is a threat, the usual outcome is to break off contact with the family due to the level of danger.

The goals of such a meeting include disclosure, or a speaking of the truth. That usually involves not simply a telling about the incest, but includes education as to its after-effects, an acknowledgement of guilt with a true apology, the beginning of a reconciliation process defined, and goals carefully set out for the family to assist them in accomplishing this. These are high goals, and again the therapist must work carefully with her client to ensure that she stay realistic in applying them to her particular family. It is difficult to find a balance between expecting far too much on the one hand, and settling for a superficial apology that the client is too quick to name repentance. Caution is needed on both sides.

The therapist's role throughout is to actively support the client, model for both the client and family how to confront and interact, as well as direct the meeting. Sessions such as these require confidence and assertiveness. They usually require saying things like, "Stop negating your daughter like that," "You need to listen to what your daughter is saying rather than simply focusing on your own feelings," "I will not allow you to demean your daughter that way as long as you are in my office." Responses such as these greatly assist the client in her own growth toward being able to assert herself with family members, without curling up, slinking away, or belittling in return.

Such sessions need to include drawing up a definite plan so that all family members have a clear idea about how the relationship is to proceed and what behaviors are appropriate. Reparative work needs to follow an apology. This can be introduced by asking your client what the family needs to do to demonstrate the professed apology.

will use these things to motivate you to pursue the subject through reading and perhaps some workshops.

The Role and Approach of the Counselor

What is the role of the therapist in this area? From my perspective, this is a huge question, one that I take very seriously. Let us remind ourselves of what we have in front of us. First of all, we have a human being who does not understand safety, love, trust, hope, truth and many other concepts. Second, we have someone who was still undeveloped in every way (physically, cognitively, emotionally, spiritually, etc.) and was taught lies repetitively during times of intense emotion with reinforcing behavior.

You do not have to be very sophisticated about the learning process to comprehend how embedded those lies are. The mind and body of a six-year-old is being repeatedly raped by an adult male who is telling her such things as: "God told me to do this," "God has daddies teach their little girls this way," "If you weren't such a whore I wouldn't have to do this," "You are nothing but trash."

Now how many times do you suppose that has to happen for that little girl to be sure those things are true? The abuse becomes the overriding experience, the abuse provides her control beliefs. God may be strong but daddy is stronger. Jesus loves little children, but not me. Those control beliefs become the basis by which all other information is processed. Again, that is why speaking the truth to a survivor, as crucial as that is, is not sufficient.

So we come again to our question, What is the role of the therapist? What response does a therapist need to give? The survivor is struggling with the most basic questions about God: Who is God? What does He think? What does He think about me? What was He thinking while daddy was raping me? Am I forgivable? Does His patience run out? Why should I have hope? Why should I believe in Him?

Be Like Christ

The therapist becomes the representative of this God to the survivor. The work of the therapist is to teach in the seen, that which is true in the unseen. The therapist's words, tone of voice, actions, body movements, responses to rage, fear, and failure all become ways that the survivor learns about God. I believe that the reputation of God Himself is at stake in the life of the therapist. We are called first and foremost, to represent Him well.

Words are how we do therapy. They are the "stuff" of the trade. Words, however, in this case are initially meaningless. What are words when you grew up hearing, "Daddy loves you," and then daddy raped you. Or when grandfather called you over to sit on his lap, and when you were afraid he said not to worry because this time it would be okay, but it never was. So the therapist says, "This is a safe place." The survivor's response? "Right." "Oh, sure." Or perhaps, she has become so desperate, words are believed no matter what actions might suggest.

And so our task becomes that of living out before them the character of God Himself. I first began to understand this early on in my work with survivors. I was working with a woman who had been chronically abused and longed for her to truly know the love of God. I tried telling her about it but realized at some point that she was politely tolerating what I was saying, but it was not going in. I clearly remember getting down on my knees before begging Him to help her see what she so desperately needed to see—that He loved her.

What I heard back from God was, "You want to know how much I love her? Then you go love her in a way that demonstrates that. You want her to know that I am trustworthy and safe? Then you go be trustworthy and safe." Demonstrate in the flesh the character of God over time so that who you are reveals God to the survivor.

That is the incarnation, isn't it? Jesus, in the flesh, explaining God to us. Jesus, bringing the unseen down into flesh and blood realities. *The survivor needs us to incarnate God* for two reasons. One, we all need that. That is why Jesus came in the flesh. He came to explain God to us. We have already spoken about the fact that human beings learn about the unseen from the seen. Jesus knew that and used countless examples in the seen to teach His disciples about the unseen.

Secondly, this need is intensified for the survivor because what has been repeatedly taught to a child in the seen is the antithesis of the truth of God. She has learned about fathers, trust, love, and refuge from one who emulated the father of lies. The unseen has been lived out before her and she has learned her lessons well.

If you want the survivor to understand that God is a refuge, then be one for her. If you want her to grasp the faithfulness of God, then be faithful to her. If you want her to understand the truthfulness of God, then never lie to her. If you want her to understand the infinite patience of God, then be patient with her. And where you are not a refuge, or are tired of being faithful, or are fudging in your answers or growing impatient with the necessary repetition, then get down on your knees and ask God to give you more of Himself so that you might represent Him well.

The second aspect of the response of the therapist is to speak truth. We have talked about the deeply embedded lies that the survivor carries within her. Such lies need to be exposed, gently and slowly, so the light of the truth of God can begin to take their place. I find it very important to learn, not just what the lies are, but also what memories taught that lie. There are usually particular aspects of certain memories that burned those lies into the brain and help keep it there.

For example, a woman who was sadistically abused told the story of being forced to kill a loved pet with her own hands or risk further pain. She was told repeatedly during childhood that she was evil and that was why no one would ever love her. Her vivid memory of killing her pet and the blood on her hands provided tangible proof of her evil and burned that lie into her brain in profound ways. It took a long, long time of carefully picking our way through that memory and all its pieces for her to even begin to grasp the subtlety and hideousness of the lies it had taught her.

Working through memories and the lies they hold is arduous and slow. It requires tremendous patience. The rewards are wonderful for you begin to see light dawn in a darkened and confused mind. It is quite different however, from simply telling someone God loves them and having them believe it. Speak it; live it; be it; repeat again.

Reflect the Man of Sorrows

The third part of the therapist's response is contained in the little book *Mister Jesus Knows All About That*. In that book the woman who wrote it is beginning to grasp that this Mister Jesus is the Man of Sorrows and acquainted with grief—*with her grief*. Mister Jesus says, "I was hurt too. The bad men took my clothes just like your daddy took yours." There is tremendous healing for survivors as they begin to study and truly grasp the suffering and death of Jesus.

He knows—that is a phenomenal revelation. I recently had a woman come in to a session who is working through some of the Scripture on the Crucifixion. She had barely sat down on the couch when she said, "They took His clothes. I never saw it before. They took His clothes." This is a woman who had many perpetrators and has countless memories of standing naked as an adolescent in a group of men. Something way down deep gets touched when such things are seen and understood.

The cross of Christ demonstrates the extent of the evil. The cross of Christ demonstrates the infinite love of God. The cross of Christ covers any evil done by the survivor herself. Any inadequacy in the cross of Christ means that none of us is safe. The cross of Christ is God with us—in our sin, our suffering, our grief, our sorrows. In order to redeem He became like us.

Self-directed client work. I do not do this work for my clients. I send them to do it. I often direct them to a particular passage or raise a specific question but I do not simply teach them about the Crucifixion. I send them to learn and study as I teach. The work has far more power when they wrestle with it themselves. This is not something I do early on in therapy. It falls more toward the end of the second phase and into the third.

One of the major reasons for this is that I find they will grasp the profound truths of the cross far more readily and deeply if they have seen some representation of those truths in their relationship with me. They have been able to speak the unspeakable. They are known. They are loved. No matter what they tell, they remain safe. I can forgive. I have hope for them. They have found in their relationship with me an aroma of the person of Christ. Out of that experience in the seen, in flesh and blood, they can then turn to the person and work of Christ and His identification with them. I have without exception found it a powerful way of teaching truth and of bringing healing.

Manage Vicarious Trauma

Any of you who have done this work or have listened carefully today have some grasp of the potential impact on the person of the therapist. We are more and more in the literature about vicarious trauma and secondary traumatic stress disorder. Those of you who heard my presentation on personhood remember that I spoke about all of us being image bearers. It is the nature of human beings that they are impacted by what they sit with. If I habitually reflect trauma or sit with trauma, I will bear the image of trauma in my person. We see this even in the person of Jesus, who though He was perfect bears in His person the image of our sin and suffering. If it was true of Him how much more so for us who are sinners ourselves!

I want to close by giving you three elements which are necessary if we are to do this work and do it well. First, know about people. Know about trauma. Understand what trauma does to human beings. And yet, in knowing, never assume you know. No matter how many survivors you see, each is unique. If we do not understand such things we will make wrong judgments. We will prematurely expect change. We will give wrong answers. We will fail to hear because we think we already know. Listen acutely. Study avidly. Live among the facts.

Second, know God. Know His Word. Be an avid student of that Word. If we are going to serve as His representative to others we need to know Him well. We are often so presumptuous and we speak for Him where we do not really know Him. We need to be so permeated by His Word that we learn to think His thoughts. May we never forget that to know His Word, according to Him, means we have woven it into our lives and live obedient to it. Where we do not live according to His Word, we do not know God.

Finally, do not do this work (or any other for that matter) without utter dependence on the Spirit of God. Where else will you find wisdom? How will you know when to speak and when to be silent? How will you discern the lies from the truth? How else will you love when you are tired or be patient when you are weary? How can you know the mind of God apart from the Spirit of God? How can you possibly expect to live as a person who demonstrates the character of God apart from the Spirit of God? How do we think that the life-giving power to the work of Christ crucified will be released into other lives unless we have allowed that cross to do its work in our own lives?

To work with sexual abuse is to work with lies, darkness, and evil. It is hell brought up from below to the earth's surface. You cannot fight the fetid litter of hell in someone's life unless you walk dependent on the Spirit of God. You cannot bring life to the place of death unless you walk dependent on the Spirit of God.

This work—in spite of its foul nature at times—is a privilege to do. It is a work that is difficult to do. The task of serving as a representative of God in the seen so that the unseen can be grasped, understood and believed in some measure, is far beyond any capability of yours or of mine. It is a work however, that if you let it, will take you to your knees with a heart hungry for more of God that you might in turn bring His presence in very concrete ways into places and lives where He has not yet been known.

Conclusion

What I have given you is a brief overview of therapy with an incest survivor. Though it is brief, you need to also see it as comprehensive in the sense that I have given you a general cognitive map or outline for how to proceed. Obviously, not all clients will proceed through all of these phases. Some will choose not to confront their family of origin, some will stay bitter, others will divorce their spouses, or terminate therapy prematurely. I have given you these stages so you can have some kind of structure in mind, some picture of what it would look like optimally. I also think this helps us not to sell our clients short. Therapists often fail to encourage further growth because they have no idea what it would look like.

Therapy with survivors is long and hard. It is inexpressibly rewarding. It is the joy of seeing someone stand up straight or find her voice for the first time in her life. It is the marvel of watching a crushed and broken human being, who has faced evil and darkness while yet a child, seek after truth and light. It is the gift of saying good-bye to someone who came to you stuck in a destructive past, and is leaving as someone who is growing and changing, with hope for a future.

It is a work that will demand much of you. However, I want to say here that anyone who attempts this without careful training and supervision is unwise, and runs a great risk of being hurtful to an already injured person. Continuing education and ongoing supervision have often not been stressed in the Christian community. I feel these tasks cannot be emphasized enough.

Therapy is an isolated experience in many ways. You sit in an office with people, one after another, day after day. You can go on and on for years with no input to challenge or stretch you. Couple that with high-stress therapy such as work with survivors and the possibility of mistakes and staleness escalate proportionately. Good therapy requires a good understanding of yourself and a growing understanding of the problems you are confronting. Humility is a key component in both.

Sexual abuse recovery is often long and difficult, but it is not impossible. It will require courage and stamina from your client and from you as well. You and your client need to remember that not only are your efforts helping her, but also the generations that will come after her. I often tell my clients that they are the "pivotal generation," for their family has faced one

SUGGESTIONS OF ABUSE
AND FALSE MEMORY SYNDROME

I would like to insert something here about the current psychotherapeutic rage: false memory syndrome. First of all, though I am saddened to say so—even reluctant—there are more than enough ineffective, unethical, and unwise therapists who work with survivors though they have no specific training in this area. Even a Ph.D. in clinical or counseling psychology does not necessarily equip one to work with sexual abuse survivors. I have no question but that some have led dependent, suggestible clients down the sexual abuse road without clinical justification.

Second, as in any area of therapy, and most certainly in this one, it is not helpful—and may even be harmful for some—to ask blatant leading questions. I have read the transcripts of some sessions and they are appalling. Did he do such and such? Even when the answer is no, or 'I don't know,' the therapist goes on to push with an implicit certainty. It is obvious that the interview is being guided by a therapist who presumptuously assumes they "know" something the client does not—that sexual abuse HAS occurred. This is arrogance, not competent therapy.

I don't care how long you have done therapy or how much you think you know, *you cannot read another person's mind, nor can you tell them what is in there.* As a matter of fact, I think the more experience we have the more aware we are of the complexity of another's mind and our inability to not only not know theirs, but our own as well. A healthy dose of humility is in order when tromping around in other people's heads.

Third, any scholar or student worth their salt knows the difference between correlation and cause and effect. It is lousy reasoning to say "if these symptoms are present, therefore *this has to be* the cause." Any time you interview a client the mindset needs to be, "It looks like this could have happened, but I need to rule out a and b first."

Good clinical reasoning engages in differential diagnosis—it is rooted in ruling out competing diagnoses and theories of causation. There must be an investigative, and even tentative quality to our approach. You can have someone with many similar symptoms to someone who has been sexually abused (distorted image of self, emotional numbing, an eating disorder, sees God as punitive) who has never been sexually abused.

Obviously asking the question, 'Have you ever been sexually abused?' is necessary. Then we must respect the answer. If it is no, and later it continues to nag at you, bring it up in a different context. Some clients may wait months to tell you, because they absolutely must believe they can trust you first.

Never tell a client "You have been sexually abused." Even with someone who *is* a survivor, to insist that there was abuse *and it must be dealt with,* when she has slipped back into denial and is not ready to proceed, is destructive and grossly unethical. It reinforces rather than heals the original trauma as it is a re-enactment of two of the major factors of abuse:

(1) coercion, and
(2) a denial of where they are.

Fourth, a good understanding of the human mind includes a keen awareness that there are some very dependent people out there who are capable of suggestibility and grave distortions. As a therapist, you are in a position of power. You have been given authority and your words will have tremendous impact. Choose them wisely and carefully.

Fifth, research has shown that memory is not usually photographic (with exceptions) and is stored concomitant with the perceiver's interpretations of that memory. Anyone who has returned to a childhood home as an adult knows this—it is amazing how small things have gotten in twenty years' time!

Sixth, a good understanding of the human heart, which Scripture clearly gives us, tells us that every heart, no matter how nice or wounded a person it dwells in, is capable of deceit, hate, and slander.

All of this is not said so you will not believe those who come to you. I always begin by accepting what they say is true. If a client says she has been abused, I believe her. If she says she has not, I do not force the issue. In over 20 years and hundreds of cases, I have encountered only two situations (to my knowledge, of course) which involved false accusations. It is my suspicion that a small proportion of those aligned with the false memory association have indeed been unjustly accused. If the human heart is capable of coming up with sexual abuse, it is certainly capable of lying about it as well.

A larger proportion of those making accusations against their parents have probably been led to do so through unwise or unethical therapy. Even if the accusations are true, I am aware of many situations where the therapist has insisted on a family confrontation when the client either did not want it or was not prepared for it. Such an encounter is inevitably a disaster.

However, since the key characteristic of a perpetrator is denial, I suspect a significant proportion of those screaming false, have been rightly accused. Some good and helpful writing has come out of the FMSF, but it is important to note that you sign up by simply saying you have been falsely accused. Membership is in no way proof of innocence.

In saying all of this I do not want to induce paranoia in the challenge of working in this difficult arena. I simply want to underscore some basic precepts of the therapeutic endeavor: your position of power, your finiteness, and the deceitfulness of the human heart. The result should be humility, wisdom and an ever-growing dependence on the Holy Spirit as you work with your clients.

way, perpetuating abuse for generations, and they are now turning in a radically different direction.

What a beautiful unfolding of God's promise that, "He who has begun a good work in you will continue to perform it..." What a marvelous privilege it is as a therapist to be a vehicle for the redemptive work of God in another's life. Because of the redemptive work of Christ, you and I have a solid basis for giving a survivor the gift of hope.

ENDNOTES

1. Jerome Kroll, *PTSD/borderlines in therapy: finding the balance* (New York: W.W. Norton & Co., 1993).
2. Diane Langberg, *Counseling survivors of sexual abuse* (Fairfax, VA: Xulon, 2003).
3. Nancy Faulkner, *Sexual abuse recognition and non-disclosure inventory of young adolescents* (Ann Arbor, MI: UMI, 1996).
4. Bagley, C., The prevalence and mental health sequelae of child sexual abuse in a community sample of women aged 18 to 27, *Canadian Journal of Community Mental Health, 10,* (1991), 103–116; D. Finkelhor, and Browne, A., Impact of child sexual abuse: A review of the research, *Psychological Bulletin, 99,*(1986), 66–77; L. Swanson, and Biaggio, M. K., Therapeutic perspectives on father-daughter incest, *American Journal of Psychiatry, 142(6),* (1985), 667–674; M. Tsai, and Wagner, N. N., Therapy groups for women sexually molested as children, *Archives of Sexual Behavior, 7* (1978), 417–427.
5. C. A. Courtois, and Watts, D. L., Counseling adult women who experienced incest in childhood or adolescence, *The Personnel and Guidance Journal* (January 1982), 275–279; B. B. Johnson, Sexual abuse prevention: A rural interdisciplinary effort, *Child Welfare, 66* (1987),165–73.
6. D. Finkelhor, Hotaling, G., Lewis, I. A., and Smith, C., Sexual abuse in a national survey of adult men and women: Prevalence, characteristics, and risk factors, *Child Abuse & Neglect, 14* (1990), 19–28.
7. C. Bagley, Development of a measure of unwanted sexual contact in childhood, for use in community mental health surveys, *Psychological Reports, 66* (1990), 401–2.
8. D. Graybill, Aggression in college students who were abused as children, *Journal of College Student Personnel 26* (1985).
9. P. Mosgofian, and Ohlschlager, G., *Sexual misconduct in counseling and ministry* (Dallas: Word, 1995).
10. R. McGee, and Schaumberg., H., *Renew: Hope for victims of sexual abuse* (Houston: Rapha, 1990).
11. N. C. Andreasen, Post-traumatic stress disorder, in H.I. Kaplan and Sadock B.J. (eds.), *Comprehensive textbook of psychiatry* 4th ed. (Baltimore: Williams and Wilkins, 1985), 38.
12. J. L. Herman, *Trauma and recovery* (New York: Basic Books, 1992), 38.
13. R. Janof-Bulman, *Shattered assumptions: Toward a new psychology of trauma* (New York: The Free Press, 1992); B. van der Kolk, McFarlane, A., and Weisaeth, L., (eds.), *Traumatic stress: The effects of overwhelming experience on mind, body, and society* (New York: The Guildford Press, 1996).

14. C. A. Courtois, and Watts, D. L., Counseling adult women who experienced incest in childhood or adolescence, *The Personnel and Guidance Journal*, (January, 1982), 275–279; D. Finkelhor, and Browne, A., Impact of child sexual abuse: A review of the research, *Psychological Bulletin, 99* (1986), 66–77.
15. American Psychiatric Association, *Diagnostic and statistical manual of mental disorders* 4th ed. (Washington, DC: 1994), 424–425.
16. S. Jones, and Yarhouse, M., *Homosexuality: The use of scientific research in the church's moral debate* (Downer's Grove, IL: InterVarsity Press, 2000).
17. See R. M. Brown, *Elie Wiesel: Messenger to all humanity* (South Bend, IN: Notre Dame University Press, 1983).

20

Abortion:

Crisis Decision and Post-Abortion Syndrome

Theresa Burke, Tim Clinton, and George Ohlschlager

Think about this for a moment. How many women do you know who have earned a college degree? Let's make it harder: how many women do you know who have been divorced? Some names come to mind, right? Now, how many women do you know who have had an abortion?

Amazingly, according to the prestigious Alan Guttmacher Institute, up to 43% of all women in America have had an abortion—as many women as are divorced, and twice as many as have earned a college degree.[1] The great disconnect on abortion is that while many talk about it as an issue, hardly anyone talks about their own abortion. Why? There are many reasons of course; the fear of judgment, stigma, and for some the shame and hurt that is inherent to post-abortion syndrome (PAS). As clinicians who have worked with women who have had abortions, we believe the problem is not just about the terminated child. We believe the problem also has to do with the pervasive suffering attached to PAS, experienced by so many women.

For more than 25 years, Judith lived with a secret. A secret she hid from everyone, including her husband: *"I spent so many years with this gnawing pain buried deep within my heart. Buried so deep, I was not even aware of what caused it. I suffered from depression, bulimia, and some serious marital problems. I felt distant from God and hated whenever the subject of abortion came up!"*

There are many women like Judith who exist in a private world of grief shrouded with loss and despair. The secret of abortion is locked tightly in the deep recess of the heart, admitted to no one. Like the leper who cringes from the sunlight, a wounded heart seeks solace in the dark. Most women simply try to forget about their abortion experience and move on with their lives. This stuffing away of secret memory strikes at the heart of one's spiritual life causing feelings of guilt, shame, self-loathing and alienation from God. Many are afraid to deal with this deep pain because they fear opening up an injury of the soul that may never stop bleeding.

Perhaps no other issue in our culture elicits the same passion and divisiveness as abortion. Friends and family are alienated, churches and communities are divided, and people everywhere are charged up on both sides of the debate. Why? Because millions of lives are affected, and millions of lives are at stake. Since the (in)famous Supreme Court decision in *Roe v. Wade* in 1973, abortion has been legal in all 50 states, and nearly 1.5 million abortions are performed in America every year.

Abortion is a medical procedure that terminates the life of an unborn child and extracts it from the mother's womb in order to end the pregnancy. These induced or "therapeutic" abortions are ostensibly performed to

- preserve the life of the mother,
- end a pregnancy that resulted from rape or incest, or to,
- prevent the birth of a deformed or genetically abnormal child.

No matter the questionable morality of "therapeutic" abortion, the cold hard fact is that only 2% of abortions meet one or more of these criteria. Fully 98% of all abortions in the United States are done essentially as an act of birth control—because having a child is "inconvenient" to the parents. Forty percent of abortions—600,000 fetuses, or 50,000 unborn lives every month—are performed on repeat patients.[2]

Violating the sanctity of life. Abortion is wrong because it is the unjust taking of human life—the deliberate death of an unborn human being. Abortion proponents deny this truth—they firmly reject God's divine act of creating human life at the moment of conception: "For you formed my inward parts; you covered me in my mother's womb. I will praise you, for I am fearfully and wonderfully made; marvelous are your works, and that my soul knows very well" (Ps. 139:13–14).

There is no excuse, for all people know very well that life is not a "biological accident"; we know deep inside that the developing fetus is more than an "unviable tissue mass." No clinical terms can dehumanize what God has created and we will neither—as individuals, nor as a nation—escape the truth that abortion is a corrupt business that "devises evil by law" in order "to condemn innocent blood" (Ps. 94: 20, 21).

The merciful reach of God. Yet our God is also a God of great and tender mercy, a God of patience and long-suffering. He has heard the cries of the innocent slaughter that piles higher year after year, and only He can bear this grief, only He can carry this great sorrow. One of the more incredible facts about our current national crisis is how so many people trapped in the deadly lie of abortion have come to know Christ, have come to be champions of life. The kingdom is filling up with former abortionists, clinic owners, abortion advocates, and abortion victims in every corner of the land.

Even in the midst of mass death, the life of Jesus shines forth. Even as the thief comes to kill, steal, and destroy, Jesus comes to give life, and give it abundantly (John 10:10). There is absolutely no doubt that God will have the last word in the abortion wars, and that Word will bring forth life, sweet life, precious life. No issue is out of His ultimate control. No person is beyond His blessed reach.

The Abortion Decision

Let's turn our attention to how the abortion decision and the abortion itself complicates and confounds the tasks of what is a natural developmental process. The decision to have an abortion depends on many factors: maturity, childhood wounds, personal and religious ethics, a law that permits and encourages the destruction of the baby in the womb, or the common pressure women feel from those who actively encourage abortion as a reasonable, responsible, and even loving thing to do.

Once a pregnancy is confirmed, the mother longs for approval, nurture and support. She is afraid of being judged or rejected for what her body has done. A younger mother will realize that she cannot raise a child on her own. She begins to imagine how her boyfriend, parents and friends will react. The real or imagined responses very much dictate the choice to keep the baby or seek an abortion.

Another significant motivation is the desire to conceal sexual activity. The abortion industry itself seeks to maintain a woman's secret autonomy by encouraging her "privacy." In turn, the end result is that women do not learn to ask for the support they need, but instead "take care of the problem" by themselves.

Many people mistakenly assume that no woman has an abortion if she does not want one. In fact, while many women believe they *need* an abortion, very few, if any, *want* an abortion. This reality is described in a rather famous line by Frederica Mathewes-Green, who wrote: "No woman wants an abortion as she wants an ice cream cone or a Porsche. She wants an abortion as an animal caught in a trap wants to gnaw off its own leg."[3] This quote was widely circulated by Planned Parenthood and other advocates of abortion,[4] but the next two sentences from Mathewes-Green's insightful commentary are not included: "Abortion is a tragic attempt to escape a desperate situation by an act of violence and self-loss. Abortion is not a sign that women are free, but a sign that they are desperate."

Many of the problems that follow abortion are not due solely to the traumatic effects of the surgery itself. Often, the problems that follow abortion are simply a magnification of problems that existed beforehand. In other cases, the problems stem back to the flawed, misinformed, compromising, self-defeating, or simply short-sighted *decision* to have an abortion. For many women, the decision to abort is itself sufficient to provoke feelings of depression, guilt, shame, and more.

Decision Making

The notion that women should be "free to choose" abortion without question or hindrance is extremely irresponsible. It is based on an ideal divorced from reality; that of a fully informed, emancipated, emotionally stable woman. In contrast, most women are not well informed about the dangers abortion poses to both their psychological and physical health, and most women are not truly "emancipated." Instead, many are emotionally dependant on or easily influenced by parents, boyfriends, husbands, counselors, employers, or others who may want them to choose abortion far more than they want to choose it for themselves. Finally, many women considering abortion are simply not emotionally stable, and this lack of stability makes them more prone to hasty, ill-considered, or self-destructive decisions.

Even if one does not have a prior psychological illness or trauma to deal with, any woman confronted with an unintended pregnancy will face feelings of shock and fear about how the birth of a child will change her life. The destabilizing effects of a surprise pregnancy are further aggravated by the great hormonal shifts that occur during early pregnancy. These chemical changes in a woman's body may make her feel more emotional, dependant, exhausted, and physically ill and weak. Any and all of these factors can degrade her ability to make an informed and well-considered decision about abortion.

For most women, abortion is an ambivalent and irresolute choice. Consider the following findings from a survey of 252 women who joined a post-abortion support group:

- Approximately 70% had a prior negative moral view of abortion and chose it in violation of their consciences;
- Between 30 and 60% had a positive desire to carry the pregnancy to term and keep their babies; Over 80% said they would have carried to term under better circumstances or with the support of loved ones;
- Fifty-three percent felt "forced" to have the abortion by other people in their lives; Sixty-four percent felt "forced by outside circumstances" to have the abortion;
- Approximately 40% were still hoping to discover some alternative to abortion when they sat down for counseling at the abortion clinic.[5]

For most women, abortion is more likely to be perceived as an "evil necessity" than a great civil right. Indeed, a major *Los Angeles Times* poll found that 74% of women who admitted having had an abortion stated that they believe abortion is morally wrong.[6]

The fact that most women having abortions see it as posing a moral dilemma is itself problematic. Moral dilemmas, by their very nature, involve emotional and intellectual conflict about the options from which one must choose. These conflicts produce tension and, for many, a powerful sense of crisis. Many women feel completely overwhelmed by their situation[7] and under such pressures many will rush into an abortion without ever examining the full range of their beliefs, needs, and feelings.

Crisis counseling experts have found that those in a state of crisis are more vulnerable to outside influences than they would otherwise be in a non-crisis situation. The state of crisis, especially when it involves moral dilemmas, causes people to have less trust in their own opinions and abilities to make the right decision. This leads them into a state of "heightened psychological accessibility" in which they become reliant on the opinions of others, especially authority figures. When faced with such a crisis situation, "a relatively minor force, acting for a relatively short time, can switch the whole balance from one side or to the other—to the side of mental health or to the side of ill health."[8]

In the case of a woman named Joanna, the abortion clinic counselor's suggestion that she needed to "decide quickly" created emotional pressure that led her to choose abortion immediately, before the opportunity to escape her crisis situation was gone. It is not a coincidence that this same tension-provoking, "choose now" approach is regularly used in marketing programs where consumers are told to "buy now" before a sale price is gone forever.

Persons in crisis "are often less in touch with reality and more vulnerable to change than [when] they are in non-crisis situations."[9] They often experience feelings of tiredness, lethargy, hopelessness, inadequacy, confusion, anxiety and disorganization. Also, a person upset and "trapped" in a crisis, like Joanna, wants to reestablish stability.[10] Thus, one is more likely to stand back and let other people (i.e. a mental health professional, family member, minister, or male partner) make their decisions for them, instead of protecting themselves from decisions that may not be in their best interests.

Uta Landy, an abortion counselor and former executive director of the National Abortion Federation, an association for abortion providers, has admitted that the decision-making processes of women seeking abortion can be temporarily impaired by feelings of crisis related to their pregnancy. Landy defines four types of defective decision-making styles which she has observed in abortion clinics:[11]

The first defective process is the "spontaneous approach," wherein the decision is made too quickly, without taking sufficient time to resolve internal conflicts or explore options.

The second defective decision-making process is the "rational-analytical approach," which focuses on the practical reasons to terminate the pregnancy (financial problems, single parenthood, etc.) without consideration of emotional needs (attachment to the pregnancy, maternal desires, etc.).

The third defective process is the "denying-procrastinating" approach which is typical of women who have delayed making a decision precisely because they have a conflicting desire to keep their babies. When such a "denying-procrastinator" finally agrees to an abortion, it is likely that she has still not resolved her internal conflicts, but is submitting to the abortion only because she has "run out of time."

Fourth, there is the "no-decision making approach," wherein a woman refuses to make her own decision but allows others, such as her male partner, parents, counselors, or physician, to make the decision for her.

Landy encourages counselors to be aware of the fact that some women's feelings about their pregnancy are not simply ambivalent but deeply confused. This confusion is not necessarily expressed in a straightforward manner, but can hide behind such outward behavior as:

1. being uncommunicative,
2. being extremely self assured,
3. being impatient (how long is this going to take, I have other important things to do),
4. being hostile (this is an awful place; you are an awful doctor, counselor, nurse; I hate being here).[12]

Despite her recognition of the fact that many women are making ill-considered decisions, Landy does not recognize any obligation on abortion providers to refuse to perform an abortion on such women, who are at higher risk of severe emotional problems later.

To escape the trap of a crisis pregnancy, women who abort must sacrifice some part of themselves. The experience of abortion is an experience of violence. The decision to expose oneself to abortion often entails a betrayal of one's own moral values or maternal instincts, and thereby a loss of some part of one's self. As the psychiatrist and abortionist Dr. Fogel observed:

"This is a part of her own life. When she destroys a pregnancy, she is destroying herself...I know that as a psychiatrist."[13]

Any number of factors can drive women to this act of desperation:

- Rejection of the pregnancy by partner or family,
- Self-doubt: perceived inability to care for a child,
- The advice or pressure of other people,
- Being driven to choose abortion by psychological compulsions, such as sexual abuse or prior abortions, which incline them to reenact previous losses through abortion.

Abortion Decision as a Symptom

With some exceptions, many crisis pregnancies are not a complete accident (unplanned or unwanted). Our propensity to permit or create crisis frequently stems from unresolved conflicts. This is why there is a need for intervention and exploration into family history and patterns. Once a woman is aware of the psychological underpinnings which provide motivation for her behaviors, only then can she redirect her life in a way that identifies life goals and a plan to reach them which is not self-destructive. Perhaps more important, is the fact that when a woman sees her abortion decision in the context of her entire life, she is often more tolerant, forgiving, and accepting of herself. This is an extremely essential ingredient to permitting God's love and grace to enter her life.

In working with women who have crisis pregnancies, an insightful therapist may also discover some very clear metaphors. Sometimes a woman is trying to resolve a past conflict or loss. Yet often, her attempts to resolve life's losses through recreating or reenacting the conflict does not succeed in changing the patterns, but rather aggravates and reinforces them. Abortion, in particular validates an already inadequate and fragile self image with the unspoken message that she is incapable and inept—that it is better to destroy the developing child than to be mothered by a woman who is not ready or can't give her child the perfect life. The nurturing, accepting and receptive qualities unique to feminine personhood have been violated.

Human beings are architects of their own misfortune, though, with the help and grace of God, can become ministers of their own healing. It is in removing our defenses, and discovering our brokenness and mistakes, that guides us toward the path of healing and redemption. Healing is not found by hiding from the truth, but by facing it with an honest courage and a humble spirit. This includes taking a look at the personal and situational factors which made one vulnerable to choose abortion in the first place.

Here are a few common examples of how crisis pregnancy and abortion can be a symptom of other conflicts:

Testing the relationship's commitment. There are women who become pregnant to test the commitment of a love relationship. When the fruit of their love is not met with wonder and excitement, the woman may turn the blame and rejection inward—and out of powerlessness she may scapegoat her developing child—to maintain peace in the relationship, or avoid embarrassment. It is not uncommon for relationships to end after abortion, and for some it gives the final excuse to be assertive once they realize there is no commitment.

Anger and control. Abortion can be a way to express anger, and it may be an attempt to punish another, or regain control. A woman may try to prove her independence and deny her need for others who have let her down. Women in this situation often disavow their need for significant others—because others in their past have disappointed or emotionally abandoned them. Their attempts to compensate for this loss are seen by outward displays of independence, abortion being one of them, though inwardly they may experience themselves as fearful, rejected children.

Absent fathers. Statistics reveal that a woman who comes from a family where her father is physically absent or emotionally distant is more likely to become pregnant as a teenager. Such women seek the affirmation and acceptance of a male or father image, but unfortunately this need for love and validation is frequently sexualized. Some women with absent fathers choose abortion because they do not want their child growing up in a home without a father. Again, the theme of choices made is an attempt to resolve a previous loss.

For the woman who invites uncaring and uncommitted men to get them pregnant, usually a fear of abandonment and a history of not having been loved can be identified. Their low self-esteem is validated through a relationship that recreates their sense of rejection. Sparing an "unwanted" child this grief by denying him life, is another painful attempt to take control of unwanted feelings of rejection.

Maternal identity. It is not uncommon for abortion to represent a rejection of mother and motherhood itself. When a woman has had a tumultuous relationship with her mother, she is often unwilling to take on that identity herself. Abortion becomes a way to redeem her from ever becoming like her mother. The relationship which craves redemption is the broken connection between mother and child—painfully recreated through abortion.

Sometimes the identity crisis is complicated by present personal problems of the mother. Our mental picture of "mother" is determined first by our own mothers. When a woman's childhood experience was one of poor or absent mothering, accepting the cloak of mother identity can be difficult.

For such a woman, becoming a mother constitutes a threat to the self. Motherhood demands that she is required now to be the caregiver, to be responsible for nurturing, supporting and loving a baby. To her picture of herself as an abandoned or abused child needing nurture, such looms like an overwhelming and impossible demand; "I didn't get enough love myself! I still want to be taken care of! How can I possibly give love and care to a baby?"

Developmental arrest. Pregnancy is an important phase in a young woman's unending task of separation and individuation from her own mother. Some women may view the pregnancy as a way to test their sexual identity and capacity to procreate. When abortion enters the picture, the next stages in the developmental process are thwarted because internal parent objects will not give permission for the woman/child to become a mother herself. The developmental phase is arrested and two critical aspects of emotional identification in pregnancy become unsalvagable: identification with her own mother and identification with the child as an acceptable part of herself.

Histories of sexual abuse. There is a remarkable clinical finding which suggests a high proportion of women have histories of molestation, sexual abuse, or incest. In such cases, an abortion is a clear metaphor of a re-creation of conflict for an internalized and damaged sense of self and sexuality, induced through sexual abuse of some kind.

In an abortion, the abortionist's hand or instrument forces her to undergo a penetrating violation deep into the protective and sacred part of her womb. Life is ended through this intrusion, similar to the death and destruction of her sense of self which commonly results from sexual abuse. In this sense, abortion can be seen as a symbolic suicide, a reenactment of this conflict acting out the rejection of the wounded inner child.

Even the grief of abortion, like the grief of sexual abuse, is held in unspoken cries of secrecy. It is a literal re-creation of the intrusion forced upon her during sexual abuse as she remains helpless and powerless consenting to the invasion while overwrought with unspoken shame and guilt, despair and grief.

Atonement baby and repeat abortions. It is not uncommon for a woman to have an atonement baby after a previous abortion. The desire to replace what was lost or make up for the lost pregnancy with another reflects the natural instinct to procreate. However, this desire is often overridden by the concept that we should all be responsible and ready for parenthood. Many times a woman will re-create the crisis of an unplanned pregnancy as an attempt to carry it out this time by getting it right, or as a symptom of psychic trauma and reenactment. Often, the woman's circumstances are still the same and she has another abortion. Repeat abortions can become a ritualized outlet for continued grief and loss. Repeat abortions are a symptom of deep psychic trauma—as repetition is one of the greatest indicators we have to demonstrate trauma. Note that 46% of all abortions are repeat abortions.

It is not uncommon to see women having 4, 5 or 6 abortions. The psychological motivation is to gain mastery over the trauma, and therefore many women become stuck in such a very self-destructive pattern. With each abortion, a woman may become more anesthetized until the process is just a routine event. In other cases, the reenactment can be a ritualized means through which a woman will intensely grieve and mourn.

Alcoholic families. The woman who chooses an abusive or alcoholic partner statistically comes from a familial history of abusive or alcoholic parents. A reenactment of conflict will include the intense desire to change him, make things better, or to continue in the familiar lifestyle of denigration and instability. When the woman becomes pregnant, abortion is a way to save the child from experiencing the pain she knew as a child. It can also be a signal to grieve her wounded and rejected "inner child" and express feelings of despair and powerlessness.

Pressure by others. It is not uncommon for women who did not want to have abortions, to experience coercion and have no voice to stop the process once it is suggested. This sense of powerlessness is frequently experienced as a type of paralysis on the abortion table—an inability to stop the procedure from happening. This indicates a lack of assertiveness, and the pain of that diminished sense of self, along with the lost child, is what is grieved after an abortion: "Why did I let them do this to my baby? How could I have gone through with this?" the woman will ask herself. The abortion is not an empowering experience, but one of complete and utter devastation upon the realization that someone talked her into violating a basic female instinct to nurture and protect her offspring. In post abortion healing, this lost sense of self must be reclaimed.

Post-Abortion Syndrome and the Conspiracy of Silence

PAS is defined as the inability to

- adequately process the painful emotions attached to abortion—especially guilt, anger, and grief;
- properly identify and grieve the loss experienced; or to
- come to peace with God, and within oneself, about the abortion.[14]

Etiology. Much controversy exists about how many women experience PAS, and to what degree. It is clear that some women who have abortions do not struggle with PAS, and that many do. The secrecy around personal disclosure and controversies associated with abortion has made gathering accurate data a difficult task. We do know that women who struggle with PAS have tended to have[15]

1. been coerced, to some degree by family or father, into having an abortion,
2. been young and immature, most between the ages of 14 and 24,
3. had a stormy relationship with little to no support from sex partner,
4. expressed psychological and moral ambivalence about it,
5. had a religious upbringing and expressed some spiritual convictions,
6. had more than one abortion,
7. had a late term abortion, in the second or third trimester,
8. had a pregnancy due to rape or incest,
9. had an abortion due to fetal or other abnormality,

10. had been awake during the abortion procedure,

11. been unable to conceive after the abortion,

12. had a recent pregnancy with a "wanted" child.

A common pattern of events that influences PAS has long been recognized by doctors and counselors working with post-abortion women: The pregnancy was a crisis event, unexpected and a source of surprise and shame for the pregnant girl and her family. The crisis precipitates a moral dilemma as abortion is considered as one way to "solve" the crisis. An abortion is performed as the expedient, though ambivalent solution, and brings a period of transient relief. The moral dilemma resurfaces, as the question is asked, "Did we do the right thing?" The pain of the act and the ensuing dilemma are dealt with poorly—by denial, suppression of feelings, and avoidance. Efforts of denial and the avoidance of pain go on for years, but erupt again to disrupt life after some event that triggers a traumatic recall of the abortion event, often a later pregnancy.[16]

Assessment and treatment. The symptomatology of PAS is remarkable for its similarity to post-traumatic stress disorder (PTSD). In fact, PAS is appropriately characterized by some as a unique form of PTSD, and we believe it is accurate to conceptualize and treat it as a trauma-based disorder. The usual pattern of symptoms include:

- *anxiety:* increased anxiety and guilt are the two "felt" emotions that dominate the feeling world of the PAS sufferer.
- *guilt:* often exacerbated and expressed as a three-strike proposition—(1) "I murdered an innocent" who was also (2) "my child," and (3) "I survived" though I did not deserve to.
- *depression:* often with all the classic symptoms—sleep disturbance, social withdrawal, helpless/hopeless syndrome, crying episodes, reduced sex and pleasure drives, amotivation, and struggles with suicide,
- *lost faith and spiritual deadness:* believing that God is enraged, or uncaring, or that one is unforgivable. Many women lose their faith and dry up spiritually following an abortion.
- *self-abuse and self-hatred:* some women become self-abusive and self-punishing, with suicidal ideation mixing together in a sometimes deadly combination.

- *flashbacks and intrusive memories:* very much like PTSD episodes where vivid dreams, memories, flashbacks, and recalls are experienced as if the event is being re-lived.
- *debilitating avoidance:* anxiety provoked behavior where people and situations with the slightest risk of eliciting a recall of the abortion are systematically avoided.
- *numbing:* when all else fails—when avoidance, self-abuse, or suicide attempts do not stop the pain—the PAS sufferer will learn to "numb out" or "flat-line" their emotional and relational lives.
- *bonding problems, including child abuse and neglect:* PAS struggles can interfere with the normal bonding process with other children—in the worst cases, child abuse and neglect is the result.
- *substance abuse:* many women abuse alcohol and drugs—including prescription medications—and quickly learn to "self-medicate" as a way to numb the pain and guilt of abortion.
- *eating disorders:* a few women, either in lieu of or in combination with drugs or other addictive agents, will develop an eating disorder of some kind.
- *barrenness and pregnancy problems:* some women transfer their psycho-spiritual distress physically, experiencing ongoing difficulty with pregnancy and fertility subsequent to an abortion.
- *anniversary reactions:* as with grief recovery, anniversaries of the abortion and related events increase emotional turmoil and distress.

Treatment planning and intervention with PAS clients concentrates on five goals:

1. *Facing the truth and accepting the loss.* The counselor must give the client permission—encourage and challenge her—to yield to what she has been fighting for months or years. She must honestly face the fact that she underwent an abortion and her child is gone. This will usually release a torrent of emotions and memories and the counselor must be able to assist the client to identify and handle each one. Telling the truth about what happened and discovering that it will not kill or crush her is a huge first step in the healing process.

2. *Deal with the guilt and renew relations with God.* No sin exists that God cannot and does not want to forgive, and to experience anew God's forgiveness and love is a wonderful renewal of spiritual and emotional life. The process of repentance and reconciliation with God is also frightening, and fraught with much unbelief and resistance, so counselors must be patient and gentle to stay with a client, not allowing her to lose focus, but acknowledging and reinforcing the evidence of God's continual entreaty to take His hand and walk together again.

3. *Address the abortion decision and deal with the anger.* Abortion represents a failure of nerve, the expedient submission to the seductive lie by the client and so many other people. The client will be angry with herself, with her sex partner, often with her parents, with the abortion doctors, counselors, clinic, and with the whole abortion system. She may want to exact vengeance or become a crusader for the right to life. Help by acknowledging her anger, working through it, checking the vengeful impulses, and affirming intent toward right action. Give her active things to do to vent the anger and reengage with the world around once again.

4. *Grieve the loss.* A child is dead. Now the client is becoming free enough to mourn the enormity of this awful truth, and to rejoice in the heavenly home of that absent child. Often the client allows herself to do what she has refused to this point—to fantasize about the child's age-appropriate behavior and interactions as if the child were still alive. It is alright to allow and facilitate this now, and to record the crying, laughter, sorrow and pain that will be elicited as the client remembers her lost child. Prepare the client to expect to experience a wide range of now "unfreezing" emotions that, at times, will surprise, even disturb the client at their appearance. All of this is normal to the grieving process and it will take much time to work through.

5. *Reconstruct a new future.* The last phase of the healing process is coming to a place of renewed commitment to living, a refreshment and release of new desires for life. Forgiveness does not mean forgetting, but the memories of the child and its absence no longer debilitate, or create despair. God is able to build palaces out of ashes. Even the pain of abortion must yield to His miraculous

restorative power—the same power that brought Jesus back to life from the grave.[17]

Further Study of Outreach and Treatment

Developing an effective and meaningful outreach to those wounded by abortion requires education of the manifestations of trauma and in the techniques grief work that have proven to be effective with this population. Reportedly, the often self-destructive behaviors after an abortion are an attempt to work through unresolved psychological conflicts and can be acted out through eating disorders, multiple abortions, obsessive compulsive rituals, anxiety over fertility, stress over maternal and sexual identity, and other physical or behavioral disturbances.

Insights into traumatic reenactments will help the counselor assist clients in interpreting their symptoms so that they can confront the trauma rooted beneath their behaviors. An illuminating work on this subject helpful to counselors and pastoral ministers is *Forbidden Grief—The Unspoken Pain of Abortion.*[18]

ENDNOTES

1. Alan Guttmacher Institute, *Facts in brief: induced abortion* (Washington, D.C., January 1997).
2. Frank Minirth, Meier, P., and Arterburn, S., Abortion, in *The complete life encyclopedia* (Nashville: Thomas Nelson, 1995).
3. Frederica Mathewes-Green, Unplanned Parenthood, *Policy Review*, (Summer 1991).
4. This quote was reprinted as "Quote of the Week" in the *Planned Parenthood Federation of America Public Affairs Action Letter*, (September 25, 1992) and as "Quote of the Month" in *The Pro-Choice Network Newsletter*, (May 1993), and reprinted in a commentary column by Ellen Goodman, "Not 'Choice,' but 'Better Choices,'" *The Baltimore Sun* (September 18, 1992).
5. David C. Reardon, *Aborted women: silent no more* (Chicago: Loyola University Press, 1987), 11–21; See also, Mary K. Zimmerman, *Passage through abortion* (New York: Praeger Publishers, 1977), 62–70; and Miller, W. B., An empirical study of the psychological antecedents and consequences of induced abortion, *J Social Issues, 48*(3), (1992), 67–93.
6. *Los Angeles Times* Poll, (March 19, 1989), question 76.
7. Vincent M. Rue and Speckhard, A. C., Informed consent and abortion: Issues in medicine and counseling, *Med. & Mind, 6*(1), (1992), 75–94.
8. Gerald Caplan, *Principals of preventive psychiatry* (New York: Basic Books, 1964).
9. Howard W. Stone, *Crisis counseling* (Fortress Press, 1976).

10. Wilbur E. Morely, Theory of crisis intervention, *Pastoral Psychology*, 21(203), (April 1970), 16.

11. Uta Landy, Abortion counseling—a new component of medical care, *Clinics in Obs/Gyn*, 13(1), (1986), 33–41.

12. Ibid.

13. Colman McCarthy, A psychological view of abortion, St. Paul Sunday Pioneer Press, *Washington Post* (March 7, 1971). Dr. Fogel, who did 20,000 abortions over the subsequent decades, reiterated the same view in a second interview with McCarthy in 1989. The real anguish of abortions, *The Washington Post* (Feb. 5, 1989).

14. T. Reisser, and Reisser, P., *A solitary sorrow: Finding healing and wholeness after abortion* (Wheaton, IL: Harold Shaw, 1999).

15. Ibid.; R. Payne, Kravitz, A., Notman, M., and Anderson, J., Outcomes following therapeutic abortion, *Archives of General Psychiatry 33*, (1976), 725; D. Reardon, *Aborted women: silent no more* (Westchester, IL: Crossway, 1987); N. Adler, Emotional responses of women following therapeutic abortion, *American Journal of Orthopsychiatry 45*, (1975), 446–454.

16. T. Reisser, and Reisser, P., *A solitary sorrow: Finding healing and wholeness after abortion* (Wheaton, IL: Harold Shaw, 1999).

17. Ibid.; T. Reisser, and Coe, J., Post-abortion counseling, in D. Benner and P. Hill, (eds.), *Baker encyclopedia of psychology and counseling*, 2nd ed. (Grand Rapids, MI: Baker, 1999).

18. Theresa Burke, with David C. Reardon, *Forbidden grief: The unspoken pain of abortion*, (Acorn Books, 2002).

Appendices

Forms and Templates for Christian Counseling

Appendix A: Professional Services Agreement

This agreement for _____services between (your practice's name) and client(s)_____shall govern all professional relations between the parties.

A. THE STAFF THERAPIST is

_____.

He or she is a professional therapist, qualified and trained as an

- ❑ LMFT, LPC, LMHC, LCPC, LCSW, LISW, licensed psychologist or psychiatrist; or
- ❑ pre-licensed intern, trainee, associate, or psychological assistant working under supervision of a licensed therapist who will know something about your case.

B. FEES AND INSURANCE POLICY.

Client fees are to be determined at the first session. Full or partial payment shall be made by the client at the end of each session. Clients agree to pay part of their fee out-of-pocket even if covered by insurance. *As a courtesy to you* we can bill insurance and other vendors on a monthly basis. We will not extend credit or schedule appointments beyond three unpaid sessions until payment is made. Clients understand that a therapist with pre-license status (as checked above) may or may not be able to receive insurance reimbursement. *Clients understand they are fully responsible for all fees if insurance or other vendor does not pay.*

C. CANCELLATION POLICY.

We agree to and ask that clients maintain responsible relations regarding appointment times. Any appointment *cancelled after 6 P.M. the day before the appointment or that the client does not show will be charged to the client at (1) half the fee rate for the first incident and (2) the full fee rate for any incidents thereafter.* Most insurances will not reimburse for this charge, *so clients understand they are responsible to pay for missed sessions per this policy.*

D. CONFIDENTIALITY POLICY.

All therapeutic communications, records, and contacts with professional and support staff will be held in strict confidence. Information may be released, in accordance with state law, only when (1) the client signs a written release of information indicating informed consent to such release; (2) the client expresses serious intent to harm himself/herself or someone else, clearly identified; (3) there is evidence or reasonable suspicion of abuse against a minor child, elder person (sixty-five years or older), or dependent adult; or (4) a subpoena or other court order is received directing the disclosure of information.

It is our policy to assert either (a) privileged communication in the event of #4 or (b) the right to consult with clients, if at all possible barring an emergency, before mandated disclosure in the event of #2 or #3. Although we cannot guarantee it, we will endeavor to apprise the client of all mandated disclosure.

Clients with any concerns or questions about this policy agree to raise them with their counselor at the earliest possible time to resolve them in the client's best interest.

E. WORK AGREEMENT.

It is agreed that the client shall make a good-faith effort at personal growth and engage in the counseling process as an important priority at this time in his or her life. Client gain is most important in professional counseling. Suspension, termination, or referral shall be discussed between counselor and client for a pattern of behavior showing disinterest or lack of commitment, or for any unresolved conflict or impasse between counselor and client.

(You or your practice's name) and client further agree that the following needs or problem issues will be addressed in both counseling sessions and in client homework, with future revisions possible as need arises:

_____

_____

_____

_____

_____

F. FEE AGREEMENT.

The agreed *fee for each intake interview session is* _____ ; and
        per 50 minute session, the fee is _____ ; and
        per 25 minute session, the fee is _____ ; and
        for each group session, the fee is _____ ; and
        for any special or emergency session, the fee is _____ .

If a sliding fee scale is elected, fill in the first two categories below:
        monthly family gross income_____
        number of persons in family _____
        sliding fee scale is _____ per session.

G. MODIFICATION & CONFLICT RESOLUTION.

It is agreed that any disputes or modifications of agreement shall be negotiated directly between the parties. If these negotiations are not satisfactory, then the parties *agree to mediate any differences with a mutual acceptable third-party mediator, considering first either the Executive Director or Associate*

Director of the practice. If these are unsatisfactory, then the parties shall move to arbitration, and then binding arbitration, choosing an arbitrator mutually agreeable to both. Litigation shall be considered only if and after all of these methods of resolution are given a good faith effort and are unsatisfactory.

Service Agreement

We, the undersigned therapist and client, have read, discussed together, and fully understand this agreement and the stated policies. We agree to honor these policies, including the commitment to negotiate and mediate as stated above, and will respect one another's views and differences in their outworking. We have also agreed to an initial definition of professional work and to the fee to be paid by the client.

Client signature_____Date_____

Therapist signature_____Date_____

Appendix B: Pastoral Counseling Services Agreement

This agreement for _____services between (your church or practice's name) and client(s)_____shall govern all counseling relations between the parties.

A. THE PASTORAL COUNSELOR is

_____. He or she is an Ordained Minister and/or Pastoral Counselor, NOT a licensed therapist, and does not provide professional counseling or psychotherapy, but only time-limited pastoral counseling interventions.

B. PASTORAL COUNSELING AT (YOUR CHURCH OR PRACTICE'S NAME) is confidential, Bible-based counseling by one trained and experienced in both pastoral and counseling ministry. Pastoral counseling will be limited to ____ sessions overall with an evaluation at the end of this program of counseling. Counseling shall then be terminated, or referral for further treatment may be made at this time, whichever is in the client's best interest.

C. FEES AND INSURANCE POLICY.

Client fees are to be determined at the first session. Full or partial payment shall be made at the end of each session by the client. Clients understand that a Pastoral Counselor will not be able to receive insurance reimbursement under most policies—clients are responsible to bill their own insurance if they believe a Pastoral Counselor is covered. We will not extend credit or schedule appointments beyond three unpaid sessions until payment is made. *Clients are fully responsible for the payment of all fees.*

D. CANCELLATION POLICY.

We agree to and ask that clients maintain responsible relations regarding appointment times. Any appointment *cancelled after 6 P.M. the day before the appointment or that the client does not show will be charged to the client at (1) half the fee rate for the first incident and (2) the full fee rate for any incidents thereafter.* Most insurance companies will not reimburse *you for this charge.*

E. CONFIDENTIALITY POLICY.

All therapeutic communications, records, and contact with professional and support staff will be held in strict confidence. Information may be released, in accordance with state law, only when (1) the client signs a written release of information indicating informed consent to such release; (2) the client expresses serious intent to harm himself/herself or someone else; (3) there is evidence or reasonable suspicion of abuse against a minor child, elder person (sixty- years or older), or dependent adult; or (4) a subpoena or other court order is received directing the disclosure of information. It is our policy to assert either (a) privileged communication in the event of #4 or (b) the right to consult with clients, if at all possible baring an emergency, before mandated disclosure in the event of #2 or #3. Although we cannot guarantee it, we will endeavor to apprise clients of all mandated disclosures.

Clients with any concerns or questions about this policy agree to raise them with their counselor at the earliest possible time to resolve them in the client's best interest.

F. WORK AGREEMENT.

It is agreed that the parishioner-client shall make a good-faith effort at change and personal growth, and engage in the counseling process as an important priority at this time in his or her life. Client gain is most important in pastoral counseling. Suspension, termination, or referral shall be discussed between counselor and client for a pattern of behavior that reveals disinterest or lack of commitment to counseling or for any unresolved conflict or impasse between counselor and client.

(Your practice's name) and client further agree that the following needs or problem issues will be addressed in both counseling sessions and in client homework, with future revisions possible as need arises:

_____

_____

_____

_____

_____

G. FEE AGREEMENT.

The agreed *fee per 50 minute session* is _____for the base rate. If the fee scale is elected, fill in the first two categories below:

 monthly family gross income_____

 number in family_____

 fee scale_____per session.

H. MODIFICATION & CONFLICT RESOLUTION.

It is agreed that any disputes or modifications of agreement shall be negotiated directly between the parties. If these negotiations are not satisfactory, then the parties *agree to mediate any differences with a mutual acceptable third-party mediator.* If these are unsatisfactory, then the parties shall move to arbitration, and then binding arbitration, choosing an arbitrator mutually agreeable to both. Litigation is not acceptable between Christians, and will only be considered if these methods of dispute resolution are given a good faith effort and are found unsatisfactory.

Service Agreement

We, the undersigned pastoral counselor and client, have read, discussed together and fully understand this agreement and the stated policies. We agree to honor these policies, including the commitment to negotiate and mediate as stated above, and will respect one another's views and differences in their outworking. We have also agreed to an initial definition of counseling work and to the fee to be paid by the client.

Client signature_____Date_____

Counselor signature_____ Date_____

Appendix C: Lay Helping Services Agreement

This agreement for lay helping services between (your church or practice's name) and parishioner(s)_____shall govern all helping ministry relations between the parties.

A. THE LAY HELPER is

_____. He or she is NOT an Ordained Minister and/or Pastoral Counselor, is NOT a licensed therapist, and does NOT provide professional counseling or psychotherapy, but only time-limited lay helping ministry.

B. LAY HELPING AT (YOUR CHURCH OR PRACTICE'S NAME) is confidential, Bible-based ministry by one trained and supervised by _____. Lay helping will be limited to ____ sessions overall with an evaluation at the end of this program of ministry. Lay helping shall then be terminated, or referral for further pastoral care or professional counseling treatment may be made at this time, whichever is in the parishioner's best interest.

C. FEES AND INSURANCE POLICY.

Lay helping is a servant's service of this church and no client fees or anything of monetary value shall be charged or given for this ministry.

D. CANCELLATION POLICY.

We agree to and ask that clients maintain responsible relations regarding appointment times.

E. CONFIDENTIALITY POLICY.

All ministry communications, records, and contact with church and support staff will be held in strict confidence. Information may be released, in accordance with church policy, only when (1) the parishioner signs a written release of information indicating informed consent to such release; (2) the parishioner expresses serious intent to harm himself/herself or someone else; (3) there is evidence or reasonable suspicion of abuse against a minor child, elder person (sixty- years or older), or dependent adult; or (4) a subpoena or other court order is received directing the disclosure of information. It is our church policy to assert either (a) privileged communication in the event of #4 or (b) the right to consult with clients, if at all possible baring an emergency, before any disclosure is made in the event of #2 or #3. Parishioners with any concerns or questions about this policy agree to raise them at the earliest possible time to resolve them in the parishioner's best interest.

F. WORK AGREEMENT.

It is agreed that the parishioner-client shall make a good-faith effort at change and personal growth, and engage in the helping process as an important priority at this time in his or her life. Parishioner growth and spiritual maturity is most important in this care-giving ministry. Suspension, termination, or referral shall be discussed between helper and parishioner for a pattern of behavior that reveals disinterest or lack of commitment, or for any unresolved conflict or impasse between helper and parishioner.

(Your church's name) and _____ further agree that the following needs or problem issues will be addressed in sessions and in any homework, with future revisions possible as need arises:

_____

_____

_____

_____

_____

G. MODIFICATION & CONFLICT RESOLUTION.

It is agreed that any disputes or modifications of agreement shall be negotiated directly between the parties. If these negotiations are not satisfactory, then the parties agree to mediate any differences with the helper's supervisor, or any other mutually acceptable third-party mediator who is a member of this church. If these are unsatisfactory, then the parties shall move to arbitration, and then binding arbitration, choosing an arbitrator mutually agreeable to both. Litigation is not acceptable between Christians, and will only be considered if these methods of dispute resolution are given a good faith effort and are found unsatisfactory.

Service Agreement

We, the undersigned lay helper and parishioner, have read, discussed together and fully understand this agreement and the stated policies. We agree to honor these policies, including the commitment to negotiate and mediate as stated above, and will respect one another's views and differences in their outworking. We have also agreed to an initial definition of counseling work.

Parishioner signature_____ Date_____

Lay Helper signature_____ Date_____

Appendix D: Client Insurance Information/Consent

A. Client's Name _____ Age _____ Birthdate_____

Address_____

              street   city   state   zip

Phone (home) _____ (work) _____

best time to call _____

If Client a Minor, Parent /Guardian name(s)

_____

Client Education _____ SSN _____ Occupation

_____

Employer Name and Address

_____

Marital Status(circle): sing wid eng mar sep div liv-tog

_____

Spouse's Name _____ Age _____

Birthdate _____

B. Family Status: List name, birthdate, sex, relationship of all children, and whether they live at home with you.

       Name   Birthdate   Sex   Relationship at Home?

_____

_____

_____

_____

_____

C. Home church(if any)_____

    Pastor _____

D. Person to call in emergency (name, phone(s), relationship)

_____

E. Referring physician name & address

_____

F. Insurance Information and Release. As a courtesy to you, we will bill your primary insurance. You are responsible for getting a physician's referral for insurance payment and are responsible for your entire bill if insurance does not pay.

At your request, we will provide you with an itemized statement so you can bill your secondary insurance.

Insured's Name_____ SSN _____
Relationship to you_____
Insured's Employer (name and address)

_____

Name of insurance_____ Policy#_____
Group# _____
Secondary insurance? _____ Policy# _____
Group# _____
2nd Insured's name _____
Birthdate _____ SSN _____
If any other person or agency will be covering the cost of counseling, give their name and address:

_____

_____

I HEREBY AUTHORIZE RELEASE OF INFORMATION NECESSARY TO FILE A CLAIM WITH MY INSURANCE COMPANY AND ASSIGN ALL MY BENEFITS TO THIS COUNSELOR.

Signature _____ Date _____

Appendix E: Client Intake Form

Today's Date_____

A. Client's Name _____
Age _____ Birthdate_____
Parent /Guardian name(s) _____
Age(s) _____
Address _____
Phone (home) _____ (work) _____ best time to call ___
Marital Status: single ____ engaged ____ married ____ (how long _____)
times married _____ separated _____ (how long _____)
divorced ____ (how long_____)
Education _____ Occupation _____ SSN _____
Spouse's Name _____ Age _____Birthdate _____
Spouse's Education_____
Spouse's Occupation _____

B. List name, birthdate, sex, relationship of all children, and whether they
live at home with you.

Name	Birthdate	Sex	Relationship at Home?
_____	_____	____	_____
_____	_____	____	_____
_____	_____	____	_____
_____	_____	____	_____

C. Who is coming for counseling? _____
Any prior counseling? Y___N___
If yes, when? _____Where? _____
With whom? _____
Why? _____

Are you or another family member currently seeing a psychiatrist or another counselor? Y_____ N_____

If so, what family member?_____

Name of helper _____

For what purpose?_____

Person to contact in emergency (name, relationship, address, phone).

_____

_____

PLEASE FILL OUT THE FOLLOWING INFORMATION AS IT APPLIES TO THE CLIENT

D. State the nature of the problem in your own words.

_____

_____

_____

_____

What is your most difficult relationship right now?

_____

What is your most difficult emotion right now?

_____

E. CRISIS INFORMATION: Any current suicidal thoughts, feelings or actions? Y_____ N_____ If yes, explain

_____

Any current homicidal or assaultive thoughts or feelings, or anger-control problems? Y_____ N_____ If yes, explain

_____

Any past problems, hospitalizations, or jailings for suicidal or assaultive behavior? Y_____ N_____ If yes, describe

_____

Any current threats of significant loss or harm (illness, divorce, custody, job loss, etc.)? Y____ N____ If yes, describe

_____

F. MEDICAL INFORMATION: Doctor's name, address and phone

_____

_____

Are you presently taking any medication? Y__N__ If so, what?_____

For what purpose?

_____

Any problems with eating_____ sleeping _____ chronic pain _____ recent weight changes _____ Describe any answers checked above_____

Any other medical problems?

_____

Have you or a family member ever been hospitalized for mental or emotional illness? Y_____ N_____

If yes, please explain—dates, where, reason:

_____

_____

G. Common problem/symptom checklist. Fill in: 0 – none, 1 – mild, 2 – moderate, 3 – severe.

___marriage	___divorce/separation	___alcohol/drugs
___God/faith	___pre-marital	___child custody
___other addictions	___church/ministry	___being single
___disabled	___grief/loss	___past hurts
___sexual issues	___work/career	___depression
___codependency	___family	___school/learning

___fear/anxiety   ___intimacy   ___children

___money/budgeting   ___anger control   ___communication

___parents   ___aging/dependency   ___loneliness

___self-esteem   ___in-laws   ___weight control

___mood swings   ___stress control

Other
(specify)_____

H. Who referred you to us? (name, relationship and phone number)

_____

_____

THANK YOU for taking the time to fill out this information sheet. Your counselor will review this with you in the first session and use it to best assist you in your counseling work. We will maintain your strict confidence regarding this information, subject to the exceptions noted in your service contract. Be sure you review and sign the elements of agreement detailed in your service contract.

Appendix F:

Helping Dangerous Clients: Clinical Care and Ethical/Legal

Management of Suicide and Homicide Risk

I. Client Information

1. Onset of suicidal ideation_____
__Recent or __Acute
__Ongoing or __Chronic

2. Lethality:
Previous attempts
__Yes: Details: How many? How did it fail? Date(s)
__No

_____

_____

_____

_____

History of family suicide completion __Yes __No
Abuse alcohol or drugs __Yes: __alcohol ___drugs __No
___in recovery: how long_____
__AA or NA : __Yes __ No Sponsored? __ Yes __No

A. __Presence of activating event that elicits
Intensity of Suicidal ideation:
__Low/somewhat troubled __Moderately troubled __Highly troubled
Frequency of ideation:
__Occasional: How often_____
__Intermittent: How often:

_____

__Daily: How long:

_____

__Feelings of sudden shame or beliefs that one is letting down the family

Intensity: __Low/ Somewhat troubled__Moderately troubled
___Highly troubled
Frequency of feelings/beliefs:
__Occasional: How often_____
__Intermittent: How often: _____
__Daily: How long: _____
__Access to lethal means (guns, medications, alcohol)
  List:

_____

Plan to deal with access_____
When_____

B. Plan __Specific __Vague __Immediate __Open ended

C. Activating Event involves: ___Personal loss (es) __Death of friend or
family member
__Financial __Home __Independent living __Employment
__Interpersonal loss/ relationship, separation /divorce, empty nest
__ Dx of terminal or chronic illness __Chronic pain

3. DSM Symptoms/Dx, check all that apply
__Major affective disorder: depression ___and/or mania__ bipolar__
__With psychosis ___with command hallucinations to harm self or others
__Severe hopelessness __Severe helplessness
__Severe loss of interest in pleasurable or highly interesting activities
__Constricted problem solving ability __ Poor coping history __Yes __No
Successful coping history __Yes __No
Rigidity __Yes __No

II. Checklist for Assessing Suicide Risk and Protective Factors

A. RISK FACTORS

Mental Health/Medical History
1 ___Mental disorder associated with suicidal behavior (angry-impulsive,
     depression, schizophrenia, alcohol dependence, substance abuse, and
     combination of mental disorders)
2 ___Communication/denial of intent
3 ___Prior suicidal behavior (e.g., suicide threats, suicide attempts)

4 ___Family history of suicidal behavior

5 ___Suicidal behavior within the past 3 months

6 ___Major medical problems, particularly chronic, incurable, or painful conditions (AIDS, brain disease, renal failure, cancer, and Huntington's disease)

7 ___Major medical problem, with prognosis/expectation of death

Psychosocial History

8 ___Unattached (never married, separated, divorced, or lack of significant relationships)

9 ___Spotty work history ___ Chronic unemployment

10 ___Childhood abuse

11 ___History of violent behavior

Psychosocial/Environmental Risk Factors

12 ___Major life stressors (e.g., physical or sexual assault, threats against life, diagnosis of serious medical problem, dissolution of significant relationship, sexual identity issues)

13 ___Any significant loss

14 ___Breakdown of support systems

15 ___Social isolation

Personal Risk Factors

16 ___Emotional instability (chronic) ___Poor problem solving
___Low stress tolerance

17 ___Impulsivity or aggression (chronic) ___Poor coping skills
___Poor judgment

18 ___Personality Disorder associated with suicide (borderline, antisocial)

19 ___ Problem thinking ___Rigid thinking ___Distorted thinking
___Irrational beliefs

Clinical Risk Factors

20 ___Specific behaviors suggestive of suicide planning (giving away possessions; writing or saying good-bye to friends/family; thinking about suicide; talking about death, suicide, or both; verbalizing specific plans to commit suicide; rehearsing suicidal act; asking about ways to die; accumulating medications; and threatening suicide)

21 ___Changes in mental status (acute deterioration in mental functioning; onset of major mental illness, particularly early phase of schizophrenia

or depression; psychosis with agitation, command hallucinations, or both; extreme anxiety, paranoia, or both; and severe depression)

22 ___Changes in behavior (social withdrawal, agitation, provocativeness, increased or decreased appetite, disturbed sleep, impulsivity, and aggressive behavior)

23 ___Changes in mood (depression, fearfulness, unfounded happiness, anger, anxiety, lability)

24 ___ Strong expression of hopelessness and/or helplessness

25 ___Changes in attitude (unrealistic, apathy, overly optimistic, overly pessimistic)

26 ___Lack of compliance with treatment

B. PROTECTIVE FACTORS

a ___Married (or committed to significant relationship)

b ___Having children who are under the age of 18 years

c ___Employed or involved in an educational or vocational training program

d ___Support system (e.g., family, friends, church, social clubs)

e ___Religious faith that is active and internalized

f ___Constructive use of leisure time (enjoyable activities)

g ___General purpose for living

h ___Overall good health/lack of chronic disorders

i ___Involved in mental health treatment

j ___Effective coping and problem-solving skills

C. RISK ASSESSMENT

Add up check-offs in section A, "Risk Factors," then subtract checks from section B, 'Protective Factors," to get risk score. Evaluate risk score against risk assessment grid below and decide on appropriate protective action, taking all client and systemic information into account.

Scores:	25 to 34	VERY HIGH RISK
	17 to 24	HIGH RISK
	9 to 16	MODERATE RISK
	8 or less	LOW RISK

D. RISK-BASED INTERVENTION

RI-1: Hospitalize or closely monitor your very high risk client.

RI-2: Closely monitor and intensify outpatient contact with your high risk client.

RI-3: Monitor and increase outpatient contact with your moderate risk client.

RI-4: Monitor your low risk client.

II: Threat/Response Matrix for Homicidal and Assaultive Clients

The Five-step Progression

1. One Principle Above All: LIFE trumps all other values—here: your commitment to confidentiality—when these important values clash. When confused, remember this first.

2. Two Key Communications to deliver at the start of all clinical and professional relations.
   a. Your unswerving commitment to honor confidentiality as far as it is allowed
   b. The limits of the rule—excepted for abuse, suicide, and homicide threats

3. Three (3x3) Conditions that trigger your duty to protect others from client harm.
   a. Direct client statements of intent to kill to seriously harm,
   b. a clearly identifiable 3rd person or group of persons,
   c. and that threatened harm is
   (1) serious, (2) imminent, and (3) doable.

4. Four Targets of Disclosure of your client's threats if duty to protect is triggered.
   a. The intended victim or group,
   b. Family or close friend of the victim if unable to contact victim
   c. Law enforcement with jurisdiction,
   d. Psychiatric/emergency response personnel.

5. Five Clinical Response Principles/Interventions with your dangerous/threatening client.
   a. Adopt a crisis mode of planning and intervention with your client (very short-term, quick-response, highly directive).
   b. Honor your legal-ethical duty to the least restrictive intervention,

but don't be slavish to it (take whatever protective action necessary to save lives).

c. Increase the frequency and intensity of your interventions in order to reduce/defuse the risk of violence.

d. Wrap 3rd party warnings into your client's therapy—use as both a "reality check" to your client about the seriousness and consequences of threats, and as a call to safety that triggers a broad range of threat-reducing actions rather than those that are threat increasing.

e. Facilitate and assist the hospitalization or law enforcement action toward your client to show that you are continuing to maintain your clinical commitment to them.

Determination of Appropriateness of outpatient or inpatient care:

_____

_____

Inpatient referral: __ Yes __No

_____

_____

Reason for decision:

_____

_____

_____

Outpatient services: __ Yes __No

Reason for decision. Note any precautions and what steps will be taken:

_____

_____

_____

Appendix G: Consent For Release Of Information

I, _____, do consent and authorize
this counselor _____ to:
(check off and fill in the blanks)

(A) release all records _____ of my (or my dependent's) counseling or
other work done by the Institute to the following person or organization

_____

(except for the record of_____).

(B) obtain all records _____of my (or my dependent's) counseling or
other work done by this person or organization

_____

(except for the records of _____)

and send to _____.

(C) exchange all records _____
(except for the records of _____)

 as may be necessary between

_____

and this person or organization_____
for the best interests of my (or my dependent's) goals in counseling or
other work.

****

This consent is valid and is to be acted on upon receipt of this form regarding the records of this client or patient:_____.

This consent will terminate without express written revocation by the client named herein on or when_____.

Client/Guardian Signature _____ Date _____

Client Address _____

Client Birthdate _____ Client Social Security Number _____

Signature of Institute Staff _____ Date _____

NOTE: *Federal regulations require ALL blanks to be filled in, including date, event, or condition that terminates consent for release of confidential client information.*

Appendix H: Authorization To Treat Minor Children

I, _____ give my permission to
    (name of parent or guardian)

_____ to see my son/daughter,
    (staff counselor)

_____ for treatment or counseling,
    (name of minor child)

with and/or without me being present in the same session. I/WE understand that we are the holder of confidential privilege—the right to withhold disclosure of private counseling information about my/our child(ren). However, in the interest of developing a trust relationship between the counselor and my/our child(ren), I/WE give the counselor permission to reveal or withhold information that in her/his clinical judgment is necessary to best help and protect my/our child(ren).

The only exception to this discretion would be in the case of :

_____

_____

_____

Parent/Guardian/Authorized Signature

_____

Date _____

Therapist/Witness _____Date _____

Appendix I: Consent For Treatment Governed
By An HMO Or Managed Care

Third party payment for this treatment of _____
is provided by _____ ,
a managed care company. Requirements of that payor include:

1. A release of information/waiver of confidentiality must be signed by the payor. In order to certify treatment, the managed care company will require the therapist to provide considerable personal information, including, but not limited to, current life situations, current and past functioning, personal and family history, past and present alcohol/drug use, previous treatment and diagnosis of mental disorder.

2. All treatment must be pre-certified. If treatment continues beyond the initial certification period, the therapist will make all reasonable efforts to arrange for continuing care without interruption. This may not always be possible. If a lapse in certification occurs, treatment may be temporarily discontinued. Alternately, the consumer may pay for sessions that are provided between or after certifications (if allowed by the managed care company involved.)

3. Any sessions that are missed without notification to this office at least 24 hours before the appointment will be the financial responsibility of the consumer.

I understand and agree to the above terms of this Consent.

_____   _____

Signature   Date

Name (printed)

_____

Appendix J: Christian Counseling Treatment Plan

Patient Name

_____

Date of
Intake_____

Referral
Source_____

Reason for
Referral_____

Medications _____

_____

_____

Physicians: _____

_____

_____

Collaborative Contacts:

_____

_____

Release of Information discussed and signed. __Yes __ No __Refused

Reason for refusal_____

Client Assessments None -Low-Average-High

Level of motivation: 0 1 2 3 4 5 6 7 8 9 10
Level of cooperation: 0 1 2 3 4 5 6 7 8 9 10

Insight into problem: 0 1 2 3 4 5 6 7 8 9 10
Level of distress: 0. 1 2 3 4 5 6 7 8 9 10

Level of hopefulness: 012345678910
Level of belief: 012345678910
Self described closeness to God: 012345678910
Level of obedience to biblical directives: 012345678910
Level of spiritual temptation: 012345678910

Level of Spiritual Disciplines

Prayer __active __fair __poor ___none
Worship __active __fair __poor ___none

Fellowship __active __fair __poor ___none
Quiet time __active __fair __poor ___none

Bible Study __active __fair __poor ___none
Service __active __fair __poor ___none

Accountability __active __fair __poor ___none
Self control __active __fair __poor ___none

Presenting Problem(s) in Clients Own Words

_____
_____
_____
_____

Onset

_____
_____

Duration

_____
_____

Previous therapy No__ Yes___
Problem focus_____

Therapist name_____

Date of service_____

Release of Information __Yes __No __Declined
Reason for refusal_____

Axis I symptom:

Cognitive:

Emotional:

Social:

Behavioral:

Physical/Medical:

Spiritual:

Axis I Primary
DX_____
Dual_____
Secondary Dx_____Comorbidity_____
Other, including V. codes that may be of clinical concern or attention.

_____

_____

Axis II
__Personality Disorder_____
__Mental Retardation_____
__No diagnosis, V.71.09

Axis III General Medical Conditions: None ____

_____

_____

Axis IV Psychosocial and/or Environmental Stressors

Stressor Chronic/Acute Mild Moderate Severe
__ with primary support group
(divorce, separation, death, illness, conflict, birth of child, discord with
family member, abuse, neglect, family member abuse of substances, child
discipline, removal from home, caring for ill or aged family member,
remarriage, estrangement, over-controlling behaviors, health or disability
problems)

__related to social environment
(a long distance move, retirement, loss of social support, death of friend,
discrimination, single parent, living alone, limited transportation, crime,
limited access to resources)

__with educational problems
(discord with teachers, academic noncompliance, bullying, and problems
with classmates, truancy, adjustment to academic disability, illiteracy, limited or restricted use of educational resources)

__with occupation
(loss of job, new job, threat of job loss, boss or coworker discord, stressful
work donations, overwork schedule, job dissatisfaction, discrimination,
demotion)

__with housing
(recent move, homelessness, overcrowding, waiting to get a home, unsafe
neighborhood, discord with neighbors, landlord, poor housing conditions,
displaced due to fire or natural disasters)

__with financiers
(poverty, loss of income, bankruptcy, inadequate finances, high credit debt,
loss of credit, creditor conflicts, loss of income due to health problems,
inadequate child or welfare support, audit, loss of business)

__health care availability
(inadequate or loss of insurance, inadequate health care services or
transportation to such, services unavailable, change in health lifestyle)

__related to legal system
(arrest, court appearance, investigation, litigation, crime victim, incarceration or incarceration of loved one, probation/parole, suspended license)

__related to medical condition
(chronic illness or disability, family member who is seriously sick, caring for ill loved one, recent physical accident, recent diagnosis of a life changing disorder, loss of appendage, physical disfigurement, or organ, miscarriage)

__ traumatic exposure
(witness to crime or accident, violent crime victim, secondary trauma, natural disaster, war, riot, severe disaster like a fire, animal attack, abortion)

Axis V. Global Assessment of Functioning Scale (GAF)

__0–10 Persistent severity of danger TO SELF OR OTHERS or inability to maintain personal hygiene.
__11–20 Some danger to self or others, occasionally fails to maintain hygiene, incoherent.
__21–30 Psychotic influence on behavior, seriously impaired judgment or communication, incapacitated in all areas of functioning.
__31–40 Minimal impairment to reality testing and communication, or major impairment in several areas of social functioning, judgment, thinking or mood.
__41–50 Serious symptoms of suicidal ideation, obsession, impulse controls, or in any serious impairment in social, occupational or school functioning.
__51–60 Moderate psychological symptoms or moderate impairment in social, occupational or school functioning.
__61–70 Mild psychological symptoms or impairment in social, occupational or school functioning. Overall functioning is adequate.
__71–80 Transient, expected symptoms to psychosocial stressors. Slight impairment in social, occupational or school functioning.
__81–90 Absent or minimal symptoms, generally satisfied with life, effective personal and social functioning.
__91–100 Superior functioning in a wide range of activities. No symptoms.

Treatment Modality: __Cognitive Behavioral Therapy
__Cognitive-Behavioral Conjoint Therapy
__Cognitive-Behavioral Family Therapy
__Cognitive-Behavioral Marital Therapy

__individual __conjoint __family __marital __group

Treatment Plan
1. Problem Focus

_____

_____

Likert Scale of severity 0 1 2 3 4 5 6 7 8 9 10
Mild——————————severe
Goal_____

Planned Interventions

_____

_____

2. Problem Focus

_____

_____

Likert Scale of severity 0 1 2 3 4 5 6 7 8 9 10

Goal_____

_____

_____

Planned Interventions

_____

_____

3. Problem Focus

_____

_____

Likert Scale of severity 1 2 3 4 5 6 7 8 9 10
Goal_____

_____

_____

Planned Interventions

_____

_____

4. Problem Focus

_____

_____

Likert Scale of severity 01 2 3 4 6 7 8 9 10

Goal_____

_____

_____

Planned Interventions

_____

_____

Estimated number of session_____ Estimated date of termination_____

Signature of therapist_____Date_____

Appendix K: Case Record Form

Client's Name_____Date_____
___Dx._____Code_____

Others present_____

Modality: Cogntive-Behavioral

Therapy/other_____

Progress/Goal #	_Progress/Goal#	_Progress/Goal #
__Completed	__Completed	__Completed
__Excellent	__Excellent	__Excellent
__Adequate	__Adequate	__Adequate
__Poor	__Poor	__ Poor
__None	__None	__ None

GAF___

Notes_____
_____

Outcome of Session_____

Plan/Homework_____

Change of Goals _____

Additional Notes _____

_____
Signature of Therapist   Date

Appendix L: Treatment Summary Form

Client's Name _____

Initial Session _____Last Session_____

Total Sessions to date____ Missed Sessions_____

Anticipated number of sessions to complete treatment_____

Referral Source_____

Medications_____

Reasons for counseling _____
_____

Final DX
Axis I _____

Axis II _____

Axis III_____

Axis IV _____

Axis V current_____at intake_____highest past year_____

Goal(s) Status
Goal 1 _____ Goal 2_____

Completed ___   Completed___
Noncompliance__   Noncompliance___

Partial completion__   Partial completion___
Relapse prevention/booster__   Relapse prevention/booster____

Goal 3_____ Goal 4_____

Completed__   Completed___
Noncompliance__   Noncompliance___
Partial completion__   Partial completion___
Relapse prevention/booster__   Relapse prevention/booster__
Relapse__   Relapse__

Intervention_____

modality __ individual __ conjoint __ family __ group___ marital___

Reasons for termination_____

_____

Referral to other therapist_____

Signature_____Date_____

Appendix M: Counseling Exit Assessment Form

Please take a few minutes to fill out this exit form. This will help us know how helpful (or not) we were to you and how to improve our services in the future. Please leave this form at the front desk or send it to

_____.

We will maintain your strict confidence about this form. Thank you.

1. Your name_____

2. Today's date_____

3. Address_____

4. Phone_____

5. Therapist(s) name_____

6. Type of service rendered: ___individual counseling/adult
___individual counseling/child   ___marital counseling
___family counseling   ___group counseling/education
___psychosocial/custody evaluation   ___separation/divorce mediation
___pre-marital   ___consultation
___education/training
___other (describe)_____

7. Approx. dates of services (mo/yr to mo/yr) _____

8. Overall, were you satisfied with the help you received from counseling or other services?
___highly satisfied   ___somewhat satisfied
___mixed feelings
___somewhat dissatisfied   ___highly dissatisfied

9. Compared to the start of counseling, how would you now rate your improvement in counseling?

____worse than before ____about the same

____slightly improved ____much improved

____greatly improved

10. If satisfied, what did you like most (one or two things)?

_____

_____

11. If dissatisfied, what is your complaint?

_____

_____

12. Did your counselor understand your problem and needs?

____yes, great understanding ____yes, mostly understood

____no, didn't understand ____not sure

13. Did your counselor respect your views and values?

____yes, greatly respected ____yes, mostly respected

____no, didn't respect ____not sure

14. Did your counselor rely on Christian resources—prayer, use of the Bible, respect for God and Christ—in helpful ways?

____yes, very helpful ____yes, somewhat helpful

____no, not helpful ____no, not wanted or appropriate

____not sure

15. Were there any problems during counseling with any of the following issues?

____fee disputes/problems ____confidentiality

____sexual actions or communications

____too passive/not enough advice

____too controlling/not enough listening and support

____lack of/inaccurate knowledge

____timely and adequate phone response

____ competent response to emergencies

____friendliness/helpfulness of office staff

____improper/incompetent treatment

____late/poor preparation for sessions

____inadequate/poor referral or consultation with other helping professionals

16. Explain any issues checked above or not listed_____

_____

_____

Appendix N: Subpoena Response Letter

GEORGE OHLSCHLAGER, J.D., LCSW
COUNSELING & PSYCHOTHERAPY · MEDIATION & PEACEMAKING
CONSULTING & SPEAKING

Date

Address

Dear Lawyer Such-and-so:

I have received your subpoena dated _____. As you are probably aware, at this stage I am duty-bound as a licensed mental health professional to assert privilege—to zealously protect the confidences of my client—about the records you demand under *Section 1010 of the California Evidence Code.* I am also instructed to assert privilege as the first step in response to legal or court demands according to sections 1–420 and 1–421 of the *AACC Christian Counseling Code of Ethics,* to which I also adhere.

Of course my assertion of privilege in no way means that I am resisting compliance with this subpoena. I am merely fulfilling the intent of any privilege statute—protecting my client's confidence and giving them the needed time he/she deserves in order to consult with a lawyer about this action. All relevant clinical records will be turned over to my client's attorney. I trust that after appropriate legal consultation, my client and his/her lawyer will respond to this subpoena as required by law.

Any further correspondence on this matter should take place directly with my client's attorney. Thank you.

Sincerely,

George Ohlschlager, JD, LCSW

Office: 3015 F Street, Eureka, CA 95501 · Mail: PO Box 6638, Eureka, CA 95502

Appendix O: Professional Christian Counseling

Definition of an Emerging Profession-Specialty

**A Proposal for Credentialing and Public Communication
to be advocated by the American Association of Christian Counselors
and the American Board of Christian Counselors**

August 2005

Base Definition

Professional Christian counseling integrates Christian spiritual formation with the best of modern mental health practice for client and community betterment. Christian counseling is holistic in that it is oriented toward a bio-psycho-social-*spiritual* assessment and intervention. Furthermore, the treatment and prevention of mental/emotional/character disorders is joined with the goal of growing up into Christian maturity. Christian counselors combine, in complementary fashion, the very best of Christian ministry and clinical mental health knowledge with dedicated, caring service to individuals, marriages, families, churches, organizations, and communities. At its best, professional Christian counseling integrates the best theory and proven methods of the mental health professions with biblical truths and spiritual practices to produce "Christ-like" character, behavior, and contentment in the lives of the people and systems served.

Professional Christian counseling, then, is Christ-centered soul-care, melding modern clinical science with ancient biblical truths to the honor of God and the wellness-maturity of clients and client systems.

Christian Counselors

Professional Christian counselors are both confessing Christians and licensed/certified/registered mental health professionals dedicated to serve others in the integrative manner described above. Whenever appropriate, these professionals bring the life of Jesus Christ into the work of counseling, psychotherapy, medical and psychiatric treatment, testing and evaluation, mediation and arbitration, counselor supervision, teaching and research, administration, consultation, speaking, and church, courtroom, and legislative testimony.

Christian counselors also—when in the client's interest, with their consent, and when appropriate in therapy—pray for and with clients, read the Bible and make reference to Scripture, encourage the confession of sin, the practice of forgiveness, the making of amends, support the practice of spiritual disciplines, and give assistance or make referral for spiritual warfare and other specialized practices. When consent does not exist, Christian counselors may be engaged in these activities silently and implicitly, always functioning in the best interests of their clients.

These spiritual practices are not illegal, unethical, or illegitimate, nor are they antagonistic to the forementioned clinical purposes and practices. Christian counseling is not dichotomized into sacred and secular compartments but, from the perspective of the mental health professions, is rightly seen as holistic, adjunctive and integrative.

This integrative work is a central aspect of the Christian counselor's lifelong challenge to become a helper of excellence and ethical integrity. Christian counseling integration is not excessively complex nor is it simplistic and reductionistic. Christian counselors understand and revere the spiritual dimension of human nature and change—best known through encountering Christ and growing in a life of faith in Him. They also diligently search for and apply the best data and practices of the behavioral and social sciences.

Tying these various threads together in clinical practice, Christian counselors understand and respect the role of cognitive, behavioral, moral, emotional, relational, and environmental forces in human and social change. They also invite God's power to transform and sanctify this change, properly using God's Word and the ministry of His church.

Common Values, Practices, and Ethics

Christian counselors accord the highest respect to the triune God revealed in the Holy Scriptures, our foundation of faith and ethical conduct. They are also dedicated to the best interests of their patients and clients, to the law and the ethical standards of their respective clinical professions, to their contractual obligations in the workplace, and to select and proven data from the bio-psycho-social sciences.

However, regardless of religious creed or preferred clinical theory, Christian counselors are bound together by these common goals:

- knowing and loving God;
- loving and serving others;
- avoiding all harm toward clients and others;
- bringing truth, healing, and agreed change into people's lives;
- helping set people free from sin, bondage, mental disorder, and emotional distress;
- making peace and doing justice; and assisting the church, community, and profession to grow to its full maturity.

Christian counselors strive to come alongside those seeking help, listen with the heart, and speak the truth-in-love. They are dedicated to listen carefully to clients, to respect them, to understand their hurts, sins, and fears, and to encourage faith, hope, and love. Christian counselors humbly challenge client distortions and wrongdoing and, by mutual agreement, help clients renounce the ways of sin and change in the direction of growth and maturity in Christ. They offer the empathic heart of understanding, the consoling voice of comfort, the guiding hope of godly reason, and the assertive challenge to change, whichever is needed at the proper time in therapy.

Christian counselors are committed to disciplined learning and faithful growth in counseling knowledge, gifts, and skills. When appropriate, Christian counselors testify to the saving grace and sanctifying power of Jesus Christ. They avoid imposing their values and beliefs on clients and, at the other extreme, they are not silent about God's love and grace. Christian counselors strive to maintain their integrity to Christ and His revelation in Scripture, while also contributing to the growth of psychosocial knowledge and clinical skill that is inherent to all professional practice and development. They are dedicated to a continual evaluation and improvement of their practices in order to fulfill the call to excellence as mental health practitioners and as Christian counselors.

Christian counselors serve clients with excellence and ethical integrity—practicing with the utmost respect, sensitivity, honesty, energy, and capability. They do not use clients for their own personal gain and strictly avoid all client harm and exploitation. They avoid activities that violate or diminish the civil and legal rights of clients and client systems. They do not discriminate in the provision of client services on the basis of gender, race, ethnicity, disability, religious creed, denomination, socio-economic status, national origin, or sexual orientation.

Aspiring to honor Christ in all things, Christian counselors are committed to moral purity and honesty, committed to maintain personal, professional, and organizational integrity. Aspiring for excellence in service, they know and respect the limits of their competence, do consult, refer, and network with other service providers, and continually study to improve their excellence in service to Christ and to others. Christian counselors maintain professional integrity in relations with the state, with state licensure boards, with the church, with professional associations, and with employers and colleagues. They understand both their duties to the state and other organizations and the limits of the authoritative powers these state and private institutions hold.

Christian counselors have the right—a right grounded in the Scriptures and protected by the religion and free speech clauses of the First Amendment and the Fourteenth Amendment to the United States Constitution—to identify publicly as Christian counselors and to always maintain this integrated clinical-spiritual practice regardless of professional association or licensure status. This right cannot be abrogated or substantially diminished by any court, state legislature, licensure board, or any professional association.

The Christian Counseling Profession

Christian counseling is a dynamic, expanding, and multidisciplinary field of practice. Over a half-century of development and growth has witnessed a complex professional-ministerial-social organism come to fruition. There are numerous Christian counseling professional associations that are national in scope at the inception of the 21st century, including the largest group, the 50,000 member *American Association of Christian Counselors* (AACC). Dozens of graduate training programs exist in all parts of the country, integrated with programs in psychology, social work, marriage and family therapy, and professional counselor training. There are at least 25,000 mental health professionals across the 50 states who also identify in some manner as Christian counselors.

More specifically, the AACC has published a *Christian Counseling Code of Ethics* and, with the *American Board of Christian Counselors,* is moving toward delivery of national practice standards and credentials in Christian counseling. Many national, refereed journals on Christian counseling now exist, over one hundred books are published annually, and training, seminar, and conference resources are mushrooming at many levels. Numerous managed care groups across America have recognized and refer specifically to Christian counselors as more and more subscribers demand this service. Finally, dubious though it may be as a mark of professional maturity, liability insurance can now be purchased for Christian counseling practice.

Christ is the bridge by which Christian counseling integrates both spiritual ministry and professional mental health practice. Since all truth is from God, Christian counseling facilitates understanding and integration between the empirical truths of general revelation and the truth of God's special revelation in Christ. Christian counseling is an emerging profession that is distinctive in its ministry to Christendom and society-at-large. Moreover, in relationship to the mental health professions it is also adjunctive and integrative, a specialty form of traditional mental health practice in every discipline—psychology, psychiatry, social work, marriage and family therapy, professional counseling, and nursing.

Christian counseling is an emerging profession wherein people are able to identify as Christian counselors and grow in their personal and professional lives. It is also an interdisciplinary organism by which professional unity is genuinely achievable in Christ. Because of Christ, the Christian counseling profession holds out the promise of overshadowing the turf-protecting enmity and professional prejudice that can otherwise infect relations between the people and disciplines of the mental health enterprise. In Christ, helpers from all recognized groups are challenged to stand together, in mutual and humble service, proclaiming both their professional distinctives and their common Christian mission.

References

Adams, J. (1970). *Competent to counsel.* United States: Presbyterian and Reformed Publishing Company.

Adler, A. (1959). *Understanding human nature.* New York: Premier Books.

Adler, A. (1963). *The practice and theory of individual psychology.* Patterson, NJ: Littlefield.

Adler, N. (1975). Emotional responses of women following therapeutic abortion. *American Journal of Orthopsychiatry, 45,* 446–454.

Ahern, J., Galea, S., Resnick, H., Kilpatrick, D., Bucuvalas, M., Gold, J., & Vlahov, D. (2002). Television images and psychological symptoms after the September 11 terrorist attacks. *Psychiatry: Interpersonal & Biological Processes, 65*(4), 289–301.

Ainsworth, M., Blehar, M. C., Waters, E., & Wall, S. (1978). *Patterns of attachment: A psychological study of the strange situation.* Hillsdale, NJ: Erlbaum.

Alacorn, R. D., Glover, S. G., & Deering, C. G. (1999). The cascade model: An alternative to comorbidity in the pathogenesis of post-traumatic stress disorder. *Psychiatry, 62,* 114–124.

Alan Guttmacher Institute. (1997, January). *Facts in brief: Induced abortion,* Washington, DC.

Alexander, J. A. (1846). *The Earlier Prophecies of Isaiah.* New York: Wiley and Putnam.

Allen, J. G. (1999). *Coping with trauma: A guide to self-understanding.* American Psychiatric Press Inc.

Allender, D. B. (1999). *The healing path: How the hurts in your past can lead you to a more abundant life.* Colorado Springs: WaterBrook.

Allender, D. B. (2005). *To be told.* Colorado Springs: WaterBrook Press.

Amen, D. (1998). *Change your brain change your life.* New York: Random House.

American Association of Christian Counselors. (2001). *AACC Christian counseling code of ethics.* Forest, VA: AACC.

American Psychiatric Association Work Group on Eating Disorders. (2000). Practical guidelines for the treatment of patients with eating disorders (revision). *American Journal of Psychiatry, 157,* (1 Suppl): 1–39.

American Psychiatric Association. (1980). *Diagnostic and statistical manual of mental disorders* (3rd ed.). Washington, DC: APA.

American Psychiatric Association. (1987). *Diagnostic and statistical manual of mental disorders* (3rd ed. revised). Washington, DC: APA.

American Psychiatric Association. (1994). *Diagnostic and statistical manual of mental disorders* (4th ed.). Washington, DC: APA.

American Psychiatric Association. (1999). *Let's talk facts about post-traumatic stress disorder.* Retrieved on June 20, 2005 from http://www.psych.org/public_info/ptsd.cfm.

American Psychiatric Association. (2000). *Diagnostic and statistical manual of mental disorders* (4th ed., text rev.). Washington, DC: APA.

Anderson, A. (1995). Eating disorders in males. In K.D. Brownell, & C G. Fairburn, (Eds.), *Eating disorders and obesity: A comprehensive handbook.* New York: The Guilford Press.

Anderson, N. T. (2003). *Discipleship counseling.* Ventura, CA: Regal Books.

Andreasen, N.C. (1985). Post-traumatic stress disorder. In H.I. Kaplan and B.J. Sadock (Eds.). *Comprehensive textbook of psychiatry* (4th ed.). Baltimore: Williams and Wilkins.

Anton, S., & Mrdenovi, S. (2005). Working ability of patients with post-traumatic stress disorder (demographic and social features): Comparative study. *Journal of Loss & Trauma. 10*(2), 155–162.

Apter, A., Kotler, M., Levy, S., Plutchik, R., Brown, S., Foster, H., Hillbrand, M., Korn, M., & van Praag, H. (1991). Correlates of risk of suicide in violent and nonviolent psychiatric patients. *American Journal of Psychiatry, 148* (7), 883–887.

Arata, C. M. (1999). Sexual revictimization and PTSD: An exploratory study. *Journal of Child Sexual Abuse. 8(1),* 49–66.

Arteburn, S. & Stoeker, F. (2000). *Every Man's Battle.* Colorado Springs, CO.: WaterBrook Press.

Arterburn, S. (2003). *Addicted to love.* United Kingdom: Vine Books.

Attig, T. (1996). *How we grieve: Relearning the world.* New York: Oxford University Press.

Backus, W. (1985). *Telling each other the truth.* Minneapolis, MN: Bethany House.

Backus, W. (1985). *Telling the truth to troubled people: A manual for Christian counselors.* Minneapolis, MN: Bethany House.

Backus, W. (2000). *What your counselor never told you: Conquer the power of sin in your life.* Minneapolis, MN: Bethany House.

Bagley, C. (1990). Development of a measure of unwanted sexual contact in childhood for use in community mental health surveys. *Psychological Reports, 66,* 401–2.

Bagley, C. (1991). The prevalence and mental health sequelae of child sexual abuse in a community sample of women aged 18 to 27. *Canadian Journal of Community Mental Health, 10,* 103–116.

Balk, D. E. (1996). Attachment and the reactions of bereaved college students: A longitudinal study. In D. Klass, P. R. Silverman, & S. L. Nickman (Eds.). *Continuing bonds: New understandings of grief* (pp. 311–328). Washington, DC: Taylor & Francis.

Barna Group. (2003, November 3). Morality continues to decay. *The Barna Update*. Retrieved from http://www.barna.org.

Bart, M. (1998, December). Spirituality in counseling finding believers. *Counseling Today*. Alexandria, VA: American Counseling Association.

Basco, M., & Rush, A. J. (1996). *Cognitive-behavioral therapy for bipolar disorder*. New York: Guilford Press.

Baucom, D.H., Epstein, N., Sayers, S., & Sher, T.G. (1989). The role of cognitions in marital relationships: Definitional, methodological, and conceptual issues. *Journal of Consulting and Clinical Psychology, 57,* 31–38.

Beattie, M. (1987). *Codependent no more*. New York: Harper/Hazelden.

Beck, A. T., Rush, A. J., Shaw, B. F., & Emery, G. (1979). *Cognitive therapy of depression*. New York: Guilford Press.

Beck, A., Brown, G., Berchick, R., Stewart, B., & Steer, R. (1990). Relationship between hopelessness and ultimate suicide: A replication with psychiatric outpatients. *American Journal of Psychiatry, 147*(2), 190–195.

Beck, A., Resnik, H., & Lettieri, D. (Eds.). (1974). *The prediction of suicide*. Bowie, Maryland: Charles Press.

Beck, A.T., Rush, A.J., Shaw, B.F., & Emery, G. (1979). *Cognitive therapy of depression*. New York: Guilford Press.

Beck, J. (1995). *Cognitive therapy: Basics and beyond*. New York: Guilford.

Becker, E. (1973). *The denial of death*. New York: The Free Press.

Becvar, D. S., and Becvar, R. J. (1993). *Family therapy: A systemic integration*. Boston: Allyn and Bacon.

Bergin, A. E. (1991). Values and religious issues in psychotherapy and mental health. *American Psychologist, 46,* 394–403.

Bergin, A. E., & Jensen, J. P. (1990). Religiosity of psychotherapists: A national survey. *Psychotherapy, 27,* 3–7.

Bisson, J. I., McFarlane, A. C., & Rose, S. (2000). Psychological debriefing. In E. B. Foa (Ed.), *Effective treatments for PTSD*, (pp. 39–59). New York: Guilford Press.

Black, D. & Winokur, G. (1986). Prospective studies of suicide and mortality in psychiatric patients. *Annals of the New York Academy of Sciences, 487,* 106–113.

Blackenhorn, D. (1995). *Fatherless America: Confronting our most urgent social problem*. New York: Basic Books.

Blank, A. S. (1993). The longitudinal course of posttraumatic stress disorder, *In Post-traumatic stress disorder: DSM IV and beyond*. Washington DC: American Psychiatric Press.

Bloomfield, H. (1998). *Healing anxiety naturally*. New York: HarperPerennial.

Bork, R. (1996). Inconvenient lives. *First Things, 68,* 13.

Bourne, E. J. (2001). *Beyond anxiety and phobia*. Oakland: New Harbinger.

Bowlby, J. (1979). *The making and breaking of affectional bonds*. New York: Routledge.

Bowlby, J. (1980). *Attachment and loss (Vol. 3). Loss: sadness and depression*. New York: Basic Books.

Bowlby, J. (1988). *A secure base: Parent-child attachment and healthy human development.* New York: Basic Books.

Brammer, L., Abrego, P., & Shostrom, E. (1998). *Therapeutic counseling and psychotherapy* (7th ed.). Englewood Cliffs, NJ: Prentice-Hall.

Breen, R.B. & Zimmerman, M. (2000). Rapid onset of pathological gambling in machine gamblers. *Department of Psychiatry and Human Behavior, Brown University School of Medicine.*

Breslau, N., & Davis, G. C. (1992). Posttraumatic stress disorder in an urban population of young adults: Risk factors for chronicity. *American Journal of Psychiatry, 149,* 671–675.

Briere, J. (1996). Treating adult survivors of severe childhood abuse and neglect: Further development of an integrative model. In *The APSAC handbook on child maltreatment, (2nd Ed.).* Newbury Park, CA: Sage Publications.

Brody, J. E. (1992, March 27). Study defines 'binge eating disorder': Report from Dr. Robert L. Spitzer at the Annual Scientific Meeting of the Society of Behavioral Medicine. *New York Times,* A16.

Broida, M. (2001). *New hope for people with depression.* Roseville, CA: Prima Publishing.

Brown, R. (1983). *Elie Wiesel: Messenger to all humanity.* South Bend, IN: Notre Dame Univ. Press.

Burke, T., & Reardon, D. C. (2002). *Forbidden grief: The unspoken pain of abortion.* USA: Acorn Books.

Burns, D. (1999). *Feeling good.* New York: William Morrow.

Caplan, G. (1964). *Principals of preventive psychiatry.* New York: Basic Books.

Carnes, P. (1984). *Out of the shadows.* Minneapolis: Comp Care.

Carnes, P. (1989). *Contrary to love.* Minneapolis: CompCare.

Carnes, P. (1991). *Don't call it love.* New York: Bantam Books.

Carnes, P. (1997). *The betrayal bond.* Deerfield Beach, FL: Health Communications, Inc.

Carnes, P., Laaser, D., & Laaser, M. (2000). *Open hearts.* Wickensburg, AZ: Gentle Path Press.

Carter, B., and McGoldrick, M. (1989). *The changing family life cycle.* Boston: Allyn and Bacon.

Centers for Disease Control and Prevention (2002). *Suicide injury fact book.* Retrieved August, 2005 from http://www.cdc.gov/ncipc/fact_book/26_Suicide.htm.

Chemtob, C., Bauer, G., Hamada, R., Pelowski, S., & Muraoka, M. (1989). Patient suicide: Occupational hazard for psychologists and psychiatrists. *Professional Psychology: Research and Practice, 20* (5), 294–300.

Chilstrom, C. (1989). Suicide and pastoral care. *The Journal of Pastoral Care, 43*(3), 199–208.

Christensen, C. M. (2003). *Power over panic: Answers for anxiety.* Colorado Springs: Life Journey.

Christensen, P. N., Cohan, S. L., & Stein, M. B. (2004). The relationship between interpersonal perception and post-traumatic stress disorder-related functional impairment: A social relations model analysis. *Cognitive Behaviour Therapy, 33*(3), 151–161.

Clemmons, A. (1991). The pastor and the institute. *Parakaleo, 3*, 1–2. Eureka, CA: The Redwood Family Institute.

Clinton, T, & Ohlschlager, G. (2002). *Competent Christian counseling, volume one: Foundations and practice of compassionate soul care.* Colorado Springs: WaterBrook Press.

Clinton, T., & Sibcy, G. (2002). *Attachments: Why you love, feel and act the way you do.* Brentwood, TN: Integrity.

Collins, G. (1995). *How to be a people helper.* USA: Tyndale.

Collins, G. R. (1988). *Christian counseling: A comprehensive guide*, rev. ed. Nashville: W Publishing Group.

Colson, C. (1995, October 2). Wanted: Christians who love. *Christianity Today, 112.*

Convissor, K. (1992). *Young widow: Learning to live again.* Grand Rapids, MI: Zondervan.

Cook, S. A. and Dworkin, D. S. (1992). *Helping the bereaved.* New York: Basic Books.

Copeland, M. E. (2001). *The depression workbook* (2nd ed.). Oakland, CA: New Harbinger.

Corey, G. (2000). *Theory and practice of counseling and psychotherapy* (6th ed.). Pacific Grove, CA: Brooks/Cole.

Corey, G., Corey, M., & Callanan, P. (1998). *Issues and ethics in the helping professions* (5th ed.). Pacific Grove, CA: Brooks/Cole.

Courtois, C. A. & Watts, D. L. (1982, January). Counseling adult women who experienced incest in childhood or adolescence. *The Personnel and Guidance Journal*, 275–279.

Crabb, L (1977). *Effective biblical counseling: A model for helping caring Christians become capable counselors.* Grand Rapids, MI: Zondervan.

Crabb, L. (1997). *Connecting.* Nashville: W Publishing Group.

Craighead, W. E., Hart, A. B., Craighead, L. W., & Ilardi, S. S. (2002). Psychosocial treatments for major depressive disorder. In P. E. Nathan & J. M. Gorman (Eds.), *A guide to treatments that work* (2nd ed., pp. 245–261). New York: Oxford University Press.

Craighead, W. E., Miklowitz, D. J., Frank, E., & Vajk, F. C. (2002). Psychosocial treatments for bipolar disorder. In P. E. Nathan & J. M. Gorman (Eds.), *A guide to treatments that work* (2nd ed., pp. 263–275). New York: Oxford University Press.

Cufee, S., Addy, C., Garrison, C., Waller, J., Jackson, K., Mckeown, R., & Chilappagari, S. (1998, February). Prevalence of PTSD in a community sample of older adolescents. *Journal of the American Academy of Child & Adolescent Psychiatry, 37*(2), 147–154.

Daud, A., Skoglund, E., Rydelius, P. (2005). Children in families of torture victims: Transgenerational transmission of parents' traumatic experiences to their children. *International Journal of Social Welfare, 14*(1), 23–33.

Davidson, G. W. (1984). *Understanding mourning: A guide for those who grieve.* Minneapolis: Augsburg.

De Bellis, M. D., Keshavan, M. S., Shifflett, H., Iyengar, S., Beers, S. R., Hall, J., & Moritz, G. (2002, December). Brain structures in pediatric maltreatment-related posttraumatic stress disorder: A sociodemographically matched study. *Biological Psychiatry, 52*(11), 1066–1079.

Desai, R. A., Dausey, D. J., Rosenheck, R. A. (2005, February). Mental health service delivery and suicide risk: The role of individual patient and facility factors. *American Journal of Psychiatry, 162*(2), 311–319.

Dissanayake, C., & Crossley, S. A. (1996, February). Proximity and sociable behaviours in autism: Evidence for attachment. *Journal of Child Psychol Psychiatry, 37*(2), 149–156.

Dobie, D. J., Kivlahan, D. R., Maynard, C., Bush, K. R., Davis, T. M., & Bradley, K. A. (2004, February). Post-traumatic stress disorder in female veterans: Association with self-reported health problems and functional impairment. *Archives of Internal Medicine, 164*(4), 394–401.

Egan, G. (1998). *The skilled helper: A problem-management approach to helping* (6th ed.). Pacific Grove, CA: Brooks/Cole.

Earle, R. & Crow, G. (1989). *Lonely all the time*. New York: Pocket.

Earle, R. H., Earle, M. R., & Osborn, K. (1995). *Sex addiction: Case studies and management*. New York, NY: Brunner/Mazel, Inc.

Ebert, A., & Dyck, M. J. (2004, October). The experience of mental death: The core feature of complex post-traumatic stress disorder. *Clinical Psychology Review, 24*(6), 617–36.

Ehrenreich, B. (1992, January). Cauldron of anger. *Life, 15*, 62–68.

Ellis, A. (1998). *The Albert Ellis reader: A guide to well-being using rational emotive behavior therapy*. NY: Citadel Press.

Engelhardt, H. T. (2000). *The foundations of Christian bioethics*. Exton, PA: Swets and Zeitlinger.

Erickson, M. (1983). *Christian theology*, Grand Rapids, MI: Baker.

Exline, J. J., Smyth, J. M., Gregory, J., Hockemeyer, J., & Tulloch, H. (2005). Religious framing by individuals with PTSD when writing about traumatic experiences. *International Journal for the Psychology of Religion, 15*(1), 17–34.

Fagan, N., & Freme, K. (2004, February). Confronting posttraumatic stress disorder. *Nursing, 34*(2), 52–54.

Faulkner, N. (1996). *Sexual abuse recognition and non-disclosure inventory of young adolescents*. Ann Arbor, MI: UMI.

Fawcett, J., Golden, B., & Rosenfeld, N. (2000). *New hope for people with bipolar disorder*. Roseville, CA: Prima Publishing.

Ferrada-Noli, M., Asberg, M., Ormstad, K., Lundin, T., & Sundbom, E. (1998, January).

Ferree, M. (2002). *No stones: Women redeemed from sexual shame*. Fairfax, VA: Xulon.

Finkelhor, D. & Browne, A. (1986). Impact of child sexual abuse: a review of the research. *Psychological Bulletin, 99*, 66–77.

Finkelhor, D., Hotaling, G., Lewis, I. A., & Smith, C. (1990). Sexual abuse in a national survey of adult men and women: Prevalence, characteristics, and risk factors. *Child Abuse & Neglect, 14*, 19–28.

Flach, F. F. (1974). *The secret strength of depression*. Philadelphia: Lippincott.

Fonagy, P. (1999). *Pathological attachments and therapeutic action*. Paper presented at the annual meeting of the California Branch of the American Academy of Child and Adolescent Psychiatry, Yosemite Valley, CA.

Forrester, K. S. (2002). *Determining the Biblical traits and spiritual disciplines Christian counselors employ in practice: A delphi study*. PhD dissertation, Southwestern Baptist Theological Seminary. Fort Worth, TX.

Foster, R. (1978). *Celebration of discipline.* San Francisco: Harper & Row.

Fraley, R. C. and Shaver, P. R. (1999). Loss and bereavement: Attachment theory and recent controversies concerning "grief work" and the nature of detachment. In J. Cassidy & P.R. Shaver (Eds.). *Handbook of attachment: Theory, research, and clinical applications.* New York: Guilford.

Frances, A., & First, A. B. (1998). *Your mental health: A layman's guide to the psychiatrist's bible.* New York: Scribner.

Frankl, V. (1984). *Man's search for meaning* (rev. ed). New York: Pocket Books.

Frans, Ö., Rimmö, P. A., Åberg, L., Fredrikson, M. (2005, April). Trauma exposure and post-traumatic stress disorder in the general population. *Acta Psychiatrica Scandinavica, 111*(4), 291–293.

Fredman, S., and Rosenbaum G. F. (n.d.). *Treatment of anxiety disorders with comorbid depression.* Retrieved from <http://www.medscape.com>

Freud, S. (1917). *Mourning and melancholia. SE,* 14:243–58.

Frommberger, U., Stieglitz, R., Nyberg, E., Richter, H., Novelli-Fischer, U., Angenendt, J., Zaninelli, R., & Berger, M. (2004, March). Comparison between paroxetine and behaviour therapy in patients with post-traumatic *stress disorder* (PTSD): A pilot study. *International Journal of Psychiatry in Clinical Practice, 8*(1), 19–24.

Frude, N. (1990). *Understanding family problems.* Chichester: J. Wiley & Sons.

Fulero, S. (1987). Insurance trust releases malpractice statistics. *State Psychological Association Affairs 19*(1), 4–5.

Gabbard, G. (1989). *Sexual exploitation in professional relationships.* Washington, DC: American Psychiatric Association.

Gallup, G., & Jones, T. (2000). *The next American spirituality: Finding God in the twenty-first century.* Colorado Springs: Victor/Cook Communications.

Garner, D.M. (1991). *Eating disorders inventory—2.* Odessa, FL: Psychological Assessment Resources.

Garner, D.M., Garfinkle, P.E., Olmstead, M.P., & Bohr, Y. (1982). The eating attitudes test: Psychometric features and clinical correlations. *Psychological Medicine, 12,* 871–878.

Gelinas, D. J. (1993). Relational patterns in incestuous families, malevolent variations, and specific interventions with the adult survivor. Pages 1–34 in P.L. Paddison (Ed.). *Treatment of adult survivors of incest,* (pp.). Washington, D.C.: American Psychiatric Press.

Germain, A., Hall, M., Krakow, B., Shear, M., & Buysse, D. J. (2005, March). A brief sleep scale for post-traumatic stress disorder: Pittsburgh Sleep Quality Index addendum for PTSD. *Journal of Anxiety Disorders, 19*(2), 233–245.

Gladding, S. T. (2005). *Counseling: A comprehensive profession* (4th ed.). Upper Saddle River, NJ: Prentice-Hall.

Gorman, C. (10 June, 2002). The science of anxiety. *Time,* 46.

Grant, J. E., Kushner, M.G., & Kim, S.W. (2002). Pathological gambling and alcohol use disorder. *Alcohol Research & Health, 26,* 143–150.

Gray, M. J., Elhai, J. D., & Frueh, B. C. (2004, December). Enhancing patient satisfaction and increasing treatment compliance: Patient education as a fundamental component of PTSD treatment. *Psychiatric Quarterly, 75*(4), 321–333.

Graybill, D. (1985). Aggression in college students who were abused as children. *Journal of College Student Personnel, 26.*

Greenberger, D., & Padeskey, C. A. (1995). *Mind over mood.* New York: Guilford Press.

Guinness, O. (1998). *The call.* Nashville: Word.

Hall, N. (n.d.). *Stress: A psychoneuroimmunological perspective.* Retrieved from www.psy-chjournal.com/interviews. *Stress and Exercise* <http://www.saluminternational.com/articleshall.htm>

Hart, A. D. (1987). *Counseling the depressed.* Waco, TX: Word.

Hart, A. D. (1995). *Adrenaline and stress.* Dallas: Word.

Hart, A. D. (1999). *The anxiety cure: You can find emotional tranquility and wholeness.* Nashville: W Publishing Group.

Hart, A. D. (2001). Has self-esteem lost its way? *Christian Counseling Today, 9*(1), 8.

Hart, A. D. (2001). *Unmasking male depression.* Nashville: W Publishing Group.

Hart, A. D., & Weber, C. H. (2002). *Unveiling depression in women: A practical guide to understanding and overcoming depression.* Grand Rapids, MI: Fleming H. Revell.

Hawkins, R., Hindson, E., & Clinton, T. (2002). Theological roots: Synthesizing and systematizing a Biblical theology of helping. In T. Clinton & G. Ohlschlager (Eds.), *Competent Christian Counseling.* Colorado Springs: WaterBrook Press.

Herman, J.L. (1992). *Trauma and recovery.* New York: Basic Books.

Hogan, N., & DeSantis, L. (1992). Adolescent sibling bereavement: An ongoing attachment. *Qualitative Health Research, 2,* 159–177.

Holtzheimer, I., Russo, P. E., Zatzick, J., Bundy, D., Roy-Byrne, C., & Peter, P. (2005, May). The impact of comorbid post-traumatic stress disorder on short-term clinical outcome
in hospitalized patients with depression. *American Journal of Psychiatry, 165*(5), 970–977.

Hunsinger, D. (2001). An interdisciplinary map for Christian counselors. In M. McMinn, & T. Phillips (Eds.), *Care for the soul: Exploring the intersection of psychology & theology* (pp. 218–240). Downers Grove, IL: InterVarsity Press.

Huppert, J. D., Moser, J. S., Gershuny, B. S., Riggs, D. S., Spokas, M., Filip, J., Hajcak, G., Parker, H. A., Baer, L., & Foa, E. B. (2005, January). The relationship between obsessive-compulsive and post-traumatic *stress* symptoms in clinical and non-clinical samples. *Journal of Anxiety Disorders, 19*(1), 127–137.

Hutchins, D. (1984). Improving the counseling relationship. *The Personnel and Guidance Journal, 62*(10), (1984), 572–575.

Hutchins, D., & Cole, C. (1992). *Helping relationships and strategies* (2nd ed.). Pacific Grove, CA: Brooks/Cole.

Janof-Bulman, R. (1992). *Shattered assumptions: Toward a new psychology of trauma.* New York: The Free Press.

Johnson, B. (1987). Sexual abuse prevention: A rural interdisciplinary effort. *Child Welfare, 66,* 165–73.

Jones, I. F. (2003). *The counsel of heaven on earth*. Manuscript submitted for publication.

Jones, S., & Yarhouse, M. (2000). *Homosexuality: The use of scientific research in the church's moral debate*. Downer's Grove, IL: InterVarsity Press.

Jordan, N. N., Hoge, C. W., Tobler, S. K., Wells, J., Dydek, G. J. Egerton, & Walter E. (2004, April). Mental health impact of 9/11 Pentagon attack: Validation of a rapid assessment tool. *American Journal of Preventive Medicine, 26*(4), 284–294.

Kellemen R. W. (2005). *Soul physicians: A theology of soul care and spiritual direction*. Taneytown, MD: RPM Books.

Kellemen, R.W. (2004). *Spiritual friends: A methodology of soul care and spiritual direction*. Taneytown MD: RPM Books.

Keller, A. S., Rosenfeld, B., Trinh-Shevrin, C., Meserve, C., Sachs, E., Leviss, J. A., Singer, M. (2004). Shame, guilt, self-hatred and remorse in the psychotherapy of Vietnam combat veterans who committed atrocities. *American Journal of Psychotherapy, 58*(4), 377–386.

Kelly, E. W. (1995). *Religion and spirituality in counseling and psychotherapy*. Alexandria, VA: American Counseling Association.

Kessler, R. C., Berglund, P., Demler, O., Jin, R., Koretz, D., Merikangas, K.R., Rush, A.J., Walters, E.E., & Wang, P.S. (2003). The epidemiology of major depressive disorder: Results from the National Comorbidity Survey Replication (NCS-R). *JAMA, 289,* 3095–3105.

Kessler, R. C., Sonnega, A., Bromet, E., Hughes, M., & Nelson, C. B. (1995, December). Post-traumatic stress disorder in the national comorbidity survey. *Archives of General Psychiatry, 52*(12), 1048–1060.

Kevorkian, J. (1996). *Prescription—medicine: The goodness of planned death*. Buffalo: Prometheus Books.

Klass, D., Silverman, P. R., & Nickman, S. L. (Eds.). (1996). *Continuing bonds: New understandings of grief*. Washington, DC: Taylor & Francis.

Klerman, G. L., Weissman, M. M., Rounsaville, B. J., & Chevron, E. S. (1984). *Interpersonal psychotherapy of depression*. New York: Basic Books.

Klosko, J. S., & Sanderson, W. C. (1999). *Cognitive-behavioral treatment of depression*. Northvale, NJ: Jason Aronson.

Kottler, J. (1993). *On being a therapist* (Rev. ed.). San Francisco: Jossey-Bass.

Kroll J. (2000). No-suicide contracts. *American Journal of Psychiatry*.

Kroll, J., (1993). *PTSD/Borderlines in therapy: Finding the balance*. New York: W.W. Norton & Co.

Kubler-Ross, E. (1969). *On death and dying*. New York: MacMillan.

Kurtz, E. (1979). *Not God: A history of Alcoholics Anonymous*. Center City, MN: Hazelden.

Laaser, M. (1996). *Faithful and true*. Grand Rapids, MI: Zondervan.

Laaser, M. (2002). *A L.I.F.E. guide: Men living in freedom everyday*. Fairfax, VA.: Xulon.

Laaser, M. (2004). *Healing the wound of sexual addiction*. Grand Rapids, MI: Zondervan.

Laaser, M. and Earle, R. (2002). *The pornography trap*. Kansas City: Beacon Hill.

L'Abate, L. (1981). Classification of counseling and therapy, theorists, method process, and goals: The E-R-A model. *The Personnel and Guidance Journal, 59*, 263–265.

Lam, D. H., Jones, S. H., Hayward, P., & Bright, J. A. (1999). *Cognitive therapy for bipolar disorder: A therapist's guide to concepts, methods, and practice.* Chichester, UK: Wiley.

Landy, U. (1986). Abortion counseling: A new component of medical care. *Clinics in Obs/Gyn, 13*(1):33–41.

Langberg, D. M. (1997). *Counseling survivors of sexual abuse.* Wheaton, IL.: Tyndale.

Langberg, D. M. (1999). *On the threshold of hope: Opening the door to healing for survivors of sexual abuse.* Wheaton, IL: Tyndale.

Lark, S. M. (1996). *Anxiety and stress.* Berkeley, CA: Celestialarts.

Lee. J., & Dade, L. (2003). The buck stops where? What is the role of the emergency physician in managing panic disorder in chest pain patients? *Journal of the Canadian Association of Emergency Physicians, 5*(4), 237–238.

Lemonick, M. (2003, January 20). How stress takes its toll. *Time.* (Special Issue).

Lerner, H. (1985). *The dance of anger.* New York: Harper & Row.

Leskela, J., Dieperink, M., & Thuras, P. (2002, June). Shame and posttraumatic stress disorder. *Journal of Traumatic Stress, 15*(3), 223–227.

Lewinsohn, P. M., Munoz, R. F., Youngren, M. A., & Zeiss, A. M. (1992). *Control your depression.* New York: Fireside/Simon and Schuster.

Lindman Port, C. Engdahl, B., & Frazier, P. (2001, September). A longitudinal and retrospective study of PTSD among older prisoners of war. *American Journal of Psychiatry, 158*(9), 1474–1480.

Los Angeles Times Poll. (1989 March 19). *Los Angeles Times,* question 76.

Lowinger, T., & Solomon, T. Z. (2004, October-December). PTSD, guilt, and shame among reckless drivers. *Journal of Loss & Trauma, 9*(4), 327–345.

Lyles, M. R. (2001). Will the real mood stabilizer please stand up? *Christian Counseling Today, 9*(3), 60–61.

Madianos, M. G., Papaghelis, M., Ioannovich, J. & Dafni, R. (2001). Psychiatric disorders in burn patients: A follow-up study. *Psychotherapy and Psychosomatics, 70*, 30–37.

Maine, M. (1999). AAMFT clinical update: Eating disorders. *A Supplement to the Family Therapy News, 1*(6), 1.

Maj, M., Akiskal, H. S., Lopez-Ibor, J. J., & Sartorius, N. (Eds.). (2002). *Bipolar disorder.* New York: Wiley.

Maris, R. (1992). Overview of the study of suicide assessment and prediction. In R. Maris, A. Berman, J. Maltsberger, and R. Yufit, (Eds.). *Assessment and prediction of suicide.* New York: Guilford.

Martell, C. R., Addis, M. E., & Jacobson, N. S. (2001). *Depression in context: Strategies for guided action.* New York: W. W. Norton.

Marty, M.E. (1998). The ethos of Christian forgiveness. In E.L. Worthington, Jr. (Ed.), *Dimensions of forgiveness: Psychological research and theological perspectives.* Philadelphia: The Templeton Foundation Press.

Mathewes-Green, F. (1991, Summer). Unplanned parenthood. *Policy Review.*

May, G. (1988). *Addiction and grace.* San Francisco: Harper and Row.

McCarthy, C. (1971, March 7). A psychological view of abortion. *Washington Post.*

McCullough, J. P. (2000). *Treatment of chronic depression: Cognitive behavioral analysis system of psychotherapy.* New York: Guilford Press.

McCullough, M. E., & Worthington, E. L., Jr. (1995). Promoting forgiveness: A comparison of two psychoeducational group interventions with a waiting-list control. *Counseling and Values, 40,* 55–68.

McCullough, M. E., Bellah, C. G., Kilpatrick, S. D., & Johnson, J. L. (2001). Vengefulness: Relationships with forgiveness, rumination, well-being, and the big five. *Personality and Social Psychology Bulletin, 27,* 601–610.

McCullough, M. E., Rachal, K. C., Sandage, S. J., Worthington, E. L. Jr., Brown, S. W., & Hight, T. L. (1998). Interpersonal forgiveness in close relationships II: Theoretical elaboration and measurement. *Journal of Personality and Social Psychology, 75,* 1586–1603.

McCullough, M. E., Sandage, S. J., & Worthington, E. L., Jr. (1997). *To forgive is human: How to put your past in the past.* Downers Grove, IL: InterVarsity Press.

McCullough, M. E., Worthington, E. L. Jr., & Rachal, K. C. (1997). Interpersonal forgiving in close relationships. *Journal of Personality and Social Psychology, 73,* 321–336.

McCullough, M.E., Fincham, F.D. & Tsang, J-A. (2003). Forgiveness, forbearance, and time: The temporal unfolding of transgression-related interpersonal motivations. *Journal of Personality and Social Psychology 84,* 540–557.

McCullough-Zander, K., & Larson, S. (2004, October). 'The fear is still in me': Caring for survivors of torture. *American Journal of Nursing, 104* (10), 54–65.

McGee, R., & Schaumberg., H. (1990). *Renew: Hope for victims of sexual abuse.* Houston: Rapha.

McMinn, M. R. (1996). *Psychology, theology, and spirituality in Christian counseling.* USA: Tyndale.

McMinn, M., & Dominguez, A. (2003). Psychology collaborating with the church. *Journal of Psychology and Christianity, 22*(4), 291–294.

Means, P. (1996). *Men's secret wars.* Grand Rapids, MI: Revell.

Meier, P., Arterburn, S., & Minirth, F. (2001). *Mood swings.* Nashville: Thomas Nelson.

Meier, P., Clinton, T., & Ohlschlager, G. (2001). Mental illness: Reducing suffering in the church.Pages 364–365. *The soul care Bible.* Nashville: Thomas Nelson,.

Mellman, T. A., & David, D. (1995, November). Sleep disturbance and its relationship to psychiatric morbidity after Hurricane Andrew. *American Journal of Psychiatry, 152*(11), 1659–1664.

Menninger, K. (1938). *Man against himself.* New York: Harcourt, Brace, & World.

Messinger. (1975). Malpractice suits—The psychiatrist's turn. *Journal of Legal Medicine, 3,* 21.

Miklowitz, . J. (2002). *The bipolar disorder survival guide.* New York: Guilford Press.

Miklowitz, D. J. & Goldstein, M. J. (1997). *Bipolar disorder: A family-focused treatment approach*. New York: Guilford Press.

Milkman H., & Sunderwirth, S. (1987). *Craving for ecstasy: The consciousness and chemistry of escape*. Lexington, MA: Lexington Books.

Milkman H., & Sunderwirth, S. (1987). *Craving for ecstasy: The consciousness and chemistry of escape*. Lexington, MA: Lexington Books.

Miller, J. (1987). *Sin: Overcoming the ultimate deadly addiction*. San Francisco: Harper and Row.

Miller, W. B. (1992). An empirical study of the psychological antecedents and consequences of induced abortion. *J Social Issues, 48*(3), 67–93.

Minirth, F., & Meier, P. (1994). *Happiness is a choice* (2nd ed.). Grand Rapids, MI: Baker.

Minirth, F., Meier, P., & Arterburn, S. (1995). Abortion. In *The complete life encyclopedia*. Nashville: Thomas Nelson.

Minuchin, S. (1974). *Families and family therapy*. London: Tavistock.

Mondimore, F. M. (1999). *Bipolar Disorder*. Baltimore: Johns Hopkins University Press.

Morely, W. E. (1970, April). Theory of crisis intervention. *Pastoral Psychology, 21*(203), 16.

Mosgofian, P., & Ohlschlager, G. (1995). *Sexual misconduct in counseling and ministry*. Dallas: Word.

Motto, J. (1992). An integrated approach to estimating suicide risk. In R. Maris, A. Berman, J. Maltsberger, and R. Yufit, (Eds.). *Assessment and Prediction of Suicide*. New York: Guilford Press.

Murray, N.D. and Pizzorno, N.D. (1998). *Encyclopedia of natural medicine*. Rocklin, California: Prima Health.

National Center for Chronic Disease Prevention and Health Promotion. (2004, September). *General alcohol information*. Retrieved May 19, 2005, from http://www.cdc.gov/alcohol/factsheets/general_information.htm.

National Center for Health Statistics. (2004). *Health, United States, 2004: With chartbook on trends in the health of Americans*. Hyattsville, Maryland: Author.

National Center for Injury Prevention and Control. (2004, November). *Intimate partner violence: Fact sheet*. Retrieved May 19, 2005, from http://www.cdc.gov/ncipc/factsheets/ipvfacts.htm.

National Center for Injury Prevention and Control. (2004, November). *Suicide: Fact sheet*. Retrieved May 2005, from www.cdc.gov/ncipc/factsheets/suifacts.htm.

National Center for Injury Prevention and Control. (2005, April). *Sexual violence: Fact sheet*. Retrieved May 19, 2005, from http://www.cdc.gov/ncipc/factsheets/svfacts.htm.

National Impact Gambling Impact Commission. (1999). *National gambling impact study commission final report*. Washington, DC.

National Institute of Mental Health (NIMH). (1999). *The numbers count*. (NIH Publication No. NIH 99–4584) [Online]. Available: http://www.NIMH.NIH.gov/pulicat/members.CFM.

National Institute of Mental Health. (2000). *Anxiety*. Retrieved May 2005, from http://www.nimh.nih.gov/publicat/anxiety.cfm#anx1.

National Institute of Mental Health. (2001). *NIMH Eating Disorders: Facts about eating disorders and the search for solutions*. NIH Publication No. 01–4901. Retrieved from http://www.nimh.nih.gov/publicat/eatingdisorder.cfm

National Institute of Mental Health. (2001). *Reliving trauma: Post-traumatic stress disorder: A brief overview of the symptoms, treatments, and research findings.*

National Institute of Mental Health. (2003). *In Harm's Way: Suicide in America.* Retrieved May 19, 2005, from http://www.nimh.nih.gov/publicat/harmaway.cfm.

National Institute on Drug Abuse. (n.d.). *NIDA's Principles of Drug Addiction Treatment: A Research-Based Guide.* Available from, http://www.nida.nih.gov/PODAT/PODATIndex.html.

National Survey on Drug Use and Health. (2003). Available from, http://oas.samhsa.gov/nhsda.htm.

Newman, C. F., Leahy, R. L., Beck, A. T., Reilly-Harrington, N. A., & Gyulai, L. (2002). *Bipolar disorder: A cognitive therapy approach.* Washington, DC: American Psychological Association.

Nishith, P., Resick, P. A., & Mueser, K. T. (2001, July). Sleep difficulties and alcohol use motives in female rape victims with post-traumatic stress disorder. *Journal of Traumatic Stress, 14*(3), 469–480.

Nixon, R., Resick, P. A., & Nishith, P. (2004, October). An exploration of comorbid depression among female victims of intimate partner violence with post-traumatic stress disorder. *Journal of Affective Disorders. 82*(2), 315–321.

Norretrander, T. (1998). *The user illusion.* New York: Viking.

O'Mathuna, D. and Larimore, W. (2001). *Alternative medicine: The Christian handbook.* Grand Rapids, MI: Zondervan.

O'Neill, R. (2002, September). *Experiments in living: The fatherless family.* Retrieved June 2005, from http://www.civitas.org.uk.

Oden, T. (1976). *Should treatment be terminated?* New York: Harper and Row.

Ohlschlager, G. & Clinton, T. (2000). Inside law and ethics: The ethics of evangelism and spiritual formation in professional counseling. *Christian Counseling Connection.* Issue 1, 6–7.

Ohlschlager, G. (1999). Avoiding ethical-legal pitfalls: Embracing conformative behavior and transformative virtues. *Christian Counseling Today, 7*(3), 40–43.

Ohlschlager, G., & Mosgofian, P. (1992). *Law for the Christian counselor: A guidebook for clinicians and pastors.* Dallas: Word.

Oliver, G. J. (1993). *Real men have feelings too.* Chicago: Moody Press.

Oliver, G. J., Hasz, M., & Richburg, M. (1997). *Promoting Change Through Brief Therapy in Christian Counseling.* Wheaton, IL: Tyndale House.

Oliver, G. J., & Wright, H. N. (1992). *When anger hits home.* Chicago: Moody Press.

Oliver, G. J., & Wright, H. N. (1996). *Good women get angry.* Ann Arbor, MI: Servant Publications.

Oquendo, M., Brent, D. A., Birmaher, B., Greenhill, L., Kolko, D., Stanley, B., Zelazny, J., Burke, A. K., Firinciogullari, S., Ellis, S. P., & Mann, J. J. (2005, March). Post-traumatic stress disorder comorbid with major depression: Factors mediating the association with suicidal behavior. *American Journal of Psychiatry, 162*(3), 560–567.

Osborne, I. (1998). *Tormenting thoughts and secret rituals: The hidden epidemic of obsessive-compulsive disorder.* New York: Dell.

Packer, J. I. (1993). *Knowing God* (rev. ed.). Downers Grove, IL: InterVarsity Press.

Papolos, D., & Papolos, J. (1997). *Overcoming depression* (3rd ed.). New York: Harper Collins.

Papolos, D., & Papolos, J. (1999). *The bipolar child*. New York: Broadway Books.

Pascal, B. (1941). *Pensèes and the provincial letters*. New York: The Modern Library.

Payne, R., Kravitz, A., Notman, M., & Anderson, J. (1976). Outcomes following therapeutic abortion. *Archives of General Psychiatry, 33,* 725.

Pearce, K. A., Schauer, A. H., Garfield, N. J., Ohlde, C. O., & Patterson, T. W. (1985). A study of post-traumatic stress disorder in Vietnam Veterans. *Journal of Clinical Psychology, 41*(1), 9–15.

Peck, S. (1997, December 18). Mission of madness. *Long Beach Telegram,* A1, A6–7.

Penzel, F. (2000). *Obsessive-compulsive disorder: A complete guide to getting well and staying well.* Oxford: New York.

Persons, J. B., Davidson, J., & Tompkins, M. A. (2001). *Essential components of cognitive-behavior therapy for depression.* Washington, DC: American Psychological Association.

Planned Parenthood Federation of America Public Affairs Action Letter. (1992 September 25). *Quote of the week.*

Pope, K., Sonne, J., & Holroyd, J. (1993). *Sexual feelings in psychotherapy: Explorations for therapists and therapists-in-training.* Washington, DC: American Psychological Association.

Population Reference Bureau. (n.d.). 2000 census data: Living arrangements profile for United States. *Analysis of Data from the U.S. Census Bureau, for The Annie E. Casey Foundation,* Retrieved May 2005, from www.aecf.org

Prochaska J. O., Norcross, J., & DiClemente C. (1994). *Changing for good.* NY: Avon Books.

Ranew, L. F., & Serritella, D. A. (1992). *Handbook of differential treatments for addictions.* Boston: Allyn and Bacon.

Reardon, D. (1987). *Aborted women: Silent no more.* Westchester, IL: Crossway.

Reisser, T., & Coe, J. (1999). Post-abortion counseling. In D. Benner & P. Hill, (Eds.). *Baker Encyclopedia of Psychology and Counseling,* 2nd ed. Grand Rapids, MI: Baker.

Reisser, T., & Reisser, P. (1999). *A solitary sorrow: Finding healing and wholeness after abortion.* Wheaton, IL: Harold Shaw.

Resnick, H. S., Kilpatrick, D. G., Dansky, B. S. Saunders, B. E., et al. (1993, December). Prevalence of civilian trauma and post-traumatic stress disorder in a representative national sample of women. *Journal of Consulting & Clinical Psychology, 61*(6), 984–991.

Richards, P.S., & Bergin, A.E. (1997). *A spiritual strategy for counseling and psychotherapy.* Washington, DC: American Psychological Association.

Ripley, J.S., & Worthington, E.L., Jr. (2002). Comparison of hope-focused communication and empathy-based forgiveness group interventions to promote marital enrichment. *Journal of Counseling and Development, 80,* 452–463.

Rogers, C. (1951). *Client centered therapy.* Boston: Houghton Mifflin.

Rogers, C. (1957). The necessary and sufficient conditions of therapeutic personality change. *Journal of Consulting Psychology, 21,* 95–103.

Rogers, C. (1961). *On becoming a person.* Boston: Houghton Mifflin.

Roth, S., Newman, E., Pelcovitz, D., Van der Kolk, B., & Mandel, F. S. (1997). Complex PTSD in victims exposed to sexual and physical abuse: Results from the DSM-IV field trial for post-traumatic stress disorder. *Journal of Traumatic Stress, 10*, 539–555.

Rue, V. M., & Speckhard, A. C. (1992). Informed consent and abortion: Issues in medicine and counseling. *Med. & Mind, 6*(1), 75–94.

Saigh, P. A. (1987, June). In vitro flooding of an adolescent's post-traumatic stress disorder. *Journal of Clinical Child Psychology, 16*(2), 147–151.

Sandage, S.J. (1997). *An ego-humility model of forgiveness: A theory-driven empirical test of group interventions.* PhD dissertation, Virginia Commonwealth University, Richmond, VA.

Sapolsky, R. M. (1998). *Why zebras don't get ulcers.* New York: W.H. Freeman and Company.

Schaeffer, B. (2000). *Is it love or is it addiction.* Center City, MN: Hazelden.

Schaeffer, F. A. (1972). *He is there and He is not silent.* Wheaton, IL: Tyndale.

Schaumburg, H. (1992). *False intimacy: Understanding the struggle of sexual addiction.* Colorado Springs: NavPress.

Scott, J. (2001). *Overcoming mood swings.* New York: New York University Press.

Seligman, M. E. P. (1975). *Helplessness: On depression, development, and death.* San Francisco: W. H. Freeman and Company.

Shaw, A., Joseph, S., & Linley, A. P. (2005, March). Religion, spirituality, and post-traumatic growth: A systematic review. *Mental Health, Religion & Culture, 8*(1), 1–11.

Shea, S. C. (1999). *The practical art of suicide assessment: A guide for mental health professionals and substance abuse counselors.* New York: John Wiley & Sons, Inc.

Sheikh, J. I., Woodward, S. H., & Leskin, G. A. (2003). Sleep in post-traumatic stress disorder and panic: Convergence and divergence. *Depression & Anxiety, 18*(4), 187–198.

Short, N., & Kitchner, N. (2002, April). Panic disorder: Nature assessment and treatment. *Continuing Professional Development.* Royal College of Nursing, *5*(7).

Sibcy, G. (2005, June). Lecture: Advanced psychopathology. Liberty University.

Silverman, P. R., Nickman, S., & Worden, J. W. (1992). Detachment revisited: The child's reconstruction of a dead parent. *American Journal of Orthopsychiatry, 62*, 494–503.

Singer, E., Smith, H., Wilkinson, J., Kim, G., Allden, K., & Ford, D. (2003, November). Mental health of detained asylum seekers. *Lancet, 362*(9397), 1721–1724.

Sire, J. (1997). *The universe next door: A basic worldview catalog* (3rd ed.). Downers Grove, IL: InterVarsity Press.

Sittser, G. L. (1996). *A grace disguised.* Grand Rapids, MI: Zondervan.

Solomon, E. P., & Heide, K. M. (2005). The biology of trauma. *Journal of Interpersonal Violence, 20*(1), 51–61.

Söndergaard, H. P., Ekblad, S., & Theorell, T. (2003, May). Screening for post-traumatic stress disorder among refugees in Stockholm. *Nordic Journal of Psychiatry, 57*(3), 185–190.

Spitzer, R.L., Yanovski, S., Wadden, T., Wing, R., Marcus, MD., Stunkard, A., Devlin, M.,

Mitchell, J., Hasin, D., & Horne, RL., (1992). Binge eating disorder: Its further validation in a multisite study. *International Journal of Eating Disorders*, 12: 137–53.

Statistics. (n.d.). *How many people have eating and exercise disorders?* Retrieved from
http://www.anred.com.

Stevenson, L. (1974). *Seven theories of human nature* (2nd ed.). New York: Oxford University Press.

Stoll, A. L. (2001). *The omega-3 connection.* New York: Simon & Schuster.

Stone, H. W. (1976). *Crisis counseling.* Fortress Press.

Strock, M., et al. (2000). Depression. *National Institute of Health Publication* No. 00–3561.
Retrieved February 25, 2005, from http://www.nimh.nih.gov/publicat/depression.cfm

Strong, S. (1968). Counseling: An interpersonal influence process. *Journal of Counseling
Psychology, 15,* 215–224.

Suicidal behavior after severe trauma. Part 1: PTSD diagnoses, psychiatric comorbidity,
and assessments of suicidal behavior. *Journal of Traumatic Stress, 11*(1), 103–113.

Sullender, R. S., & Malony, H. N. (1990). Should clergy counsel suicidal persons? *The
Journal of Pastoral Care, 44* (3), 203–211, 204–206.

Sullivan, P.F. (1995). Mortality in anorexia nervosa. *American Journal of Psychiatry* 152(7):
1073–1074.

Sutcliffe, P., Tufnell, G., & Cornish, U. (Eds.). (1998). *Working with the dying and bereaved.*
New York: Routledge.

Swanson, L., & Biaggio, M. K. (1985). Therapeutic perspectives on father-daughter
incest. *American Journal of Psychiatry, 142,* (6), 667–674.

Swenson R. A. (1995). *Margin.* Colorado Springs, CO: NavPress.

Swenson, R.A. (1992). *Margin: Restoring emotional, physical, financial, and time reserves to
overloaded lives.* Colorado Springs, CO: NavPress.

Tada, J. E. (1997). Decision-making and dad. Pages 471–475 in G. Stewart & T. Demy
(Eds.). *Suicide: A Christian response, crucial considerations for choosing life.* Grand
Rapids, MI: Kregel.

Tan, S.-Y. (2000). *Rest: Experiencing God's peace in a restless world.* Ann Arbor, MI: Vine
Books.

Tan, S.-Y., & Gregg, D. H. (1997). *Disciplines of the Holy Spirit.* Grand Rapids, MI:
Zondervan.

Tan, S.-Y., & Ortberg, J., Jr. (1995a). *Coping with depression.* Grand Rapids, MI: Baker.

Tan, S.-Y., & Ortberg, J., Jr. (1995b). *Understanding depression.* Grand Rapids, MI: Baker.

Taub. (1983). Psychiatric malpractice in the 1980's: A look at some areas of concern. *Law,
Medicine and Health Care,* 97.

Taylor, S., Thordarson, D. S., Fedoroff, I. C., Maxfield, L., & Ogrodniczuk, J. (2003, April).
Comparative efficacy, speed, and adverse effects of three PTSD treatments: Exposure
therapy, EMDR, and relaxation training. *Journal of Consulting & Clinical Psychology,
71*(2), 330–339.

Teicher, M. H., Andersen, S. L., Polcari, A., Anderson, C. M., Navalta, C. P., & Kim, D. M. (2003). The neurobiological consequences of early stress and childhood maltreatment. *Neuroscience & Biobehavioral Reviews, 27*(1/2), 33–45.

The Barna Group. (2004, September). Born again Christians just as likely to divorce as non-Christians. The Barna Update. Retrieved May 2005, from http://www.barna.org.

The leadership survey on pastors and internet pornography. (2001). *Leadership Journal,* 001.

The National Center for Fathering. (n.d.). *National surveys on fathers and fathering.* Retrieved June 2005, from http://www.fathers.com/research.

The National Center for Fathering. (n.d.). *The consequences of fatherlessness.* Retrieved June 2005, from http://www.fathers.com/research/consequences.html.

The twelve steps: A spiritual journey. (1988). San Diego: Recovery Publications.

Thelen, M.H. Farmer, J., Wonderlich, S., & Smith, M. (1991). A revision of the bulimic test: The BULIT-R. *Psychological Assessment: A Journal of Consulting and Clinical Psychology, 3,* 119–124.

Thomas, J. M. (1995). Traumatic stress disorder presents as hyperactivity and disruptive behavior: Case presentation, diagnoses, and treatment. *Infant Mental Health Journal, 16*(4), 306–318.

Thurman, C. (1991). *The lies we believe.* Nashville: Thomas Nelson.

Thurman, C. (1995). *The lies we believe workbook.* Nashville: Thomas Nelson.

Thurman, C. (2001). Perfectionism. In T. Clinton, E. Hindson, & G. Ohlschlager (Eds.), *The soul care Bible.* Nashville: Thomas Nelson.

Torrey, E. F., & Knable, M. B. (2002). *Surviving manic depression.* New York: Basic Books.

True, W. R., Rice, J., Eisen, S. A., Heath, A. C., Goldberg, J., Lyons, M. J., & Nowak J. (n.d.). A twin study of genetic and environmental contributions to liability for post-traumatic stress symptoms. *JAMA & Archives, Archives of General Psychiatry, accessed June 20, 2005 from* http://archpsyc.ama-assn.org/cgi/content/abstract/50/4/257

Tsai, M., & Wagner, N. N. (1978). Therapy groups for women sexually molested as children. *Archives of Sexual Behavior, 7,* 417–427.

Tyson-Rawson, K. (1996). Relationship and heritage: Manifestations of ongoing attachment following father death. Pages 125–145 in D. Klass, P.R. Silverman, & S. L. Nickman (Eds.). *Continuing bonds: New understandings of grief.* Washington DC: Taylor & Francis.

van der Kolk, B., McFarlane, A., & Weisaeth, L. (Eds.). (1996). *Traumatic stress: The effects of overwhelming experience on mind, body, and society.* New York: The Guildford Press.

Van Leeuwin, M.S. (1985). *The Person in psychology: A contemporary Christian appraisal.* Grand Rapids, MI: Eerdmans.

Vandereycken, W. (1995). The families of patients with an eating disorder, in K.D. Brownell, & C.G. Fairburn (Eds.), *Eating disorders and obesity: A comprehensive handbook.* New York: The Guilford Press.

Vernick, L. (2000). *The TRUTH principle: A life changing model for spiritual growth and renewal.* Colorado Springs, CO: WaterBrook Press.

Vitz, P. (1994). *Psychology as religion: The cult of self worship* (2nd ed.). Grand Rapids, MI: Eerdmans.

Volberg, R.A. (2003). *Gambling and problem gambling in Arizona: Report to the Arizona lottery.* Retrieved from http://www.problemgambling.az.gov/prevalencestudy.pdf.

Wade, N.G., & Worthington, E.L., Jr. (2003a). Overcoming interpersonal offenses: Is forgiveness the only way to deal with unforgiveness? *Journal of Counseling and Development, 81*, 343–353.

Wade, N.G., & Worthington, E.L., Jr. (2003b). *Content and meta-analysis of interventions to promote forgiveness.* Manuscript under editorial review, Virginia Commonwealth University, Richmond.

Wald, J., Taylor, S. (2005). Interoceptive exposure therapy combined with trauma-related exposure therapy for post-traumatic stress disorder: A case report. *Cognitive Behaviour Therapy, 34*(1), 34–41.

Wallerstein, J. S., & Blakeslee, S. (1995). *The good marriage: How & why love lasts.* New York: Houghton Mifflin Company.

Walsh, F., and McGoldrick, M. (1998). A family systems perspective on loss, recovery and resilience. In P. Sutcliffe, G. Tufnell, & U. Cornish. *Working with the dying and bereaved.* New York: Routledge.

Walters, R. (1981). *Anger: Yours & mine & what to do about it.* Grand Rapids, MI: Zondervan.

WebMD Health On-line. (n.d.). What are eating disorders? Retrieved from http://www.webmd.com.

Weishaar, M. & Beck, A. (1992). Clinical and cognitive predictors of suicide. In R. Maris, A. Berman, J. Maltsberger, & R. Yufit (Eds.). *Assessment and prediction of suicide.* New York: Guilford Press.

Weiss, J. (1998, March 7). Wounded Heroes. *The Dallas News.* Retrieved May, 2005, from http://www.dallasnews.com.

Weissman, M. M., Markowitz, J. C., & Klerman G. L. (2000). *Comprehensive guide to interpersonal psychotherapy.* New York: Basic Books.

Weissman, M.M. (1993). The epidemiology of personality disorders: A 1990 update. *Journal of Personality Disorders, Supplement, Spring,* 44–62.

Wells, D. (1994). *God in the wasteland: The reality of truth in a world of fading dreams.* Grand Rapids, MI: Eerdmans.

Welte, J.W., Wieczorek, W.F., Barnes, G.M, Tidwell, M.C., & Hoffman, J.H. (2003). The relationship of ecological and geographic factors to gambling behavior and pathology. (Accepted for publication by the *Journal of Gambling Studies*).

Whealin, J. M. (n.d.). *Complex PTSD a national center for PTSD fact sheet.* Retrieved on June 20, 2005 from http://www.ncptsd.va.gov/facts/specific/fs_complex_ptsd.html.

Willard, D. (1988). *The spirit of the disciplines: Understanding how God changes lives.* San Francisco, CA: Harper and Row.

Willingham, R. (1999). *Breaking free.* Downers Grove, IL: InterVarsity.

Wilson, E. (2002). *Steering clear.* Downers Grove, IL: InterVarsity.

Wolterstorff, N. (1984). *Reason within the bounds of religion: 2nd edition.* Grand Rapids, MI: Eerdmans.

Wolterstorff, N. (1987). *Lament for a son.* Grand Rapids, MI: Eerdmans.

Worthington, E. (1988). Understanding the values of religious clients: A model and its application to counseling. *Journal of Counseling Psychology, 35*(2), 166–174.

Worthington, E. L., Jr. (1998). An empathy-humility-commitment model of forgiveness applied within family dyads. *Journal of Family Therapy, 20,* 59–76.

Worthington, E. L., Jr. (2000b). On chaos, fractals, and stress: Response to Fincham's "Optimism and the Family." In J. Gillam (Ed.), *The science of optimism and hope.* Philadelphia: The Templeton Foundation Press.

Worthington, E.L., Jr. (1999). *Hope-focused marriage counseling.* Downers Grove, IL: Inter-Varsity Press.

Worthington, E.L., Jr. (2000a). Is there a place for forgiveness in the justice system? *Fordham Urban Law Journal, 27,* 1721–1734.

Worthington, E.L., Jr. (2001a). Unforgiveness, forgiveness, and reconciliation in societies. In Raymond G. Helmick & Rodney L. Petersen (Eds.), *Forgiveness and reconciliation: Religion, public policy, and conflict transformation.* Philadelphia: The Templeton Foundation Press.

Worthington, E.L., Jr. (2001b). *Five steps to forgiveness: The art and science of forgiving.* New York: Crown Publishers.

Worthington, E.L., Jr. (2003). *Forgiving and reconciling: Bridges to wholeness and hope.* Downers Rove, IL: InterVarsity Press

Worthington, E.L., Jr., & Scherer, M. (2003). Forgiveness is an emotion-focused coping strategy that can reduce health risks and promote health resilience: Theory, review, and hypotheses. *Psychology and Health, 19,* 385–405.

Worthington, E.L., Jr., & Wade, N.G. (1999). The social psychology of unforgiveness and forgiveness and implications for clinical practice. *Journal of Social and Clinical Psychology, 18,* 385–418.

Worthington, E.L., Jr., Berry, J.W., & Parrott, L. III. (2001). Unforgiveness, forgiveness, religion, and health. In T. G. Plante & A. Sherman (Eds.), *Faith and health: Psychological perspectives.* New York: Guilford Press.

Worthington, E.L., Jr., Kurusu, T., McCullough, M.E., & Sandage, S. (1996). Empirical research on religion and psychotherapeutic processes and outcomes: A 10-year review and research prospectus. *Psychological Bulletin, 199,* 448–487.

Worthington, E.L., Jr., Sandage, S. J., & Berry, J.W. (2000). Group interventions to promote forgiveness: What researchers and clinicians ought to know. In M.E. McCullough, K.I. Pargament, & C.E. Thoresen (Eds.), *Forgiveness: Theory, research and practice.* New York: Guilford Press.

Yalom, I. D. (1995). *The theory and practice of group psychotherapy,* New York: Basic Books.

Yalom, I. D. (2002). *The gift of therapy: An open letter to a new generation of therapists and their patients.* NY: HarperCollins.

Young, E. J. (1965). *The book of Isaiah: The English text, with introduction, exposition, and notes*. In R. K. Harrison (Ed.), *New International Commentary on the Old Testament*. Grand Rapids, MI: Eerdmans.

Young, J. (1999). *Cognitive therapy for personality disorders: A schema-focused approach: 3rd Ed*. Sarasota, FL: Professional Resource Press.

Zimmerman, M. K. (1977). *Passage through abortion*. New York: Praeger Publishers.

Index

LaVergne, TN USA
15 March 2011
220023LV00004B/1-6/P